HISTORICAL DICTIONARY

The historical dictionaries present essential information on a broad range of subjects, including American and world history, art, business, cities, countries, cultures, customs, film, global conflicts, international relations, literature, music, philosophy, religion, sports, and theater. Written by experts, all contain highly informative introductory essays of the topic and detailed chronologies that, in some cases, cover vast historical time periods but still manage to heavily feature more recent events.

Brief A–Z entries describe the main people, events, politics, social issues, institutions, and policies that make the topic unique, and entries are cross-referenced for ease of browsing. Extensive bibliographies are divided into several general subject areas, providing excellent access points for students, researchers, and anyone wanting to know more. Additionally, maps, photographs, and appendixes of supplemental information aid high school and college students doing term papers or introductory research projects. In short, the historical dictionaries are the perfect starting point for anyone looking to research in these fields.

HISTORICAL DICTIONARIES OF LITERATURE AND THE ARTS

Jon Woronoff, Series Editor

Science Fiction Literature, by Brian Stableford, 2004.

Hong Kong Cinema, by Lisa Odham Stokes, 2007.

American Radio Soap Operas, by Jim Cox, 2005.

Japanese Traditional Theatre, by Samuel L. Leiter, 2006.

Fantasy Literature, by Brian Stableford, 2005.

Australian and New Zealand Cinema, by Albert Moran and Errol Vieth, 2006.

African-American Television, by Kathleen Fearn-Banks, 2006.

Lesbian Literature, by Meredith Miller, 2006.

Scandinavian Literature and Theater, by Jan Sjåvik, 2006.

British Radio, by Seán Street, 2006.

German Theater, by William Grange, 2006.

African American Cinema, by S. Torriano Berry and Venise Berry, 2006.

Sacred Music, by Joseph P. Swain, 2006.

Russian Theater, by Laurence Senelick, 2007.

French Cinema, by Dayna Oscherwitz and MaryEllen Higgins, 2007.

Postmodernist Literature and Theater, by Fran Mason, 2007.

Irish Cinema, by Roderick Flynn and Pat Brereton, 2007.

Australian Radio and Television, by Albert Moran and Chris Keating, 2007.

Polish Cinema, by Marek Haltof, 2007.

Old Time Radio, by Robert C. Reinehr and Jon D. Swartz, 2008.

Renaissance Art, by Lilian H. Zirpolo, 2008.

Broadway Musical, by William A. Everett and Paul R. Laird, 2008.

American Theater: Modernism, by James Fisher and Felicia Hardison Londré, 2008.

German Cinema, by Robert C. Reimer and Carol J. Reimer, 2008.

Horror Cinema, by Peter Hutchings, 2008.

Westerns in Cinema, by Paul Varner, 2008.

Chinese Theater, by Tan Ye, 2008.

Italian Cinema, by Gino Moliterno, 2008.

Architecture, by Allison Lee Palmer, 2008.

Russian and Soviet Cinema, by Peter Rollberg, 2008.

African American Theater, by Anthony D. Hill, 2009.

Postwar German Literature, by William Grange, 2009.

Modern Japanese Literature and Theater, by J. Scott Miller, 2009.

Animation and Cartoons, by Nichola Dobson, 2009.

Modern Chinese Literature, by Li-hua Ying, 2010.

Middle Eastern Cinema, by Terri Ginsberg and Chris Lippard, 2010.

Historical Dictionary of Opera

Scott L. Balthazar

The Scarecrow Press, Inc.
Lanham • Toronto • Plymouth, UK
2013

Published by Scarecrow Press, Inc.
A wholly owned subsidiary of The Rowman & Littlefield Publishing Group, Inc.
4501 Forbes Boulevard, Suite 200, Lanham, Maryland 20706
http://www.scarecrowpress.com

10 Thornbury Road, Plymouth PL6 7PP, United Kingdom

British Library Cataloguing in Publication Information Available

Library of Congress Cataloging-in-Publication Data

Balthazar, Scott Leslie.
Historical dictionary of opera / Scott L. Balthazar.
pages cm. — (Historical dictionaries of literature and the arts)
Includes bibliographical references.
ISBN 978-0-8108-6768-0 (cloth : alk. paper) — ISBN 978-0-8108-7943-0 (ebook)
1. Opera—Dictionaries. I. Title.
ML102.O6B28 2013
782.103—dc23
2013004536

Printed in the United States of America.

Contents

Editor's Foreword

If you don't know Italian, you may actually have a better idea of what opera is, since you judge it by what it is rather than as a simple word that just means a "work," which does not tell us much. For what an extraordinary work it is! Combining music and dance, story and acting, scenery, costumes, and more, the final result can be enjoyed by countless audiences who may not know Italian—although that skill can come in handy—but who appreciate the incredible talent of a long line of composers and librettists whose work has been performed and is still being performed by remarkable casts of singers, dancers, musicians, set designers, and others ever since the late 16th century. Moreover, opera is a "work in progress," having evolved over centuries as it was fashioned by different cultures and countries, with Italian, French, German, English, Russian, American, and many other varieties, and reshaped by different currents and tastes, from the baroque through the classical and romantic periods, and more recently influenced by neo-classicism, serialism, minimalism, and whatever comes next. Will opera still be around for another century? That is a question that will not be answered here, but this book does give us every reason to hope so.

This *Historical Dictionary of Opera* looks back on a very long history and follows it to the present time, starting with an introduction that provides a deep and also a broad overview, helping us to make sense of the many different and sometimes contradictory influences and trends. Since there are so many events and persons, an occasional look at the chronology can help readers keep track. Even more helpful is the dictionary section, with numerous entries on composers, librettists, singers, and conductors, as well as essential terminology, stylistic movements, and some of the major features of opera. For the former, it goes beyond mere biodata and looks into the careers of pivotal persons, and for the latter, it does more than offer a simple definition but also explains what they mean in practice, offering suitable examples. So, more than just information, there is a degree of insight that can be gleaned from what is hardly a dull compendium of facts. And those who want to know more can always look up some of the many articles and books included in the bibliography.

This obviously was a very demanding and time-consuming task, which required more than merely an ability to track down the facts but to understand them, put them in context, and explain what they mean for opera per se. And that is not the sort of knowledge that can be accumulated just for the purposes of writing a book. Indeed, in a sense the author has been writing this book for decades, ever since he started his career almost 30 years ago, and especially during his long tenure as professor of music history at West Chester University of Pennsylvania, where he has been teaching since 1991. His specialization is 19th-century Italian opera as well as contemporary theories of instrumental form in the 18th and 19th centuries, but his interests range far wider. In addition to lecturing, he has written articles and reviews for various specialized music journals and has contributed to the *New Grove Dictionary of Opera*, the *New Grove Dictionary of Music*, the *Cambridge Companion to Verdi*, and most recently the *Cambridge Verdi Encyclopedia*. Unlike the above, this historical dictionary is not a composite work but the work of one person, one person who is very clearly fascinated by and knowledgeable about opera and also able to pass this fascination and knowledge along to others.

Jon Woronoff
Series Editor

Preface

The *Historical Dictionary of Opera* is a one-volume encyclopedia covering the history of the genre from ca. 1600 to the present in its major regional traditions (Italian, French, German, eastern European nationalist, and British), as well as touching on several that are peripheral (e.g., Spanish and Chinese). Although it is directed primarily at students—and consequently assumes basic knowledge of European music history and some familiarity with general musical terms and techniques—it may be useful to all opera lovers, performers, and composers who seek information about the development of the genre in a compact format. In consideration of series goals, guidelines for length, and the scope of the subject, and unlike publications such as the comprehensive four-volume *New Grove Dictionary of Opera* (the authoritative reference for professionals) or trade-book opera dictionaries, it is conceived as a textbook in alphabetical format. It helps the reader identify central figures, works, concepts, and trends in the history of opera through selectively chosen entries that provide essential information and integrate that content within broad social or stylistic narratives. Most entries fall into the following five categories:

Composers. Although they vary in length and detail depending on the importance of an individual for the history of opera, most composer entries deal with education and musical training, patronage, appointments and important commissions, and artistic influences that contributed to their style and success as opera composers and illustrate the development of the profession. Significant operas are characterized briefly (unless they merit their own individual articles) in relation to the composer's musical style and the nature of librettos they set.

Other individuals. Entries on particularly significant librettists, performers, impresarios, publishers, commentators, and the like focus on their contributions to the evolution of musical style, performance standards, poetry, the opera profession, and the role of opera in society.

Individual keystone operas. Highly selective entries for landmark operas include basic information regarding composition and initial production, brief plot summaries, and discussions of ways in which these works represent broad trends in musical and textual style and illustrate the categories of opera and various technical features.

Cities. Several entries cover locales that have been central to the development of opera; identify important patrons, theaters, conservatories, and composers based there; and briefly chronicle their rise to prominence (and decline if appropriate). Thus they provide geographical context and reference points for other topics.

Terms. This multifarious category ranges from vocabulary to broader topics, including aspects of musical, poetic, and dramatic style; form, technique, and genre; performance practice; production; social and business concerns; and pertinent artistic and literary movements.

Individual topics within these categories have been selected for their importance to historical trajectories, and topics that are less central have been left out. In addition, certain categories of entries—for example, those on subjects, themes, or characters shared by multiple operas—have been excluded, mostly because of limited space. For the same reason, a necessarily arbitrary division has been drawn between "true opera" and lighter satellite genres, such as operetta and musical theater, which receive minimal coverage.

This volume also includes several supplements. A historical introduction links topics through a sketch of broad tendencies and introduces names and terms to provide novice readers with access points to specific entries. Similarly, a timeline contributes a second chronological pathway for exploring the dictionary. Cross-references, indicated by boldface in the text, by direct citation (e.g., *see* PARIS), or by reference to related entries (e.g., *see also* SOPRANO; CASTRATO) then open up further avenues of investigation. Readers interested in learning more should certainly consult the extended bibliography of further readings at the back of this volume.

Such a sizable project could not have been completed without generous grants of alternate work assignment from the West Chester University Faculty Grants Development Committee, the Provost's Stimulus Grant Program, and the Sabbatical Leave Committee. Series editor Jon Woronoff made countless invaluable suggestions. Thanks go to my West Chester University colleagues Julian Onderdonk, Thomas Winters, Maria Purciello, and Ann Hiloski-Fowler for their support and interest, and for their flexibility in accommodating my schedule. Judy, Dave, Herb, and Penny were always there for me, lifting my spirits and keeping me going throughout the lengthy process of writing this dictionary.

Chronology

1550 Emilio de' Cavalieri (composer, ca. 1550–1602) born Rome

1551 Giulio Caccini (composer, 1551–1618) born Rome

1561 Jacopo Peri (composer, 1561–1633) born Rome or Florence

1567 Claudio Monteverdi (composer, 1567–1643) born Cremona

1573 First Florentine Camerata, led by Giovanni de' Bardi, active ca. 1573–1587

1587 Francesca Caccini (composer and singer, 1587–after 1641) born Florence

1589 Spectacular *intermedi* performed for the wedding of Ferdinando de' Medici and Christine of Lorraine

1592 Second Florentine academy, led by Jacopo Corsi, active ca. 1592–after 1600

1595 Francesco Manelli (producer and composer, after 1595–1667) born Tivoli

1597 Virgilio Mazzocchi (composer, 1597–1646) born Civita Castellana

1598 Peri's *Dafne*, the first complete opera, performed Florence

1600 Giulio Rospigliosi (librettist, 1600–1669) born Pistoia; Cavalieri's *Rappresentatione di Anima et di Corpo* staged Rome; Loreto Vittori (singer, 1600–1670) born Spoleto; Peri and Caccini's *L'Euridice*, the first surviving complete opera, staged Florence

1602 Francesco Cavalli (composer, 1602–1676) born Crema; Caccini's *Le nuove musiche* published Florence

1607 Monteverdi's *L'Orfeo* performed Mantua

1608 Giacomo Torelli (theater designer, 1608–1678) born (probably) Fano

1614 Juan Hidalgo (composer, 1614–1685) born Madrid

1620 Anna Renzi (singer, ca. 1620–after 1661) born Rome

1623 Antonio Cesti (composer, 1623–1669) born Arezzo

1625 Francesca Caccini's *La liberazione di Ruggiero dall'isola d'Alcina*, the first surviving opera by a female composer, performed Florence

1626 Atto Melani (singer, 1626–1714) born Pistoia

1627 Heinrich Schütz's (1585–1672) *Dafne*, the first German-language opera, performed Torgau; Filippo Piccinini's (composer, died 1648) *La selva sin amor*, the first opera produced in Spain, performed Madrid

1628 Robert Cambert (composer, ca. 1628–1677) born Paris

1631 Stefano Landi's (1587–1639) *Sant' Alessio* performed Rome

1632 Jean-Baptiste Lully (composer, 1632–1687) born Florence

1635 Philippe Quinault (librettist, 1635–1688) born Paris

1637 Manelli's *Andromeda*, the first public, commercial opera, performed Venice; Mazzocchi and Marco Marazzoli's (ca. 1602–1662) *Chi soffre speri*, the earliest surviving prominent comic opera, performed Rome

1643 Monteverdi's *L'incoronazione di Poppea* performed Venice; Marc-Antoine Charpentier (composer, 1643–1704) born Paris

1644 Tomás de Torrejón y Velasco (composer, 1644–1728) born Villarrobledo (probably), Spain; Sigmund Staden's (1607–1655) sacred Singspiel *Seelewig*, the earliest surviving complete German opera, performed Nuremberg

1645 Francesco Sacrati's (1605–1650) *La finta pazza* (originally 1641), the earliest Italian opera imported to France, performed Paris

1649 Cavalli's *Giasone* performed Venice; John Blow (composer, 1649–1708) born Newark, England

1653 Siface (singer, 1653–1697), born Chiesina Uzzanese

1656 Cesti's *Orontea* performed Innsbruck; *The Siege of Rhodes*, by various composers, the first true English opera (music lost), performed London

1657 Hidalgo's *El laurel de Apolo*, one of the earliest zarzuelas, performed

1659 Henry Purcell (composer, 1659–1695) born London

1660 Hidalgo's *La púrpura de la rosa*, the first all-sung Spanish opera by a Spanish composer, performed Madrid; Alessandro Scarlatti (composer, 1660–1725) born Palermo; André Campra (composer, 1660–1744) born Aix-en-Provence; Hidalgo's *Celos aun del aire matan*, the earliest extant complete Spanish opera sung throughout, performed Madrid

1665 Luis Grabu (composer) active ca. 1665–1694

1668 Cesti's *Il pomo d'oro* performed Vienna; Apostolo Zeno (1668–1750) born Venice

1671 Cambert's *Pomone*, the first true French opera, performed Paris; Antonio Caldara (ca. 1671–1736) born Venice

1672 Académie Royale de Musique established by Lully in Paris

1673 Lully's *Cadmus et Hermione*, the first *tragédie en musique*, performed Paris

1674 Lully's *Alceste, ou Le triomphe d'Alcide* performed Paris

1678 Antonio Vivaldi (composer, 1678–1741) born Venice

1683 Jean-Philippe Rameau (composer, 1683–1764) born Dijon; Blow's *Venus and Adonis* (ca. 1683), the first surviving all-sung English stage work, performed London or Windsor

1684 Francesco Durante (teacher, 1684–1755) born Frattamaggiore

1685 George Frideric Handel (composer, 1685–1759) born Halle; Grabu's *Albion and Albanius*, the earliest surviving full-scale English-language opera, performed London

1686 Nicola Porpora (composer, 1686–1768) born Naples

1689 Purcell's *Dido and Aeneas* performed Chelsea, England

1690 Arcadian Academy founded in Rome

1694 Leonardo Leo (composer, 1694–1744) born San Vito degli Schiavoni

1696 Leonardo Vinci (composer, ca. 1696–1730) born Strongoli; Francesca Cuzzoni (singer, 1696–1778) born Parma

1697 Faustina Bordoni (singer, 1697–1781) born Venice; Campra's *L'Europe galante*, the first *opéra-ballet*, performed Paris

1698 Pietro Metastasio (librettist, 1698–1782) born Rome

1699 Johann Adolf Hasse (composer, 1699–1783) born Bergedorf

1701 Torrejón y Velasco's *La púrpura de la rosa* (1701), the first surviving opera written and premiered in the Americas, performed Lima

1704 Carl Heinrich Graun (composer, 1704–1759) born Wahrenbrück

1705 Farinelli (singer, 1705–1782) born Andria

1706 *Frappolone e Florinetta* (probably composed by Francesco Gasparini, 1661–1727, music lost), the first known intermezzo, performed Venice; Baldassare Galuppi (composer, 1706–1785) born Burano

1707 Scarlatti's *Mitridate Eupatore* performed Venice; Carlo Goldoni (librettist, 1707–1793) born Venice; Michelangelo Faggioli's (1666–1733) *La Cilla*, the first known comic opera in Neapolitan dialect, performed Naples

1708 Egidio Duni (composer, 1708–1775) born Matera; Tomaso Albinoni's (1671–1751) *Pimpinone*, the earliest surviving intermezzo, performed Venice

1710 Giovanni Battista Pergolesi (composer, 1710–1736) born Lesi; Thomas Augustine Arne (composer, 1710–1778) born London

1711 Handel's *Rinaldo*, the first Italian opera written for England, performed London

1712 Francesco Algarotti (writer on opera, 1712–1764) born Venice

1714 Christoph Willibald Gluck (composer, 1714–1787) born Erasbach; Niccolò Jommelli (composer, 1714–1774) born Aversa; Ranieri Calzabigi (librettist, 1714–1795) born Livorno

1715 Alain-René Lesage's (writer, 1668–1747) parody of André Destouches's (1672–1749) *Télémaque et Calypso* (1714), the first work to be designated opéra comique, performed Paris

1717 David Garrick (actor and producer, 1717–1779) born Hereford

1719 Handel's first Royal Academy of Music (1719–1729) founded London

1724 Handel's *Giulio Cesare in Egitto* performed London

1726 François-André Danican Philidor (composer, 1726–1795) born Dreux

1727 Tommaso Traetta (composer, 1727–1779) born Bitonto

1728 Niccolò Piccinni (composer, 1728–1800) born Bari; Johann Christoph Pepusch (1667–1752) and John Gay's (playwright, 1685–1732) *The Beggar's Opera*, the first ballad opera, performed London; Johann Adam Hiller (composer, 1728–1804) born Wendisch-Ossig

1729 Handel's Second Academy (1729–1734) established London

1730 Mattia Verazi (librettist, ca. 1730–1794) born Rome (probably)

1732 Joseph Haydn (composer, 1732–1809) born Rohrau, Austria

1733 Pergolesi's *La serva padrona* performed Naples; Rameau's *Hippolyte et Aricie* performed Paris

1737 San Carlo Theater constructed Naples

1739 Joseph Legros (singer, 1739–1793) born Monampteuil; Carl Ditters von Dittersdorf (composer, 1739–1799) born Vienna

1740 Giovanni Paisiello (composer, 1740–1816) born Roccaforzata

1741 André-Ernest-Modeste Grétry (composer, 1741–1813) born Liège

1749 Lorenzo Da Ponte (librettist, 1749–1838) born Ceneda, currently Vittorio Veneto; Domenico Cimarosa (composer, 1749–1801) born Aversa

1750 Antonio Salieri (composer, 1750–1825) born Legnago

1752 The War of the Comedians (1752–1754) begins in Paris; Johann Standfuss's (died after ca. 1759) version of *Der Teufel is los*, the first singspiel in the modern sense of the word, performed Leipzig; Jean-Jacques Rousseau's (writer/composer, 1712–1778) *Le devin du village* performed Fontainebleau (1752) and Paris (1753)

1755 Catarina Cavalieri (singer, 1755–1801) born Vienna

1756 Wolfgang Amadeus Mozart (composer, 1756–1791) born Salzburg

1760 Luigi Cherubini (composer, 1760–1842) born Florence; Arne's *Thomas and Sally, or The Sailor's Return*, the first all-sung English comic opera, performed London

1762 Stephen Storace (composer, 1762–1796) born London; Gluck's *Orfeo ed Euridice* performed Vienna

1763 Etienne-Nicolas Méhul (composer, 1763–1817) born Givet

1767 Gluck's *Alceste* performed Vienna

1771 Ferdinando Paer (composer, 1771–1839) born Parma

1776 Ernst Theodor Amadeus Hoffmann (composer, 1776–1822) born Königsberg

1778 La Scala Theater opens Milan; Domenico Barbaia (impresario, ca. 1778–1841) born Milan

1781 Mozart's *Idomeneo, re di Creta* performed Munich

1782 Daniel-François-Esprit Auber (composer, 1782–1871) born Caen; Paisiello's *Il barbiere di Siviglia* performed St. Petersburg

1783 Filippo Galli (singer, 1783–1853) born Rome

1785 Isabella Colbran (singer, 1785–1845) born Madrid

1786 Mozart's *Le nozze di Figaro* performed Vienna; Carl Maria Von Weber (composer, 1786–1826) born Eutin, Germany

1787 Mozart's *Don Giovanni* performed Prague

1788 Felice Romani (librettist, 1788–1865) born Genoa

1789 Paisiello's *Nina, o sia La pazza per amore* performed Caserta

1790 Giovanni Davide (singer, 1790–1864) born Naples

1791 Giacomo Meyerbeer (composer, 1791–1864) born Vogelsdorf; Mozart's *Die Zauberflöte* performed Vienna; Eugène Scribe (librettist, 1791–1861) born Paris

1792 Cimarosa's *Il matrimonio segreto* performed Vienna; Gioachino Rossini (composer, 1792–1868) born Pesaro

1794 Giovanni Battista Rubini (singer, 1794–1854) born Romano

1795 Heinrich Marschner (composer, 1795–1861) born Zittau; Saverio Mercadante (composer, 1795–1870) born Altamura

1796 Giovanni Pacini (composer, 1796–1867) born Catania

1797 Giuditta Pasta (singer, 1797–1865) born Saronno; Gaetano Donizetti (composer, 1797–1848) born Bergamo

1799 Fromental Halévy (composer, 1799–1862) born Paris

1801 Vincenzo Bellini (composer, 1801–1835) born Catania

1803 Hector Berlioz (composer, 1803–1869) born La Côte-Saint-André

1804 Mikhail Ivanovich Glinka (composer, 1804–1857) born Novospasskoye, Russia

1805 Luigi Ricci (composer, 1805–1859) born Naples (probably); Ludwig van Beethoven's (1770–1827) *Fidelio* performed Vienna

1808 Ricordi publishing house established Milan

1809 Federico Ricci (composer, 1809–1877) born Naples

1810 Francesco Maria Piave (librettist, 1810–1876) born Murano; Otto Nicolai (composer, 1810–1849) born Königsberg; Giorgio Ronconi (singer, 1810–1890) born Milan; Ferenc Erkel (composer, 1810–1893) born Gyula, Hungary

1811 Ambroise Thomas (composer, 1811–1896) born Metz

1813 Richard Wagner (composer and librettist, 1813–1883) born Leipzig; Giuseppe Verdi (composer, 1813–1901) born Roncole

1816 Rossini's *Il barbiere di Siviglia* performed Rome

1818 Charles-François Gounod (composer, 1818–1893) born Paris

1819 Stanislaw Moniuszko (composer, 1819–1872) born Ubiel, near Minsk; Jacques Offenbach (composer, 1819–1880) born Cologne

1820 Jenny Lind (singer, 1820–1887) born Stockholm

1821 Pauline Viardot (singer, 1821–1910) born Paris; Weber's *Der Freischütz* performed Berlin; Angelo Mariani (conductor, 1821–1873) born Ravenna

1823 Rossini's *Semiramide* performed Venice

1824 Bedřich Smetana (composer, 1824–1884) born Litomyšl, Bohemia

1825 Léon Carvalho (theater director, 1825–1897) born Mauritius

1829 Rossini's *Guillaume Tell* performed Paris

1831 Bellini's *Norma* performed Milan

1833 Aleksandr Porfir'yevich Borodin (composer, 1833–1887) born St. Petersburg

1834 Amilcare Ponchielli (composer, 1834–1886) born Paderno Fasolaro

1835 Donizetti's *Lucia Di Lammermoor* performed Naples; Camille Saint-Saëns (composer, 1835–1921) born Paris

1836 Meyerbeer's *Les Huguenots* performed Paris; Carlos Gomes (composer, 1836–1896) born Campinas, Brazil; William Schwenck Gilbert (librettist, 1836–1911) born London

1838 Georges Bizet (composer, 1838–1875) born Paris

1839 Modest Petrovich Musorgsky (composer, 1839–1881) born Karevo, Russia

1840 Pyotr Il'yich Tchaikovsky (composer, 1840–1893) born Votkinsk, Russia

1841 Antonin Dvořák (composer, 1841–1904) born Nelahozeves, Bohemia

1842 Arrigo Boito (librettist and composer, 1842–1918) born Padua; Verdi's *Nabucco* performed Milan; Jules Massenet (composer, 1842–1912) born Montaud, France; Arthur Sullivan (composer, 1842–1900) born London

1843 Wagner's *Der fliegende Holländer* performed Dresden; Donizetti's *Don Pasquale* performed Paris

1844 Nikolay Andreyevich Rimsky-Korsakov (composer, 1844–1908) born Tikhvin, Russia

1845 Wagner's *Tannhäuser und der Sängerkrieg auf Wartburg* performed Dresden

1847 Giuseppe Giacosa (librettist, 1847–1906) born Colleretto Parella

1851 Verdi's *Rigoletto* performed Venice

1854 Alfredo Catalani (composer, 1854–1893) born Lucca; Leoš Janáček (composer, 1854–1928) born Hukvaldy, Moravia

1857 Ruggero Leoncavallo (composer, 1857–1919) born Naples; Luigi Illica (librettist, 1857–1919) born Castell'Arquato

1858 Giacomo Puccini (composer, 1858–1924) born Lucca

1859 Gounod's *Faust* performed Paris

1862 Claude Debussy (composer, 1862–1918) born St. Germain-en-Laye

1863 Pietro Mascagni (composer, 1863–1945) born Livorno

1864 Richard Strauss (composer, 1864–1949) born Munich

1865 Wagner's *Tristan und Isolde* performed Munich

1867 Arturo Toscanini (conductor, 1867–1957) born Parma; Umberto Giordano (composer, 1867–1948) born Foggia

1870 Franz Lehár (composer, 1870–1948) born Komáron, Hungary

1871 Verdi's *Aida* performed Cairo, Egypt

1872 Ralph Vaughan Williams (composer, 1872–1958) born Down Ampney, England

1873 Fyodor Chaliapin (singer, 1873–1938) born Kazan, Russia; Enrico Caruso (singer, 1873–1921) born Naples

1874 Musorgsky's *Boris Godunov* performed St. Petersburg; Mary Garden (singer, 1874–1967) born Aberdeen, Scotland; Arnold Schoenberg (composer, 1874–1951) born Vienna

1875 Bizet's *Carmen* performed Paris; Maurice Ravel (composer, 1875–1937) born Ciboure

1876 Bayreuth Festival House (1876) opens; Wagner's *Der Ring des Nibelungen* performed Bayreuth

1881 Tchaikovsky's *Yevgeny Onegin* performed Moscow; Béla Bartók (composer, 1881–1945) born Nagyszentmiklós, Hungary

1882 Gian Francesco Malipiero (composer, 1882–1973) born Venice; Igor Stravinsky (composer, 1882–1971) born Oranienbaum, Russia; Zoltán Kodály (composer, 1882–1967) born Kecskemét, Hungary

1885 Alban Berg (composer, 1885–1935) born Vienna

1887 Verdi's *Otello* performed Milan

1890 Mascagni's *Cavalleria rusticana* performed Rome

1892 Massenet's *Werther* performed Vienna; Leoncavallo's *Pagliacci* performed Milan; Darius Milhaud (composer, 1892–1974) born Marseilles

1893 Alois Hába (composer, 1893–1973) born Vizovice, Moravia

1895 Kirsten Flagstad (singer, 1895–1962) born Hamar, Norway; Paul Hindemith (composer, 1895–1963) born Hanau, Germany

1896 Puccini's *La bohème* performed Turin

1899 Francis Poulenc (composer, 1899–1963) born Paris

1900 Puccini's *Tosca* performed Rome; Kurt Weill (composer, 1900–1950) born Dessau

1902 William Walton (composer, 1902–1983) born Oldham, England; Debussy's *Pelléas et Mélisande* performed Paris

1904 Luigi Dallapiccola (composer, 1904–1975) born Pisino d'Istria, Croatia

1905 Michael Tippett (composer, 1905–1998) born London; Richard Strauss's *Salome* performed Dresden

1906 Dmitry Shostakovich (composer, 1906–1975) born St. Petersburg

1911 Richard Strauss's *Der Rosenkavalier* performed Dresden; Gian Carlo Menotti (1911–2007) born Cadegliano

1913 Benjamin Britten (composer, 1913–1976) born Lowestoft

1918 Leonard Bernstein (composer, 1918–1990) born Lawrence, Massachusetts

1923 György Ligeti (composer, 1923–2006) born Diciosânmartin, Romania; Maria Callas (singer, 1923–1977) born New York

1925 Berg's *Wozzeck* performed Berlin

1926 Hans Werner Henze (composer, 1926–) born Gütersloh, Germany; Joan Sutherland (singer, 1926–2010) born Sydney

1928 Weill's *Die Dreigroschenoper* performed Berlin

1929 Henri Pousseur (composer, 1929–2009) born Malmedy, Belgium

1933 Krzysztof Penderecki (composer, 1933–) born Dębica, Poland

1934 Marilyn Horne (singer, 1934–) born Bradford, Pennsylvania; Harrison Birtwistle (1934–) born Accrington, England

1935 John C. Eaton (composer, 1935–) born Bryn Mawr, Pennsylvania; Luciano Pavarotti (singer, 1935–2007) born Modena

1937 Philip Glass (composer, 1937–) born Baltimore

1945 Britten's *Peter Grimes* performed London

1947 John Adams (composer, 1947–) born Worcester, Massachusetts

1949 Dallapiccola's *Il prigioniero* broadcast Radio Audizioni Italiane (stage premier Florence, 1950)

1950 Menotti's *The Consul* performed Philadelphia

1951 Stravinsky's *The Rake's Progress* performed Venice; Britten's *Billy Budd* performed London; Menotti's *Amahl and the Night Visitors* broadcast National Broadcasting Company

1954 Walton's *Troilus and Cressida* performed London

1956 Bernstein's *Candide* performed New York

1957 Tan Dun (composer, 1957–) born Simao, Hunan; Peter Sellars (director, 1957–) born Pittsburg

1958 Menotti's Festival of the Two Worlds founded Spoleto, Italy

1959 Poulenc's *La voix humaine* performed Paris

1963 Shostakovich's *Ledi Makbet Mtsenskogo uyezda* (*Lady Macbeth of the Mtsensk District*, composed 1930–1932, premiered 1934) revived as *Katerina Izmaylova* and performed Moscow

1966 Metropolitan Opera Company moves to Lincoln Center

1968 Dallapiccola's *Ulisse* performed Berlin

1969 Pousseur's *Votre Faust* (written 1960–1967) performed Milan; Penderecki's *The Devils of Loudun* performed Hamburg

1970 Tippett's *The Knot Garden* performed London

1973 Britten's *Death in Venice* performed Snape Maltings, England

1976 Glass's *Einstein on the Beach* performed Avignon, France

1978 Ligeti's *Le Grand Macabre* performed Stockholm

1980 Eaton's *The Cry of Clytaemnestra* performed Bloomington, Indiana

1981 Karlheinz Stockhausen's (1928–2007) *Licht* cycle of seven operas created 1977–2003, staged individually 1981–2011 in Milan, Leipzig, Amsterdam, Stuttgart, Munich, and Cologne

1983 Bernstein's *A Quiet Place* performed with *Trouble in Tahiti* in Houston

1986 Birtwistle's *The Mask of Orpheus* performed London

1987 Adams's *Nixon in China* performed Houston

1991 Meredith Monk's (1942–) *Atlas* performed Houston; Adams's *The Death of Klinghoffer* performed Brussels

1994 Birtwistle's *The Second Mrs. Kong* performed Glyndebourne

1998 Tan's *Peony Pavilion* performed Vienna

2003 Thea Musgrave's (1928–) *Pontalba* performed New Orleans, Louisiana; Teatro La Fenice reopens (rebuilt 2001–2003 following 1996 fire)

2004 Teatro alla Scala reopens after extensive renovations (2002–2004)

2005 Adams's *Doctor Atomic* performed San Francisco

2006 Tan's *The First Emperor* performed New York

2009 Glass's *Kepler* performed Linz

2010 Henze's *Gisela! or The Strange and Memorable Ways of Happiness* performed Gladbeck, Germany

2011 Judith Weir's (1954–) *Miss Fortune* premiered Bregenz, Austria

Introduction

Opera, at its finest one of humankind's most sublime artistic achievements, is an often high-minded theatrical entertainment in which a play enacted onstage is sung either entirely or to a significant extent. The most encompassing art form, it combines music (both vocal and instrumental), poetry and/or prose (the libretto), acting, and related media such as dance, mime, set painting, costuming, stage machinery, lighting, and other special effects. And its diverse elements are unified by plot, dramatic theme, or broad artistic conception. The proportion of sung versus recited lines varies, a number of subspecies such as French opéra comique and German singspiel alternating spoken dialogue and songs, as does the level of artistic ambition. Consequently the distinction between opera and popular musical theater is sometimes unclear. The term was first connected with musical drama in the early 17th century through the designation *opera scenica* (scenic or theatrical work), one of numerous alternatives for the more common *dramma per musica*.

THE 17TH CENTURY

Apart from the liturgical dramas of the 12th century, which may be viewed as a distant predecessor, opera arrived relatively late in the history of European music. Born of Humanist hubris, ambition, and optimism, its invention required a quarter century of discussions concerning the power of ancient Greek music and experimentation in private and public entertainments with recapturing the intense expressive effect of ancient tragedy through a rhetorical combination of music and poetry. This creative process involved two successive artistic academies in Florence. Giovanni de' Bardi's first Florentine Camerata conceptualized opera in the 1570s and 1580s and devised the *stile rappresentativo*, later termed recitative, as the means by which dialogue could be sung. Jacopo Corsi's second Camerata would put theory into practice in the 1590s to produce the first complete operas, beginning with *Dafne* by Jacopo Peri, Giulio Caccini, and others, and with Peri's version of *Euridice*. These early works grew out of established traditions—those of the *intermedio* and the pastoral play with music, for example—in which music enhanced often lavish aristocratic theatrical productions that celebrated important occasions with splendid effect to convey the power of the court.

Stories were drawn from classical mythology, in which the associations of Apollo and Orpheus with music rationalized their singing, as did the pastoral affinities of other characters.

The earnestness of these initial attempts and their relegation of music to a supporting role dominated by recitative hamstrung the new genre, as Florence's elite continued to prefer more elaborate alternatives. This perceived shortcoming was addressed by Claudio Monteverdi in his first opera for the court of Mantua, *Orfeo*, which enlarged the role of songlike *canzonette* and madrigals, instrumental music, dances, and stage effects, combined in large-scale scene complexes. However, as in Florence, other types of musical entertainments like *intermedi* and ballets, as well as spoken plays and outdoor spectacles, remained far more frequent and popular. Sacred opera had been introduced in Rome simultaneously with the first Florentine productions by Emilio de' Cavalieri through his *Rappresentatione di Anima et di Corpo*. It flourished there when the Barberini family was in power from the 1620s through the 1650s (except for the decade 1644–53, when their extravagant spending on such entertainments contributed to their banishment). Its development was led by the librettist Giulio Rospigliosi, whose humanized treatments of the lives of saints and medieval epics incorporated comic *contrascene* and were often staged to spectacular effect.

Opera was transplanted to Venice and its inauguration as a public entertainment supported by ticket sales begun by the composer/singer Francesco Manelli and his librettist Benedetto Ferrari, starting with *Andromeda* in 1637. It quickly became one of the city's premier attractions for local nobles, diplomats, wealthy businessmen, and tourists. Its new brand of classical historical opera—Monteverdi's *L'incoronazione di Poppea* appears to have been the first example—catered to the taste of public audiences, symbolizing the greatness of Venice by analogy to ancient Rome and combining heroic and comic elements in plot-driven librettos. The introduction of more human characters in historical rather than mythological contexts raised the perpetual issue of plausibility in sung theater. Commercial success brought about the initial development of the Italian operatic system, spawning numerous competing theaters opened by enterprising aristocrats and a calendar of operatic seasons that catered to its audiences' schedules, and accelerated the pace of operatic creation, making opera a persistent enterprise. This success saw the emergence of the entrepreneurial impresario and advances in theater design, set construction, and stage machinery, led by the architect Giacomo Torelli. And it contributed to the rise of specialist composers such as Francesco Cavalli and Antonio Cesti who cultivated "aria opera" dominated by virtuoso performances that featured singing in the new bel canto style. The operatic castrato rose in prominence during this period: by 1680 the male lead in serious drama was normally a castrato, this remarkable vocal type being considered ideal for heroic parts. In short, this line of development tipped the balance of artistic purpose from idealized aesthetic enrichment toward quasi-popular entertainment.

Beginning in the 1640s, opera was disseminated across Italy, particularly in Naples, and to the rest of Europe by Venetian touring companies, including a group or groups known as the Febiarmonici, following the example of commedia dell'arte troupes. Their productions, pervaded by Cavalli's operas in the 1650s and 1660s, would secure the dominance of bel canto concert opera during that period. As opera spread, composers' careers became more cosmopolitan: Cesti, an Italian who spent the majority of his adult life in Austria, provides the most prominent example. Through this process, Italian opera became the springboard for the development of localized styles elsewhere, notably in France and England.

French operatic activity centered on the court of Versailles and associated theaters in Paris, developing there in rivalry with imported Italian opera, which arrived under the endorsement of Cardinal Mazarin in 1645 and eventually featured operas by Cavalli and others. In an effort to control political content and maintain quality, Louis XIV granted a patent initially to Pierre Perrin and Robert Cambert in 1669, then to Jean-Baptiste Lully and Philippe Quinault, to establish the Académie d'Opéra (the Académie Royale de Musique under Lully) along the lines of other academies that had been launched in the 1660s. In their *tragédies en musique*, beginning with *Cadmus et Hermione* (1673) and including such masterpieces as *Alceste, ou Le triomphe d'Alcide*, Lully and Quinault combined elements of the court ballet (*ballet de cour*), the comédie-ballet (a spoken play with musical interpolations), the pastorale (a pastoral play with music), and spoken tragedy, emphasizing dance, chorus, and special effects in an attempt to outdo the Italians and create a style aligned with court taste. Owing to Lully's patent, these pioneering works entrenched conventions such as the French overture and the divertissement that would govern *tragédie lyrique* through the middle of the 18th century until the arrival of Christoph Willibald Gluck and others in the 1770s.

The French style was almost immediately carried to England by the expatriates Luis Grabu and Robert Cambert, where it received a congenial welcome in part because Charles II had spent part of his exile in Paris during the Commonwealth. In England it combined with features of Italian opera, which had been known there through musical scores (though probably not performed) since the 1650s, and the long-standing tradition of the masque. Composers, most notably John Blow and Henry Purcell, synthesized these styles into their semi-operas (plays with masque) and all-sung operas, resulting most prominently in Purcell's masterpiece *Dido and Aeneas*.

THE 18TH CENTURY

During the 18th century the preeminent operatic genre in Italy and through-out most of Europe was the *dramma per musica*, now more commonly termed opera seria, which was cultivated in court settings as well as independent theaters run by coalitions of aristocrats as elevated, edifying entertainment. It represented a classicizing reform of the Venetian style, which was viewed in some circles as undisciplined and coarse. The agenda for this reform was set beginning in the 1690s by Apostolo Zeno's Accademia degli Animosi and by the Arcadian Academy, which eventually included Pietro Metastasio, the most revered librettist of the century. Amounting to an elegant simplification of language and form that rejected the mannerisms of the poet Giambattista Marino and his followers—their bizarre, sometimes licentious subjects, distortions of syntax, and indulgent metaphors—and advocating instead a more reasoned style informed by Homer, Dante, and Petrarch, it attempted to reclaim for opera the high ground of moral edification.

Beginning with Alessandro Scarlatti, the development of a correspondingly direct and dignified musical style was particularly associated with Naples and the composers and singers who worked there, many of them products of its system of orphanage conservatories. Its most illustrious graduates included Nicola Porpora, Leonardo Vinci, Leonardo Leo, and Giovanni Battista Pergolesi in the first half of the century and extended through Niccolò Jommelli, Tommaso Traetta, Giovanni Paisiello, and Domenico Cimarosa in the second half to Saverio Mercadante and Vincenzo Bellini in the 19th century. The *galant* bel canto music most associated with the Arcadian style in the early to mid-18th century, which was invented by Vinci, Pergolesi, the German Johann Adolf Hasse, and numerous others, projected a corresponding aesthetic of naturalness, decorum, and simplicity. The style's good manners were reinforced by its grounding in broadly accepted poetic, dramatic, and musical norms such as standardized stanzaic forms and rhyme schemes; the unities of time, place, and action; and the conventional alternation of recitatives and da capo arias, as well as stylized, symbolic expressions of emotion guided by the doctrine of the affections. Opera seria dominated the aristocratic theater not only in Italy but also in major cities elsewhere (apart from France), for example London, Vienna, Berlin, and Dresden.

Across the second half of the century, these conventions were challenged increasingly by new generations of librettists and composers, including the critic Francesco Algarotti, librettists Mattia Verazi and Ranieri Calzabigi, and composers such as Jommelli, Traetta, and Christoph Willibald Gluck, whose novelties were nurtured by sympathetic theater managers, performers, and aristocratic patrons. These innovators, who were influenced by the more diverse resources and spectacle of French opera and by the archeological rediscovery of classical architecture, and who were averse to the perceived expressive restrictions imposed by Arcadian conventions and Metastasio's hegemony and disaffected with aria opera and the Italian castrato star system, adopted the goals of greater verisimilitude, naturalness, and dramatic conviction.

Their efforts met the least resistance outside of the doctrinaire Italian orbit in artistically open-minded, often Francophile courts like Vienna, Mannheim, Stuttgart, Dresden, St. Petersburg, and Parma. And initially novelties appeared most frequently in anything-goes genres like the *festa teatrale* and *azione teatrale* (for example, Gluck's *Orfeo ed Euridice* for Vienna). But by the 1780s even formal opera seria routinely included progressive features: exploration of new, nonclassical subjects; staged deaths; more duets and other ensembles—including act-ending finales—at the expense of arias; less static set-piece forms like the *rondò*; increased presence of chorus and ballet; larger orchestras and more colorful scoring; more frequent obbligato recitative; and recitative-like declamation within arias. Thus it embodied compromises between the French and Italian and the old and new manners, exemplified in various works by Antonio Salieri, Niccolò Piccinni, and Wolfgang Amadeus Mozart (e.g., in *Idomeneo, re di Creta*). This transformative movement eventually infiltrated even the more hidebound Italian centers such as Naples, with Venice playing a leading role in replacing the Metastasian *lieto fine* with tragic endings, paving the way for 19th-century tragic *melodramma*.

In France, even after Lully's death his *tragédies en musiques* dominated the repertory in revivals until Gluck's operas appeared in Paris in the 1770s. Their primacy, buttressed by the Académie Royale de Musique, was challenged mainly by Jean-Philippe Rameau's operas of the 1730s and 1740s, which revived the genre as new works were becoming less frequent, and by isolated productions by other composers, for example Marc-Antoine Charpentier's *Médée*. Rameau's works sparked notable controversy by shifting the text-music balance toward music while keeping the Italianate *galant* style at arm's length through their complex harmonic progressions, and by his adherence to Lully's fluid interplay between lyrical melody and declamation and his emphasis on spectacle, chorus, and dance. During the same period, new types, such as the less formalized, less high-minded *opéra-ballet* popularized by André Campra, also gained an increasing presence.

Although *tragédie en musique* was attacked by the liberal philosophes during the War of the Comedians in the 1750s for its antiquated musical style and its associations with the French academies and the cultural status quo, it still contributed to mid-18th-century adaptations of Italian opera by Gluck and others. And, ironically, the controversy prompted a short-lived renewal of interest in the genre. Importation of Italian opera buffa and intermezzo sparked a prickly rivalry between advocates of the French and Italian styles, and reciprocal influences occurred as composers sought compromises and enriched their resources by drawing on competing idioms. The arrivals of Gluck and Piccinni in the 1770s brought a rapprochement between the French and Italian traditions, establishing a more international musical language that prevailed in French serious opera into the 19th century and prefigured 19th-century syntheses in France, Italy, Germany, and elsewhere.

Despite the continuing importance of opera seria and *tragédie en musique* in the 18th century, the most progressive aspect of 18th-century opera—and the aspect most in tune with Enlightenment ideals and the democratization of culture—was the development of lighter alternatives to historical or mythological heroic opera. These new comic genres incorporated more current, familiar, and culturally relevant subject matter directed toward a socially diverse audience, and in some cases forged a local connection through the use of regional dialects. Their music was less affected, and in certain respects more "natural" and popular in style, putting less emphasis on individual vocal agility and more on convincing delivery of lines and the intricacies of ensemble interaction. Unencumbered by costly prima donnas and castratos, comic opera was less expensive to produce and therefore more susceptible to revivals and longer production seasons and more affordable for audiences. Because the stakes were lower, it often served as a proving ground for young composers who then alternated between serious and comic opera for the remainder of their careers.

The birth of comic opera in Italy coincided with and likely resulted in large measure from shedding comic scenes from opera seria pursuant to the Arcadian reforms. It began with intermezzos performed between acts of serious operas in Venice as early as 1706, a practice transplanted to Naples by the 1720s, resulting in the most famous work in the genre, Pergolesi's *La serva padrona* (1733). Full-length comic opera (eventually termed opera buffa) developed simultaneously but took the opposite geographical path, appearing initially in Naples in the first decade of the century, often featuring parts for commoners in Neapolitan dialect, and spread to Venice and elsewhere by the 1740s. Although invented by lesser lights, it was soon taken up by such established composers of opera seria as Alessandro Scarlatti (a single *commedia*), Leonardo Vinci, and Leonardo Leo.

Both the intermezzo and opera buffa explored issues of class and social mores, often in contemporary domestic settings. Based initially on the lowbrow themes of the commedia dell-arte, its situations and plots were treated with increasing maturity in midcentury Venice in the librettos of Carlo Goldoni, who humanized its characterization of individuals and emphasized ensemble interaction in duets and most notably in central finales occurring at the end of act 1 or 2. Such composers as Baldassare Galuppi became adept at writing rhythmically energized music sufficiently pliable in phrase structure to facilitate natural banter. During the second half of the century, successful comic operas were quickly exported as far away as Lisbon and St. Petersburg and were responsible for establishing the international reputations of such composers as Piccinni, Paisiello, and Cimarosa. Composers competed to enlarge the central finale as their command of flexible dialogue and dynamic pacing increased, and they escalated comic mannerisms such as patter song in establishing the vernacular of the buffo bass and other vocal types. While much of this development went on in Italian theaters, the emergence of opera buffa as a vehicle for sophisticated political, social, and cultural commentary centered on Vienna's Burgtheater in the 1780s. With Joseph II's backing, the company assembled a world-class cast of singing actors to perform opere buffe by Wolfgang Amadeus Mozart and others, notably *Le nozze di Figaro*, *Don Giovanni*, *Così fan tutte*, and (under Leopold II) Cimarosa's *Il matrimonio segreto*.

In Paris, opéra comique grew out of the *comédies en vaudevilles* of the annual fair theaters, which adapted popular songs for insertion within spoken plays. Its development was sparked in the 1750s by an Italian troupe performing intermezzos—most famously *La serva padrona*—and opere buffe and by the success of Jean-Jacques Rousseau's *Le devin du village*, a knock-off of the Italian intermezzo. By the 1760s, newly composed, often Italianate songs termed *ariettes* replaced the borrowed vaudeville melodies, resulting in opéra comique as currently defined, which alternates spoken dialogue with newly composed songs and which was initially promoted by Egidio Duni and François-André Danican Philidor and epitomized in the 1780s by André-Ernest-Modeste Grétry. Following the Revolution, opéra comique supplanted the *tragédie lyrique* as the preeminent French genre and adopted its seriousness of purpose, grandeur, expansive use of chorus, imposing orchestration, and spectacular scenic effects in presenting melodramatic, politicized, moralizing topics that served republican ideals.

English ballad opera developed under the influence of imported French *comédies en vaudevilles*, beginning with John Gay's *The Beggar's Opera* in 1728, and featured a similar combination of spoken dialogue and borrowed popular melodies. The musical pasticcio, in which arias from different operas, often by different composers, combined with new recitatives, dominated theaters in the middle of the century. However, beginning in the 1760s, England also saw experiments with operas by single composers having either spoken dialogue or, more rarely, composed-out recitatives, notably Thomas Arne's *Thomas and Sally*. Although serious opera in German had appeared in the 17th century and was supported by a stable company in Hamburg, it was far less common than opera imported from Italy or France. Thus singspiel (at first an existing spoken play to which adapted melodies were added, later a newly written play sporting increasingly ambitious original music), which took its cue from translated ballad opera and later rustic sentimental opera, became the first native genre that received widespread performance during the second half of the century. It began in Leipzig, then took root particularly in Berlin and in southern Germany and Vienna, where it competed with opera buffa and opéra comique. Joseph II's National-Singspiel (established 1778) and a subsequent enterprise treated it with the same seriousness of purpose as its rival genres in an effort to bolster German-language theater. While significant successes were few and far between, these efforts produced several monumental representatives of the type, most prominently Mozart's *Die Entführung aus dem Serail* and *Die Zauberflöte*.

By the end of the 18th century the various brands of comic opera far surpassed their serious counterparts in frequency of performance and social relevance. And their predominance is reflected in their assimilation of serious elements in such mixed types as sentimental opera, *opera semiseria*, and rescue opera, as well as in the more heroic, melodramatic, and spectacular treatments of opéra comique.

THE 19TH CENTURY

During the 19th century, Paris would become the glittering operatic jewel of Europe, a beacon for composers, librettists, performers, and audiences alike. The French Revolution had temporarily ended the government monopoly on opera and dissolved the theatrical hierarchy dominated by the orthodox Opéra, allowing new theaters to open and encouraging the innovative Opéra-Comique and other companies to pursue different subjects and genres that addressed a more diverse range of social constituencies, at least until Napoleon reestablished the Opéra as the preeminent state-sponsored venue and took greater control of the Opéra-Comique prior to 1810. Works that idealized Republican Rome and served as democratic parables, *faits historiques* that centered on recent events and glorified the heroism of commoners, and adventure plots featuring gloomy Gothic settings were enhanced by a new level of realism in the scenery, costuming, and cataclysmic and picturesque special effects of their productions, prefiguring *grand opéra* of the 1830s and the *Gesamtkunstwerk* of Richard Wagner. Escalating Italian influence surfaced in French operas at the Opéra-Comique and Opéra by the expatriates Luigi Cherubini and Gaspare Spontini, as well as those of native son Étienne-Nicolas Méhul. This tendency was reinforced by Napoleon's support of imported Italian operas at the new Théâtre-Italien, which would eventually showcase works by Gioachino Rossini, Gaetano Donizetti, Vincenzo Bellini, and numerous others. Their synthesis of Italianate lyricism with such traditional French characteristics as fluid vocal declamation and flexible phrasing, piquant orchestration, and harmonic enrichment became institutionalized in state-sponsored *grand opéra* in the late 1820s and 1830s, led by giants such as Rossini, Daniel-François-Esprit Auber, Giacomo Meyerbeer, and the librettist Eugène Scribe.

Targeted to dazzle its audience of passably cultured, socially and artistically conservative bourgeoisie, *grand opéra* deployed historical plots in an expansive five-act format, entwining human interrelationships with a panoramic political and religious background and treating multiple choruses as social cohorts that interact on a personal level with the principals. Standards for the genre were unreasonably high, each premier expected to outdo previous productions in its spectacular crowd scenes, sets, costuming, ballets, and cataclysmic special effects. Thus in contrast to the lighter, more modest opéras comiques concurrently promoted by Auber and Fromental Halévy to complement its appeal, it was the most prohibitively costly type of opera ever produced, limiting numbers of productions and creating a discouragingly exclusive creative environment dominated by a coterie of privileged individuals led by Meyerbeer.

Other composers as prominent as Hector Berlioz and Richard Wagner tested the waters with limited success, and the growing perception that the Opéra was inbred, corrupt, and indulgent caused a backlash after the Revolutions of 1848. It fostered the development of new genres and theaters, such as operetta at Jacques Offenbach's Bouffes-Parisiens and *opéra lyrique* at Léon Carvalho's Théâtre-Lyrique, and the more intimate, psychologically introspective, personalized works of Charles Gounod, Auber, Halévy, Georges Bizet, and Jules Massenet. By the 1860s, the excesses of *grand opéra* would mostly succumb to naturalism and more modest scale. Reduced spectacle, musical continuity created through emphasis of flexible declamation and recurring motifs linked to literary theme and characterization, subtle orchestral tone color, and chromatic harmony—characteristics in part influenced by Wagner—combined at the end of the century with fin-de-siècle sensuality and decadence to humanize characters and their situations and rouse empathy for their misfortunes.

As noted above, Italian opera was gaining an increasingly secure and influential presence in Paris and continued to dominate stages elsewhere across Europe. In Italy, political disruptions caused by Napoleon's advances, along with romantic agitation for a renewal of Italian literature and culture, broke Metastasio's perennial stranglehold at the more conservative courts and supplied the grist for a range of new plots for opera buffa, opera seria, and *opera semiseria*, many showing resemblances to post-revolutionary opéra comique. Disruption of the court system, as in France, also facilitated theater openings, initially increasing the demand for new operas, although financial constraints would eventually lead to reliance on repertory operas to flesh out seasons more frugally.

At the turn of the century, Simon Mayr and Ferdinando Paer made mainstream practice out of modifications to opera seria that had been tested in the second half of the 18th century. And they introduced new expressive and structural conventions, which would be consolidated and popularized by Rossini in the 1810s and 1820s and by immediate successors such as Donizetti and Bellini. With their librettists, they explored recent French, English, and German literary subjects and advanced the process of humanizing tragic catharsis through increasingly complex and subtle psychological interrelationships, building on precedents from *opera semiseria* and opéra comique in replacing opera seria with tragic *melodramma*. Dialogues, no longer confined primarily to recitative scenas, gained a more prominent profile in lyric set pieces, both in an expanding proportion of ensembles devoted to that purpose and even in primarily solo numbers, thanks to new multimovement formal schemata for the grand aria, duet, *introduzione*, and finale that created a balance between interaction and reflection, passionate declamation and vocalism. More populist-sounding melodies based on the lyric prototype made opera aesthetically accessible to a broader public and helped *melodramma* push opera buffa into the background (and virtual extinction by midcentury), its potential for further comic intensification having been exhausted by Rossini and others in such masterworks as *Il barbiere di Siviglia*.

By the 1840s composers and librettists began to resist in earnest the constriction of structural options imposed by the now-conventional scene forms by truncating, expanding, and otherwise modifying both their individual movements and their broad designs to adapt them to increasingly diverse dramatic situations. Giuseppe Verdi, the dominant figure in Italian opera from the 1840s through at least the 1870s, played a significant role in steering this trend, as well as in loosening the conventions for distributing time onstage among primary, secondary, and supporting roles, particularly as his clout increased with his skyrocketing reputation in the 1850s. And he became more selective about choosing original subject matter, holding out for innovative and uniquely characteristic situations that allowed him to create individualized works, each evoking a particular color in its psychological, musical, social, and visual ambience. In this endeavor he drew heavily on French opera, exploiting glaring clashes between comic and serious elements, integrating small forms into broad scene complexes, and fusing French and Italian vocal styles, enlarging his orchestral palette in a complex synthesis that would characterize Italian opera into the 20th century. He also put an end to traditional number opera by demanding unaccustomed respect for the musical integrity and cohesiveness of entire works. Verdi's intimidating presence imposed virtually insurmountable hurdles for lesser composers of his own generation and the next (e.g., Saverio Mercadante and Amilcare Ponchielli), and even the *giovane scuola* of the 1890s numbered mainly one-hit verismo composers such as Pietro Mascagni and Ruggero Leoncavallo.

Only Giacomo Puccini was able to establish himself as a viable successor to Verdi by combining aspects of verismo, domestic tragedy, and light opera across the turn of the century.

In Germany and Austria, singspiel embraced the artistic ambition modeled by *Die Zauberflöte*, adopting attributes of rescue opera (as in Ludwig van Beethoven's *Fidelio*) and themes of northern European romanticism (as in Louis Spohr's *Faust*), while a more comic strain continued to be cultivated by Otto Nicolai and others. Composers and librettists combined set pieces into more substantial scene complexes; unified their music with recurring melodies and motifs; expanded the roles of solo ensembles, choruses, and dance; and provided for stunning special effects. They embraced such weighty literary themes as the relationship between material and spiritual existence, the reunion of mankind with nature, and redemption through self-denial, as well as the romantic supernatural and other elements of anti-rationalism, nature worship, nostalgia, and nationalist folklore. Periodic attempts to substitute composed-out recitative for spoken dialogue converted singspiel into romantic grand opera. These tendencies, seen in the first half of the 19th century in works by E. T. A. Hoffmann and Heinrich Marschner, were popularized particularly by Carl Maria von Weber's *Der Freischütz* and reached their apex in the early operas of Wagner.

Wagner began his career attempting to cultivate German operas modeled on a broad range of established genres, from German romantic opera (*Die Feen, Der fliegende Holländer*) to Italian and French comic opera (*Das Liebesverbot*) and French *grand opéra* (*Rienzi, Tannhäuser*, and *Lohengrin*). His sabbatical in exile during the late 1840s and early 1850s allowed him to hold forth in print on a host of issues concerning historical and contemporary religion, politics, and society and their relationships to art and to formulate what he regarded as a superior, more encompassing category of opera, the *Gesamtkunstwerk*. It was to synthesize existing operatic models and put equivalent emphasis on all aspects of the theatrical experience—music, poetry, dance, mime, and various aspects of staging (set design, costuming, and special effects)—in presenting mythic parables based on northern European folklore that would resonate with his German audience. The resulting music dramas—*Der Ring des Nibelungen, Tristan und Isolde, Die Meistersinger von Nürnberg*, and *Parsifal*—spearheaded his crusade of promoting German pride and ambition and redeeming humanity through quasi-religious didactic/philosophical artistic experiences. Wagner's legacy loomed over subsequent generations of composers and artists in all fields, although his operatic successes were never equaled during the remainder of the 19th century, and it was co-opted for various political agendas through the first half of the 20th century and World War II.

Efforts to establish a distinct identity for Germanic opera and to counteract domination by Italian, and to a lesser extent French opera, were in due course duplicated by composers in other countries. While Spain and Scandinavia were unable to detach themselves decisively from the Italian and German traditions respectively, composers in Russia, Czechoslovakia/Bohemia, Poland, and Hungary had successes of more or less long-standing duration. Operas had been performed in those regions as early as the first half of the 17th century, and a range of traditions and genres from Italian opera seria and opera buffa to German singspiel and French opéra comique and *grand opéra* became widely familiar by the 18th. Although the first vernacular operas appeared in the 18th century, they were isolated occurrences mostly created by foreigners.

Cultivation of nationalist traditions depended variously on levels of aristocratic support; perceived need for artistic reinforcement of social, political, cultural, and ethnic identity (often related to the impetus for political, social, and cultural independence); and regard for the indigenous language. Regional styles of opera involved local historical and mythic/heroic subject matter—normally chronologically distanced from contemporary politics, although parallels were apparent—set among the historical aristocracy or in idealized rural settings that resonate with native, folkloric culture. Their music quotes from or reinterprets both native dance and song traditions, either as they currently existed or as they had been co-opted and diluted for salon settings, and ersatz stereotypes associated wrongly or not with ethnic localities (for example *verbunkos* music in Hungary). Ultimately adaptations of non-major-minor modalities and whole-tone and pentatonic scales, mimicry of traditional instruments, and brilliant late 19th-century orchestration evoking exotic or fantastic settings (for example, in the works of Nikolay Andreyevich Rimsky-Korsakov) gave a culturally idiosyncratic color to styles that to one extent or another remained rooted in international conventions for organization, vocal writing, and casting of various categories of characters.

Apart from vernacular operas in foreign styles having little ethnic identity, the first real nationalist successes came in the mid-19th century with works by Mikhail Ivanovich Glinka in Russia, Bedřich Smetana in Bohemia/Czechoslovakia, Stanislaw Moniuszko in Poland, and Ferenc Erkel in Hungary. While Moniuszko and Erkel remained isolated figures who found no prominent successors during the 19th century, the Russian and Czech traditions were more permanent, later involving on the one hand Modest Petrovich Musorgsky, Pyotr Il'yich Tchaikovsky, Rimsky-Korsakov, and Aleksandr Porfir'yevich Borodin, and on the other Antonin Dvořák and Leoš Janáček, among others. The Russian development of "realist" declamation by Aleksandr Sergeyevich Dargomïzhsky and Musorgsky in direct settings of literature by the likes of Aleksandr Sergeyevich Pushkin (*Literaturoper*) established precedents for more mainstream composers at the turn of the century.

THE 20TH CENTURY

Innovation in the 20th century took place in the context of an ingrained repertory of several dozen historical works composed mainly in the 19th century, which dominated the major opera houses. This stock-in-trade was enriched sparingly as years went by through increased attention to Mozart and through revival of works from the baroque, primarily operas of Handel and Monteverdi. Relatively few new operas entered this repertory, mainly those of such composers as Puccini, Richard Strauss, and Benjamin Britten, whose musical styles maintained ties to traditional approaches while diversifying their subject matter. Various other factors undermined support for new works: belt-tightening from the economic and social traumas of the period delineated by the two world wars; the displacement of support from the aristocracy to the state, private donations, and ticket revenues; the lack of appeal and perceived relevance in middle- and lower-class markets of a genre linked to elitist culture; the advent of "difficult" modernist styles that made extraordinary demands on listeners and performers alike; and competition from more contemporary forms of entertainment such as movies, television, popular music, and popular musical theater. The cult of novelty among the most progressive composers and their development of styles that are difficult to sustain across multiple long works (e.g., expressionism) further reduced output and contributed to the decline of the specialist opera composer and of common international and nationalist styles, which were replaced by a remarkable array of individual voices.

Composers and their librettists addressed these challenges with a gamut of strategies, extending the trend toward individualizing operas that had begun in the 19th century and had been piloted by Wagner and Verdi. Approaches ranged from miniaturism, chamber opera, and neo-classical number opera, which abandon Wagnerian grandeur and embrace the opportunities provided by smaller theaters and academic workshops (for example Paul Hindemith's *Hin und Zurück*), and comic and light opera, which attempt to bridge the gap with popular culture (for example Kurt Weill's *Die Dreigroschenoper*), to gigantism, most notably in Karlheinz Stockhausen's cycle *Licht*, which takes Wagnerian monumentality to its logical endpoint while also embracing the avant-garde deconstructive experiments that challenged traditional naturalist values and confronted the preconceptions of a conservative mainstream.

This centrifugal tendency toward idiosyncrasy, which makes many 20th-century operas resistant to categorization, is evident in their broad dispersion of subject matter. Alongside the inertia represented by various traditionalist neo-romantic and neo-verismo styles, which remained in the mix during the early 20th century and were particularly promoted by totalitarian regimes in the 1930s and 1940s, progressive composers and librettists confronted topics that had been only sporadically explored at the end of the 19th century, departing from Italianate and French naturalism and Wagnerian philosophical idealism and epic heroism partly in an effort to find subjects appropriate for their new musical resources. Symbolist and expressionist composers such as Claude Debussy, Arnold Schoenberg, and Alban Berg directed their alternately understated/allusive and hyperbolic/exaggerated musical languages toward advancing the preoccupation of Wagner's music dramas with inner motivations and psychology under the influence of Freudian and Jungian psychoanalysis. Neuroses and psychoses—frequently embodied disturbingly in female leads—were now separated from broader philosophical, religious, historical, mythical, and heroic ideals. The morbid dissociation of Debussy's *Pelléas et Mélisande*; the hallucinatory derangement of Berg's *Wozzeck*; and the sexual violence, promiscuity, and incest of Strauss's *Salome* led almost inevitably to exploration of such taboos as homosexuality, bisexuality, transgendering, and cross-dressing, as in Francis Poulenc's surreal parody *Les mamelles de Tirésias* or Britten's psychodrama *Death in Venice*. Simultaneously, a revival of comedy and operetta (e.g., Strauss's *Der Rosenkavalier* or Franz Lehár's *The Merry Widow*) provided an escapist antidote to more emotionally invested alternatives.

In other cases the range of 20th-century orchestral, harmonic, and melodic resources facilitated the projection of exotic, fantastic, or self-consciously artificial worlds having satiric goals or a comic orientation, as in such Russian folk operas as Rimsky-Korsakov's *The Golden Cockerel* and Igor Stravinsky's *The Nightingale*, or later in more grotesque manifestations such as Dmitry Shostakovich's *The Nose*. Nationalism remains a factor in these fanciful, folkloric topics, in historical operas such as Sergey Prokofiev's *War and Peace*, and in social or political satires, whether historical or current, for example Weill's *Aufstieg und Fall der Stadt Mahagonny* or Luigi Dallapiccola's *Il prigioniero*. *Zeitopern*, beginning between the wars, served up parodies of contemporary life, manners, and mores; mocked political oppression; and in certain instances examined the role of the artist, art and music, and even opera itself in contemporary society, as in Weill's *Jonny spielt auf*, as do their recent progeny, "CNN operas" such as John Adams's *Nixon in China* and *The Death of Klinghoffer*. In contrast, such cultural specificity is rejected in favor of a more universalizing agenda, and traditional linear narrative is replaced by ritual and ceremony, in operas that adapt classical myths and allegories (Stravinsky's *Oedipus rex* and Harrison Birtwistle's *The Mask of Orpheus*), which detach themselves from contemporary reality by focusing on timeless, universal themes of the human condition. So too do radical avant-garde works beginning in the 1960s, which dispense with linear plotting, empathy, catharsis, and resolution in favor of more abstract collages of ideas, sounds, and images, distancing the audience from action onstage, for example Philip Glass's cycle of portrait operas, which includes *Einstein on the Beach*, descendents of numerous other 20th-century portrait operas (e.g., Hindemith's *Mathis der Maler*).

Twentieth-century operatic music frequently derived from broader stylistic movements that were not primarily operatic but equally involved various other instrumental and vocal genres, which served as inspiration for composers seeking new directions. At the turn of the century the most prominent trends may be viewed to one extent or another as extensions of Wagnerian principles—inner drama, emphasis of poetry and other dramatic components apart from music, minimization of lyricism and vocality, and structural continuity—with which progressive musical languages were merged. The most patent connections to Wagner were seen in spin-offs appearing shortly after the composer's death (notably Engelbert Humperdinck's *Hansel und Gretel*, 1893, and Strauss's *Guntram*, 1894), many of which closely imitated his style and were guided and constrained by injunctions from Bayreuth.

More modernist adaptations took Wagnerian precepts in new directions. The symbolist works of Debussy, Paul Dukas, and Béla Bartók, beginning with *Pelléas et Mélisande*, accosted middle-class, traditionalist values, rejecting the Germanic pretense of the music drama (as well as the exhibitionism of French *opéra* and Italian *melodramma*, the sentimentality and histrionics of verismo, and the mundaneness and bleak social criticism of naturalism) and forgoing theatrical realism. Instead they concentrated entirely on psychological allusiveness conveyed by a non-Germanic musical idiom, while treating idiomatic declamation of text as a badge of non-Germanic cultural identity and increasing the importance of sonic and associative qualities of words separated from syntax and meaning.

Following its appearance in 1890s in poetry, the visual arts, and music, symbolism gained a pan-European presence and exerted particular influence in Germany (through the poet Stefan George) on the development of expressionism among the composers of the Second Viennese School and of other modernist styles. Like symbolism, operatic expressionism, exemplified by such works as Schoenberg's monodrama *Erwartung*, emphasizes inner drama. However, it operates at a much higher pitch of intensity, exaggerating the psychological trauma previously essayed, for example, in Kundry's music from Wagner's *Parsifal*. Appropriately for its subject matter, it utilizes new musical resources that are even more fervid in their effect: chromatic, atonal harmony; pervasive dissonance; and new sonic resources, among them the speechlike style of *Sprechstimme*. In combination, they create a spontaneous stream of dreamlike ecstasy and hysteria, camouflaging the constructivism of Wagner's leitmotif technique in a continuum of motivic development and, eventually, serial procedures, assiduously avoiding traditional formalism. The musical and theatrical influence of expressionism cast a long shadow, playing a seminal role in the development of modernist dramatic and musical languages in opera.

Russian and other eastern European traditions, which persisted into the first quarter of the 20th century as represented by Rimsky-Korsakov, Shostakovich, Dvořák, Janáček, and Zoltán Kodály, also incorporated elements of post-Wagnerian music drama, *grand opéra*, and other 19th-century genres. International characteristics combine with historical, epic, folkloric, and fantastic plots; elements of realism and the supernatural; nationalist preoccupations with rhythmic accentuation and pitch shapes that convey the essence of the vernacular language; and ethnically tinged adaptations—in some cases exaggerated parodies—of mainstream musical developments. Russian operas by Musorgsky, Borodin, and Stravinsky accompanied the ballet to Paris in the second decade of the century. Alongside the Spanish music of Isaac Albéniz and Manuel de Falla, oriental exoticisms, and American popular music, they exerted a profound influence on developments between the world wars, particularly in modernist stagings by Sergey Diaghilev and Vsevolod Meyerhold, which featured dehumanized figures that encouraged emotional detachment by the audience. Similarly in Italy, the international expansion of options, which had begun with the *scapigliati* in the last quarter of the 19th century and continued until opera was eventually superseded by film music and ballet, included a judicious internalization of Wagnerian formal and expressive approaches. Continuity, emphasis of the orchestra, reminiscence motifs, progressive harmony, and plastically constructed, motivically oriented melody—tinged with elements of symbolism and expressionism—are heard to varying degrees, for example in Gian Francesco Malipiero's operas of the 1920s.

Between the world wars, operatic innovation turned against post-Wagnerian approaches, particularly post-romantic expressive extremes and extravagances of casting, orchestration, and production, as well as the apparent disdain for structure and (at times) morality that was associated with symbolism and expressionism. The economic realities of the time encouraged composers to blunt modernist idioms and adapt them to the more familiar and accessible environments of comedy and musical theater, while they addressed structural concerns by reconsidering traditional forms. These tendencies were represented by the neo-classicisms of Stravinsky and others, their nostalgic, often parodistic recollection of past musical styles and number opera, whether baroque, classical, or romantic, variously implying criticism of present-day culture and distancing their audiences from the theatrical experience. Similarly, the *Zeitopern* of Weill, Hindemith, and Ernst Krenek, which examined current subjects from modern, generally urban society with an ironic detachment often reinforced by their stagings, delivered political or social critiques that made them as popular with their Weimar Republic audiences as they were unpopular with the Nazi regime. The United States became a center for operatic experimentation—part of its broader emergence in music and the arts generally in the 20th century—as it provided a refuge from the Nazis (and later the Stalinists) for numerous composers (for example Schoenberg, Weill, Krenek, Hindemith, and Stravinsky).

Following World War II the leading modernists—the serialist composers of the Darmstadt school and their followers, represented most prominently by Pierre Boulez early in his career—largely abandoned opera. They questioned the validity of the genre and its associations with the bourgeoisie and conventional values, viewing music as an abstract constructivist enterprise unsuited to traditional theater and adopting an anti-melodic dogma and a consequent restriction of traditional expressive resources unsuited to most operagoers. They ceded the field, in part, to composers who adopted existing post-Wagnerian, post-verismo, neo-expressionist, neo-classical, and *Zeitoper* styles, embracing them either in sequence across their careers or interweaving them in eclectic mixtures within individual works, as in the oeuvres of Harrison Birtwistle and Hans Werner Henze. A tendency toward conservatism was particularly pronounced in the Soviet Union and its satellites under Joseph Stalin owing to government censorship of "modernist formalism" and anything that smacked of political dissent (e.g., condemnation of Dmitry Shostakovich in the 1930s) and to forcible promotion of socialist realism in politicized operas on contemporary or historical subjects that glorified proletarian heroism and the nation, the most successful of which was *War and Peace*. Works in more progressive styles (for example those by the Hungarian György Ligeti and the Pole Krzysztof Penderecki) appeared outside the Soviet Union or following its demise.

At the same time, postmodernist composers challenged the nature of opera and its traditional preconceptions, reimagining it under the influences of alternative theater, performance art, and the "happenings" of the beat period, film and television, and non-European musical, ritual, and ceremonial traditions, while incorporating electronic resources developed after World War II. They regarded the crux of opera as conceptual originality and consequently extended their exploration of available options to the brink of generic disintegration, at which point the designation "opera" becomes inappropriate or meaningless.

These radical reinventions of the medium appear among the works of such composers as Ligeti, Luciano Berio, Karlheinz Stockhausen, and Birtwistle, and in the most prominent, original, and influential postmodernist style, the minimalism (or process music) of Glass (and to a much lesser extent the post-minimalist adaptations of John Adams). They involve the replacement of linear narrative with a collage-like assemblage of static scenes that explore abstract, often metaphysical ideas like the nature of time, space, and existence and disjunctions between representational expression and nonrepresentational expression, between immersion and detached contemplation. Their incorporation of interactive relationships with their audience (beyond the evaluative feedback that had long been a part of the operatic experience) and introduction of aleatory (randomness), improvisation, and other indeterminate elements at various times breaks the fourth wall, erasing the lines between art and reality, stagecraft and illusion; contradicts 19th-century assumptions regarding art's preeminent role and the sanctity of the operatic experience; and calls into question the value of the opera composer in contemporary society.

Such progressive works mix various styles from within Western art music and juxtapose idioms from the European classical tradition with those of non-Western cultures, folk, jazz, and pop. They magnify the importance of dance and mime, which are often enlisted for their primitivist or folklike associations, allowing presentation of dramatic characters or ideas in multiple dimensions as singers, instruments, puppets, and so on (e.g., Birtwistle's *Mask of Orpheus*) and even inviting instrumentalists to take roles onstage, sometimes in costume (Glass's *Einstein on the Beach*). And they demand a new vocal and instrumental virtuosity of rhythmic and metrical complexity, nontraditional tuning, innovative timbres, improvisation, chance relationships, and interaction with electronic media, as well as the acting chops necessary to convey mercurial changes of mood, psychology, and personality, requiring performers to dedicate themselves to scores that sometimes put them at a disadvantage.

At the turn of the 21st century, opera faces significant challenges. While state subsidies and private endowments continue in the United States and particularly in Europe, they have suffered against other political priorities and have fallen off sharply since the economic downturn of 2008. The importance of new operas is dwindling, and the live theater continues to be dominated by the late 18th- and 19th-century repertory revolving around Mozart, Verdi, and Wagner. Puccini, Strauss, Britten, and Prokofiev count among a relatively few 20th-century composers making headway, and only a small collection of works written after World War II (e.g., *The Rake's Progress* and *Peter Grimes*) have been produced repeatedly. Novelty in the Age of the Director has largely involved reassessment and reinterpretation of aging masterpieces—recontextualizations and contemporary displacements, frequently with nonrepresentational sets—much more than launching new ones. Despite engagement with opera by numerous composers, difficulty of entry has resulted in the extinction of the specialist opera composer, at least in the sense familiar from the Italian and French traditions, with rare exceptions such as Gian Carlo Menotti, Britten, and Henze. As noted above, cross-pollination of opera with musical theater and avant-garde performance art dissolved its traditional boundaries and threatened its identity as a genre, promoting radical reinterpretations that eventually exhausted the possibilities for violating its conventions, pointing toward a creative dead end and reducing audience appeal. As a result, opera has been vastly surpassed by musical theater in the United States and elsewhere in terms of popularity, productions of new works, and financial success.

Yet grounds remain for guarded optimism. Despite financial stringencies, many companies, even major houses, have embraced the role of periodically fielding new operas as an alternative to repertory standards, and numerous composers have made at least one foray. Belt-tightening has encouraged them to create more accessible dramas and comedies involving traditional storytelling that are aesthetically inviting and can be produced with modest means. Improvements in transportation across the last quarter of the 20th century have allowed an elite cadre of devotees to pursue premiers, performers, and productions of repertory works to far-flung locales. And for the rest of us, the proliferation of recording technologies from phonograph records to audiocassettes, compact discs, video tapes, digital versatile discs, and online videos and websites has had beneficial effects. It has provided access to the panorama of contemporary styles and has contributed, among other things, to decreasing domination of the field by male composers, to revival of baroque and other operas outside the canon, and to consideration of issues of authentic performance practice (e.g., the use of period instruments or replicas, historical vocal ornamentation, and reduced vibrato). While it has reinforced the system of star performers by prioritizing commercially marketable voices enhanced by studio editing, it has also allowed new talents to be seen and heard and raised expectations regarding quality of performance across the board. And it has facilitated comparison of various productions and highlighted the advantages and disadvantages of traditional versus deconstructionist approaches.

A burgeoning calendar of opera festivals, concert programs of opera arias or other excerpts, concert performances (unstaged or partially staged) of entire operas, and movie theater simulcasts by a host of companies have also provided opportunities for younger singers, brought opera to different venues, and broadened its exposure to a new public. The introduction of subtitles in video recordings and surtitles or supertitles in the opera house has demystified the art form and made experiencing it in the original languages more feasible and appealing for a wider audience. And scholarly interest in and regard for opera has grown prodigiously since the 1970s. In short, while obstacles are numerous, opera maintains its viability and shows every sign of remaining robust as it enters its fifth century.

ACTING. A perennial butt of disparagement, operatic acting has varied considerably in its goals, style, and effectiveness throughout its history. Reflecting the high ideals of opera's initial creators (*see* FLORENTINE CAMERATA), early acting reportedly showed a commitment to psychologically moving representation of the action and its emotional substance through affective facial expressions and other physical gestures. Stage movement was apparently limited to positioning oneself in a prominent location for vocal passages and repositioning during ritornellos and other instrumental interludes. **Chorus** members were expected to act their parts in a manner supportive of the leads, adopting geometrically patterned arrangements, often an encompassing semicircle, without seeming rigid or unnatural.

Expectations for sensitive acting declined with the advent of **aria** opera in the Venetian public theater ca. 1640–60, even more so in conjunction with the cult of virtuosity in the 18th century, when **castratos** like **Farinelli** and **Senesino** made only token efforts to amplify their singing, and passionate performers like Nicolo Grimaldi ("Nicolini," 1673–1732) and **Faustina Bordoni** were exceptional. Still, theater critics advocated appropriate facial expressions and gestures, noble bearing in imitation of classicizing painting and sculpture, and dramatic engagement with other performers. And they warned against inappropriate onstage behavior, such as unnatural, exaggerated breathing or spitting; breaking character during ritornellos; interacting with members of the audience or orchestra when idle; and indulging personal habits like taking snuff. French standards for acting, which had been ambitious under **Jean-Baptiste Lully**'s domineering hand, similarly receded in the early 18th century as Italianate virtuosity gained increasing prominence, although the best performers, such as the French **bass** Claude Louis Dominique Chassé (1699–1786), still gave stirring performances. While the chorus had a much greater presence in France than in Italy, it was treated largely as spectacular décor, entering ostentatiously from the wings and arranging itself in a semicircular configuration, its members often masked and their arms folded.

The style of operatic acting and its aspirations experienced a fundamental shift in the direction of emotiveness and naturally paced interaction among characters in conjunction with the rise of comic opera (*see* CATEGORIES OF OPERA) and the popularization of artistic ideals associated with late 18th-century reforms. **Christoph Willibald Gluck** was himself credited with facilitating passionate acting by both soloists and chorus through the emotional immediacy of his music and its relaxation of conventions, potential unlocked by the **alto castrato Gaetano Guadagni**, said to have created the title role of *Orfeo ed Euridice* under the tutelage of the famous actor **David Garrick**.

Numerous other contributions could be cited, among them **Mattia Verazi**'s nuanced stage directions in his **librettos** and his detailed involvement in every aspect of the **productions** he directed; **Wolfgang Amadeus Mozart**'s investment in naturally paced comic dialogue; the increased attention given to **duets** and other ensembles in the late 18th and 19th centuries; treatment of the chorus as an interactive presence; the internalized characterization demonstrated by such innovators as the dramatically gifted **soprano** Wilhelmine Schröder-Devrient (1804–1860) under the guidance of **Carl Maria von Weber** and others; and the illusionistic approach promoted by **Richard Wagner** and his followers at the Bayreuth **Festival**. Konstantin Stanislavsky's (1863–1938) system of method acting, in which performers immerse themselves in the characters they play, was developed at the Moscow Art Theater (founded 1898) and applied to opera at his Bol'shoy Theater Opera Studio (founded 1918, later renamed the Stanislavsky Opera Theater Studio), resulting in a number of influential productions in the 1920s and 1930s that integrated singing and movement (including *La bohème*, 1927, and *Carmen*, 1935). The relatively recent involvement of theater and film directors such as Franco Zeffirelli (1923–) and Jean-Pierre Ponnelle (1932–1988) in productions crafted for video recording have continued to raise expectations regarding the realism and subtlety of operatic acting.

See also CHALIAPIN, FYODOR; COLBRAN, ISABELLA; GALLI, FILIPPO; GARDEN, MARY; PRODUCTION; VERISMO; VIARDOT, PAULINE.

ADAMS, JOHN. (Born 1947, Worcester, Massachusetts.) American **minimalist**/post-minimalist **composer** of five operatic works (beginning 1983) and other vocal and instrumental music. Trained initially as a clarinetist, Adams studied composition at Harvard University with teachers including Roger Sessions (1896–1985) and David Del Tredici (born 1937). He taught at the San Francisco Conservatory (1972–82) and was composer in residence for the San Francisco Symphony Orchestra (1982–85). From the late 1980s to the present, Adams has served as artistic director for music **festivals** in

California, conducted an array of major world orchestras, and received numerous awards, including multiple Grammys, a Pulitzer Prize (2003), and an honorary doctorate from Cambridge University.

To date, Adams's operas have with one exception been based on events, sometimes controversial, from the 20th century and have all been produced in collaboration with the American director **Peter Sellars**: *Nixon in China* (1987), on the president's 1972 meeting with Mao Zedong; *The Death of Klinghoffer* (1991), a reenactment of the 1985 hijacking by terrorists of the cruise ship *Achille Lauro* and the murder of one of its passengers; *I Was Looking at the Ceiling and Then I Saw the Sky* (1995), a love story and social parody set in the aftermath of the 1994 Los Angeles earthquake presented in 25 pop songs accompanied by synthesizer and rock band; *Doctor Atomic* (2005), concerning the Manhattan Project of the 1940s; and *A Flowering Tree* (2006), based on a south Indian folktale of the awakening of moral consciousness and showing similarities to *Die Zauberflöte*. Adams has deployed elements of his eclectic postmodernist style, which ranges from such popular idioms as rock, gospel, and rap to traditional operatic lyricism, postminimalist repetitive constructions, and atonal chromaticism, to bridge the gap between low and high art and provide sensitive and powerful readings of broad-ranging contemporary situations.

AIDA. Opera; music by **Giuseppe Verdi**, **libretto** by Antonio Ghislanzoni (1824–1893) based on a scenario by Auguste Mariette (1821–1881); four acts; premiered Cairo, Egypt, Opera House, December 1871. One of Verdi's most magnificent and familiar operas, it culminated his synthesis of French and Italian features beginning in the late 1840s.

Having declined an offer from the khedive (colonial governor) of Egypt to compose an ode for the inauguration of the Suez Canal in 1869, Verdi agreed to an opera for the new Cairo Opera House after he received the scenario for *Aida* created by Mariette, the French-born Egyptian director of antiquities. As was increasingly his custom, Verdi took an active role in expanding the scenario and revising the verses supplied by Ghislanzoni. Its scheduled January opening delayed because delivery of the imported **sets** and costumes was held up during the siege of Paris in the Franco-Prussian War, *Aida* eventually saw acclaimed premiers in Cairo and Milan (1872) and joined the general European repertory almost immediately.

Aida sets its love triangle in ancient Egypt, which faces invasion by Ethiopia. The Egyptian commander Radames loves the prisoner Aida, daughter of the Ethiopian king Amonasro, and is loved by the jealous Egyptian princess Amneris. As rewards for leading his army to victory over the advancing Ethiopians, the king grants Radames's request to free the captives, who include Amonasro, over the objections of Ramfis and his militant Egyptian priests, but also makes Amneris his unwelcome prize. Torn between love and homeland, Radames agrees to flee with Aida and reveals—when she prods him as her father has coached her to do—the route the Egyptians will take to pursue the rejuvenated Ethiopian army, information Amonasro needs to set up an ambush. However, Amneris and Ramfis overhear and arrest him immediately for treason. Amneris's love eventually overcomes her jealousy, but the implacable priests sentence Radames to entombment. Aida, who has concealed herself in the underground vault, joins him, while Amneris prays for their souls in the chamber above.

Verdi's fusion of French and Italian characteristics addressed inadequacies of both **grand opéra** and numerous Italian subjects he had rejected during the 1860s. Monumental beyond any other Verdi opera, *Aida*'s evocative locale and panoramic, quasi-historical religious and political background give multiple opportunities for spectacular tableaux in the French style. These exotic and often patriotic entertainments marshal multiple, lavishly costumed **choruses** and corps of dancers representing priests, maidens, soldiers, and slaves in front of elaborate, innovative sets, including the spectacular split stage for the entombment scene (Act 4). To evoke a Middle Eastern *tinta*, Verdi enlisted a French musical dialect consisting of modal and pentatonic scales, chromatic harmony and nonfunctional chord juxtapositions, and instrumentation charged with winds, brass, and harp. Spontaneously unfolding melodies in the French style convey psychological deflections phrase by phrase, as in Aida's prayer "Numi, pietà" (Act 1). Structural cohesion and unity of characterization is created by thematic linkages stemming from French practice. These techniques include framing recapitulations of melodies within scenes; reminiscences of melodies between scenes, such as "Su! del Nilo" and "Numi, pietà" (Acts 1 and 2); and returns of motifs associated with Amneris's cloying and vindictive alter egos, Aida's love for Radames, and the dogmatism of the priests (the latter two ideas introduced in the prelude to the opera—*see* OVERTURE).

More Italianate is the intensely personalized projection of the consequences of the political background in the love triangle and in the mind games leading to Radames's treason. **Bel canto** melody, most famously Radames's one-movement *romanza* "Celeste Aida" (Act 1), and impassioned **arioso**, for example Amneris's monologues during the trial scene (Act 4), humanize the characters and provide more intimate foreground communication against the epic background. Underneath the comparatively continuous surface, Verdi continued to rely to one extent or another on the schematic forms of Italian set pieces. These appear occasionally in their entirety, as in Aida and Radames's four-movement love **duet** "Pur ti riveggo, mia dolce Aida" (Act 3). Or following general trends in Verdi's usage, they occur more commonly in adaptations, in which they are abridged and their movements joined to more idiosyncratic sections. Amneris's confrontation with Aida (Act 2) begins with a **tempo d'attacco** "Fu la sorte dell'armi" and slow second-movement "Pietà ti prenda del mio dolore." But then the **women** sing on top of the offstage reprise of the patriotic hymn "Su! del Nilo" from Act 1, combining the typical intrusion that occurs in *tempi di mezzo* with a pseudo-**cabaletta**, followed by Aida's imploring reprise of her Act 1 prayer "Numi, pietà."

This amalgamation of French and Italian traits is represented magnificently by the grand **finale** of Act 2, in which the Ethiopian slaves are paraded before the Egyptians and eventually pardoned. It begins with a colossal choral processional and **ballet** constructed of numerous patriotic, martial, religious, and exotic melodies—the instrumental march preceding the ballet being one of Verdi's biggest hits—arranged in telescoped ABA patterns. This preface introduces an Italianate **recitative** and three-movement ensemble structured traditionally in important respects. Amonasro steps forward and pleads for his people in the *largo concertato* "Anch'io pugnai? . . . Ma tu, Re"; Radames wins their freedom, and his betrothal is proclaimed in the *tempo di mezzo* "Re: pei sacri numi"; and a colossal reprise of several of the opening choruses with the leads singing rapturous counterpoint takes the role of a **stretta** and frames the entire scene.

AIR. Term used somewhat inconsistently in 17th-century French opera for any type of distinguishable set piece. Airs fall into three main categories established in **Jean-Baptiste Lully**'s *tragédies en musique* in the 1670s. Occurring as relatively minor elements of dramatic scenes dominated by **recitative**, vocal airs (*airs à chanter*) may be solos or **duets**, trios, larger ensembles, or **choruses**, or even distinctive passages of recitative (until the mid-18th century). In **divertissements**, vocal airs, dance airs (*airs de movement*, which may or may not include singing), and instrumental airs (*airs à jouer*, **overtures** and descriptive instrumental pieces) constitute the bulk of the music. This range of options served *tragédie en musique* and *opéra-ballet* through the mid-18th century.

The *air à chanter* typically adopts a simple, unornamented, more or less lyrical style of melody in which the vocal rhythms emphasize proper accentuation of the poetry. The most common forms are binary and ternary variants and the rondeau (ABACA . . .), although more complex designs involving recitative also occur. The *air à chanter* may present monologue or dialogue and attend to a broad range of dramatic functions, from real-time action to parenthetical reflection. In many cases it lacks regular meter, obbligato accompaniment, conventional form, or definitive closure to distinguish it from its recitative context, causing contemporary critics to complain about the monotony of dramatic **scenes** in French opera.

In the early 18th century, shorter declamatory airs in binary form in the French style were distinguished from longer Italianate *ariettes*, which gave music greater prominence. More substantial, normally accompanied by **or-**

chestra and cast in versions of da capo form (*see* ARIA), and characterized by regular meter and virtuosic **coloratura ornamentation**, these *ariettes* began appearing in *opéra-ballets* of the 1710s and infiltrated *tragédie en musique* as early as **André Campra**'s *Télèphe* (1713), becoming a feature of **Jean-Philippe Rameau**'s style in the 1730s (e.g., in ***Hippolyte et Aricie***). Air and *ariette* were further distinguished from *couplets* (strophic songs), *cavatines* (short songs lacking a reprise), and **romances**. Beginning in the 1750s, *ariette* also designated newly composed set pieces (as opposed to **vaudevilles**) for one or more singers in the *comédie mêlée d'ariettes* (*see* OPÉRA COMIQUE).

By the end of the century the designation "air" was mostly limited to solo songs, while dances were termed *air de ballet* or *air de danse*, and other types of instrumental numbers received descriptive titles. It continued to be used in the 19th century as the preferred title for French solo set pieces, which sometimes borrowed features of their designs from the Italian grand aria.

ALCESTE. *Tragedia*; music by **Christoph Willibald Gluck**, **libretto** by **Ranieri Calzabigi** based on Euripides; three acts; premiered **Vienna**, Burgtheater, December 1767. Written between ***Orfeo ed Euridice*** and *Paride ed Elena* (1770), *Alceste* was the second of Gluck's three "reform" operas created with Calzabigi before Gluck relocated to **Paris** in the 1770s. A resounding hit in Vienna, it was revised extensively with a new libretto by Marie François Louis Gand Leblanc, Bailli du Roullet (1716–1786), for Paris (1776) to fulfill obligations for that city. Gluck cut, altered, and redistributed material from Vienna and added many new sections, particularly in the second and third acts, including a new role for Hercules in Act 3.

Currently *Alceste* is best known for its preface, probably written primarily by Calzabigi for the published score (1769), which constitutes a kind of manifesto of the reform movement in late 18th-century Italian opera that was shaped in great part by French tendencies. It promotes the classicizing goals of "noble simplicity" and musical enhancement of dramatic and poetic expression over the traditional subservience of Italian music to the vanity of singers and to expectations by the audience merely to be entertained. Opposing both hidebound conventions and any misplaced emphasis on novelty that undermines dramatic truth, Gluck and Calzabigi rejected impediments to the flow of the action, such as virtuoso passagework and **ornamentation**, long ritornellos, unmotivated repetitions of text caused by the conventions of the da capo **aria**, and discontinuities created by simple **recitative**. And they advocated the employment of a broad range of moods and styles to convey different situations, in particular the contribution of the **overture** and other instrumental music to dramatic atmosphere.

Alceste deploys these principles on a much grander scale than *Orfeo*. Its economical plot, devoid of Italianate intrigues, shifts emphasis from the twists of **opera seria** to the impassioned reactions of its very human characters to their grievous situation. An oracle proclaims the imminent death of Admeto (Admetus), king of Thessaly, unless someone takes his place. His wife Alceste (Alcestis) volunteers, resulting in Admeto's recovery and despair when he learns about her sacrifice. Happily she is rescued—by Apollo in the Viennese version and by Hercule (Hercules), who fights the demons of Hades to reclaim her, in the Parisian version. Amplification of this minimal narrative across an opera of approximately three hours places unaccustomed demands on dramatic singing; on visual elements such as scenery, costuming, and choreography; and on a **chorus** capable of characterizing both the Thessalian people and the denizens of the underworld.

See also WOMEN AND OPERA.

ALCESTE, OU LE TRIOMPHE D'ALCIDE. *Tragédie en musique*; music by **Jean-Baptiste Lully**, libretto by **Philippe Quinault** based on Euripides; **prologue** and five acts; premiered **Paris**, Opéra, January 1674.

Alcestis, or The Triumph of Alcides debuted amidst extended celebrations of Louis XIV's return in 1674 from the Dutch War (1672–78), during which dikes were breached to impede the French advance. Like other *tragédies en musique*, it constituted an apotheosis of the king through allegorical representation of his presumably illustrious participation in the campaign, which had also been the subject of countless news reports and other artworks. Following a prologue in which the Nymph of the Seine laments Louis's absence in pursuit of Glory, the opera presents the saga of Alceste (Alcestis), wife of Admète (Admetus, king of Thessaly), who is loved by Alcide (Hercules) and Lycomède (Lycomedes). Lycomède kidnaps Alceste, taking her by ship to his fortified island, Scyros, his escape abetted by the sea nymph Thétis, who temporarily impedes his pursuers Admète and Alcide with a storm. Admète, wounded in the battle to reclaim Alceste, will die unless she takes his place in Hades. Alcide agrees to rescue her there if Admète allows him to claim her. He then enters Hades through a portal revealed by the goddess Diana, makes fast work of the boatman Charon and the three-headed beast Cerberus, and charms Proserpine, who persuades Pluto to release Alceste. Returning to life, Alcide sets aside his own prerogatives and gives Alceste back to Admète, a union blessed by Apollo.

At its premier, *Alceste* prevailed over organized opposition rooted in jealousy of Lully's power at court and enjoyed regular revivals through the 1750s, setting the standard for *tragédie en musique* well into the 18th century. Its mythological plot, cast with gods and demigods, ignores the **unities of time, place, and action**, encompassing geographically detached locales, an extended time frame, and a secondary, comic love triangle involving companions of the principal characters. In particular, Alceste's confidant Céphise receives a disproportionate number of **airs**. And it encourages comparisons with contemporary events—Lycomède personifies Holland's illegitimate challenge to France, the siege of Scyros represents the Dutch War, Thétis's storm parallels the Dutch flood defense, and so on—while idolizing Louis XIV by equating him (as often was done) with the dauntless and righteous Hercules.

Alceste also follows the standard format of five acts, each of which centers on one main event: the abduction of Alceste, the defeat of Lycomède, the death of Alceste, her rescue from Hades, and her return to Admète. Each of these acts includes a **ballet divertissement** that presents spectacular scenic action integrated into the plot and depicted by a descriptive orchestral accompaniment (Act 1, storm; Act 2, battle; Act 3, funeral; Act 4, infernal dance; and Act 5, celebration). Choruses appear prominently throughout (e.g., the three choruses of water nymphs and gods, Thessalians, and sea nymphs and tritons in Act 1). Varying styles of **recitative** declamation convey diverging personalities, from Lycomède's belligerent arrogance to Alcide's temperate heroism. Unlike Italian **arias**, Lully's short, syllabic, dance-based airs, though numerous, avoid virtuosic display and play a relatively modest role in the drama (as in Céphise's songs in Act 2). The opera begins with a French **overture** in the conventional style that Lully had originated in his *ballets de cours* (*see* BALLET).

See also WOMEN AND OPERA.

ALGAROTTI, FRANCESCO. (1712, Venice–1764, Pisa.) Italian theater, music, and art critic and **librettist**, one of the most influential writers on opera of the mid-18th century. After training in the liberal arts in **Rome** and Bologna, Algarotti became involved in literary and scientific discourse in **Paris** (1732), where he befriended Voltaire, and in **London** (1734). In the 1740s and early 1750s he served in advisory positions to Frederick the Great in Berlin and Augustus III in Dresden. In both cities he adapted **librettos** to local tastes, and in Dresden he frequented the same classicizing artistic circles as **Johann Adolf Hasse**.

After returning to Italy in 1753 (**Venice**, then Pisa), Algarotti published his *Saggio sopra l'opera in musica* (1755), in which he criticized the lack of decorum in Italian theaters and the hegemony of singers, particularly **castratos**, and of music in general over dramatic poetry. He favored a partnership between **composer** and librettist like that of **Jean-Baptiste Lully** and **Philippe Quinault** in adapting exotic subjects susceptible to stylized operatic treatment and spectacular staging, simplifying the plot and situation, and integrating **choruses** and **ballets** in the French manner. He attached to the *Saggio* an *Iphigénie en Aulide* libretto that seems to have influenced **Christoph Willibald Gluck**'s version (Paris, 1774) and other late 18th-century "reform" operas. He was also probably involved to some extent with **Tommaso Traetta**'s Italian-French fusion operas for Parma ca. 1760. An early neoclassicist, Algarotti advocated less ornate, classically inspired opera houses incorporating stadium seating to optimize clear acoustics and sight lines, anticipating **Richard Wagner**'s Bayreuth **Festival** Theater.

ALTO. *See* CONTRALTO.

ARCADIAN ACADEMY. Roman literary academy of aristocrats, writers, artists, and musicians founded to restore good taste in the arts. Its precepts guided the development of Italian opera in the 18th century.

The Accademia degli Arcadi was established after the death of Queen Christina of Sweden in 1689 to honor her patronage of the arts in **Rome** following her arrival there in the 1650s. Under the protection of Cardinal Pietro Ottoboni (1667–1740) and the leadership of Giovanni Maria Crescimbeni (1663–1728), the Arcadians began meeting in 1690 in a woods on the Janiculum, a hill on the outskirts of Rome, and subsequently relocated among the rooms, theaters, and gardens of various palaces over the next decades. **Librettists** who belonged to the academy included the founding members Gian Vincenzo Gravina (1664–1718) and Silvio Stampiglia (1664–1725), as well as **Pietro Metastasio**, student of Gravina and one of the most influential playwrights of the 18th century, and **Ranieri Calzabigi**, author of the **Christoph Willibald Gluck** reforms of the 1760s. **Apostolo Zeno** was a member of the Accademia degli Animosi, after 1698 a branch of the Arcadian Academy that shared similar aims. The opera **composers Alessandro Scarlatti** and **Niccolò Jommelli** were Arcadians—as was Arcangelo Corelli (1653–1713)—and **George Frideric Handel** attended and composed music for their meetings (1707–08). Although it faced opposition and various crises, particularly during the French Revolution owing to its aristocratic associations, the academy survived into the 20th century, when it was reconstituted as the Accademia Litteraria Italiana.

At its inception, the Arcadian Academy attempted to reform the style of Italian poetry to reflect the simplicity and naturalness of **pastoral** literature, in contrast to the contrived complexity, formality, virtuosity, and embellishment, and the mixture of serious and comic elements, of 17th-century poetry and theater. In particular, it opposed the mannered poetry of Giambattista Marino (1569–1625) and his followers, which featured bizarre, sometimes licentious subjects, distortions of syntax, and indulgent metaphors, advocating instead a more classicizing, reasoned, elevated style theoretically informed by Homer, Dante, and Petrarch. According to these principles, poets associated with the academy and their many imitators developed conventions of genre, form, and language that would govern Italian **opera seria** through the 18th century and would precipitate the development of **opera buffa** and the comic **intermezzo**.

ARCHILEI, VITTORIA. (Active 1582–1620.) Italian **soprano** known as "La Romanina," Archilei was one of the most famous singers at the turn of the 17th century. **Emilio de' Cavalieri** mentored her in **Rome**, and she followed him to Florence in the late 1580s, where she remained in the service of the Medici family through the end of her career. She performed in the *intermedi* for several important wedding celebrations, including that of Ferdinando de' Medici in 1589, as well as other stage works including Cavalieri's *Disperazione di Fileno*, her passionate singing reportedly bringing tears from the audience. **Giulio Caccini** and **Jacopo Peri** both claimed she had sung their new music and praised her brilliant and sometimes subtle **ornamentation**. Although the death of a famous singer named Vittoria was reported as early as 1614, she probably lived into the early 1640s.

See also WOMEN AND OPERA.

ARIA. In opera, a song for one singer, normally setting Italian lyric poetry as opposed to **recitative** verse (*see* VERSIFICATION), accompanied by **orchestra** and/or **basso continuo**.

In the early 17th century the term distinguished solos in strophic form, in which successive stanzas of poetry (strophes) are set to the same music (AAA . . .) or similar music (strophic variations, AA'A" . . .), from throughcomposed **madrigals**. These arias are **monodies** accompanied by basso continuo, although ritornellos (short instrumental passages) for small orchestras of strings and other instruments frequently separate stanzas (e.g., ARAR . . . or ARA'RA" . . .). Examples, which are relatively few in number and share the stage with lengthy recitatives, madrigals, various ensembles, and **choruses**, include dance songs (*see* CANZONETTA), such as Orfeo's "Vi ricorda," and more emotionally invested, metrically flexible pieces in various recitative styles, such as the strophic variations for Music's "Dal mio Permesso amato" and Orfeo's "Possente spirto" (*Orfeo*, Act 2, **Prologue**, and Act 3, respectively).

In the Venetian-style works of the mid-17th century, **bel canto** arias in triple meter came to dominate, multiplying to as many as 50 per opera, and began to take a standardized position at the end of a **scene** following a recitative. While strophic forms remained common, **librettists** tended to reduce the number of strophes to two, and conventionalized internal forms developed for the individual strophes (ABB' and ABA'), creating the complete forms ABB'R ABB'R and ABA'R ABA'R. Although continuo accompaniment for the voice with intervening orchestral ritornellos remained standard, concertato arias in which instruments accompany the voice or punctuate its phrases appeared beginning in the 1640s and include the popular trumpet arias of the 1670s. As written, their vocal lines appear relatively plain but in practice were doubtless elaborately ornamented. By this time conventional categories of aria—comic arias, love arias, and the like—had begun to develop. One particularly important type was the lament—an aria expressing grief or remorse—which had appeared as early as *Euridice* and had become a shopworn cliché by the 1660s, many of **Francesco Cavalli**'s and **Antonio Cesti**'s operas including multiple examples. Dido's lament (*Dido and Aeneas*, Act 3) provides the most famous Italianate (though not Italian) example from later in the century. As early as 1638, **Claudio Monteverdi**'s madrigal *Lamento della ninfa* included a basso ostinato (a short **bass** melody, normally a diatonic or chromatic descent from tonic to dominant, repeated numerous times) over which the vocal melody unfolds, and later laments (including Dido's) followed suit.

Prior to 1690 the ABA'R ABA'R form lost its second strophe and became the da capo aria ABA, in which the reprise of the opening section, rather than being written out, was indicated by the instruction "da capo" ("from the head": AB da capo). The form took root first in **Venice**, after which it and its variants dominated **opera seria** during the 18th century and also served in **opera buffa**. Valuing its stable symmetry, classicizing poets connected to the **Arcadian Academy** and **composers** working in **Naples**, most visibly **Alessandro Scarlatti**, institutionalized its conventions, including its function of providing parenthetical summation, reflection, or moralizing commentary detached temporally from the real-time action presented in recitative. This purpose, which has been compared to that of the chorus in Greek tragedy, is often achieved through a poetic metaphor (simile aria). The continuo aria all but disappears by the 1720s, orchestral accompaniment reinforcing the vocal passages throughout. And arias were commonly categorized according to affect or topoi/topic (for example, "rage" arias or "military" arias, *see* DOCTRINE OF THE AFFECTIONS) or by vocal type (the virtuosic *aria di bravura* or the more lyrical *aria cantabile*). Aside from occasional entrance arias (for example Caesar's "Presti omai," *Giulio Cesare in Egitto*, Act 1), da capo arias typically follow recitatives and conclude the scenes in which they occur, their singers leaving the stage to applause (hopefully) following their so-called exit arias.

The length of arias progressively increased as the da capo form incorporated additional subdivisions, resulting in the Neapolitan five-part da capo form. The A and B sections each set a short stanza of poetry (most often four lines long). In the A section (and subsequently in the da capo) the opening stanza is sung twice framed by ritornellos (RAR'A'R"), while the B section sets the second stanza one or more times without ritornellos. The complete form plays out RAR'A'R" B RAR'A'R", the vocal passages constituting the five parts: AA' B AA'. In the opening section, the first vocal passage (A) normally modulates from the home key to the dominant (or to the relative major in minor keys), the new key being confirmed by the second ritornello (R'), while the second vocal passage (A') returns to the home key, which is confirmed by the final ritornello (R"), making the opening section tonally closed. The B section ranges further afield, modulating between more distantly related keys in music that contrasts to a greater or lesser degree with that of the A section.

By midcentury, variations of the standard form abounded. Before 1750 they leaned toward greater length and complexity through expanding and increasing the number of vocal passages in the opening section, interpolating recitative in the middle section, and intensifying the contrast between the A and B sections through changes of musical theme, tempo, and meter. (*Giulio Cesare* includes examples such as Cleopatra's "V'adoro, pupille," Act 2.) However, by midcentury—and to a limited extent as early as the 1720s— composers also tended to simplify the form in a number of ways. In the dal segno aria, the instruction da capo dal segno ("from the head, from the sign") directs performers to begin the reprise of the A section not at the opening, but at an internal point indicated by a sign, which may appear anywhere from near the beginning of the opening ritornello to the beginning of the second vocal passage, resulting sometimes in drastic abridgements (RAR'A'R" B A'R"). The opening A section could also be shortened by eliminating its second vocal passage and writing out the reprise (RAR' B A'R") so that the opening vocal passage moves from tonic to dominant and its return remains in the tonic, mimicking the exposition and recapitulation of sonata form, while the B section stands in for the development.

Alternative forms that were particularly common in opera buffa were the so-called cavatina, which consisted in effect of only the opening section of the da capo form (RAR'A'R" without B or the da capo) and the binary form AB A'B', sometimes with a final faster section (**stretta**). By the 1780s composers were increasingly turning to episodic arias consisting of a series of different melodies and textures often framed by recapitulation of the opening idea, as in Figaro's "Se vuol ballare" (*Le nozze di Figaro*, Act 1), which privileged natural psychological movement through varying moods and points of view—and dramatic progression—over classical balance and closure. Similar concerns probably contributed to the popularity of the two-movement, slow-fast *rondò*, the shift between tempos conveying a change of focus or mood on the part of the character singing (for example, Idamantes, "Non ho colpa," *Idomeneo*, Act 1). Such arias are normally dramatic, expressive, and technical tours de forces for principal characters, so naturally they were adapted and parodied in lighter genres, for example Leporello's catalog aria "Madamina, il catalogo è questo" (*Don Giovanni*, Act 1) which reverses the tempos.

At the end of the 18th century, **duets** and larger ensembles increased in importance, and the number of arias declined, encouraging cultivation of an aria form that could showcase the various capabilities of the singer within a single set piece. Consequently in the 19th century the da capo aria was replaced by the multimovement grand aria, which developed out of the two-tempo *rondò* through the definition of an additional distinct middle section. In its most elaborate form, the grand aria consisted of three separate movements: a reflective lyrical slow movement, a more energetic, dramatically active *tempo di mezzo* that incorporated an event, announcement, or change of focus that at least theoretically motivated the final reflective movement, a fast, vocally dazzling **cabaletta**. Whereas slow movements of **Gioachino Rossini**'s era typically consisted of an episodic melody that proceeded from disconnected, highly embellished phrases to more integrated coloratura passagework, beginning with **Vincenzo Bellini**'s generation it comprised a single lyrical melody that adopted a version of the **lyric prototype**. This complex of movements set multiple stanzas of lyric verse and normally followed a scena (*see* SCENE) in recitative style, which in the most extended examples was preceded by a chorus. A well-known illustration of the three-movement form with chorus and scena is Norma's "Casta diva" (*Norma*, Act 1). Through the 1830s a two-movement version of this form without the *tempo di mezzo* also appeared frequently, for example in Arsace's "Ah quel giorno" (*Semiramide*, Act 1). In the 19th century an aria for a character's first appearance onstage is called a cavatina (compare the 18th-century usage designating a shortened da capo aria)—as in the aforementioned arias for Norma and Arsace—and a principal character's aria at the end of an opera is their *rondò finale*.

The 19th-century grand aria had the advantage of incorporating a range of vocal modalities—lyrical, dramatic, and virtuosic—in its three movements, respectively. The *tempo di mezzo* also revived the real-time action within the set piece and often included chorus and *pertichini* (secondary characters), who might also sing in the opening movement and cabaletta, linking it to the dramatic matrix of the scena. As a result of the Rossini craze of the 1810s and 1820s, the form was widely imitated, often loosely, in France (*see* AIR) and Germany, for example in Marguerite's "O beau pays" (*Les Huguenots*, Act 2) and Agathe's "Leise, leise" (*Der Freischütz*, Act 2).

After ca. 1850, however, effective motivation of the cabaletta and the perceived unnaturalness of the monolithic conventionalized structure led composers like **Giuseppe Verdi** and their librettists to rely on one-movement arias like the canzone (a quasi popular song), *ballata* (a dance song), *preghiera* (prayer), *racconto* (narrative), and *romanza* (see ROMANCE) with increasing frequency, either embedded within flexibly constructed ensemble scenes or as stand-alone solos. For these arias, composers adopted a variety of forms, from conventional strophic and ternary (ABA') forms to progressing episodic arrangements, treated the lyric prototype with greater flexibility, and included frequent impassioned declamation, increasingly allowing the music to emerge seamlessly from its context and deflect through a series of spontaneously organized vocal phrases and orchestral motifs in response to the words. By **Giacomo Puccini**'s day, typically only the applause break at the end of an aria distinguishes it from its surroundings and from other monologues.

In the 20th century, unless the designation is broadened sufficiently to include any extended vocal solo, "aria" has a much more limited application than in previous eras, owing literally to the scarcity of Italian opera after Puccini. But language aside, one may legitimately question whether the diverse solos scattered among number operas like *Der Rosenkavalier*, *Wozzeck*, *Die Dreigroschenoper*, *Peter Grimes*, or *The Rake's Progress*—the ruminative monologues, the narratives, stage songs, pseudo-pop songs, or the ironic parodies of traditional archetypes—really serve the same dramatic, performative, or structural functions as the distinct virtuosic or emotive centerpieces of past ages, to which the term properly applies.

ARIETTE. *See* AIR.

ARIOSO. Operatic singing that is "**aria**-like," but not a formal aria. In the 17th and 18th centuries, arioso occurred within **recitatives**, setting recitative verse (*see* VERSIFICATION), hence the term *recitativo arioso*. Arioso is more melodious than typical recitative, often having a more patterned and fully notated accompaniment, and is performed in stricter meter and tempo. It sometimes appears at the end of a recitative to create a transition with the following aria. In the 18th century, short arias were sometimes called "arioso." Conversely, the terms "cavata" and "cavatina" were sometimes used to denote extended, clearly defined sections of arioso within recitatives. In the 19th century, the turn to multipart set pieces that include dramatically active declamatory movements meant that arioso could occur within a formal aria (or **duet** or ensemble) in a movement that was not primarily lyrical, especially the *tempo di mezzo*. In French opera beginning with **Jean-Baptiste Lully**, *récitatif mesuré* often fits the definition of arioso, as do many passages in 19th-century German operas by **Richard Wagner** and others.

ARNE, THOMAS AUGUSTINE. (1710, London–1778, London.) The most prominent English theater **composer** of the mid-18th century. Arne made his livelihood a family affair, composing music for a succession of **London** troupes that included his younger sister (Susanna, 1714–1766) and brother (Richard), who were actor-singers; his father, who handled business concerns; his brother-in-law and manager Theophilus Cibber; and probably more than one mistress among his female protégées. In addition to copious music for spoken plays, pantomimes, **masques**, and **ballets**, Arne wrote approximately 20 operas of various **categories** from the 1730s through the 1770s. They run the gamut from **ballad opera**, including a remake of *The Beggar's Opera* (1759); to English comic opera either with spoken dialogue or with music throughout, as in *Thomas and Sally, or The Sailor's Return* (1760), the first all-sung English comic opera; to fully composed serious opera with **recitatives**, for example, the three-act allegorical historical opera *Eliza* (1754), concerning Elizabeth I and the Spanish Armada, and *Artaxerxes* (1762), an English-language **opera seria** based on **Pietro Metastasio**'s *Artaserse* (1730).

AUBER, DANIEL-FRANÇOIS-ESPRIT. (1782, Caen–1871, Paris.) French **composer** of approximately 50 operas mostly from the 1810s through the 1860s (the majority **opéras comiques**) and instrumental and other vocal music, teacher, and writer on music theory. Auber is credited with originating the genre of French *grand opéra*.

The son of a well-to-do merchant, Auber was trained as a pianist, string player, and singer. Having returned from a trip to London (1802–03) in connection with the family business, Auber lived in **Paris** the remainder of his life, pursing his musical career at first as a dilettante supported by his father. After a number of string concertos, he composed his first opera, the one-act comedy *Julie* (1805), for an amateur academy that included painter and lifelong friend Jean-Auguste-Dominique Ingres. He also began composition lessons with **Luigi Cherubini** and associated with a Belgian prince residing in Paris, for whom he accompanied touring virtuosos in the prince's salon and composed the opéra comique *Jean de Chimay* (1812). After his father's death he took a more professional approach to music and made a name for himself at the Opéra-Comique (and in Germany) with *La bergère châtelaine* (1820) and *Emma* (1821).

Auber's long-standing collaboration with the **librettist Eugène Scribe**, which produced more than three dozen works, began with the opéra comique *Leicester, ou Le château de Kenilworth* (1823). Their ninth project, *La muette de Portici* (1825) on a **libretto** heavily rewritten by Scribe, is considered to be the first *grand opéra*, a story of revolution set in 17th-century **Naples** and its environs as the Neapolitans suffer under the Spanish viceroy. Its mute heroine, who has been seduced and abandoned by the viceroy's son, is sister to the leader of an unexpectedly bloody rebellion. When he is poisoned by fanatical followers, she commits suicide by magma as Vesuvius erupts.

La muette established many of the conventions of the new genre as it would develop in the 1830s: the five-act structure, specificity of historical context and locale, spectacular tableaux that involve huge crowd scenes and dazzling special effects requiring state-of-the-art technology, visual **acting** (the female lead dances and mimes her role), a broad spectrum of musical idioms from **coloratura** in the manner of **Gioachino Rossini** to exuberant songs and dances in a popular style, and a network of dramatically motivated melodic reminiscences. Alongside **Giacomo Meyerbeer**'s operas, it became one of the most performed stage works of the 19th century in Paris and elsewhere.

On the heels of *La muette*, Auber cemented his reputation with the opéras comiques *La fiancée* (1829), *Fra diavolo, ou L'hôtellerie de Terracine* (1830, supposedly based on the escapades of a recent Italian brigand), and *Le domino noir* (1837), as well as the *opéra historique Gustave III, ou Le bal masqué* (1833), all on Scribe librettos. The last, recounting the historical assassination of an 18th-century king of Sweden, was staged including a ballroom scene of 300 participants and is the antecedent to **Giuseppe Verdi**'s *Un ballo in maschera* (1859). Riding this wave of success, Auber became director of the Paris Conservatoire (1842) and sacred music director for Napoleon III during the 1850s and 1860s. And he received numerous awards, beginning with the Legion of Honor (1825). Despite his other duties, Auber continued to write operas frequently until about 1860, most prominently the biblical *L'enfant prodigue* (1850) and the opéra comique *Manon Lescaut* (1856), a domestic tragedy in the style of ***opéra lyrique***, its naturalistic depictions of urban life and its heroine's onstage death anticipating ***Carmen*** and **verismo**. Auber's last international success was *Le premier jour de bonheur* (1868).

AZIONE TEATRALE. *See* FESTA TEATRALE.

BALLAD OPERA. Eighteenth-century English comic opera (*see* CATE-
GORIES OF OPERA) that combines spoken dialogue and satirical or sentimental songs having melodies from folk or popular music, opera, oratorio, or
instrumental music provided with new words that give them a relationship to
the plot. In this respect, ballad opera shows similarities to French **vaudeville**
and German **singspiel**. Composers of art music melodies assembled in ballad
operas include Arcangelo Corelli (1653–1713), **John Blow**, **Henry Purcell**,
George Frideric Handel, and many others. The string orchestras available at
theaters that performed these works may have provided accompaniments.

Ballad opera began with John Gay's (1685–1732) *The Beggar's Opera* in
1728, and dozens of works were created from the late 1720s into the 1740s.
Sources for the genre included 17th-century plays performed with songs and
instrumental music, rare English musical satires of Italian operas, and the
comédies en vaudevilles (*see* OPÉRA COMIQUE) of the Parisian fair theaters, which included pirated melodies and were performed in London between 1718 and 1726. Gay and his arranger Johann Christoph Pepusch
(1667–1862) separated ballad opera from these other entertainments by balancing the quantities of spoken text and music and by using preexisting
music exclusively. Like *The Beggar's Opera*, other early ballad operas were
originally performed as "mainpieces" in three acts, but were often abridged
in subsequent **productions**. These and new, shorter works were increasingly
performed as "afterpieces" to spoken plays.

Ballad operas often parody British high society and politics, contemporary
values and mores, theater life and management, **opera seria**, or subjects from
folklore, history, or mythology while glorifying or sentimentalizing the lower
classes in the city or country. These themes appear in *The Beggar's Opera*,
as well as Thomas Cooke's (1703–56) *Penelope* (1728), in which the heroine
and Ulysses are lowlife Londoners. Though known primarily for his novels
Shamela (1741), a parody of Samuel Richardson's *Pamela*, and *Tom Jones*
(1749), Henry Fielding (1707–1754) was the leading author of ballad operas
(about 10) in the 1730s and 1740s following Gay's death, many tailored to

the Irish ballad opera specialist Kitty Clive (1711–1785). They include *The Mock Doctor* (1732, after Molière) and *Eurydice* (1737), whose heroine opts to remain in the underworld.

A few popular ballad operas remained in the repertory through the 18th century, and their descendants beginning in the 1760s—for example, **Thomas Arne**'s *Thomas and Sally* (1760)—point toward the operettas of **William Schwenck Gilbert and Arthur Sullivan**. Until the 1790s, ballad operas (and **pasticcios**) were the only operas heard in the American English colonies.

See also ERKEL, FERENC; VAUGHAN WILLIAMS, RALPH.

BALLATA. *See* ARIA; STAGE SONG.

BALLET. A theatrical entertainment involving dance or mime; in conjunction with opera, it may be self-contained or integrated into the action. A ballet is performed in costume and choreographed in styles ranging from formalized steps and gestures to more abstract expressive movements. In opera it typically involves a separate company of trained soloists and/or a chorus of dancers instead of the singers (or in addition to them). And while no decisive line may be drawn between ballet and less ambitious types of operatic dancing, the term is normally reserved for extended, formalized entertainment in a particularly artful style rather than a brief recreation of folk or ballroom dancing. In general parlance, the term may also refer to the musical score for a ballet or to the company of dancers.

Ballet and other types of dancing were associated with opera from the beginning, in part because of their importance in such predecessors as the Italian *intermedio*, the French *ballet de cour* (court ballet), and the English **masque**. In Italian operas of the 17th and 18th centuries, ballets occurred most frequently between acts and at the ends of operas, while shorter dances happened during the instrumental ritornellos and sinfonias of **pastoral** scenes. Although their music is seldom present in operatic scores, ballets performed between acts were frequently indicated in **librettos** from the 17th century onward. And in the 18th and 19th centuries, increasingly detailed information was provided regarding their plots—which were tangentially related to the associated opera if at all—and the names of participants, including the choreographer and other contributors to the **production**, the dancers, and the composer (normally not the composer of the opera).

Dances contained within acts are more closely tied to the opera's plot, illustrating aspects of the situation, reacting to events, providing scenic enhancement, and contributing to ambiance, for example the pastoral dances in Acts 1 and 2 of **Claudio Monteverdi**'s *Orfeo* and the *moresca* (Moorish dance) of its 1609 ending. Such integrated ballets continued in **Rome** through the 1620s and 1630s as well as in **Venice**. Although their presence declined in the increasingly **aria**-driven and cost-conscious public operas, they retained their prominence in court spectacles, for example, in Italian works for **Vienna**, notably *Il pomo d'oro*.

Ballet also played an integral role in French *tragédie en musique* from its inception, particularly in the **divertissements** that embellished many acts, illustrating scenic events such as storms, battles, ceremonies, and celebrations (*see ALCESTE, OU LE TRIOMPHE D'ALCIDE*). The role of the divertissement, and consequently of ballet, increased in the *opéras-ballets* of the early 18th century. English Restoration opera was also saturated with dance owing to its roots in the masque. Beginning in the second half of the 18th century, the efforts of choreographers led by Jean-Georges Noverre (1727–1810) to give ballet a more integral dramatic role led to the concept of the *ballet d'action*, elements of which are evident in **Christoph Willibald Gluck**'s *Orfeo ed Euridice*, which incorporates ballets into the plots of both the Tartarean and Elysian scenes of Act 2.

In the 19th century, dances ranging from lengthy ballets to brief interludes occurred frequently as spectacular elements, particularly in French Napoleonic opera (*see* SPONTINI, GASPARE) and *grand opéra* (for example the ballet of spectral debauched nuns in Act 3 of **Giacomo Meyerbeer**'s *Robert le diable*, 1831, and the *choeurs dansés* of bathers and gypsies in *Les Huguenots*, Acts 2 and 3, respectively). They also played important roles in French-influenced works of other nations, for example, the gypsies and matadors of the Act 2 finale in **Giuseppe Verdi**'s *La traviata* (1853) and the religious and political ceremonies in *Aida*. Attuned to French taste, composers habitually added dances for Parisian revivals of works premiered elsewhere, for example Verdi's *Le trouvère* in 1857 (originally *Il trovatore*, 1853, Rome) and **Richard Wagner's** *Tannhäuser* in 1861 (originally 1845, Dresden).

Incorporation of ethnic dances served as an embodiment of nationalism beginning in the middle of the 19th century, sometimes distinguishing social classes or rival ethnicities, as in **Mikhail Ivanovich Glinka**'s *A Life for the Tsar* (1836). Other examples of regionally based dances or dance-inspired vocal or instrumental music come readily to mind: the Spanish dances in the *tonadilla* (late 18th century); peasant dances in *Der Freischütz* and Aennchen's polonaise-derived "Kommt ein schlanker Bursch gegangen" (Act 2); Italian dance songs like the Duke's *ballata* "Questa o quella," *Rigoletto*, Act 1; **Ferenc Erkel**'s adaptations of the Hungarian military *verbunkos* style; the Russian or Polish folk songs and dances of **Boris Godunov**; various **stage songs** in *Carmen*; the waltzes of Viennese **operettas**; and the Russian peasant dances and songs and the ballroom dances in *Yevgeny Onegin*. In some instances a dance-infused atmosphere may be suggested primarily through orchestral music with minimal dancing, as in Verdi's party scenes (e.g., *Rigoletto*, Act 1; *La traviata*, Acts 1 and 2). In rare but prominent cases the female lead is developed most memorably through her dances, as in the mimed role of Fenella in **Daniel-François-Esprit Auber**'s *La Muette de Portici*, 1828, and the lead in *Salome*.

Dance remains a critical element of 20th- and 21st-century opera. Well-known examples include the fanciful anthropomorphisms of **Maurice Ravel**'s *L'enfant et les sortilèges* (1925) and the interpolation of the communist ballet *The Red Detachment of Women* into *Nixon in China*. Dance and mime pervade such works as Sergey Diaghilev's (1872–1929) **Paris** production of **Nikolay Andreyevich Rimsky-Korsakov**'s *The Golden Cockerel* (1914, originally 1909), which marginalized the singers while dancers took center stage; Igor Stravinsky's hybrid ballet operas *The Nightingale* (1914) and *Perséphone* (1934); **Benjamin Britten**'s *Death in Venice* (1973); **Philip Glass**'s **Einstein on the Beach**; **Harrison Birtwistle**'s *The Mask of Orpheus* (1986); and Karlheinz Stockhausen's (1928–2007) **Licht**. And they play an integral role in the genre of **Beijing opera**.

See also FESTA TEATRALE.

BARBAIA, DOMENICO. (ca. 1778, Milan–1841, Posillipo.) The most powerful **impresario** of the early 19th century. A dynamic entrepreneur, Barbaia rose from kitchen servant in taverns to wealthy coffeehouse proprietor by popularizing cappuccino and café mocha, and sold weapons during the Napoleonic Wars. He entered the theater world by running the gambling operations at La Scala (beginning 1806; *see* THEATER DESIGN). His success led to appointment as manager of the opera houses in **Naples** from 1809 to 1824, where he rebuilt the San Carlo after it was destroyed by fire in 1816. Barbaia ran the Kärntnertortheater and the Theater an der Wien in **Vienna** (1821–28) and La Scala and the Teatro Cannobiana in Milan (beginning 1826).

Barbaia possessed an acute eye for talent. He signed **Gioachino Rossini**, **Saverio Mercadante**, **Giovanni Pacini**, and **Gaetano Donizetti** to long-term contracts; brought **Vincenzo Bellini** to La Scala (*Il pirata*, 1827); and commissioned **Carl Maria von Weber**'s *Euryanthe* (1823) for Vienna. He also promoted the careers of some of the great singers of the period, among them the tenors **Giovanni Davide** and **Giovanni Battista Rubini** and the soprano **Isabella Colbran**, his mistress until he lost her to Rossini.

IL BARBIERE DI SIVIGLIA **(PASIELLO).** *Dramma giocoso* (*see* OPERA BUFFA); music by **Giovanni Paisiello**, **libretto** probably by Giuseppe Petrosellini (1727 to after 1797) adapted from Pierre-Augustin Beaumarchais's (1732–1799) play *Le barbier de Séville* (1773); four acts; premiered St. Petersburg, Hermitage, September 1782. The most popular opera buffa of the late 18th century.

Paisiello's treatment of the first of Beaumarchais's three Figaro plays, which had been performed in St. Petersburg two years earlier by Catherine the Great's talented Italian company, was an unparalleled success, staged almost instantaneously across Europe, translated into French and German, and frequently parodied. In **Vienna**, where **Wolfgang Amadeus Mozart** would have seen it before setting the second play of the trilogy as *Le nozze di Figaro*, it was heard nearly 100 times in five theaters between 1783 and 1804. **Gioachino Rossini** courted Paisiello's approval when he launched his own *Barbiere* in 1816.

The victory of Beaumarchais's and Petrosellini's nobly born Rosina and her beau Almaviva—with help from their servants—over their middle-class nemesis Bartolo celebrates sentimental marriage for love (*see* SENTIMEN-TAL OPERA) and testifies to the continued dominance of the aristocracy and the validity of social stratification. Following Figaro's advice, Almaviva enters Dr. Bartolo's house disguised as a drunken soldier and exchanges letters with his intended sweetheart Rosina, who is Bartolo's ward and the object of his unwanted attentions. Initially unsuccessful in rescuing Rosina, Almaviva tries again disguised as Alonso, pretended assistant to her singing teacher Don Basilio, who is reportedly ill. In the confusion that ensues, Figaro manages to steal a key to her window, but this second gambit also ends in chaos. Bartolo strikes back, temporarily convincing Rosina that her lover is unfaithful. But Almaviva makes a third appearance in time to prove otherwise, and he and Figaro pull off an impromptu wedding before Bartolo can stop it.

As in other contemporary comic operas, most of Paisiello's characters may be traced to **commedia dell'arte** prototypes: Figaro as Arlecchino; the pairs of *innamorati* (Almaviva and Rosina), *vecchi* (Dr. Bartolo and Don Basilio), and *zanni* (the incongruously named old man Giovinetto [Young Boy] and sleepy Svegliato [Awake]); and Almaviva's tipsy alter ego, the Capitano. And much of *Il barbiere*'s humor resides in slapstick opera buffa and commedia dell'arte staples: Figaro's **patter songs**, *lazzi* such as Giovanetto's and Svegliato's sneezing and yawning fits (Act 2), Almaviva's drunken **sortita** (also Act 2), and Bartolo's shave (Act 3), along with Basilio's slander *tirata* (Act 2, and two other tirade arias) and Rosina's mock **da capo aria** (Act 3). Conforming to trends in late 18th-century comic opera, roughly half the score involves **duets** or ensembles, culminating in the lengthy episodic **finale** of Act 4, and the music includes touches of local color (e.g., Bartolo's Act 3 "Seghidiglia spagnuola"). Also typical is Paisiello's translucent, string-dominated orchestration against which woodwinds serve specific connotative roles (for example, **pastoral** flutes or romantic clarinets).

IL BARBIERE DI SIVIGLIA (ROSSINI). *Commedia* originally titled *Almaviva, ossia L'inutile precauzione* (*Almaviva, or The Useless Precaution*); music by **Gioachino Rossini**, **libretto** by Cesare Sterbini (1784–1831) based on Pierre-Augustin Beaumarchais's (1732–1799) play *Le Barbier de Séville* (1773) and (probably) Giuseppe Petrosellini's (1727–after 1797) libretto (1782) set by **Giovanni Paisiello**; two acts; premiered **Rome**, Teatro Argentina, February 1816. *The Barber of Seville* is Rossini's most familiar opera and one of the most popular **opera buffas** of all time.

To offset any perceived hubris in venturing a remake of Paisiello's revered masterpiece, Rossini proffered various apologias, and Sterbini downplayed comedic scenes that Paisiello had made famous. *Barbiere* was created on an even shorter timetable than most operas of the period—Rossini agreed to write it two months before it opened and supposedly finished the score in as little as nine days—and suffered a disastrous premier plagued by miscues and heckling by Paisiello loyalists. Nonetheless, it quickly gained a following in Italy and abroad and has remained a standby of the repertory to the present day.

In contrast to Beaumarchais's aristocratic heroine, Rossini and Sterbini's Rosina comes off more as an enterprising commoner who shares her aristocratic suitor's victory over her possessive guardian and would-be husband Dr. Bartolo, but whose success may be viewed as a triumph of middle-class upward mobility. As characters introduce themselves through a series of **arias**, Figaro advises the Count Almaviva to make contact with his sweetheart by disguising himself as a soldier and garrisoning himself in Bartolo's house. In the Act 1 **finale**, Almaviva makes his entrance pretending to be drunk and slips Rosina a letter, but withdraws when real soldiers come to quell the ruckus. His first attempt to infiltrate only partly successful, Almaviva appears again in Act 2 pretending to cover for her "ailing" music teacher Don Basilio. In the confusion created by Basilio's unexpected arrival, Figaro steals a key to her balcony that can be used by the couple to elope later. Although Bartolo subsequently gains the advantage by producing a letter that incriminates her suitor, Figaro and Almaviva smooth things over, and the count marries Rosina before Bartolo can derail their improvised wedding.

Barbiere's effectiveness results from Rossini's exaggerated delineation of his characters through the manic energy of much of his music. Sparkling orchestration, frolicsome orchestral motives that underlie passages of *parlante* and *nota e parola*, breakneck **coloratura** for the singers (sometimes mimicked by the orchestra), frenetic **patter song** for the buffo characters and Almaviva, obsessive repetitions of driving cadential formulas, the obligatory "Rossinian" crescendos, and incisive differentiation of the various sections of episodic arias and ensembles contribute to countless slapstick tours de force. Rossini's comedic gifts are evident in some of the most familiar buffo numbers in the repertory, for example arias of self-characterization such as

Figaro's famous cavatina (*see* ARIA) "Largo al factotum" and the *lazzi* (*see* COMMEDIA DELL'ARTE) for Basilio ("La calunia") and Bartolo ("A un dottore," all in Act 1); the Act 1 finale (Almaviva's inebriated intrusion); and the Act 2 quintet, in which Almaviva and Rosina plot her escape while Figaro shaves Bartolo. Rossini also broadens his spectrum of musical characterization by adapting the florid **bel canto** singing and the conventional multimovement aria forms (with or without ***tempo di mezzo***) of his **opera serias** for the romantic leads to represent Rosina's frivolity, in her cavatina "Una voce poco fa" (Act 1) and music lesson "Contro un cor" (Act 2), and Almaviva's ardor in his romantic **stage songs** (the two-tempo "Ecco, ridente in cielo" and the strophic canzone "Se il mio nome," both Act 1).

In shifting focus from social satire to farcical humor by pushing the comedic envelope, Rossini raised expectations for his performers, making opera buffa a test of **acting** skill and its own brand of vocal virtuosity as exacting in their demands as those of serious opera. Thus he turned his back on the cornerstones of late 18th-century comic opera—humanity and sly wit coupled with stylistic grace and simplicity—and reinforced its infiltration by slapstick and bel canto. Ironically, in his landmark essay, Rossini essentially exhausted the possibilities of the genre and likely precipitated its inevitable decline.

BAROQUE. Term for the period in music (and the other arts) from roughly 1600 to 1750, and for the array of expressively intense styles current during that time. Baroque opera developed in Florence, **Rome**, Mantua, **Venice**, and **Naples** prior to the advent of 18th-century Metastasian **opera seria** (*see* ARCADIAN ACADEMY; METASTASIO, PIETRO) and various types of comic opera (*see* CATEGORIES OF OPERA), which were more attuned to Enlightenment ideals.

Originally a pejorative French term derived from the Portuguese "barroco" referring to a misshapen pearl, it was applied after the fact in the mid-18th century to purportedly outmoded music characterized by angular, motivically based melody; complex counterpoint; and bold harmony featuring harsh dissonance, frequent modulation, and chromatic chord progressions. Directed toward the arts first in a 1734 critique of **Jean-Philippe Rameau**'s *Hippolyte et Aricie*, *musique barroque* was subsequently (1746) contrasted by the French priest and writer Noël-Antoine Pluche (1688–1761) in his widely read *Spectacle de la nature* against the newer *musique chantante* (lyrical, melodious music) in the *galant* style. Related, more contemporaneous terms include *seconda pratica* and *stile moderno* (as opposed to the conservative *prima pratica* and *stile antico* of 16th-century church composers). "Baroque" came into widespread music-historical usage only in the mid-20th century. (It had been established in the visual arts by the late 19th century.)

Baroque music displays such common denominators as the combination of voices and instruments in *concertato* ensembles (in contrast to the a cappella style of 16th-century sacred vocal music) and the adoption of **basso continuo** support for treble melody and the resulting polarized texture (led by melodies in the soprano and bass ranges with the middle of the texture playing a supporting role), both essential to early opera. However, efforts to convey variegated emotions in a broad range of performative circumstances led to polarities—in music as in the other arts—which discourage unilateral characterization. In opera, for example, this diversity is demonstrated by contrasts involving the metered, dance-based style of the **aria** versus the more flexible, speech-based style of **recitative**, the extravagant lengths of entire operas versus the more modest scale of individual scenes and set pieces, the intermixture of serious and comic scenes, and the broad expressive and structural range of arias and other lyric numbers.

Like the other arts, opera advanced and benefitted from current political, literary, and scientific tendencies. Born in the Age of Absolutism, it originated and flourished thanks to aristocratic patronage and served as an emblem of aristocratic wealth, power, and cultural refinement. It embodied the concurrent revival of classical rhetoric—the art of persuasive communication—in assuming that music could and should convey the meaning of the words; that various melodic gestures, ornaments, and harmonic progressions could intensify dramatic meaning; and that expressive communication could be constructed in terms of established categories (topoi/topics) of genre and expression. And the conscious attempt to relate these categories—and musical expression in general—to new theories of human psychology (*see* DOCTRINE OF THE AFFECTIONS) represents a way in which composers and **librettists** embraced the scientific leanings of their time.

BARTÓK, BÉLA. (1881, Nagyszentmiklós, Hungary–1945, New York.) Internationally acclaimed Hungarian **composer** of instrumental and vocal music, including one important opera. Bartók began musical training with his mother, then chose the Budapest Academy, where he studied piano and composition (1899–1903), over a scholarship to the **Vienna Conservatory**. Soon after graduating (1904) he began his lifelong collection, edition, and adaptation of Hungarian folk music, often collaborating with the composer **Zoltán Kodály**.

Bartók's **symbolist** opera *A Kékszakállú herceg vára* (*Bluebeard's Castle*, composed 1911, premiered 1918) distills the fairy tale previously told in Paul Dukas (1865–1935) and Maurice Maeterlinck's (1862–1949) *Ariane et Barbe-bleue* (1907) into a one-act dialogue with spoken **prologue** for Bluebeard and his new wife Judith and recasts it as a horrifying love story. A ritual opening of seven doors inside the castle—dramatized with colored beams of light and a dissonant "blood" motif—reveals his secrets, culminating in his reunion with his three former wives, whom Judith joins in their imprisonment behind the last door. Judith's comparative lyricism and richer modal language, which contrast Bluebeard's declamation and the pentatonic writing associated with his castle, suggests her incompatibility with his world. Beyond *Bluebeard*, Bartók's contributions to the stage were limited to a **ballet** and the pantomime *A csodálatos mandarin* (*The Miraculous Mandarin*, composed 1918–19, premiered 1926).

BASS. Lowest male voice, covering the range from about F two octaves below middle c' to e' above middle c'.

In early Italian opera the bass voice was largely confined to secondary roles as gods (primarily gods of the underworld) or other infernal types (e.g., Pluto and Charon in **Claudio Monteverdi**'s *Orfeo*), often accompanied by low brass, or learned old men (Seneca in *L'incoronazione di Poppea*). In the late 17th and early 18th centuries, basses occasionally played more mainstream supporting parts as aristocrats or military leaders, and in comic *contrascene* they also developed conventionalized characters adapted from the **commedia dell'arte**, for example, drunken servants; bumbling, sexually inappropriate old men; and ethnic villains. They would become the buffo basses of 18th-century **opera buffa** and **intermezzo**, by the beginning of the century already demonstrating many of their stereotypical musical attributes (for example, preposterously large leaps, uncomfortable vocal ranges, incipient **patter song**, and clumsy **ornamentation**).

In France the deep bass was valued more than in Italy for its contrast with higher parts, and basses appeared in serious lead roles as early as the hero of **Francesco Cavalli**'s *Ercole amante* (1662, **Paris**). However, for the most part **Jean-Baptiste Lully** followed the tradition of using basses for gods (both heavenly and infernal) and as comic accessories. In the early 18th century, **Jean-Philippe Rameau** may well have initiated the development of the high bass or baritone tessitura (*basse-taille* or low **tenor**) extending to f' above middle c' beginning with Theseus in *Hippolyte et Aricie*. The bass gained even greater importance in **Christoph Willibald Gluck**'s Parisian operas of the 1770s, for example Hercules in the French *Alceste* (1776).

Although basses were generally neglected in 18th-century **opera seria**, the buffo bass took center stage in comic opera (e.g., Uberto in *La serva padrona*; *see* CATEGORIES OF OPERA). It would remain prominent throughout the century (Bartolo in *Le nozze di Figaro*) and into the 19th (the lead in *Don Pasquale*). Basses also play important roles in late 18th-century **singspiel** as villains or sages (Osmin in **Wolfgang Amadeus Mozart**'s *Die Entführung aus dem Serail*, 1782; Sarastro in *Die Zauberflöte*).

Nineteenth-century use of the bass voice to depict serious, mature male characters—particularly authority figures (the Israelite Priest Zaccaria in *Nabucco*, the Egyptian king and the high priest Ramfis in *Aida*) or villains, and even the devil (Mephistopheles in *Faust*)—led to its increased presence, for example in **Giuseppe Verdi**'s *Simon Boccanegra* (1857, revised 1881), which includes four important bass or baritone roles versus one for tenor. This prominence contributed to differentiation of various subspecialties within the voice type that remain to the present day, among them the *basso cantante* (French *basse chantante*), a bass having a high or lighter legato voice suitable for the lyrical bass or bass-baritone roles of **Vincenzo Bellini** and **Gaetano Donizetti** (Oroveso in *Norma*) and others such as Escamillo in *Carmen*, and the *basso profondo* (French *basse noble* or *basse profonde*), an exceptionally resonant, powerful, and deep voice that can extend as far as D two octaves below middle c' for roles such as Osmin.

Once the baritone designation came into common usage in the 19th century—for midrange voices extending approximately from the pitch A two octaves below middle c' to f' above middle c'—subspecies comparable to those of the bass voice were recognized, such as the lyric baritone, an alternative to the buffo bass for more sympathetic leads (Figaro in Rossini's *Il barbiere di Siviglia*, Marcello in *La bohème*) and the dramatic or so-called Verdi baritone, represented by **Giorgio Ronconi**, one of the premier singers of the 19th century and the creator of the role of Nabucco, which emphasizes the upper tessitura absent vocal ornamentation (**Rigoletto**, Amonasro in *Aida*, and Iago in *Otello*). Familiar bass or baritone roles in 20th-century operas include Baron Ochs in *Der Rosenkavalier*; the barrister Swallow in *Peter Grimes*; Arkel, Pelléas, and Golaud in *Pelléas et Mélisande*, and the title character in *Wozzeck*.

See also BASSO CONTINUO; CHALIAPIN, FYODOR; GALLI, FILIPPO; MANELLI, FRANCESCO.

BASSO CONTINUO. **Baroque** "continuous **bass**" technique for improvising ("realizing") an accompaniment (or part of the accompaniment) for operatic music beginning with early 17th-century **monody** and persisting in simple **recitatives** (in **opera buffa**) as late as the mid-19th century, as well as for various types of other vocal and instrumental music. The notes of the bass line, and often numbers and natural, flat, and sharp signs in a so-called "figured bass," indicate harmonies to be supplied by the performer. Depending on the historical and musical context, a realization may range from sparse chords to counterpoint or elaborate passagework.

Basso continuo originated in late 16th-century sacred music, in which an organ doubled the harmonies of the voices and instruments, and in solo arrangements of 16th-century secular a cappella vocal music, in which a **lute** or **harpsichord** would double or replace the lower voices. It was an integral element of early opera: **Emilio de' Cavalieri**'s *Rappresentatione di Anima, et di Corpo* (published 1600) and **Jacopo Peri**'s *Euridice* both included basso continuo with figured bass lines. Among a startling array of possibilities, the theorbo/*chitarrone* and archlute (*see* LUTE) were the most popular continuo instruments in 17th-century opera (normally played alone, without a melody instrument doubling the bass line), and remained part of the continuo group into the 18th century. After 1700 the preferred arrangement became one or two **harpsichords**, cello, and probably double bass (doubling the bass line), and possibly an archlute (at least early in the century). In the 19th century the piano seems largely to have replaced the harpsichord.

THE BEGGAR'S OPERA. **Ballad opera**; **overture** probably composed by Johann Christoph Pepusch (1667–1752), who also assembled and possibly arranged the songs, **libretto** by John Gay (1685–1732), likely suggested by Jonathan Swift; three acts; premiered **London**, Lincoln's Inn Fields, January 1728. With *The Beggar's Opera*, Gay is credited with inventing and popularizing a new genre. Its spoken dialogue alternates with 69 **airs**, which take their melodies from English, Irish, Scottish, and French folk and popular melodies, "Greensleeves" among them, and songs by **Henry Purcell**, **George Frideric Handel**, and numerous other composers.

The lowlife plot of *The Beggar's Opera* unremittingly transgresses the elevated, moralizing conventions of **Arcadian opera seria**. The bandit and lothario Macheath has married Polly unbeknownst to her father Peachum, a fence and snitch whose name references the latter occupation. Peachum turns Macheath over to the authorities, but the smitten Lucy, daughter of the turnkey Lockit, helps him escape even after discovering his infidelity. Following a second arrest, Macheath is spared execution by operatic convention, which precludes tragedy.

Throughout the opera, spoken repartee and songs parody Italian opera seria staged by Handel at the Royal Academy; the British government, particularly the mistrusted, scandal-prone first Prime Minister Sir Robert Walpole; and virtually every other aspect of contemporary London society. Its unprecedented popularity helped torpedo Handel's First Academy, sparked a revival of German **singspiel**, and spawned pirated versions and merchandizing rivaling modern hit movies. Gay attempted to capitalize on its success with the sequel *Polly*, which was banned prior to its premier (1728). Performed in London and myriad other locations including America throughout the century, after falling out of fashion in the 19th century, *The Beggar's Opera* regained its popularity beginning in the 1920s. **Kurt Weill** and Bertolt Brecht's (1898–1956) *Die Dreigroschenoper* was based on it.

BEIJING OPERA. The most prominent and sophisticated type of Chinese opera. Also known as Peking opera, Beijing opera combines stylized singing, instrumental music, acting, mime, dance, acrobatics, and martial arts weaponry. Elaborately and beautifully costumed characters, some having painted faces, represent four main categories of conventional roles as well as numerous subcategories, enacting stories based on Chinese history, folk literature, and more recently contemporary life. Major companies are active in Beijing, Shanghai, Taiwan, and elsewhere.

Beijing opera originated as a court entertainment in 1790 during the Quing (Manchu) dynasty (1644–1912) when performers from Anhui province appeared for an imperial birthday celebration. The Anhui troupes were joined in 1828 by troupes from Hubei, combining Hubei *xipi* music and Anhui *erhuang* music into the *pihuang* system central to the style, in which traditional types of arias and melodies are supported by an orchestra of bowed and plucked **lutes**, shawms, and percussion instruments such as drums, clappers, gongs, and cymbals. The status of Beijing opera was enhanced through important imperial performances in 1860 and 1884. By the 1870s, **women**, who had been banned from the stage since the 18th century, began taking roles alongside men, and several specifically female troupes were in place by the end of the 19th century, resulting eventually in elimination of the ban (1912). The art form reached a peak of popularity and creativity in the early 20th century prior to the invasion of China by Japan in 1937.

Opera was treated as an instrument of political and social reform beginning with the Beijing opera reform movement (ca. 1908–17), which resulted in innovative works that addressed contemporary social issues. After World War II the communist regime regarded opera as a tool of ideological indoctrination, suppressing the existing repertory as bourgeois during the Cultural Revolution (1966–76) and replacing it with the eight model plays devised by Jiang Qing (wife of Mao Zedong). They included five new Beijing operas having communist themes and contemporary staging (e.g., *The Legend of the Red Lantern*). In the 1980s traditional subjects returned to the stage.

BEL CANTO. A mostly retrospective, 19th-century Italian term meaning "beautiful singing" that has been subject to various interpretations. It may refer to a style of singing that is fluidly lyrical, light, agile, and often profusely embellished with ornamentation and passagework. Vibrato is introduced sparingly as an expressive coloration, and tone production is focused in the head rather than the chest (*see* SINGING STYLE). It may also denote a musical style that showcases this type of singing through idiomatic vocal writing and subdued accompaniments.

The term appears to have come into use by the mid-1800s to lament a lost vocal art following the shift in Italian singing ca. 1830 to a heavier, more overtly dramatic style dominated by chest voice in all registers and constant vibrato. It also had nationalistic associations, distinguishing—either positively, by praising simple lyricism, or pejoratively, by deriding trivial tunefulness and vocalization—the Italian style from the German. Although sometimes confined in usage to the era of Gioachino Rossini, Vincenzo Bellini, and Gaetano Donizetti, as a compositional and vocal style, bel canto originated at least as early as the aria-dominated operas and other vocal works of the 1640s (e.g., those of Francesco Cavalli) and can be traced back even further to the solo madrigals of the late 16th century. Furthermore, while examples of traditional bel canto music continue to appear in Bellini and Donizetti ("Casta Diva" from *Norma* is an obvious example), the switch to the heavier style of singing was already taking place during their era. The bel canto compositional style outlived the singing style, and the term is often extended to the more vocally oriented set pieces of Giuseppe Verdi and even Giacomo Puccini.

BELLINI, VINCENZO. (1801, Catania–1835, Puteaux.) Italian **composer** of 10 operas (1825–35) and the last great product of the 18th-century Neapolitan **conservatory** system. His career demonstrates the emerging preeminence of northern Italy in the early 19th century, since all eight of his mature operas premiered in Milan, Parma, and **Venice** (as well as **Paris**).

Born into a family of musicians, Bellini displayed a precocious talent rivaling **Wolfgang Amadeus Mozart**'s, reportedly having sung an **aria** when he was 18 months old, conducted a church service at age three, and composed at age six. Shortly thereafter, he began formal composition lessons with his grandfather, who had trained in **Naples**. Then he himself entered the Real Collegio di Musica in Naples in 1819, where he studied with the iconic opera composer Niccolò Zingarelli (1752–1837). At the theater he was impressed by **Gioachino Rossini**'s late Italian works. Following his initial *opera semiseria* *Adelson e Salvini* (1825), a graduation project performed at the conservatory, his second major work, the *melodramma* *Bianca e Gernando* (1826), premiered at the San Carlo Theater as a prize for his standing as the year's leading graduate.

In 1827, Bellini left Naples and his lifelong friend, correspondent, and eventual biographer Francesco Florimo (1800–1888) for the burgeoning center of Milan. There he began his collaboration with the house poet at La Scala, **Felice Romani**, his **librettist** for all but the last of his remaining operas. Romani's poetry was uniquely inspiring to Bellini, and he allowed Bellini unaccustomed input in creating his **librettos**. However, his nonchalant work habits were a constant source of friction. In the case of *La sonnambula* (1831), his foot-dragging forced Bellini to compose Act 2 in two weeks. For *Beatrice di Tenda* (1833), the Venetian police were enlisted to strongarm Romani into completing the libretto for a premier delayed by a month, ending Bellini's partnership with him.

Bellini's first commission after his move north, *Il pirata* (1827), was a monumental success reinforced by *La straniera* in 1829. His prestige garnered him a record fee when *La sonnambula* and *Norma* were commissioned in 1831, and gave him unparalleled input regarding casting and other aspects of **production**, setting a precedent for **Giuseppe Verdi**'s autocratic approach later on. Following the *Beatrice* debacle, Bellini took a sabbatical in 1833, returning to Naples after a six-year absence and making long trips to **London** (1834) and Paris (1833 and 1834), in the latter case with the apparent aim of landing a contract at the Opéra. Unsuccessful, he settled for the Théâtre Italien for the premier of *I puritani* (1835). The annoyance of wet-nursing the inexperienced librettist Carlo Pepoli (1796–1881) through the creative process nonetheless afforded him unprecedented control over poetic tone and dramatic design. That, the opportunity to adapt to French conventions and flexibilities, and probably Rossini's advice (at least concerning orchestration) contributed to its unique "*tinta*," unconventional melodic and scenic structures, rich sound, increased atmospheric action and presence of **chorus**, and melodic recurrences, all more typical of French opera than Italian.

Famous for his limpid lyricism, Bellini gradually streamlined Rossini's sprawling multipart melodies and developed the simpler, more populist song form—the **lyric prototype**—which is particularly evident in his **cabalettas**. It appears less concisely and frequently in his slow movements, which feature the long outpourings so famously admired by Verdi. At the same time, he challenged Rossini's florid **bel canto** style through his use of syllabic, declamatory singing in traditionally lyrical movements, and of **arioso** for **recitative** verse (*see* VERSIFICATION), occasionally incorporating brief dialogues into lyric slow movements. This trend peaked in *La straniera*, which sparked debate on this count at its premiere (1829), perhaps leading Bellini to backpedal by including more **coloratura** in later works. Many of Bellini's operas depart from the classicizing norms of Neapolitan **opera seria** in their **romantic** settings that abandon classical mythological or historical situations: gloomy castles, seacoasts, Druid temples, and forts populated by outlaws, a sleepwalker, Shakespearean feuding neighbors, and civil war combatants. They also tend to replace plot intrigues with static love triangles that emphasize raw emotions (*see NORMA*).

Exacting in his work, Bellini appears to have labored over details more than other Italian composers, he took an especially active role in rehearsals, and he supported a new, more overtly impassioned style of performance. Like many composers, he reused music from unsuccessful works in one city for later successes in another, notably music from *Zaira* (unsuccessful in Parma, 1829) for *I Capuleti e i Montecchi* (Venice, 1830), *Norma*, and *Beatrice di Tenda*.

BERG, ALBAN. (1885, Vienna–1935, Vienna.) Leading operatic **composer** of the Second Viennese School. His two **expressionist** operas are landmarks of 20th-century modernism.

Born in **Vienna** to a well-to-do middle-class family, Berg took piano lessons with his governess and composed music at an early age. Although he performed poorly in school, by his late teens he involved himself in Viennese artistic culture and befriended many of its leading figures, including the erotic **symbolist** painter and leader of the Viennese Succession movement Gustav Klimt; the expressionist painter, poet, and playwright Oskar Kokoschka; and the novelist and playwright Stefan Zweig. He also studied composition with **Arnold Schoenberg** (beginning 1904) as he was pressing late 19th-century chromatic harmony toward atonality.

Berg began work on his first opera, *Wozzeck*, prior to World War I while supporting himself as an arranger of piano-vocal scores and continued following military service during the war while managing Schoenberg's society for contemporary music (beginning 1918). Completed in 1922 and first performed in 1925, *Wozzeck* was the first large-scale atonal opera. After assimilating Schoenberg's twelve-tone procedure and writing two major instrumental works in that style, Berg turned in 1928 to the pair of erotic "Lulu" plays by Frank Wedekind—*Der Erdgeist* (*Earth Spirit*, 1895) and *Die Büchse der Pandora* (*Pandora's Box*, 1904)—which chart the rise and fall of an alluring harlot and dancer. *Lulu*'s emotionally vacant, narcissistic sociopath, fixated on her ill-gotten wealth and social status and unmoved by the deaths that result from her series of affairs, is arrested after shooting her latest husband. She escapes from prison where she has contracted cholera, beginning her free fall into poverty and prostitution. *Lulu* (composed 1928–35, completed and premiered 1979) is the first full-scale twelve-tone opera, in which rows serve as **leitmotifs** for characters and concepts. Berg organized its set pieces into a long-range palindromic (mirror) structure paralleling Lulu's ascent and decline, which is centered on a silent film interlude depicting her trial. Completion and performance of the opera, left unfinished at Berg's death, was obstructed by his widow until she died in 1976.

See also CENSORSHIP.

BERLIOZ, HECTOR. (1803, La Côte-Saint-André–1869, Paris.) French **composer** of orchestral music, six operas (three of them significant), other vocal music, and innovative concert works that combine symphonic and operatic elements, as well as the **librettist** for two of his operas, conductor, and writer on music.

In **Paris** beginning in 1821, Berlioz spent two years as an unenthusiastic medical student before devoting himself to music against his parents' wishes, studying composition with Jean-François Le Sueur (1760–1837), first privately (beginning 1822), then enrolled at the Conservatoire from 1826. An insatiable operagoer, his encounters with works by **Christoph Willibald Gluck** and **Gaspare Spontini** were particularly meaningful. While a student, he explored a number of operatic projects including *Les francs-juges* (composed 1825–26, unperformed), parts of which reappeared in works like the *Symphonie fantastique* (1830). Berlioz won the Prix de Rome on his fourth try in 1830, which for two years allowed him to attend operas in Italian cities from **Naples** to Milan, most of which failed to impress him.

Returning to Paris in 1832 full of ambition, Berlioz established himself as a writer at the *Journal des débats*. And he won a following as a conductor of his own orchestral concerts, including performances of the *Symphonie fantastique* (1832), the dramatic symphony *Roméo et Juliette* (1839), and the concert opera *La damnation de Faust* (1846). He also directed operas by other composers such as **Carl Maria von Weber**'s *Der Freischütz*, performed in 1841 as *Le Freyschutz*, with its spoken dialogues set as recitatives by Berlioz, and Gluck's *Orphée* and *Alceste* in 1859 and 1861, respectively (originally 1774 and 1776). But the Opéra was the true gateway to fame, and he began his ultimately fruitless campaign to conquer it with the semiserious *Benvenuto Cellini*, which occupied him beginning in 1834 and was finally performed unsuccessfully at the Opéra (1838). Based on the life of the brilliant 16th-century mannerist artist and musician pardoned for murder when he completes a magnificent statue commissioned by the pope, this technically daunting, miniature ***grand opéra*** is constructed in four tableaux and dominated by massed crowd scenes.

After an ill-fated stint as music director for Louis Jullien's (1812–1860) Drury Lane opera company in **London** (1847–48), for which his expected long-term contract ended after nine months, he toured extensively across Europe through the mid-1850s. Again aiming at the Opéra, he composed *Les Troyens* on his own **libretto** from 1856 to 1858, then spent five years or so trying to arrange its **production** at that theater, finally performing a trimmed-down, three-act version—*Les Troyens à Carthage*—at **Léon Carvalho**'s Théâtre Lyrique in 1863, a premier that fared better than *Cellini*'s had. In its complete, five-act version, *Les Troyens* is an epic *grand opéra* based on Virgil's *Aeneid*, beginning with the Trojan horse episode and sack of Troy, the planned spectacular crowd scenes that were cut at the Théâtre Lyrique, then segueing to Dido and Aeneas in Carthage for the last three acts. Berlioz's operatic career ended with the brilliantly scored domestic comedy *Béatrice et Bénédict*, his own adaptation of William Shakespeare's *Much Ado about Nothing*, composed while negotiating the production of *Les Troyens* and performed to open a new summer theater in Baden-Baden, Germany (1862).

BERNSTEIN, LEONARD. (1918, Lawrence, Massachusetts–1990, New York.) American **composer** of instrumental and vocal music, including works for the Broadway stage, an **operetta**, and two true operas, and **librettist** (or contributor to the **libretto**) for several of them.

Trained at Harvard University (1935–39), the Curtis Institute (1939–41), and the incipient Berkshire Music Center (1940 and 1941, now Tanglewood) in composition, orchestration, and conducting, Bernstein directed the New York Philharmonic Orchestra (1958–69) and made notable conducting appearances, including the American premier of *Peter Grimes* (Tanglewood, 1946) and other operas in **New York**, Milan, and **Vienna**. His long list of awards boasts 11 Emmys, and Grammy and Kennedy Center lifetime achievement awards.

Like **Gian Carlo Menotti**, Bernstein bridged the divide between opera and popular theater, expanding the stylistic range of the musical in such works as *On the Town* (1944), *Wonderful Town* (1953), and *West Side Story* (1957) and incorporating elements of jazz, musical theater, and other popular idioms in his eclectic operas. In his first, *Trouble in Tahiti* (1952, on Bernstein's libretto), at the end of a typical day a couple escapes to an exotic movie to avoid resolving their problems. *Candide* (1956, libretto by Lillian Hellman, 1905–1984, and others including Bernstein), an operetta reminiscent of **Jacques Offenbach** and others, traces the misadventures of Voltaire's unlikely hero, who discovers El Dorado. *A Quiet Place* (1983), the controversial one-act sequel to *Trouble in Tahiti*, with which it was originally paired and which in the 1984 revision was included as a flashback in its second act, revisits the same couple at the wife's funeral and shares musical materials with the earlier opera, although it adopts a more modern style. A soap opera depicting the troubled family reunion of brother and sister, her husband (who is also her brother's ex-lover), and their father, it explores uncomfortable interpersonal relationships involving homosexuality and psychological abnormalities.

BIRTWISTLE, HARRISON. (Born 1934, Accrington, England.) The most prominent English opera **composer** of the late 20th century. Birtwistle trained in clarinet and composition at the Royal Manchester College of Music (1952–55), the Royal Academy of Music (1957–58), and Princeton University (after 1966) and co-founded the New Music Manchester Group (1953), which performed music of the Second Viennese School and the modernist avant-garde. He served as musical director of the Royal National Theater in London (1975–82) and as professor of composition at King's College (1994–2001).

From the late 1960s through 2008, Birtwistle produced eight nontraditional operas on familiar subjects, which link ritualized scenes in nonlinear narratives. Among them, *Punch and Judy* (1968), a tragicomedy commissioned by the English Opera Group (founded by **Benjamin Britten**), depicts the puppet character Punch as a homicidal maniac who somehow escapes execution. Over the next several years, Birtwistle used nonoperatic compositions to chart new directions for his first large-scale opera *The Mask of Orpheus*

(1986), a layered account of the myth that provides varying versions of events from different perspectives, representing each of the main characters by a singer, a mime, and a puppet. In the chamber opera *Yan Tan Tethera* (1986), shepherds count sheep using a traditional British rhyme. The title character of *Gawain* (1991) decapitates the green knight at their first combat, then cheats death at their rematch using a magic sash and is burdened by guilt. Birtwistle's *The Second Mrs. Kong* (1994) constructs a surreal afterlife in which historical figures (Nicolò Paganini and Johannes Vermeer) and fictional ones (the Sphinx, Orpheus, and King Kong) collaborate in a second, even more bizarre retelling of the Orpheus legend.

BIZET, GEORGES. (1838, Paris–1875, Bougival.) French **composer** of eight completed operas and **operettas** from the 1850s through the mid-1870s, other vocal and instrumental music, and arranger. A gifted melodist and orchestrator whose talent remained unfulfilled owing to his apparent artistic indecisiveness and untimely death, Bizet is remembered primarily for two operas, *Les pêcheurs de perles* (*The Pearl Fishers*, 1863) and *Carmen*, as well as a handful of popular instrumental works.

Born into a musical family in **Paris**, Bizet received early training from his mother, then entered the Conservatoire at age nine. There he studied piano, organ, and composition with **Fromental Halévy** and others and won numerous prizes, including the Prix de Rome (1857). While still at the Conservatoire he wrote his first **opéra comique** *La maison du docteur* (ca. 1855, not performed) and an operetta, *Le docteur Miracle* (1856), for a competition designed to promote the genre, for which Bizet shared the first prize. A phenomenal score reader at the keyboard, he began a career as an arranger of other composers' operas and orchestral music (for piano, piano four hands, and piano-vocal scores), his first major assignment (1855) being the vocal score of **Charles-François Gounod**'s *La nonne sanglante* (1854), hack work that sapped his time but nonetheless provided a secure source of income and acquainted him intimately with recent repertory.

Bizet's three years in **Rome** (1857–60), which caused him to miss the premier of *Faust* in 1859, were an agreeably unfocused and minimally productive time in which his reluctance to commit to projects, sometimes poor judgment, and weak follow-through became evident. His output included an outdated Italianate **opera buffa**, *Don Procopio*, written 1858–59 after false starts on a *grand opéra* and an opéra comique, which had little chance of being performed. Between *Don Procopio* and the completion of the exotic *opéra lyrique Les pêcheurs de perles*, he left seven projected operas incomplete, including the *grands opéras Don Quichotte* and *Ivan IV*, the latter lacking only part of Act 5. Passages from these aborted projects were absorbed into later works, including *Les pêcheurs*. Conceived as an opéra comique with spoken dialogues that were replaced by **recitatives** prior to performance at the Théâtre Lyrique, its plot carries overtones of *Norma*. A love triangle set in Ceylon, its heroine, a priestess, is accused of breaking her vow of chastity and condemned to death along with her beloved until their persecutor recants. Displaying Bizet's gift for colorful atmospheric orchestration and now known primarily for its friendship **duet** for Zurga and Nadir (Act 1), *Les pêcheurs* received a respectable number of performances but was panned unfairly by critics and considered a disappointment by the composer.

Following another abandoned project, Bizet completed the lyric opera *La jolie fille de Perth* (1867), based on Walter Scott's novel (1828). Projected for performance during the Parisian International Exposition in the summer of 1867, it was displaced to December by Gounod's *Roméo et Juliette* and failed to draw as well as Bizet had hoped. Following his contribution of Act 1 to the composite operetta *Marlbrough s'en va-t-en guerre* the same year, he began and set aside eight operas over the next four years until the one-act opéra comique *Djamileh* received a poor performance in 1871 and failed. Following another incomplete project, Bizet redeemed himself in 1874 with *Carmen* and achieved the potential that Halévy, Gounod, and the director of the Théâtre Lyrique **Léon Carvalho** had all discerned. Despite initial misgivings by management and resistance from the **orchestra** and **chorus** regarding its risqué subject matter, demanding scoring, and unconventional **acting** responsibilities, and despite initial shock at the first performances, *Carmen* won over audiences across Europe with its emotional intensity, naturalistic ambiance, and appealing tunes, and stands as one of the most popular and influential operas of all time. Bizet died the evening of its 33rd performance.

BLOW, JOHN. (1649, Newark, England–1708, London.) English **composer** of vocal music, including one particularly significant opera, *Venus and Adonis* (ca. 1683), as well as incidental music for spoken plays and instrumental music, and organist. Blow began his career as a choirboy in the Chapel Royal choir and served as organist at Westminster Abbey (1668–79 and 1695–1708, ceding the position to his student **Henry Purcell** in the intervening years). *Venus and Adonis*, in which the goddess loses her lover, who is killed by a wild boar, is the first entirely sung English stage work (all-sung **masque**) that survives. It betrays its origins in the masque tradition through its brevity, emphasis of dance and chorus, and scarcity of **arias**. Originally a private entertainment for King Charles II, it was also produced (1684) at Josias Priest's boarding school, where Purcell's *Dido and Aeneas* (with which it shares telling similarities) would later be performed.

BOHÈME, LA. Opera; music by **Giacomo Puccini, libretto** by **Luigi Illica and Giuseppe Giacosa** based on Henri Murger's (1822–1861) collection of stories *Scènes de la vie de bohème* (*Scenes of Bohemian Life*, 1851); four acts; premiered Turin, Teatro Regio, February 1896. Puccini's aim of setting Murger's subject, which had autobiographical resonances from his early years, brought him into well-publicized contention over creative precedence with **Ruggero Leoncavallo**, whose *La bohème* would appear a year after Puccini's (1897). Composition of the opera (beginning 1894) was delayed by Puccini's indecision about a possible adaptation of Giovanni Verga's short story *La lupa* (*The She-Wolf*, 1880), by his involvement in **productions** of *Manon Lescaut* (1893), and by numerous well-chosen revisions, including the addition of Rodolfo and Mimì's self-portraits and **duet** in Act 1 and the high jinks that open Act 4. Although its premier, conducted by **Arturo Toscanini**, received mixed reactions from the public and critics, *Bohème* quickly entered the repertory and has become Puccini's most-produced opera.

Probably more than any other Puccini opera, *La bohème* adheres to the **verismo** ethos and diverges from traditional *melodramma* by making social indifference and the vagaries of life itself, rather than a villain like Iago or Scarpia, the agents of tragedy. On Christmas Eve, after briefly celebrating with friends and burning his most recent play for heat, the impoverished poet Rodolfo meets and falls in love with the ailing embroiderer Mimì, who visits his garret to have her candle relit. They debut as a couple at a sidewalk café, where they are rescued by the gold-digging singer Musetta, who pays their bill. As Mimì's illness worsens, Rodolfo persuades her to leave him for a man who can better afford to care for her, but at death's door she returns to him and dies among her friends.

Despite obvious similarities to **Giuseppe Verdi**'s *La traviata* (1853)—both center on beauties who die of consumption—*La bohème* provides a counterpoise, because its proletarian lovers forsake their relationship not for social niceties but for Mimì's survival, and because poverty is the root cause of the heroine's illness and death. And while both **women** (and Musetta) prostitute themselves in one way or another, Mimì's modesty contrasts with Violetta's theatricality. Unlike *La traviata*'s comfortable mansions, *Bohème*'s wintry settings amidst the ramshackle garrets, outdoor cafés, and city walls of **Paris**—the bleakness of the environment so effectively captured in the prelude (*see* OVERTURE) to Act 3—underscore Mimì's cruel circumstances, the hand warmer shared by Musetta symbolizing the relief from poverty that comes too late to save her. Attention to menial details in the garret and café scenes—for example the philosopher Colline's sentimental eulogy over his winter coat to be bartered to help Mimì ("Vecchia zimarra")—enlists the audience to soldier along with them.

Like Puccini's other operas, *La bohème* testifies to the composer's gift for supplely interweaving characteristic orchestral motives, which convey mood and a sense of place, with naturally paced lyrical or declamatory vocal phrases, as in the jocular banter of the café scene and the openings of Acts 1 and 4 or the ominous stillness to start Act 3. Spontaneous recycling of these associative calling cards across scenes and from act to act, for example the "Bohemian" motive of the opening scene or motives from Rodolfo and Mimì's meeting recalled poignantly in their Act 4 deathbed duet, obviously contributes to long-range coherence. And it also facilitates local continuity by helping to embed solos realistically in the flow of conversation, for example, Rodolfo's "Che gelida manina" followed by Mimì's reply "Mi chiamano Mimì," in effect the slow movement of their ongoing duet, or Musetta's famous **stage song** waltz "Quando me'n vo" (Act 2), which spawns an ensemble. By minimizing set pieces and making each act a unified scene, Puccini achieved the verismo goals of realistic action and audience immersion that have made *La bohème* such an appealing masterwork.

BOITO, ARRIGO. (1842, Padua–1918, Milan.) Italian **librettist** who collaborated with **Giuseppe Verdi** on *Otello* and *Falstaff* (1893), music critic, and **composer** of the historically important *scapigliatura* opera *Mefistofele* (1868).

Raised in **Venice**, where he received his first musical training, Boito attended the Milan **Conservatory** (1853–61). There he met his lifelong friend the **conductor** and composer Franco Faccio (1840–1891) and trained under Alberto Mazzucato (1813–1877), principal conductor at La Scala, composer, and later director of the conservatory. While in **Paris** with Faccio, funded by a grant from the conservatory, he wrote the poetry for Verdi's *Inno delle nazione* (1862). Back in Milan the next year, Boito famously offended Verdi at a dinner celebrating Faccio's first opera, creating a rift that would last almost two decades. With his senior colleague present, he read his ode *All'arte italiana*, in which he advanced the *scapigliatura* agenda of abandoning outmoded, allegedly provincial artistic styles, a clear reference to Verdi's personification of the artistic establishment.

During the 1860s, Boito supported himself as a music and drama critic and as co-editor of the progressive journal *Il Figaro*. Work on the opera *Mefistofele* (on his own **libretto**), which he had begun at the conservatory, was put on hold by the success of **Charles-François Gounod**'s *Faust* at La Scala (1862, originally 1859) and interrupted by service in Giuseppe Garibaldi's army in 1866. By 1868 it had proceeded sufficiently for its devastatingly unsuccessful La Scala premier, where it was panned for being too long and heavily orchestrated. Boito himself conducted after refusing to make well-advised cuts Mazzucato had demanded, causing the maestro to resign from the project.

Withdrawing temporarily from composing, Boito wrote essays on opera and other topics; translated lieder and French, German, and Russian operas; and wrote a number of librettos, including *Ero e Leandro* (eventually completed in 1896 by Luigi Mancinelli, 1848–1921) and *La Gioconda* (1876) for **Amilcare Ponchielli**. He also plucked up sufficient courage to revise and abbreviate *Mefistofele*, which had a successful showing in Bologna (1875) and was even revived in Milan (1881). Relentless diplomacy by Faccio and Giulio **Ricordi** resulted in a momentous partnership between Boito and Verdi. After Verdi turned down a Nero libretto (which Boito completed as *Nerone* and partially set to music, and which was finished by a consortium that included **Arturo Toscanini** and was performed in 1924), they collaborated on the revision of *Simon Boccanegra* (1881) and on *Otello* and *Falstaff*. Boito was awarded an honorary doctorate from Cambridge University in 1893 and served in the Italian parliament (beginning 1912).

BORDONI, FAUSTINA. (1697, Venice–1781, Venice.) A leading Italian mezzo-**soprano** during the first half of the 18th century, she debuted in 1716 in **Venice**, where she spent the next decade. Bordoni appeared in **London** during the closing years (1726–28) of **George Frideric Handel**'s first Royal Academy, where she created five roles for his operas, performing alongside **Senesino**, **Francesca Cuzzoni**, and other notables. After marrying **Johann Adolf Hasse** in 1730, she moved with him to Dresden, where she sang at least 15 of his operas, while also circulating among **Naples**, Venice, and other cities in works by her husband, **Leonardo Vinci**, **Nicola Porpora**, and **Giovanni Battista Pergolesi**. Bordoni retired from the stage in 1751, though she retained her position in Dresden as *virtuosa da camera* for a dozen more years, and moved with her husband to **Vienna** by the mid-1760s, then to Venice in 1773. Famed as a dramatic singer and skilled actress, she was blessed with brilliant velocity and rapid diction well suited for virtuoso **coloratura arias**. In **London** she shared an infamous rivalry—in one instance, blows were reportedly struck during a performance—with Cuzzoni, who specialized in slower, poignant arias and whose skills were said to complement Bordoni's.
See also WOMEN AND OPERA.

BORIS GODUNOV. Opera; music by **Modest Petrovich Musorgsky, libretto** by the **composer** based on the play (written 1825) by Aleksandr Pushkin (1799–1837) and on accounts of Russian history; originally seven **scenes** in four parts, revised as nine scenes in a **prologue** and four acts; composed 1868–69, revised 1871–72, premiered St. Petersburg, Mariinsky Theater, February 1874; standard version supplemented by **Nikolay Andrey-**

evich **Rimsky-Korsakov**, premiered **Paris**, Opéra, May 1908. *Boris* is Musorgsky's only completed opera and the only Russian historical opera to remain in the standard repertory.

Conceived as a ***Literaturoper*** set in the Russian realist style of continuous recitative—Musorgsky termed it *"opéra dialogué"* ("dialogue" or "recitative" opera)—*Boris* originally consisted almost entirely of extracts from Pushkin, all but two of the seven scenes involving the title character. After the imperial theaters' governing board rejected the opera in 1871, Musorgsky expanded it to incorporate the Polish Act 3, text for which was newly written (as were other passages), and broadened its musical style to include more lyrical **arioso**. The opera entered the international repertory in Rimsky-Korsakov's thoroughgoing revision, its lead role becoming a notable **bass**/baritone vehicle for singers like **Fyodor Chaliapin**. Since the 1970s new productions have relied more on Musorgsky's original.

Boris's tenuously connected episodes, which take place in Russia and Poland ca. 1600, depict the lead as both perpetrator and victim of a ruthless political environment and humanize him through his domestic interactions with his children. Prior to the opera, Boris, regent for Ivan the Terrible's dimwitted heir, the Tsar Fyodor, had arranged the assassination of Fyodor's half-brother Dmitry, who was Ivan's last successor. In the prologue, following Fyodor's death and absent a viable heir, Boris manipulates popular opinion to grab the throne himself. The monk Pimen, a former soldier familiar with Dmitry's death, tells the novice Grigory about Boris's complicity in the murder. Realizing that he could pass for the murdered tsarevitch, Grigory decides to avenge Dmitry and cultivate his own dormant sense of adventure and political ambition by leaving the monastery, taking Dmitry's name, traveling to Poland, and returning with an army to depose Boris. In Lithuania he is seduced by the daughter of the provincial governor (Marina), who convinces him to marry her, make her tsarina, and promote the Roman Catholic agenda of her advisor Rangoni in exchange for her enlistment of military support. Russian poverty, increasing awareness of Boris's culpability, and his guilt-driven hallucinations, which are witnessed by his disloyal advisor Shuysky and the assembly of boyars, erode Boris's support. As the false Dimitry and his army approach, Boris dies of a stroke while abdicating to his son, leaving Russia in chaos.

The revised *Boris* represents a partial retreat from the pervasive realist declamation of the original version and of such earlier, incomplete works as *Salammbô* (1863–66, passages of which were incorporated into *Boris*) and particularly *Zhenit'ba* (*The Marriage*, 1868) and a return to a more traditional spontaneous lyricism aligned with ***opéra lyrique*** and exemplified by the **duet** for Grigory/False Dimitry and Marina in Act 3. Musorgsky may have effected this compromise—verging on the mainstream while adhering to syllabic text setting and avoiding **coloratura** display—better to woo the theater directorate and to give his tragedy additional gravitas by dissociating it from comic banter. Numerous Russian or Polish folk songs and dances—some of them identifiable quotations or adaptations—also enrich the score, as in the "Gnat Song," "Handclapping Game," and "Parrot Song" in Act 2 or the series of numbers that constitute the bulk of the final scene. These set pieces contribute to broad scenic tableaux, either domestic (as in Act 2, which depicts Boris as a doting father) or public and spectacular (for example, the demonstration and Boris's coronation in the prologue or the Act 4 uprising), which juxtapose personal interactions against political background and history in the manner of *grand opéra*. **Richard Wagner**'s influence is also evident in the **leitmotifs** associated with each character (several in Boris's case), which occur most densely in the scenes retained from the original version.

BORODIN, ALEKSANDR PORFIR'YEVICH. (1833, St. Petersburg–1887, St. Petersburg.) Russian chemist and nationalist **composer** of instrumental and vocal works and one very significant opera.

The illegitimate son of an aristocrat, Borodin was raised in luxury and tutored privately in the liberal arts, languages, and music. After studying chemistry in Germany, he pursued a noteworthy career as a professor and administrator (beginning 1864) at the St. Petersburg Medico-Surgical Academy. Mily Alekseyevich Balakirev (1837–1910) introduced him to the Russian nationalist group known as The Five (the Kuchka or Mighty Handful). Borodin's first opera, *Bogatïri* (*The Heroic Warriors*), a **pasticcio** farce in the style of **Jacques Offenbach**, which appropriated music from Offenbach, **Giacomo Meyerbeer**, and **Giuseppe Verdi**, parodied both traditional Russian rustic regionalism and late 19th-century naturalism. It received one performance in 1867.

Borodin worked on *Knyaz' Igor* (*Prince Igor*), for which he wrote the **libretto**, periodically from 1869 until his unexpected death, incorporating music from two other operatic projects. Based on a 12th-century epic (or possibly an 18th-century forgery), *Igor* is a Russian *grand opéra*, in which aristocratic individual and family tribulations play out against a background of war and social disintegration. It is regarded as a flawed landmark of Russian nationalism, in which Borodin's music vastly surpasses its plot, and a fitting successor to **Mikhail Ivanovich Glinka**'s *Ruslan and Lyudmila* (1842). Nowadays its best-known music is the set of *Polovtsian Dances* performed in Act 2 for Igor and his captors. At his death Borodin left a miscellany of finished scores (partially orchestrated) and sketches that were revised and completed (1887–88) by **Nikolay Andreyevich Rimsky-Korsakov** and Aleksandr Glazunov (1865–1936) and performed in St. Petersburg in 1890.

BRITTEN, BENJAMIN. (1913, Lowestoft–1976, Aldeburgh.) British **composer** of 15 operatic works from ca. 1940 to the mid-1970s, and other vocal and instrumental music. Like **Gian Carlo Menotti** and **Hans Werner Henze**, Britten was a rare opera specialist in the 20th century who contributed more than any other English composer to the current repertory.

Born to well-to-do middle-class parents, Britten took piano and viola lessons and showed prodigious aptitude as a composer at an early age. As a teenager he studied composition privately in **London** while receiving a preparatory school education, then at the Royal College of Music (1930–33). He began his career writing music for movies, plays, and radio productions (some 70 projects, mostly 1935–45). His pacifist stance led him to immigrate to the United States in 1939 with his future artistic collaborator, co-founder of the English Opera Group (beginning 1947), and life partner, **tenor** Peter Pears (1910–1986). He produced his first theatrical work, the **operetta** *Paul Bunyan*, at Columbia University in New York (1941).

Throughout his career, Britten for the most part resisted modernist atonality, pervasive dissonance, and melodic fragmentation—although he adopted these techniques as appropriate for expressive purposes—and his style remained grounded in tonality. Structurally his operas are also comparatively traditional: they tend to be organized in set pieces, including large ensembles, which sometimes allude to Italian designs and make room for richly accompanied emotive lyricism attuned to the inflections of the English language.

Britten's three large-scale works, which involve expansive casts and premiered at major venues, set their ostracized protagonists, victims of rumors and arguably unjust accusations, against grotesquely depicted persecutors. In *Peter Grimes* (London, Sadler's Wells Theater), one of the most-performed 20th-century operas, a fisherman accused of murdering his apprentice kills himself by scuttling his own boat. *Billy Budd* (premiered Covent Garden) was commissioned by the British government for the national exhibition of 1951. Based on Herman Melville's novella, its tale of an inarticulate sailor unable to defend himself, who is executed after killing a shipmate who had vindictively accused him of mutiny, is narrated as a flashback by an aging British naval captain who failed to intervene. *Gloriana* (1953, commissioned by Covent Garden) was a rare failure for Britten in part because of its unflattering portrayal of the aging Elizabeth I, who betrays the Earl of Essex against a background of court politics, impending rebellion, and historicist allusions to period music.

A number of Britten's remaining operas, written for smaller companies—in particular his English Opera Group—also explore aspects of "otherness": *The Rape of Lucretia* (1946), in which a Roman general's wife kills herself after their ruling prince violates her; *Albert Herring* (1947, after a short story by Guy de Maupassant), a comic chamber opera in which a shy boy dominated by his mother breaks out of his shell in a night of drunken debauchery; *The Turn of the Screw* (1954, based on the novella by Henry James), a bizarre psychodrama involving a governess tormented by spirits who threaten her wards, in which Britten employed a twelve-tone row that conveys her emotional instability; and *Death in Venice* (1973), based on the Thomas Mann novella of homoerotic and pedophilic yearnings.

BUSENELLO, GIOVANNI FRANCESCO. (1598, Venice–1659, Legnaro.) Lawyer, poet, and prominent **librettist**, Busenello wrote five operas for **Venice** set by **Claudio Monteverdi** and **Francesco Cavalli**, including *L'incoronazione di Poppea*. He participated in several Venetian academies, the most important being the hedonistic Accademia degli Incogniti (Academy of the Unknowns), founded by the young Giovanni Francesco Loredano in 1630. This politically powerful literary society, which claimed as members the most prominent Venetian writers of the second quarter of the century, including Cavalli's librettist Giacinto Andrea Cicognini (1606–ca. 1650), essentially set the agenda for Italian **librettos** in the 1640s. They also played a major role in Venetian public opera through their management of the Teatro Novissimo (1641–45) for which the architect **Giacomo Torelli** worked his magic.

Emulating their hero, the iconoclastic poet Giambattista Marino (1569–1625), Busenello and his fellow Incogniti rebelled against academic authority and took artistic whim and audience gratification as their overriding values. They constructed more complicated, inventive plots and subplots derived from sources broadened to include such Romans as Ovid, Plutarch, and Virgil and to include historical subjects in addition to mythology. Defying theatrical conventions, they intermixed tragedy, comedy, and satire; rejected the Aristotelian unities; and mesmerized their audiences with intrigues, disguises, intricate networks of lovers, and spectacle. Having turned their backs on humanist idealism and optimism, they wrote librettos rife with erotic sensuality that indulged in exaggerated rhetoric and the virtuosity of overwrought metaphor.

C

CABALETTA. Conventional, usually fast final movement of Italian multi-movement **arias** and **duets** in the 19th century. In its standard configuration, the cabaletta showcases a catchy, often virtuosic main theme (A), which is reprised as a whole or in part following an energetic transition, and concludes with a rousing, applause-inducing coda often adapted from the transition: A–transition–A–coda. A familiar example is Norma's "Ah! bello, a me ritorna," which ends her aria "Casta diva" (*Norma*, Act 1).

In duet cabalettas, each singer normally takes a solo prior to the transition, usually repeating the same theme, although by midcentury contrasting themes also occur. Following the transition, **Gioachino Rossini** normally repeated the two solos prior to the coda: Solo A (first singer)–Solo A (second singer)–transition–Solo A (first singer)–Solo A (second singer)–coda (together). By the 1830s, **Vincenzo Bellini** and others abridged the duet reprise by having it sung simultaneously: Solo A (first singer)–Solo A (second singer)–transition–A (together)–coda (together); or alternatively Solo A (first singer)–Solo B (second singer)–transition–A or B (together)–coda (together).

Traditionally a reflective movement, the cabaletta reacts to events in the preceding movement (*tempo di mezzo*). Although the repetition of its main melody inherently lacks dramatic justification, in the age of **bel canto** singing, it provided an opportunity for flashy improvised ornamentation. In two-movement arias the cabaletta as a whole often wants for motivation, in part because its conventionally brilliant character limits its range of moods. And even in three-movement arias, **librettists** all too often failed to engineer decisive shifts in the *tempo di mezzo* to trigger it, making both movements superfluous. By midcentury—as dramatic plausibility became a preoccupation—composers and librettists addressed the cabaletta's shortcomings by abbreviating its reprise, exploring a broader range of musical affects, concocting more dynamic situations, or omitting it (and the *tempo di mezzo*) entirely.

CACCINI, FRANCESCA. (1587, Florence–after 1641.) Italian singer, **composer** of several operas (one of which survives), songs, *intermedi*, **ballets**, and incidental music for plays, and poet. Daughter of the singer and composer **Giulio Caccini**, she is the first known female opera composer.

Trained in voice, keyboard, and other instruments, Francesca also received sufficient liberal education to write poetry in Italian and Latin. She debuted as a singer at the Florentine wedding of Maria de' Medici in 1600, probably playing a role in **Jacopo Peri**'s *Euridice*. She was subsequently offered a position at Maria's court in France but was denied permission to leave Florence. Following her father, Francesca served the Medici family in Florence throughout most of her career, except for a sojourn in Lucca (1627–33), when she married an aristocrat there. Her one extant opera, *La liberazione di Ruggiero dall'isola d'Alcina*, which pits good and evil sorceresses against each other, the latter seducing and bewitching knights and then turning them into various plants, animals, and objects, was composed in 1625 for the visit of a Polish prince, who commissioned two additional operas the next year. It is the earliest surviving opera composed by a **woman**.

CACCINI, GIULIO. (1551, Rome–1618, Florence.) Italian **tenor** and **composer** also known for his proficiency on the **lute** and other instruments. Although in the late 1580s and 1590s attempts were made to lure him to Ferrara, Genoa, and **Rome**, his activities centered in Florence throughout his career, where he played a prominent role as a singer and composer in numerous court spectacles and joined in the **Florentine Cameratas** of Giovanni de' Bardi and Jacopo Corsi. For the festivities celebrating the wedding of Maria de' Medici and Henry IV of France in 1600, he composed pieces written for his associates to replace sections of **Jacopo Peri**'s *Euridice*. He quickly completed his own version, arranging for it to be printed before Peri's so that he could claim to have invented **recitative**. He also wrote most of the music for a dramatic *intermedio*, *Il rapimento di Cefalo*, the centerpiece of the entertainment.

Caccini's greatest accomplishment was the singing manual *Le nuove musiche* (*New Pieces of Music*, 1602), perhaps the most important printed collection of solo **madrigals**, *canzonette*, and strophic variation **arias**. Caccini's famous preface provides a window into the style and execution of *seconda pratica* **monody**. It is characterized by *sprezzatura* ([aristocratic] nonchalance), a flexible, expressively responsive approach to rhythm, meter, and tempo that mimics the pacing and inflections of speech (a form of rubato), combined with a casual treatment of dissonance. Despite this freedom, Caccini discouraged the apparently common practice of indiscriminately elaborating vocal melodies to the detriment of musical and poetic expression.

As an antidote, he discussed the realization and tasteful deployment of a repertory of **ornaments** and illustrated their usage by printing properly embellished versions of his songs.

By all accounts an unpleasant, self-promoting individual, Caccini was involved in numerous court intrigues and disputes. Among these, he may have contributed to unmasking an affair, leading to the murder of Pietro de' Medici's adulterous wife Eleonora; hijacked the 1600 wedding festivities, probably engineering the demotion of **Emilio de' Cavalieri** as music director; and made various untenable artistic claims, for example implying in his prefaces to *Euridice* and *Le nuove musiche* that he invented the *stile rappresentativo*, **basso continuo**, and opera.

CADENZA. In opera, unaccompanied embellishment in a free tempo of the final cadence of an **aria** or a section of an aria, or occasionally a movement of a 19th-century **duet**. The cadenza is often signaled by a fermata (held note) and may be either improvised or notated. Vocal cadenzas were considerably shorter than instrumental cadenzas: according to 18th-century theorists they were to be sung on a single breath, although in reality singers took liberties with that rule.

The term was first applied to an ornamented cadence in the early 16th century, and melismatic final cadences became common in early 17th-century **monodies**. In the late 17th and early 18th centuries the rise of **bel canto** operatic singing and the dominance of the da capo aria encouraged such improvised **ornamentation** as the cadenza provided. Singers commonly performed cadenzas in da capo arias to end the three main sections, but virtuosos such as **Farinelli** reportedly shoehorned as many as seven into a single aria. In the late 18th century, two-movement *rondò* cadenzas are heard commonly before thematic reprises and at the end of the slow first movement. Similar opportunities exist in the 19th-century three-movement aria at the end of the slow movement and before the reprise of the **cabaletta** melody. By midcentury, particularly as the cabaletta declined, cadenzas were confined mostly to the ends of slow movements. And increasingly the virtuosic runs, leaps, trills, and other ornaments were replaced with impassioned declamation, particularly in male arias. Operatic cadenzas essentially disappeared after 1875.

CALDARA, ANTONIO. (Probably 1671, Venice–1736, Vienna.) One of the most prolific **composers** of the early 18th century, he wrote more than 75 operas from the 1690s through the 1730s, in addition to other stage works, oratorios, and a sizable corpus of instrumental music. Caldara began his career as a choirboy and cellist at St. Mark's Basilica in **Venice** (before 1699) and wrote four operas for that city (1689–98) in addition to trio sonatas and chamber cantatas. His first prestigious appointment was as *maestro di* *cappella* at Mantua (1699–1707) under the last duke of the Gonzagas, a family that had employed opera composers since **Claudio Monteverdi**. Unfortunately the War of the Spanish Succession and Habsburg invasion limited the number of productions there as elsewhere in northern Italy. Following a stint as choirmaster at Prince Francesco Ruspoli's court in Rome (1709–16), where he concentrated on oratorios and cantatas, he acknowledged political inevitability and joined the court of Emperor Charles VI in **Vienna** as vice Kapellmeister (1716 until his death). During his 20 years there, he took over, for the most part, the theatrical duties of the legendary Kapellmeister Johann Fux (1660–1741) and wrote an astonishing three dozen plus theatrical works for name days and birthdays of the emperor and empress and other celebrations, as well as 10 or more for Salzburg and a number for other locations.

Owing largely to his duties in Vienna, Caldara was one of the most productive composers of operas on **librettos** by the early members of the **Arcadian Academy**: **Apostolo Zeno** (about 20 operas, many of them inaugural settings) and **Pietro Metastasio** (10 operas, all inaugural settings, including *L'olimpiade*, 1733; *Demofoonte*, 1733; and *La clemenza di Tito*, 1734, later remade by **Wolfgang Amadeus Mozart**). Caldara was most conservative when working for the Viennese court, indulging Charles's taste for high-minded subjects, elaborate da capo **arias** slathered in **coloratura** and densely accompanied by contrapuntal string ensembles, and patience-testing **recitatives**. His operas for other cities—Venice and Salzburg, primarily—tend to be lighter in their subject matter and style and more varied in the forms and textures of their arias.

CALLAS, MARIA. (1923, New York–1977, Paris.) American-born **soprano** of Greek descent (originally Kalogeropoulou). Callas trained in Athens in the early 1940s and debuted there as Tosca (*see TOSCA*; 1942). Her appearance in **Amilcare Ponchielli**'s *La Gioconda* (Verona, 1947; originally 1876) began an extremely versatile Italian career. She ranged from such emotionally and vocally taxing roles as Aida (*see AIDA*), Isolda (*see TRISTAN UND ISOLDE*), and Tosca to lighter ones in the **bel canto** tradition, such as Lucia in *Lucia di Lammermoor* and Gilda in *Rigoletto*, to more rarified parts in such operas as **Christoph Willibald Gluck**'s *Alceste* and **Luigi Cherubini**'s *Médée* (1797). By the 1950s the most famous singer in the world, Callas was in constant demand for such warhorse leads as **Norma**, Violetta in **Giuseppe Verdi**'s *La traviata* (1853), and Tosca.

Reputedly an uncompromising perfectionist and petulant collaborator who increasingly canceled appearances as her long-standing vocal problems worsened in the 1960s, Callas was renowned, despite various technical shortcomings, as an incisive dramatic interpreter. She possessed a distinctly per-

sonal voice capable of both breathtaking changes of timbre and dazzling displays of acrobatic **coloratura**. Ending where she began, her last operatic role was Tosca (**London**, 1965).
See also WOMEN AND OPERA.

CALZABIGI, RANIERI. (1714, Livorno–1795, Naples.) Italian **librettist** and writer, author of 13 **librettos** from the 1740s to the 1790s and the most dedicated proponent of fusing French and Italian elements in serious opera to reform **Pietro Metastasio**'s conventions (*see* ARCADIAN ACADEMY). Having completed a Jesuit education in the 1720s, Calzabigi collected books and began his literary career while working in his family's business in Livorno (from 1733), joining the Arcadian Academy by 1740. Exiled from Tuscany, possibly in connection with a poisoning, he relocated to **Naples** in 1741, where his first librettos (starting with *La gara fra l'Amore e la Virtù*, 1745, not performed and now lost) were courtly occasional pieces that already showed his tendencies toward naturalness and unconventionality. He spent the early 1750s in **Paris** as a companion of Giacomo Casanova, where he absorbed the French theatrical style and edited the complete works of Metastasio (1755) prefaced with an essay on the poet's plays that criticized traditional *tragédie en musique* but advocated incorporating French **choruses**, **ballets**, and spectacular scenery in Italian **opera seria**.

Ejected from France, possibly because of a misguided business venture with Casanova, Calzabigi traveled for several years, arriving in **Vienna** in 1761. There he experienced a strained relationship with the court poet Metastasio as he joined forces with **Christoph Willibald Gluck** in staging the so-called reform operas *Orfeo ed Euridice* (1762); *Alceste* (1767), published in 1769 with a preface explicating their reforms; and *Paride ed Elena* (1770). Public acceptance of Calzabigi's intensive innovations may be credited to the familiarity of his Viennese audience with French theater and the looser conventions of the *festa teatrale*, their artistic open-mindedness in general, and his fortunate collaboration with a like-minded composer. Owing to Gluck's increasing absences, economic circumstances, and local artistic squabbles, he left Vienna in 1773 for Italy and reestablished himself in Naples by 1780, where he continued to write librettos until 1794, including two for **Giovanni Paisiello**.

CAMBERT, ROBERT. (ca. 1628, Paris–1677, London.) French **composer** of four operatic works, including the first extant French opera.

Cambert began his career as a church organist in **Paris**, where he rose to fame at the court of Louis XIV. His elegy *La muette ingratte* (1658, lost) was his earliest attempt to mimic Italian operatic music, leading to increasingly ambitious projects. The *Pastorale d'Issy* (1659, privately performed, music lost), the first of three collaborations with the poet Pierre Perrin (ca. 1620–1675), was his first full-length (though relatively brief) opera, lasting approximately 90 minutes, and according to Perrin the first French opera (probably a spurious claim). The *comédie en musique Ariane, ou Le mariage de Bacchus* (1659, unperformed, music lost) led eventually to the award of the initial royal privilege (monopoly) for musical spectacles to Perrin in 1669.

Cambert and Perrin's **pastorale** *Pomone* (1671, music partly lost), in which the god of autumn courts the goddess of fruits (Pomona) by taking the identities of other gods, was the more successful of only two Cambert operas produced under the privilege. It initiated the royal Académies d'Opéra and established enduring conventions including its mythological subject, five-act design, and prominent use of **ballets** and stage machinery for special effects. A critical and popular triumph, it is widely considered the first legitimate French opera, and at least the first to have its music preserved. After Perrin lost his monopoly to **Jean-Baptiste Lully** the next year, Cambert immigrated to **London**, where he composed music for King Charles II.

CAMPRA, ANDRÉ. (1660, Aix-en-Provence–1744, Versailles.) French **composer** of more than 15 operas (most from the late 1690s through the 1710s), as well as **ballets** and sacred music. The leading composer of French opera between **Jean-Baptiste Lully** and **Jean-Philippe Rameau**, Campra is credited with creating the genre of *opéra-ballet*.

As a church music director, Campra rose through provincial ranks to the post of *maître de musique* at the Cathedral of Notre Dame in **Paris** (beginning 1694), where he also composed music for elaborate Latin plays at the Jesuit College of Louis-le-Grand. His first full-length opera, the *opéra-ballet L'Europe galante* (1697), inaugurated a new type, to which he made four additional contributions. Following a **prologue**, *L'Europe galante*'s four comic or semiserious entrées (acts) present unconnected, ethnically stereotyped vignettes of love in France, Spain, Italy, and Turkey. Campra also wrote about twice as many examples of the established *tragédie en musique*, beginning with *Hésione* (1700) and including his masterwork, *Tancrède* (1702). He returned primarily to sacred music from the 1720s on.

CANTO DECLAMATO. *See* SINGING STYLE.

CANZONE. *See* ARIA; STAGE SONG.

CANZONETTA. A short, lively, dancelike song in early 17th-century opera, a poetic and musical outgrowth of the popular *frottola* tradition and related 16th-century genres like the villanella. Its poetry presents emotionally inconsequential subject matter in a series of short stanzas that feature clear meter, lively accentuation, and patterned rhymes. The correspondingly popular, tuneful, and lighthearted music sets the text in strophic form or strophic variations (*see* ARIA). A relationship to Renaissance dance is heard in the *canzonetta*'s emphatically metrical patterned rhythms, often energized by hemiola (e.g., alternation of 6/8 and 3/4 meter) and other types of syncopation, and regular phrase lengths. *Canzonette* appeared in opera as early as Tirsi's "Nel pur ardor" (Jacopo Peri, *Euridice*, scene 2). Claudio Monteverdi employed this style for various arrangements of voices, from solo songs with basso continuo to choruses, in the festive episodes of *Orfeo*, for example the wedding celebrations that begin Act 2 (see the well-known "Vi ricorda"). In early opera, the *canzonetta* represents the opposite end of the spectrum of text-setting styles from the expressively ornamented fluid melody of madrigals and the rhetorical intensity of the various types of recitative.

CARMEN. **Opéra comique**; music by **Georges Bizet**, **libretto** by Henri Meilhac (1831–1897) and Ludovic Halévy (1834–1908) based on Prosper Mérimée's (1803–1870) novella (1845); four acts; premiered **Paris**, Opéra-Comique, March 1875. Currently the most familiar opera in the repertory, its popularity has been ensured by the showstopping tunefulness of many of its numbers and its risqué plot. It contributed to the synthesis of opéra comique with more serious genres in the late 19th century and provided a prototype for Italian **verismo** opera in the 1890s.

The opera's subject, championed by Bizet and his **librettists**, led to the resignation of one of the theater directors, the one who stayed on (Camille Du Locle, 1832–1903) had reservations about its realism and musical exoticisms, and its sometimes difficult ensemble writing provoked objections by the **orchestra** and **chorus**. The original production met with outrage from the press and conservative members of the audience, suffered dwindling attendance, and was almost withdrawn after a few showings. Sustained by critics and composers who recognized its importance, *Carmen* gradually gained a cult following in Paris and spread by way of **Vienna** throughout the world during the decade following its premier.

Working in and around Seville, the gypsy smuggler and serial seductress Carmen abandons the lieutenant Zuniga and takes up with the corporal Don José, whom she subsequently replaces with the bullfighter Escamillo. Don José has joined the army to avoid imprisonment for a crime committed at home but is jailed for helping Carmen escape arrest after she slashes a woman at the tobacco factory where she sometimes works. Micaëla, his hometown sweetheart, tries to save him from Carmen's clutches and his self-destructive impulses: her news of his mother's forgiveness and impending death lures him home temporarily. But tragically he returns and, overcome by jealousy, stabs his tormenter in a final confrontation.

Carmen was considered inappropriate for a respectable, family-friendly theater owing to any number of its frank realisms: the presence of coarse women who work in factories, smoke cigars, and commit crimes; Carmen's sexual empowerment and resistance to personal commitment and social restraints; the hero's unredeemable moral and psychological disintegration; and the heroine's resulting murder onstage. Yet while its dark side precludes conventional categorization, it nonetheless abounds in traditional elements of opéra comique and French opera in general. In its original version, spoken dialogues alternated with its concise, self-contained, melodically engaging set pieces. (Spoken dialogues were replaced by **recitatives** for the 1875 production in Vienna.) Local color, represented by the score's famous dance songs—Carmen's habanera (a Cuban dance widely exported in the 19th century), "L'amour est un oiseau rebelle," her vocalization at her arrest, and her seguidilla (a Spanish dance similar to the bolero), "Près des ramparts de Séville" (all Act 1)—exploits the vogue for exoticism in contemporary French opera.

The emphasis on self-portraiture and atmosphere represented by Carmen's music as well as set pieces for the factory girls, the children playing soldier, Escamillo, and the smugglers is stock in trade for opéra comique. So too is the slapstick compression of otherwise serious events in Acts 1 and 2, for example, the soldiers' harassment of Michaëla, Carmen's jailbreak, and the smugglers' disarmament of Zuniga (as well as their predominantly jocular demeanor), although this comic nonchalance disappears in Acts 3 and 4. Popular tunefulness is joined at times by a saccharine lyricism—in Micaëla's duet with Don José (Act 1) or her air "Je dis que rein" (Act 3)—reminiscent of **Charles Gounod** and *opéra lyrique*. Bizet made prominent use of recurring associative motifs, as was common in French opera: Carmen's fatalism theme and Escamillo's Toreador Song ("Votre toast," Act 2), introduced in the **overture** along with those preceding the bullfight in Act 4, as well as Micaëla's love theme from her Act 1 duet with Don José. And he relied frequently on traditional French schemata: strophes for the characteristic songs for Carmen and Escamillo; ternary forms for more sophisticated numbers (the introduction to Act 1, in which the soldiers' ennui chorus frames Micaëla's dialogue with the corporal Moralès, the Act 2 quintet for the gypsies and smugglers, and Micaëla's air in Act 3); and a rondo-like arrangement for the fortune-telling scene in Act 3.

See also WOMEN AND OPERA.

CARUSO, ENRICO. (1873, Naples–1921, Naples.) Italian **tenor**, among the most acclaimed singers of the 20th century.

After early experiences singing in church as a boy **soprano**, Caruso trained in **Naples**, debuted there in the little-known Mario Morelli's *L'amico francesco* (1894), and sang in a number of provincial theaters to mixed reviews until he finally gained public notice in a performance of **Amilcare Ponchielli**'s *La Gioconda* in Palermo (1897, originally 1876). He cemented his reputation with premieres of Francesco Cilea's (1866–1950) *L'arlesiana* (1897) and *Adriana Lecouvreur* (1902) and **Umberto Giordano**'s *Fedora* (1898). Following notable performances in Buenos Aires, **Rome** (both 1899), Milan (1900–01), and **London** (1902), he began a long-standing association with **New York**'s Metropolitan Opera, taking his first bows as the Duke in *Rigoletto* (1903). Caruso's love affair with the Met numbered over 800 appearances in approximately 40 operas and included the premier of **Giacomo Puccini**'s *La fanciulla del West* (1910, the Met's first world premier) under **Arturo Toscanini**.

Once Caruso developed his upper register early in his career, his voice combined the richness of a baritone (*see* BASS) with the brilliance of a tenor. Known for precise intonation and unmatched breath control, which allowed sustained phrasings and liquid legato and portamento (sliding) connections between notes, Caruso dominated a wide repertory that ranged from Verdian warhorses, to Puccinian and other late 19th-century Italian repertory, to French ***grand opéra*** and ***opéra lyrique***.

CARVALHO, LÉON. (1825, Mauritius–1897, Paris.) Progressive foreign-born French theater director and baritone (*see* BASS). Carvalho moved to **Paris** as a youth and trained at the Conservatoire, after which he performed minor roles at the Opéra-Comique (beginning 1848). He was hired as director of the struggling Théâtre-Lyrique in 1856 soon after his wife, **soprano** Marie Miolan-Carvalho (1827–1895), became the premier attraction there. Carvalho made the house a legitimate rival of the Opéra and Opéra-Comique and courageously championed the works of forward-looking composers such as **Hector Berlioz**, **Charles-François Gounod**, and **Georges Bizet**, as well as historical **opéra comique** and Italian and German operas. He ran the Opéra-Comique from 1876 to1887, again supporting innovators like Léo Delibes (1836–1891, *Lakmé*, 1883) and **Jules Massenet**, and later, after legal troubles resulting from a theater fire were resolved, from 1891 until the end of his career.

CASTRATO. Adult male **soprano** or **contralto** singer castrated before puberty to retain his high range while other aspects of his anatomy, particularly his chest size and lung capacity, continued to expand, often disproportionately. The castrato's unique physiology and extended training that continued through adolescence resulted, in the best circumstances, in unique power, otherworldly and brilliant tone quality, a range as great as three octaves or more, astonishing breath control, astounding agility and velocity for florid **ornamentation** and acrobatic passagework, and exceptional musicality and expressiveness.

Castration of singers originated to provide high male voices in 16th-century Italy after the range of sacred choir music had expanded upward, because **women** were prohibited from singing in churches outside of convents. Castratos were preferred over boy sopranos, who could serve for only a few years before their voices broke, and over contratenor falsetto singers, particularly in the uppermost register. They were employed in the Sistine Chapel choir by 1565, were formally sanctioned by Pope Sixtus V after 1589, became particularly important for oratorios and other types of *concertato* music (music combining voices and instruments) in the 17th and 18th centuries, and were active in Rome as late as 1914 (Alessandro Moreschi, 1858–1922).

Engaging castratos for stage productions was a natural step, and they performed in some of the earliest operas. Giovanni Magli (died 1625) and possibly Giovanni Bacchini (active 1588–1607), both castratos, played female roles in **Claudio Monteverdi**'s *Orfeo*. In *L'incoronazione di Poppea*, Nero, the Page, and probably Ottone were castrato roles. The operatic castrato rose in prominence across the 17th century: by 1680 the male lead in an **opera seria** was normally a castrato, because this dominant vocal type was considered ideal for heroic parts. The spread of Italian opera across Europe by ca. 1800 made castratos prized, lavishly compensated performers everywhere except France, where they were banned from opera. **Senesino** and **Farinelli** were two of the most esteemed and popular among hundreds who performed in the late 17th and 18th centuries. During the Enlightenment, castration of singers was increasingly criticized and ridiculed, and the number of castratos declined. After 1800 their parts were replaced first by female pants roles (*see* TRAVESTY; for example, Arsace in **Gioachino Rossini**'s *Semiramide*) and eventually by **tenor** heroes. **Giacomo Meyerbeer**'s *Il crociato in Egitto* (1824) was the last important opera to feature a castrato part (Armando).

See also GUADAGNI, GAETANO; MELANI, ATTO; SIFACE; VELLUTI, GIOVANNI BATTISTA; VITTORI, LORETO.

CATALANI, ALFREDO. (1854, Lucca–1893, Milan.) Italian **composer** of five operas and leader of the underachieving generation active in the 1870s and 1880s prior to **verismo**. Born into a musical family, Catalani received elite training at **conservatories** in Lucca, **Paris**, and Milan and met proponents of the avant-garde *scapigliatura* movement at the Milanese salon of **Giuseppe Verdi**'s confidante Clarina Maffei. His graduation opera *La falce* (1875) set a **libretto** by one of their leaders, **Arrigo Boito**, who would later write Verdi's last two librettos, *Otello* and *Falstaff* (1893). While serving as composition professor at the Milan Conservatory (beginning 1888), Catalani premiered his last opera, *La Wally* (1892), at La Scala, his only contribution to the modern repertory. A pulmonary inflammation that plagued him from his teens interfered with his productivity and finally killed him at 39.

Though undeniably talented and admired by the likes of the young **Arturo Toscanini** and Gustav Mahler (1860–1911), Catalani never realized his potential—his relatively meager output attributable to his ill health and other factors—contributing to his morbid jealousy of **Ruggero Leoncavallo, Giacomo Puccini**, and others. Although he collaborated with the three most important **librettists** of his day—Boito; Antonio Ghislanzoni (1824–1893), who versified **Aida**; and **Luigi Illica**—he never found a loyal partner like **Vincenzo Bellini**'s **Felice Romani** or Verdi's **Francesco Maria Piave**. And the **Ricordi** Publishing House, which had a stranglehold on Milan, gave him indifferent support.

Catalani's involvement with *scapigliatura* proved to be a dead end, as his **Wagnerism** put him out of step with public taste in Italy in the late 1880s and 1890s. A number of his operas show Germanic traits: northern mythological and supernatural references (*Elda* on the Lorelei legend, 1880); Germanic locales—*La Wally* is an alpine romantic tragedy, in which the heroine throws herself off a cliff after her lover is killed by an avalanche; Wagnerian treatment of characters as symbols rather than human individuals; nontraditional harmonic progressions and voice leading; and dedication to the orchestra, to the extent that Catalani wrote a tone poem (*Ero e Leandro*, 1884) and several other orchestral works, and incorporated extended symphonic sections in his operas. In avoiding the ostentation of **grand opèra** (except in *Dejanice*, 1883), Catalani failed to discover an alternative source of structural cohesion and direction until he turned to a network of developing and recurring motives in *La Wally* (1892) akin to those of late Verdi (in *Aida*, *Otello*, and *Falstaff*), Puccini, and **Richard Wagner**.

CATEGORIES OF OPERA. Throughout their history, operas have been categorized according to diverse criteria. Designations for these categories have appeared in **librettos**, scores, contemporaneous accounts, and dictionaries and histories (both old and new).

The broadest divisions are delineated by subject matter, characterization, and emotional intensity: serious versus comic or semiserious opera. Various subcategories of serious opera—*festa teatrale*, *grand opéra*, *melodramma*, music drama (*see* WAGNER, RICHARD), **opera seria**, *tragédie lyrique*, and many others—of comic opera—**ballad opera**, *farsa*, **intermezzo**, **opera buffa**, **opéra comique**, **operetta**, **singspiel**, *tonadilla*, and **zarzuela**—and of hybrids such as *opéra lyrique* and *opera semiseria* are further distinguished by location and language, structural and other stylistic conventions (such as length, number of acts, cast size, whether or not spoken dialogue is employed), period of compositional activity, mode of presentation (e.g., self-standing versus intermission entertainment), prestige, and associations with different theaters and target audiences. Several of these subcategories (particularly opéra comique) accommodated a broad range of stylistic options and requirements that shifted over time and crossed broader boundaries. And their names sometimes shifted from initial historical designations (*dramma per musica* and **tragédie en musique**) to historical terms applied during later phases of development (the late 18th-century *tragédie lyrique* replacing the 17th-century *tragédie en musique*), to modern terms ("opera seria" for the more contemporaneous *dramma per musica*). A host of more precise ad hoc historical or modern descriptors that define sub-subcategories have also been applied, for example *dramma tragicomico* or *dramma eroicomico* (tragic-comic or heroic-comic drama) for *opera semiseria*, or mythological, historical, or heroic opera, etc., for opera seria. Other designations may address even more specific aspects of plot or situation, such as fantasy opera (e.g., those of **Nikolay Andreyevich Rimsky-Korsakov**), **pastoral** opera, *rappresentazione sacra*, **rescue opera**, or *Zeitoper*.

Categories are sometimes associated with an individual or group and their aesthetic goals or style, such as Arcadian or Metastasian opera (*see* ARCADIAN ACADEMY and METASTASIO, PIETRO); reform opera (*see* ALCESTE, GLUCK, CHRISTOPH WILLIBALD, and *ORFEO ED EURIDICE*); or Mozartian opera, Verdian opera, Wagnerian opera, and the like. They may relate to a broader historical, aesthetic, artistic, or musical style, period, or movement, as in **baroque** opera, **expressionist** opera, *galant* opera, **minimalist** opera, **neo-classical** opera, **romantic** opera, **sentimental opera**, **symbolist** opera, or **verismo** opera. They may reflect municipal, regional, or national identities (sometimes within a specific timeframe): **Beijing opera**, Florentine opera (*see* FLORENTINE CAMERATA), Neapolitan opera (*see* NAPLES), 17th-century Roman opera (*see* ROME), 17th-century Venetian opera (*see* VENICE), or French, German, Italian, or Russian opera. Or they may emphasize a single specific aspect of creation, execution, or style, for example, **bel canto** opera, court opera, *Literaturoper*, **masque**, **melodrama**, **number opera**, *opéra-ballet*, **pasticcio**, public opera, **puppet opera**, **serenata**, or television opera (*see* KRENEK, ERNST; MENOTTI, GIAN CARLO).

CAVALIERI, CATARINA. (1755, Vienna–1801, Vienna.) Leading Austrian **soprano** whose career centered almost exclusively on her home city of **Vienna**, where she was mentored by the court opera composer **Antonio Salieri**. She sang numerous German roles at the National-**Singspiel**, and **opera buffa** leads at the Burgtheater after 1783. A specialist in extended coloratura **arias**, she had extraordinary endurance, agility, and power throughout her range, which extended to high d", although its top end was often judged unpleasant. Her acting and delivery of spoken dialogue were less effective. She is notable for creating the role of Konstanze in **Wolfgang Amadeus Mozart**'s *Die Entführung aus dem Serail* (1782), for which Mozart provided two display arias tailored to her abilities ("Ach ich liebte" and "Martern aller Arten"). She also played Donna Elvira and the Countess in Viennese productions of *Don Giovanni* (1788, originally Prague 1787) and *Le nozze di Figaro* (1789, originally 1786), respectively.

CAVALIERI, EMILIO DE'. (ca. 1550, Rome–1602, Rome.) Italian **composer**, musician, theatrical producer, and diplomat. Cavalieri was involved in music making for the Oratorio del Santissimo Crocifisso in **Rome** (beginning 1578). He followed his patron Cardinal Ferdinando de' Medici to Florence when he became Grand Duke of Tuscany, and as his agent in the 1590s, Cavalieri contributed to intrigues involving the elections of several popes. Ferdinando appointed him superintendent of artists and musicians at court in 1588. For Ferdinando's wedding in 1589, Cavalieri coordinated a stable of poets—including Giovanni de' Bardi (1534–1612, patron of the first **Florentine Camerata**); Ottavio Rinuccini (1562–1621, later author of the earliest operas *Dafne* and *Euridice*); and his own **librettist** Laura Guidiccioni Lucchesini (1550–ca. 1597)—and composers—among them the madrigalist Luca Marenzio (ca. 1553–1599), his rivals **Giulio Caccini** and **Jacopo Peri**, and himself—producing the most famous and extravagant collection of *intermedi* that Florence would ever see. In the 1590s, his adaptations of poems by Torquato Tasso and Giovanni Battista Guarini popularized **pastoral** topics that anticipate the earliest operas.

Though elbowed aside by Caccini as director of Maria de' Medici's wedding celebration in 1600, Cavalieri composed *La contesa fra Giunone e Minerva* (lost) and most likely produced Peri's *Euridice*. Disgusted at the betrayal, Cavalieri retreated to Rome, where earlier that year he had produced his most famous work, the *rappresentazione sacra Rappresentatione di Anima, et di Corpo* (Rome, February 1600). Predating Peri's *Euridice* by half a year, it is the earliest surviving play set completely to polyphonic music and the first work to be published with figured **bass** (*see* BASSO CONTINUO). Like Caccini, Cavalieri claimed to have invented the new theatrical style and applied it first to opera.

CAVALLERIA RUSTICANA. *Melodramma*; music by **Pietro Mascagni**, **libretto** by Giovanni Targioni-Tozzetti (1863–1934) and Guido Menasci (1867–1925), based on a short story (1880) and play (1884) by the Italian realist author Giovanni Verga (1840–1922); one act with orchestral **intermezzo**; premiered **Rome**, Teatro Costanzi, May 1890. *Rustic Chivalry* is the first noteworthy **verismo** opera and Mascagni's only lasting success. It won the second (1888) of four competitions held by the Milanese publisher Sonzogno to cultivate new talent and expand the Italian side of their French-dominated catalog. Having enjoyed phenomenal success at its premier, it has remained a repertory staple to the present day, frequently appearing on a double bill with **Ruggero Leoncavallo**'s *Pagliacci*.

A prototype for verismo operas by Leoncavallo, **Giacomo Puccini**, and others, *Cavalleria* turns its back on **romantic pastoralism**, instead exposing the tragic realities of the lives of its rustic commoners against a backdrop of contemporary Sicilian village life. Its concise plot unfolds in a condensed format, lasting a little over an hour, its brevity allowing sustained intensity. Prior to the opera, while the peasant Turiddu had been serving in the army, his fiancée Lola married the prosperous tradesman Alfio. Out of spite, Turiddu seduced the innocent Santuzza but abandoned her for an affair with his former lover. Against a backdrop of Easter festivities, he rejects Santuzza's plea to reclaim her, so she betrays his adultery with Lola to Alfio. As the congregation leaves Mass, Alfio refuses Turiddu's invitation to drink, provoking a duel and Turiddu's death.

Scenic stage songs and instrumental music—the pastoral instrumental prelude, the opening Easter **chorus** "Gli aranci olezzano sui verdi margini" with its botanical imagery, Alfio's teamster's *sortita* "Il cavallo scalpita," and the choral hymn "Regina coeli"—establish the local color of peasant Easter celebrations, the Mass and floral imagery providing metaphors for Santuzza's (and modern society's) lost purity. They also serve as a broadly paced point of departure for the intensification of action that leads to the **duets** for Santuzza, in which Turiddu rejects her and she betrays him to Alfio. Similarly, the momentary respite of the intermezzo, the chorus "A casa, amici" following the Mass, and Turiddu's *brindisi* (*see* STAGE SONG) with Alfio and chorus "Viva il vino spumeggiante" begin a gradual buildup toward the challenge and offstage duel and murder.

CAVALLI, FRANCESCO. (1602, Crema–1676, Venice.) Italian **composer** of more than 30 operas (largely from the 1640s through the 1660s), which provide the most comprehensive documentation of the midcentury Venetian style, and other vocal music, singer, and organist; along with **Antonio Cesti**, a central figure in the development of 17th-century **bel canto**. Born Francesco Caletti, he took the name of his first patron ca. 1630. Cavalli began his career as a **soprano**, then **tenor** in the choir of St. Mark's Basilica in **Venice** in 1616 under the direction of **Claudio Monteverdi**. He also served as organist at the church of Saints Giovanni e Paolo beginning in 1620, then at St. Mark's from 1639 through the end of his career, where he became *maestro di cappella* in 1668.

Cavalli was financially well seated owing to a profitable marriage in 1630, which allowed him to bankroll his own early operatic productions in Venice. In just the third season of Venetian public opera he not only composed but produced and partly financed his first opera, *Le nozze di Teti e di Peleo* (1639), beginning a series of collaborations with the **librettists Giovanni Francesco Busenello** (who would also write *L'incoronazione di Poppea* for Monteverdi), Giovanni Faustini (1615–1651), and Giacinto Andrea Cicognini (1606–ca. 1650) that would boast the triumphs *Didone* (1641), *Egisto* (1643), and *Giasone*. These operas and the later *Xerse* (1655) would serve the repertories of touring companies who disseminated opera in the 1650s and 1660s throughout Italy, particularly in **Naples**, and elsewhere. And they would secure the dominance of bel canto, **aria**-dominated opera during that period.

Cavalli spent 1660–62 in France arranging a revival of *Xerse* and, after disruptions and delays, the new opera *Ercole amante*, originally planned for the marriage of Louis XIV and Maria Theresa of Spain. A six-hour entertainment that took place in a cavernous, acoustically barren theater, it featured **ballets** by **Jean-Baptiste Lully** that were danced by aristocrats including the bride and groom. Thus Cavalli played an important role in introducing opera to France prior to Lully's hegemony. He died a wealthy man, leaving an estate valued at more than the annual budget of the St. Mark's choir.

CAVATINA. *See* ARIA.

CENSORSHIP. Political intervention in one form or another was a fact of life in opera from the earliest days. For the most part it focused on subject matter, wording, and aspects of **production**, although in the 20th century it was also directed at times toward artists and musical style.

By comparison with plays and books, operas generally represented less threatening representations of their subjects owing both to the condensation of language necessary to make room for music and perhaps to the reduced intelligibility of sung text. For example *Le nozze di Figaro* was tolerated in **Vienna**, whereas Pierre-Augustin Beaumarchais's (1732–1799) play had been banned. Nonetheless, operas were also subjected to various restrictions. In the 17th and 18th centuries, and in some locations as late as the 19th, such control was to a large extent a matter of self-censorship. It was exerted within the internal management structure of specific theaters through aristocratic oversight by court officials or coalitions of noble investors working in conjunction with an impresario and a house **librettist**, who for the most part understood local expectations. Examples include **Giulio Rospigliosi**'s Roman sacred operas for the Barberini family; the productions of such early Venetian theaters as the Santi Giovanni e Paulo and the San Giovanni Grisostomo managed by the Grimani family (*see* VENICE); **Jean-Baptiste Lully**'s operatic monopoly run in collaboration with the royal academies; **Pietro Metastasio**'s **opera seria librettos** promoting social order and the status quo; the production syndicate at Eszterháza during **Joseph Haydn**'s service as music director, over which Prince Nikolaus ("The Magnificent") dictated artistic policy; and the interaction between theater managers and the government commissions supervising French *grand opéra* during the 1830s and 1840s.

External censorship of specific works or elements of specific works was directed more toward independently run public theaters. In the 18th century the newly developing comic genres (*see* CATEGORIES OF OPERA)— **intermezzo, opera buffa, opéra comique**, and **ballad opera**—were particularly troubling to the authorities owing to their proclivity toward parody and satire and their tendency to clarify intentions through stagings not apparent in librettos. Government interference with serious opera increased in the late 18th century and the first half of the 19th century in response both to the political instability of revolutionary and restoration cycles and to the exploration of novel, more cathartic and less distanced, often antiestablishment subject matter to replace the remote, conventionalized topics of opera seria. For example, censors targeted potentially seditious rhetoric or rebellious acts, implicit criticism of high-ranking aristocrats and the clergy through their involvement in unseemly activities, supernatural and satanic imagery, uncomfortable levels of social realism, and sex and violence.

Rigoletto provides a familiar example of this meddling. Initially titled *La maledizione* (*The Curse*), it was based on Victor Hugo's play *Le roi s'amuse*, which had been banned in Paris and elsewhere. Intended for the Teatro La Fenice in **Venice** within the kingdom of Lombardy-Venetia, which was controlled by the Austrian Habsburgs following the Congress of Vienna, the military governor prohibited performance of the subject in any form owing to its perceived immorality, obscenity, and triviality. Carlo Marzari, president of the theater, and the house poet **Francesco Maria Piave** negotiated with censors represented by their comparatively sympathetic director (Luigi Martelli) to devise a revision that mediated between their requirements and **Giuseppe Verdi**'s artistic conscience and theatrical intuitions. The censors originally wanted the French king of the play depicted as an upstanding citizen who finds himself at Sparafucile's inn accidentally, instead of a carousing libertine, and they objected to Rigoletto's deformity and to the ignominious delivery of the nearly dead Gilda to her father in a sack. The ensuing compromise shifted the location from the French royal court to a nondescript duchy of indeterminate location, kept Hugo's characters but changed their names (e.g., Hugo's Triboulet to Rigoletto, the King to the Duke), omitted a scene in which the Duke rakishly flourishes a key necessary to enter a palace room and ravish Gilda, and had the Duke lured to Sparaficile's inn rather than arriving there on his regular rounds.

A final category of censorship involves dictatorial bans on individual **composers**, librettists, or other creators or performers (in many cases for their ethnicity, religion, politics, or lifestyle orientation) or on specific types of opera or musical styles. For example, through its Reichsmusikkammer (1933–45), the Nazi regime prohibited "degenerate art" linked to American and "Jewish" influences (jazz, **operetta**, the individualism embodied in **romanticism**, and Second Viennese School modernism), and excluded artists representing these tendencies (for example, **Alban Berg**, **Paul Hindemith**, **Arnold Schoenberg**, and **Kurt Weill**), particularly non-Aryans. Stalin's Soviet Union advocated the style of socialist realism and its presentation of the human condition in relation to the collective purpose using a populist style. Consequently it condemned formalism in music and allegedly bourgeois-decadent idioms that focus on individual experience absent the collective background, an orientation that famously resulted in the suppression of **Dmitry Shostakovich**'s *Lady Macbeth of the Mtsensk District* (originally 1934, censured 1936). During the Cultural Revolution in China, the traditional repertory of the **Beijing opera** was replaced by the propagandistic model operas.

See also HENZE, HANS WERNER; KRENEK, ERNST; MALIPIERO, GIAN FRANCESCO; STRAUSS, RICHARD.

CESTI, ANTONIO. (1623, Arezzo–1669, Florence.) Italian **composer** of at least a dozen operatic works during the 1650s and 1660s and other vocal music, **tenor**, and organist; his *Orontea* is a landmark 17th-century opera. Cesti made his living as a singer, organist, and *maestro di cappella* in Arezzo, Volterra, Pisa, and nearby Florence through the 1640s and took Franciscan orders in 1637.

Cesti's turn to secular music in the late 1640s was supported by the Medici family and members of the Florentine Accademia dei Percossi, which included the prominent **librettist** Giacinto Andrea Cicognini (1606–ca. 1650). Cesti began singing in operas (probably including **Francesco Cavalli**'s *Giasone*) in 1650 and quickly became a star, his celebrity status, and at least one notorious love affair, earning a reprimand from his monastery in Arezzo. Cesti's first opera, *Alessandro vincitor di se stesso*, premiered in 1651 in **Venice** followed by *Il Cesare amante* later that year. These Venetian successes led to an appointment in 1652 at the Innsbruck court of Archduke Ferdinand Karl as director of a virtuoso ensemble of Italian singers (*Kammermusiker*) that performed operas, cantatas, and other vocal music at the ducal court.

Aside from two relatively brief absences—a trip to Venice (ca. 1655) to recruit talent for the Innsbruck court, during which he touched off a feud leading to the murder of a Venetian nobleman, and a lavishly praised stint in the papal choir (1659–61)—Cesti spent the remainder of his career in Austria. His first operatic production for Innsbruck was a revival of *Cesare amante* (1651–52) as *Cleopatra* (1654), which led to four new operas between 1655 and 1662. The second and third of these, **Orontea** and *La Dori* (1657), became staples of the repertory, were revived numerous times into the 1680s in various cities, and played a central role in establishing the emerging Venetian **bel canto** style.

Following the death of Ferdinand Karl's successor in 1665 and imperial annexation of the Innsbruck court, Cesti composed five operas for **Vienna** (1666–68) as Leopold I's director of theater music, including the gargantuan *Il pomo d'oro* for Leopold's marriage, a spectacular machine opera that boasted 23 different stage sets. During this period, Cesti wrote only one new opera for Venice, *Il Tito* (1666), though several of his operas were revived there. Although he intended to end his career in Venice, Cesti died as *maestro di cappella* for the Florentine court, where he was rumored (unsubstantiated) to have been poisoned by enemies.

CHALIAPIN, FYODOR. (1873, Kazan, Russia–1938, Paris.) Russian dramatic **bass**, who also excelled in such baritone roles as **Yevgeny Onegin**. Chaliapin has been credited with bringing a new level of realism and emotional subtlety to operatic **acting**. Mostly self-trained, he cut his teeth in provincial companies before formal study in Tbilisi opened the door to acclaimed performances of such demanding roles as **Boris Godunov** with the St. Petersburg Imperial Opera (1894–96) and the Mamontov Private Russian Opera (1896–98) and Bol'shoy Opera (1899–1914) in Moscow. Chaliapin established an international career beginning in 1901 as Mefistofele in **Arrigo Boito**'s opera and excelled not only in serious parts but also in such lighter roles as Don Basilio (**Gioachino Rossini**, *Il barbiere di Siviglia*). His numerous recordings and two films of his riveting performances demonstrate his breadth of vocal color and highly emotive yet naturalistic style of acting.

CHARPENTIER, MARC-ANTOINE. (1643, Paris–1704, Paris.) French **composer** of sacred music, a handful of operatic works (mostly during the 1680s and 1690s, many of them lost), and other vocal music.

Charpentier studied with the oratorio composer Giacomo Carissimi (1605–1674) in Rome in the mid-1660s, and after returning to **Paris** ca. 1670 drew on his experiences in Italy by importing Italian music to France, setting Italian songs, and introducing Italianate characteristics in his own works. Skirting **Jean-Baptiste Lully**'s royal monopoly for *tragédie en musique* (1672–87), he cultivated a range of other genres. In the service of Marie de Lorraine, a cousin of Louis XIV who maintained one of the finest corps of singers and instrumentalists in France, he wrote **pastoral** operas including *Les arts florissants* (1685–86) and *La descente d'Orphée aux enfers* (1686).

In 1672, probably owing in part to Marie's intervention, he began a collaboration with Molière and his Troupe du Roy (later the Comédie-Française) after Molière's partnership with Lully foundered, replacing incidental music written by Lully and providing interpolations for Molière's last comedy *Le malade imaginaire* (1673) and for new plays by other authors, continuing in this role until 1686. He also contributed music for Jesuit sacred dramas in the 1680s, for example *David et Jonathas* (1688).

In the 1680s and 1690s, Charpentier served Louis the dauphin and Philippe II d'Orléans (later regent of France after Louis XIV's death), setting the latter's **libretto** *Philomèle* (lost). These connections at court no doubt helped him gain a production of his only *tragédie en musique*, *Médée* (1693), at the Académie Royale de Musique. Widely praised as the most important new French opera in the decade after Lully's death, it is the most prominent early example of the assimilation of Italian elements in French opera made possible by his absence.

CHERUBINI, LUIGI. (1760, Florence–1842, Paris.) Italian **composer** of over 30 Italian and French operas, mainly **opera seria** and **opéra comique** from the 1780s through the mid-1810s, as well as other vocal and instrumental music; teacher; and **conservatory** administrator.

Trained initially by his father, a keyboardist at the Pergola theater, and other musicians in Florence, in 1778 Cherubini went to study with the prominent opera composer Giuseppe Sarti (1729–1802) in Bologna and Milan. While learning his craft by composing **arias** for Sarti's operas, he internalized progressive tendencies in Italian opera that had been initiated by **Niccolò Jommelli** and **Tommaso Traetta** in the middle of the century. Over the next decade he wrote 10 opere serie from *Il Quinto Fabio* (1780) through *Ifigenia in Aulide* (1788), several on adaptations of warhorse **librettos** by **Pietro Metastasio**. Having succeeded in several major Italian centers, including Florence, **Rome**, and **Venice**, he tried **London**, where he premiered an **opera buffa**, *La finta principessa* (1785), and an opera seria, *Il Giulio Sabino* (1786), and met the famous violinist Giovanni Battista Viotti (1755–1824).

Viotti introduced Cherubini to the French royal court and Paris, where he spent the rest of his career, and helped him become music director of the new Théâtre de Monsieur (1789), which relocated as the Théâtre Feydeau (1791). This appointment provided a steady income while he learned French and licked his wounds over the mediocre reception of his Parisian debut the previous year, the *tragédie lyrique* (*see* TRAGÉDIE EN MUSIQUE) *Démophon* for the Opéra. At the Feydeau, Cherubini produced six operas over the next decade, including several of his most famous, the *comédie-héroïque* *Lodoïska* (1791), the opéra comique *Médée* (1797), and the *comédie lyrique* *Les deux journées* (1800).

In the years following the Revolution, Cherubini managed to adapt successfully to volatile political circumstances. He was hired in 1794 by the recently founded Institut National de Musique (1792), eventually named the Conservatoire National de Musique, or Conservatoire, for which he would serve as director from 1822 until 1842. He fulfilled a number of commissions for the provisional government and the First Empire, including an appointment as director of music in French-occupied **Vienna** (1805–06). During the Restoration he was director of the royal chapel (1814–30), at which time his operatic output declined dramatically in favor of sacred music. His theater career ended with the successful exotic *grand opéra Ali-Baba, ou Les quarante voleurs* (1833).

Considered by many of his contemporaries to be the greatest composer of his day, Cherubini spearheaded the post-Revolutionary transformation and ascendancy of opéra comique, which retained its traditional spoken dialogue but otherwise usurped the role of *tragédie lyrique* as the preeminent operatic vehicle and adopted many of its features: serious, sometimes mythological and even horrific plots, allegorical political messages, and scenic spectacle. For example, in *Lodoïska*, the heroine and her lover are imprisoned by an evil baron but are rescued by their allies during a battle that destroys his castle (*see* RESCUE OPERA). Like other composers of serious French opera, Cherubini preferred intense emotional characterization; sophisticated counterpoint; prominent, richly colored orchestration; and a wealth of ensembles, **choruses**, and orchestral pieces (their flexible forms responding to dramatic situation) to **bel canto** lyricism and structural routine.

CHORUS. Vocal group in which more than one person sings each part; alternatively a set piece performed by such a group. Operatic choruses represent assemblages of various social classes, occupations, and ethnicities, ranging from friends and confidants to religious congregations and armies, and often define an opera's ambience and its broad conflicts and allegiances. They may interact in dialogue with the principals as participants in the action or comment as a corps of detached observers. Operatic choruses are normally scored in two to six parts arranged in unison, chordal, or imitative (fugal) textures, or divided into subgroups that alternate and respond to each other, and may be segregated by gender or mixed (see the choruses in *Norma*).

In the earliest Florentine, Mantuan, and Roman operas, brief choruses in the styles of **madrigals** or *canzonette* involving probably no more than a dozen or so singers occur frequently. They portray companions to the leads and comment in the manner of a Greek chorus on prior action, contributing an alternative style to the prevailing **monody** (as in **Claudio Monteverdi**'s *Orfeo*). In mid-17th-century Venetian-style public opera (e.g., *Giasone*), the chorus essentially disappeared for reasons of thrift, the new focus on **arias**, and waning interest in the seminal operatic goal of recreating Greek tragedy.

(It did, however, remain an ingredient in Italianate spectacular court operas in Germanic cities such as **Vienna**, for example, *Il pomo d'oro*.) From this point until the late 18th century, many pieces designated *coro* were, in fact, modest ensembles performed by soloists (the final chorus of *Rinaldo*).

Choruses played an integral role in the French *tragédie en musique* from its start in the 1670s, particularly in the spectacular **divertissements** that frequently interrupt the action (for example in *Alceste, ou Le triomphe d'Alcide*) and remained central to the French aesthetic through the *grands opéras* of the mid-19th century. Initially comparable to those of early Italian operas in their modest numbers of performers, French choral forces sometimes reached staggering proportions by the late 18th century and involved multiple cadres standing in for various social and political groups (as in *Les Huguenots*). Choruses also appear in late 17th-century **masque**-based English opera (*Dido and Aeneas*) and in 18th-century **opéra comique** as early as *Le devin du village*.

Through the influence of French opera and Italian festival opera (*Orfeo ed Euridice*), the chorus was reintroduced into **opera seria** by the end of the 18th century, particularly in *introduzioni*, where an opening chorus might serve as the finale for the overture, and in multipart **finales** (*Idomeneo, re di Creta*, Act 2). In the 19th century it became a standard component of scenes involving arias and ensembles larger than **duets**. For example it often precedes the **recitative** scena (*see* SCENE) and participates in the *tempo di mezzo* and the transition and coda of the **cabaletta** of the three-movement Italian grand aria (e.g., Norma's "Casta diva"). Choruses were often written in *parlante* style, the orchestra playing the lead melody while singers of modest ability enlisted for the task joined in with supporting chords. **Giuseppe Verdi** made a virtue out of unison choruses that embodied the populist tunefulness of the mid-19th century and became calling cards for their operas (the anvil chorus "Chi del gitano," *Il trovatore*, 1853, Part 2), earning him the title "padre del coro." Italian choruses having patriotic overtones ("Va, pensiero," *Nabucco*, Part 3) were joined by choruses having a nationalistic character, particularly in eastern Europe in such operas as *Boris Godunov* and *Yevgeny Onegin*. Although **Richard Wagner** used chorus extensively in his early operas (for example *Der fliegende Holländer* and *Tannhäuser*), they became infrequent in his music dramas, apart from *Die Meistersinger von Nürnberg* (1868). Following his lead, the chorus subsequently receded in importance, although notable examples occur in the 20th century such as the ship's crew of **Benjamin Britten**'s *Billy Budd* (1951) and the nuns of **Francis Poulenc**'s *Dialogues des Carmélites* (1957).

CILLA, LA. *Commedia pe'museca*; music by Michelangelo Faggioli (1666–1733), **libretto** by Francesco Antonio Tullio (1660–1737); premiered **Naples**, Palazzo Carafa, December 1707; music lost. Possibly performed as early as 1706, *La Cilla* is the first known comic opera (*see* CATEGORIES OF OPERA) in Neapolitan dialect, the starting point for **opera buffa** in the 18th century. A **pastoral** romantic comedy, its libretto provides for more than five dozen short set pieces. After *La Cilla*, its **librettist** Tullio became particularly active in the late 1710s when he wrote six comedies for the Teatro dei Fiorentini, which had begun to specialize in comic opera. He remained involved in Neapolitan comic opera until the end of his life.

CIMAROSA, DOMENICO. (1749, Aversa–1801, Venice.) **Composer** of approximately 65 operas, the majority comic (*see* CATEGORIES OF OPERA), from the 1770s through the 1790s; alongside **Giovanni Paisiello**, he was one of the most significant Italian composers of his time.

Following lessons at a local monastery, Cimarosa trained at the venerable Santa Maria di Loreto Conservatory in **Naples** (1761–71) as a violinist, keyboard player, and singer, and likely studied composition subsequently with the prominent opera composer **Niccolò Piccinni**. He debuted with the **opera buffa** with *farsa Le stravaganze del conte* (Naples, 1772), initiating an almost 30-year career that produced over 50 comic operas of various types (opera buffa, **intermezzo**, *farsa*, *dramma giocoso*) and 16 serious operas on **librettos** by **Pietro Metastasio** and others. The vast majority premiered in Naples, but he also wrote significant numbers for such other major centers as Rome, **Venice**, St. Petersburg, and **Vienna**.

Cimarosa taught at a Venetian orphanage **conservatory** (probably beginning 1782) and served from 1787 to 1791 as *maestro di cappella* for Catherine the Great in St. Petersburg, following Paisiello and Giuseppe Sarti (1729–1802) in that position. His most enduring work, the sentimental comedy *Il matrimonio segreto*, appeared during his subsequent appointment as *maestro di cappella* (1791–93) for Emperor Leopold II, premiering in Vienna with the emperor in attendance (1792). After Cimarosa returned to Naples in 1793, *Gli Orazi ed i Curiazi* (1796), his greatest heroic opera, betrayed his post-revolutionary Republican sympathies. He supported both the French occupation of Venice (1796) and establishment of the short-lived Parthenopean Republic in Naples (1799), after which the Bourbon restoration resulted in his imprisonment and threatened execution.

An opera buffa composer at heart, Cimarosa developed a light, charming style unconvincing in heroic opera but congenial to the **sentimental arias** and tangled multisection comic ensembles of the late 18th century. His operas were restaged across Europe from London and Lisbon to St. Petersburg and were favorites in Vienna and at the Hungarian court of Eszterháza, where **Joseph Haydn** mounted them frequently. They remained in the repertory until they were eclipsed by **Gioachino Rossini** in the 1810s and were praised by such illustrious figures as Johann Wolfgang von Goethe, Stendhal, and Eugène Delacroix.

CLAQUE. Organized corps of mercenary attendees (*claqueurs*, from French for "clap") at a play or opera recruited with free tickets or hired outright to reinforce support for allied productions and artists or to disrupt rivals. The practice began as early as ancient **Rome** and was reinstituted in the 16th century. The modern claque, which is distinct from the factions that formed naturally in Italian theaters in the 18th century, developed in 19th-century theaters dominated by unsophisticated middle-class audiences who attended primarily for social reasons. It was regimented as a business in **Paris** in the 1820s, where theater managers could order up claques of varying sizes. They were organized under a leader (*chef de claque*) who directed their demonstrations and were manned by specialists in clapping, crying, laughing, or enlisting allegiance by alerting patrons to highlights of the show. Performers commonly bribed the *chef de claque* to avoid being booed. Claques spread to Italy (particularly at La Scala), **Vienna**, **London**, and **New York** (at the Metropolitan Opera) and continued to exist well into the 20th century.

CNN OPERA. *See* ZEITOPER.

COLBRAN, ISABELLA. (1785, Madrid–1845, Bologna.) Premier Spanish **soprano** of the first quarter of the 19th century. Colbran was noted for the brilliance and strength of her voice, an astonishing three-octave range reaching e''' (three octaves above middle c'), and her powerful acting. She made a name for herself singing tragic operas by **Gaspare Spontini** and **Simon Mayr** and created lead roles tailored to her strengths in the majority of **Gioachino Rossini**'s dramas of the 1810s and 1820s, from *Elisabetta, regina d'Inghilterra* (1815) and *Otello* (1816) to *La donna del lago* (1819) and *Semiramide*. The onetime mistress of the Neapolitan impresario **Domenico Barbaia**, she jilted him for Rossini, whom she married in 1822. Colbran retired from the stage in 1824 following a failed performance of Rossini's *Zelmira* (originally 1822) in London.

COLORATURA. Term originating as early as the 17th century for vocal (or instrumental) **ornamentation** or passagework ("coloring"). It currently refers to such figuration, roles that feature such figuration, and singers who favor such roles. While coloratura roles for **sopranos** (both females and male **castratos**) were especially prevalent from the 17th century through the first half of the 19th, such roles for **tenor** and **bass** also appear in **bel canto** opera, for example Idomeneo in *Idomeneo, re di Creta* and Assur in *Semiramide*, respectively.

COMMEDIA DELL'ARTE. Itinerant improvised theater especially active in the 16th and early 17th centuries, which continued to exist through the 17th and 18th centuries and even up to the present day. It made important contributions to comic opera (*see* CATEGORIES OF OPERA), especially in Italy.

Commedia dell'arte performances were based on a repertory of conventional plotlines and a stable of stock character types combined in domestic comedies centering on attitudes toward marriage, love and lust, and character flaws. Their slapstick humor involved sight gags, dancing and acrobatics (a specialty of the servant Arlecchino), sometimes lewd or cross-gendered costuming, and standardized set pieces such as the *burla* (practical joke), *lazzo* (a mimic "schtick" often exploiting maladies such as a sneezing fit or heart attack), or *tirata* (a long-winded tirade) that could be worked into multiple situations. Characters included lecherous, pedantic, miserly old aristocrats, doctors, lawyers, or guardians (*vecchi* such as Pantalone and the Dottore); abusive masters, spouses, or servants (e.g., Brighella); pompous military officers or swashbucklers (Capitano or Scaramuccia); gossipy old women (La Ruffiana); comic servants (*zanni*); saucy maids or peasants (Columbina, later the soubrette in opera; *see* SOPRANO); and pairs of lovers (*innamorati*). The male characters, other than the *innamorato* or aristocrats, wore masks and adopted standard quirks associated with the regions of Italy where they had originated (Pantalone of **Venice**). In one typical commedia dell'arte scenario, the *vecchi* plot against the *inammorati*, who eventually marry with the help of the *zanni*.

Many commedia dell'arte performers were also skilled musicians, and their plays often included songs and dances. Offspring of commedia dell'arte situations, themes, and characters are conspicuous in 17th-century operatic *contrascene* (for example, in *Giasone*), the 18th-century **intermezzo (*La serva padrona*)**, **opera buffa (*Le nozze di Figaro*)**, and **singspiel (*Die Zauberflöte*)**, as well as much later works (**Giuseppe Verdi**'s *Falstaff*, 1893, and **Ruggero Leoncavallo**'s *Pagliacci*).

COMPOSER. The creator of the musical score for an opera (or other work of music).

In the 17th century, with rare exceptions (e.g., Jacopo Corsi, 1561–1602, *see* FLORENTINE CAMERATA), opera composers hailed from the ranks of the nonaristocratic classes: **Giulio Caccini** was the son of a carpenter, **Jean-Baptiste Lully** probably a peasant, and **Jacopo Peri** claimed aristocratic descent but by 12 was singing in a convent. They began their training as choirboys and/or organists, lutenists (*see* LUTE), or violinists, most often with local clergy or more rarely with family members in the profession (Lully, **Alessandro Scarlatti, André Campra**). Having demonstrated exceptional talent and proficiency and possibly gained the support of an aristocratic patron, they apprenticed with a more prominent maestro (**Claudio Monteverdi** with Marc'Antonio Ingegneri, ca. 1535–1592).

Young professionals found employment as singers, organists, lutenists, and/or string players (**Francesco Cavalli**, **Antonio Cesti**, and many others), either in church or at court, and to the extent possible used their social graces and political savvy (notably Lully) to rise in rank to some sort of supervisory position: *maestro di cappella* (Cavalli and a host of other Italians); *maître de musique* (Lully, Campra); court composer (Monteverdi); or instrument keeper (**Henry Purcell**). Since they were seldom sufficiently well heeled to quit their day jobs and risk it all on a fledgling occupation, writing operas was only one of many activities in which they were involved. Cavalli was a rare exception in gaining financial independence in his late twenties through a propitious marriage, but he nonetheless remained organist and *maestro di cappella* at St. Mark's Basilica in **Venice** until his death. Nor was there abundant demand for opera until the system of regular **seasons** coalesced in the Venetian public theaters in the second half of the century. Consequently early operatic portfolios were modest: Caccini had two operas performed; Peri four; Monteverdi six or so (three, of course, iconic masterpieces); **Francesco Manelli** eight; Cesti twelve; and even Lully, who held a monopoly for 15 years, just one per year. Only Cavalli, who could finance his own productions and composed operas through his sixties, put up numbers (about three dozen) that pointed toward the output of specialist composers in the next century.

In the 18th century, particularly outside of Italy, the church remained a primary option for initial musical service as a choirboy (**Joseph Haydn**, **André-Ernest-Modeste Grétry**) or organist (**Jean-Philippe Rameau**), alongside studying with family members in the trade (**Antonio Vivaldi**, **Wolfgang Amadeus Mozart**) or taking lessons from court musicians, often thanks to aristocratic intervention for a promising talent (**George Frideric Handel**, **Antonio Salieri**). This period also saw a modest increase in the number of composers who received an advanced education apart from clerical studies (Handel, **Christoph Willibald Gluck**, Grétry). However, in Italy the vast majority of professional musicians (**Giovanni Battista Pergolesi**, **Niccolò Jommelli**, **Tommaso Traetta**, **Giovanni Paisiello**, **Domenico Cimarosa**, etc.) now trained in the burgeoning Neapolitan system of church-affiliated **conservatories**, which at their height were capable of providing a complete course of instruction, both nurturing early talent and availing the most gifted with advanced mentoring by renowned maestros.

As in the past, 18th-century opera composers typically held various salaried positions throughout their careers in the church—as singers, instrumentalists, or *maestri di cappella*—or at secular courts in similar capacities (Paisiello and hosts of others), where they also benefitted from aristocratic largesse and succeeded in part owing to their social and political skills (the chess master and composer **François-André Danican Philidor**, Salieri). In addition, new employment opportunities came from the conservatories in **Naples** and Venice—most of the prominent Italians were maestri and/or administrators at one time or another (notably Vivaldi)—and by the various theaters who hired in-house composers to write operas on a specified schedule and often to assume responsibilities connected with rehearsal and production (Vivaldi, Handel, **Nicola Porpora**, **Thomas Augustine Arne**). The new comic **categories**—opera buffa, intermezzo, *farsa*, opéra comique, and ballad opera—provided a comparatively low-risk proving ground for young composers, where they could cut their teeth before tackling more substantial fare. By the 18th century, opera theaters holding regular seasons were firmly entrenched across Europe in dozens of locations, providing a sufficient operatic market for composers to specialize, making opera composition, rather than church or court jobs, their primary occupation rather than a sideline. Improvements in transportation brought wider-ranging travel and employment opportunities, for example Handel's and Porpora's moves to London, Traetta's and Paisiello's to St. Petersburg, and the beginnings of the influx into Paris (Gluck and **Niccolò Piccinni**).

Benefiting from the increased conventionalization of opera and the formulaic compositional style taught in Neapolitan conservatories, specialists boasting enormous facility produced staggering numbers of operas on a regular basis: Niccolò Piccinni about 110, **Baldassare Galuppi** 100, Paisiello 90, **Antonio Caldara** 75, Jommelli and Cimarosa 65 each, and so on. That productivity still depended to a certain extent on circumstances (the nature of positions held, involvement with other categories of music, life span) is demonstrated by the modest operatic portfolios of such notables as Mozart and Haydn (about 20 operas each) and Pergolesi (about 10).

In the 19th century the status of opera composers rose dramatically. Long considered secondary collaborators of **librettists**, who frequently received top billing, composers became stars and even national icons like **Gioachino Rossini**, **Richard Wagner**, and **Giuseppe Verdi**. Their elevation both reflected and encouraged expansion of their artistic roles, which now included service as their own librettists for some—or in Wagner's case all—of their works (**Hector Berlioz, Aleksandr Porfir'yevich Borodin, Modest Petrovich Musorgsky, Pyotr Il'yich Tchaikovsky, Arrigo Boito, Nikolay Andreyevich Rimsky-Korsakov, Ruggero Leoncavallo**), or at least substantive contributions to **librettos** (**Giacomo Meyerbeer, Vincenzo Bellini**, Verdi), and active engagement with aspects of production, rehearsal, and direction (**Carl Maria von Weber, Gaetano Donizetti**, Bellini, Wagner, Verdi). They drew higher fees for commissions and were better able to maintain the integrity of their scores and control their transmission and subsequent production. Non-European (**Carlos Gomes**) and female (*see* WOMEN AND OPERA) composers of stature remained rare in the 19th century.

As in the past, 19th-century composers entered the field through a variety of portals, harking in some cases from obscure origins (**Saverio Mercadante**, Donizetti) or from musical families (Rossini, Bellini, **Georges Bizet**, **Giacomo Puccini**), some of them demonstrating precocious talent (Meyerbeer, Donizetti, Bellini, **Charles-François Gounod**, **Amilcare Ponchielli**, **Otto Nicolai**). Many began their instruction with clergy (**Franz Schubert**, Donizetti, Verdi) and/or family members, whether professionals (Rossini, **Giovanni Pacini**, Bellini, Nicolai, Puccini, **Richard Strauss**, **Franz Léhar**) or accomplished amateurs (Musorgsky, **Jules Massenet**), or with other musicians who happened to be available (**Ernst Theodor Amadeus Hoffmann**, Weber). A number of them received excellent liberal educations along the way (Schubert, Leoncavallo), and several trained for nonmusical professions (Hoffmann, Borodin, Musorgsky). Some carried out their studies under the wing of prominent independent teachers, and most familiarized themselves with operatic conventions by haunting local opera houses (e.g., **Mikhail Ivanovich Glinka**). However, the establishment of conservatories on the Neapolitan model across Italy and the rest of western Europe (and elsewhere) made that course of advanced training with prestigious maestros routine for composers from Naples (Mercadante, Bellini, Leoncavallo) to Milan (Ponchielli, Puccini, **Pietro Mascagni**); Bologna (Rossini); Paris (Berlioz, Bizet, Gounod, Massenet, **Camille Saint-Saens**), where the Prix de Rome launched a number of careers; Prague (Léhar); and even as far away as Rio de Janeiro (Gomes).

Increasingly—and particularly in the second half of the century—leading opera composers engaged in an expanding array of alternative activities, some traditional sidelines related to opera, others outside the field. Some were generalists equally (or more) active in other genres of music (Berlioz, Saint-Saëns, Tchaikovsky, **Antonin Dvořák**). A few still held traditional positions as church composers (Pacini, Ponchielli, Rimsky-Korsakov) or court composers (Meyerbeer, Donizetti), many others depending to one extent or another on aristocratic (or upper-middle-class) benevolence (Wagner, Verdi, Tchaikovsky). A host of them were performers at one point or another as orchestra musicians (Dvořák, Massenet); pianists or organists (Weber, Meyerbeer, Nicolai, **Ferenc Erkel**, Ponchielli); and/or conductors (Weber, Berlioz, Nicolai, Erkel, **Bedřich Smetana**, Rimsky-Korsakov, Mascagni). **Jacques Offenbach** was a virtuoso cellist. They became music directors of theaters and opera companies, taking positions that could involve conducting, directing, negotiating contracts with singers, sparring with censors (*see* CENSORSHIP), and various other activities (**Ferdinando Paer**, Weber, Rossini, Pacini, Donizetti, Erkel). They were teachers or directors at music schools or conservatories (**Simon Mayr**, Mercadante, Pacini, Ponchielli, Tchaikovsky, Rimsky-Korsakov). Even after they had made their fortunes, some of them still supplemented their incomes by giving music lessons and making appearances in salons or aristocratic soirees. As authors or journalists they critiqued new music and concert and theater performances and took integral parts in the aesthetic debates of their day (Hoffmann, Berlioz, Wagner, Boito). Several found opportunities in the expanding music-publishing industry and supplemented their incomes (particularly as they were starting off) by supplying arrangements of symphonic music and piano-vocal scores of operas to publishers (Bizet) or orchestrating works by other composers (Rimsky-Korsakov). A few, particularly the Russian nationalists, had independent careers entirely outside of music (Borodin, Musorgsky).

During the first half of the 19th century the output of specialist composers, particularly the leading Italians, remained high (Mayr approximately 70 operas, Mercadante 60, Pacini 80, Donizetti 65), the short life spans of individuals like Bellini (10 operas), Weber (10), and Schubert (8), as well as involvement with other categories of music in the latter two cases, limiting their productivity. However, by midcentury, portfolios tended to shrink owing to the diversification of activities noted above and to such factors as the growth of repertory opera, the **romantic** cult of originality, which encouraged the abandonment of **number opera** and various structural and melodic conventions, the more deliberate selection of librettos, new complexities of musical language and structure, and higher production costs associated with *grand opéra* and its offshoots. Declines in aristocratic patronage were only partly offset by increased involvement of publishers in commissioning and producing operas (e.g., opera competitions like the four sponsored by Sonzogno, 1883–1902, the second of which was won by Mascagni, and the negotiations brokered by Giulio **Ricordi** late in Verdi's career). Aside from rare exceptions like Offenbach (about 90 works), whose audiences showed an insatiable appetite for new **operettas**, numbers of new operas seem relatively modest compared to those of the previous century: Verdi 28, only 12 of them during the 42 years from 1851 until he stopped composing for the theater in 1893; Wagner 13; Ponchielli 9; Mascagni 17; Leoncavallo 20 (a number of them operettas); and Puccini 12.

Few 20th-century composers have started their career paths in choir lofts—**Leoš Janáček** and **William Walton** are rare throwbacks—or have claimed humble origins (**Claude Debussy**, **Arnold Schoenberg**, **Zoltán Kodály**). Instead the standard trajectory begins when budding talents, who come more often than not from the ranks of the educated upper middle class (**Igor Stravinsky**, **Alban Berg**, **Darius Milhaud**, **Benjamin Britten**), start their music lessons with family members, family friends, a tutor or governess (Berg), or more prominent musicians (Schoenberg, Stravinsky, **Michael Tippett**, Britten, **Philip Glass**), setting out initially as instrumentalists but soon turning to composition (**Maurice Ravel**, **John Adams**, and many others). And while a number of 20th-century composers were self-taught in one or more aspects of composition (**Francis Poulenc**, **Luigi Dallapiccola**) and became acquainted with current trends through immersion in progressive artistic circles (Berg, Poulenc, Walton), they by and large completed their advanced training at colleges, universities, and/or conservatories. Music **festivals**, which have supplanted aristocratic courts or urban salons as access points (**Leonard Bernstein**, Glass), have allowed young professionals to broaden their horizons through mentoring by prominent composers. Elite patronage (and to a certain extent commissions from theaters and opera companies) has been replaced by more egalitarian academic, government, media, private, or foundation fellowships, grants, and prizes at the undergraduate, graduate, postgraduate, and professional levels. Modern educational opportunities have opened doors for increasing numbers of women and minorities, as have gender- and ethnicity-informed hiring practices in academia.

University or conservatory teaching and administration (or much more rarely secondary education) has become the occupation of choice for composers (Janáček, Schoenberg, Kodály, **Paul Hindemith**, **Harrison Birtwistle**, **John Eaton**, Adams). But opera composers have also served as directors of music societies, theaters or opera companies, and festivals (Strauss, **Gian Carlo Menotti**, Birtwistle, Adams), and some have been noted instrumentalists (Hindemith, Poulenc, Dallapiccola) and conductors (Janáček, Strauss, Hindemith, Tippett, Bernstein, Adams). They have written music for film, theater, radio, and television productions (Poulenc, Britten, Bernstein, Glass, Adams), and even film scripts (Menotti), and have developed secondary careers outside music (Janáček, writing and editing; Schoenberg, painting). Continuing the trend begun in the 19th century, a growing number of composers have created or contributed to at least some of their own librettos (Janáček, Strauss, Schoenberg, Stravinsky, Hindemith, Poulenc, **Ernst Krenek**, Menotti, Bernstein, **Karlheinz Stockhausen**, **Henri Pousseur**, Glass, etc.).

By the 20th century, the heyday of the specialist opera composer had largely passed. Among other things, full-time teaching, the dominance of repertory seasons that limit new productions, and the modernist obsession with conceptual innovation has made opera specialists like Strauss (15), Krenek, Menotti, and Glass (about two dozen each), and **Hans Werner Henze** (more than a dozen) rare birds, and even their productivity falls far short of that seen in the heyday that ended ca. 1850. Some of the most iconic works of the 20th century have come from generalist composers who have staged limited numbers of operas: Debussy (1), Schoenberg (4), **Béla Bartók** (1), Berg (2), Hindemith (about a dozen), **Dmitry Shostakovich** (2 full-scale operas), Birtwistle (6), Adams (5). And while the fraternity of opera composers remains an exclusive one, academic employment has provided a measure of financial security that encourages the necessary experimentation and investment of time and energy, while diverse media have facilitated exposure to the genre, allowing democratic access by many talents who could never have participated previously and enabling composers to acquaint themselves with the entire spectrum of the art form to an extent never before possible.

See also AUBER, DANIEL-FRANÇOIS-ESPRIT; CAMBERT, ROBERT; CATALANI, ALFREDO; CAVALIERI, EMILIO DE'; CHARPENTIER, MARC-ANTOINE; DITTERSDORF, CARL DITTERS VON; DUNI, EGIDIO; GIORDANO, UMBERTO; GRABU, LUIS; GRAUN, CARL HEINRICH; HÁBA, ALOIS; HIDALGO, JUAN; HILLER, JOHANN ADAM; LEO, LEONARDO; LIGETI, GYÖRGY; MALIPIERO, GIAN FRANCESCO; MARSCHNER, HEINRICH; MONIUSZKO, STANISLAW; PENDERECKI, KRZYSZTOF; RICCI, LUIGI AND FEDERICO; SPONTINI, GASPARE; THOMAS, AMBROISE; TORREJÓN Y VELASCO, TOMÁS DE; VAUGHAN WILLIAMS, RALPH; VINCI, LEONARDO.

CONDUCTOR. The development of the modern conductor and his involvement with opera performance and **production** was an extended process. By the 17th century, beating time in choral music had long been commonplace and may well have occurred in the earliest operas. For example, an illustration of the premier of **Jean-Baptiste Lully**'s *Alceste* (1674) suggests that at least in France from the beginnings of *tragédie en musique*, an individual (the *batteur de mesure*, "time beater"), possibly the composer himself, stood either on the stage apron (in front of the proscenium arch) or amidst the **orchestra** facing the singers and marked time with his hand, a rolled-up manuscript, or the type of staff that would later fell Lully (during a performance of sacred music). Probably focused on coordinating dancers and the **chorus**, this practice remained in place at the Opéra into the 19th century.

In 18th-century Italy, direction of a performance was often divided between the **basso continuo** harpsichordist (*see* HARPSICHORD)—often the composer, at least for a production's initial performances—who apparently was responsible for performers onstage and who might periodically indicate the tempo with his arms or feet, and the first violinist, who primarily directed the orchestra by playing with exaggerated motions. This shared responsibility continued in Italy and elsewhere in productions of Italian opera through the middle of the 19th century. The transition to the baton conductor apparently began as early as the 1790s with the keyboardist or first violinist rising to direct with his hands or bow, for example Bernhard Anselm Weber (1764–1821, music director of the Berlin National Theater 1796–1820) and François-Antoine Habeneck (1781–1849, conductor of the Paris Opéra 1824–46), respectively. Conductors who also managed opera companies, notably **Carl Maria von Weber** in Dresden (1817–21), merged the professional responsibilities of musical performance with choosing repertory, directing **acting** and stage movement, and supervising various other aspects of production and set a precedent for broader conceptual involvement by the conductor. This expanded interpretive role was reinforced in the second half of the 19th century by figures such as **Richard Wagner**, **Angelo Mariani**, and Franco Faccio (1840–1891, principal conductor at La Scala 1871–90), who paved the way for such virtuoso conductors as **Arturo Toscanini**.

See also BERLIOZ, HECTOR; BERNSTEIN, LEONARD; ERKEL, FERENC; HINDEMITH, PAUL; HOFFMANN, ERNST THEODOR AMADEUS; JANÁČEK, LEOŠ; LEHÁR, FRANZ; MASCAGNI, PIETRO; MERCADANTE, SAVERIO; MEYERBEER, GIACOMO; NICOLAI, OTTO; OFFENBACH, JACQUES; PENDERECKI, KRZYSZTOF; RIMSKY-KORSAKOV, NIKOLAY ANDREYEVICH; SAINT-SAËNS, CAMILLE; SMETANA, BEDŘICH; SPONTINI, GASPARE; STRAUSS, RICHARD; TIPPETT, MICHAEL.

CONSERVATORY. School that specializes in training musicians. Beginning in the 1600s, Italian conservatories in **Naples** (for boys) and **Venice** (*ospedali* for girls) provided an alternative to the vocal instruction that had occurred previously in church choir schools and through individual apprenticeships with family members or other professionals. They responded to a number of factors: the increased demand for both singers and instrumentalists resulting from the rise of sacred *concertato* music, instrumental music, and opera; competition among cities noted for their music; after 1700 the decline of monasteries and church schools; and the humanist view of the value of music in a liberal education. Conservatories developed among the numerous orphanages of these cities, many of which by 1600 had become schools directed and staffed by clergy. Their faculty normally included a music teacher, in some cases musicians of some repute, such as **Antonio Vivaldi** or those drawn from the choir of the Basilica of St. Mark.

In Naples, orphanages found that music students could earn their keep by singing sacred music in the streets for contributions, by performing for civic and ecclesiastical functions, and by supplementing reduced music making in the churches during Lent with in-house performances of oratorios and other large-scale works, which included sacred music dramas as early as the 1650s. Music faculties were expanded during the 17th century to incorporate string, brass, and vocal teachers (including **castratos**) and eventually provided instruction in figured bass (*see* BASSO CONTINUO) and composition. As these conservatories gained notoriety in the late 17th century, demand for instruction increased and they began admitting fee payers, often aristocratic children. And they organized their expanded staffs more formally, distributing instruction among established *maestri* (masters) and their senior students, who taught beginners. After 1700, senior students in Naples were composing operas and religious works and were performing frequently in public.

By the 18th century the four main Neapolitan schools (the Santa Maria di Loreto, Santa Maria della Pietà dei Turchini, Poveri di Gesù Christo, and San Onofrio a Capuana), had become a prodigious industry that manufactured singers, instrumentalists, and composers at a rate exceeding local demand and increasingly exported them across Europe. Many of Italy's leading composers trained in this system, beginning with **Nicola Porpora, Leonardo Vinci**, and **Leonardo Leo** at the start of the century and extending through **Giovanni Battista Pergolesi, Niccolò Jommelli, Tommaso Traetta, Giovanni Paisiello**, and **Domenico Cimarosa** to **Saverio Mercadante** and **Vincenzo Bellini** in the 19th century. Whereas Naples became Italy's premier operatic center, once-dominant Venice declined partly because it began this process in earnest only in the first half of the 18th century, and its conservatories specialized in training girls, whose career paths were limited, making success stories like **Faustina Bordoni** rare exceptions.

The Neapolitan juggernaut lost momentum in the late 18th century. Quality deteriorated partly owing to overcrowded facilities that necessitated communal practicing in large rooms, parents opposed exploitation of their children for opera **choruses** and other public functions, and fiscal and political instabilities following the French Revolution reduced enrollments and led church and state to appropriate facilities. The surviving conservatories were consolidated into a single state-run institution after 1806, the Real Collegio di Musica, eventually directed by Niccolò Zingarelli (1752–1837), himself a product of the Neapolitan system.

The Italian method set a standard for professional music education that guided a more modern, comprehensive program developed by the **Paris** Conservatoire (the Conservatoire National Supérieur de Musique et de Danse, chartered 1795), which included music theory and history alongside practical instruction for singers, instrumentalists, and composers; took as its broader mission preservation of French musical culture; and subsumed existing schools elsewhere in France and Belgium. Conservatories that opened in numerous cities adopted the French model to varying degrees: Milan (1808); Prague (founded 1808, opened 1811); Vienna (1817); **London** (Royal Academy of Music, 1823, and Royal College of Music, 1883); Leipzig (1843); St. Petersburg (1862); Moscow (1866); Boston (Boston Conservatory and New England Conservatory, 1867); Berlin (1869); Philadelphia (Philadelphia Musical Academy and Philadelphia Conservatory of Music, 1870, Curtis Institute, 1924); and **New York** (New York College of Music, 1878, Juilliard School, 1905).

CONTRALTO. A singer having a range from about f below middle c' to (potentially) f'' above middle c' and the lowest of the three principal female vocal types, lying below the **soprano** and mezzo-soprano and above the **tenor**. The term "contralto," which derives from the 15th-century designation *contratenor altus* (the part singing against and above the tenor), is the standard one for a soloist, as opposed to the equivalent choral part (alto). It may be used for female or male singers (**castratos**, falsettists of various types, and very high tenors like the French *haute-contre*). Introduction of the designation "mezzo-soprano" in the 19th century after the soprano's range was extended upward has contributed to ambiguities of usage, since the ranges and certain operatic roles for contraltos and mezzo-sopranos overlap. However, for female contraltos the tessitura—the most used or comfortable part of the total range—lies at the low end and the color is usually darker.

In the 17th century contraltos most frequently played old **women** (e.g., Arnalta in *L'incoronazione di Poppea*) and by the late 17th century typically served as the counterpart to a comic bass. Eventually more serious roles appeared, particularly in **George Frideric Handel**'s operas, such as the grieving widow Cornelia in *Giulio Cesare in Egitto*. Early 19th-century female contraltos in **travesty** replaced castratos as **coloratura** male heroic leads (sometimes taking the designation *musico* from the castratos they superseded), for example, Arsace in *Semiramide* (**coloratura** contralto or mezzo-soprano) and also appeared in comic roles (Rosina in **Gioachino Rossini**'s *Il barbiere di Siviglia*). During the 19th century, although both the lighter, brighter mezzo-soprano vocal type and its designation received increasing usage at the expense of the contralto, dramatic contralto roles continued to appear occasionally, particularly in Russia and France (for example, Ol'ga in *Yevgeny Onegin* or the mother Fidès in **Giacomo Meyerbeer**'s *Le prophète*, 1849), and more rarely in Italy and Germany (the gypsy Ulrica in **Giuseppe Verdi**'s *Un ballo in maschera*, 1859, or the old woman Mary in *Der fliegende Holländer*). Prominent 20th-century contralto roles include character parts like Marie's friend Margret in **Wozzeck** and the tavern mistress Auntie in **Peter Grimes**.

See also GUADAGNI, GAETANO; MELANI, ATTO; SENESINO.

CONTRASCENA. A contrasting comic scene in serious, historical, or mythological operas (*see* CATEGORIES OF OPERA) of the 17th and early 18th centuries. Initially *contrascene* were populated by secondary characters from the working classes, such as servants, nurses, and lower-ranking soldiers. Men in drag often played the female roles, and the humor, such as it was, seldom rose above insults, complaints, sexual innuendos, and fisticuffs. Although the majority of these scenes were at best tenuously related to the main plotlines, in some cases they contributed to the realism of historically based operas by providing different perspectives on, contexts for, and often parodies of the main characters and their situations. In **Claudio Monteverdi**'s *L'incoronazione di Poppea*, the disgruntled soldiers of Act 1, and the amorous page and lady and the bickering page and nurse in Act 2, provide early examples of *contrascene*. By ca. 1700, the humor of the *contrascena* had become less vulgar and lowbrow; the characters tended to resemble **commedia dell'arte** types, particularly the sly female servant and the fatuous old aristocrat; and women were singing the female roles.

In the 17th century, a *contrascena* at the end of an act had sometimes intersected with an ***intermedio*** performed between acts, its singers participating alongside the dancers, creating an antecedent for the 18th-century comic **intermezzo**. In the first decades of the 18th century, **librettists** such as **Apostolo Zeno** increasingly marginalized *contrascene* by reducing their numbers and pushing them to the ends of acts as de facto intermezzos (for example, in the operas of **Alessandro Scarlatti**), and later librettists like **Pietro Metastasio** virtually eliminated them from **opera seria**. Their roles of comic entertainment and sardonic social commentary were then usurped by the intermezzo, **opera buffa**, and other genres of comic opera.

CUZZONI, FRANCESCA. (1696, Parma–1778, Bologna.) One of the more notorious Italian **sopranos** of the second quarter of the 18th century. Following her first known appearance (Parma, 1714), she became *virtuosa di camera* to the Grand Princess of Tuscany in Florence in 1717. The next year she debuted in **Venice** in Carlo Francesco Pollarolo's (ca. 1653–1723) *Ariodante* (premiered 1716) alongside **Faustina Bordoni**, initiating a lifelong rivalry. Recruited for **George Frideric Handel**'s Royal Academy in **London**, she sang in every opera produced between her debut in Handel's *Ottone* (1723) and the company's closing in 1728, including Cleopatra in *Giulio Cesare* (1724). She began her stormy tenure by refusing to rehearse her first **aria** in *Ottone*, until Handel allegedly threatened to throw her out a window. And the drama continued through repeated squabbles with **Senesino** and his supporters and the infamous onstage catfight with Bordoni during a performance of Giovani Bononcini's (1670–1747) *Astianatte* (1727), which led to her temporary dismissal. After an exasperated Handel ignored her for the second Royal Academy, in 1734 she joined the rival Opera of the Nobility with **Farinelli** and Senesino. Cuzzoni was a specialist in slow, cantabile arias who used rubato in performance to telling effect. While not noted for the velocity of her passagework, she reportedly had a unique ability to negotiate intricate figuration and ornamentation. After her voice and reputation gradually declined in the 1740s, financial problems mounted. She was imprisoned for debt at least once (1750) and reportedly subsisted late in life by making buttons.

D

DA CAPO ARIA. *See* ARIA.

DA PONTE, LORENZO. (1749, Ceneda, currently Vittorio Veneto–1838, New York.) Italian born, late 18th-century **librettist**; with **Wolfgang Amadeus Mozart** and other **composers** he was one of the key figures responsible for the pinnacle of **opera buffa** development reached in **Vienna** during the 1780s at the end of Joseph II's reign.

Information concerning Da Ponte's life comes largely from his own memoires, which are partly self-serving novelizations. His early studies for the priesthood and his ordination in 1773 fell victim to his supposedly libertine attitudes and womanizing (he befriended Giacomo Casanova in the 1780s), leading to his exile from **Venice** (1779–86). In Dresden he learned the theater trade by assisting the librettist Caterino Mazzolà (1745–1806), who recommended him to **Antonio Salieri** in Vienna.

A smooth operator, after his arrival in 1781, Da Ponte came to the attention of Joseph II and, despite his lack of operatic experience, was appointed poet to the court theater after Joseph lost interest in **singspiel** and restarted his Italian company in 1783. He began by preparing existing **librettos** for Viennese productions—his first projects in 1783 were an adaptation of Mazzolà's *La scuola degli gelosi* for Salieri and a translation of **Christoph Willibald Gluck**'s *Iphigénie en Tauride* (originally Paris, 1779). His reputation in Vienna was secured in 1786 by a series of six successful librettos, which included Mozart's *Le nozze di Figaro* and the even more popular *Una cosa rara* for Vicente Martin y Soler (1754–1806), followed by others including Mozart's *Don Giovanni* (1787) and *Così fan tutte* (1790). After Joseph's death (1790), intrigues, rivalries, and indiscretions resulted in his firing and exile from Vienna in 1791. Over the next 14 years he attempted to find a new home, stopping briefly in politically volatile **Paris**, working intermittently in **London** for the King's Theater, and unsuccessfully attempting to implant Italian opera in the Low Countries. He eventually fled his creditors to America in 1805, where he became a grocer and bookseller in **New York** and Philadelphia, and eventually professor of Italian at Columbia College (later Columbia University).

Of his three main collaborators in Vienna, he professed greater esteem for Martin y Soler and Salieri than for Mozart. A unique talent who instinctively understood operatic pacing and theatrical effect, Da Ponte adroitly distilled situations and characters, tailoring their treatments to the specific strengths of composers working alongside him. Blessed with a remarkably liberal political environment in Vienna, Da Ponte tested the boundaries of sociopolitical commentary and satire that represented the fulfillment of Enlightened culture prior to the Revolution.

DAFNE **(PERI).** **Pastoral** opera; music by **Jacopo Peri**, **libretto** by Ottavio Rinuccini (1562–1621) based on the myth of the nymph Daphne's flight from Apollo and escape through transformation into a laurel tree; **prologue** and six scenes; premiered Florence, Palazzo Jacopo Corsi, 1598; most music lost. Assumed to be the earliest opera, its creation began as early as 1594 and involved Jacopo Corsi (1561–1602) and **Giulio Caccini**, as well as Peri, who was responsible for most of the final score. It was further revised for performances in 1599, 1600, and 1604, in some of which Peri played Apollo. Its printed libretto is the first extant.

DAFNE **(SCHÜTZ).** Opera; music by Heinrich Schütz (1585–1672), **libretto** by Martin Opitz (1597–1639) adapted from Ottavio Rinuccini's (1562–1621) libretto for **Jacopo Peri**; premiered Torgau, April 1627; music lost. Considered the first opera in the German language, comments by Schütz and inferences from early German librettos indicate that the work involved spoken dialogue with strophic songs interspersed. Sigmund Theophil Staden's (1607–1655) sacred **singspiel** *Seelewig* (1644) is the earliest German opera to survive intact.

DAL SEGNO ARIA. *See* ARIA.

DALLAPICCOLA, LUIGI. (1904, Pisino d'Istria, Croatia–1975, Florence.) Premier Italian **composer** of four modernist operas as well as other vocal and instrumental music, and **librettist** for his own works. Dallapiccola received a broad classical education at a school run by his father. When his family was interned in Graz during World War I, he was able to attend operas and became fond of those of **Wolfgang Amadeus Mozart** and **Richard Wagner**, particularly *Der fliegende Holländer*. After the war he was decisively influenced by **Claude Debussy**, including *Pelléas et Mélisande*, and **Claudio Monteverdi**. In 1922, he relocated to Florence, where he would base his activities the remainder of his life. He trained in composition at the conservatory and taught himself the twelve-tone method, leading to his eventual stylistic fusion of German constructivism—serial technique and processive development—with Italianate lyricism.

In one way or another, each of Dallapiccola's operas deals with a loss of personal liberty and hope that tests faith. *Volo di notte* (premiered 1940) reflects Italian futurist preoccupations with technology and its impact on human existence: an Argentinian airfield manager's obsession with timely delivery of the mail leads him to order night flights, one of which wanders off course, runs out of fuel, and crashes, widowing the pilot's wife of six weeks. In *Il prigioniero* (premiered 1949 on radio), a twelve-tone work in which musical motifs represent hope, prayer, and liberty, a victim of the 16th-century Inquisition escapes temporarily, regains his faith, but ultimately is recaptured and burned alive. Dallapiccola's *rappresentazione sacra Job* (1950) combines his long-standing interest in Italian early music—it incorporates a plainchant cantus firmus—with serialism in his first extended work based on a single twelve-tone row. *Ulisse* (1968), an account of the hero's struggles and restoration of faith through a vision of God, draws on 12 twelve-tone rows as sources for a network of referential motifs within a broad, symmetrically structured series of closed scenes.

DANCE. *See* BALLET.

DAVIDE, GIOVANNI. (1790, Naples–1864, St. Petersburg.) Premier Italian **tenor** of the first quarter of the 19th century. Davide was noted for his acrobatic agility and an astonishing three-octave range reaching b-flat" (two octaves above middle c') in falsetto, which suited late **bel canto** tenor roles. He began his career singing operas by **Simon Mayr**, then created lead roles in **Gioachino Rossini**'s *Il turco in Italia* (1814); *Otello* (1816 as Roderigo, as Otello in revivals); *Ricciardo e Zoraide* (1818); *Ermione* (1819); *La donna del lago* (1819); and *Zelmira* (1822). He also appeared in numerous others by Rossini, **Vincenzo Bellini**, and **Gaetano Donizetti** through the late 1820s. Already past his prime when he arrived in **Paris** and **London** in the early 1830s, he ended his theater career managing the Italian opera in St. Petersburg.

DEBUSSY, CLAUDE. (1862, St. Germain-en-Laye–1918, Paris.) French **composer** of instrumental and vocal music, including one landmark opera performed during his lifetime and approximately a dozen incomplete or planned operatic projects from the 1880s through the second decade of the 20th century.

Debussy was born to modest means—his father, a shopkeeper who had served in the military and who would be arrested for activities in the Commune of 1871, intended him for the navy—and lacked early formal education. With the help of the **symbolist** poet Paul Verlaine's mother-in-law, he entered the Conservatoire (1872), where he studied piano and composition, and won the Prix de **Rome** in 1884. Following his return to **Paris** in 1887, he felt an affinity toward the symbolist poets he met in cafés; made two pilgrimages to Bayreuth (1888 and 1889); was influenced by the Javanese gamelan music he heard at the Universal Exposition (1889, Paris); and met the poet Stéphane Mallarmé, leading to his greatest early success, the *Prélude à l'après-midi d'un faune* (1894).

Debussy's first attempted opera, *Rodrigue et Chimène* (1890–93), was a relatively conventional post-Wagnerian melodrama based on the legend of *El Cid*, which he abandoned after attending the premier of Maurice Maeterlinck's symbolist play **Pelléas et Mélisande** in 1893. Debussy set it as an abbreviated **Literaturoper** (1893–95), completing the orchestration in 1901 after a production was arranged. Reluctant simply to tread theatrical water, he sought out different subject matter, beginning operas on two short stories by Edgar Allan Poe, *The Devil in the Belfry* (*Le diable dans le beffroi*, 1902 –12) and *The Fall of the House of Usher* (*La chute de la maison Usher*, 1908–17), but left them incomplete.

LE DEVIN DU VILLAGE. *Intermède* (related to the Italian **intermezzo**); music by Jean-Jacques Rousseau (1712–1778), **libretto** by the **composer** on an original story; one act; premiered Fontainebleau, 1752, and **Paris**, Opéra, 1753. First presented on the public stage during the **War of the Comedians**, the *Village Fortune Teller* was Rousseau's attempt to create a French equivalent to the simple, lyrical, *galant* style of imported Italian comic opera (*see* CATEGORIES OF OPERA) that he supported. Its story is a rustic parable of Enlightened sentimentality (*see* SENTIMENTAL OPERA) and naturalness. The shepherd Colin is momentarily beguiled by his sophisticated aristocratic mistress, but he comes to his senses and returns to his true love Colette, thanks in part to the sage counsel of the local Soothsayer. Immensely successful, *Le devin* was produced more than 500 times between 1753 and 1829, when **Hector Berlioz** reportedly ridiculed it in the theater and ended its career. **Wolfgang Amadeus Mozart**'s third opera, the **singspiel** *Bastien und Bastienne* (1768), was based on a parody of *Le devin* entitled *Les amours de Bastien et Bastienne* (Paris, 1753).

DIDO AND AENEAS. Tragic opera (all-sung **masque**); music by **Henry Purcell**, **libretto** by Nahum Tate (1652–1715) based on his play *Brutus of Alba* (1678) and Virgil's *Aeneid*; **prologue** (music lost) and three acts with spoken epilogue; probably premiered Chelsea (**London**), girls' boarding school of Josias Priest, 1689. Although the only confirmed performance in Purcell's time occurred at Priest's school, various issues—contradictory evidence of style, cast, staging, and topical and allegorical references; inconsistencies between the Chelsea libretto and the earliest surviving manuscript score; and circumstantial similarities to **John Blow**'s *Venus and Adonis* (ca. 1683)—open the possibility that the opera was written for private presentation in the chambers of Charles II (ca. 1684) and then revised for amateur performance.

Dido, Queen of Carthage, reluctantly accepts the courtship of the Trojan hero Aeneas. Motivated by hatred for Dido and all who prosper, a coven of witches led by an evil Sorceress sends an elf disguised as Mercury to beguile Aeneas by ordering him to leave Carthage to found Rome, resulting in Dido's death. Lacking English operatic precedents beyond *Venus and Adonis*, Purcell combined elements common to Venetian opera (its basso ostinato set pieces, most famously Dido's "When I Am Laid in Earth"), French opera (its French **overture**, spectacular supernatural plot, heavily inflected **arioso recitatives**, and frequent **choruses**) and the English masque and antimasque traditions (its modest size, allegorical/mythological orientation, and plot-driven, scene-ending **ballets**—including grotesque ones for the witches), creating a masterpiece of telling effect.

DITTERSDORF, CARL DITTERS VON. (1739, Vienna–1799, Neuhof, Bohemia.) Austrian **composer** of about three dozen Italian and German comic operas (*see* CATEGORIES OF OPERA) from the 1770s through the early 1790s, as well as other vocal and instrumental music. Dittersdorf was the most visible composer of **singspiels** during the 1780s.

A violin prodigy, Dittersdorf trained as a youth with musicians employed in **Vienna** by a Saxon prince (1750–61), after which he worked in the Imperial court theater (1761–64). He then moved on to Grosswardein (now Oradea, Romania, 1764–69), where he composed a *dramma giocoso* (*see* OPERA BUFFA) and an **intermezzo**, and Johannisberg, Germany (near Frankfurt), where he established a small opera company (1769–76) and wrote nine Italian comic works, several of which were performed at Eszterháza (*see* HAYDN, JOSEPH). He returned to Vienna as early as 1784 and in 1786 began writing singspiels for the second incarnation of the imperial troupe at the Burgtheater and the Kärntnertortheater. His first and most successful of these was *Der Apotheker und der Doktor* (*The Pharmacist and the Doctor*, 1786), in which a young couple and their friend conspire to outwit their feuding fathers and marry despite her parents' efforts to arrange another match.

After a fiasco involving his opera buffa *Democrito corretto* (1787), Dittersdorf turned entirely to German opera, writing six of them for Vienna, Brno, and Breslau between 1787 and 1791. His popularity declining in Vienna, sidelined by gout, and semiretired in Bohemia after 1794, he nonetheless composed almost a dozen more works for Duke Friedrich August of Oels in Silesia (1794–98), where he enjoyed a loyal following, beginning with *Das Gespenst mit der Trommel* (*The Ghost with the Drum*). Dittersdorf's German operas are notable for incorporating action into musical numbers—in particular for adapting the extended, multisection opera buffa **finale** to singspiel, as in Act 1 of *Die Liebe im Narrenhause* (1787)—and for their Viennese melodic fecundity.

DIVERTISSEMENT. French term that designates a range of musical entertainments in the 17th and 18th centuries, particularly during the reign of Louis XIV, from **ballets** and other court spectacles to chamber and keyboard music. The operatic divertissement, to which the term was applied by ca. 1700, was normally a distinct section related to the main action. It consisted of **airs** and *ariettes*, vocal ensembles, **choruses**, and dances performed by secondary characters, as well as other instrumental music, and frequently employed machinery for special effects. Divertissements could occur on multiple occasions at any point within an opera as an enhancement of an ongoing situation, defining cohorts of characters who react to circumstances and depicting scenic events such as storms or celebrations.

Divertissements appear in **Jean-Baptiste Lully**'s earliest *tragédies en musiques* (*see ALCESTE, OU LE TRIOMPHE D'ALCIDE*), take an expanded role in the *opéras-ballets* of **André Campra,** and in **Jean-Philippe Rameau**'s operas serve as climaxes for almost every act (*see HIPPOLYTE ET ARICIE*), where they often included florid *ariettes* in the Italian style. They became less frequent in the late 18th century partly because of the renewed emphasis on naturalistic drama by **Christoph Willibald Gluck** and others but still serve as atmospheric enhancements, as in the opening of Euridice's scene in Elysium (*Orfeo ed Euridice*, Act 2). In 19th-century *grand opéra*, elements of the divertissement are integrated within massive scenic tableaux to create spectacle, establish a sense of place, emphasize different constituencies and their relationships to one another, and intensify conflicts (*see LES HUGUENOTS* and *AIDA*), sometimes to bizarre effect, as in *Robert le diable*'s Act 3 ballet of spectral debauched nuns (Giacomo Meyerbeer, 1831).

DOCTRINE OF THE AFFECTIONS. Quasi-scientific German music criticism (originally *Affektenlehre*) beginning ca. 1700 that attempted to apply a rational conceptual framework to musical expression. Discussions by numerous writers, most prominently Johann Mattheson (1681–1764) in his *Der* *vollkommene Capellmeister* (*The Complete Music Master*, 1739), were grounded in 17th-century psychological and physiological theories extending back to René Descartes' *Les passions de l'âme* (*The Passions of the Soul*, 1649) and to ancient Greek and Roman concepts of rhetoric.

According to the doctrine of the affections, opera **arias** (and other types of music) are capable of communicating an array of more than two dozen specific affects—for example, joy, sadness, love, and rage—which may be named and classified. Our emotional reactions result from musical stimulation of the bodily humors and conveyance of physical experiences such as calm versus agitation or pleasure versus pain. In conjunction with the meaning of the text, elements of music including tempo, rhythmic activity, melodic contour, vocal range, dynamics, major or minor mode, and instrumentation, as well as conventional symbols such as specific ornaments, melodic gestures (e.g., the lament bass; *see* ARIA), and rhythmic patterns (for example, those associated with particular types of dances) either directly prompt physical-psychological responses or conjure associative topics (military, celebratory, etc.) that in turn elicit those responses. According to this theory, single moods should be maintained throughout an aria (or an extended section of an aria), and consecutive arias should display contrasting affects for maximum impact. The sequence of arias in the first scene of **George Frideric Handel**'s *Giulio Cesare in Egitto* illustrates this principle: "Presti omai" (joy), "Empio dirò" (rage), "Priva son" (sadness), and so forth.

DON GIOVANNI. Opera buffa; music by **Wolfgang Amadeus Mozart**, libretto by **Lorenzo Da Ponte**; two acts; premiered Prague, National Theater, October 1787. Commissioned to capitalize on the success of *Le nozze di Figaro* (originally **Vienna**, 1786), performed in Prague during the previous Carnival **season**, Mozart's *Don Giovanni* likely took as its starting point Giovanni Bertati's (1735–ca. 1815) one-act libretto set by Giuseppe Gazzaniga (1743–1818) for **Venice** in early 1787 and incorporated versions of the story by Molière and other playwrights. Acclaimed in Prague, when it was reprised in Vienna in 1788 it received more performances than *Figaro* had. Frequently adapted as a **singspiel** in Germany, it was heard as far away as St. Petersburg by the end of the century, in Italy (Bergamo and **Rome**) in 1811, and in the United States (with Da Ponte's participation) in 1826. It is currently Mozart's most familiar opera.

Don Giovanni illustrates the growing infusion of serious elements into comic opera (*see* CATEGORIES OF OPERA) and prefigures the rise of *opera semiseria* in the late 18th century. An allegorical social satire in which Don Juan's unbridled libido represents the abuse of absolute power and the decline of morality in post-Enlightenment society, its plot centers on the seductions of four women: Donna Elvira, a previous conquest who still loves him and is mocked for her continued devotion; the Commendatore's daughter Donna Anna, whom Giovanni attempts to seduce disguised as her fiancé Don Ottavio and for whom her father dies defending her honor; Zerlina, a peasant girl preparing her wedding to Masetto, whom a frustrated Giovanni attempts to take by force, pinning the blame on his servant Leporello when caught in the act; and Elvira's maid, saved from his attentions by the arrival of Masetto's posse, bent on revenge. The predatory cycle ends when Giovanni mocks the Commendatore by inviting his memorial statue to dinner. The "stone guest" obliges, arriving accompanied by infernal demons who drag the unrepentant lothario to his punishment.

Giovanni's increasingly ignominious and unrewarding trysts—from his apparently straightforward seduction of the aristocrat Elvira to the deception of the aristocrat Anna, the attempted rape of a peasant, and the aborted advance on a servant—serve as a parable of aristocratic decline. His lack of a distinct musical identity and willingness to adopt the language of his prey— he even trades clothes with Leporello to chase Elvira's maid—betrays his lack of social and moral compass. Aristocratic ineptness and impotence is evident in the inability of Anna and Ottavio initially to see through his flimsy disguise and to catch him once she identifies him midway through the first act, in the futility of Elvira's attempt to reform him, and in their ultimate reliance on supernatural intervention. Their weakness contrasts with the courage and resiliency of their subjects, demonstrated by Leporello's habitual insubordination, the **chorus** of "Viva la libertà!" that greets the aristocrats at Giovanni's party, and Masetto's efforts to impose justice. And whereas Leporello, Zerlina, and Masetto shrug off the nasty experience, the aristocrats are devastated, Donna Anna and Don Ottavio postponing their wedding, Elvira retreating to the convent, and Giovanni succumbing to his fate.

Mozart's music incorporates a corresponding mixture of light and shadow, beginning with the **overture**, which precedes its brilliant D major sonata form with music that later accompanies the Commendatore's arrival in the Act 2 **finale**, implementing **Christoph Willibald Gluck**'s prescription for overtures that initiate the drama. The action of the opening *introduzione*, which leads directly from the overture without a break, is extraordinarily complex and intense and juxtaposes comic and serious sections. It extends from Leporello's complaint *sortita*, through trios in which Giovanni escapes from Anna's palace (while Leporello cowers) and kills her father, a simple **recitative** in which the sidekicks take stock after the murder, and an obbligato recitative for Anna's discovery of her father's corpse and her revenge **duet** with Ottavio, which invoke the posturing of **opera seria**. The range of moods is even more pronounced in the graveyard scene (Act 2), in which Giovanni and Leporello respond to the statue's rebukes with a comic duet, and the **finale** *ultimo*, which contrasts the zany energy of the banquet with the sepulchral music that follows the statue's entrance, and the meditative epilogue. One notable illustration of this musical enrichment occurs midway through the Act 1 finale (beginning "Da bravi, via ballate"), a contrapuntal tour de force in which three **stage bands** accompany *parlante* dialogue with simultaneous dances in different meters.

DON PASQUALE. *Dramma buffo*; music by **Gaetano Donizetti**, **libretto** by Giovanni Ruffini (1807–1881) based on the libretto by Angelo Anelli (1761–1820) for Stefano Pavesi's (1779–1850) *Ser Marcantonio* (1810); three acts; premiered **Paris**, Théâtre Italien, January 1843. The last glittering masterpiece of **opera buffa** in an era of decline.

The plot of *Don Pasquale* shows a simplification of cast and intrigue paralleling that of early 19th-century *melodramma*. And it personifies the ascendency of the middle class, represented by the triumph of Ernesto, Norina, and Malatesta over the antiquated, self-styled aristocrat Pasquale, reflecting their aspirations during the liberal reign of King Louis-Philippe. Pasquale plans to disinherit Ernesto, because he disapproves of his nephew's involvement with Norina, a young widow of modest means whom he has not yet met, intending to father his own heir by a new bride. His doctor, Malatesta, who is loyal to Ernesto and Norina, hatches a plot to pass off Norina as his convent-reared sister Sofronia. Smitten by Sofronia/Norina, who feigns naiveté, Pasquale marries her on the spot, signing a bogus contract that makes her mistress of his household. Her prey ensnared, Sofronia turns into a domineering, adulterous, spendthrift shrew, leading Pasquale to beg Ernesto to marry Norina so that she can replace Sofronia as head of his house. By blessing the marriage even after the hoax is revealed, Pasquale puts love before social and financial advantage and meekly accepts the irrelevance of rank.

Don Pasquale extends the tendency of opera buffa to absorb musical features of serious opera (*see* CATEGORIES OF OPERA)—and for *melodramma* to assimilate elements of light opera—which along with the deterioration of opera buffa as a vehicle for social satire would soon make the genre superfluous. Like serious opera since the 1810s, *Don Pasquale* relies exclusively on orchestrally accompanied, obbligato **recitative** throughout. It replaces single-movement buffo character **arias** with multimovement forms (for example, Norina's cavatina, Act 1), or combines one-movement arias into longer set pieces (Malatesta's slow "Bella siccome un angelo" and Pasquale's **cabaletta** "Un foco insolito" with intervening *tempo di mezzo*). Like Rossini's ensembles, it distills multiple phases of interaction and reflection into the conventional forms of the **duet** (Ernesto and Pasquale Act 1) and **finale** (Act 2). And despite Donizetti's continued reliance on witty *parlante* and furious **patter** for comic effect (the duet for Pasquale and Ernesto, Act 1; the Act 2 finale; and the duet for Pasquale and Malatesta, Act 3), the increased presence of lyric vocal writing for characters other than Pasquale, the only true buffo part (e.g., "Bella siccome un angelo"), points ahead to the rare Italian comic operas of the late 19th century (for example, **Giuseppe Verdi**'s *Falstaff*, 1893).

DONI, GIOVANNI BATTISTA. (1595, Florence–1647, Florence.) Italian classicist, music historian, and the most prominent contemporary music theorist writing on early opera. Trained in the humanities and, reluctantly, the law, he served the Catholic Church, eventually rising to the position of secretary of the College of Cardinals (1629). Following the death of his brother in 1633, he turned for comfort to his true calling, the study of Greek language and music, teaching himself to read Greek notation and eventually winning a faculty position at the University of Florence in 1640. Though influenced by Girolamo Mei (1519–1594) and Vincenzo Galilei (late 1520s–1591; *see* FLORENTINE CAMERATA), Doni's readings of the Greek theoretical sources led him to differing conclusions in his *Trattato della musica scenica* (*Treatise on Theatrical Music*, 1633–35) and elsewhere. Believing that Greek dialogues were spoken, not sung, he argued that modern operas should follow suit, with composers saving their efforts for expressive **arias**, streamlining their operas, and increasing the potential for effective **acting**. He also advocated richer, more contrapuntal operatic accompaniments that surpass simple **basso continuo**. In taking these positions, Doni anticipated trends toward simplification of **recitative**, concentration of musical expression in arias, and development of the operatic **orchestra**. He also provided unique discussions and classifications of different types of early 17th-century recitative.

DONIZETTI, GAETANO. (1797, Bergamo–1848, Bergamo.) Alongside **Vincenzo Bellini**, the preeminent **composer** of Italian opera in the 1820s and 1830s. Though less revered than Bellini, his output of about 65 completed operas far surpassed that of his short-lived rival, and he was equally proficient in both comic and serious genres (*see* CATEGORIES OF OPERA). He also composed a substantial body of sacred works, cantatas, and occasional music at various points in his career.

Born into a lower-class family having no musical pedigree, Donizetti was discovered and mentored by the locally based, internationally renowned opera composer **Simon Mayr** at the school he created to train musicians for the cathedral in Bergamo. Mayr began Donizetti's composition lessons and arranged his continued studies in Bologna with Padrei Stanislao Mattei (1750–1825), who had been **Gioachino Rossini**'s teacher. Donizetti's first commission was *Enrico di Borgogna* (1818) for a minor theater in **Venice**. By 1821 his reputation had extended outside of northern Italy, resulting, probably with some help from Mayr, in commissions for **Rome** and **Naples**, where he would center his activities from 1822 to 1838. Contracts with **Domenico Barbaia**, the most powerful **impresario** of the period, would demand as many as four operas per year—including *L'esule di Roma* (1828), his most successful early work—and eventually lead to his appointment as director of the Teatro Nuovo in Naples (1827) and director of royal theaters there (1828–38), including the Teatro San Carlo. During the 1820s he set **librettos** by and formed important connections with important **librettists**, among them Andrea Leone Tottola (died 1831), one of Rossini's poets; the innovator Domenico Gilardoni (1798–1831); and **Felice Romani**, Bellini's collaborator and the greatest librettist of his day.

The 1830s brought international acclaim, beginning with *Anna Bolena* (1830), staged in the same **season** at the Teatro Carcano in Milan that saw the premier of Bellini's *La sonnambula*, one of several occasions that put Donizetti in direct competition with his contemporary. *Anna Bolena* was soon taken to **Paris**, sowing the seeds for his eventual move there. It was among more than two dozen new operas written between 1830 and 1838, which include several that remain popular: *L'elisir d'amore* (1832), *Lucrezia Borgia* (1833), *Maria Stuarda* (1835), and *Lucia di Lammermoor*. During this period, Donizetti befriended a number of leading singers—**Giuditta Pasta**, **Giovanni Rubini**, and **Giorgio Ronconi**—who would nurture his career and influence his compositional style. This support and his burgeoning fame allowed him to take greater control of both new productions and revivals in aspects ranging from the libretto to casting and staging. With broader involvement came more work and travel, and an array of headaches. He increasingly encountered unauthorized, uncompensated, often inaccurate performances created by orchestrating published piano-vocal scores, a practice that triggered the development of copyright laws in the 19th century. He butted heads with Naples' infamously conservative and intractable censors (*see* CENSORSHIP). And he and his performers suffered under the financially inept and artistically intrusive committee that supervised him as director of theaters.

Probably owing to these last two concerns, in 1835 Donizetti jumped at Rossini's commission for *Marino Faliero* for the Théâtre Italien in Paris, competing successfully with Bellini's *I puritani* in the same season. While ambivalent about the French **grand opéra** he witnessed in Paris, he saw the potential for its enrichment through Italian lyricism and for adaptation of its grandiose historical backgrounds, **choruses**, and **ballets**. His wife's death in childbirth left no reason to stay in Naples, so he moved to Paris in 1838. Following an understandable ebb of activity that saw only revivals of earlier works, he regained his stride with his revision of *Poliuto* (banned in Naples) as *Les martyrs*, *La fille du régiment*, and *La favorite* (all 1840). These works were followed by Italian commissions and appointment as *Hofkapellmiester* and imperial court composer in **Vienna** (1842), which required very little effort and produced only two operas, *Linda di Chamounix* (*opera semiseria*, 1842) and *Maria di Rohan* (1843). ***Don Pasquale***, an enduring favorite, and *Dom Sébastien, roi de Portugal*, his last opera, were composed for Paris in 1843. Syphilis, the first symptoms of which had appeared as soon as the late 1820s, precipitously stifled his productivity after 1843. He was institutionalized in 1846 before being released to relatives who moved him back to Bergamo for his final year.

Neapolitan conservatism is typically blamed for Donizetti's initial adherence to Rossini's florid melodic style, set piece forms, and exaggerated comedic mannerisms, as well as the orientation of his early output toward *farsa*, **opera buffa**, and *opera semiseria*. His almost exclusive concentration on *melodramma* and other serious genres after about 1830 and his more consistent adoption of progressive approaches, paralleling Bellini, probably resulted from the success of *Anna Bolena* and his status and responsibilities as director of theaters. Resembling Bellini's melodies, Donizetti's in the 1830s tend to abandon Rossini's episodic multipart forms, show increasing reliance on the popular **lyric prototype,** and give less play to **coloratura** (especially in male roles) and more emphasis to motivic coherence. Like Bellini, he took initial steps toward streamlining **recitatives** and lyric movements and using **arioso** and *parlante* to reduce the disjunction between scena (*see* SCENE) and lyric set piece. And he integrated the lyric movements of **duets** and larger ensembles into an ongoing dialogue through the displacement of simultaneous singing to the ends of movements and by beginning with successive solos, which often introduce different melodies that define the characters.

Although Donizetti, more than Bellini, remained comfortable with conservative, classicizing librettos, his progressive works adopt the Italian **romantic** agenda of literary revival through assimilation of nontraditional sources, among them the works of Miguel de Cervantes (for *Il furioso nel isola di San Domingo*, 1833); Lord Byron (for example, *Parisina*, 1833); Victor Hugo (*Lucrezia Borgia*); and Sir Walter Scott (for example, *Lucia di Lammermoor*). He and his librettists also began to undercut the workload *convenienze*, in particular the traditional series of introductory "portrait gallery" arias beginning Act 1 (*see NORMA*). At the end of his career he successfully embraced the prerequisites of **opéra comique** and of French *grand opéra*—its formal freedoms, ballets and choral tableaux, strophic **arias**, enriched orchestration, and declamatory vocal style—for his Parisian operas, while reverting necessarily to more Italianate idioms for commissions in Italy and (to a lesser extent) Vienna.

DIE DREIGROSCHENOPER. Play with music; music by **Kurt Weill, libretto** by the playwright Bertolt Brecht (1898–1956), translated by the author Elisabeth Hauptmann (1897–1973), based on ***The Beggar's Opera***; pro-

logue and three acts; premiered Berlin, Theater am Schiffbauerdamm, August 1928. Weill's second, and by far most popular, of several collaborations with Brecht.

After hearing about a successful revival of *The Beggar's Opera* in **London** (1920), Brecht had Hauptmann translate it (1927–28) and proposed Weill's almost totally new setting of his adaptation—Weill wrote original music for all but one song—to a fledgling theater company in Berlin. Eventually renamed *Die Dreigroschenoper* (*The Threepenny Opera*), its premiere showcased the singing actress and Weill's recent bride Lotte Lenya (1898–1981) and was accompanied by a seven-person jazz band, later enlarged to 23. After an initially standoffish reception, it became extremely popular in Germany and was translated into many languages for thousands of international performances, setting a record for longest-running musical play with over 2,600 shows in **New York** (beginning 1956), in a production featuring Lenya and the familiar American actors Ed Asner, Bea Arthur, and Jerry Stiller.

Although the plot closely parallels Gay's original, it begins with a departure, a street performance of the most famous song in the show, the "Ballad of Mac the Knife," which introduces the cad Macheath (Mac the Knife), leader of a gang of thieves. He marries Polly, whose hypocritical father, the purportedly respectable shopkeeper Jonathan Peachum, disapproves of her groom despite his own shifty sideline of extorting money from London's beggars as he outfits them and runs their operation. Targeted by the law, Macheath is betrayed twice by whores who are hiding him—Peachum first bribes Macheath's ex-lover Jenny, then blackmails the constable Tiger into making the whores snitch—and jailed. Freed initially by another ex-lover, Tiger's daughter Lucy, he narrowly escapes a second time when, as the gallows beckon, a messenger of the new king brings his reprieve, probably through Tiger's intervention.

The Threepenny Opera is the best known of Weill's politically charged, socially relevant *Zeitopern*. It invites a Marxist interpretation owing to its sympathetic depiction of lower-class life as experienced by its beggars, thieves, and whores and its critical appraisal of family dynamics, business, government, and the legal system. It avoids (and, in the case of the *lieto fine*, parodies) the artifices and pretenses of traditional opera, replacing them with a sophisticated, jazz-influenced pseudo-popular idiom that blurs the boundary between opera and musical theater. In particular, it rejects post-Wagnerian neo-**romanticism** by adopting such **neo-classical** features as an 18th-century source; distinct set pieces (including brief songs and **duets**, along with formal **finales** for each act); and music detached from and sometimes contradictory to textual meaning. And by embracing Brecht's program of epic theater (*see* WEILL, KURT), in which disconnected scenes are self-consciously announced by brief descriptions of characters, situations, and action on placards, it rebuilds the "fourth wall" between audience and stage and encourages a more detached and analytic response to the theatrical experience.

DUET. In opera, a lyric set piece (as opposed to **recitative** dialogue) for two singers, normally accompanied by **orchestra** and/or **basso continuo**.

Operatic duets appear in Italy as early as **Claudio Monteverdi**'s *Orfeo*. In 17th-century operas they may involve any pair of singers—from principals to secondary characters—and occur at any point within an opera, although their roles in the comic *contrascene* of serious operas (*see* CATEGORIES OF OPERA) and as concluding affirmations for lovers are common. As it would throughout its development, the duet tends to parallel forms heard currently in **arias** and (later) ensembles. Early 17th-century duets resemble the *canzonetta* or **madrigal**, and composers soon adopted strophic, basso ostinato (e.g., the final duet for Nero and Poppea in *L'incoronazione di Poppea*), ABB, and ABA' schemata (*see* ARIA). The ensemble module, in which interaction through parallel solos or quicker dialogue (or both) precedes more reflective simultaneous singing (*see* FINALE), is present in rudimentary fashion as early as the shepherds' duet near the start of *Orfeo*, Act 2.

During the first three quarters of the 18th century, duets became less frequent in aria-dominated **opera seria**, in brief **intermezzos**, and in early **opera buffa**. One or two duets per opera served mainly as the final scenes of acts and were confined to romantic leads or confidants. Like contemporary arias, they tend to reinforce positions established through prior action or to provide summary reactions. Da capo forms or variants (dal segno or cavatina abridgements) in which the ensemble module plays some role are frequent. For example, the A section (and possibly B) may begin with successive solos followed by quicker exchanges that lead to simultaneous singing (for example, Cornelia and Sesto's commiseration duet ending Act 1 of *Giulio Cesare in Egitto*). Or the textural shift from dialogue to singing together may happen twice within a single section, as in Serpina and Uberto's duet ending Part 1 of *La serva padrona*.

By the late 18th century, duets became more prominent again and involved a broader range of characters, particularly in opera buffa, as romantic couples and sympathetic confidants were joined by various rivals and antagonists. Da capo forms were replaced by through-composed forms that proceed through a series of sections without large-scale recapitulations. And particularly in comic duets, interactive passages make increasing contributions to plot and character development. These characteristics may be observed in the role pairings and themes of the five duets from *Don Giovanni*: Anna/Ottavio (allied lovers, grief and planned revenge); Giovanni/Zerlina (master and peasant, seduction); Giovanni/Leporello (master and servant, comic confrontation); Zerlina/Leporello in the Vienna version (peasant and servant, threatened revenge); and Giovanni/Leporello with the Commendatore's statue (master and servant, comic supernatural encounter). This diversification in the late 18th century opened the way for the duets of 19th-century *melodramma* to embrace an unlimited range of situations involving nontraditional pairs of characters. Couples at all stages of their relationships, amatory or political rivals or allies, and loving or feuding family members appear with equal frequency, as suggested by the duets of **Giuseppe Verdi**'s *Luisa Miller* (1849): Federica/Rodolfo (cousins, unrequited love); Walter/Wurm (master and servant, conspiracy and loyalty); and Miller/Luisa (father and daughter, revelation and reconciliation).

Duets in *melodramma*, and increasingly in the waning genre of opera buffa, normally follow all or part of the grand duet form, which presents two ensemble modules in a four-movement schema: an interactive *tempo d'attacco*, reflective lyrical slow movement, interactive *tempo di mezzo*, and reflective **cabaletta**. These expansive episodic structures facilitate progressing action, allowing 19th-century duets not only to reinforce positions established previously in the scene, but also to propel the action forward and develop the situation and relationships between characters. Composers like Gaetano Donizetti and Verdi exploited this new potential by giving duets an expanded dramatic presence. Verdi's *Rigoletto* and *Aida*, in which duets carry the lion's share of the action, illustrate the dominant role of the duet by the middle of the century.

Non-Italian duets may imitate Italian models or take different approaches. For example, composers of *tragédie en musique* from **Jean-Baptiste Lully** to **Jean-Philippe Rameau** emphasized the duet more than their Italian contemporaries, including three or four per opera, sometimes embedding them in broader scene complexes, creating more diverse pairings (including secondary characters) and situations, and drawing on binary and cyclical rondeau forms as well as Italianate da capo variants. A similar variety of purpose and frequency of appearance characterizes duets of **opéra comique** in the second half of the 18th century. Nineteenth-century French duets may freely adapt the Italian four-movement design, or follow more idiosyncratic forms that respond flexibly to the progress of the plot, a "French manner" that influenced both German and Italian composers. Although self-standing duets continue to occur in the late 19th century, they are often absorbed into the flow of action as continuous dramatic dialogues (e.g., Siegmund and Sieglinde's love duet, **Richard Wagner**, *Die Walküre*, Act 1; *see DER RING DES NIBELUNGEN*). In the 20th century, duets are rarely featured as set pieces distinct from broader dialogues, except in retrospective works like *Der Rosenkavalier*, **Giacomo Puccini**'s *Turandot* (1926), and *The Rake's Progress*.

DUNI, EGIDIO. (1708, Matera, Italy–1775, Paris.) Italian **composer** of over 30 **opera serias** and **opéras comiques** from the 1730s through the 1760s, during which time, alongside **François-André Danican Philidor**, he transformed the latter genre. Duni trained in **Naples** and wrote about a dozen Italian operas, mostly serious ones on texts by **Pietro Metastasio**, between 1735 and 1756 for **Rome**, Milan, **London**, Florence, Genoa, and Parma. As court *maestro di cappella* in Francophile Parma, he became acquainted with opéra comique and may have attempted two of them before trying his luck in **Paris** with *Le peintre amoureux de son modèle* (*The Painter in Love with His Model*, 1757). Produced in the aftermath of the **War of the Comedians**, it discredited the claim by the pro-Italian faction that the French language was inappropriate for opera by accompanying much of its **libretto** with new Italianate music.

While in Paris, Duni wrote approximately 20 comic operas, many of them for the Comédie-Italienne, for which he served as music director (1761–68). A number of his collaborations with the prominent **librettists** Louis Anseaume (ca. 1721–1784)—for example, *Le peintre* and *L'école de la jeunesse* (1765)—and Charles-Simon Favart (1710–1792)—*La fée Urgèle* (1765) and *Les moissonneurs* (1768)—were extremely popular and traveled extensively across Europe. Duni is historically important primarily for leading the transition in opéra comique from the *comédie en vaudevilles* to the *comédie mêlée d'ariettes* (beginning with *Le peintre* and *La fille mal gardée, ou Le pédant amoureux*, 1757; *see* OPÉRA COMIQUE), and for incorporating multisectional ensembles modeled on those of **opera buffa**, for example in *L'isle des foux* (1760).

DURANTE, FRANCESCO. (1684, Frattamaggiore–1755, Naples.) Italian composer of sacred vocal and instrumental music, violinist, and internationally reputed teacher in the Neapolitan orphanage **conservatory** system, who trained many important 18th-century opera composers. Durante studied composition and violin at the Conservatorio di Sant' Onofrio a Capuana in **Naples** with his uncle, Don Angelo Durante (ca. 1650–after 1704) and others from 1699 to 1705. Francesco taught briefly at the Sant' Onofrio (1710–11) and subsequently may have spent time as a maestro in **Rome**. After returning to Naples he served as primo maestro of the Conservatorio dei Poveri di Gesù Cristo (1728–39) and later simultaneously at the Conservatorio di Santa Maria di Loreto (beginning 1742) and again at the Sant' Onofrio (beginning 1745) for the last decade of his life. His students, who seemingly venerated him, included **Giovanni Pergolesi**, **Niccolò Piccinni** (Durante's favorite), and **Giovanni Paisiello**.

DURAZZO, GIACOMO. (1717, Genoa–1794, Padua.) Italian aristocrat, theater director, **librettist**, and diplomat; alongside **Francesco Algarotti** an ardent advocate for operatic reform in the mid-18th century. Influenced by French culture through business and political connections, Durazzo began his operatic activities with a plan in 1748 to adapt **Jean-Baptiste Lully**'s *Armide* (originally 1686) as a progressive Italian opera (set by **Tommaso Traetta** and produced in 1761). He established ties to **Vienna** in 1749 as an envoy and subsequently married a local aristocrat. In Vienna, Durazzo performed in French plays and eventually became director of court theaters under Maria Theresa (1754), raising the quality of their offerings and cultivating their **ballets**; wrote **librettos** for **Christoph Willibald Gluck** and others; and enhanced Vienna's theatrical profile across Europe. Durazzo had hired Gluck to direct public concerts and theater works, to provide additional music for French **opéras comiques**, and to write new ones, and gave him experience composing ballet music essential to his later reform operas. Durazzo likely matched up Gluck with **Ranieri Calzabigi** when the latter arrived in 1761, and supported the development of innovative works such as Gluck's *Orfeo ed Euridice*, which synthesized French and Italian characteristics, while balancing those novelties against more traditional projects supported by **Pietro Metastasio** and his circle. He was eventually let go (1764) owing to court intrigues and an alleged affair with a dancer and spent the last two decades of his career as an emissary to **Venice**.

DVOŘÁK, ANTONIN. (1841, Nelahozeves, Bohemia, now Czech Republic–1904, Prague.) Czech **composer** of instrumental music, 10 operas from the 1870s through the first decade of the 20th century (both serious and comic—*see* CATEGORIES OF OPERA) and other vocal music; one of the most prominent and productive opera composers of the 19th-century nationalist movement.

Dvořák graduated from the Prague Organ School in 1859, then earned a living for more than a decade as a violist, from 1862 to 1871 in the orchestra of the Prague Provisional Theater, which was directed by **Bedřich Smetana** after 1866. There he internalized a repertory of works from Italy, France, and Germany and participated in premiers of native operas by Smetana (including *The Bartered Bride*, 1866, standard version 1870) and others. He acquainted himself with **Richard Wagner**'s works, which were not programmed, primarily through borrowed scores.

Dvořák's first opera, *Alfred der Grosse* (completed by 1870), was not staged until 1938. His second, *Král a uhlíř* (*King and Charcoal Burner*), premiered at the Provisional Theater in 1874 after he rewrote it to make it easier to perform. *Šelma sedlák* (*The Cunning Peasant*, 1878) was Dvořák's first unqualified success. Like *King and Charcoal Burner* a rustic comedy modeled on *The Bartered Bride*, it closed his most productive period of operatic composition, during which he had produced five operas in eight years. His invigoration of its traditional comic plot, which resembles *Le nozze di Figaro* in some respects, through engaging comic ensembles, apt characterization, and thematic recollections deployed for dramatic effect helped to make it almost as popular as *The Bartered Bride* during the five years following its premier.

The Cunning Peasant remained popular until pushed aside by Dvořák's next comic opera, the sentimental love story *The Jacobin* (1889, revised 1898), the high-water mark of his slim output of new operas from the late 1870s until the late 1890s, which included only *Dimitrij* (1882, revised 1885) and revisions of several earlier works. This lacuna resulted from his attention to instrumental and choral music and time spent abroad. During his extended trip to the United States (1892–95), he wrote only instrumental music, declining a potential Hiawatha opera.

In Dvořák's last three operas, written at the turn of the century, his continued adherence to **romantic** and nationalist subjects set him apart from the **verismo** mainstream. And although he turned partly away from traditional set piece construction and toward Wagnerian continuity of action and increased use of motivic reminiscence, he was less committed to Wagner's program than that of his Czech contemporary Zdeněk Fibich (1850–1900), and his style remained rooted in traditional **number opera**. *Čert a Káča* (*The Devil and Kate*, 1899) is based on a Czech folktale about a shrew who prefers hell over the real world. The lyric fairy tale *Rusalka* (1901), in which a lovesick water nymph yearns to be human, has been Dvořák's most popular opera at home and abroad. It is currently the second-most performed Czech opera after *The Bartered Bride* and, apart from the much less prominent *The Devil and Kate*, is his only opera still produced outside the Czech Republic. Dvořák's take on the familiar medieval epic *Armida* (1904) premiered in Prague with little success shortly before his death.

EATON, JOHN C. (Born 1935, Bryn Mawr, Pennsylvania.) American **composer** of about 15 operas and other theater pieces from the 1950s through the first decade of the 21st century, as well as other vocal and instrumental music. Eaton studied composition at Princeton University (graduated 1957) with Roger Sessions (1896–1985), then spent a decade composing in **Rome** supported by three Prix de Rome and two Guggenheim fellowships. He subsequently taught composition at the University of Indiana (1970s and 1980s) and the University of Chicago (beginning 1989).

Following the lead of **Alois Hába** and others, Eaton's style incorporates microtonal tuning, which involves intervals smaller than semitones (quarter tones and sixth tones), as well as synthesized and electronically modified sounds, applied in his operas to nontraditional treatments of a range of literary and historical subjects. Eaton first drew on these expanded resources for the television opera *Myshkin* (written 1970, based on Fyodor Dostoyevsky's *The Idiot*), in which the psychological vagaries of the title character are experienced first person through the camera's lens and are represented musically by quarter-tone versus sixth-tone vocabularies. In *Danton and Robespierre* (1978), which depicts the betrayals and executions of political rivals during the Reign of Terror following the French Revolution, quarter-tone tuning in equal temperament versus just intonation distinguishes the two adversaries.

Eaton's best-regarded work, *The Cry of Clytaemnestra* (1980), accompanied by chamber orchestra and electric tape, presents a compressed account of the Trojan War from the perspective of Agamemnon's wife, including his sacrifice of her daughter to enable his voyage, their mutual infidelities, and his murder, in which episodes of the plot are punctuated by wails of the title character. Eaton's prominent later operas include *The Tempest* (1985), which incorporates synthesizers, electronically modified instruments and voices, and Renaissance and jazz trios; his other Shakespeare adaptation *King Lear* (composed 2003–04); and a CNN opera (*see* ZEITOPER), *The Reverend Jim Jones* (1989), concerning the mass cult suicide in Jonestown, Guyana (1978).

EINSTEIN ON THE BEACH. Opera by **Philip Glass** and director Robert Wilson (born 1941), **libretto** by Christopher Knowles (born 1959), Lucinda Childs (born 1940), and Samuel M. Johnson; four acts and five "knee plays"; premiered Avignon, France, July 1976.

Einstein is the first of Glass's trilogy concerning pivotal historical figures. An expansive work, it runs without intermission for somewhat less than five hours, during which time the audience is free to come and go as they please. Its four acts consist of two or three extended **scenes** each and are framed by five shorter interludes ("knee plays," referring to their joining function), the first ongoing as the audience enters the theater. One of the best known postmodernist operas of the late 20th century, it was staged in several locations including **Paris** and **New York** during the year of its premier, has been revived several times, and was the subject of a documentary film.

More than Glass's other operas, *Einstein* explores a nonnarrative conception of theater that depends equally on visual and acoustical elements: scenography, staging, choreography, text, and music are all indispensable for meaning and were conceived concurrently. The scenario created prior to the **production** outlined a series of visual images that thematically reference the scientist's work. Scenes allude, for example, to trains, which Einstein used to explain relativity; a clock, whose representation of time is vulnerable to Einstein's theories; a bed, where Einstein's dreams served as inspirations; a spaceship, representing travel enabled by Einstein's discoveries; and a nuclear holocaust. Texts to be spoken or sung were assembled during rehearsals and consist of numbers, solfège syllables, abstruse poems by Christopher Knowles, and brief passages by the choreographer Childs and the actor Johnson, who played parts in the opera. They reference contemporary pop culture and current events, including the Beatles, 1970s teen heartthrob David Cassidy of *The Partridge Family* sitcom, current radio shows, Patricia Hearst (an heiress on trial for armed robbery), and pop songs.

Glass constructed his music according to **minimalist** principles involving methodical, repetitive variation of short patterns; additive processes, in which notes are added and subtracted from these patterns; and cyclical processes, in which patterns of different lengths are repeated simultaneously so that their unequal durations cause them to diverge and converge, finishing a cycle when their starting points again coincide. Compared to earlier minimalist works, Glass somewhat deradicalized these approaches in *Einstein* through enrichment of their harmonic underpinning and more expressive melodic writing. The opera is performed by two women, a man, and a boy in speaking roles; a 16-person chamber choir with **soprano** and **tenor** soloists; the Philip Glass Ensemble (two keyboards, three wind players on multiple parts, and soprano soloist); and a violinist dressed as Einstein located between the stage and the orchestra.

Einstein allows its audience to experience the scientist's theories by engaging their perception of time passing at different rates of speed. Music, staging, and visual imagery emphasize the polarity between rapid foreground events and extended background processes, as in the disparity between melodic 16th notes energizing slowly paced cycles or between rapid hand gestures by the actors and their slower, broader body movements. This stratification encourages the audience to construct individualized ways of processing time and to experience the present in a dreamlike state.

ENSEMBLE. *See* FINALE.

ERKEL, FERENC. (1810, Gyula, Hungary–1893, Budapest.) The most important **composer** of Hungarian 19th-century opera (nine works between 1840 and 1885). Erkel trained as a pianist and composer in Pozsony (now Bratislava, Slovakia). He began his theatrical career as the first **conductor** of the Hungarian theater company of Buda (1835–36) and of the newly formed Hungarian Theater (from 1838).

Erkel's operas combine Italian, French, and Viennese influences with nationalist plots and musical elements of Hungarian folk music and the *verbunkos* style of military recruiting dances: "Hungarian" scales, rhythms, cadence motifs, three-part form, and affects. This approach appears as early as his first opera, *Bátori Mária* (1840). Two of Erkel's operas had an immediate impact, remained in the repertory of the Budapest opera, and enjoyed some success outside Hungary, particularly in Vienna: *Hunyadi László* (1844), a 15th-century political tragedy that features recurring themes and extended ensemble **finales**, and the chamber opera *Bánk bán* (1861), centered on a medieval Hungarian revolt against foreign oppression. Erkel also popularized a new type of opera, the *népszínmü*—a Hungarian equivalent of English **ballad opera**—in *Két pisztoly* (1844) and *A rab* (1845).

Late in his career Erkel wrote both rustic comic operas (*see* CATEGORIES OF OPERA) like *Sarolta* (1862) and pseudo-**Wagnerian**, continuous music drama, represented by *Brankovics György* (premiered 1874, written in collaboration with his two sons), considered his masterpiece by contemporaries. Erkel served in the 1870s and 1880s as principal conductor of the National Hungarian Choral Association (1868–81), music director of the Royal Hungarian Opera House, and director of the Academy of Music in Budapest.

EURIDICE. **Libretto** by Ottavio Rinuccini (1562–1621) based on Ovid's *Metamorphoses*; **prologue** and five scenes; setting by **Jacopo Peri** with insertions by **Giulio Caccini**, premiered Florence, Palazzo Pitti, October 1600; setting by Caccini, premiered Florence, Palazzo Pitti, December 1602. Peri's version of *Euridice* was the first true opera having a coherent plot, for which all the music still exists. It was produced in a palace apartment by Jacopo Corsi, patron of the second **Florentine Camerata**, as a minor entertainment during the festivities for the wedding (in absentia) of Maria de' Medici to Henry IV of France. Peri himself played the **tenor** role of the mythical singer Orpheus, while his rival Caccini supplied substitute **arias** and **choruses** for singers belonging to his own retinue, including the original Euridice. **Emilio de' Cavalieri** probably supervised the production.

Befitting the celebration, Rinuccini modified the story so that Pluto imposes no conditions, and Orpheus successfully rescues his wife, Euridice, from the underworld. In contrast to the *intermedi* and other lavish entertainments that dominated such celebrations—and would guarantee Peri's unassuming offering a lukewarm reception—*Euridice* presents a coherent plot using dialogue. And unlike **pastoral** plays, its dialogue was sung throughout using the *stile rappresentativo* developed by the Camerata. Respecting their agenda, Rinuccini gave the prologue to Tragedy (rather than Music) to emphasize her priority, and Peri limited lyric set pieces to a very few strophic songs (e.g., Tirsi's "Nel pur ardor," scene 2) and reflective, scene-ending ensembles in the manner of Greek choruses. Most of these resemble strophic *canzonette*, and some include solo passages. The tiny orchestra comprised **basso continuo** instruments and possibly a violin and recorders.

Caccini published his version of *Euridice* in 1601 prior to its premier (1602) and just weeks before Peri's printed score was ready, apparently so that he could claim to have invented opera.

EXIT ARIA. *See* ARIA.

EXPRESSIONISM. Predominantly Austro-German post-**romantic**, proto-modernist style of literature, painting, and music during the first quarter of the 20th century that conveys exaggerated psychological turmoil or abnormality. The term was first applied in the visual arts to the French Fauves and the German Brücke and Blaue Reiter movements and subsequently to progressive music in the second decade of the century.

In music, expressionism is generally viewed as an outgrowth of late 19th-century expressive intensification involving increased chromaticism, dissonance, melodic disintegration, and tonal decay, heard in the sorceress Kundry's music in **Richard Wagner**'s *Parsifal* (1882) and in **Richard Strauss**'s early operas *Salome* and *Elektra* (1909). The style is associated particularly with the Second Viennese School: **Arnold Schoenberg**'s song cycle *Das Buch der hängenden Gärten* (1908–09) is regarded as the earliest true expressionist work, and his opera *Erwartung* (composed 1909, premiered 1924) is considered a paradigm. Expressionism takes the goal of communicating inner reality espoused by Wagner and nurtured less stridently by the **symbol-**

ists to an unsettling extreme. An anti-bourgeois affirmation of individualism over conventionality, its adherents justified its jarring disjunctions of mood and absence of apparent formal logic as resulting from creative compulsion rather than training or conventional standards of beauty.

The expressionist aesthetic of relentless intensity, instability, and disorder was difficult to sustain across extended compositions, resulting, for example, in the miniaturization of the one-act *Erwartung* or the short scenes of **Alban Berg**'s *Wozzeck* and *Lulu* (composed 1928–35, completed and premiered 1979). It was also difficult to sustain across a corpus of works, leading eventually to reliance by its practitioners on various constructivist elements (e.g., developing variation, set theory, serial procedures, and traditional forms). During the period between the world wars, expressionism faced challenges from alternative approaches—most prominently 20th-century **neoclassicisms**, the Parisian avant-garde, and Bertolt Brecht's "epic theater" (*see* WEILL, KURT)—aimed at reviving order and accessibility while distancing their audiences from extremes of cathartic immersion. After World War II, expressionism enjoyed a revival in Germany as its gestures were subsumed within the international compositional language.

F

FARINELLI. (1705, Andria–1782, Bologna.) Legendary 18th-century **soprano castrato**, composer of **arias** and keyboard works, and theatrical producer, born Carlo Broschi. His older brother Riccardo Broschi (ca. 1698–1756), also a composer, probably started his music lessons in **Naples** (ca. 1711), and the famed vocal coach **Nicola Porpora** took him on in 1717. His stage name came from an early patron, a Neapolitan magistrate named Farina.

After debuting in a minor role in Porpora's setting of **Pietro Metastasio**'s *Angelica e Medoro* (1720), Farinelli established himself after 1722 in Naples and **Rome**, frequently playing female leads, then extended his successes to the major northern Italian cities. With the help of the English ambassador to Turin, the Opera of the Nobility (*see* HANDEL, GEORGE FRIDERIC) drew him to **London** in 1734 where he performed operas by **Johann Adolf Hasse**, Porpora, and others, including his brother, to ecstatic acclaim. In 1737 the Queen Consort of Spain brought Farinelli to Madrid to rehabilitate her enfeebled husband Philip V by singing arias to him in the evening. Following the king's death in 1746, Farinelli became artistic director of court theaters in Madrid, for which he partnered with his close friend Metastasio on numerous spectacular productions, some involving horses and ships. Farinelli was famed for both his sensitive musicianship and his unworldly technique: a phenomenal range of over three octaves (reportedly from as low as c below middle c' to soprano high c''' or d'''); prodigious breath control and sustaining ability, including an exquisite messa di voce (crescendo and decrescendo on an extended note); and remarkable agility negotiating electrifying passagework, rapid wide leaps, and trills and other **ornaments**.

FARSA. A type of comic opera (*see* CATEGORIES OF OPERA), most often in one act, generally sung throughout, but occasionally set in the manner of French **opéra comique** with spoken dialogues between musical set pieces. Two *farse* were typically presented together in an evening along with two **ballets**. Development of the genre, which centered on the San Moisè theater in **Venice**, occurred in the 1790s and seems to have run its course by

1820, although stragglers appeared as late as **Giovanni Pacini**'s *Don Giovanni Tenorio* (1832). A *farsa* is structured like a miniaturized two-act **opera buffa** with the equivalent of a central **finale** in the middle, but no intermission. It includes fewer scenes, a smaller cast, and no **chorus**, and involves few if any set changes and no special effects. Economical to produce in a post-Revolutionary economy, like other comic operas, *farse* frequently reappeared from year to year to fill out **seasons**, and young composers cut their teeth on them. Five of **Gioachino Rossini**'s first nine operas were *farse* for the San Moisè theater, among them *L'inganno felice* (1812), his first real success, and *Il signor Bruschino* (1813), one of his best early operas. The term *farsetta* had also been used for **intermezzos** by the mid-18th century.

See also CIMAROSA, DOMENICO; DONIZETTI, GAETANO; MAYR, SIMON; RICCI, LUIGI AND FEDERICO.

FAUST. *Opéra*; music by **Charles-François Gounod**, **libretto** by Jules Barbier (1825–1901) and Michel Carré (1822–1872) based on Carré's play *Faust et Marguerite* (1850) and Johann Wolfgang von Goethe's (1749–1832) *Faust*, Part 1 (1808); five acts; premiered **Paris**, Théâtre Lyrique, March 1859.

The outcome of Gounod's long-standing fascination with the Faust legend—he became acquainted with the subject during his Prix de **Rome** years (1839–42) and worked on the church scene (Act 4) in 1849—the project took wing following his introduction in 1855 to the collaborators Barbier and Carré, who added several new scenes to Carré's play (the duel, the witches' sabbath, the dungeon scene, and Marguerite's redemption). Despite major cuts and other modifications during dress rehearsals and replacement of the lead on three weeks' notice, *Faust* was a solid success at its premier. Although initially criticized from some quarters as **Wagnerian**, and still regarded in Germanic countries as unworthy of Goethe and performed as *Margarete*, it came to be regarded by many as a decisive advance for French opera and a symbol of national prestige on the world stage.

A prototype for *opéra lyrique*, *Faust* explores at a more personal level than normally encountered in **grand opéra** such weighty **romantic** themes as the meaning of existence, unbounded passion and the spiritual limitations of physical love, satanism, and redemption through religious faith. Discontented with his studies, the scholar Faust turns to the demon Méphistophélès, bargaining his soul for youth and the beautiful Marguerite. Méphistophélès helps Faust ward off his rival Siébel by plying Marguerite with jewels, and goads him to continue his courtship when she demurely rejects him. Marguerite's brother, the soldier Valentin, returns from war to find her an unwed mother shunned by society and curses her as he dies after losing his duel with Faust. When her prayers go unanswered, Marguerite kills her infant and is sentenced to death. After Faust declines the enticements of a satanic afterlife—witches celebrating Walpurgis Night conjure a dazzling banquet of legendary queens and courtesans—he and Méphistophélès seek out the imprisoned Marguerite and urge her to escape with them. Rewarded for her resistance, she is delivered to heaven.

Faust illustrates the type of generic and stylistic fusion cultivated at the Théâtre Lyrique, which specialized in comic opera, modern novelties, and foreign imports. Though cast as an *opéra* in five acts, it premiered with spoken dialogue between set pieces in the manner of **opéra comique**. (Gounod provided **recitatives** for later productions in other French cities and eventually the Paris Opéra, 1869.) Spectacular, freely constructed **divertissements** are plentiful, for example the fair scene comprising all of Act 2, in which a single event, Marguerite's rebuff, is overshadowed by multiple **choruses** of soldiers and townspeople eventually joined simultaneously in a showstopping climax, Méphistophélès' paean to greed "Le veau d'or" ("Song of the Golden Calf"), his rebuke by the chorus (the chorale "De l'enfer") after he magically shatters Valentin's sword, and the waltzing chorus. Acts 4 and 5 are similarly embellished by atmospheric choruses, instrumental interludes, and dances. Yet these spectacles are counterbalanced in more private scenes by intimate moments such as Faust's famous ternary **aria** in the French style "Salut! demeure chaste et pure" (Act 3) and by Italianate multimovement set pieces such as Marguerite's three-section aria ("Il était un roi de Thulé") that ends with the waltz-like **cabaletta** "Ah! je ris de me voir") or her love **duet** with Faust near the end of the act.

Similarly, Gounod's tuneful melodic style leans in the direction of opéra comique, for example in the gaiety of the soldiers' chorus "Gloire immortelle" (Act 4), the vivacity of the witches' chorus, or the more earnest—some might say saccharine—lyricism of solos like Faust's Act 3 aria. However, his approximations of Beethovenian fury and gloom in the Act 4 duel or Act 5 dungeon scene and the measured quality of the interpolated recitatives reflect the more heroic aims of the Opéra. Also indebted to both *grand opéra* and opéra comique is the thematic integration provided by frequent reminiscences of earlier music, for example the themes from Marguerite and Faust's courtship recalled in their Act 5 reunion duet, or the musical apotheosis that ends Act 3, a device that prefigures **Amilcare Ponchielli**, **Giacomo Puccini**, and others.

FEBIARMONICI. Mid-17th-century itinerant company or companies of **composers**, **librettists**, singers, instrumentalists, and set and costume designers, operatic counterparts to troupes of the spoken **commedia dell'arte**. These "musicians of Apollo" disseminated opera throughout Italy during the 1640s and 1650s by performing works in the Venetian style in leased theaters that normally hosted plays. The first recorded performance by Febiarmonici occurred in Piacenza in 1644 (*La finta pazza*, originally 1641, probably by

Francesco Sacrati). A Roman company introduced opera to **Naples** at the behest of the viceroy as early as 1650 with performances of **Francesco Cavalli**'s *Didone* (originally 1641) and **Claudio Monteverdi**'s *L'incoronazione di Poppea*, among others, beginning the cultivation of opera in that city. Financial pressures led the Febiarmonici to economize and to broaden their audience by employing smaller casts and orchestras, cheaper scenery and stage equipment, more varied and popular subjects, and increased numbers of arias and shorter recitatives, helping to promote the late 17th-century public theater style.

FESTA TEATRALE. "Theatrical celebration" popular at **Vienna**'s imperial court and elsewhere in the Habsburg territories for commemorating state events such as aristocratic weddings and birthdays. Most often mythological, allegorical, and/or **pastoral**, *feste teatrali* are populated by the gods, demigods, shepherds, and nymphs of Arcadia, heaven, the underworld, and elsewhere. Comprising from one to five acts (most often two), they display greater structural liberty and less linear plotting than **opera seria** and often involve expanded resources like **choruses**, **ballets**, large **orchestras**, and special effects. In their unconventionality they resemble the **serenata**, a partially staged secular cantata performed outdoors at night, and the *azione teatrale*, which was performed indoors and, theoretically at least, had more of a story. *Feste teatrali* include **Antonio Cesti**'s *Il pomo d'oro* and **Wolfgang Amadeus Mozart**'s *Ascanio in Alba* (Milan, 1771). **George Frideric Handel**'s, *Acis and Galatea* (1718) was likely performed as a serenata, while **Christoph Willibald Gluck**'s *Orfeo ed Euridice* was designated an *azione teatrale*, partly explaining its progressive features. The fluidity of these designations is illustrated by Mozart's *Il sogno di Scipione*, entitled *azione teatrale* but probably performed as a serenata (Salzburg, 1772). **Pietro Metastasio** wrote numerous **librettos** falling into these **categories**.

FESTIVAL. A short off-season series of operatic productions (or other types of concerts), normally held in the summer, often at scenic vacation spots or historic sites. Performances may occur in outdoor pavilions or arenas. Festivals embrace a wide range of missions and formats. Increasing numbers of audio and video recordings from those that emphasize innovative repertory have been particularly important for drawing greater attention to obscure works.

The most prominent early festival, and the most significant point of departure for those that have proliferated mostly in the 20th century, is the annual Bayreuth Festival conceived by **Richard Wagner** for *Der Ring des Nibelungen* and *Parsifal* (originally 1882) in the Festspielhaus designed and built especially for that purpose. Launched in 1876 with the support of various

Wagner societies, King Ludwig of Bavaria, the philosopher Friedrich Nietzsche, and composers including Franz Liszt (1811–1886), it was eventually broadened to include all of the last 10 of Wagner's completed operas. It has been administered by members of the Wagner family up to the present day. Despite its importance, however, the Bayreuth Festival was not unique in the 19th century. A festival that predated it was the Chorégies d'Orange, held outside of Marseille since 1869. Envisioned as a Roman festival centering on habitual performances of **Étienne-Nicolas Méhul**'s *Joseph* (originally 1807) in a Roman arena, it included plays and concerts until 1970, then primarily operas. The Munich Opera Festival, administered by the Bavarian State Opera, also opened about the same time as Bayreuth.

Like Bayreuth, a number of festivals showcase works of a single composer or national tradition. In 1913 the Arena di Verona festival initiated performances in a Roman amphitheater to commemorate the birth centenary of **Giuseppe Verdi** with *Aida*, and has concentrated on Verdi and a mostly Italian operatic repertory, while also offering **ballets** and concerts. The Salzburg Festival (founded 1920), which has staged operas since 1922, mounted a complete **Wolfgang Amadeus Mozart** cycle in 2006. The Festival Puccini (Torre del Lago, Italy, beginning 1930) debuted in a temporary lakeside theater in front of **Giacomo Puccini**'s house. Held on the grounds of an English country house since 1934, the Glyndebourne Festival Opera specializes in Mozart and has issued frequent recordings. **George Frideric Handel** operas have been presented at the London Handel Festival (founded 1978) for about 20 years. The Rossini Opera Festival (Pesaro Italy, Teatro Rossini and other venues), established in 1980 in collaboration with the **Ricordi** Publishing House and partly in conjunction with the publication of the **Gioachino Rossini** critical edition, has revived many of the composer's lesser-known works. Undertaken more recently (starting in 2001), the Miskolc Opera Festival (Miskolc, Hungary) has focused each season on works of **Béla Bartók** and one other composer.

As noted above, festivals have played an important role in broadening the operatic repertory for modern audiences. Several have specialized in pre-19th-century works (e.g., the Bayreuth Baroque Festival, **baroque** operas and orchestral, chamber, and vocal music 2002–09, currently on hiatus; the biennial Boston Early Music Festival, beginning 1980, which has staged a baroque opera each season since 1995; and the Drottningholm Festival, which mounts historically based performances of Handel, **Christoph Willibald Gluck**, **Joseph Haydn**, and Mozart operas in a historic year-round theater in Stockholm); in rare operas (the Irish Wexford Festival Opera, which has performed little-known works by familiar composers since 1951); or in new music (the Munich Biennale, founded in 1988 by **Hans Werner Henze** for premiers of contemporary theater music). Others treat opera as one element of a broader cultural program, for example the Chatauqua Opera in southwestern New York State, the oldest continuously active summer opera company in the United States, which opened (1929) in conjunction with the religious and artistic Chatauqua Institution. The Festival dei Due Mondi (Festival of the Two Worlds, from 1958 in Spoleto, Italy) and its sister Spoleto Festival USA (from 1977 in Charleston, South Carolina), founded by composer **Gian Carlo Menotti** to highlight the intersection between European and American culture, include opera along with classical and jazz concerts, spoken drama, dance, visual art, and (in Italy) scientific programs. Still others—such as the Aspen [Colorado] Music Festival (beginning 1949); the Wolf Trap Opera Company (beginning 1971), based at the Wolf Trap National Park for the Performing Arts (Vienna, Virginia), the lone national park for the performing arts (established in 1966 as Wolf Trap Farm Park); and the London Handel Festival's Handel Singing Competition (since 2002)—have dedicated themselves to cultivating new talent.

Summer festivals are rarely the primary season for a permanent company, as in the case of the Santa Fe [New Mexico] Opera (founded 1956 on the site of a former guest ranch and specializing in the operas of **Richard Strauss**) or even the off-season home for a year-round company. However, a number of primarily orchestral festivals have added opera to their schedules, for example the Ravinia Festival (Highland Park, Illinois), the oldest outdoor music festival in the United States and since 1936 the summer home of the Chicago Symphony Orchestra; the Tanglewood Music Festival (Lenox, Massachusetts), summer home of the Boston Symphony Orchestra since 1937; and Opera Saratoga (Saratoga Springs, New York, formerly the Lake George Opera) founded in 1962, the summer home for the Philadelphia Orchestra and the New York City Ballet. The number of festivals held in locations other than Europe or the United States, such as the International PuntaClassic Festival (Punta del Este, Uruguay), is growing.

FIDELIO. Opera (singspiel); music by Ludwig van Beethoven (1770–1827), **libretto** by Joseph von Sonnleithner (1766–1835) based on Jean-Nicolas Bouilly's (1763–1842) *Léonore, ou L'amour conjugal* (1798); three versions, two (originally three) acts; premiered **Vienna**, Theater an der Wien, November 1805. Beethoven's only completed opera.

Its 1805 premier dampened by the presence of Napoleon's occupying army and the resulting flight of a number of Beethoven's patrons, the first *Fidelio* was also judged too long, and cuts were made for subsequent revivals in 1806 and 1814, the last revision becoming the definitive version. Different **overtures** were used for each **production**, now designated *Leonore* Overtures Nos. 2 and 3 and the *Fidelio* Overture, respectively, *Leonore* No. 1 having been written for an intended staging in Prague (1807).

Fidelio continues the ambitious philosophical and aesthetic program of singspiel development set out by **Die Zauberflöte**. Its story, supposedly based on a real event, had been treated previously as a *fait historique* (1798; *see* OPÉRA COMIQUE) by Pierre Gaveaux (1760–1825), a *dramma semiserio* (1804) by **Ferdinando Paer**, and a *farsa sentimentale* (1805) by **Simon Mayr**. The hero Florestan has been imprisoned for political reasons by the villainous Don Pizarro and is guarded by the well-intentioned jailer Rocco. His wife Leonora has infiltrated the prison disguised as the boy Fidelio, hoping to free her husband. Rocco's daughter Marzelline loves Fidelio but is courted by Rocco's assistant Jaquino. Anticipating an impending inquiry by the benevolent nobleman Don Fernando, Pizarro decides to kill Florestan immediately and orders Rocco to prepare his grave, Rocco taking Fidelio into the underground dungeon to help. When Pizarro attempts to murder Florestan, Leonora reveals her true identity and protects Florestan long enough for Fernando to arrive and free the prisoners.

Like many turn-of-the-century **opéras comiques** and operas of mixed type (*see* OPERA SEMISERIA), it combines light action—Leonora's cross-gendered disguise, her unwitting pursuit by Marzelline, and Jaquino's frustration—with darker elements: a Gothic setting; an imperiled hero; a harrowing rescue; post-revolutionary themes of liberty, universal brotherhood, and conjugal devotion; and a fortuitous intervention to seal the happy ending and avert tragedy. Set pieces beginning the first act belong to the lighter traditions of singspiel (Marzelline's strophic **aria** "O wär ich schon"), **opera buffa** (the canonic quartet of misunderstanding "Mir ist so wunderbar"), or a combination of the two (Rocco's episodic buffo aria in strophic form "Hat man nicht auch Gold"). However, Beethoven's music increases in intensity as the danger becomes imminent, involving more symphonic and evocative orchestration, more declamatory and spontaneously impassioned vocal writing, more elaborate forms, and increased presence of action ensembles. In Act 2, notable examples include Florestan's elaborate dungeon scene—it includes a somber orchestral introduction, pathos-infused obbligato **recitative**, and aria ("In des Lebens") in *rondò* form in which the change of tempos reflects his shift from doomed resignation to hope as he senses Leonore's presence—and the climactic quartet "Er sterbe" in which she fends off Pizarro.

FINALE. The concluding set piece of an opera (*finale ultimo*) or of an act or part of an opera (central finale). The term may also refer to the last movement of an instrumental work.

The finale was not conventionalized in Italian 17th-century opera and may range from **arias** through various types of ensembles and **choruses**, for example the trio with chorus that ends **Jacopo Peri**'s *Euridice* and the two endings of **Claudio Monteverdi**'s *Orfeo* (the 1607 solos with chorus by the

Bacchantes and the 1609 virtuoso **duet** for Orfeo and Apollo, chorus of nymphs and shepherds, and *moresca* for shepherds). By the early 18th century, act-ending arias or duets became common, and operas often conclude with a *coro* of principals (***Giulio Cesare in Egitto***) that moralizes on the outcome. The *concertato* central finale for solo ensemble and sometimes chorus originated in Venetian comic operas of the mid-18th century, its development generally credited to the **librettist Carlo Goldoni** and **composer Baldassare Galuppi**. It incorporated real-time interaction and a progressing situation as early as their *Arcadia in Brenta* (1749) and consisted mainly of dialogue with a final ensemble section.

The characteristic central finale of the second half of the century is the episodic "chain" finale, which consists of a series of sections—and eventually separate movements in different tempos and meters—that articulate phases of the action. Each section or movement comprises one or more comic ensemble modules, which consist of a passage of interactive dialogue and real-time action, often in declamatory, ***parlante***, or *nota e parola* style, followed by simultaneous parenthetical reflection in a more lyrical idiom. These finales normally close the first chapter of the plot by disrupting an initial intrigue. Unexpected entrances or revelations either mesmerize the characters and prompt a hushed reaction (the sotto voce ensemble, ancestor to the ***largo concertato*** of the 19th century) or send them into a hyperactive frenzy (a concluding **stretta**) descended from the *gliuòmmari* (comic tangles) of the **commedia dell'arte**. Progressively extended and elaborated during the late 1700s, chain finales reached a peak of development in operas of the 1780s and 1790s in **Vienna** by **Antonio Salieri, Carl Ditters von Dittersdorf,** and **Wolfgang Amadeus Mozart (*Le nozze di Figaro*,** Act 2, and ***Don Giovanni*,** Act 1). They made their way into **opera seria** ca. 1770 in the **librettos** of **Mattia Verazi** (e.g., **Niccolò Jommelli**'s *Fetonte*, 1768) initially as the *finale ultimo*, either in new operas or attached to existing librettos by **Pietro Metastasio** and others, and became common in that position (as well as in earlier acts) by the 1790s (*see IDOMENEO, RE DI CRETA*, Act 2).

By the generation of **Simon Mayr** ca. 1800, the last three sections of the chain finale—a slow passage of static reflection, a resumption of the action in dialogue, and a fast reactive conclusion—were expanded into three substantial movements, the *largo concertato*, ***tempo di mezzo***, and stretta. In the conventional schema popularized by **Gioachino Rossini**, these movements were preceded by an interactive ***tempo d'attacco***. However, in practice the opening section of the finale could be more complicated than a single movement and could be introduced by a chorus and comprise multiple phases of dialogue, **stage songs** and other solos, dances, and choruses. By the mid-19th century, composers like **Giuseppe Verdi** often omitted either the stretta alone, leaving the action of the *tempo di mezzo* to resonate into the intermission, or both the *tempo di mezzo* and stretta, ending with the *largo concertato*

(*La traviata*, 1853, Act 2). The stretta could also be modified to include recapitulations of musical themes heard earlier (*Aida*, Act 2). During the first half of the 19th century, a common option for the *finale ultimo* in **melodramma** was the *rondò finale*, which centers on an extended multimovement aria, sometimes in two-movement slow-fast form. By midcentury this finale, often a death scene for the hero or heroine, took the form of a duet or trio of principals and possibly other participants, which centered on a substantial slow movement framed by dialogue (see the final scenes of **Rigoletto** and *Un ballo in maschera*, 1859).

In French opera, development of the finale took a different course. **Jean-Baptiste Lully**'s *tragédies en musiques* (and **Jean-Philippe Rameau**'s in the next century) normally ended acts, including the last, with freely constructed **divertissements** involving **ballet**, chorus, and **airs**. In the earliest **opéras comiques** (ca. 1750–75), acts prior to the last typically concluded with ensembles, frequently duets or trios but occasionally larger ones, most often a single movement, the first chain finale occurring in **André-Ernest-Modeste Grétry**'s *Le magnifique* (1773). **Vaudeville** finales were popular to end opéras comiques and were adopted in **opera buffa** as well (*Don Giovanni*). Choruses also occur frequently to end French and Italian operas by the late 1700s.

Nineteenth-century French **grands opéras** loosely adapted the Italian format for central finales, an extended opening phase of action incorporating local color or ceremony (**Les Huguenots**, Act 3). Spectacular, often catastrophic events were common in the last act (see Act 5). **Richard Wagner** followed suit in his French-influenced operas (e.g., **Tannhäuser**), although more spontaneous confrontations or action scenes were also possible in German opera (**Der Freischütz**, Act 2). By the late 19th century, even in Italy traditional formal conventions were often obscured (Verdi, *Falstaff*, 1893, Act 2) or absent entirely (**Tosca**, Acts 1 and 2), and the range of options for situations and organization essentially became unlimited. Compare, for example, the extended monologue of Wotan's farewell to Brünnhilde (*Die Walküre*, Act 3; *see DER RING DES NIBELUNGEN*), which includes the spectacular element of Loge's magic fire, to the spontaneously constructed continuous dialogue in Siegmund and Sieglinde's love duet (Act 1) and in the confrontation between Siegmund and Hunding (Act 2), a quartet of sorts that also involves Wotan and Brünnhilde. In the 20th century, with rare exceptions like those found in retrospective number operas (the "Threepenny Finales" of **Die Dreigroschenoper**, the vaudeville finale of **The Rake's Progress**), final scenes show little distinction in cast, structure, and style from other ones (see those in **Pelléas et Mélisande** or **Peter Grimes**), tend to subside rather than amass forces (for example in **Wozzeck**), and, aside from their location, shed their identity as a specific type of set piece.

FLAGSTAD, KIRSTEN. (1895, Hamar, Norway–1962, Oslo.) Norwegian singer and opera manager considered by some to be the premier representative of the **Wagnerian soprano.** Flagstad trained in Oslo and made her debut in 1913 at its National Theater. She performed for the next 18 years exclusively in Scandinavia, first in lyric roles such as Marguerite (*Faust*), when she gained renown for her ability to learn parts quickly. Her turn to more dramatic roles such as **Tosca** and **Aida** around 1930 prepared her for her emergence as a heroic soprano. Following Flagstad's Wagnerian debut as Isolde (*see TRISTAN UND ISOLDE*) in Oslo (1932), the Swedish soprano Ellen Gulbranson (1863–1947) recommended her to Bayreuth, where she sang Sieglinde and Gutrune in 1934 (*see DER RING DES NIBELUNGEN*). Flagstad gained worldwide attention with performances at the **New York** Metropolitan Opera (beginning 1935) as Isolde and Brünnhilde and was enormously successful there despite flare-ups with costars and management. She also appeared frequently in Wagnerian roles at Covent Garden, **London** (1936–37).

Flagstad raised eyebrows when she returned to German-occupied Norway during World War II to reunite with her second husband, a timber magnate who was arrested after the war for collaborating with the Nazis. She herself was tried and acquitted, having performed during the war only in nonoccupied countries. Flagstad made her return to the stage through Covent Garden (1948–51) and gave the world premier of **Richard Strauss**'s *Vier letzte Lieder* in London (1950). After ending her Wagnerian career with Isolde in 1951 at Covent Garden, she lightened her repertory, taking up such roles as Dido (*see DIDO AND AENEAS*) and **Christoph Willibald Gluck**'s **Alceste** until her last appearance in 1953. Flagstad finished her career as the first director of the Norwegian State Opera (1958–60).

See also WOMEN AND OPERA.

DER FLIEGENDE HOLLÄNDER. *Romantische Oper*; music by **Richard Wagner**, **libretto** by the **composer** based on Heinrich Heine's (1797–1856) *Aus den Memoiren des Herren von Schnabelewopski* (1831); three continuous acts; premiered Dresden, Königliches Sächsisches Hoftheater, January 1843. Wagner claimed that he conceived *The Flying Dutchman* during his tempestuous voyage from Riga to **London** in 1839, the Act 3 sailors' **chorus** "Steuermann! Lass die Wacht" purportedly inspired by sea chanties. The experience likely colored the helmsman's song "Mit Gewitter und Sturm" (Act 1) and the Dutchman and storm motives of Senta's ballad ("Johohe," Act 2) as well. Composition began in mid-1840 starting with the ballad and choruses; the libretto was written and the score completed in 1841. Wagner sold his prose scenario to the Paris Opéra, but the subject was reassigned to French poets, who based their own libretto on other sources, and to the

French composer Louis Dietsch (1808–1865). It was produced as *Le vaisseau fantôme* (1842), leading Wagner to change the locale from Scotland to Norway when *Dutchman* went into production at about the same time.

Originally conceived in a single act, perhaps as the opener of a double bill with a **ballet** at the Opéra, Wagner subsequently divided it into three acts to be performed continuously with orchestral transitions, initiating Wagner's agenda of continuity for audience immersion. It eventually premiered—conducted by Wagner—in three separate acts. The Dutchman, a sea captain betrayed by his wife, is a lost soul doomed to sail eternally because he swore an oath to Satan while attempting to round a stormy cape. He can be redeemed only by winning a **woman**'s unselfish love when he disembarks once every seven years. He meets the Norwegian captain Daland when their ships are becalmed at sea. The greedy Daland barters a night's accommodations—and his daughter Senta—for the Dutchman's treasure. Senta, who already knows the Dutchman's legend, cherishes his portrait and counts herself his soul mate, ignoring the advances of the hunter Erik. When she meets the Dutchman, she vows to redeem him. As he casts off to resume his journey, having released her from her promise, she testifies to her loyalty by diving into the sea, uniting with him in death.

Rooted in English nautical folklore, *Dutchman*'s plot is steeped in **romantic** imagery of the natural sublime (storms at sea) and the supernatural (the Dutchman and his crew). And it raises philosophical issues that would preoccupy Wagner throughout his career: the validity of irrational, intuitive behavior (Senta's love); corruption through materialism and ambition (Daland's greed and the Dutchman's oath); transcendence over bourgeois complacency (Erik's ordinariness); redemption of men's ambitions by women's self-renunciation (Senta's sacrifice); and the quest for spiritual unity (Senta and the Dutchman's apotheosis).

Dutchman's music demonstrates an adaptation and synthesis of German, French, and Italian elements that would inform Wagner's operas through *Lohengrin* (1850) and in some ways anticipate his later music dramas. Its **arias** and choruses are rooted in the strophic lieder that had long characterized German opera. The many examples include the helmsman's song mentioned earlier, the spinning chorus, Senta's ballad, Erik's "Mein Herz voll Treue," Daland's "Mögst du, mein Kind" (all Act 2), and the Norwegian Sailor's Chorus (Act 3). Yet all show the Wagnerian tendency to loosen schematic forms by interspersing dialogue between their stanzas. And in Senta's ballad, Wagner replaced homogeneous melody with an episodic succession of associative ideas—the Dutchman's open fifths, the wave- and wind-tossed account of his legend, and the redemption motif that gradually seduces the girls listening to the song—all of which convey textual content and Senta's obsessive mentality. Frequent textually prompted recurrences of these ideas, in addition to anticipations and recollections of melodies from the choruses, expose the roots of Wagner's later **leitmotif** technique in his saturated application of reminiscence motives informed by French opera.

The atmospheric choruses for the girls and sailors belong to the tradition of characteristic **stage songs** for picturesque cohorts featured in **opéra comique** and such German romantic predecessors as *Der Freischütz*. Wagner adopted a similarly folkish style for the conventional bourgeois musical personas of Daland and Erik, their tuneful, square phrases, diatonic major-key harmonic progressions, and formulaic turns to the dominant at times suggesting town band music. And while their melodies become less symmetrical and predictable as they proceed, their foursquare openings sufficiently distinguish them from the ethos of the Dutchman's and Senta's music, its chromatic vocabulary and spontaneous, motivically oriented construction suggesting their more visionary understanding of life and death and foreshadowing Wagner's future style.

Wagner's initial attempt to groom *Dutchman* for the Opéra is evident in such French elements as the construction of Act 1 as a grand tableau, in which the Dutchman's entrance is framed by sailors' choruses, and the composer's attentiveness to details of orchestration and variations of sonority, for example the a cappella Helmsman's song (Act 1). The same rationale could be cited for the Italianate impulse, probably filtered through **Giacomo Meyerbeer**, to construct scenes around a substantial slow movement followed by a fast movement reminiscent of a **cabaletta** or **stretta**. Examples are plentiful: Daland's duet with the Dutchman (Act 1); in Act 2 Senta's ballad followed by the chatty women's chorus, Senta's duet with the Dutchman, and the trio stretta that closes the act; and in Act 3 Erik's "Willst jenes Tags" and the stretta for him, Senta, and the Dutchman. Yet even in the earliest work of his maturity, Wagner employs this schema less obtrusively than in Italian or even French operas, interrupting the ends of movements or entire set pieces or dissolving them into transitions.

FLORENTINE CAMERATA. Academy (intellectual society) of primarily aristocratic musicians, poets, scientists, and others who met informally at the palace of Count Giovanni de' Bardi (1534–1612) in Florence ca. 1573–87 to discuss a range of scientific, philosophical, and aesthetic subjects; to perform music; and most famously to investigate and recreate the legendary expressive power of ancient Greek music in tragic plays. In addition to Bardi, himself an amateur **composer**, the group included at least three prominent musicians: the singer and composer **Giulio Caccini**; the lutenist (*see* LUTE), composer, and music theorist Vincenzo Galilei (late 1520s–1591), father of the astronomer Galileo Galilei; and the amateur composer Piero Strozzi (ca. 1550–ca. 1609).

The Camerata's discussions of Greek music were based on the work of the classical historian Girolamo Mei (1519–1594), who had recently completed his monumental treatise *De modis musicis antiquorum* (*On the Manner of Ancient Music*, ca. 1568–73) and would correspond extensively with Galilei from Rome about his theories while the Camerata was active. Mei and Galilei agreed that Greek music had involved a single melody set in a relatively narrow range, in contrast to modern polyphony, which pits competing melodies in different ranges against one another. Greek rhythms and contours had enhanced the inflections of speech that characterize particular emotional affects. And Greek tragedies were sung throughout, so that music continuously reinforced dramatic pathos. Galilei's *Dialogo della musica antica et della moderna* (*Dialogue Concerning Ancient and Modern Music*, 1581) recommended that modern composers imitate these characteristics and also discouraged the musical depictions of specific textual images often heard in polyphonic **madrigals** (so-called "madrigalisms," such as dissonance on the word "sorrow"), instead advocating impassioned declamation.

These principles were applied to several documented works performed for the Camerata, and Caccini credited the Camerata with inspiring his professed invention of a new style of "musical speech" (*in armonia favellare*, later termed "**recitative**") for the first operas. However, the music that resulted from the Camerata's immediate activities might better be considered an adaptation and reinforcement of the Italian use of melodic formulas to sing long poems as "recitational arias," which dated back at least to 1500. Furthermore, Bardi's Camerata played no direct role in the creation of the first operas, having ceased activities probably a decade or so earlier. Instead, a second academy, led by the aristocratic composer Jacopo Corsi (1561–1602) beginning ca. 1692, which included Caccini, Galilei, and Strozzi, as well as the younger singer/composer **Jacopo Peri** and the aristocratic poet Ottavio Rinuccini (1562–1621), would claim this honor with *Dafne* and *Euridice*.

DER FREISCHÜTZ. *Romantische Oper* (**singspiel**); music by **Carl Maria von Weber**, **libretto** by Johann Friedrich Kind (1768–1843) based on a story from Johann August Apel (1771–1816) and Friedrich August Schulze's (1770–1849) *Gespensterbuch* (1811–15); three acts; premiered Berlin, Schauspielhaus, June 1821. The most familiar and influential German **romantic** opera prior to **Richard Wagner**, its Act 2 **finale**, the Wolf's Glen **scene**, was famed for its innovative lighting and other special effects. *Der Freischütz* (loosely *The Free Shot*) emerged from the literary circle in Dresden with which Weber associated, as part of his effort to energize German opera. Having triumphed in Berlin as the first opera to be produced at the new theater there, it was soon translated into most European languages including English and French and produced in locations as distant as Brazil and Australia.

Set in a bucolic woodland village, *Der Freischütz* offers a nationalistic, nostalgic vision of rustic life in 17th-century Bohemia saturated with such romantic themes as magic and the supernatural, the macabre, and nature worship and religious pantheism. The simpleminded but good-hearted hunter Max needs to win a shooting contest to claim his bride Agathe, daughter of the head woodsman Cuno, and despairs as his marksmanship inexplicably deteriorates. The villainous Caspar, who has struck a Faustian bargain with the Devil's henchman Samiel and wants to trade another soul for his own, approaches Max with the promise of magic bullets. Seven are to be cast in the malignant Wolf's Glen, a hell mouth deep in the forest: six infallibly hit the shooter's mark, while Samiel guides the seventh. Caspar intends this final bullet for Agathe, banking that grief over her death will erode Max's religious faith, allowing his soul to be claimed. However, because Samiel holds no lien on the virtuous peasant, Max's errant trial shot finds Caspar instead of Agathe. After Max confesses and a wise hermit intervenes on his behalf, the shooting contest is abolished, and the couple are permitted to marry following Max's year-long probation.

Although Weber and Kind drew on foreign models—their familiarity with **opéra comique** is evident in their many picturesque **choruses** and dances, the Wolf Glen's Gothic hue, the insouciance of Agathe's companion Aennchen, and the flexible approach to form, while Agathe's Act 2 aria adapts the Rossinian (*see* ROSSINI, GIOACHINO) slow-movement **cabaletta** schema (*see* ARIA)—Weber's score is distinctly Germanic. It takes inspiration from the descriptive precision, expressive intensity, and dramatic tension and pacing of Ludwig van Beethoven's (1770–1827) symphonic music and the text painting of romantic lieder, particularly in Agathe's Act 2 scena (*see* SCENE) and aria, in which she responds to nature's voice as she waits for Max to return from the hunt, and in the bullet-casting sequence of the Wolf's Glen scene, in which the **orchestra** describes increasingly perilous natural and supernatural reactions as each bullet is created in a precisely calibrated crescendo of terror.

Weber's music also sharply distinguishes the realms of good and evil. The songs and dances of jovial peasants (the victory and laughing choruses and the waltz in Act 1, Aennchen's polonaise arietta in Act 2, and the bridesmaids' and hunters' choruses in Act 3) caricature rustic folk music through their engaging melodies, some resembling Männerchor singing or yodeling, oompah accompaniments, uncomplicated major-mode chord progressions, horn-brightened instrumentation, and strophic lied forms. Caspar and Samiel's sinister ethos, represented by the former's bizarre drinking song ("Hier im ird'schen Jammerthal") and grim celebratory aria ("Schweig, schweig," both Act 1), and the Wolf's Glen scene, depends on a more sophisticated chromatic harmonic language in minor mode, scored with low strings and woodwinds (see the start of the Wolf's Glen music). The villains use the technique of **melodrama** to establish a hierarchy of evil, the most villainous character speaking while others sing. Frequent musical foreshadowings and reminiscences—for example, connections among the **overture**, Caspar's songs in Act 1, the Wolf's Glen scene, and the Act 3 finale—further intensify the air of foreboding.

G

GALANT. Eighteenth-century French term for post-**baroque** (even anti-baroque) styles in literature, the visual arts, music, and manners that are modern, pleasing, natural, and occasionally mildly erotic, as illustrated by the *fêtes galantes* paintings of Antoine Watteau or the ***opéras-ballets*** of **Jean-Philippe Rameau**. In music it distinguished a free, lyrical, theatrical, or chamber idiom, subject in theory to no rules other than those of good taste, from the strict, learned, contrapuntal baroque church style, and is ably represented in Italy by the keyboard compositions of Domenico Scarlatti (1685–1757), the ensemble works of Giovanni Battista Sammartini (ca. 1700–1775), and operas by such composers as **Leonardo Vinci**, **Giovanni Battista Pergolesi**, and **Johann Adolf Hasse**.

In opera, the *galant* style dominated mid-18th-century **bel canto** as it was cultivated by the leading **castratos** such as **Farinelli**. It is characterized by lightly accompanied, short melodies constructed with brief, often repetitive phrases probably derived from dance, the articulations of which coincide with line or couplet changes in the poetry being sung. Its lilting triple meters, triplet figures, backwards dotted rhythms, limited use of **coloratura** passagework, and frequent appoggiaturas contribute to a light, graceful affect. Relatively slow chord changes within simple, functional, diatonic harmonic progressions, *Trommelbass* accompaniments (repeated notes in the bass) and other devices that enliven harmonically static passages, and weak-beat cadences abandon the intensity of baroque harmony. Eighteenth-century singers utilized subtle dynamic shadings, smooth transitions of vocal range, variation of tempo (rubato), and nimble **ornamentation** to project a humanized antidote to baroque gravity.

In the late 18th century, as the *galant* came to be considered artificial, effeminate, and negatively aristocratic, it was transformed into the more introspective *Empfindsamer Stil* championed by Carl Philipp Emanuel Bach (1714–1788), and it remained an important color in the diverse, dramatic Viennese classical style of **Joseph Haydn**, **Wolfgang Amadeus Mozart**, and others.

GALLI, FILIPPO. (1783, Rome–1853, Paris.) Preeminent Italian **bass** of the era of **Gioachino Rossini**, acclaimed for his agility, wide range, and acting prowess. Galli debuted as a buffo **tenor** in 1801, but by 1811 had retrained, possibly on the advice of **Giovanni Paisiello**, as a bass and debuted a second time in Rossini's *farsa* La cambiale di matrimonio (originally 1810). Over the next 12 years he created eight Rossinian bass leads in *L'inganno felice* (1812), *La pietra del paragone* (1812), *L'italiana in Algeri* (1813), *Il turco in Italia* (1814), *Torvaldo e Dorliska* (1815), *La gazza ladra* (1817), *Maometto II* (1820), and *Semiramide* (1823). Galli's career demonstrates the astonishing workloads of successful early 19th-century singers: he appeared in roughly 70 different productions from the 1810s through 1825, seven operas in 1814 alone. Galli later sang in **London** for five years (1827–33) and in Mexico and Spain throughout the 1830s. He ended his career as a teacher at the **Paris** Conservatoire.

GALUPPI, BALDASSARE. (1706, Burano–1785, Venice.) Prolific **composer** of **opera seria** (over 60 from the late 1720s into the 1770s, many on **Pietro Metastasio**'s **librettos**, approximately 100 operas total) and, with the **librettist Carlo Goldoni**, the leading developer of the *dramma giocoso* (*see* OPERA BUFFA) and the multisection comic **finale** in the 1750s and 1760s, paving the way for those of **Wolfgang Amadeus Mozart** and others; also an important composer of sacred music and keyboard music, keyboard player, and arranger.

Trained in **Venice** near his hometown, Galuppi wrote his first 11 operas (1722–37) almost exclusively for that city, after which his works received wider play. Beginning in 1740, he took a conservatory appointment after finding the Venetian theaters still dominated by Neapolitans and local hero **Antonio Vivaldi**, then traveled to **London** (1741) where he supervised productions (including his own) to mixed reviews at the King's Theater. Back in Italy again (1743), he continued his steady stream of serious operas while he familiarized himself with Neapolitan opera buffa by adapting imports for Venice and wrote his first *dramma giocoso*, *La forza d'amore* (1745).

From 1749 to 1772, Galuppi devoted more attention to his own comic operas (*see* CATEGORIES OF OPERA), many of them with Goldoni. Beginning their collaboration with *L'Arcadia in Brenta* (1749), they produced well more than a dozen that were widely performed internationally. *Il filosofo di campagna* (1754) led the way, making Galuppi one of the most popular composers across Europe. Recognition at home came through prestigious appointments as *maestro di coro* at St. Mark's Basilica and at the Ospedale degli Incurabili orphanage **conservatory** (both 1762). Galuppi spent 1765 to 1768 in Catherine the Great's St. Petersburg where he premiered at least one new opera and introduced his Italianate idiom to Russian sacred music. He returned to Venice (1768) and resumed work at the conservatory, producing only a handful of new operas between 1769 and 1773.

GARDEN, MARY. (1874, Aberdeen, Scotland–1967, Inverurie, Scotland.) Preeminent Scottish **soprano**-actress of the early 20th century. After relocating to the United States in 1883, her vocal studies in Chicago and **Paris** were funded by wealthy philanthropists through the end of the century. She debuted as an understudy at the Opéra-Comique (*see* PARIS) in Gustave Charpentier's (1860–1956) *Louise* (1900) and rose to stardom by creating the role of Mélisande in *Pelléas et Mélisande* (1902). In **London** (1902–03) and Paris through the first decade of the 20th century, she flourished on a diet of late 19th-century French parts by **Ambroise Thomas**, **Charles-François Gounod**, **Camille Saint-Saëns**, and **Jules Massenet**. She premiered Massenet's *Chérubin* (1905), as well as works by lesser composers. Famed for her prodigious **acting** ability—her style was said to have been influenced by Sarah Bernhardt—her notoriously erotic rendition of **Salome** for the fledgling Manhattan Opera House (1909; *see* NEW YORK CITY) made her famous in the United States, leading to her long-standing employment by a series of companies in Chicago (1910–34), beginning with the Chicago Grand Opera, as a performer and director.

GARRICK, DAVID. (1717, Hereford–1779, London.) English actor; producer of plays, operas, and **ballets**; and playwright; the most important Shakespearean of his day. Garrick debuted as a professional actor in 1741 and shortly thereafter created his first Shakespearean role as Richard III, and later Lear and Hamlet. He assumed control of **London**'s Drury Lane Theater in 1747, retaining that position until his retirement in 1776. According to contemporary accounts, Garrick's style was similar in many respects to modern **acting**, though apparently more exaggerated in his gestures and vocal inflections. His example encouraged opera singers to abandon the traditional manner of assuming a static, conventionalized pose and facial expression that caricatured the current affect of one's role in favor of freer, more subtle, and more inventive mimic gestures coupled with more emotionally transparent delivery of his lines.

Garrick's unconventionally natural, psychologically immediate style of acting influenced such progressives as the Italian theater critic **Francesco Algarotti**, the philosophe Denis Diderot, and the French choreographer Jean-Georges Noverre, and his management of Drury Lane shaped numerous careers. In the late 1740s he reportedly taught the **castrato Gaetano Guadagni**, who subsequently created the title role in **Christoph Willibald Gluck**'s *Orfeo ed Euridice*.

GIACOSA, GIUSEPPE. *See* ILLICA, LUIGI, AND GIUSEPPE GIACO-SA.

GIASONE. Dramma musicale; music by **Francesco Cavalli**, **libretto** by Giacinto Andrea Cicognini (1606–ca. 1650) based on Apollonius of Rhodes's account of Jason and the Argonauts; **prologue** and three acts; premiered **Venice**, Teatro San Cassiano, January 1649. The most widely performed opera of the 17th century.

Cicognini's libretto is characteristic of mid-17th-century Venetian opera in the complexity of its plot, which involves adultery, attempted murder, assisted suicide (unsuccessful), theft and conquest, divine intervention, magic, disguises and mistaken identities, spectacle, and occasionally tasteless humor through the intermixture of comic *contrascene* involving a nurse, a lady-in-waiting, a captain of the guard, and the stuttering, hunchback dwarf Demo. In line with other contemporary operas, the myth of Jason and Medea becomes an allegorical contest between Fate (personified by Apollo) and Love over Giasone's heroic and amorous pursuits. Giasone has fathered twins first with Isifile (Hypsipyle) and later with Medea (without knowing her true identity). She helps him steal the Golden Fleece from Giove (Jove) by invoking the infernal spirit Volano, who gives Giasone a magic ring. As Giasone and Medea sail away, Giove and the wind god Eolo attempt to sink Giasone's ship but are duped by Amore (Love) into swamping his pursuers, Egeo (Aegeus—Isifile's former lover) and his servant Demo. Having escaped, Giasone promises Medea that he will have her rival Isifile killed, but Medea is mistakenly almost drowned instead. Egeo saves Medea, who marries him, and Giasone marries Isifile rather that kill her as she requests.

As its tortuous plot proceeds, *Giasone* demonstrates the spectrum of standard scenes and set pieces in Venetian opera: comic **aria** (Medea's nurse Delfa, Acts 1 and 3); trumpet aria (for Alinda, Act 2, also comic); love **duet** (Giasone and Medea, Act 2); sleep scene (Egeo's intended murder of Giasone, Act 3, one of five such scenes); invocation (Medea and Volano, Act 1); lament (three sung by Isifile); and scenes that reference music and madness. And it displays midcentury trends toward **recitatives** and arias that are discrete in musical style and dramatic function, standard aria forms, and an emerging comic style of **patter song**.

In the four decades following its premier, *Giasone* was popularized by touring companies through more than 20 revivals and adaptations. Its prominence as a landmark of the Venetian style made it a target for the **Arcadian Academy**'s reformers, who objected to its mixture of comic and serious topics, its unconventional poetry, and its lack of realism owing to the abandonment of classical dramatic **unities** and the superabundance of arias.

GILBERT, WILLIAM SCHWENCK, AND ARTHUR SULLIVAN.

(Gilbert: 1836, London–1911, Grim's Dyke, Harrow Weald; Sullivan: 1842, London–1900, London.) **Librettist** and **composer**, respectively, of 14 **operettas** (mostly during the 1870s and 1880s), many of them among the most beloved and frequently performed works of the light musical stage. While both worked at times with other artists, they never achieved independent success comparable to their collaborations. In addition to his operettas, Sullivan also wrote in a wide range of other genres, including incidental music for plays, choral and orchestral music, and songs.

Gilbert, who began his career as a humorous journalist and lawyer, became a surgical parodist of Victorian politics and society in lyrics beloved for his virtuosic handling of poetic meter and rhyme and ingenious wordplay. Sullivan, a member of the Chapel Royal at age 12 and scholarship student at the Royal Academy of Music and the Leipzig Conservatory, made a name as a composer of orchestral and choral works and songs and brought to popular theater an unaccustomed technical polish; sophisticated tunefulness; sensitivity to locale, atmosphere, and characterization of social cohorts; and knack for spoofing the pretenses of grand opera.

Their introduction in 1869 resulted in the modestly successful *Thespis, or The Gods Grown Old* (1871, mostly lost) and later the immediately popular *Trial by Jury* (1875), their first surviving operetta together, which was instigated by Richard D'Oyly Carte (1844–1901) for his Royalty Theater in **London**. A lukewarm response to Sullivan's next work with a different librettist possibly led to his long-term alliance with Gilbert and Carte, beginning with *The Sorcerer* (1877), *H.M.S. Pinafore, or The Lass That Loved a Sailor* (1878), and *The Pirates of Penzance, or The Slave of Duty*, which premiered in New York (1879) to establish copyright and preempt the increasingly frequent unauthorized productions occurring in the United States. In 1881, Carte built the Savoy Theater, which was dedicated to performances of Gilbert and Sullivan operettas and which opened midway through a production of *Patience, or Bunthorne's Bride*. Their first premier there was *Iolanthe, or the Peer and the Peri* (1882).

The mixed reception of *Princess Ida, or Castle Adamant* (1884), artistic differences, and Sullivan's apparently inferior standing with the public frayed the collaboration briefly. But he and Gilbert set aside their differences in 1885 with *The Mikado, or the Town of Titipu*, considered their best work, and five other productions, including *Ruddigore, or the Witch's Curse* (1887); *The Yeomen of the Guard, or the Merryman and His Maid* (1888); and their final success, the late triumph *The Gondoliers, or The King of Barataria* (1889). Their partnership ended after the failure of *The Grand Duke, or The Statutory Duel* in 1896. Sullivan and Gilbert were knighted in 1883 and 1907, respectively.

GIORDANO, UMBERTO. (1867, Foggia–1948, Milan.) Prominent member of the *giovane scuola*, he composed 12 operas (mostly from the 1890s through the first quarter of the 20th century) as well as other vocal and instrumental music. While Giordano was a student at the **Naples** Conservatory, his one-act opera *Marina* (ca. 1889, not performed) placed sixth in the Sonzogno competition of 1889, the year **Pietro Mascagni**'s *Cavalleria rusticana* won, beginning a long-standing relationship with the publisher. With his first staged work, *Mala vita* (1892), about a factory worker, his mistress, and a prostitute, Giordano dove into **verismo** headfirst and scandalized Italian audiences.

Following this rocky start, his career peaked at the turn of the century with three straight triumphs: the verismo opera *Andrea Chénier* (1896), which culminates in the guillotining of the poet and his lover; *Fedora* (1898), cast with **Enrico Caruso** as **tenor** lead; and *Siberia* (1903), which premiered in Milan and later gained international notice at the **Paris** Opéra (1911). Subsequently he experienced a series of failures in the first decades of the 20th century, relieved only by the temporary success of his masterpiece, *La cena delle beffe* (1924), a twisted account of humiliation, infidelity, and murder in Renaissance Florence. His last opera, *Il re*, appeared in 1929. Giordano is noted among the **composers** of the *giovane scuola* for his fluent adaptation of atmospheric regional musical idioms such as Neapolitan dances and Russian folk songs.

GIOVANE SCUOLA. The "Young School" of Italian **composers**, rivals and successors to **Giuseppe Verdi** born after 1850 and active primarily from the 1890s on. The best-known individuals identified with this group are **Alfredo Catalani**, **Ruggero Leoncavallo**, **Giacomo Puccini**, **Pietro Mascagni**, and **Umberto Giordano**. Most of them embraced the nontraditional subjects, frank emotional intensity, and structural freedoms of the verismo style.

GIULIO CESARE IN EGITTO. **Opera seria**; music by **George Frideric Handel**, **libretto** by Nicola Francesco Haym (1678–1729) based on Giacomo Francesco Bussani's (active 1673–80) libretto of the same name (1677); three acts; premiered London, King's Theater, February 1724. Handel's extremely successful fifth opera for the Royal Academy of Music featured the eminent **castrato Senesino** as Caesar and soprano **Francesca Cuzzoni** as Cleopatra. It was revived three times during the first and second academies. Its staging by the **New York** City Opera in 1966 with Beverly Sills as Cleopatra was a landmark in the modern revival of **baroque** opera.

After Cesare (Caesar) invades Egypt in successful pursuit of his Roman rival Pompey, both Cleopatra and her brother Tolomeo (Ptolemy) seek separate alliances with him. Whereas Tolomeo alienates Cesare by offering the head of Pompey as tribute, Cleopatra beguiles him by disguising herself as the disenfranchised noblewoman Lidia and making her entrance costumed as Virtue framed by Mt. Parnassus. A succession of fruitless intrigues drives the bulk of the plot: Cornelia's and her son Sesto's (Sextus) multiple suicide attempts; rebuffed advances toward her by Tolomeo, the Egyptian general and confidant Achilla (Achillas), and the Roman tribune Curio (Curius); her thwarted efforts to kill Tolomeo; and Achilla's unsuccessful plan to kill Cesare. Political and social order is restored when Achilla, betrayed by Tolomeo and mortally wounded in battle, turns his troops over to Cesare, Sesto assassinates Tolomeo, and Cesare triumphantly crowns Cleopatra queen, promising renewed tranquility.

Although *Giulio Cesare* shows many similarities to then-current **Arcadian** opera seria, it also retains such remnants of 17th-century Venetian public opera as plot complexity, disguise and mistaken identity, *contrascene* (Cesare's contest of wills with the obbligato violin in his first **aria** in Act 2), and modest spectacle (Cleopatra's introduction to Cesare, and the battle symphony and harbor scene in Act 3). Handel's music outshines that of his Italian contemporaries in its inventive treatment of conventional affect in arias (*see* DOCTRINE OF THE AFFECTIONS) and its rich orchestration.

GLASS, PHILIP. (Born 1937, Baltimore.) Highly regarded American **minimalist composer** of over two dozen operatic works and other theater pieces (from the mid-1970s to the present)—three of which are well known—incidental music for plays, film music, as well as other vocal and instrumental music.

Glass began lessons on violin and flute while in elementary school and started composing at age 12, finding inspiration in the cutout bins at his father's record store. He entered the University of Chicago at age 15 in an early-admissions program (1952–56) and earned a master's degree at the Julliard Conservatory (1962). His teachers included Vincent Persichetti (1915–87) at Julliard; **Darius Milhaud** at the Aspen Music School (1960; *see* FESTIVAL), whom he regarded as a decisive influence; and Nadia Boulanger (1887–1979) in **Paris** on a Fulbright scholarship (1964–66). He also spent a year (1966–67) studying in India. Returning to **New York** in 1967, he adopted the minimalist style of Terry Riley (born 1935) and Stephen Reich (born 1936), and founded the Philip Glass Ensemble of amplified woodwinds, keyboard synthesizers, and **soprano** voice in 1968 as an outlet for his compositions. Decisive influences on his style include the musics of Anton Webern (1883–1945), Milhaud, the sitar player Ravi Shankar (1920–2012), and the tabla player Alla Rakha (1919–2000), and the films of Jean Cocteau.

The music of Glass's operas represents an enrichment of the short repeating melodic and rhythmic patterns of 1960s minimalism through the employment of more clearly directed harmony, more elaborate textures, and richer timbres to create a less distant, more expressive style. Glass's best-known works belong to his so-called portrait trilogy involving pivotal historical figures presented using languages not usually heard in opera, which Glass viewed as a cohesive theatrical cycle. His first opera, *Einstein on the Beach*, is his largest and least traditional. Lacking a discernible plot, its visual images and sound references to the physicist's life and theories accompany a heterogeneous collage of numerals, sight-singing syllables, and short poems and other texts that reference contemporary popular culture. The more traditional *Satyagraha* (1980), which is more indicative of Glass's later style, enlists an extensive cast of solo singers, full **chorus**, and **orchestra** of strings and woodwinds and references in its music a number of traditional opera composers, including **Gioachino Rossini** and **Richard Wagner**. Its text, assembled from Hindu scripture and sung in the original Sanskrit, evokes scenes from Mohandas Gandhi's life during a period of fighting social inequity in South Africa (1893–1914), which are surveyed by silent representations of Leo Tolstoy, the Bengali poet-musician Rabindranath Tagore, and Martin Luther King Jr. in a kind of sacred ritual play. *Akhnaten* (1984), based on the life of the Egyptian reformer who, according to some accounts, was deposed by his people, sets a text in English, Hebrew, and Egyptian using the composer's most chromatic and dissonant incarnation of minimalist style.

Among Glass's operas composed since *Akhnaten* are two chamber works—*The Juniper Tree* (1985, after the Brothers Grimm) and *The Fall of the House of Usher* (1988, after Edgar Allan Poe); the homage trilogy to Cocteau—*Orphée* (1993), *La belle et la bête* (1994), and *Les enfants terribles* (1996); and the full-length operas *The Making of the Representative for Planet 8* (written 1985–86, premiered 1988), *Galileo Galilei* (2002), *Waiting for the Barbarians* (2005), *Appomattox* (2007), and *Kepler* (2009). Glass's most recent opera is *The Lost* (2013).

GLINKA, MIKHAIL IVANOVICH. (1804, Novospasskoye, Russia–1857, Berlin.) Russian **composer** of two major operas (and other vocal and instrumental music) that established a European presence for the Russian nationalist movement in music.

Glinka spent his youth on his aristocratic family's estate, where he became familiar with peasant songs and dances, heard Western art music played by his uncle's serf orchestra, and studied piano and string instruments with his governess and one of the orchestra musicians. He continued his training in St. Petersburg (beginning 1818) while attending the opera, studying voice, beginning to compose sets of variations, and conducting the serf **orchestra** on visits to Novospasskoye. An unsuccessful venture to establish a resident

Italian opera company in St. Petersburg (beginning 1828) ended after three seasons, but it allowed Glinka to absorb the conventions of **Gioachino Rossini**'s operas, leading him to travel in the early 1830s to Milan, where he met **Vincenzo Bellini** and **Gaetano Donizetti**, and Berlin.

Having completed his self-guided studies, Glinka embarked in 1834 on creating the first opera on a Russian text and subject set entirely to music, the patriotic heroic-tragic opera *Zhizn' za tsarya* (*A Life for the Tsar*), which enjoyed an epochal premier in St. Petersburg (1836), eventual performances in Prague (1866) and elsewhere, and enshrinement in the Russian repertory. Its **libretto** by the aristocratic poet Yegor Fyodorovich Rozen (1800–1860) on a topic championed by the Russian **romantic** poet Vasily Andreyevich Zhukovsky (1783–1852) reflects a concept of patriotic nationalism promoted under Nicholas I, which emphasized servile self-sacrifice for and quasi-religious worship of the homeland personified by the tsar. Paralleling historical accounts, the peasant Ivan Susanin conceals the location of the 16-year-old tsar Mikhail Romanov from Polish invaders despite their intimidation and his eventual death, a saga that recalled the more recent resistance of partisan serfs against Napoleon in 1812. Opposition between Russians and Poles is represented by their different musical styles, Russian folk songs quoted verbatim or filtered through Italianate adaptations of their idiom for the St. Petersburg salons contrasting with conventionalized polonaises and mazurkas, the Russian references playing a central dramatic role rather than serving merely to provide local color. Elements of French *grand opéra*—the five-act structure, historical emphasis, massed crowd scenes, musical differentiation of social cohorts, and a network of recurring themes—combine with a framework of Rossinian set piece forms and prevalent lyricism.

An unexpectedly successful performance of Rossini's *Semiramide* the same year had assembled a cast capable of managing Glinka's monumental creation, but also ushered in a craze for Italian opera that deflected attention away from the nationalist movement and ultimately dampened reception of his fantastical opera *Ruslan i Lyudmila* (1842), in which the knight Ruslan defeats a giant and sorcerers to rescue his beloved Lyudmila, its score alternating exotic and magical references against an Italianate matrix. Initially successful, its fortunes faded with the reestablishment of an Italian company in 1843, and it eventually disappeared. Unproductive following this perceived betrayal, Glinka departed Russia in disgust in 1856 and died the next year in Berlin.

GLUCK, CHRISTOPH WILLIBALD. (1714, Erasbach–1787, Vienna.) Bohemian **composer** of about 50 operas (18 on **librettos** by **Pietro Metastasio**) and **ballets**, and virtuoso glass harmonica player. With the **librettist Ranieri Calzabigi**, he decisively advanced the agenda of operatic reform initiated in the mid-18th century by such composers as **Niccolò Jommelli**

and **Tommaso Traeta**, combining Italian and French characteristics and shaping the subsequent development of serious opera (*see* CATEGORIES OF OPERA). Although Metastasio and **George Frideric Handel** were derisive toward him, his influence on numerous other notables such as **Wolfgang Amadeus Mozart**, **Simon Mayr**, and **Richard Wagner** is evident.

Gluck received his initial musical instruction in his hometown, then studied mathematics and logic at the University of Prague beginning in 1731, where he heard Italian opera and oratorio and played the organ in church. He also studied music in Milan after 1737 with the symphony composer Giovanni Battista Sammartini (ca. 1700–1775), likely mastering orchestration, an essential tool in his eventual reform style. At the ducal theater he would have heard Italian operas with ballets performed during the intermissions. His first opera (one of many versions of Metastasio's *Artaserse*, 1741) began a run of four consecutive heroic operas for the prestigious Carnival **season** in Milan as well as others for several northern Italian cities (five in total on librettos by Metastasio). Through aristocratic and professional connections, Gluck moved to **London** as composer for the King's Theater in 1745 during the second Jacobite rebellion, where he became acquainted with the realistic style of **David Garrick**'s acting and Handel's tone painting, further influences on his reform style. His two operas for London—*La caduta de' giganti* and *Artamene* (both 1746)—show his penchant for borrowing music from his own previous operas (and works by others) that would continue throughout his career.

After a stop in Dresden (1747), Gluck made a splashy entry onto the Viennese musical scene with a remake of Metastasio's *Semiramide riconosciuta* (1748) for the birthday of the empress Maria Theresa and the opening of the renovated Burgtheater (court theater). The poet—never one of Gluck's fans—credited himself for succeeding despite the barbaric music. Gluck resumed his travels over the next four years, moving first to Hamburg, where he became orchestra director for an **opera buffa** troupe and caught a sexually transmitted disease from its lead **soprano**, then staging operas in Copenhagen, Prague, and **Naples**, all on Metastasio's librettos. By the time he married the wealthy daughter of a deceased Viennese businessman in 1750, Gluck was back in **Vienna**, which would serve as his base of operations for the next two decades.

During his initial Viennese employment by the music-loving Prince Joseph Friedrich von Sachsen-Hildburghausen, Gluck was introduced to local and visiting singers and instrumentalists and gained recognition from the imperial court, in particular for his remake of Metastasio's *Le cinesi* (1754), paving the way for his appointment at the Burgtheater. Although **Giacomo Durazzo**, the count and theatrical producer who spearheaded his hiring, probably had enlisted Gluck to enact his own program of uniting French ballet, **chorus**, and special effects with the lyricism of Italian poetry and melody, he was initially employed as director of concerts (ca. 1756) and later as composer of ballets for other theaters. Despite the limitations of these appointments, Gluck was nonetheless involved with a rich and varied repertory that included, in addition to the theatrical menu of spoken plays, modified **opéras comiques**, ballets, and a few Italian heroic operas. Gluck's concert repertory consisted of oratorios, operatic music, and instrumental music of all sorts, for which he had an excellent orchestra and soloists at his disposal. Among his numerous commissions for Italian operas and opéras comiques for the Burgtheater and elsewhere, the *festa teatrale L'innocenza giustificata* (1755) on a libretto by Durazzo and Metastasio advanced Durazzo's agenda by integrating choruses, ballets, and more freely structured scenes.

The arrival in 1761 of Calzabigi, who, like Durazzo, had previously advocated synthesizing French and Italian opera, gave further impetus to Gluck's efforts, resulting in the iconic reform opera *Orfeo ed Euridice* (1762). To a greater degree than *L'innocenza* or any other previous work, it mediates between French spectacle and Italian lyricism, integrating chorus and ballet, minimizing **coloratura**, eliminating *recitativo semplice* (*see* RECITATIVE), and abandoning the structural conventions of **opera seria**. An immediate success in Vienna, *Orfeo* also impressed French musicians when the score appeared in **Paris** and attracted attention at the liberal-minded Francophile court of Parma. Gluck and Calzabigi's next collaboration was *Alceste* (1767), intended for Maria Theresa as an allegory of her devotion to her recently deceased husband. When it appeared in print (1769), it included one of the seminal documents in the history of opera, a preface attributed to Gluck but probably written by Calzabigi, which provides a rationale for the novelties in *Alceste* and *Orfeo*.

By 1772, having survived a harrowing experiment in theater management (1769–70) and experienced snubs including the lukewarm reception of his third and final collaboration with Calzabigi, *Paride ed Elena* (1770), Gluck looked for new opportunities in Paris, where he relocated in 1773 and produced four French adaptations of previous operas—including *Orphée et Eurydice* (1774) and the French *Alceste* (1776)—and five new works, including his two *Iphigénie* operas (1774 and 1779), *Armide* (1777), *Echo et Narcisse* (1779), and an opéra comique. Though championed by the likes of Jean-Jacques Rousseau (1712–1778) and Voltaire, he was assaulted by proponents of traditional opera, French and Italian alike. Following a stroke in 1779 he moved back to Vienna, where he adapted earlier works but wrote no new operas. Additional strokes led to his death.

GOLDONI, CARLO. (1707, Venice–1793, Paris.) Playwright and the most important comic **librettist** of the mid-18th century. In the 1730s and 1740s he vacillated between an intermittent legal career and (beginning 1734) theater work. He served both as an assistant to Domenico Lalli (1679–1741, house poet and impresario for the prestigious **Venetian** Teatro San Giovanni Grisostomo), revising **librettos** for and staging a half dozen **opera serias** between 1735 and 1741, and as a playwright for a **commedia dell'arte** troupe, creating scenarios for improvised spoken plays and librettos for sung **intermezzos**. In 1748 he joined a second commedia dell'arte company, for which he began creating plays that were entirely written out, establishing himself in a genre that would win him literary repute. Although his famous collaboration with the **composer Baldassare Galuppi** had begun in 1740 with the opera seria *Gustavo I, re di Svezia*, it caught fire in 1749 with the *dramma giocoso* (*see* OPERA BUFFA) *L'Arcadia in Brenta*. And it extended through at least 15 operas until 1766, including two of his most popular librettos, *Il filosofo di campagna* (with Galuppi, 1754) and *La buona figliuola*, set originally by **Egidio Duni** in 1756, and reset four years later to international acclaim by **Niccolò Piccinni**. He moved to **Paris** in 1762, where he spent the remainder of his life.

Blessed with incomparable facility and reportedly capable of delivering a play in as little as four days, Goldoni produced approximately 80 librettos from the 1730s through the 1770s, mostly intermezzos and opere buffe, in addition to dozens of spoken plays. They were set and reset by the leading composers of the second half of the century, the most prominent of whom (in addition to Galuppi and Piccinni) were **Tommaso Traeta**, **Domenico Cimarosa**, **Giovanni Paisiello**, **Antonio Salieri**, **Wolfgang Amadeus Mozart** (*La finta semplice*, 1769), and **Joseph Haydn** (*Il mondo della luna*, 1777). Goldoni regarded his spoken plays far more highly than his librettos, which served as a profitable avocation and were released under a pseudonym once he had a reputation. He popularized the designation *dramma giocoso* for opere buffe that characterize aristocrats and members of the lower classes as individuals and treat relationships between them as grist for social criticism. In tandem with Galuppi, he was instrumental in increasing the presence of ensembles in comic opera, particularly lengthy multisectional **finales** to end acts 1 and 2. Operatic adaptations of several of his plays occurred in the 20th century, for example the *Tre commedie goldoniane* (1926) of **Gian Francesco Malipiero**.

GOMES, CARLOS. (1836, Campinas, Brazil–1896, Belém, Brazil.) Brazilian **composer** of 11 stage works and other vocal music. Gomes stands next to **Amilcare Ponchielli** and **Alfredo Catalani** in the line of development from **romantic** *melodramma* to the *giovane scuola*. He is a rare example prior to the 20th century of a non-European opera composer who achieved significant success in Europe.

Trained at the Imperial Conservatory of Music in Rio de Janeiro (beginning ca. 1859), Gomes familiarized himself with operas of the Italian mainstream from **Gioachino Rossini** through **Giuseppe Verdi**. Following two successful premiers in the early 1860s, the government funded travel to Italy, where he studied at the Milan Conservatory with the composers Lauro Rossi (1812–1885, the conservatory director) and Alberto Mazzucato (1813–1877, who also taught **Arrigo Boito**). After graduating in 1866, Gomes produced seven stage works for Italy and two for Brazil, among which the opera-ballet *Il Guarany* (1870) brought him international notice, and the grand operas *Salvator Rosa* (1874) and *Lo schiavo* (Rio de Janeiro, 1889) were important successes.

GOUNOD, CHARLES-FRANÇOIS. (1818, Paris–1893, St. Cloud.) Apart from **Giacomo Meyerbeer**, the most prominent **composer** of French operas during the third quarter of the 19th century, as well as sacred music, songs, and instrumental music. Alongside **Ambroise Thomas**, his popularization of *opéra lyrique* set the course for **Georges Bizet**, **Jules Massenet**, and others.

Against the wishes of his mother, who wanted him to have a legal career, Gounod studied music at the **Paris** Conservatoire (beginning 1836) with Antoine Reicha (1770–1836), **Fromental Halévy**, and Jean-François Le Sueur (1760–1837). He won the Prix de **Rome** in 1839, during which he explored Palestrina-style counterpoint, finding it revelatory, and acquainted himself with a broad spectrum of music in **Vienna** and Leipzig (1842–43) at the end of his grant. After focusing on sacred music early in his career and briefly contemplating the priesthood, Gounod turned to the stage in 1848. An unknown quantity, he won a commission in 1849 for the *grand opéra Sapho* (1851) on the recommendation of the singer **Pauline Viardot**, who sang the title role. It failed despite positive reviews, as did three other attempts at the Opéra: *La nonne sanglante* (1854), on a **libretto** by **Eugène Scribe** previously rejected by **Hector Berlioz** and **Giuseppe Verdi**; *Ivan le terrible*, which was canceled after the attempted assassination of Louis Napoleon at the Opéra in 1858; and a revision of *Sapho* the same year.

Despite Gounod's dubious track record, **Léon Carvalho**, the new manager of the emergent Théâtre Lyrique, took up his standard and persevered even after the **opéra comique** *Le médecin malgré lui* (1858) garnered critical praise but failed to win an audience. He was rewarded with *Faust* (1859), which conquered Paris (after some initial standoffishness) and the rest of Europe and remains one of the mainstays of 19th-century French opera. His next four projects failed to capitalize on *Faust*'s success, although *Philémon et Baucis* (1860), a sentimental rejoinder to the debauchery of **Jacques Offenbach**'s recent *Orphée aux enfers* (1858), and a revamped version of the rustic epic *Mireille* (1864), sometimes viewed as a precursor to **Carmen** and other late 19th-century naturalist operas, eventually won followings in France.

Gounod's fortunes turned with *Roméo et Juliette*, which premiered at the Théâtre Lyrique during the International Exposition of 1867, a triumph that outshone Verdi's *Don Carlos*, given simultaneously at the Opéra. Following a hiatus in England (1870–74)—he fled initially because of the Franco-Prussian War—his last three operas received negative press, and after the depressing failure of *Le tribut de Zamora* (1881) he bowed to public opinion and ended his opera career, turning to other genres.

Gounod's charm resulted from his abandonment of *grand opéra* in the late 1850s and 1860s for a more personal style suited to his temperament and abilities. His *opéras lyriques* feature sensitive musical delineations of multidimensional characters facilitated by his distinctive style of light melody and chromatic harmony, his cultivation of a French version of **parlante** texture, and his flexible treatment of form in his set pieces. Gounod's memorable love **duets**—four in *Roméo et Juliette* alone—set an example that would guide Bizet, Massenet, and others throughout the century.

GRABU, LUIS. (Active ca. 1665–1694). Spanish **composer** active in **London**. Grabu studied in **Paris**, probably with **Robert Cambert** and **Jean-Baptiste Lully**. He appeared in England by 1665 in the service of Charles II, becoming Master of the King's Music (1666), where he directed and contributed new music for a revision of Cambert's *Ariane, ou Le mariage de Bacchus* (1674, originally 1659, music lost), probably the first professionally staged all-sung opera in England. The subject of considerable disparagement at court, Grabu was dismissed in 1674 and later migrated to France to avoid political agitation against Catholics (1679), but he was brought back in 1683 to create an English equivalent of the **tragédies en musique** with which he had become familiar in Paris. *Albion and Albanius* (1685), an allegorical glorification of the reign of Charles II in the French style on a **libretto** by the poet laureate John Dryden (1631–1700), is the earliest surviving full-length English-language opera. After Grabu left England in 1693, his whereabouts are unknown.

GRAND OPÉRA. Spectacular, mostly historical French serious opera set to music throughout and performed at the **Paris** Opéra, in contrast to **opéra comique**, which has spoken dialogue and was normally performed at lesser theaters. Although the term had occasionally been applied to **Jean-Baptiste Lully**'s *tragédies en musique*, it first appeared frequently after the turn of the 19th century in connection with the *opéras* of **Christoph Willibald Gluck**, **Niccolò Piccinni**, and **Gaspare Spontini**, and entered common parlance when the genre became a Parisian bourgeois social institution and a center of attention across Europe after ca. 1830. At its height, *grand opéra* was represented most prominently by the works of the **librettist Eugène Scribe** and the composers **Daniel-François-Esprit Auber** (*La muette de Portici*, 1828); **Gioachino Rossini (*Guillaume Tell*)**; **Fromental Halévy** (*La Juive*, 1835); and particularly **Giacomo Meyerbeer (*Les Huguenots*)**. In scores and **librettos**, *grands opéras* are most often designated *opéra historique* or simply *opéra*.

Taking works of the post-Revolutionary era as models for combining Italianate lyricism and passionate French declamation, emphasizing spectacular massed-scene complexes that integrate **chorus** and dance, adopting increasingly melodramatic and violent nonclassical subjects from recent history, and assuming a government-sanctioned social and political function, *grand opéra* became the premier blockbuster entertainment for polite upper-middle-class society. Standards of quality and propriety were maintained by an entrepreneurial theater manager contracted by the state—most notably Louis Véron (1798–1867)—who hired the composers and librettists, performers, and **production** staff and assumed financial obligations, and by a government-appointed commission that reviewed and authorized the manager's decisions. Through this arrangement, the state guarded against unflattering messages and polished its own image while minimizing the financial risks of an extraordinarily demanding and expensive style of theater.

Owing to high costs, new productions were infrequent—no more than one per year—and consequently expectations of opulence, spectacle, and innovation ran high. Across five lengthy acts (or less ideally four) lasting four to five hours, individuals enact their personal conflicts and love interests, marching inevitably toward disaster against an epic backdrop of post-classical historical conflict. Huge casts numbering a dozen or more soloists and multiple choruses and **ballet** corps, which represented various social/political cohorts, recreate this historical panorama. And the principle of *actualité* (veracity) demanded that **sets**, costumes, lighting, and stage machinery for special effects be created afresh for each new opera and painstakingly researched to mimic specific periods, locales, and even times of day. The best scenographers (among them Pierre-Luc-Charles Ciceri, 1782–1868), lighting directors, and machinists were recruited to stage the climactic cataclysms (explosions, fires, volcanic eruptions, shipwrecks, and massacres) and other special effects (sunrises, ice skating, and risqué bathing scenes) for which *grand opéra* was famous.

The demands of entertainment, innovation, and realism weighed equally on music. To engage their bourgeois audiences, composers adopted vocal idioms ranging from the pompous declamation and syllabic airs descended from *tragédie en musique* to the emotive lyricism and **coloratura** of Italian *melodramma*, the *parlante* dialogue and **patter song** of **opera buffa**, and the sprightly tunefulness of opéra comique. While relationships to Italian structural components like the *largo concertato* and **stretta** and French strophic and ternary forms are evident, *grand opéra* avoids rigid schemata that interfere with continuous dramatic flow. Instead, composers arranged set pieces to accommodate spontaneous series of events and unorthodox, showstopping situations. Consequently, acts tend to comprise a relatively small number of huge scenes, each a tableau in numerous sections consisting primarily of scenic music related to traditional French **divertissements** that conveys a sense of place for a single major event. Framing returns of distinctive music create order and sometimes occur simultaneously in contrapuntal layers or in juxtaposition to produce dazzling climaxes that were lauded by contemporary audiences. Serving the principle of *lisibilité* ("legibility"), music provided audible representations of dramatic content and clarified plot, situation, and characterization through transparent expression of emotions, picturesque depiction of locales, and recurring signature themes and sonorities that designate various characters and cohorts. And the French operatic **orchestra** became a proving ground for novel sonorities as composers expanded its array of instruments and novel colors to convey idiosyncratic environments.

French *grand opéra* remained an active and consequential genre in Paris as late as Meyerbeer's *L'Africaine* (1865) and **Giuseppe Verdi**'s *Don Carlos* (1867) and had a wide-ranging impact throughout the 19th century. For composers across Europe, and from true representatives of the genre such as Verdi's *Les vêpres siciliennes* (1855) to works that embrace its influences (e.g., *La traviata*, 1853; *Aida*; and *Tannhäuser*), it served as a wellspring of musical and dramatic enrichment and a prototype for cultivating the entirety of operatic spectacle.

See also BERLIOZ, HECTOR; BIZET, GEORGES; *BORIS GODUNOV*; CATEGORIES OF OPERA; CENSORSHIP; GOUNOD, CHARLES-FRANÇOIS; GRÉTRY, ANDRÉ-ERNEST-MODESTE; MASSENET, JULES; MONIUSZKO, STANISLAW; PONCHIELLI, AMILCARE; SAINT-SAËNS, CAMILLE; STAGE SONG; WAGNER, RICHARD.

GRAUN, CARL HEINRICH. (ca. 1703, Wahrenbrück–1759, Berlin.) German **composer** of almost three dozen operas, mostly **opera seria** written from the 1730s through the 1750s on **librettos** by **Apostolo Zeno**, **Pietro Metastasio,** and the Prussian court poet Leopoldo de Villati (1701–1752), as well as other vocal and instrumental music, and **tenor**. Trained in Dresden (1714–17) and at the University of Leipzig (1718–19), Graun based his early career in Dresden, where he assimilated the modern Italianate *galant* style. He wrote six operas for the court of Brunswick-Wolfenbüttel as a tenor and composer (from 1724) and vice Kapellmeister (beginning 1731).

With dim hopes for further advancement in Brunswick, he moved to Prussia in 1735 in the service of Crown Prince Frederick. After Frederick became king in 1740, he charged Graun with establishing a Berlin court opera and promoted him to court Kapellmeister (1741). He inaugurated the new company with performances of *Rodelinda, regina de' Langobardi* (1741) and *Cleopatra e Cesare* (1742), the latter in the new court theater, which saw productions of two dozen of his operas over the next 14 years. In accordance with the vision of Frederick's theatrical advisor **Francesco Algarotti**, Graun gradually distanced his operas from **Johann Adolf Hasse**'s **Arcadian** style in Dresden by adopting tragic or mythological subjects, emphasizing ensembles, incorporating **ballets** within acts, and displacing da capo **arias** in favor of other forms, particularly the cavatina. Frederick considered *Montezuma* (1755, on the king's libretto), which paints an unflattering portrait of rapacious Catholic conquistadors, to be a masterpiece in the new Berlin style.

GRÉTRY, ANDRÉ-ERNEST-MODESTE. (1741, Liège–1813, Montmorency.) Belgian-French **composer** of over 65 operas from the 1760s to ca. 1800, and other vocal and instrumental music. Grétry was the most prominent, prolific, and influential composer of **opéra comique** of the late 18th century.

Grétry began his musical training at the choir school of St. Denis in Liège and took private lessons in counterpoint and composition. As a student he was influenced by the **opera buffa** troupe of Giovanni Francesco Crosa (ca. 1700–1771), which made an extended stopover in Liège (1754–55) while Crosa was fleeing **London** creditors. Through St. Denis, Grétry gained admission to the Collège Darchis in **Rome** (beginning 1760), where he produced his first opera (two **intermezzos**) *La vendemmiatrice* (1765). The next year he relocated in Geneva, met Voltaire, saw opéra comique for the first time, and wrote one of his own, *Isabelle et Gertrude, ou Les sylphes supposés*. He arrived in **Paris** in 1767, where he spent the remainder of his career.

Grétry gained a reputation with the Parisian public through six opéras comiques for the Comédie-Italienne from 1768 to 1770 on **librettos** by Jean-François Marmontel (1723–1799) and Louis Anseaume (ca. 1721–1784)—who had collaborated with **Jean-Philippe Rameau** and **Egidio Duni**, respectively—among which *Le tableau parlant* (*The Talking Picture*, 1769) stands out. These public productions, as well as others at palaces of well-placed aristocrats, brought him to the attention of the royal family, who commissioned two operas (*Les deux avares* and *L'amitié à l'épreuve*, both 1770) for the wedding of the future Louis XVI and Marie Antoinette. They were among a half dozen works produced for the royals from 1770 to 1773 that also included *Zémire et Azor* (on the "Beauty and the Beast" story, 1771), which led to his appointment as the queen's personal music director (1774).

Grétry's career peaked during the mid-1780s with a series of triumphs at the Opéra—the *opéra-ballet Le caravane du Caire* (1783) and the *comédie lyrique Panurge dans l'île des lanternes* (1785)—and the Comédie-Italienne: the *opéras comiques L'épreuve villageoise* and *Richard Coeur-de-lion* (both 1784), the latter the pinnacle of Grétry's popularity. Revived constantly, *Richard* remained the best-known 18th-century opéra comique during the 1800s. A **rescue opera** based on the English king's return from the Third Crusade, it explores Enlightened themes like aristocratic abuse of power while glorifying a symbol of regal virtue. *Richard* may be regarded as an early prototype for 19th-century French *grand opéra* owing to its historical subject, musical contribution to vivid depiction of a medieval community, humanized characters, and structural sophistication, including the dramatically targeted returns of Richard's **romance** "Une fièvre brûlante."

Grétry's operas of the 1770s and 1780s significantly expanded the dramatic and musical range of French opera and advanced the reconciliation of French and Italian styles in opéra comique begun by Egidio Duni and his contemporaries in a manner agreeable to Parisian audiences. They encompass a broad array of topics, from rustic **sentimentality** (*L'epreuve villageoise* [*The Rustic Trial*]) to classical mythology (*Amphitryon*, 1786), history (*Les mariages samnites* [*The Samnite Marriages*], 1776, set during the Roman Republic; *Guillaume Tell*, 1791); Gothic melodrama (*Richard Coeurde-lion*); and dark comedy (*Raoul Barbe-bleue*, 1789, in which the title character dies). Grétry developed an Italianate style of melody sensitive to the rhythms of the French language and deployed it in freely constructed set pieces, including **duets** and Italianate multisectional **finales**, that favor progressing episodic forms rather than conventional schemata. He energized the **orchestra** by enhancing its colors, particularly winds, brass, and percussion, by exploring the possibility of pantomime and by giving a cogent dramatic role to idiosyncratically constructed **overtures** (for example in *Le magnifique*, 1773). And as noted above, his efforts to increase the depth of pre-Revolutionary opéra comique opened the door to developments in French opera in the 19th century.

Grétry's popularity declined shortly before the Revolution as public support turned to Nicolas-Marie Dalayrac (1753–1809), whom he had mentored. His adaptations to changing tastes brought only periodic successes, for example with *Raoul Barbe-bleue* and *Guillaume Tell*. His career ended with the *comédie lyrique Delphis et Mopsa* (1803).

GUADAGNI, GAETANO. (1728, Lodi–1792, Padua.) **Contralto castrato** noted for his exceptionally effective **acting**. Guadagni began his career in 1746 as a church singer in Padua and opera singer in **Venice**. In **London** from 1748 he performed parts in comic operas (*see* CATEGORIES OF OPERA) and in **George Frideric Handel**'s oratorios, including the *Messiah*

(1750, originally 1742). After establishing himself internationally in the 1750s through a series of appearances in Lisbon, **Paris**, Venice, **Naples**, and elsewhere, he moved to **Vienna** in 1762, where he created the title role in **Christoph Willibald Gluck**'s *Orfeo ed Euridice*, by which he became a household name. Distinguished by his graceful gestures and refined face and figure, Guadagni was renowned for his acting abilities, which were reportedly honed by **David Garrick**. Although capable of breathtaking passagework, he was known for singing simply with exacting intonation in service of dramatic characterization, allowing himself infrequent expressive embellishments. Through the early 1770s he performed in several **pasticcio** remakes of *Orfeo* and remained popular for aristocratic commemorations of weddings, coronations, and other events and in concert performances. However, he disappointed audiences with his unwillingness to break character by acknowledging applause or singing encores, and his direct style was overshadowed by the bravura performances of his contemporaries. Having entered semiretirement as a chapel singer in Padua (1768), he abandoned the stage entirely in 1781.

GUILLAUME TELL. *Opéra*; music by **Gioachino Rossini**, **libretto** by Étienne de Jouy (1764–1846), Hippolyte-Louis-Florent Bis (1789–1855), the composer, and others based on Friedrich Schiller's (1759–1805) play (1804); four acts; premiered **Paris**, Opéra, August 1829. The subject had previously been set by **André-Ernest-Modeste Grétry** (1791).

Rossini's final opera, and his only entirely original opera in French, *Tell* was projected as the start of a long career in Paris, supported by a lifetime salary and a contract for five operas over the next decade. Derailment of these agreements by the Revolution of 1830 and other factors broke his stride, and he subsequently retired from the stage. Rossini chose the subject after rejecting two librettos by **Eugène Scribe**, which were later set prominently as **Daniel-François-Esprit Auber**'s *Gustave III* (1833, later adapted as **Giuseppe Verdi**'s *Un ballo in maschera*, 1859) and **Fromental Halévy**'s *La Juive* (1835). Though often abridged, *Tell* became a stalwart of the Opéra, receiving its 500th Parisian staging before Rossini's death in 1868, and has been revived periodically outside France, primarily in Italian translation.

Along with Auber's *La muette de Portici* (1828), *Tell* served as a crucial prototype for French **grand opéra**. An offshoot of **rescue opera**, its plot incorporates **sentimental** and **romantic** themes of aristocratic abuse and benevolence; nationalistic rebellion against oppression; troubled relationships between politically conflicted lovers, fathers and offspring, and a husband and wife; and rustic Alpine **pastoralism**. In medieval Switzerland under Austrian rule, Tell leads resistance against the sadistic governor Gesler, attempting to enlist Arnold, son of the village elder Melcthal, who loves the Austrian princess Mathilde. Celebration of an impending wedding, during which Tell's son Jemmy wins a shooting contest, is interrupted by the shepherd Leuthold, fleeing after killing his daughter's attempted rapist, an Austrian. Tell braves rapids and a brewing storm to row him to safety. The vindictive Austrians take Melcthal hostage and ultimately execute him after the villagers refuse to identify Tell as Leuthold's accomplice, impelling Arnold to renounce Mathilde and join Tell's rebels. When Gesler and his soldiers occupy the town, demanding a show of submission, Tell refuses, and Gessler famously forces him to risk his son Jemmy's life by shooting an apple off his head. Tell succeeds but is arrested after the Austrians discover he has hedged his bet by concealing a second arrow for Gesler in case Jemmy died. Mathilde proposes to offer herself in trade for Tell before he manages to escape while piloting his captors' boat across treacherous waters during a storm. He returns to kill Gesler and joins Arnold and other patriots after Arnold signals their revolt by torching his own house.

Tell's music illustrates the synthesis of French and Italian elements that typifies early 19th-century *opéra*. Here Rossini's sparing vocal writing stands in stark contrast to the lavish **coloratura** of his Italian works. Even its most engagingly lyrical Italianate melodies are only modestly embellished (e.g., Arnold's "Ah! Mathilde," Act 1). And its most expressive passages rely instead on impassioned declamation. For example "Sois immobile," Tell's climactic warning to his son before the Act 3 trial shot, is a paradigm of French melodic responsiveness to nuances of the text. Its accompaniment by solo cello also illustrates Rossini's uncharacteristically sophisticated use of the enriched resources of the Opéra's **orchestra** (including two harps, four horns, and three trombones) for both intimate chamber arrangements and massed effects. This rich palette is evident in Rossini's scenic **overture** cum programmatic symphonic poem: its pastoral first and third sections (the former an ode for five solo cellos on Alpine tranquility, the latter Rossini's famous "spring song"), an intervening storm, and a triumphant cavalry charge immediately convey the regional inspiration for patriotic action that drives the opera.

The opera's organization also represents a compromise between Italian convention and French spontaneity. It contains surprisingly few independent **airs**—Arnold's "Asil héréditaire" (Act 4) stands out—and instead relies on ensembles to carry the action and on numerous **choruses** and **ballets** in extended massed-crowd scenes to create ambience; define dramatically active cohorts of villagers, patriots, and soldiers; and provide a panoramic, quasi-historical backdrop for interpersonal relationships. Set piece forms combine Italian and French approaches, a practice that would be institutionalized by **Giacomo Meyerbeer**. Compare, for example, Mathilde's strophic, French-styled love song "Sombre forêt" (Act 2) to Arnold's Italianate three-movement grand **aria**. Ensembles also show varying reliance on Italian forms. In Act 2 the love **duet** ("Oui, vous l'arrachez") and men's trio

("Quand l'Helvétie") may both be read as standard four-movement designs. However, the **finale** takes greater liberties: its three opening choruses, which individuate the rebels of Unterwalden, Uri, and Schwyz, are interspersed with dialogue; its mostly declamatory oath only alludes to a ***largo concertato***; and the call to arms in a foreshortened ***tempo di mezzo*** elicits a mostly orchestral **stretta**. The finale of Act 3, the trial shot, is even less conventional, Tell's monologue "Sois immobile" replacing the *largo concertato*, and its stretta ("Quand l'orgueil"), in which Gesler is cursed, providing the only clear remnant of the Italian form.

H

HÁBA, ALOIS. (1893, Vizovice, Moravia–1973, Prague.) Czech **composer** of three operas (from the late 1920s to the early 1940s) as well as other vocal and instrumental music, and **librettist** for two works. Hába was the leading proponent of microtonal tuning, which involves intervals smaller than a semitone (quarter tones and sixth tones), between the wars and one of few opera composers—probably the first—to employ it. He grew up singing and playing string instruments in his father's folk band and learned Moravian peasant songs from his mother, music which included microtonal inflections, and studied composition at the Prague Conservatory (1914–15), where he learned to set modal folk melodies.

Hába began using quarter tones with the *Suite for String Orchestra* (1917). His quarter-tone opera *Matka* (*The Mother*, 1929, premiered 1931), his only stage work to be performed, centers on a loving second wife who provides a moral compass for her husband, children, and stepchildren. Hába's other two operas never saw the light of day: *Nová země* (*The New Land*), composed 1935–36 in traditional semitones, and *Přijd' království tvé* (*Thy Kingdom Come*) a sixth-tone opera composed 1932–42.

HALÉVY, FROMENTAL. (1799, Paris–1862, Nice.) French **composer** of about three dozen *grands opéras* and **opéras comiques** (mostly from the 1820s through the 1850s, many on **librettos** by **Eugène Scribe**) and of other vocal music; teacher and author. Halévy's family, of Jewish descent, changed their name from Levy (1807). Admitted to the **Paris** Conservatoire in 1810, he studied composition with **Luigi Cherubini** and **Étienne-Nicolas Méhul**, and won the Prix de **Rome** in 1819, writing his first opera, *Les bohémiennes* (1819–20), before leaving for Italy.

Halévy began teaching at the Conservatoire in 1827 and eventually instructed **Charles-François Gounod**, **Georges Bizet**, and **Camille Saint-Saëns**. His most important work was the *grand opéra La Juive* (1835), his first operatic collaboration with Scribe. Immensely popular from its premier, it was staged frequently alongside **Giacomo Meyerbeer**'s operas. In it, a Jewish goldsmith's adopted daughter, presumed inaccurately to be Jewish

herself, falls in love with a Catholic prince in a society that prohibits inter-
marriage, and she and her father are boiled alive for her supposedly forbidden affair. Its local color includes an offstage Te Deum accompanied by
organ and a Passover Seder. After the pinnacle reached by *La Juive*, Halévy's unremarkable, sometimes repetitive operas became staples at the Opéra
and Opéra-Comique, where they appealed to the complacent bourgeois audiences who frequented those theaters.

HANDEL, GEORGE FRIDERIC. (1685, Halle–1759, London.) Preeminent German-born **composer** of the early 18th century. Although now best
known for his oratorios and instrumental music, Handel wrote over 40 operas, mostly **opera serias** for **London** from the 1710s through the 1730s. In the
20th century they became centerpieces in the revival of baroque opera, beginning with productions in Göttingen in the 1920s, and the majority had
been restaged by the 1990s.

The son of a barber-surgeon who intended him for a legal career, Handel
received musical training after his lord, the Duke of Saxe-Weissenfels, heard
him play the organ as a boy. While studying at the University of Halle in
1702, he served as organist for a year at the Protestant Cathedral and may
have been introduced to opera during a trip to Berlin. In 1703 Handel moved
to Hamburg, which had the only permanent public opera theater in Germany,
the Oper am Gänsemarkt featuring the German operas of Reinhard Keiser
(1674–1739), where he worked as a violinist and **harpsichord basso continuo** player. After Keiser fled debtors in 1704, Handel successfully staged his
first opera *Almira* (1705) and at least three others (all on German **librettos**).

In 1706 the Florentine prince Ferdinando de' Medici introduced Handel to
scores of Italian operas and persuaded him to come to Florence. From that
base, Handel also made extended visits to **Rome**, where he gained the support of several influential cardinals, and to **Venice** and **Naples** (1707–09). He
composed sacred music and secular cantatas, which taught him to set Italian
texts, and produced his first two Italian operas, *Rodrigo* (1707) and *Agrippina* (1709). The latter premiered before a Carnival audience of visiting luminaries and made Handel an international sensation overnight. In attendance
were Prince Ernst Georg of Hanover, brother of the elector of Hanover (soon
to be George I of England and Handel's patron in London), and the Duke of
Manchester, the English ambassador, who would entice Handel first to Hanover, where he became electoral Kapellmeister, and then to London for an
initial visit in 1710–11. Amidst the arrangements and **pasticcios** of Italian
operas in English translation that had been popular for about five years
before Handel arrived, his ***Rinaldo*** (1711) was the first Italian opera conceived for London and performed by an Italian company that included **castrato** singers.

After returning to Hanover (1711–12), Handel made a second trip to London beginning in late 1712, which was expected to be temporary but became permanent, owing in part to the Elector of Hanover's succession to the English throne as George I (1714). During the first phase of this relocation, which included the famous *Water Music Suites* (1717), Handel produced four new operas: the **Arcadian** *Il pastor fido* (1712), which reportedly underwhelmed its viewers, and the more heroic and enthusiastically received *Teseo* (1713); *Silla* (possibly not staged); and *Amadigi* (1715). Handel also wrote replacement **arias** for his own revivals and for that of the **Alessandro Scarlatti** opera *Pirro e Demetrio* (originally 1694). Short-lived employment with the Earl of Carnarvon at his estate outside of London resulted in the **masque** *Acis and Galatea*, Handel's most widely performed theatrical work during his lifetime, and the oratorio *Esther* (both 1718), revivals of which would eventually lead Handel to specialize in the genre.

Having whetted the appetite of the London elite for Italian opera, Handel, with the Swiss-born house manager John Jacob Heidegger (1666–1749), founded the Royal Academy of Music in 1719, a subscription series at the King's Theater underwritten by George I and overseen by a board of directors consisting of aristocrats and landed gentry committed to establishing world-class opera in England. The academy contracted four premier singers, including the castrato **Senesino** and the **soprano** Margherita Durastanti (active 1700–1734), who had sung Handel's *Agrippina* in Venice, as well as the composer Giovanni Bononcini (1670–1747), and gave Handel the position master of the **orchestra**. After a makeshift spring **season** (1720) that included the dazzling premier of Handel's *Radamisto*, attended by George I and Frederick, Prince of Wales, the academy began in earnest in the fall with Bononcini's initial opera and Senesino's unveiling.

Handel composed 14 operas for the academy, 13 of them with house **librettists** Paolo Antonio Rolli (1687–1765), who like his fellow Catholic Bononcini was removed subsequent to the suppression of the Jacobites in 1722, and Nicola Francesco Haym (1678–1729). Among these, *Giulio Cesare in Egitto*, *Tamerlano* (1724), and *Rodelinda, regina de' Longobardi* (1725) were the greatest artistic triumphs. Addition of the prima donnas **Francesca Cuzzoni**, who first appeared in Handel's *Ottone* (1723), and **Faustina Bordoni**, who debuted in his *Alessandro* (1726), created an inflammatory rivalry that contributed to the eventual demise of the enterprise, despite Handel's efforts to accommodate the prickly sopranos' vocal requirements, exploit their complementary strengths, and balance their workloads in such operas as *Alessandro* and *Admeto* (1727). Factionalism among their supporters, financial losses, and ultimately ridicule of the company by John Gay's (1685–1732) *The Beggar's Opera* led backers to distance themselves from the undertaking and from Italian opera in general. The last operas were given in 1728, and the academy was dissolved 1729 with an agreement to allow Heidegger and Handel to continue on their own at the King's Theater for the next five years.

For his so-called Second Academy (1729–34), Handel hired a new company of singers that included the soprano Anna Maria Strada del Pò (active 1719–41), who would appear frequently in Handel's productions until 1737, and eventually Senesino and the esteemed **bass** Antonio Montagnana (active 1730–1750). The seven Handel operas and several pasticcios presented by the academy, beginning with *Lotario* (1729) and ending with *Arianna in Creta* (1734), received mostly lukewarm responses. While an exceptionally fine work, which featured Montagnana and Senesino, *Orlando* (1733) hardly fared better than the rest and possibly exacerbated the conflict that led to the castrato's dismissal. A revival of *Esther* and the premier of another oratorio, *Deborah* (1733), paved the way for Handel's eventual concentration on that genre.

In 1733, discomfited by the commoner Handel's de facto monopoly on Italian opera in England, a coalition of aristocrats and gentry allied with Frederick established a rival Opera of the Nobility, hiring the venerable composer **Nicola Porpora** as its director and the sensational **Farinelli** as its drawing card (beginning in 1734) and hijacking most of Handel's singers (including Senesino). After Handel's contract with Heidegger expired in 1734, the Opera of the Nobility took over the King's Theater and began offering Italian operas in the new *galant* style by Porpora, **Johann Adolf Hasse**, and others.

Handel responded by hiring yet another corps of singers and moving to the recently opened Covent Garden theater, where his operas featuring **ballets**, which were performed by a troupe led by the French choreographer Marie Sallé (ca. 1707–1756), alternated two nights a week with the theater's spoken plays. He inaugurated the new location with a revival of *Il pastor fido* and premiers of two of his best operas, *Ariodante* and *Alcina* (both 1735), among six new works performed at that theater through 1737. Fighting a losing financial battle with his aristocratic rivals, Handel turned increasingly to oratorios, other nonoperatic vocal music, and organ concertos to flesh out his playbills in 1735 and 1736.

After his own company and the Opera of the Nobility both closed in 1737, Handel launched four new works (two of them pasticcios) at the King's Theater and Covent Garden with little success, beginning with *Faramondo* (1738) and including *Serse* (also 1738), the standout of this last phase. Following the failure of *Deidamia* (1741), he abandoned opera seria entirely and concentrated on the English oratorio and other genres. By the time he retired from the operatic stage, Handel was idolized in England and Germany, he was bestowed with numerous honors including a London statue erected in his honor, and his operas received numerous revivals during his lifetime.

Broadly speaking, Handel adhered to the conventions of Arcadian opera seria. Although a few operas prior to and after the first academy set librettos having magical or comical elements reminiscent of the Venetian style (e.g., *Rinaldo* and *Orlando*), most present heroic, classical subjects (*Giulio Cesare*) and in some cases are adapted from librettos by **Apostolo Zeno** or **Pietro Metastasio**. Each of three acts presents several extended **scenes**, each of which combines up to a dozen small scenes consisting of **recitative** alone or recitative followed by a da capo exit aria. Standards for hierarchical distribution of arias among singers and characters of different ranks are carefully observed. And ensembles are rare, comprising a very few **duets** to end acts and epigrammatic concluding "**choruses**" of soloists to end operas.

However, Handel also benefitted both from his training in Hamburg under the influence of Keiser and from the less ingrained expectations of his London audiences to vary and enrich their theatrical experience. He exploited the expressive possibilities of obbligato recitative more than his Italian contemporaries. Delineating the affects (*see* DOCTRINE OF THE AFFECTIONS) of his arias more sharply than most of his rivals, Handel juxtaposed drastic shifts of mood in successive scenes and alternated Germanic quasi-instrumental vocal writing in his virtuoso showpieces with the more liquid melodies of the new Italian *galant* style. And he treated the Neapolitan da capo form with greater freedom, varying the number of ritornellos and solo passages in the outer (A) section, incorporating more decisive contrasts between the outer and inner (B) sections, and employing with some frequency shortened versions of the form like the cavatina or continuous designs, even interjecting brief passages of recitative between sections. The synthetic, international orientation of Handel's style is particularly apparent in his commitment to the orchestra: the rich, varied, and appropriately cast accompaniments of his arias; his efforts to introduce French ballet spectacle in his late operas; his adoption of the French **overture** and French dance types; and his incorporation of notable examples of scenic descriptive music.

HARPSICHORD. Keyboard instrument having a wing shape (like a grand piano), in which the strings are perpendicular to the keyboard. It is distinguished from other stringed keyboard instruments by its mechanism for plucking the strings with plectrums mounted on jacks attached to the ends of pivoting keys rather than striking them with metal bars (clavichord) or hammers (piano). Harpsichords typically have one or two keyboards (manuals) ranging from four to five octaves, which may be combined through the use of stops and levers to vary dynamics and tone color. Dating from ca. 1400, the harpsichord was the primary **basso continuo** instrument in opera from the late 17th century through the early 19th century, when it was replaced by the piano. Its use was renewed in the 20th century in conjunction with the revival of **baroque** opera.

HASSE, JOHANN ADOLF. (1699, Bergedorf–1783, Venice.) Along with **Niccolò Jommelli**, one of the most esteemed **composers** of **opera seria** (almost 50) and *festa teatrale* (a half dozen) in Italy, Germany, and Austria during the 1720s through the 1760s, and **tenor**. Although he wrote about 10 early **intermezzos** for **Naples**, Hasse mostly avoided comic opera (*see* CATEGORIES OF OPERA), perhaps because it offered little opportunity for his lyrical style of writing. Apart from **Antonio Caldara**, he was the most dedicated composer of operas on original or adapted **librettos** by **Pietro Metastasio**.

Hasse began his career in Germany as a singer, then moved to Naples ca. 1722, where he studied with **Alessandro Scarlatti** and possibly **Nicola Porpora**, quickly becoming one of the most active composers living there. In **Venice** by 1730, he married **Faustina Bordoni**, one of the premier singers of her day who performed many of his operas, and wrote his first (adapted) Metastasian opera (*Artaserse*, 1730). He returned to Germany as Kapellmeister to the royal court of Dresden in 1731—an event marked by the premier of *Cleofide* on a revised libretto by Metastasio, which was attended by Johann Sebastian Bach (1685–1750) and his son Wilhelm Friedemann (1710–1784)—and later became *Ober-Kapellmeister* in 1750.

In the 1740s, Hasse likely joined a group of classicizing intellectuals, artists, and musicians, including the poet and theater critic **Francesco Algarotti** and the classical archaeologist Johann Joachim Winckelmann, who may have encouraged his admiration for Metastasio's poetry. He befriended the poet in the early 1740s while premiering two of his librettos (*Antigono*, 1743, and *Ipermestra*, 1744) and eventually set all but one of them. Based, at least nominally, in Dresden until 1763, Hasse and his wife made frequent visits to Naples, Venice, **Paris**, **Vienna**, Warsaw (the second home of the Saxon electors), and elsewhere. Faced with economic belt-tightening during and after the Seven Years' War (1756–63)—he wrote no new operas for Dresden following Frederick the Great's invasion of Saxony in 1756—Hasse turned his attentions increasingly to Vienna in the 1760s, where he staged several opere serie and *feste teatrali* and wrote numerous sacred works. Plagued by gout after 1752 and having been dismissed without pension by the Saxon court, Hasse retired to Venice with his wife in 1773.

Hasse was renowned for his subtly expressive and psychologically individualized treatment of the *galant* **bel canto** style in da capo and dal segno **arias** tailored to individual performers, an approach that influenced numerous other composers. Already in the 1730s his arias were heard as far away as London, performed at **George Frideric Handel**'s Second Academy and at the rival Opera of the Nobility by such notables as **Farinelli**. The conservative classicism of Hasse and Metastasio, which for the most part avoided midcentury innovations and gave alternating prominence to poetry in **recitatives** and music in arias, is often contrasted with the reforming classicism of

Christoph Willibald Gluck and **Ranieri Calzabigi**, which rejects convention and subordinates both music and poetry to theatrical effect. Most of Hasse's **productions** were scenically modest, in the **Arcadian** style. However, several received spectacular stagings in Dresden and Vienna. *Solimano* (1753) and a remake of *Ezio* (1755, originally 1730) involved hundreds of supernumeraries and animals as exotic as elephants and camels, the stage opening onto a candlelit outdoor area. And Hasse and Metastasio's Viennese *festa teatrale Alcide al bivio* (1760) for the wedding of Joseph, the emperor-to-be, shows an expansion of resources and emphasis of **chorus**, **ballet**, **orchestral** color, and scenery similar to that of Gluck's subsequent "reform" operas, a rich spectacle that may have also influenced **Joseph Haydn** at Eszterháza.

HAYDN, JOSEPH. (1732, Rohrau, Austria–1809, Vienna.) Known nowadays primarily as an icon of late 18th-century Viennese classical instrumental music, Haydn was also an active **composer** of light operas for the Esterházy family theaters from the 1760s through the 1780s.

After his dismissal from the choir school of St. Stephen's Cathedral in **Vienna** ca. 1749, Haydn embarked unwillingly on a career as a freelance musician, associating with **Pietro Metastasio** and apprenticing with and serving as accompanist for the composer **Nicola Porpora**. He wrote his first opera, the **singspiel** *Der krumme Teufel* (lost), ca. 1752. Having established a reputation in Vienna over the next decade, he obtained appointments as Kapellmeister to the Bohemian Count Carl Morzin (1759) and to the Esterházy family (1761), for whom he worked most of the remainder of his life. Hungary's wealthiest princes at the time Haydn joined them under Paul Anton and particularly under his successor Nikolaus ("the Magnificent") from 1762–90, the family maintained an extensive musical establishment that included an orchestra and opera company, and—after Nikolaus built the Eszterháza palace beginning in the 1760s—an opera house (1768) and a marionette theater (1773). Haydn's first opera in Italian was the *festa teatrale Alcide* (1762, adapted from Metastasio) for the Esterházy ancestral home of Eisenstadt.

In all, Haydn wrote at least 16 operas for Eisenstadt and Eszterháza up to Nikolaus's death in 1790. Most belong to lighter **categories**—singspiel, *festa teatrale*, *comedia*, **intermezzo**, *dramma giocoso* (*see* OPERA BUFFA), *burletta*, **puppet opera**, and *drama eroicomico* (*see* OPERA SEMISERIA)— apart from the *drama eroico Armida* (1783), followed later by the *dramma per musica* (*see* OPERA SERIA) *L'anima del filosofo, ossia Orfeo ed Euridice* written for **London** in 1791 but not performed until 1951. Operas that have been revived with some success in modern times include *L'infedeltà* *delusa* (1773), *Il mondo della luna* (1777), and *La fedeltà premiata* (1781), one of Haydn's best-received works in his own day. He also wrote numerous **arias** for use in operas by other composers at the Esterházy estates.

HENZE, HANS WERNER. (Born 1926, Gütersloh.) Prolific German **composer** of about 20 operas and musical theater works, as well as other vocal and instrumental music. In the wake of **Giacomo Puccini** and **Richard Strauss**, and alongside **Benjamin Britten** and **Gian Carlo Menotti**, one of the most productive opera composers of the 20th century.

As a youth, Henze studied piano and music theory locally and was composing by age 12, eventually entering the Brunswick State Music School (beginning 1942). Limited in his exposure to contemporary music by the political and cultural restrictions of Nazi Germany, he managed surreptitiously to listen to classical music on the radio, a pursuit facilitated, ironically, by BBC broadcasts heard as a prisoner at the end of World War II. Following the war, Henze was able to take formal composition lessons with Wolfgang Fortner (1907–1987) at the Heidelberg Institute of Church Music, where he studied works by **Paul Hindemith**, **Béla Bartók**, and **Igor Stravinsky**. He attended the first Darmstadt summer institute for new music in 1946, after which he explored ways of integrating the serialist techniques cultivated there with Stravinskian **neo-classicism**, jazz, and other influences. This heterodoxy alienated him from modernist composers but put him at the forefront of the postmodern eclecticism that is already evident in his first true opera, *Boulevard Solitude* (1952), which adapts twelve-tone technique to the traditional forms of **number opera**.

Henze's operas have synthesized a variety of different idioms, among them a version of Italianate lyricism beginning with his next full-scale opera *König Hirsch* (composed 1953–55, premiered 1956), a five-hour epic fantasy that embraces the scale, if not the musical language, of **Wagnerian** music drama. This break with the modernist mainstream led to and was reinforced by a move to Italy in 1953, which produced operas in the mold of *opera semiseria* (*Der Prinz von Homburg*, 1960) and **opera buffa** (*Der junge Lord*, 1965). In contrast to the light scorings of those works and of *Elegy for Young Lovers* (1961), *The Bassarids* (1966), Henze's best-received opera, is more wholeheartedly symphonic in its scoring and its design in four extended "movements." Beginning in the late 1960s, Henze's operas, like other works such as his requiem for Che Guevara (*Das Floß der Medusa*, premiered 1971), became politicized, reflecting his socialist leanings, and adopted a more **expressionist** musical language: *We Come to the River* (1976), *The English Cat* (1983), and *Das verratene Meer* (1990). Henze's most recent opera is *Gisela! or The Strange and Memorable Ways of Happiness* (2010), a modern love story redolent of the **commedia dell'arte** and **romantic *melodramma***.

See also CENSORSHIP.

HIDALGO, JUAN. (1614, Madrid–1685, Madrid.) The most significant Spanish **composer** of the 17th century, and harpist. He wrote at least 15 theatrical works, including songs for spoken comedies, **zarzuelas**, semi-operas (*see* MASQUE), and two all-sung operas and other vocal music.

Hidalgo started his career as a harpist for the Spanish royal chapel (ca. 1630), composed secular and sacred songs beginning in the 1640s, and was working in the theater by the 1650s. He collaborated with the poet and **librettist** Pedro Calderón de la Barca (1600–1681), the leading Spanish dramatist, on probably the earliest zarzuelas, for example, *El laurel de Apolo* (1657). The pair also created two historically important operas written for celebrations of the Treaty of the Pyrenees (1659) and the marriage of Louis XIV and Maria Theresa, ending the French-Spanish conflict that had begun during the Thirty Years' War. *La púrpura de la rosa* (*The Blood of the Rose*, 1660, music lost) was the first Spanish opera by a Spanish composer, and the first opera produced in Spain since the unique experiment *La selva sin amor* (*The Forest without Love*, 1627, the first opera produced in Spain) by the Italian Filippo Piccinini (died 1648). And *Celos aun del aire matan* (*Jealousy, Even of the Air, Kills*, 1660) is the earliest extant complete Spanish opera sung throughout. Hidalgo is believed to have worked independently of Italian influences, and his **airs**, rather than **recitatives** (which are few in number), often carry the action and show the influence of traditional Spanish dances and songs.

HILLER, JOHANN ADAM. (1728, Wendisch-Ossig–1804, Leipzig.) German **composer** of approximately a dozen **singspiels** from the late 1760s through the 1770s, as well as other vocal works, and writer on music. Hiller received informal training in music and a classical education leading to legal studies locally, in Dresden, where he became familiar with the *galant* **opera serias** of **Johann Adolf Hasse**, and in Leipzig (beginning 1751). Attaching himself to a theatrical troupe in Leipzig (1766), Hiller began a long-standing collaboration with the playwright Christian Felix Weisse (1726–1804) with a remake of *Die verwandelten Weiber, oder Der Teufel ist los*, for which he refined songs composed by Johann Standfuss (died after ca. 1759) and wrote new ones, leading to 10 operas over the next decade. Hiller and Weisse expanded the range of singspiel subjects to include medieval (*Lisuart und Dariolette*, 1766), rustic sentimental (*Lottchen am Hofe*, 1767, and *Die Jagd*, 1770), and classical (*Die Muse*, 1767) stories. Hiller also led the development of the German narrative *Romanze* (*see* ROMANCE). After the company moved to Berlin in 1773 and Hiller and Weisse's *Die Jubelhochzeit* was performed there that year, their relationship with it ended and their collaboration waned as Hiller turned to other activities.

HINDEMITH, PAUL. (1895, Hanau, near Frankfurt–1963, Frankfurt.) German **composer** of about a dozen operatic works from ca. 1920 to 1960, as well as other vocal and instrumental music, **librettist** for two of his operas, and **conductor**. Along with **Kurt Weill** the most significant German theater composer between the world wars.

Born to a working-class family, Hindemith received a scholarship to train as a violinist and composer at the Frankfurt **Conservatory** (1909–17). While employed in the **orchestra** of the Frankfurt Opera (1915–23), he also played in taverns and movie houses, a formative experience that influenced his later style. Hindemith held teaching positions in Berlin (1927–37); New Haven, Connecticut (emigrating during World War II following his censure by the Nazis, 1938, and taking a position at Yale University, 1940–53); and the University of Zürich after the war (1951–56). He began conducting in 1953.

Hindemith's first complete operas, each of one act, branded him as the bad boy of German stage music. *Mörder, Hoffnung der Frauen* (*Murderer, Hope of Women*, composed 1919, premiered 1921), a *Literaturoper* on a minimally modified play by Oscar Kokoschka, and *Sancta Susanna* (1922) present **expressionist** erotic subjects using post-**romantic** chromatic and impressionist idioms and bear resemblances to **Richard Strauss**'s *Salome* and *Elektra* (1909) and **Alban Berg**'s *Lulu* (composed 1928–35, completed and premiered 1979). During the same period, Hindemith's fully staged setting of a **puppet** play, *Das Nusch-Nuschi* (1921), which mocks *Tristan und Isolde*, distanced him from **Richard Wagner**'s followers. This anti-Wagnerian stance shaped his first full-length stage work, *Cardillac* (1926), a macabre tale based on **Ernst Theodor Amadeus Hoffmann**, in which an obsessively possessive, homicidal goldsmith murders his own customers. Displaying a **neo-classical** detachment of music from action, it made Hindemith the leading new composer in Germany. Hindemith's scandalous reputation was reinforced by his "divorce opera" *Neues vom Tage* (1929), which drew Adolf Hitler's disdain for its lead **soprano**'s bathing scene.

Hindemith's concentration on *Sing-und-Spielmusik* ("music for singing and playing") also termed *Gebrauchsmusik* ("music for use")—pieces for amateur performance as a social activity—during the years 1927–32 informed *Hin und zurück* (*Away and Back*, 1927), a 12-minute chamber opera in which a series of set pieces depicting a crime of passion is played forward, then reversed at the midpoint of the opera in a pseudo-palindrome (mirror) structure, as well as the children's opera *Wir bauen eine Stadt* (*We Build a City*, 1930).

Two of Hindemith's last operas, both historically based philosophical journeys on his own **librettos**, and both interconnected with symphonies sharing their titles, are generally considered to be his best work in the genre. In *Mathis der Maler* (*Matthias the Painter*, composed 1933–35, premiered 1938), the German Renaissance artist Matthias Grünewald becomes involved in a peasant uprising and is tempted like St. Anthony, who is depicted in his famous *Isenheim Altarpiece*. Well established in the current repertory and considered Hindemith's operatic masterpiece, *Mathis* represents a weightier application of the *Gebrauchsmusik* concept, in which adaptations of folk and sacred music humanize and individualize the main characters. After two decades without an opera, in part due to scarce opportunities for productions in the United States during the 1940s, Hindemith brought out *Die Harmonie der Welt* (1957), on the search by the 17th-century astronomer Johannes Kepler for the key to cosmic harmony. In 1961, Hindemith collaborated with the American playwright Thornton Wilder on a final one-act opera, *Das lange Weinachtsmahl* (*The Long Christmas Dinner*), in which a holiday meal provides the lens for viewing 90 years of relationships within a stable, prosperous, and altogether unremarkable American family.

See also CENSORSHIP.

HIPPOLYTE ET ARICIE. *Tragédie en musique*; music by **Jean-Philippe Rameau**, **libretto** by Simon-Joseph Pellegrin (1663–1745) based on Jean Racine's (1639–1699) *Phèdre* (1677) and accounts by Euripides and Seneca; **prologue** and five acts; premiered **Paris**, Opéra, October 1733. The preeminent masterpiece of early 18th-century French opera.

Hippolyte is unmistakably French in style. Its story, presented in the standard format of a prologue and five acts, comes from classical mythology. Aricie (Aricia) falls in love with Hippolyte (Hippolytos) despite having vowed chastity as a priestess of Diana to his father Thésée (Theseus), king of Athens. Thésée has killed her family but spared her on that condition. With Thésée absent, in Hades to rescue his companion Peirithous, Phèdre (Phaedra), his second wife, attempts to seduce her stepson. When Thésée returns to find them together, she lets him believe that Hippolyte has threatened her, but eventually she confesses and kills herself.

In contrast to Italian **opera seria**, *Hippolyte*'s freely constructed scenes are extended tableaux consisting of numerous miniature sections and incorporating a nonconventional mixture of **airs**, *ariettes*, **duets** and other ensembles, **choruses**, and descriptive instrumental music accompanying mimed action and dance. Its **recitatives** have more distinctive musical profiles than their Italian counterparts, and its mostly syllabic airs draw on dance rhythms in the French manner. Each act includes a spectacular **divertissement**: celebrations of Diana (Acts 1 and 4); Thésée's return (Act 3, and his trial in the underworld, Act 2); and Hippolyte and Aricie's union (Act 5).

At the same time, *Hippolyte* differs from **Jean-Baptiste Lully**'s treatment of the *tragédie en musique* in striking a compromise with Italian aesthetics. Less obviously a paean to French royalty—in its prologue the goddess Diana promises to serve Love instead of extolling Louis XV, who lacks an unambiguous counterpart in the cast—it advances *galant* personal issues like emotional attachments and human failings. This new focus is reflected in the expanded role of music to intensify personal expression in impassioned solo scenes such as Aricie's tortured soliloquy "Temple sacré" (Act 1) and Phèdre's conflicted monologue before her confrontation with Hippolyte (Act 3). And Rameau's Italianate leanings appear in the more lyrical and virtuosic vocal lines of its *ariettes* and in the vigorous descriptive string writing (likely influenced by **Antonio Vivaldi**) of passages like the thunder symphony in Act 1, which interrupts the destruction of Diana's temple by Phèdre's guards. Although relatively mild, these stylistic departures from Lully's precedents were sufficient to incite revolt among his loyalists, who were apparently concerned that the upstart would eclipse their hero.

HOFFMANN, ERNST THEODOR AMADEUS. (1776, Königsberg, now Kaliningrad–1822, Berlin.) German lawyer; writer; journalist; **conductor**; **composer** of nine **singspiels** and other operas, as well as other stage, instrumental, and vocal music; and artist. E. T. A. Hoffman was an important early exponent of German **romantic** opera.

Hoffmann followed his father unwillingly into the legal profession, studying law at Königsberg University (1792–95), and worked for a decade as a lawyer, judge, and government bureaucrat in decreasingly prestigious positions in Berlin (beginning 1798), Posen (now Poznań, beginning 1800), and Plock (beginning 1802), the last two in Poland. Initially trained by his uncle in music and other fields, he continued to study piano, violin, counterpoint, composition, and art in Königsberg and Berlin and enjoyed Italian and German operas. His earliest surviving composition is the singspiel *Die Maske* (1799, not performed); his first opera given in public was the singspiel *Scherz, List, und Rache* (1801, lost).

Reassigned to Warsaw in 1804, he found opportunities in music temporarily plentiful and immediately abandoned government service. He premiered the singspiel *Die lustigen Musikanten* (1805), published a piano sonata, and helped direct a local music society, composing music for its concerts, conducting its **orchestra**, and performing as a pianist and singer until the society disbanded during Napoleon's occupation in 1806. With prospects in Warsaw declining, he took a job as director (briefly) and composer for a financially precarious theater company in Bamberg, Germany (1808–13), writing incidental music for plays, designing and painting sets, and earning most of his living as a voice and piano teacher. During a brief period of solvency for the theater, he wrote the grand romantic opera *Aurora* (composed 1811–12), which was not performed. He also began his association (1809–15) with the music journal the *Allgemeine musikalische Zeitung* of Leipzig, for which he wrote short stories and reviews of music that established him as a leader of the romantic movement, and secured a local contract to publish his collected essays as *Fantasiestücke in Callots Manier* (1814).

Hoffmann's misfortunes in the theater continued when he was dismissed after less than a year as conductor for an opera company based in Dresden and Leipzig (1813–14), and he rejoined the Prussian bureaucracy, returning full circle to the Berlin High Court. He managed during moments of free time to finish the magic opera *Undine* (1816), the first of numerous adaptations of a novella (1811) by Friedrich de la Motte Fouqué, which he had conceived as early as 1812. An arch-romantic predecessor to **Carl Maria von Weber**'s *Euryanthe* (1823) and **Richard Wagner**'s *Lohengrin* (1850), it sets the story of a water spirit who marries and is betrayed by a knight to music reminiscent of **Wolfgang Amadeus Mozart**, **Christoph Willibald Gluck**, and Ludwig van Beethoven (1770–1827). A triumph from the start, its potentially long run ended after 14 performances when the playhouse burned down.

Aside from *Undine*, Hoffmann is best known today for his magical and supernatural stories, including *Nussknacker und Mausekönig* (*Nutcracker and Mouse King*, 1816, the source for **Pyotr Il'yich Tchaikovsky**'s **ballet** *The Nutcracker*) and for his reviews extolling Beethoven's works.

HORNE, MARILYN. (Born 1934, Bradford, Pennsylvania.) Preeminent American **coloratura** mezzo-**soprano** of the second half of the 20th century, noted for her impressive range, clear and powerful chest register, and brilliant but rich passagework. As a youth, Horne moved with her parents to California, where she sang in the Los Angeles Concert Youth **Chorus** and the Long Beach St. Luke's Choir and trained at the University of Southern California. She debuted in Los Angeles (1954) in **Bedřich Smetana**'s *The Bartered Bride* (originally 1870) and the same year dubbed for the lead in the movie *Carmen Jones*. Throughout her career Horne specialized in **bel canto** roles in operas by **Gioachino Rossini** and **Vincenzo Bellini**, frequently appearing opposite soprano **Joan Sutherland** (for example as Adalgisa to Sutherland's **Norma**; *see NORMA*), but also sang a broader repertory that included the leads in *Rinaldo*, *Carmen*, and **Camille Saint-Saëns**'s *Samson et Dalila* (1877).

See also WOMEN AND OPERA.

***LES HUGUENOTS**. **Grand opéra**;* music by **Giacomo Meyerbeer**, **libretto** by **Eugène Scribe**, revised by Emile Deschamps (1791–1871), based on the historical St. Bartholomew's Day Massacre (1572); five acts; premiered **Paris**, Opéra, February 1836. An epochal success, *Les Huguenots* received more than a thousand performances at the Opéra and almost universal critical acclaim, establishing parameters that would guide numerous composers, including **Giuseppe Verdi** and **Richard Wagner**, as they created their own conceptions of *grand opéra*.

The French Wars of Religion (1562–98) had already served as the subject for several plays, a novel, and an **opéra comique**. A turning point in those wars, the infamous slaughter by Catholics of prominent aristocratic Huguenot leaders gathered to celebrate the wedding of King Charles IX's sister Margaret of Valois to the future King Henry IV, a Huguenot, was an event in which Charles's mother, Catherine de' Medici, had been implicated. Engaging a volatile subject in a politically unsettled era, Scribe's libretto faced modifications to address **censorship** and the sensibilities of its bourgeois audience. For example, owing to government opposition to negative portrayals of the monarchy, Catherine's alleged role in the incident was reassigned to the Catholic nobleman St. Bris, the depiction of the heroine Valentine's adultery was toned down, and in some subsequent productions the Catholic-Protestant conflict was recast to involve other groups.

At a banquet held by the Catholic libertine Count of Nevers, the Huguenot Raoul de Nangis reveals that he has fallen in love with an unknown woman he previously rescued from highwaymen, but changes his mind when she appears, presumably as his friend's mistress. Called to a secret rendezvous, Queen Marguerite informs him that he is to marry Valentine, daughter of the ardent Catholic militant St. Bris, to defuse the religious conflict. However, he declines the match when he recognizes his bride-to-be from Nevers's palace, exacerbating tensions the arranged marriage was designed to subdue. When St. Bris plots Raoul's ambush to avenge the affront, Valentine warns Raoul's henchman Marcel, and Huguenots rescue him from certain death. As the ensuing massacre of Huguenots begins, Nevers is murdered by fellow Catholics for refusing to participate, leaving Valentine free to marry Raoul (after adopting his religion) in an impromptu ceremony conducted by Marcel outside a church sheltering the Huguenots. In the midst of their rampage, Catholics led by St. Bris slaughter the Huguenots, including Raoul and his own daughter, before Marguerite can intervene to end the bloodshed.

In *Les Huguenots*, Meyerbeer and Scribe achieved an ideal synthesis of appealing elements that they themselves were never able to duplicate successfully. A paradigm for its genre, *Les Huguenots* amply met standards for grandeur, luxury, and spectacle. Presented in five acts, its plot sets individual amorous entanglements and familial, religious, and political conflicts against a panoramic historical background. It features a huge cast of seven principals and multiple **choruses** and **ballet** corps, sometimes layered against each other. It was staged with **sets** and costumes carefully researched to recreate specific historical locations (e.g., the gardens of Catherine de' Medici's residence, the Château de Chenonceau) and attire. Its requisite spectacular

scenes include Nevers's banquet (Act 1), a ballet chorus of bathing beauties (Act 2), a street scene including exteriors of a tavern and a Catholic church and graced by a wedding procession (Act 3), the consecration of swords by Catholic conspirators (Act 4), and the ballroom scene and slaughter of Protestants outside their church (Act 5).

Les Huguenots also satisfied generic expectations of innovation, realism, and engaging entertainment in its music. Meyerbeer's inventive palette of orchestral sonorities contributes to atmosphere and characterization. Cases in point are the lumbering, socially challenged Marcel's signature bassoons and double basses; his army song "Piff, paff" accompanied by piccolo, bassoon, and percussion (Act 1); the unaccompanied viola and flute obbligatos in Raoul's romantic "Plus blanche" (Act 1); and Marguerite's **pastoral** "O beau pays" (Act 2), respectively, and the bass clarinet accompaniment of Raoul and Valentine's ersatz wedding (Act 5). Loose versions of conventional Italianate scene forms occur with some frequency, for example in Act 2 Marguerite's three-movement **aria**, her four-movement **duet** with Raoul, and the aborted betrothal in the **finale**, which centers on a conciliatory **largo concertato** and a **stretta** that renews Catholic and Huguenot discord. However, in departures from Italian practice, most of the relatively few **airs** are single movements (Raoul's two solos in Act 1) in strophic or ternary forms, and the acts consist mainly of single huge scenes in which the set pieces emerge spontaneously from their contexts. Sustained engagement of a musically unsophisticated audience inspired an impressive array of vocal idioms ranging from Marguerite's **coloratura** *sortita* "O beau Pays" to Marcel's character piece "Piff, paff" (both Act 1), and naturalness is served by a fluid mixture of metered and free **recitative**, *parlante*, and **arioso** in dialogues. Ingratiating elements of opéra comique are prevalent to a surprising degree, particularly at the start of the opera in the Act 1 banquet, where Nevers's Catholic friends relentlessly tease the Huguenots and show inappropriate interest in Valentine, and in Urbain's voyeurism during the bathing scene (Act 2).

I

IDOMENEO, RE DI CRETA. *Dramma per musica* (*see* OPERA SERIA); music by **Wolfgang Amadeus Mozart**, **libretto** by the Salzburg clergyman Giovanni Battista Varesco (1735–1805) based on Antoine Danchet's (1671–1748) libretto *Idomenée* (1712); three acts; premiered Munich, Residenztheater, January 1781. Sexagenarian **tenor** Anton Raaff (1714–1797), for whom the title role was his last, probably recommended the young Mozart for the commission. Though Mozart eventually adapted the part of Idamante for tenor (Vienna 1781), it was originally sung by **soprano castrato** Vincenzo dal Prato (1756–1828).

Currently considered the most successful example of reform tendencies in true opera seria of the late 18th century, *Idomeneo* steers a middle course between the radical innovations of **Christoph Willibald Gluck**'s *Orfeo ed Euridice* and traditional **Metastasian** opera, a compromise probably influenced by Mozart and Varesco's familiarity with **Niccolò Piccinni**'s progressive works. Although the plot is comparatively economical, it includes the subsidiary complication of a love triangle alongside the hero's central quandary (cf. Gluck's simpler *Alceste*). Idomeneo (Idomeneus), king of Mycenaean Crete returning from the Trojan War, has saved his storm-ravaged fleet by promising to sacrifice the first person he encounters on arriving. His son Idamante (Idamantes) welcomes him onshore, becoming his unforeseen victim. Idamante loves the Trojan prisoner Ilia, daughter of Priam, and is pursued by Elettra (Electra), daughter of the deceased king Agamemnon of Argos. In a vain attempt to save Idamante, Idomeneo orders him to take Elettra home to Argos, but a sea monster heralded by a storm blocks his escape and ravages the countryside. Idomeneo bows to duty and prepares to sacrifice Idamante, who has killed the monster but accepts his fate nonetheless. Neptune's oracle saves him, commanding Idomeneo to step aside for Idamante, who will rule with Ilia as his queen. Elettra consigns herself to Hades rather than submit to her rival.

Various other aspects of Mozart and Varesco's approach mediate between conventional **number opera** and more modern trends. Whereas **arias** dominate in Act 1 and the opening **scenes** of Act 2—the storm and **chorus** of shipwrecked sailors being the main exception—ensemble, choral, and descriptive instrumental music take center stage beginning in the port scene that ends Act 2 (march, maritime chorus, farewell trio, tempest with monster, Idomeneo's confession in obbligato **recitative**, and chorus of terror) and in all of Act 3. In that act, even the confessional garden scene centers on a **duet** and the great quartet "Andrò, ramingo e solo," while the subsequent scenes in the palace square and Neptune's temple create, in effect, an extended tableau. In the French manner, substantial ballet **divertissements** end Acts 1 and 3.

Even relatively traditional set pieces show this balance between old and new. In conveying a conventional lexicon of 18th-century affects (*see* DOCTRINE OF THE AFFECTIONS) in arias and other set pieces—military for Idomeneo, rage for Electra, sentimental for the lovers Idamante and Ilia, pastoral and tempestuous for choruses—Mozart created extraordinarily rich contrapuntal accompaniments infused with wind and brass solos. Although his arias still reach sizable proportions, include extensive **coloratura**, and start with full-fledged ritornellos, they do so within late 18th-century abbreviations of da capo form (e.g., Idomeneo's bravura aria "Fuor del mar," Act 2). Like their predecessors, Mozart's arias mostly follow and react to recitatives. Yet characters often remain onstage after their ovations rather than automatically exiting, participating in the ongoing action and fusing their individual scenes into larger complexes. And although simple recitatives with **harpsichord** remain essential for plot development, obbligato recitatives with **orchestra** are prevalent, raising the emotional pitch and enhancing continuity.

Having already made extensive modifications for the first performance, Mozart apparently intended to revise *Idomeneo* again to further emphasize French elements, but his plans never came to fruition. After modest success in the 18th century, it was revived sporadically in the 19th and 20th centuries but has never entered the standard repertory.

ILLICA, LUIGI, AND GIUSEPPE GIACOSA. (Illica: 1857, Castell'Arquato–1919, Colombarone; Giacosa: 1847, Colleretto Parella–1906, Colleretto Parella.) Team of **librettists** responsible for three of **Giacomo Puccini**'s most successful operas: *La bohème*, *Tosca*, and *Madama Butterfly* (1904).

Illica, a soldier/adventurer in the 1870s, made a name for himself as an avant-garde writer and literary critic in Milan in the 1880s. *Il vassallo di Szigeth* (1889) for the *scapigliatura* composer Antonio Smareglia (1854–1929), was his first of about three dozen **librettos** that range in style from **verismo** to **symbolism**. Illica's initial collaboration with Puccini involved completing the vexed libretto for *Manon Lescaut* (1893), which had already expended three other librettists (including **Ruggero Leoncavallo**) and eventually incorporated contributions by Giulio **Ricordi** and Puccini himself. Trained as a lawyer, Giacosa began a literary career in 1873 in conjunction with **Arrigo Boito**'s *scapigliati*, taught literature at the Milan Conservatory (1888–94), and by the end of the century had earned a reputation as the preeminent contemporary Italian playwright. Ricordi matched him with Illica in 1893. In the resulting division of labor, Illica devised plots and sketched dialogue, which Giacosa turned into finished poetry. Following Giacosa's death, Illica wrote one other libretto for Puccini, *Maria Antonietta*, for which the composer wrote no known music.

IMPRESARIO. Director of an opera **season** at a particular theater. In the late 19th and 20th centuries, the term also came to be used for agents who handled artists and touring theater companies. Originally Italian "entrepreneurs" who provided services in various fields such as tax collection, impresarios began managing opera seasons in **Venice** when the aristocratic owners of public theaters contracted them to avoid both the aggravation of running theaters themselves and the lavish expenditures expected of the nobility. By the 18th century the practice spread to the rest of Europe except for France.

Impresarios like **Domenico Barbaia** worked under a detailed contract, which stipulated the number and types of operas and various aspects of the quality of productions, and normally under supervision by a board of directors consisting of aristocrats or wealthy citizens. They were responsible for hiring personnel including **librettists**, **composers**, choreographers, **set** and costume designers, singers, dancers, **chorus** and **orchestra** members, and miscellaneous theater staff. An impresario commissioned new operas and **ballets**, selecting subjects that would suit the available cast, appeal to local audiences, and avoid political conflicts, and filled out the season with revivals of appropriate repertory works. He handled finances, balancing costs against estimated revenues from ticket sales and box rentals, and negotiated details with the board, local bureaucrats, and **censors** as necessary.

Though often subsidized by theater owners, impresarios operated on narrow margins and sometimes failed to meet costs, occasionally fleeing creditors midseason. Expenses escalated rapidly in the 1820s, because fees for the most famous composers and singers had more than doubled since the 18th century, larger choruses and orchestras cost more, and revenue dropped when **theater** casinos were closed following the Restoration. Issues of this sort exacerbated the struggle to make ends meet, forced impresarios to raise ticket prices and fees for box rentals, and made them prey to audience whims. Wars, fires, deaths of aristocratic patrons, and other calamities honed the razor's edge on which impresarios operated.

L'INCORONAZIONE DI POPPEA. *Dramma musicale*; music by **Claudio Monteverdi** and other **composers**, **libretto** by **Giovanni Francesco Busenello** based on accounts by Publius Tacitus and other Roman writers of Poppaea Sabina's seduction of the Emperor Nero; **prologue** and three acts; premiered **Venice**, Teatro Santi Giovanni e Paolo, Carnival 1642–43. Variations in the existing scores indicate that substantial portions of the music performed nowadays were probably written by Francesco Sacrati (1605–1650), **Francesco Cavalli**, and Benedetto Ferrari (after 1603–1681), who also wrote the text for at least the final Nero-Poppea **duet**. Castratos took several roles, including Nero and Ottone, and the noted **soprano Anna Renzi** sang Ottavia.

A masterpiece of early public opera, *Poppea* is credited with being the first Roman historical opera, a type that traded on Venetian posturing as the new Roman Republic and would become increasingly popular in the 1650s. Like other works of the period, it relies on an intricate network of intrigues to engage its unsophisticated audience. Following a prologue in which Love claims precedence over Fortune and Virtue, its characters play out a chain of infatuations: Druisilla for Ottone, Ottone for Poppea, and Poppea for Nero and the position of empress. Poppea manipulates Nero to betray his wife Ottavia and his counselor Seneca, who opposes their adultery. Ottavia strikes back, coercing Ottone to assassinate Poppea dressed in drag (*see* TRAVESTY). Having lent her dress as a disguise, Druisilla is falsely accused and sentenced to death when Ottone fails and flees the crime scene. Ottone eventually confesses to save her and reveals Ottavia's role, resulting in the exile of the three conspirators and Poppea's victory.

Though not a court opera, *Poppea* still presents elements of spectacle, such as Mercury's appearance to herald Seneca's suicide, Cupid's intervention to prevent Poppea's murder, and the attendance of Cupid and other angels, Venus, and the Graces at her coronation. And like other Venetian operas, *Poppea* includes comic *contrascene*, derived partly from the **commedia dell'arte**, involving Nero's guards, Poppea's and Octavia's nurses, and a page. The immoral triumph of desire and social ambition over reason and virtue reflects the cynical, heterodox philosophy of the Venetian Accademia degli Incogniti, in which Busenello was a leading figure.

In its architecture, *Poppea* anticipates later conventions by displacing the extended tableaux of *Orfeo* with series of small **scenes** in which the location of lyric set pieces varies and **arioso** passages create transitions between those set pieces and **recitatives**. Although no standardized distinction between verse types for **arias** and recitatives yet existed (*see* VERSIFICATION), the transformation of the virtuoso continuo **madrigal** into **coloratura bel canto** arias and duets punctuated by ritornellos takes a decisive step toward the aria operas of the generation of Cavalli and **Antonio Cesti**. At the same time, while Monteverdi expanded the range of text-setting styles to create madrigalistic responses to psychological shifts and humanize his characters, he continued to rely on recitative as the most emotionally incisive mode of communication.

INTERMEDIO. Italian musical entertainment, often very elaborate, performed between acts of spoken plays from the 15th century (beginning in Ferrara) through the 17th; a crucial antecedent of early opera. The most lavish court spectacles involved singers, dancers, and mimic actors accompanied by instruments, who performed in costume with scenery and complex stage machinery for special effects. They enacted a static **pastoral**, mythological, and/or allegorical episode, sometimes clarifying the situation or symbolism through spoken recitation. Often the set of four to six *intermedi* created for a typical five-act play were unified by a narrative theme: each, for example, might depict one the elements—earth, air, fire, and water—or times of day. Polyphonic **madrigals** (performed by ensembles or as solos with instruments taking the lower parts), continuo madrigals, dance songs of various types (such as *canzonette*), and choral dialogues, as well as various instrumental dances and processionals, played roles in these productions.

Beginning with the wedding of Cosimo de' Medici and Eleonora of Toledo in 1539, *intermedi* were cultivated extensively in Florence for celebrations of state events as allegorical enactments of the power and legitimacy of the ruling family. They became increasingly extravagant in their musical resources, which could extend to sizable instrumental ensembles involving multiple organs, **harpsichords**, **lutes**, viols, and hosts of wind instruments, and *concertato* madrigals involving as many as 60 singers. This trend culminated in blockbuster *intermedi* for the wedding of Ferdinando de' Medici and Christine of Lorraine in 1589, which received repeated performances with three different plays. Three poets collaborated on the texts, including Giovanni de' Bardi (1534–1612), host of the **Florentine Camerata**, and Ottavio Rinuccini (1562–1621), later **librettist** for **Jacopo Peri**'s *Dafne* and *Euridice*. The six *intermedi* depicted mythological **scenes** extolling the power of ancient music, an allegorical celebration of the spouses' anticipated role (and presumably that of dramatic music) in reviving a lost golden age. At least seven **composers** contributed, including the important madrigalist Luca Marenzio (ca. 1553–1599), Peri, **Giulio Caccini**, and **Emilio de' Cavalieri**. For the same festivities, a sacred play, *L'esaltazione della croce*, was also performed with six *intermedi* of its own.

The most elaborate musical precedent among the influences on the Camerata, the *intermedio* fused familiar genres of instrumental and vocal music with dance and stagecraft in presenting mythological scenarios and conventional infernal, pastoral, rescue, and apotheosis scenes. A number of early operas (*Dafne*, for example) may be regarded as elaborations of episodes from *intermedi*. Yet *intermedi* lacked important operatic ingredients like extended dialogue, sustained plots, and musical **recitative**, and constituted mainly tableaux composed of self-contained components. Though the *intermedio* declined following the advent of opera, it remained an important genre, continuing to be performed between the acts of operas as well as spoken plays, for example in Roman remakes of Venetian operas as late as the 1670s. A French equivalent (*intermède*) was also cultivated through the third quarter of the 17th century.

See also INTERMEZZO.

INTERMEZZO. A brief Italian comic opera, most often in two parts, but sometimes three, connected by a single plot and cast; alternatively an instrumental interlude (*see CAVALLERIA RUSTICANA*), movement, or independent piece. It was performed between acts of a three-act **opera seria** (and before the final scene if the intermezzo had three acts) and in some cases between acts of a spoken play. Thus it may trace its roots in part to the 17th-century **intermedio**. Common sources for plots, which involved domestic contests of will or parodies of the conventions of opera seria or social mores, included spoken comedies (e.g., Molière's) and conventional **commedia dell'arte** scenarios. The cast normally included only two or three singing characters, such as a saucy servant or peasant girl (soubrette; *see* SOPRANO); a lecherous, befuddled old noblemen, lawyer, doctor, or guardian; or a cowardly, braggart soldier. Each part of the intermezzo generally gives an **aria** or two to each character and closes with a **duet**. *Recitativo semplice* (*see* RECITATIVE) carries the action, while rare examples of obbligato recitative parody the self-importance of the male leads.

The intermezzo replaced the comic *contrascene* of 17th-century serious operas, which increasingly disappeared in accordance with the reforms of the **Arcadian Academy** ca. 1700, and provided an outlet for buffo actor-singers. It developed first in **Venice**, centered on the Teatro San Cassiano, the first known example being *Frappolone e Florinetta* (likely by Francesco Gasparini, 1661–1727, music lost), performed between acts of Gasparini's *Statira* (1706). The earliest surviving intermezzo is Tomaso Albinoni's (1671–1751) *Pimpinone* (1708). The intermezzo detached from opera seria in **Naples** after ca. 1720, where it developed under **Johann Adolf Hasse, Giovanni Battista Pergolesi**, and others, with Pergolesi's *La serva padrona* (1733) emerging as the paradigm for the genre. Beginning in the 1710s, specialist singers carried the intermezzo from Venice and Naples throughout Europe, reaching **Paris** by 1752, where intermezzo and **opera buffa** performances ignited the **War of the Comedians**. After ca. 1750, **ballets** largely replaced intermezzi as entertainment between acts of serious operas, while opera buffa continued to develop as the preeminent comic genre in Italy.

See also BASS; FARSA; GOLDONI, CARLO; HAYDN, JOSEPH; OPÉRA COMIQUE; PICCINNI, NICCOLÒ.

INTRODUZIONE. A lyric set piece normally involving **chorus** that introduces an act in late 18th- or 19th-century Italian opera. For *introduzioni* that begin operas, a range of options is defined by two types. The term sometimes designates a chorus, which is normally followed by a scena (*see* SCENE) and **aria** (often designated as a cavatina) for the male lead. Alternatively, it is applied to a much more complicated, multisectional scene featuring chorus, which in the 19th century is modeled on the ensemble **finale**.

These two options were popularized by **Gioachino Rossini**, as illustrated by the opening scenes of *Otello* (1816) and ***Semiramide***, respectively. A familiar example of the chorus-plus-aria type in **Giuseppe Verdi**'s works is the *introduzione* of *Ernani* (1844). The ensemble type, which becomes prevalent in Verdi, occurs in ***Rigoletto***, *La traviata* (1853), and elsewhere. Multisectional Act 1 *introduzioni* were already present in the last quarter of the 18th century, for example in **Wolfgang Amadeus Mozart**'s ***Don Giovanni***. *Introduzioni* of later acts are normally choruses, which may stand alone or introduce arias.

J

JANÁČEK, LEOŠ. (1854, Hukvaldy, Moravia–1928, Moravská Ostrava.) Prominent Czech **composer** of 10 operas (1880s–1920s) as well as other vocal and instrumental music, **librettist** for the majority of his own operas, teacher, choir director, and journalist.

Trained initially by his family of provincial schoolteacher musicians, Janáček moved to Brno as a choirboy in 1865 and eventually attended the Prague Organ School (1874–75 and 1877) and **conservatories** in Leipzig (1879–80) and **Vienna** (1880), where the operas he infrequently attended failed to impress him. Returning to Brno, he taught at various schools (1880–1904), founded and directed the Brno Organ School (1881–1919), conducted two choral societies, and established the music journal *Hudební listy* (1884–88), for which he reviewed operas performed in Brno. This new exposure to the genre led to his first foray, *Šárka* (composed beginning 1887, premiered 1925), a **romantic** nationalist opera on a Czech myth in which Bohemian amazons drug their male enemies and slaughter them while they sleep.

Janáček began collecting Moravian music in 1888, an interest reflected in *Počátek románu* (*The Beginning of a Romance*, premiered 1894), which is dominated by folk songs and dances. *Jenůfa* (composed beginning 1894, premiered 1904) inaugurates a more integrated treatment of this ethnic influence, which avoids direct quotations. Instead, Janáček assimilated melodic and rhythmic elements and the modal palette of folk music into a style he termed "speech melody," in which the vocal lines accentuate the movement and intonations of spoken language, an approach akin to the declamatory realism of **Modest Petrovich Musorgsky** and the Russian Kuchka. *Jenůfa* unravels the tangled familial interrelationships of a Czech village: the heroine's illegitimate child by one of her cousins is killed by her stepmother so that she can marry another of her cousins, half-brother of her former lover, who has abandoned her. The opera became popular in Prague after 1916 and in Germany after 1924, establishing Janáček's international reputation as an opera composer very late in his career.

Příhody Lišky Bystroušky (*The Cunning Little Vixen*, premiered 1924) is Janáček's lightest opera, despite the death of the heroine, and currently his best known. It is a parable of the circle of life, in which a female fox raised as a pet by a forester escapes, marries and has cubs, and is shot by a poacher, her pelt recognized by the forester at the poacher's wedding. Although less familiar, two of Janáček's other late works are major entries of notable originality: *Věc Makropulos* (*The Makropulos Affair*, premiered 1926) presents a remarkably convoluted mystery in which a beguiling opera singer resolves a probate case by clarifying lines of inheritance, because she has lived for more than 300 years thanks to a 16th-century potion; *Zmrtvého domu* (*From the House of the Dead*, premiered 1930) is based on a novel by Fyodor Dostoyevsky set in a Siberian prison camp.

JOMMELLI, NICCOLÒ. (1714, Aversa–1774, Naples). Though universally ignored by modern companies, Jommelli, author of over 65 mostly heroic operas (*see* CATEGORIES OF OPERA) from the 1730s through the 1770s, was considered by many contemporaries to be the preeminent Italian **composer** of the mid-18th century. Alongside **Tommaso Traetta**, he broke earliest and most visibly with the conventions of 18th-century **opera seria** and anticipated numerous innovations of **Christoph Willibald Gluck**. Despite these unorthodoxies, **Pietro Metastasio** ardently supported Jommelli, in contrast to his disdain for Gluck. Jommelli's devotion to Metastasio, in keeping with the mania of the day, is demonstrated by numerous settings of his **librettos** (normally remodeled), in some cases in as many as four versions (*Demofoonte* and *Ezio*).

Jommelli trained with the local choir director in Aversa and at conservatories in **Naples** (late 1720s), where the opera composers **Leonardo Leo** and **Johann Adolf Hasse** were dominant influences, and later with Giovanni Battista ("Padre") Martini (1706–1784) in Bologna (1741). He debuted in Naples with the **opera buffa** *L'errore amorosa* (1737), and his first opera seria, *Ricimero re di Goti*, premiered in **Rome** (1740). Despite his residency in **Venice** and regular position as musical director at one of its orphanage **conservatories** (beginning ca. 1745), the 1740s were a blur of work and travel. He wrote 27 new operas from 1740 to 1750 for most of the major Italian centers, including Rome, Bologna, Venice, Turin, Ferrara, Padua, Crema, Naples, Parma, and **Vienna**. In some cases there were two operas for the same Carnival **season**, and 1749 saw six operas for Rome, Parma, Vienna, and Venice. A revised version of his Venetian **intermezzo** *L'uccellatrice* of 1750 was later performed in Paris (1753) during the **War of the Comedians**.

Jommelli gravitated toward Rome beginning in 1747, and an appointment as *maestro di cappella* at St. Peter's Basilica (probably in late 1749) brought nonoperatic responsibilities, a temporary decrease in both travel and operatic productivity, and membership in the **Arcadian Academy**. Beginning with *Ifigenia in Aulide* (1751), with one exception his next operas (through January 1753) were for Rome. His burgeoning reputation garnered offers from Lisbon and Manheim (declined) before Carl Eugen, the Francophile Duke of Württemberg, recruited him for the new theater in Stuttgart, where he became *Ober-Kapellmeister* in 1754. Benefitting from the duke's deep pockets, Jommelli developed one of the finest **orchestras** in Europe to accompany his premier corps of singers, dancers, and scenographers, over whom he apparently exerted absolute control. Jommelli's Stuttgart appointment produced, among more than two dozen operas, one of the most admired settings of Metastasio's *L'Olimpiade* (1761), and perhaps Jommelli's most innovative opera *Fetonte* (1768), as well as religious music for special occasions.

Intrigues brewing at Karl Eugen's court encouraged Jommelli to hedge his bets by reconnecting with Lisbon in 1769, but on leave from Stuttgart he was abruptly dismissed without further compensation and without access to the scores he had created there. He returned to Naples, where he resumed an extremely demanding schedule that resulted in seven operas between May 1770 and July 1771, beginning with *Armida abbandonata*. A stroke in 1771 physically incapacitated Jommelli, although he managed to eke out a number of additional scores during his final years.

Jommelli diverged from most contemporaries by treating opera as a dramatic medium (in addition to a concert medium) and by expanding the range of the prevailing *galant* **bel canto** style, leading some contemporaries to view him as "Germanic." He developed the middle ground between simple **recitative** and **aria** by exploring the dramatic potential of more frequent obbligato recitatives (probably influenced by Hasse and by French opera) and by including emotive declamation in arias. He gave the orchestra a greater voice through more expressive recitative and aria accompaniments, expanded use of woodwinds, more independent part writing for the middle strings, instrumental motivic connections between scena (*see* SCENE) and aria, and occasional tone painting and programmatic interludes. He challenged Arcadian conventions by developing a broader repertory of aria forms, from abbreviated dal segno variants to monumental structures which differentiate the functions of their extended themes in ritornellos and solo sections along the lines of sonata form. Nontraditional scene structures, possibly encouraged by involvement with Francophile Vienna and Stuttgart, incorporate substantial ensembles, **ballet**, and **chorus**. Jommelli's scores show trenchant harmonic progressions and modulations, frequent and precise dynamic indications, and a command of counterpoint uncharacteristic of his Italian colleagues.

K

KODÁLY, ZOLTÁN. (1882, Kecskemét–1967, Budapest.) Hungarian **composer** of three **singspiels** (1920s–40s), as well as incidental music for plays and other vocal and instrumental music, and music educator. The son of a provincial railway stationmaster, Kodály learned piano and string instruments at home and heard folk melodies sung in school. He trained in composition at the Budapest Academy of Music (1900–05), where he was employed (beginning 1907) as a composition teacher and a deputy director (1918–19) during the Hungarian Democratic Republic, after which he was dismissed when the revolution was put down. Following World War II, Kodály became an icon of Hungarian music education, serving as president of the Budapest Academy of Music, the Hungarian Council of the Arts, and the Hungarian Academy of Sciences. The Kodály pedagogical method is still used internationally.

Beginning in 1905, Kodály had joined **Béla Bartók** in collecting and editing eastern European folk music, and his style synthesizes folk-song elements with adaptations of **Claude Debussy**'s harmonic style and aspects of early music. As an opera composer, Kodály is known primarily for the singspiel *Háry János* (1926), which enacts the apocryphal adventures of an Austrian war veteran who brags that he rescued the kaiser's daughter, was promoted to general and defeated Napoleon, and won the affections of the emperor's wife, but returned to his humble village life. Its music incorporates Hungarian songs and military recruiting dances (*verbunkos*), some of which were extracted for the orchestral *Háry János Suite* (1927), which gained him international recognition. Kodály's other two operas *Székely fonó* (*The Transylvanian Spinning Room*, first version 1924), its dialogue replaced with mimed action for the 1932 revision, and *Czinka Panna* (1948) have received little attention.

KRENEK, ERNST. (1900, Vienna–1991, Palm Springs, California.) Prolific Austrian **composer** of some 20 operatic works from the 1920s through the early 1970s (most on his own **librettos**), as well as other vocal and instrumental music. Krenec studied piano from age six and composition from age

16, pursuits he was able to continue while assigned to military service in **Vienna** during World War I. His first staged opera, the comic *Der Sprung über den Schatten* (*The Leap over the Shadow*), appeared in 1923.

Krenek is known primarily for the enormously popular and frequently performed *Jonny spielt auf* (*Jonny Strikes up the Band*, 1927), the archetypal Weimar Republic **Zeitoper** dealing with contemporary issues of social freedom and artistic relevance. Composed in a popular tonal style infused with Italianate lyricism and jazz idioms, its title character, an African American jazz musician who symbolizes freedom from social and artistic inhibitions, steals a rare violin from a virtuoso involved in a love triangle with an opera composer and his prima donna. Contrasts between opera and popular music, as well as parodies of **romantic** nature worship and the Second Viennese School **expressionism** of **Arnold Schoenberg** and his followers, contribute to the dialectic between tradition and novelty.

Krenec fled Vienna for the United States following the Nazi invasion in 1938. Along with **Gian Carlo Menotti** he became an originator of television opera (*see* CATEGORIES OF OPERA) with *Ausgerechnet und verspielt* (1961) and two other works over the next decade.

See also CENSORSHIP.

L

LARGO CONCERTATO. Slow, reflective movement and melodious focal point of a 19th-century Italian ensemble involving three or more singers, such as a central **finale**, in which all the characters onstage react—often in a so-called "frozen moment" of reflection—to the situation or to a specific event. In the standard form, the *largo concertato* is the second movement, following the ***tempo d'attacco***. Characters may sing simultaneously throughout the movement, or the leads may build up the texture gradually with successive solos prior to singing together with the rest of the cast in a groundswell to a melodic climax. As in the slow movement of a **duet**, the solos may repeat the same melody in a pseudo canon (for example, "Freddo ed immobile" from the Act 1 finale of ***Il barbiere di Siviglia***). Or more frequently, different melodies may segregate characters according to their relationships with one another and depict their individual dispositions ("Bella figlia dell'amore," ***Rigoletto***, Act 3 quartet prior to Gilda's murder).

The *largo concertato* developed primarily as an expansion of the penultimate reflective passage in late 18th-century finales, for example, "Questo birbo mi toglie il cervello" in the *andante ma non troppo* "Vostre dunque saran queste carte" (***Le nozze di Figaro***, Act 2, finale). Still present in the late operas of **Giuseppe Verdi** (for example "A terra! . . . sì . . . nel livido fango" in the Act 3 finale of ***Otello***), the *largo concertato* was largely abandoned by the ***giovane scuola***, with surreptitious exceptions such as "Quando me'n vo" (***La bohème***, Act 2) and "Bevo al tuo fresco sorriso," the former an outgrowth of Musetta's waltz, the latter rationalized as a drinking song in Act 2 of **Giacomo Puccini**'s rather old-fashioned *La rondine* (1917).

LEGROS, JOSEPH. (1739, Monampteuil–1793, La Rochelle.) Leading French *haute-contre* (high **tenor**) of the 1760s and 1770s. Trained as choirboy at the Laon cathedral, Legros's **Paris** debut in 1764 began a career that spanned two decades (to 1783). He starred in revivals of all of **Jean-Philippe Rameau**'s major ***tragédies en musiques*** and created lead roles in most of **Christoph Willibald Gluck**'s serious operas (*see* CATEGORIES OF OPERA) for Paris. Gluck adjusted the **castrato** part of Orpheus in the French

Orphée et Eurydice (1774) for him—it still reaches soprano e-flat"—and he sang in premiers of Gluck's four subsequent *opéras*. In these and works by **Niccolò Piccinni** and Antonio Sacchini (1730–1786), Legros proved adaptable to the lyrical Italianate style that was infiltrating French opera in the second half of the century. At the end of his career he directed the Concert Spirituel (from 1777), advancing the music of **Joseph Haydn** and **Wolfgang Amadeus Mozart** in Paris.

LEHÁR, FRANZ. (1870, Komáron, Hungary–1948, Bad Ischl, Austria.) Hungarian-born Austrian **composer** of more than two dozen stage works, mostly **operettas** created during the first three decades of the 20th century; **conductor**; and violinist. Lehár trained with his father, a military bandmaster, and uncle, a provincial **orchestra** director, and at the Prague **Conservatory**, where he had contact with **Antonin Dvořák**. He started his career as a theater musician and military bandmaster (1888–1902), during which time he composed dances and marches, several of which became popular; had the opera *Kukuška* (1896) mounted (unsuccessfully) in Leipzig; and began two operettas.

Lehár's first complete operettas were performed in **Vienna** in 1902, *Der Rastelbinder* gaining particular notice, and his crowning achievement in the genre came three years later. *Die lustige Witwe* (*The Merry Widow*, 1905), in which dignitaries from an impoverished Balkan duchy try to make a local match for a wealthy widow so that she and her riches will remain in the country, sparked a revival of Viennese operetta locally and abroad. In short order he fortified this resurgence with *Der Graf von Luxemburg* (1909) and *Zigeunerliebe* (1910).

Although World War I and the postwar infusion of popular music from the United States temporarily broke the spell, Lehár enjoyed renewed popularity in the 1920s in a collaboration with the **tenor** Richard Tauber (1891–1948) that started in 1921 with a production of *Zigeunerliebe* and culminated in Lehár's final triumph *Das Land des Lächelns* (1929, revision for Tauber of *Die gelbe Jacke*, 1923). Lehár spent the end of his life (beginning 1935) as a publisher of his own works and was faulted internationally for his apparent indifference to Nazi atrocities.

LEITMOTIF. A "leading motif" is a distinctive musical melody or melodic fragment, harmonic progression, or sonority associated with a person, place, object, emotion, concept, or other dramatic element that returns periodically over the course of an opera (or cycle of operas) or other musical work (especially a programmatic symphony or symphonic poem).

Use of leitmotifs is most associated with **Richard Wagner**'s music dramas (e.g., ***Der Ring des Nibelungen***, ***Tristan und Isolde***, and *Parsifal*, 1882) and with the operas and orchestral works of the so-called New German School, led by Franz Liszt (1811–1886), and its followers such as **Richard Strauss**. Yet the term originated not with Wagner but with commentators such as the Austrian music historian August Wilhelm Ambros (1816–1876) beginning in the 1860s. Wagner himself used other terms to refer to recurring ideas, such as *Erinnerungsmotiv* (reminiscence motif) and *Hauptmotiv* (head motif).

The technique had its roots in the thematic reappearances that contributed to the enlargement of the role of music in the late 18th-century **opéras comiques** of **André-Ernest-Modeste Grétry** (most notably *Richard Coeur-de-lion*, 1784), **Étienne-Nicolas Méhul**, and **Luigi Cherubini** and continued to appear in the French ***grands opéras*** of **Giacomo Meyerbeer** (e.g., *Les Huguenots*) and the German **romantic** operas of **Carl Maria von Weber** (***Der Freischütz***), **Heinrich Marschner**, and Wagner's operas prior to the *Ring* (for example, ***Der fliegende Holländer*** and ***Tannhäuser***). It continued to develop in various ways throughout the 20th century in the hands of art-music composers—for example **Alban Berg** in *Wozzeck* and *Lulu* (composed 1929–35, completed and first performed 1979)—and composers of film scores.

As Wagner employed them in his music dramas, leitmotifs are far more pervasive than the associative motifs of prior composers or of mid- to late 19th-century composers in Italy and France such as **Giuseppe Verdi**, **Georges Bizet**, or **Giacomo Puccini**. They may debut or return in either the vocal parts or in the **orchestra**—although the orchestra carries most of the weight—and in many cases originate through transformation of existing materials. Consequently they often constitute integrated families within which they share musical characteristics and related associations, such as the *Ring* motifs for "renunciation of love" and the "ring" or Loge's "fire" and Brünnhilde's "magic sleep." They may occur, with or without specific textual prompts, to draw attention to immediate events or stated viewpoints, to connect current dramatic events to events in the past or future, or to reveal unarticulated attitudes, meanings, or implications. Connections between leitmotifs and other dramatic elements are often ambiguous and ambivalent, both when motifs first appear and as they develop across a score and their identities become more complex. Once in place, they often assume a second, primarily musical function and contribute to design and expression independent from any textual associations.

LEO, LEONARDO. (1694, San Vito degli Schiavoni–1744, Naples.) One of the leading **composers** of Neapolitan **opera seria**, **opera buffa**, and oratorio, and the dominant musical figure in **Naples** from 1830 until his death.

Despite his reportedly unreliable work habits, he produced approximately 60 operas and numerous works in other theatrical genera like the *festa teatrale* and **serenata**. Leo trained in Naples (beginning 1709), possibly under **Alessandro Scarlatti**, and rose progressively through the viceregal and royal chapels from organist in 1713 to *maestro di cappella* shortly before his death. Late in his career, as a maestro in several of Naples' **conservatories**, he mentored **Niccolò Jommelli** and **Niccolò Piccinni**.

Alongside Vinci, **Antonio Caldara**, and **Nicola Porpora**, Leo was one of the leading composers of opera seria on **librettos** by the first- and second-generation **Arcadians Apostolo Zeno**, Silvio Stampiglia (1664–1725), and **Pietro Metastasio**. However, unlike his contemporaries, he favored a more traditional, studied, contrapuntal style reminiscent of Scarlatti over the modern *galant* style. Leo is also noted for his contribution to raising the standards of Neapolitan comic opera in its fledgling era.

LEONCAVALLO, RUGGERO. (1857, Naples–1919, Montecatini.) **Composer** of about 20 Italian operas from, with one exception, the 1890s through the 1920s, and poet who wrote many of his own **librettos**, following the Wagnerian precepts of the *giovane scuola*. Though Leoncavallo was best known for two **verismo** works, *Pagliacci* and *Zazà* (1900), much of his output was lighter in style.

Leoncavallo studied piano and composition in **Naples** (1866–76) and poetry with the Wagnerian (*see* WAGNERISM) Giosuè Carducci at the University of Bologna (1876–77). At this time he was inspired by performances of **Arrigo Boito**'s *Mefistofele* (originally 1868) and **Richard Wagner**'s *Rienzi* (originally 1842) and *Der fliegende Holländer*, and he responded with his first opera, *Chatterton* (ca. 1876). After abortive trips to Egypt and **Paris**, he turned to Milan, where his first-performed opera—and the most successful of his career—the verismo manifesto *Pagliacci* premiered in 1892. He also contributed to the libretto of **Giacomo Puccini**'s *Manon Lescaut* (1893). Leoncavallo's *commedia lirica La bohème* (1897), which followed Puccini's more famous *Bohème* by a year and was based on the same source, competed with it for a time, creating friction with Puccini and his publisher **Ricordi**. After the international success of his *commedia lirica Zazà* (1900), like *La bohème* a portrait of Parisian Bohemianism, Leoncavallo's troubles with publishers escalated, and his works received fewer performances in Italy. In Germany, however, his popularity continued unabated, leading to numerous revivals and a new opera, *Der Roland von Berlin* (1904). Beginning with *La jeunesse de Figaro* for **New York** (1906), he focused primarily on comic operas (*see* CATEGORIES OF OPERA) and **operettas**.

LIBRETTIST. Creator of the **libretto** for an opera or other type of dramatic vocal work.

Although most librettists had some type of liberal education and early exposure to literature and poetry, they have come from a variety of backgrounds and trained in a number of different fields including clerical studies (for example, **Giulio Rospigliosi, Lorenzo Da Ponte**) and the law (**Giovanni Francesco Busenello, Philippe Quinault, Pietro Metastasio, Carlo Goldoni**, and Giuseppe Giacosa; *see* ILLICA, LUIGI, AND GIUSEPPE GIACOSA). **Francesco Maria Piave** started off in his family's glass business and then worked as a printer's proofreader. Frequently budding librettists apprenticed with established theater poets (Goldoni, Da Ponte) and cut their teeth adapting existing librettos to local taste or new styles.

Even after their careers took off, most librettists held other responsibilities. The earliest were typically aristocrats, government functionaries, and other courtiers (e.g., the first opera librettist, Ottavio Rinuccini, 1562–1621; Alessandro Striggio, ca. 1573–1630; Quinault; **Ranieri Calzabigi**) or clergy—Rospigliosi was Pope Clement IX—and they participated in various literary and artistic academies (Busenello; *see also* FLORENTINE CAMERATA). Many had steady work as theater or court poets (e.g., Metastasio, Goldoni, **Mattia Verazi**, Piave), in which their duties could involve supervising aspects of rehearsal and production and negotiating with censors (*see* CENSORSHIP). Outside the world of opera, some were poets and playwrights of considerable repute, notably Metastasio, Goldoni, **Eugène Scribe**, and Giacosa, while others were lawyers (Busenello, Goldoni); writers, journalist-critics, and editors (**Francesco Algarotti**, Calzabigi, **Felice Romani, Arrigo Boito**, Illica); theater managers (**Giacomo Durazzo**); and teachers (Da Ponte, Giacosa). Following **Richard Wagner**'s lead, increasing numbers of composers have written at least some of their own librettos—or librettists have written their own scores (Boito)—particularly in the 20th century (**Richard Strauss, Arnold Schoenberg, Gian Carlo Menotti**) or have contributed scenarios, poetic drafts of scenes or set pieces, or profuse and detailed feedback (**Vincenzo Bellini** with Romani and **Giuseppe Verdi** with Piave).

Specialist librettists at times demonstrated tremendous facility, in extreme cases completing full-scale works in a matter of a week or two—Goldoni claimed he produced comic librettos in four days—and assembled huge portfolios across long careers (for example, Goldoni's approximately 80 librettos and Romani's 90). Although some were known primarily for particular genres (Quinault for *tragédie en musique*, Metastasio for heroic **opera seria**, Goldoni for comedy; *see* CATEGORIES OF OPERA), most cast broad nets and, in addition to opera librettos of various types, also crafted librettos for **melodramas** and other sorts of theatrical entertainment, ballet scenarios (Scribe), and scenarios and written-out plays for the **commedia dell'arte** and other troupes. Others dabbled more or less successfully and were involved in relatively few operatic production (e.g., Antonio Somma, 1809–1864, author of apparently only two librettos, the incomplete *Re Lear* and *Un ballo in maschera*, 1859, both for Verdi). In the 20th century, librettists were increasingly established authors who wrote librettos as a sideline (Bertolt Brecht, 1898–1956—*see* WEILL, KURT—and W. H. Auden, 1907–1973). Consequently, librettists varied in their level of experience with, understanding of, and success in handling the many conventions of operatic drama, **versification**, and musical form and the nuances of characterization, language, diction, pacing, timing, and the interaction of words and music.

A number of librettists enjoyed (or endured) long-standing associations with prominent composers, notably Quinault with **Jean-Baptiste Lully**, Goldoni with **Baldassare Galuppi**, Da Ponte with **Wolfgang Amadeus Mozart**, Romani with Bellini, Piave with Verdi, **William Schwenck Gilbert** with Arthur Sullivan, Illica and Giacosa with **Giacomo Puccini**, and Hugo von Hofmannsthal (1874–1929) with Richard Strauss. In several cases, librettists were at least equal partners in innovations normally credited to the composers with whom they collaborated (Verazi with **Niccolò Jommelli** and Calzabigi with **Christoph Willibald Gluck**).

See also ZENO, APOSTOLO.

LIBRETTO. A "little book," normally printed pocket size, containing the text of an opera or other vocal work, as well as other information. The term also refers to the text of an opera, independent from the published artifact. The author of a libretto is the **librettist**.

The first existing printed libretto appeared in 1600 for Ottavio Rinuccini (1562–1621) and **Jacopo Peri**'s *Dafne* (originally 1598). The earliest librettos published for German, French, and English operas, respectively, were Heinrich Schütz's (1585–1672) *Dafne* (published 1627), Michel de La Guerre's (ca. 1606–1679) *Le triomphe de l'amour* (published 1654), and John Gay's (1685–1732) *The Beggar's Opera* (published 1728).

For most of the 17th, 18th, and 19th centuries, librettos were printed for individual productions and sold at the theater for reference during performances, which was facilitated by undimmed house lights. They provided the text and, for foreign-language operas, often included a translation. The layout of poetic **versification** was respected: for example, Italian librettos normally offset stanzas of *versi lirici* for set pieces from *versi sciolti* for **recitatives**. Such theatrical librettos were bare bones, utilitarian publications produced on a short timetable and consequently boast few decorative frills, give only perfunctory stage directions, and suffer from numerous errors. By the late 19th century, the introduction of electricity, which allowed lights to be extinguished during performances, and the dominance of repertory operas with which the majority of the audience was already familiar made theater librettos superfluous.

Librettos have also been sold for use outside the theater. For example, commemorative librettos printed after the fact tend to be more elaborate than theater librettos and often include illustrations (e.g., engravings of set designs) and descriptions of prior performances. Librettos were also published—sometimes under pseudonyms by poets who had reputations to protect and joined their contemporaries in regarding the libretto as an inferior genre—as literature to be read or performed as spoken plays with the **aria** texts removed (*see* GOLDONI, CARLO; METASTASIO, PIETRO). Since the 20th century, librettos have mostly been produced independently of theaters by publishers and by the manufacturers of vinyl LPs, audiotapes, and compact discs.

As Italian librettos developed across the 18th and 19th centuries, they incorporated an increasing wealth of historically significant detail regarding the productions for which they were printed. Beyond basic information concerning authorship (librettist and **composer**) and publication (publisher, location, and date), they may provide guides to content (lists of characters and scenes, an *argomento*—"argument"—explaining any historical or fictional background, and synopses of **ballets** performed between acts or as part of the opera) and cast lists including singers, their understudies, solo dancers, **orchestra** section leaders, and sometimes the entire personnel of the ballet corps, orchestra, and **chorus**. They often name theater managers (**impresario** and music director) and the **production** crew (**set**, costume, and stage machinery designers; lighting director; choreographer; prompter; machinery operators; and other stagehands). They may append a dedication or tribute to a patron or reigning aristocrat; a prefatory rationale for a new genre, style, or aesthetic orientation; a salute to the audience; or a disclaimer that the action is fictional and not necessarily reflective of the poet's beliefs. And they may note deleted passages (not set to music or cut in performance) and supply texts for alternate arias. Librettos outside of Italy tended to follow suit, although German and Viennese librettos are generally less illuminating and—in the case of **singspiels**—sometimes omit the spoken dialogues. Librettos of comic operas (for example **ballad operas**) may provide notated melodies for some or all of the songs.

The stories of librettos have seldom been entirely new. Instead they have drawn on myths or legends, historical episodes, folktales, and original stories found in existing histories, the Bible, poems, plays, novels, short stories, previous librettos, newspaper stories, or other accounts written from ancient to more recent times, the most literal borrowings occurring in *Literaturopern* of the late 19th and 20th centuries. Only in the 20th century have original librettos become at all common, ranging from the *Zeitopern* of the period between the wars to various avant-garde, anti-narrative constructions of the second half of the century. (For examples of libretto plots, see entries for individual operas; brief summaries of important works are also given in individual composer entries.)

Librettos were most often written ahead of time—though not always as far ahead of time as the composer might have preferred—and delivered to the composer complete. However, on a tight deadline or when composers and librettists (and perhaps others involved in the production) collaborated closely, the creation of text and score could happen more or less simultaneously, individual scenes being set to music as they were received. Occasionally the text was spontaneously conceived in conjunction with music and other elements (*see EINSTEIN ON THE BEACH*). During the 17th and much of the 18th centuries, the libretto was considered the primary component of an opera's identity: versions of librettos were set repeatedly by different composers, and their authors received top billing. While few would argue that even a great libretto could compensate for a poor score or weak production— **Pietro Metastasio**'s claim that **Christoph Willibald Gluck**'s remake of his *Semiramide riconosciuta* (1748, originally 1729) triumphed despite dreadful music seems a tad self-serving—a weak libretto could mar an otherwise fine effort (e.g., **Carl Maria von Weber**'s *Euryanthe*, 1823, or **Amilcare Ponchielli**'s *I promessi sposi*, 1856) and undermine its longevity.

LICHT. Cycle of seven operas by Karlheinz Stockhausen (1928–2007), **librettos** by the **composer**; created 1977–2003; *Donnerstag, Samstag,* and *Montag* staged individually Milan, La Scala, 1981, 1984, and 1988; *Dienstag* and *Freitag* staged individually Leipzig, Opera, 1993 and 1996; *Mittwoch* presented in parts in Amsterdam, Stuttgart, and Munich, 1995–98; *Sonntag* staged Cologne, 2011.

Licht is the most ambitious operatic cycle (or theatrical work) ever conceived. It combines Judeo-Christian elements—the main characters are the archangel Michael (the creator), Lucifer (his nemesis), and Eve (the regenerative source of mankind)—the ancient Indian Vedic religion, the 20th-century *Urantia Book* of cosmic spiritual philosophy, and Japanese classical Noh theater. Its mammoth series of existential meditations, presented in operas named for the days of the week, lasts more than 29 hours. In addition to its length, serial format, and metaphysical orientation, it bears obvious relationships to **Richard Wagner**'s *Der Ring des Nibelungen* in its reuse of melodic formulas in the manner of **leitmotifs**; the prominence of instruments, which represent each of the main characters; the creation by the composer of not only the score, but also poetry and directions for staging and choreography; and consequently the equivalent status given to all those elements.

LIETO FINE. The virtually obligatory happy ending for a play or opera in the 17th and 18th centuries. The *lieto fine* frequently arrived implausibly through a deus ex machina (the unexpected appearance of a god or goddess through stage machinery—for example, Neptune's oracle in *Idomeneo, re di Creta*) or intervention by a benevolent nobleman playing that part (Fernando in *Fidelio*), and was confirmed by a celebratory or moralizing ensemble or love **duet**. It typically involved rescuing imperiled heroes and heroines (Caesar and Cleopatra in *Giulio Cesare in Egitto*), compensating them through their apotheosis (**Claudio Monteverdi**'s *Orfeo*), reuniting estranged couples (**Wolfgang Amadeus Mozart**'s *Così fan tutte*, 1790), or reconciling adversaries through clemency or reasoned negotiation (Mozart's *La clemenza di Tito*, 1791).

The *lieto fine* became a keystone of the didactic, moralizing agenda of **Arcadian opera seria** by rewarding wisdom, charity, justice, and virtuous, reasoned acts and by promoting social stability and aristocratic rule. In the process it glorified aristocrats by analogy, reinforced the congratulatory mood of their festivities (for example, *Il pomo d'oro*), and turned potential tragedy into escapist entertainment. Following the French Revolution and the Congress of Vienna, Enlightened optimism gave way to a more pessimistic, **romantic** vision of the human condition and a more cathartic aesthetic, which were embodied in often violent, tragic endings.

LIGETI, GYÖRGY. (1923, Diciosânmartin, Romania–2006, Vienna.) Prominent **composer** of one complete opera, as well as experimental theater pieces and other vocal and instrumental music. **Conservatory** trained in Kolozsvár, Romania, and Budapest during the 1940s, and having begun his career as a disciple of **Béla Bartók**, Ligeti fled Hungary during the revolution of 1956 and relocated in Cologne and **Vienna**, where he joined the musical avant-garde and became one of their leading exponents.

Ligeti's *Le Grand Macabre* (premiered 1978) is a surrealist exposé of life and death set in a fictional kingdom modeled on the paintings of Peter Bruegel the Elder and populated by a menagerie of bizarre characters that includes a satanic prophet of doom (the Grand Macabre) and his drunken sidekick, young lovers (originally dubbed Spermando and Clitoria) who copulate in a tomb, and a cross-dressing astrologer and his dominatrix wife. The score includes an **overture** for automobile horns and offers distorted parodies of the music of **Claudio Monteverdi** and Ludwig van Beethoven (1770–1827) and beer hall dances. Ligeti began, but left incomplete, operas on the Oedipus myth (1971–72) and William Shakespeare's *The Tempest*.

LIND, JENNY. (1820, Stockholm–1887, Wynds Point, England.) **Coloratura soprano** nicknamed the "Swedish Nightingale." Noted for her upper range, which reached high g''', Lind was arguably the most famous singer outside of Italy in the 19th century. Trained in Stockholm, she debuted at age 18 as Agathe in *Der Freischütz*. Her voice already frayed by 1841, she relearned her technique with the noted teacher Manuel Garcia (1805–1906) in **Paris**, allowing her to return to the stage after a yearlong hiatus.

During the 1840s, Lind toured extensively in Sweden, Germany (at times with Felix Mendelssohn, 1809–1847), Austria, and England—where she debuted for Queen Victoria and Prince Albert—building her career on such roles as Alice in **Giacomo Meyerbeer**'s *Robert le diable* (1831), **Vincenzo Bellini**'s **Norma** and Amina in *La sonnambula* (1831), and Marie in **Gaetano Donizetti**'s *La fille du régiment* (1840). Following her retirement from opera in 1849—and at Phineas Taylor Barnum's invitation—she sang in 93 cities in the United States in 1850, then continued to perform in concerts and oratorios in Europe until her last appearance in 1883. She finished her career as a philanthropist and a professor of singing at **London**'s Royal College of Music.

LITERATUROPER. Modern term for an opera that uses the (normally) abridged text of a preexisting book or play as its **libretto**. Aleksandr Sergeyevich Dargomïzhsky's (1813–1869) *The Stone Guest* (1872), a setting almost verbatim of Alexander Sergeyevich Pushkin's play (1830), is probably the earliest *Literaturoper*. Other familiar examples are **Pietro Mascagni**'s *Guglielmo Ratcliff* (1895), which limits itself to four scenes from Andrea Maffei's translation of Heinrich Heine's play *Wilhelm Ratcliff* (1822), and **Claude Debussy**'s *Pelléas et Mélisande* (1902), an abridgement of Maurice Maeterlinck's play (1892).

See also CATEGORIES OF OPERA; *SALOME*; *YEVGENY ONEGIN*.

LONDON. British capital, the locus of operatic development in England during the 17th and 18th centuries and a world-class center for operatic performance from the 18th century to the present day.

Royal patronage of musical theater in England was curtailed after the second English Civil War, which had been incited partly by the extravagance of the **masque** under Charles I, and which led to abolition of the monarchy, Charles's execution, and the establishment of the Commonwealth (beginning 1649). As a result, opera in England began primarily as a public, commercial enterprise managed by **impresarios** or aristocratic coalitions and operated at private expense, though often under government regulation. In the 17th century, several rival companies, often short-lived, periodically performed masques and semi-operas as an enrichment of their normal repertories of spoken plays and plays with music.

Following the Restoration of the monarchy (beginning 1660) under Charles II, the **librettist** and manager William Davenant (1606–1668) converted an indoor tennis court into the Lincoln's Inn Fields Theater (the Duke's Theater, active 1661–74 and 1695–1705, torn down and rebuilt 1714, closed for opera 1734), the first English playhouse having a proscenium arch and movable **sets**. He inaugurated it with a remake of his *The Siege of Rhodes*, the first true opera in England (music by several composers on Davenant's **libretto**, originally performed in an aristocratic palace in 1656, music lost). The King's Company built the rival Royal Theater in 1663, rebuilt after it burned (1672) as the Drury Lane Theater (1674; torn down 1791 and rebuilt 1794; burned 1809 and rebuilt 1812; still active). Davenant's Duke's Company moved to a new theater, Dorset Garden (1671, closed 1709), capable of spectacular effects, where all-sung operas and semi-operas were given occasionally, including **Luis Grabu**'s *Albion and Albanius* (1685), the first surviving English opera, and later, under the United Company (a merger of the Duke's and King's Companies in 1682), **Henry Purcell**'s *King Arthur* (1691) and *The Fairy Queen* (1692). The Patent Company under Christopher Rich (1657–1714) became active at Dorset Garden and Drury Lane (1695–1701) performing semi-operas including Purcell's *The Indian Queen* (1695). In response, Thomas Betterton (1635–1710, previously co-manager of the Duke's Company beginning 1668 and manager of the United Company) reopened the Lincoln's Inn Fields (1695) for masques.

This instability was exacerbated by the introduction of Italian opera to London in the early 18th century. The architect and manager John Vanbrugh (1664–1726) designed and built the Queen's Theater (after 1714 the first King's Theater) in the Haymarket (opened 1705, modified 1709, burned 1789). An order of the Lord Chamberlain (1707) restricting spoken plays to Rich at Drury Lane and opera to Vanbrugh at the Haymarket allowed Vanbrugh to attempt the first entire **season** of opera in early 1708, which fielded translated **pasticcios** performed by **castratos** who were unable to sing capably in English. A disaster, it resulted in Vanbrugh's bankruptcy and succession by the Irish impresario Owen Swiney (1676–1754), whose company switched to Italian in 1710.

Italian opera written for England and sung in Italian by Italian singers began in 1711 with **George Frideric Handel**'s *Rinaldo* and experienced mixed success, while Rich continued to offer semi-operas and all-sung operas in English at Lincoln's Inn Fields and masques as afterpieces to plays at Drury Lane. Lavishly staged Italian opera featuring star singers became a centerpiece of London culture with the establishment of the Royal Academy (1719–29), bankrolled primarily by aristocratic shareholders with modest royal support and led by Handel and the Swiss impresario John Jacob Heidegger (1666–1749), who had succeeded Swiney at the Haymarket in 1713. Handel and Heidegger's company was restructured as the Second Academy (1729–34), which saw competition from the Opera of the Nobility beginning in 1733 at Lincoln's Inn Fields. Dislodged from the Haymarket by their rivals after their contract expired, Handel and Heidegger moved in 1734 to the recently built Covent Garden Theater (opened 1732 by Rich; burned and rebuilt 1808–09; remodeled as the Royal Italian Opera, 1847; burned and rebuilt 1856–58; renamed the Royal Opera House, 1892; extensively remodeled 1996–2000 and still active). Both companies failed in 1737, merging at the King's Theater and failing again in 1738, at which point Handel shifted his focus from opera to oratorio.

Adding to the complementary problems of excessive expenditures by both companies for star singers like **Senesino** and **Farinelli** coupled with insufficient demand, the advent of **ballad opera**, spearheaded by John Gay's (1685–1732) *The Beggar's Opera* at Lincoln's Inn Fields drew attention back to English opera in the 1730s. After 1740 the King's Theater turned increasingly to pasticcios and comic opera and **ballet**, laboring through operatic performances of declining quality. Efforts by Drury Lane and Covent Garden eventually culminated in a resurgence of opera sung in English in the 1760s, beginning with **Thomas Augustine Arne**'s *Artaxerxes* (1762), an adaptation of a **Pietro Metastasio opera seria** libretto, as well as original comic operas and pasticcios.

In 1778 the owners of Covent Garden and Drury Lane bought the King's Theater and remodeled it (1782) to no avail. It burned down in 1789 (the fire set deliberately) and was rebuilt and enlarged 1790–91 as the second King's Theater (opened 1791; burned and rebuilt 1867–68; remodeled 1877; demolished and rebuilt as the current Her Majesty's Theater, opened 1897, no longer specializing in opera). They enlisted **Joseph Haydn**, who wrote one opera for it, *L'anima del filosofo* (1791, possibly incomplete), which was never staged. A second consortium that set up at the Pantheon Theater, a grandiose multipurpose hall remodeled for opera, with the intention of staging opera seria subsidized with **opera buffa**, attempted unsuccessfully to hire **Wolfgang Amadeus Mozart** in rivalry with Haydn. They put on one financially disastrous season (1790–91), and the theater burned down shortly into the second, probably victim to arson.

Despite the elimination of competition from the Pantheon, the King's Theater in the Haymarket continued to struggle against English opera staged at Covent Garden and Drury Lane. It turned in the 19th century increasingly to Italian repertory operas, notably those of Mozart and **Gioachino Rossini**, **Vincenzo Bellini**, and **Gaetano Donizetti**, and German and French works by **Carl Maria von Weber**, **Giacomo Meyerbeer**, and others, and to ballet in the 1830s and 1840s. Covent Garden also began to cultivate imported opera, leading to the establishment of the Royal Italian Opera in 1847, which eventually surpassed the Haymarket as the preeminent foreign opera house. At both theaters, non-Italian works were translated into Italian, except in productions by international touring companies, until the 1890s, when performances in the original languages began at Covent Garden and its company was renamed the Royal Opera.

During the early 19th century, Drury Lane continued its allegiance to English works or English-language adaptations of foreign ones. Various other efforts in the 19th century to promote native British opera had limited impact: the Lyceum Theater (opened for opera 1809; remodeled as the English Opera House, 1816; burned 1830 and reopened nearby as the Theatre Royal Lyceum and English Opera House, 1834, for spoken and sung works; remodeled 1904; closed 1986; restored 1996 and still active); the Royal English Opera (1858–64); the Carl Rosa Opera Company at the Princess's Theater (1875–1960); and the stillborn Grand National Opera House (1875, superseded at its site by the current Scotland Yard). The most vigorous native musical theater was the Savoy (opened 1881, remodeled 1929, burned and rebuilt 1993, still active) and its D'Oyly Carte Opera Company promoting the **operettas** of **William Schwenck Gilbert and Arthur Sullivan**.

Covent Garden has survived into the 21st century as the home of the Royal Opera (founded in 1946 as the Covent Garden Opera Company), led by such esteemed musical directors as Karl Rankl (1946–51), Rafael Kubelík (1955–58), Georg Solti (1961–71), and Colin Davis (1971–86). One of the world's premier venues for opera, it and other theaters in and within striking distance of London contributed mightily to the English "musical renaissance" of the 20th century by hosting numerous premiers of major works: at Covent Garden, **Ralph Vaughan Williams**'s *The Pilgrim's Progress* (1951), **William Walton**'s *Troilus and Cressida* (1954), **Benjamin Britten**'s *Billy Budd* (1951) and *Gloriana* (1953), **Michael Tippett**'s *The Midsummer Marriage* (1955), *King Priam* (1962), *The Knot Garden* (1970), and *The Ice Break* (1977), and **Harrison Birtwistle**'s *Gawain* (1991); the Royal College of Music, Ralph Vaughan Williams's *Hugh the Drover, or Love in the Stocks* (1924), *Sir John in Love* (1929), and *Riders to the Sea* (1937); Sadler's Wells Theater, Britten's *Peter Grimes*; the Coliseum Theater, Birtwistle's *The Mask of Orpheus* (1986); Queen Elizabeth Hall, Birtwistle's *Yan Tan Tethera* (1986); the Glyndebourne **Festival**, Britten's *The Rape of Lucretia* (1946) and *Albert Herring* (1947) and Birtwistle's *The Second Mrs. Kong* (1994); and the Aldeburg Festival, Britten's *Death in Venice* (1973) and Birtwistle's *Punch and Judy* (1968).

LUCIA DI LAMMERMOOR. *Dramma tragico*; music by **Gaetano Donizetti**, **libretto** by Salvadore Cammarano (1801–1852) based on Sir Walter Scott's (1771–1832) novel *The Bride of Lammermoor* (1819); three acts; **Naples**, Teatro San Carlo, September 1835.

Donizetti and Cammarano's choice of subject matter reflects the trend in early 19th-century Italy toward adoption of northern **romantic** sources instead of Greek mythology or Roman history, Scott's novel having already been tapped for three previous librettos. *Lucia* quickly gained a foothold in Italy, leading Donizetti to create a translated version with numerous adjustments of the score for **Paris** (1839), and within a decade was heard extensively in France, England, and the United States. Far from Donizetti's most radical opera, it nonetheless held the tightest grip on the 19th-century repertory and the romantic imagination, its prominence demonstrated by a pivotal appearance in Gustave Flaubert's novel *Madame Bovary* (1857). Its mad **scene** became a showcase for **coloratura sopranos** such as **Maria Callas**, and it remains one of Donizetti's most frequently performed operas.

Set in 17th-century Scotland during the reign of William and Mary, *Lucia* trades on the shopworn **sentimental** theme of marriage for love versus financial or social advantage, but intensifies the traditional love triangle (*see NORMA*) by introducing more idiosyncratic relationships (Enrico and Lucia), Gothic backdrops (Edgardo's ruined castle and its cemetery), and lurid violence. Lucia loves Edgardo of Ravenswood, longtime enemy of her brother Enrico of Lammermoor, who is depending on her arranged marriage to Lord Arturo Bucklaw for financial security. Before Edgardo departs for France to assist the exiled James II, he and Lucia take private marriage vows and exchange rings. However, during his absence, Enrico and his henchman Normanno intercept his letters and counterfeit a new one that deceives her into believing that Edgardo has betrayed her. Browbeaten by her brother, Lucia signs a marriage contract with Arturo just as Edgardo returns, interrupting the wedding, cursing her, and trampling her ring. Unable to cope, Lucia kills Arturo in their bedroom, appearing before revelers in her blood-soaked nightgown for her mad scene, and Edgardo later stabs himself after hearing that she has died.

Lucia anticipates works of the next decades in its concise presentation of the action through frugal distribution of set pieces—Edgardo's **aria finale** in Act 3 is his first major solo—and compression of individual movements within the standard forms. Frequent *racconti* (*see* STAGE SONG) make short work of narrative background, for example the chorus reporting Edgardo's presence during the *tempo di mezzo* of Enrico's cavatina, Lucia's ominous account of her ancestor's murder in the slow movement of her own cavatina (both Act 1), and the minister Raimondo's report of Arturo's demise ("Dalle stanze ove Lucia," Act 3).

In line with tendencies to rein in **bel canto** vocal pyrotechnics, Donizetti mostly abandoned coloratura, generally relying on currently fashionable syllabic melody, which confines ornaments to rhythmic hiccups at the ends of phrases. Yet by combining *canto declamato* (*see* SINGING STYLE) with judiciously deployed vocalization, Donizetti created two of the most emotionally taxing and cathartic scenes of the second quarter of the century, Lucia's mad scene ("Il dolce suono") and Edgardo's suicide (both Act 3). And *Lucia*, of course, boasts a wealth of ingratiating melody, including "Verranno a te sull'aure," the slow **cabaletta** of Lucia and Edgardo's love **duet** (Act 1), and "Chi me frena," the showstopping *largo concertato* of the Act 2 finale. Some of Donizetti's most innovative experiments in orchestration—the harp prelude to Lucia's cavatina and the flute (originally glass harmonica) solo introducing her mad scene; the cello solo that exchanges phrases with Edgardo in his breathless repeat of the cabaletta "Tu che a Dio" after he stabs himself during the transition—join his melodies in creating the atmosphere of bleak foreboding suggested by Scott's novel. And Enrico's manipulation of Lucia in their Act 2 duet demonstrates Donizetti's capacity for representing nuanced psychological interplay that anticipates **Giuseppe Verdi** (e.g., Germont and Violetta in *La traviata*, 1853, or Amonasro and Aida in *Aida*).

LULLY, JEAN-BAPTISTE. (1632, Florence–1687, Paris.) Italian-born French **composer** of 15 operas during the 1670s and 1680s, as well as numerous **ballets** and other theatrical works, and other vocal and instrumental music; violinist. With the **librettist Philippe Quinault**, Lully originated the genre of *tragédie en musique*.

Son of a prosperous miller, Lully appears to have taken guitar and violin lessons with local Franciscan friars. Then, for unknown reasons, he was chosen to travel to **Paris** as a page to teach Italian to one of Louis XIV's cousins (1646–52). In Paris he studied violin, and probably composition, keyboard, and dance, with various artists, became a violin virtuoso, and had the opportunity to attend the most important production of Italian opera in France to date, Luigi Rossi's (ca. 1597–1653) *Orfeo* (1647). He met the young king when dancing with him in the *Ballet royal de la nuit* (1653), leading to a series of court positions: composer of instrumental music (1653), which involved writing ballets, including entrées inserted between scenes of Italian operas given at court; leader of the Petits Violons (1655), a counterpart to Louis XIV's 24 Violons, to which Lully brought a military style of discipline that impressed the king; superintendent of the king's chamber music (1661), which led him to take French citizenship; and music master to the royal family (1662). Beginning in 1664, he collaborated with Molière on a series of *comédies-ballets*, which combined dances and songs with spoken comedy, most notably *Le bourgeois gentilhomme* (1670).

Although Lully had claimed that opera was unsuited to the French language when Pierre Perrin (ca. 1620–1675) was granted exclusive rights to produce French opera (1669), he maneuvered to have the monopoly transferred to him in 1672 when Perrin was in debtors' prison. Having gained exclusive rights to produce any all-sung dramatic work involving more than two singers and six instrumentalists anywhere in France, he established the Académie Royale de Musique (the Opéra) in Paris and made it a central social institution. **Productions** were to occur consecutively at the royal court (Saint Germain-en-Laye, Fountainebleau, or Versailles) and in Paris for a broader public at the theater of the Palais Royal, where Lully used the facility and shared **sets**, costumes, and machinery from court productions at no cost.

Lully collaborated in this venture with the librettist Philippe Quinault, with whom had already written two ballets, beginning with the pastorale (*see* PASTORALISM) *Les fêtes de l'Amour et de Bacchus* (1672), then produced about an opera per year until his death, exerting obsessive control over all aspects of production and demanding the highest standards of performance. Beginning with their second opera, *Cadmus et Hermione* (1673), Lully and Quinault combined elements of ballet, *comédie-ballet*, spoken tragedy, and theatrical special effects to establish the new type of *tragédie en musique*. Lully wrote 13 *tragédies* in total, the majority based on Ovid's *Metamorphoses*. Eleven with Quinault include **Alceste, ou Le triomphe d'Alcide** (after Euripides' *Alcestis*), now considered his most representative contribution to the genre; *Thésée* (1675); *Atys* (1676, after Ovid's *Fasti*); *Proserpine* (1680); and *Armide* (1686, after Torquato Tasso's *Gerusalemme liberata*). He also teamed with Thomas Corneille (1625–1709, younger brother of the more famous Pierre) when Quinault was in disfavor at court in 1678–79 (*Psyché*, 1678, and *Bellérophon*, 1679). Lully's last completed opera was the heroic pastorale *Acis et Galatée* (1686). An immensely successful and wealthy entrepreneur, Lully bought the office of secrétaire du roi, and the aristocratic title that came with it, in 1681.

LUTE. Plucked gut-string instrument having a half-teardrop-shaped body, fretted fingerboard, and tuning pegbox angled back from its neck. A standard six-course lute (six single or double strings) was typically tuned in fourths beginning on low G or A with a third between the middle strings. The lute was introduced to Europe from the Middle East through Spain during the Middle Ages. After 1500 it was plucked with the fingers (as opposed to a plectrum), allowing more varied chords and counterpoint to be played, and was used to perform both solo music and accompaniments. During the first half of the 17th century, the lute rather than the **harpsichord** was the primary **basso continuo** instrument in opera and other secular music. Two types of large lutes—the theorbo (alternatively termed *chitarrone* ca. 1580 to 1650) and the archlute—having as many as eight additional unstopped bass strings, which were tuned using a separate pegbox in diatonic steps within the octave from G' to G, emerged primarily for this task. Lutes participated in some basso continuo consorts into the 18th century.

LYRIC PROTOTYPE. Modern term for "song form" melodies in mid-19th-century Italian opera. Melodies in this style set eight lines of lyric poetry (*see* VERSIFICATION) to four four-measure (or eight-measure) musical phrases, two or three of which may be similar: A (lines 1–2), A' (lines 3–4), B (lines 5–6), and A" or C (lines 7–8). A familiar example is the Duke's "Questa o quella" (***Rigoletto***, Act 1). The lyric prototype came into use as early as the **cabalettas** of **Gioachino Rossini**'s late operas, replacing more complicated, multisection melodies, and was popularized in **Vincenzo Bellini**'s cabalettas and (later) slow movements, hence the term "Bellinian lyric form." This schema could be stretched or compressed to fit different numbers of lines by adding or subtracting musical phrases, lengthening or shortening them, or joining an incomplete melody (often in minor mode) to a second one in major (e.g., Violetta's "Ah fors'è lui," **Giuseppe Verdi**, *La traviata*, 1853, Act 1).

M

MADRIGAL. Italian (or English ca. 1600) sophisticated secular art song. Its poetry consists of a single stanza that emphasizes eleven-syllable lines, often in irregular alternation with seven-syllable lines. It is distinguished from **recitative** poetry (*versi di selva* in the early 17th century; *see* VERSIFICA-TION) by its more patterned rhymes, and from *canzonetta* poetry by its looser meter, absence of multiple stanzas, and more elevated content. In the mid-16th century the madrigal developed as polyphonic, a cappella music characterized by vivid madrigalisms (word painting). Continuo madrigals—solo (or more rarely **duet**) madrigals having **basso continuo** accompaniment—evolved in the late 16th century as a type of **monody**. They developed from arrangements of a cappella madrigals in which the top voice was sung while the lower parts were adapted for the **lute** and eventually simplified even further as a figured bass. Madrigalisms are less characteristic of the continuo madrigal than the a cappella madrigal. In its music, the continuo madrigal is distinguished from the *canzonetta* by its more fluid, flexibly phrased, and expressive melody, which may at times resemble narrative or expressive recitative, frequent chromatic harmonies, and lavish, often virtuosic **ornamentation** and passagework. In early opera, the madrigal represents the opposite end of the spectrum of lyric styles from the popular tunefulness of the *canzonetta*. **Claudio Monteverdi**'s *Orfeo* incorporates the madrigal idiom in monologues ("Possente spirto," Act 3), duets ("Chi ne consola"), and **choruses** ("Ahi, caso acerbo," both Act 2).

MALIBRAN, MARIA. (1808, Paris–1836, Manchester.) French-born mezzo-**soprano** of Spanish descent, sister of **Pauline Viardot**. One of the most famous singers of the 19th century, Malibran gained cult status after her premature death at 28.

Malibran was trained by her father, Manuel García (1775–1832), a notable **composer** and tenor who had created roles in such operas as *Il barbiere di Siviglia*. She began her career in **London**, debuting at age 17 (1825) as Rosina in *Il barbiere* as a stand-in for **Giuditta Pasta** and also singing in **Giacomo Meyerbeer**'s *Il crociato in Egitto* (originally 1824). She appeared later that year in **New York** with her father's touring company in operas by **Gioachino Rossini** and **Wolfgang Amadeus Mozart** beginning with *Il barbiere*, the first opera performed in Italian in the United States. She sang mainly in **Paris** and London between 1828 and 1832, when she relocated to Italy, where she performed in revivals of operas by **Vincenzo Bellini**, Ludwig van Beethoven (1770–1827), **Giovanni Pacini**, and others, including *I Capuleti e i Montecchi* (the **travesty** part Romeo), *La sonnambula*, *Norma*, and *Fidelio*. In creating the title role of **Gaetano Donizetti**'s *Maria Stuarda* (1835), she notoriously ignored changes imposed by **censors** in Milan.

Malibran was famed for her prodigious range from g below middle c to high e '", agility, and power. Having ended an ill-conceived May-December marriage to the middle-aged Eugène Malibran, a banker who subsequently lost his wealth and needed to be supported by her singing, she died after falling off a horse while pregnant by her second husband and refusing to rest and recuperate.

MALIPIERO, GIAN FRANCESCO. (1882, Venice–1973, Treviso.) Italian **composer** of instrumental music and about three dozen operatic works (mostly from the 1910s through the 1960s), **librettist** for virtually all of his mature works, and musicologist who edited music of 16th- and 17th-century Italian composers, including the complete works of **Claudio Monteverdi** (1926–42). He was the most important Italian operatic innovator of the late 1910s and 1920s.

Malipiero received **conservatory** training in **Venice** and Bologna under Marco Enrico Bossi (1861–1925) and apprenticed with the blind composer and **Richard Wagner** proponent Antonio Smareglia (1854–1929), from whom he learned orchestration. His first significant opera, *Sogno d'un tramonto d'autunno* (1913), a *Literaturoper* on an abridged play by Gabriele d'Annunzio (1863–1938), reflects his early interests in **Claude Debussy**, **Richard Strauss**, Paul Dukas (1865–1935), and **Igor Stravinsky**.

The period 1917–29 brought Malipiero's most radical involvement with avant-garde theater in a series of works that involved diverse experimentation with genre, form, length, narrative, cast, and musical style and premiered mostly outside conservative Italy. In *Pantea* (composed 1917–19, premiered 1932), a mute dancer is beset by hallucinations and the specter of death to the accompaniment of an offstage vocalizing **chorus** and baritone (*see* BASS) soloist. *Sette canzoni* (1920) consists of seven miniature operas unrelated in their stories, each centering on a single song but otherwise mimed, totaling three-quarters of an hour. *Tre commedie goldoniane* (composed 1919–22, premiered 1926) recombines characters from several **Carlo Goldoni** plays (many of them mute) who stage cartoonishly accelerated action and allude to traditional **opera buffa** devices like *recitativo secco* (*see* RECITATIVE) in a distinctively Venetian setting. The modal contrapuntal style of *San Francesco d'Assisi* (composed 1920–21, staged 1949) reflects Malipiero's interest in early music.

In the 1930s, at the zenith of Benito Mussolini's dictatorship, Malipiero retreated into a more conservative, diatonic and lyrical style and attempted a reconciliation with the Fascists, for example, in his *Giulio Cesare* (1936, based on William Shakespeare's play), especially after *La favola del figlio cambiato* (1934) was banned in Germany and Italy (*see* CENSORSHIP). Following World War II, he readopted a more chromatic musical style and returned partly to adventurous experimentation, as in *Gli eroi di Bonaventura*, a miniaturist pastiche of scenes from his earlier operas, and *Il marescalco* (both 1969).

MANELLI, FRANCESCO. (After 1595, Tivoli–1667, Parma.) Italian singer, **composer**, poet, and **impresario**. Manelli, who trained as a church singer and apprenticed with the Roman opera composer Stefano Landi (1587–1639), was employed throughout his career as a **bass** (notably at St. Mark's in **Venice** beginning 1638) and choirmaster. In the 1630s he followed his wife, herself a singer, to northern Italy, where they were involved in writing, producing, and performing early operas at Padua (1636), Bologna (1640), Parma (after 1645), and most importantly Venice. There, with the **librettist** Benedetto Ferrari (after 1603–1681), Manelli wrote, produced, and he and Maddalena sang multiple roles in *Andromeda* (1637). Staged, according to Ferrari, without aristocratic financial support and dependant on ticket sales to cover expenses, *Andromeda* was the first public commercial opera, inaugurating the new industry in Venice.

MARIANI, ANGELO. (1821, Ravenna–1873, Genoa.) Italian virtuoso **conductor**, violinist, and **composer**. Trained as a violinist, Mariani began his career as a provincial bandmaster (1842) near his hometown. In the 1840s he studied composition briefly in Bologna (1844) and supported himself as a journeyman orchestral string player, teacher, and, increasingly, music director and conductor, appearing in far-flung cities that included **Naples**, Milan (where he was censured by the Austrian authorities for a purportedly seditious reading of *Nabucco* in 1847), Copenhagen (where he turned down the position of director of the Danish royal chapel), and Constantinople. His unique artistry was recognized by **Gioachino Rossini**, **Giacomo Meyerbeer**, **Saverio Mercadante**, and **Giuseppe Verdi**.

Mariani settled in Genoa (1852) as resident conductor of the Teatro Carlo Fenice, while making regular appearances at Bologna. Possibly as early as the premier of Verdi's *Aroldo* in Rimini (1857)—at least during its virtuosic *burrasca* (storm, Act 4)—Mariani apparently had begun directing from a podium with a baton, instead of from his seat as first violinist, becoming the first prominent Italian opera conductor. He began a professional and personal relationship with Verdi while preparing *Aroldo*, at a time when the composer came to regard the conductor as an equal partner in crafting the artistic vision of an operatic **production**. Their friendship ended in 1871 after Verdi engaged another conductor for the premier of *Aida* in Cairo. In the 1860s Mariani popularized Meyerbeer's *grands opéras* in Italy and in his last years played a central role in introducing **Richard Wagner**'s works to Italy, conducting the Italian premiers of *Lohengrin* (originally 1850) and *Tannhäuser* in Bologna (1871 and 1872, respectively).

MARSCHNER, HEINRICH. (1795, Zittau–1861, Hanover.) German **composer** of about 20 operas in various genres from the 1810s through the 1850s, as well as incidental music for plays, **ballets**, solo and choral lieder, and instrumental music; he was the most prominent composer of German **romantic** opera between **Carl Maria von Weber** and **Richard Wagner**.

Marschner studied composition in Prague with the Bohemian composer Václav Tomášek (1774–1850) beginning in 1813. Subsequently in Leipzig he ignored the legal studies endorsed by his father in favor of socializing with musicians and music critics, and he met Ludwig van Beethoven (1770–1827) in Vienna (1815). Marschner held positions in Dresden (as Weber's assistant, 1823–26); Danzig (as music director, 1826); and Hanover (as court music director, 1831–59). His first produced opera, *Der Kiffhaeuser Berg* (1816), in which the absence of the heroine's father as a result of a dwarf's potion complicates her wedding plans, already manifests his lifelong commitment to northern romantic themes.

Marschner attempted a number of genres from **opera seria** to German approximations of historical *grand opéra*. But his reputation rests on his romantic **singspiels**, principally three works created in quick succession around 1830: *Der Vampyr* (1828), a successor to Weber's *Der Freischütz* in which the Scottish vampire must sacrifice three virgins to remain on earth; *Der Templer und die Jüdin* (1829), based indirectly on Sir Walter Scott's *Ivanhoe*; and *Hans Heiling* (1833), in which the king of subterranean gnomes is rejected by his beautiful human bride-to-be. Marschner's singspiels move in the direction of *Der fliegende Holländer* in his fusion of set pieces into **scene** complexes (on the example of *Der Freischütz*), development of conflicted protagonists, enlargement of the **orchestra** (particularly in the low registers), and intensification of melodic and harmonic chromaticism.

MASCAGNI, PIETRO. (1863, Livorno–1945, Rome.) Italian **composer** of 17 operas and **operettas** (mostly from the 1890s through the 1910s) and **conductor**. He began the vogue of **verismo** opera with *Cavalleria rusticana*.

Compositions written in his teens earned Mascagni aristocratic backing to attend the Milan **Conservatory** (1882–85), where he trained under **Amilcare Ponchielli** and boarded with **Giacomo Puccini**. After traveling for a year conducting operettas, he settled in Cerignola with his new bride (1886) and worked as a teacher. Mascagni won the second Sonzogno competition in 1888 with his masterpiece, the inaugural verismo opera *Cavalleria rusticana*, which premiered in Rome in 1890 and swept Europe and the United States.

Mascagni spent the remainder of his career attempting both to trade on and to emancipate himself from this success, reinventing his persona numerous times and demonstrating his prodigious versatility in such works as the *commedia lirica L'amico Fritz* (1891); two tragic *Literaturopern*, *Guglielmo Ratcliff* (begun 1883, premiered 1895) and *Parisina* (1913); the orientalizing *melodramma Iris* (1898; a precursor to Puccini's *Madama Butterfly*, 1904), which, like *L'Amico Fritz*, is still performed in Italy; the medieval Lady Godiva legend *Isabeau* (1911); the **sentimental** lyric opera (*see* OPÉRA LYRIQUE) *Lodoletta* (1917); and the late verismo opera *Il piccolo Marat* (1921). Beginning in the 1890s, Mascagni also established himself as a conductor of world repute. After he replaced **Arturo Toscanini** at La Scala (1929), he became a favorite of the Fascists, who bankrolled the production of his final opera, the political allegory *Nerone* (1935).

MASQUE. An English court masque was a set of descriptive dances on an allegorical or mythological subject performed mainly by aristocrats to celebrate a state event such as a wedding or birthday. It originated during the first half of the 16th century at the court of Henry VIII in social dancing organized around an allegorical pretext. The masque became a more formalized art form during the reign of James I (1603–25), best represented by collaborations among the poet Ben Johnson (1572–1637), poet-**composer** Thomas Campion (1567–1620), and architect–stage designer Inigo Jones (1573–1652). Masques became increasingly extravagant during the next quarter century under Charles I, probably contributing to Puritan opposition and the English Civil War, after which the masque retreated into less ostentatious **productions** known as school masques, "moral representations," and "private entertainments."

Early masques often used songs to introduce the dances. *Cupid and Death* (1653)—text by James Shirley (1596–1666), music by Christopher Gibbons (1615–1676) and Matthew Locke (ca. 1622–1677)—extended experiments in the 1630s directed at including even more continuous vocal music. This process led to the famous all-sung masques *Venus and Adonis* (ca. 1683) by John Blow (1649–1708) and **Henry Purcell**'s *Dido and Aeneas*, which constitute the native English operas of the late 17th century.

Two other important English genres are related to the masque. The anti-masque, a comic or grotesque dance depicting disreputable characters, animals, or witches and other supernatural beings, was performed within a masque near its end by professional dancers, providing the obvious prototype for the witches' scenes in *Dido and Aeneas*. The play-with-masque or semi-opera—a spoken play interrupted by masques involving song, dance, instrumental music, and special effects—is exemplified by Purcell's ***The Fairy Queen*** (1692), which provides masques for an adaptation of William Shakespeare's *A Midsummer Night's Dream*. Semi-opera was also cultivated in Spain by the playwright Pedro Calderón de la Barca (1600–1681) and the composer **Juan Hidalgo**.

MASSENET, JULES. (1842, Montaud–1912, Paris.) **Composer** of some three dozen operas representing each of the French genres from the 1860s until his death, as well as **ballets**, incidental music, and other instrumental and vocal music. Massenet was the most prominent French opera composer during the last quarter of the 19th century after **Charles Gounod**'s decline and **Georges Bizet**'s death.

Pursuing a standard line of development that began with early piano lessons from his mother, Massenet trained at the **Paris** Conservatoire (1852–62) in piano and in composition with **Ambroise Thomas**. Playing timpani at the Théâtre Lyrique acquainted him with the works of Gounod and other French contemporaries, as well as those of **Christoph Willibald Gluck** and other classical masters. He won the Prix de Rome in 1863.

After his return to Paris in 1866 he enjoyed a stable, prestigious, and extremely productive career, supported by Thomas and the publisher Georges Hartmann, in which he succeeded in all types of music. Thomas encouraged the Opéra-Comique to commission Massenet's first staged opera, *La grand'tante* (1867), after which, over the next decade, he built a reputation as a composer of orchestral, piano, and vocal music. Three well-received operas beginning in 1872 led to the ***grand opéra Le roi de Lahore*** (1877), a Parisian and international success that was particularly influential in Italy. An exotic opera set in India, it exploited—as Massenet would continue to do—the late 19th-century vogue for oriental subjects, depicting a love triangle that violates Hindu codes and the death, reward in paradise, reincarnation, and second death of its king.

Massenet's success led to his appointment as composition professor at the Conservatoire (1878–96) and to frequent operatic productions, a number of them familiar to modern listeners. His Salomé opera *Hérodiade* (1881), performed in Brussels after the Paris Opéra turned it down on moral and aesthetic grounds, is a spectacular work very different from **Richard Strauss**'s ***Salome***. Replete with crowd scenes in the manner of *grand opéra*, its heroine, who truly loves John the Baptist, kills herself after her stepfather executes him. The **opéra comique** *Manon* (1884), a second international success on the same subject as **Daniel-François-Esprit Auber**'s and **Giacomo Puccini**'s *Manon Lescaut* operas (1856 and 1893, respectively), adopts a more personal style of tragedy akin to *opéra lyrique*. It and the first Parisian performance of *Hérodiade* at the Théâtre Italien that same year were followed closely by *Le Cid* (1885), an epic *grand opéra* in which a medieval Spanish knight kills his beloved's father in a duel over his own father's honor.

Werther, though not an immediate triumph, is now considered Massenet's operatic masterpiece, a skillful adaptation of Johann Wolfgang von Goethe's novel similar to *Manon* in its domestic realism and psychological intimacy. *Esclarmonde* (1889) was written for Massenet's current infatuation, the American **soprano** Sibyl Sanderson (1865–1903), while awaiting production of *Werther*. Deemed Massenet's most **Wagnerian** score owing to its subject matter—a Byzantine heroine with magic powers is won at a joust by her beloved—it returns to *grand opéra* with spectacular medieval effects. Massenet also wrote the lyric comedy *Thaïs*, a paradigm of fin-de-siècle decadence and sensuality, for Sanderson, who played a redeemed courtesan. The last of Massenet's works still to be revived with any frequency, it appeared during the tremendously productive year of 1894, which also saw premiers of two other operas.

Massenet's style strikes nuanced compromises between the historical pageantry, massed crowd scenes, noisy orchestration and **choruses**, and lavish stagings of *grand opéra*, and the sensationalistic situations and personal intimacy of *opéra lyrique* and opéra comique. As well as any of his contemporaries, he pandered to late 19th-century Parisian taste for the exotic and for salaciousness and violence balanced against religious moralizing and individual redemption. And like Gounod, he embraced the expressive resources of Italianate lyricism in a French context, deploying the full range of late 19th-century harmonic effects—from diatonic functional progressions to whole-tone scales and Debussian parallel 9th chords—as well as orchestration enhanced by the selective introduction of extra brass, winds, percussion, organ, and even saxophone on occasion, to enrich his melodies and project a distinctive sense of place.

IL MATRIMONIO SEGRETO. *Melodramma giocoso* (*see* OPERA BUFFA); music by **Domenico Cimarosa**, **libretto** by Giovanni Bertati (1735–ca. 1815) based on George Colman the Elder (1732–1794) and **David Garrick**'s *The Clandestine Marriage* (1766), itself influenced by etchings of William Hogarth's *Marriage à la mode*, and on two earlier **opéras comiques**; two acts; premiered **Vienna**, Burgtheater, February 1792.

The Secret Marriage is said to have concluded the golden age of late 18th-century **opera buffa**, sharing the summit with **Giovanni Paisiello**'s *Il barbiere di Siviglia* and **Wolfgang Amadeus Mozart**'s late comedies (*see* CATEGORIES OF OPERA). Exceptionally successful at its premier, it was privately encored the same night for Leopold II after a cast dinner at his palace. More popular in Vienna than any of Mozart's operas, it conquered Europe in a matter of months, and it holds the rare distinction among 18th-century non-Mozartian opere buffe of revival in the 20th century.

Matrimonio segreto is a **sentimental opera** that simultaneously endorses conjugal love and lampoons social climbing, arranged marriages, and the aristocracy. Paolino has secretly married Carolina and has matched her older and less attractive sister, Elisetta, with Count Robinson, hoping that Carolina's father, Geronimo, will thus accept his younger daughter's marriage to a commoner. The situation is complicated by Geronimo's sister, Fidalma, who fancies Paolino, and by the count's attraction to Carolina. Following a failed elopement, Paolino and Carolina confess, the count agrees to marry Elisetta, and Geronimo blesses the headstrong couple. Amidst these amorous complications, Bertati lampoons such easy targets as Geronimo's deafness, catfights between the sisters, and the count's self-importance. In the late 18th-century manner, the action proceeds in frequent episodic **duets** and **ensembles** enlivened by comic *parlante*, *nota e parola*, and **patter song**.

MAYR, SIMON. (1763, Mendorf–1845, Bergamo.) German-born **composer** of almost 70 Italian operas, mostly from the mid-1790s to ca. 1820, and sacred music; teacher and music theorist. His operas constitute an important link between 18th-century **opera seria** and 19th-century Rossinian *melodramma*, and he contributed to the development of *opera semiseria* and *farsa*.

An accomplished pianist and composer at a young age, Mayr nonetheless received a traditional general education that led him to begin legal and theological training in nearby Ingolstadt while continuing to study music. Influential patrons took him first to Bergamo (1789) and then to **Venice**, where he was exposed to a spectrum of vocal and instrumental music and was encouraged by **Niccolò Piccinni** and the fellow German composer Peter Winter (1754–1825) to compose operas. His second, *La Lodoiska* (1796), vaulted him to the highest rank among Italian composers and, along with other early works, established a relationship with Venice and the north that resulted in at least 30 operas for that city over the course of his career, as well as more than a dozen for Milan and other regional centers. Operas for **Rome** and **Naples** came later in his career, among them the *melodramma Medea in Corinto* (1813), perhaps his most influential work, famous as the earliest opera for Italy to use obbligato **recitative** exclusively throughout.

Mayr devoted himself to the city of Bergamo, in 1805 helping to found a free school of music where he was the director and professor of music theory and composition, writing numerous treatises for his students, and where **Gaetano Donizetti** studied for a number of years. He also established a charity for impoverished musicians and their families and an academy for the performance of Italian and Viennese music. His loyalty to Bergamo and distaste for artistic politics and intrigue caused him to refuse numerous lucrative positions in larger, more prominent cities such as St. Petersburg, **Paris**, **London**, Dresden, and Bologna.

Mayr's works constitute one of the most important connections between **Christoph Willibald Gluck** and **Gioachino Rossini**. Adhering to Gluck's agenda and his early Germanic training, his style features motivically oriented melodies and accompaniments; colorful, wind-infused orchestration; chromatic harmony and often abrupt modulations; expansive **choruses**; and atmospheric sinfonias (*see* OVERTURE) and other instrumental passages. Mayr also contributed to the early development of dramatically progressing multimovement **arias** and ensembles that prefigure Rossinian formal conventions.

MAZZOCCHI, VIRGILIO. (1597, Civita Castellana–1646, Civita Castellana.) Italian clergyman and **composer** of sacred music and four operatic works from the 1630s and 1640s. Mazzocchi moved to nearby **Rome** in the 1620s and entered the service of Cardinal Francesco Barberini, nephew of Pope Urban VIII, ca. 1625. With Francesco's support he rose quickly through ecclesiastical ranks to the post of *maestro di cappella* at St. Peter's Basilica (1629), where he spent the remainder of his career composing music for the Church and for Barberini theatrical productions on **librettos** by **Giulio Rospigliosi**.

Mazzocchi is best known for the *commedia musicale* based on Boccaccio, *Chi soffre speri* (*He Who Suffers May Hope*, originally *L'Egisto*, 1637), which was mounted in 1639 with *intermedi* by Marco Marazzoli (after 1602–1662). A moral allegory in which a poor aristocrat courts a rich widow by making sacrifices that ultimately restore his wealth and the health of her sickly son, more than half of its **scenes** include servants modeled on **commedia dell'arte** characters who converse in dialect. Their antics, the realistic contemporary scenario, and the absence of chorus, mythological characters, and machinery for special effects make *Chi soffre speri* the earliest prominent comic opera (*see* CATEGORIES OF OPERA) to survive. Mazzocchi also wrote three Christian allegories for large casts of boys (e.g., *La Genoinda, ovvero L'innocenza difesa*, 1641) that exemplify the sacred drama cultivated more broadly by Rospigliosi.

MÉHUL, ÉTIENNE-NICOLAS. (1763, Givet–1817, Paris.) French **composer** of more than 30 operas from the 1790s through the mid-1810s, as well as other vocal and instrumental music. Along with **Luigi Cherubini** and **Gaspare Spontini**, Méhul was one of the foremost Parisian composers during the Revolutionary and Napoleonic eras in the generation following **André-Ernest-Modeste Grétry**.

Méhul moved to **Paris** ca. 1778, where he studied keyboard instruments and composition privately and cultivated associations with Parisian musical society while earning a living as a teacher and organist. He started writing operas with *Cora* (begun 1785), which premiered unsuccessfully at the Opéra in 1791 following numerous delays, and *Euphrosine, ou Le tyran corrigé* (1790), his first staged opera, which began a decade-long collaboration with the **librettist** François Benoît Hoffman (1760–1828).

Alongside Cherubini, Méhul led the development of French serious opera with spoken dialogue (*see* OPÉRA COMIQUE) written primarily for the Opéra-Comique, departing in his *drames lyriques* and similar works from the good-natured *comédies mêlée d'ariettes*. Similar in their melodramatic plots to Italian *opera semiseria*, many of these operas center on destructive love triangles that are eventually resolved, often through benevolent action: the *comédie héroïque Stratonice* (1792), in which the hero loves his father's fiancée; the *drame lyrique Mélidore et Phrosine* (1794), in which the heroine's brother is the (incestuous) rival; and the chivalric drama *Ariodant* (1799), considered Méhul's best and most inventive work from this period. Although his popularity waned in Paris after the turn of the century as audiences again turned to lighter fare, he continued to produce significant operas in his serious manner. Most successful among these were the **romantic** opéra *Uthal* (1806), after James Macpherson's Ossianic power struggle between the title character and his royal father-in-law, who is supported by the mythic hero Fingal. The biblical *drame mêlé de chants Joseph* (1807), which initially exploited the Egyptomania that followed Napoleon's conquest of North Africa and the post-Revolutionary religious revival, remained admired through the 19th century and is the composer's most enduring success.

In these works, Méhul and his librettists integrated the texts of musical numbers (*see* NUMBER OPERA) into the plot and consequently gave music an essential role in dramatic exposition. Adhering to French tradition, he prioritized effective delivery of the text over melody and enlisted all elements of music for expressive purposes, including startling dissonance, innovative orchestration involving unaccustomed instruments (harp and serpent) and focusing on the middle register—famously omitting violins in *Uthal*—and structural cohesion through dramatically relevant thematic reminiscences and arrangements of keys. Action flows freely through extended ensembles and **scene** complexes studded with **choruses**.

Though Méhul flirted with public censure in *Le jeune Henri* (1797), viewed by detractors as unpatriotic in its depiction of Henry IV—and by analogy Louis XVI—as a courageous virtuous youth, he remained a darling of the Revolutionary and Napoleonic governments owing to his contribution of numerous patriotic songs and choruses and Revolutionary festival music. His prestigious government awards and honors included membership in the newly formed Légion d'Honneur (1804) and a prize from Napoleon for *Joseph* as the best production at the Opéra-Comique during the first decade of the 19th century. And he wrote music including the opera *Les troubadours, ou La fête au château* (not performed) for Napoleon's wedding to Marie-Louise of Austria in 1810.

MELANI, ATTO. (1626, Pistoia–1714, Paris.) **Contralto castrato** singer and **composer**, one of the premier virtuosos of the mid-17th century. In the service of Prince Mattias de' Medici of Siena, Melani went to **Rome** (1644) to train with the opera composer Luigi Rossi (ca. 1597–1653), then to the royal court in **Paris**, where he performed in early productions of imported Italian operas, for example Rossi's *Orfeo* (1647) and **Francesco Cavalli's** *Xerxes* (1660). He also served as a clandestine diplomatic emissary and was deported following an embezzlement scandal involving the minister of finance in 1661. Melani entered the service of the clergyman-**librettist** Cardinal **Giulio Rospigliosi** in Rome as a Catholic political operative for almost two decades, then returned to France in 1679.

MELODRAMA. Style of text setting in which a spoken monologue or dialogue is accompanied by the **orchestra**, which creates atmosphere or provides emotional reinforcement or commentary (in contrast to *melodramma*). Also a play employing this approach extensively. Operatic genres that include speech, such as **opéra comique** and **singspiel**, allow for this technique.

Jean-Jacques Rousseau (1712–1778) is often credited with inventing *mélodrame* in his *scène lyrique Pygmalion* (composed ca. 1762, first performed 1770), although at least one previous example exists, and various combinations of speech and music probably date much earlier. Familiar melodramas occur in the dungeon scene of Ludwig van Beethoven's (1770–1827) *Fidelio* (1805) and the Wolf's Glen scene of *Der Freischütz* (1821); **Wolfgang Amadeus Mozart** included extended melodramas in the singspiel *Zaide* (1780). Numerous adaptations occur in 20th-century opera, for example in **Alban Berg's** *Wozzeck* and *Lulu* (composed 1929–35).

MELODRAMMA. Term used nowadays as a generic designation for 19th-century tragic opera emphasizing overwrought emotional relationships, straightforward plotting, and cathartic deaths of protagonists, in contrast to

18th-century heroic **opera seria** featuring elevated reflection, convoluted intrigues, and moralizing happy endings. In the 19th century, *melodramma* literally meant "musical drama" in designating the **librettos** of comic operas (**Gioachino Rossini**'s *melodramma giocoso La pietra del paragone*, 1812) as well as semiserious (his *melodramma La gazza ladra*, 1817) and serious works (his *melodramma eroico Tancredi*, 1813, and *melodramma tragico Semiramide*, 1823). For serious operas it occurs interchangeably throughout the 19th century with such other terms as the traditional *dramma* and the increasingly prevalent *dramma lirico, tragedia lirica,* and *opera.* Compare, for example, **Giuseppe Verdi**'s *melodramma* **Rigoletto**, his *dramma Il trovatore* (1853), *opera La traviata* (1853), *dramma lirico* **Otello**, and **Vincenzo Bellini**'s *tragedia lirica* **Norma**.

MENOTTI, GIAN CARLO. (1911, Cadegliano–2007, Monte Carlo.) Italian-born American **composer** and **librettist**, and extraordinarily productive opera specialist (more than two dozen stage works from the mid-1930s through the mid-1990s), a rarity in the 20th century. Like Aaron Copland (1900–1990) and **Leonard Bernstein**, Menotti was an avowed popularizer. He brought classical art music to a broad audience and helped raise the artistic ambitions of the Broadway musical by adapting highbrow opera for the general public and merging it with musical theater.

Menotti started his training at the Milan **Conservatory** at age 13, then four years later entered the Curtis Institute in Philadelphia. There he began a lifelong companionship with fellow student Samuel Barber (1910–1981). His first opera, the comedy *Amelia al ballo*, premiered in Philadelphia as *Amelia Goes to the Ball* (1937) and was performed within a week in **New York** so successfully that the Metropolitan Opera scheduled it the following year.

Menotti waited out World War II in the United States with Barber, from 1943 at their 40-year home "Capricorn" in Mount Kisco, New York. The postwar years brought his greatest acclaim. His fifth opera, the macabre tragedy *The Medium* (1945), was filmed in 1951 (directed by Menotti and conducted by Thomas Schippers, 1930–1977). Sent on tour in 1955 by the U.S. State Department along with his comedy *The Telephone* (1946), it became his first international success. Menotti created *The Consul* (1950), his most telling drama about a family seeking political asylum, from materials developed for Metro-Goldwyn-Mayer. The Hollywood studio had hired the versatile composer—he wrote his own **librettos**—to do film scripts, none of which were produced. *The Consul* received the Pulitzer Prize and the Drama Critics' Circle Award and was translated into a dozen languages for performances in 20 countries. It and his next two operas, *Amahl and the Night Visitors* (1951), the first opera written specifically for television, and *The*

Saint of Bleeker Street (1954), which won a second Pulitzer, a Drama Critics' Circle Award for best play, and a New York Music Critics' Circle Award for best opera, are said to represent the peak of Menotti's output.

Menotti founded the original Italian branch of the Spoleto **Festival** of the Two Worlds in 1958, its American cousin in South Carolina following in 1977. From the 1950s through the 1980s he continued his cultivation of new populist operatic genres begun with the television opera *Amahl* and the radio opera *The Old Maid and the Thief* (1939). He created the unique madrigal fable *The Unicorn, the Gorgon, and the Manticore* (1956) and numerous children's operas, beginning with *Martin's Lie* (1964) and *Help, Help, the Globolinks!* (1968). In 1984, Menotti received a Kennedy Center Honor for lifetime achievement in the arts.

MERCADANTE, SAVERIO. (1795, Altamura–1870, Naples.) Italian **composer** of more than 60 operas—mostly from 1820 through the 1840s—and of sacred and instrumental music; **conductor** and teacher. For brief periods in the mid-1820s and late 1830s, Mercadante was considered to be the leading Italian composer. As a Neapolitan **conservatory** director beginning in the 1840s, he led the revival of Italian instrumental music.

The son of an aristocrat and his maid, Mercadante was adopted by his father, who moved to **Naples** in 1806, where Mercadante received conservatory training in violin, flute, voice, counterpoint, and composition from, among others, Niccolò Zingarelli (1752–1837); directed the conservatory **orchestra**; and wrote a flute concerto that is still played. With the conservatory system in decline in the early 1800s, following his graduation in 1817 he was considered the best prospect for a Neapolitan revival. Known initially as an orchestra director and composer of instrumental music, Mercadante soon turned to opera with *L'apoteosi d'Ercole* (1819), an allegory of the Bourbon restoration and an anticipated return of Naples to musical preeminence.

Mercadante's status declined after his support of the Carbonari revolution (1820–21), which forced him to focus on productions in northern Italy such as the ***opera semiseria*** *Elisa e Claudio* (1821), its plot reminiscent of **Domenico Cimarosa**'s *Il matrimonio segreto*, and the tragic ***melodramma*** *Amleto* (1822), both for Milan. He secured the position of house composer for the San Carlo theater (1823) as no better than the third choice of the **impresario Domenico Barbaia**, who hired Mercadante planning to promote him as the next **Gioachino Rossini** but replaced him with **Giovanni Pacini** after three years when the latter's career took off.

Following this setback, Mercadante reassessed his style, as he would several times; found inspiration in Rossini's progressive Neapolitan scores; and wrote the psychologically nuanced revolutionary allegory *Caritea, regina di Spagna* (1826), a success largely because the lead resists foreign aggression (and learns to love). He spent 1826 to 1831 primarily in Madrid, Lisbon, and

Cádiz as music director of their opera houses, studying and producing **Vincenzo Bellini**'s operas, continuing to modernize his own style in a handful of new works, and raising his stock back in Italy, where he emerged again as a leading composer with *Gabriella di Vergy* (1832). Exposure to French opera in **Paris** (1835–36)—in particular **Giacomo Meyerbeer**'s *Les Huguenots*, the premier of which eclipsed that of his own *I briganti* (1836)—led to another stylistic reorientation that resulted in his masterpiece *Il giuramento* (1837), which tells the same story as **Amilcare Ponchielli**'s later *La Gioconda* (1876). Setting the tone for his other operas of this period (including *Elena da Feltre* and *Il bravo* of 1839 and *La vestale* of 1840)—and anticipating **Giuseppe Verdi** in certain respects—*Il giuramento* minimizes **bel canto coloratura** and provides more dramatic musical expression of its text, including **cabalettas** that replace virtuosic passagework with dramatic declamation. Its better-individuated characters participate in a forward-looking linear plot. And it shows more thoughtful and flexible treatment of set piece forms, enlarges the active movements of individual set pieces, emphasizes dramatically active ensembles and choruses, and expands the expressive role of orchestration. Mercadante also insisted that the production respect the artistic integrity of the notated score.

The success of *La vestale* won Mercadante an offer from Rossini in Bologna that he used to leverage directorship of the Naples Conservatory (beating out **Gaetano Donizetti**). There he positioned himself again as championing the revival of the Neapolitan school, this time through development of instrumental music influenced by French and German composers and promotion of a pedagogy suited to the modern style of dramatic singing (*see* SINGING STYLE). He also served as music director at the San Carlo Theater (beginning 1844). Although *Leonora* (1844) and *Orazi e Curiazi* (1846) were late successes, Mercadante's theatrical output slowed considerably at this point and ended after several premiers fell flat in the early 1850s, leading him to concentrate instead on instrumental, sacred, and occasional music.

METASTASIO, PIETRO. (1698, Rome–1782, Vienna.) Poet, philosopher, second-generation member of the **Arcadian Academy**, and the most esteemed Italian **librettist** in the history of opera. He is best known for 27 **opera seria librettos** (most written from the mid-1720s through the mid-1740s) and other works that were set dozens of times each by legions of composers—sometimes in several versions by the same individual—progressively modified to suit later tastes. **Niccolò Jommelli**, for example, composed four versions of Metastasio's *Demofoonte* and *Ezio*. They were also read and performed as plays and circulated widely in dozens of printed editions.

Born Pietro Trapassi, his early supporters included Cardinal Pietro Ottoboni (1667–1740), founding patron of the Arcadian Academy, and Gian Vincenzo Gravina (1664–1718), another founder of the academy, who adopted the boy, provided for his education, changed his name to the Greek equivalent, and left him a rich inheritance when he died in 1718. During the 1720s, Metastasio premiered half a dozen operas (and many other works), beginning with *Didone abbandonata*, set in 1724 by Domenico Sarro (1679–1744). Boasting music by such Neapolitan luminaries as Leonardo Vinci (1696–1730) and Nicola Porpora (1686–1768), they triumphed in the operatic meccas of **Naples**, **Venice**, and **Rome**, securing the young poet's reputation.

Marianna Pignatelli, lady-in-waiting to the Viennese empress, admired Metastasio's libretto for her brother's wedding opera and joined **Apostolo Zeno** (yet another Arcadian) in recommending him as imperial Italian court poet in **Vienna** when Zeno resigned to return to Venice in 1729. The first decade of Metastasio's imperial appointment was the apex of his productivity and artistic dominance, when his emblematic Arcadian style reigned over heroic Italian opera. He wrote 11 opera seria librettos during this decade, most appearing first with music by the court composer **Antonio Caldara**, in addition to seven oratorios and numerous lyric poems. These included four of his most frequently set plays: *Demetrio* (1731), *L'olimpiade* (1733), *Demofoonte* (1733), and *La clemenza di Tito* (1734, adaptation set by **Wolfgang Amadeus Mozart** in 1791). Following the death of Emperor Charles VI (1740), Metastasio retained his position and his veneration at the court and across Europe. But in Vienna fashion shifted from the Italian opera seria on which he had built his career toward French theater—both spoken plays and opera—and **opera buffa** and **singspiel** after Joseph II became emperor in 1765. Consequently the bulk of his remaining major works premiered outside the imperial capital. Metastasio's last libretto, *Il Ruggiero, ovvero L'eroica grattitudine* (1771), was set by **Johann Adolf Hasse** for Milan.

Metastasio's opera seria librettos championed the classical, ethical ideals of the Arcadian Academy and the psychological theories of René Descartes. He directed them toward moving the emotions, conveying pleasure, and promoting morality over immorality, reason over passion, and political stability over reform. Serving these goals, they juxtapose the real-time actions of idealized historical or mythological heroes and heroines in **recitatives** against timeless, universalizing commentary in arias that feature eloquent metaphors and other turns of phrase. Such didactic **arias** and the *lieto fine*, which rewards the just and the rightfully entitled, are indispensible elements of this moralizing art form.

Like his fellow Arcadians, Metastasio valued the classical simplicity, clarity, conciseness, elegance, and subtle emotional nuance of language modeled in more recent times by Francesco Petrarch, Torquato Tasso, Giovanni Battista Guarini, and others. He also promoted clarity and simplicity through structural conventions. Standardized aria texts in two stanzas serve the prevailing da capo aria. The conventionalized small **scene**, defined by the complement of characters onstage, consists at minimum of a recitative dialogue followed in many cases by a concluding exit aria or, more rarely, preceded by an entrance aria. Such small scenes tend to combine in much larger dramatic trajectories. Extended scenes defined by a fixed locale begin with a series of dialogue recitatives and occasional entrance arias that bring characters onstage, then proceed to exit arias that gradually eliminate characters until no one is left and the scene concludes. At the ends of acts, these accretion-attrition scenes may finish with **duets** or very rarely more populous ensembles or **choruses**. Metastasio also contributed to establishing rules for distributing singers' workloads—proportional numbers of arias, duets, and obbligato recitative monologues—among roles of different stature.

Despite Metastasio's increasing marginalization at the Viennese court, he remained an icon to whom composers and performers paid homage, and versions of his operas continued to appear frequently as late as the 1830s. Even such a reformer as **Christoph Willibald Gluck** cut his teeth setting Metastasio's librettos. And Gluck's collaborator **Ranieri Calzabigi** had edited Metastasio's plays and defended him against his critics before coming to Vienna.

MEYERBEER, GIACOMO. (1791, Vogelsdorf–1864, Paris.) German-born **composer** of 16 German, Italian, and French operas from the 1810s through the 1860s, and pianist. Meyerbeer is known principally for four French *grands opéras* on **librettos** by **Eugène Scribe**, which were performed hundreds of times in **Paris** and across Europe during the 19th century, setting the standard for the genre.

Son of a wealthy industrialist, Meyerbeer was educated in the liberal arts by private tutors and trained in music by Georg Joseph (Abbé) Vogler (1749–1814) among others. Famous initially (by age 11) as a piano prodigy, he turned to composition in his twenties. Following favorable reviews of an oratorio in 1811, he wrote his first opera, *Jephtas Gelübde* (1812), on a biblical subject, which was produced in Munich at Vogler's recommendation.

Better to familiarize himself with current operatic trends, he journeyed to Paris (1814–15) and to Italy (1816), where, after acquainting himself with **Gioachino Rossini**'s operas in particular, he set three plays by the ubiquitous Gaetano Rossi (1774–1855), one of Rossini's **librettists**. Their efforts culminated in the *melodramma* eroico *Emma di Resburgo* (1819), a major Venetian success that established him as Rossini's most serious rival. Its acclaim was surpassed the following year by *Margherita d'Anjou* (libretto by **Felice Romani**, 1820) and subsequently by *Il crociato in Egitto* (1824), the last important opera having a **castrato** role. Praised for effectively merging Italian lyricism with German intensity, it positioned Meyerbeer briefly as the preeminent composer in Italy immediately following Rossini's departure in 1823.

By this point Meyerbeer's operas were performed widely throughout Italy and north of the Alps, bringing him international attention. Courted by the Paris Opéra since 1823, his introduction to the French capital occurred in 1825 through productions of *Il crociato* (organized by Rossini at the Théâtre Italien) and *Margherita*. Meyerbeer's historic collaboration with Scribe, one of the most famous literary figures of the 19th century, and with the Opéra began with *Robert le diable* (1831), originally intended for the Opéra-Comique. It was based tangentially on a medieval Norman chivalric legend in which Robert's evil companion—eventually revealed to be his father—tries to claim his soul by offering him a magic branch to help him seduce his beloved. *Robert* resonated with contemporary Parisian taste, represented by the current popularity of English Gothic novels, **Carl Maria von Weber's** *Der Freischütz*, a recent translation of Johann Wolfgang von Goethe's *Faust*, Louis Daguerre's moody dioramas, and various similarly themed plays staged in boulevard theaters.

Regarded by some as a watershed in the history of art, *Robert* traveled across Europe, and instrumental arrangements of its greatest hits (including Fryderyk Chopin's duo for cello and piano, 1831) were widely distributed, making Meyerbeer's increasingly rare premiers into breathlessly awaited, pan-European phenomena. In 1832, he arranged with the Opéra for a second project with Scribe that would become *Les Huguenots*, in which the troubled affair of the Protestant Raoul and the Catholic Valentine unfolds against preliminaries to the slaughter of French Protestants in the St. Bartholomew's Day Massacre of 1572. After it triumphantly premiered in 1836, following contractual complications and **censorship** involving its religious subject matter, it became the most influential of Meyerbeer's operas.

New subjects immediately came his way, including two for librettos by Scribe. After drafting one act of *L'Africane*, based on Portuguese explorer Vasco da Gama's explorations of India, Meyerbeer turned to *Le prophète* in 1838, for which negotiations extended over the next decade owing to delays involving new management at the Opéra and casting issues. During this period, Meyerbeer replaced **Gaspare Spontini** as Prussian general music director in Berlin (1842), for which he conducted the court orchestra, supervised their concert schedule, and wrote a **singspiel** (*Ein Feldlager in Schlesien*, 1844). *Le prophète* finally premiered in Paris, 1849, with **Giuseppe Verdi** and numerous other luminaries present. Its subject, the 16th-century Dutch Anabaptist John of Leiden, leads an anti-aristocratic German uprising, disavowing his own mother in the process of becoming emperor, but ultimately is betrayed by his followers and killed when his palace explodes. Among other special effects, *Le prophète* featured an ice-skating scene simulated by roller-skaters and a dazzling sunrise created through the first theatrical use of an electric spotlight. Following the Revolutions of 1848, conservatives took comfort in the opera as a parable of the dangers of social disorder fed by fanatics.

Once *Le prophète* had taken off, Meyerbeer resumed work on *L'Africaine* (1865). As with other works, the road to completion was long, interrupted by, among other things, revision of *Feldlager* as the **opéra comique** *L'etoile du Nord* (1854). The score essentially completed by 1863, Meyerbeer fell ill during rehearsals, entrusting the final touches to his friend, the musicologist and composer François-Joseph Fétis (1784–1871), and died the next year. The most exotic and spectacular of Meyerbeer's *grands opéras*, it features a scene in an Inquisition prison, an Asian garden boasting a poisonous tree, and a shipwreck scene that required one of the first revolving stage sets.

With Scribe, Meyerbeer built on precedents set by **Daniel-François-Esprit Auber**'s *La muette de Portici* (1828) and Rossini's *Guillaume Tell* to create a model of *grand opéra* that would shape its development by Verdi, **Richard Wagner**, and various others across the second half of the 19th century. Better, perhaps, than any other team they managed to fulfill the diverse mandates of the genre by providing something for everyone, from historical grandeur, spectacle, and local color to emotional intimacy, and from heroic, popular, and atmospheric music to dramatically targeted **coloratura**.

MILHAUD, DARIUS. (1892, Marseilles–1974, Geneva.) French **composer** of 16 operatic works (half during the 1920s), **ballets**, incidental music for plays, and film and radio scores, as well as other vocal and instrumental music.

Milhaud took violin lessons as a boy and was composing music in his teens, becoming familiar with the folk songs of Provence from the women who worked in his father's almond business. He trained at the **Paris** Conservatoire (1909–15) with Paul Dukas (1865–1935), among others, and composed his first opera, the folksy *La brebis égarée* (*The Stray Sheep*, composed 1910–14, premiered 1923) as a student. Despite his continued appreciation for the music of **Claude Debussy,** he chose an alternative stylistic path: following a stint in Rio de Janeiro (1916–18) as secretary to the playwright Paul Claudel, for whom he had composed incidental music, Milhaud returned to Paris and joined the avant-garde circle of Erik Satie (1866–1925) and Les Six, seconding them in snubbing traditional art music and experimenting with polytonality (simultaneous layers of music in different keys), American jazz, percussion effects, and aleatoric techniques involving music left unspecified by the composer.

Milhaud's iconoclasm is demonstrated in three "Opéras-minutes" (1927–28) of about 10 minutes each: *L'enlèvement d'Europe*, *L'abandon d'Ariane*, and *La délivrance de Thésée*. *Les malheurs d'Orphée* (1926), the first of Milhaud's chamber operas, is a rustic domestication of the Orpheus legend, in which he and Eurydice are forced to flee their relatives, who oppose their marriage, she dies of illness, and Orpheus is killed by her three sisters after he returns home. His best-known opera, *Le pauvre matelot* (*The Poor Sailor*, 1927), is another miniature from this period, widely performed owing to its small cast, chamber orchestration (in the revised version), inexpensive sets and costumes, and appealingly melodious style. Its title character, returning from a long voyage, assumes a new identity so that he can surreptitiously observe his wife's fidelity. His plan backfires when he tells her that her spouse is imprisoned, leading her to kill him and steal his money to ransom her supposed "husband."

Other prominent operas by Milhaud include *Christophe Colomb* (1930), a nonlinear narrative of short flashback scenes from Columbus's life examined from different points of view and set with resources comparable to **grand opéra**, including four demanding solo roles, an enormous **chorus**, pit **orchestra** and offstage instrumental ensemble, and projected film images. One of Milhaud's late works, *La mère coupable* (*The Guilty Mother*, 1966), a comedy of manners based on the third play of Pierre-Augustin Beaumarchais's trilogy that includes *The Barber of Seville* and *The Marriage of Figaro*, unfortunately suffers from heavy-handed orchestration that covers the dialogue and consequently obscures the complex plot.

MINIMALISM. Postmodernist musical style developed in the 1960s and 1970s in the American counterculture hotbeds of Berkeley, California, and downtown **New York City** by Terry Riley (born 1935), La Monte Young (born 1935), Steve Reich (born 1936), and **Philip Glass**. Related to minimalism in the visual arts and influenced by rock, jazz, and non-Western musics, it rejects the rarified complexity of post–World War II serialist approaches (e.g., of Pierre Boulez, born 1925) and the indeterminacy of composers like John Cage (1912–1992) by adopting simplified musical materials to promote broader accessibility and audience appeal. Minimalism embraces versions of diatonic tonality; rhythmic regularity and a steady, energized pulse; and timbral experimentation using nontraditional treatments of customary instruments and voices, non-Western instruments, and various acoustic and electronic sound effects. Its highly simplified, abstract musical ideas are obsessively repeated, often in conjunction with gradual variation of those ideas (shortening or lengthening) and of their rhythmic and metrical interactions with one another ("phasing") in transparent layered textures that explore relationships between foreground and background musical events. Minimalist composers have been invested in integrating different types of music and different artistic media and therefore have been involved in various alternative forms of musical theater.

Among minimalist composers, Glass has produced distinctive full-scale operas that have found a level of commercial success despite their unconventionality, most prominently *Einstein on the Beach*. His anti-narrative, ritualistic creations evoke a spiritual, metaphysical environment in part by utilizing language as a nonreferential sound source, drawing on non-European dialects and nonsense syllables. The post-minimalist composer **John Adams** has adapted the musical style to more traditional, humanized storytelling in so-called CNN operas (*see* ZEITOPER) that take their stories from contemporary events, for example *Nixon in China*.

See also TAN DUN.

IL MITRIDATE EUPATORE. *Tragedia in musica*; music by **Alessandro Scarlatti**, **libretto** by Girolamo Frigimelica Roberti (1653–1732) based loosely on Aeschylus's account of the exploits of Mithridates VI, king of Pontus, as well as the *Electra* plays of Euripides and Sophocles; five acts; premiered **Venice**, Teatro San Giovanni Grisostomo, January 1707. Although it initially received a hostile reception from parochial Venetian critics, it influenced **George Frideric Handel** and is currently considered to be Scarlatti's masterpiece.

Mitridate Eupatore is an early adaptation of a frequent 18th-century operatic subject, various episodes of which served numerous operas, among them **Wolfgang Amadeus Mozart**'s *Mitridate, re di Ponto* (1770). By the standards of early 18th-century **opera seria**, it presents a particularly grisly drama of intrigue. Stratonica, Eupatore's mother, has murdered Eupatore's father and married Farnace, who now rules Pontus. To overthrow their rivals, Eupatore and his wife Issicratea (Hypsicrateia), pretending to be Egyptian ambassadors, offer the head of Eupatore to Stratonica and Farnace to finalize a treaty between Egypt and Pontus. When Farnace arrives to see the head, Eupatore kills him and presents Farnace's head to Stratonica. She is killed by Issicratea, clearing Eupatore's path to the throne.

MONIUSZKO, STANISLAW. (1819, Ubiel, near Minsk in present-day Belarus–1872, Warsaw.) Polish **composer** of some two dozen operas (mostly during the 1840s and 1850s), as well as other vocal and instrumental music. Moniuszko was the most successful Polish opera composer of the 19th century.

Member of an affluent family, Moniuszko began piano lessons with his mother before continuing his musical studies (1827–39) in Warsaw, back in Minsk near his hometown, and in Berlin. On his own at age 20, he pieced together a living teaching piano, playing the organ, and **conducting**, and wrote compositions that included his first staged opera *Nocleg w Apeninach* (*A Night in the Apennines*, 1839). Among Moniuszko's works of the 1840s, the light opera *Loteria* (*The Lottery*, 1843) and particularly the Polish **grand opéra** *Halka* (written 1846–47, first staged 1854, Vilnius) represent his best efforts. In *Halka*, after the title character, a peasant girl, is seduced and abandoned by a nobleman, she throws herself off a cliff during his wedding to her rival. Following its enlargement and **production** in Warsaw (1858), *Halka* became the most popular Polish opera, and Moniuszko was famous. An international tour led to his appointment as opera director at the Wielki Theater in Warsaw and productions of his remaining half dozen operas. **Censorship** following the January Uprising against Russian rule (1863–64) stifled theatrical opportunities in Warsaw and contributed to a downturn in Moniuszko's productivity for the remainder of his life.

MONODY. Term currently used for Italian solo song accompanied by **basso continuo** ca. 1600–40. In opera, it may apply to set pieces, such as **madrigals**, *canzonette*, and strophic variations (*see* ARIA), and to **recitatives**, and may denote either a piece of music (a madrigal may be a "monody") or its style of text setting (a "monodic" madrigal, for example). It is also used, where appropriate, for such early 17th-century nonoperatic genera as solo motets and cantatas. Monodies apparently originated in the 16th-century practice of arranging polyphonic a cappella music for solo voice with a **lute** accompaniment that simplified the counterpoint. Normally true monodies are distinguished from their antecedents because they further reduce the accompaniment to a figured bass. Florence was an early center of monody, and **Giulio Caccini**'s *Le nuove musiche* sparked the craze in the first decades of the 17th century. However, the fashion also developed in **Venice**, **Rome**, and elsewhere. Use of the term has broadened considerably since **Giovanni Battista Doni** equated "stylus monodicus" with the *stile recitativo* in 1640.

MONTEVERDI, CLAUDIO. (1567, Cremona–1643, Venice.) Italian **composer**, string player, and lutenist (*see* LUTE); a leading composer of **madrigals** and about a half dozen early operas, his *Orfeo* is regarded as the first operatic masterwork.

Monteverdi studied with Marc'Antonio Ingegneri (ca. 1535–1592), *maestro di cappella* of the Cremona cathedral, and showed extraordinary talent at an early age, publishing a volume of sacred music at 15. Ca. 1590 he was appointed as a violin and viol player at the court of Duke Vincenzo Gonzaga in Mantua as part of a general reinforcement of his court's musical forces. Vincenzo established a virtuoso vocal group in imitation of the famed *concerto delle donne*, a trio of **women** singers in Ferrara. They performed madrigals and other songs using dramatic facial and hand gestures and inflections of dynamics and tempo, the influence of which may be seen in some of Monteverdi's madrigals from the 1590s and which is one likely source for the intensity of his theatrical music. Although documentation is lacking, Monteverdi would have contributed to musical entertainments for numerous court festivities that took place in Mantua in the 1590s, including **ballets** and *intermedi*, another probable influence on his rich and diverse operatic style. His fourth and fifth books of published madrigals (1603 and 1605) demonstrate the experience gained from writing dramatic music for soloists with **basso continuo** accompaniment, including his development of nontraditional melodic contours and dissonance treatments that served emotional expression (*see* SECONDA PRATICA), a characteristic that brought him into conflict with the conservative theorist Giovanni Maria Artusi (ca. 1540–1613).

Having started near the bottom, Monteverdi's status in Mantua (and his reputation from Ferrara to as far away as Copenhagen) rose quickly. He led the three musicians accompanying Vincenzo on his campaign against the Turks (1595), during which he probably made the acquaintance of Giovanni de' Bardi (1534–1612, patron of the **Florentine Camerata**), and no doubt went with him to the Florentine wedding of Maria de' Medici (1600), where he would have heard **Jacopo Peri**'s *Euridice*. Ca. 1601 he was appointed court music director, in charge of the duke's weekly concerts and other secular music. Monteverdi's first opera, *Orfeo* (1607), on a **libretto** by the diplomat and poet-musician Alessandro Striggio (ca. 1573–1630), Monteverdi's protector in Mantua, likely ensued from court rivalry with Florence. Commissioned by the duke's son Francesco, it was staged for Carnival (*see* SEASON) and was subsequently deemed sufficiently important for publication in **Venice** in 1609.

Immediately following the death of his wife, Claudia, in 1607, Monteverdi began two dramatic works for Francesco's marriage in 1608, the opera *Arianna* (music lost except for Arianna's famous lament, which had a telling effect on its audience) and a ballet, and probably contributed to several *intermedi*. Complications caused by an accelerated timetable, the untimely death of the original lead singer from smallpox, and interference by the duchess brought Monteverdi to the point of a nervous breakdown, leading him to resign his position. After he was ordered back to Mantua and his contract renegotiated (1609), relations with the court continued to deteriorate. Owing to a combination of financial considerations, Monteverdi's recalcitrance, and intrigues by a rival musician, he was dismissed by Francesco after his father's death in 1612.

Monteverdi's luck changed in 1613 with the passing of the *maestro di cappella* of St. Mark's Basilica in Venice. By winning the premier position, which had been held by a series of Italy's great madrigal and church music composers, Monteverdi became one of the most powerful musicians in Italy.

It required him to write music for the church and provide sacred and secular compositions for civic events. Although the Venetian budget offered little support for theater music, he continued to receive numerous invitations from Mantua (several aborted), among them the completed operas *Andromeda* (1620, music lost) and *Armida* (1626, known only from letters). He also nurtured connections with the imperial court in **Vienna** during the 1620s and 1630s, and he provided music for the wedding of the Duke of Parma in 1628. The greatest support for Monteverdi's theater music in Venice in the 1620s came from the aristocratic patron Girolamo Mocenigo, an ardent champion of Monteverdi's music and of music in general. For Mocenigo, Monteverdi wrote the theatrical madrigal *Il combattimento di Tancredi e Clorinda* (1624 or 25), in which he inaugurated his *stile concitato* ("excited style"), and the *favola Proserpina rapita* for the wedding of Mocenigo's daughter (1630).

Monteverdi's activities are virtually uncharted during the 1630s, although we know that he became a priest in 1632 and corresponded with the theorist **Giovanni Battista Doni** about a projected treatise on the *seconda pratica*. No evidence exists that Monteverdi was involved with **Francesco Manelli**'s *Andromeda*, the first public opera, staged in Venice in 1637, though he must have been aware of it. For he was quick to take advantage of the new commercial opportunity, reviving *Arianna* for Venice in 1640 and bringing out three new operas in quick succession: *Il ritorno d'Ulisse in patria* (1640); *Le nozze d'Enea in Lavinia* (1641, music lost); and *L'incoronazione di Poppea* (1643, probably including some music not by Monteverdi). In these operas, written in his seventies, Monteverdi charted the course for the development of the **bel canto** style by midcentury composers such as **Francesco Cavalli** and **Antonio Cesti**.

MOZART, WOLFGANG AMADEUS. (1756, Salzburg–1791, Vienna.) Iconic late 18th-century composer, creator of 18 completed theatrical works (from 1767 until his death), which are distributed equally among the three central **categories** of **opera buffa** (five), **singspiel** (four), and **opera seria** (four), in which he was a consummate master, and other (mostly early) examples of subordinate genres (Latin **intermezzo**, *festa teatrale*/**serenata**, and incidental music), as well as instrumental and other vocal music.

Mozart's career played out in two main phases. During the first, his hometown, the archbishopric of Salzburg, served as a base for travels to the major musical centers of Europe. He served two prince-archbishops: Sigismund III, Count of Schrattenbach (1698–1771), a popular, generous patron of the arts who granted liberal leaves for the Mozart family to pursue their fortunes; and Count Hieronymus Colloredo (1732–1812), who succeeded him in 1772, a less popular ruler despite notable social reforms, who curtailed support for musical activities and demanded greater attention to duties at court. In the second phase of his career (beginning 1781), Mozart broke with Salzburg and earned a living as a freelance musician based in **Vienna**.

Mozart's father, Leopold (1719–1787), who would serve as vice Kapell-meister in Salzburg (beginning 1763), trained Wolfgang and his equally pre-cocious sister Maria Anna ("Nannerl") in music and general studies—Wolf-gang's earliest compositions date from 1761—and introduced the children to serenatas, plays with incidental music, and opere buffe performed by im-ported companies. The family's travels began with an unverified trip to Mu-nich (1762) and another to Vienna later that year, in which Wolfgang and Nannerl played the harpsichord for the Empress Maria Theresa and were invited to Versailles by the French ambassador. They followed up with a much more extended tour (1763–66), in which the family traveled northwest through Germany to Brussels and **Paris** (where the children entertained Louis XV and gave public concerts), to England (where they stayed for a year and performed for George III), east through Ghent and Antwerp to the Hague and Amsterdam, back to Paris (1766) and home through Switzerland.

A heady, formative experience for a child, the parade of concerts, theaters, composers, performers, and new scores that must have dazzled Wolfgang on these trips gave him both the command of musical fundamentals and contem-porary operatic style and the necessary confidence to launch his theater ca-reer the following year with the Latin intermezzo *Apollo et Hyacinthus*. Mozart composed his first two true operas during a second excursion to Vienna (1767–68) that was initially diverted because of a smallpox outbreak in which both children suffered mild cases. The much-sought Viennese pre-mier of his first opera buffa *La finta semplice* (*The Pretended Simpleton*, composed 1768) never left the ground and needed to be postponed and relo-cated to Salzburg (1769), reportedly because of court intrigues. However, his first operatic **production**, the singspiel *Bastien und Bastienne* (1768), prob-ably took place at the Vienna home of Dr. Franz Anton Mesmer, the notori-ous proponent of "animal magnetism" (mesmerism).

After spending most of 1769 in Salzburg, Leopold and Wolfgang headed to Italy, with the goal of establishing the teenager as an opera composer and raising his profile as a performer. Following performances at the home of the Austrian ambassador to Milan, Count Karl Firmian (early 1770), he received a commission for his first opera seria, *Mitridate, re di Ponto* (*Mithridates, King of Pontus*). The pair traveled south as far as **Naples**, and among other accomplishments Wolfgang was named Knight of the Golden Spur by the pope and inducted into the Accademia Filarmonica in Bologna. When they returned to Milan in October, *Mitridate* was composed and staged with great success (December 1770), receiving about two dozen performances. Widely noted in the German, Austrian, and Italian press, the tour gained the fledgling composer invaluable international notoriety, and he returned to Salzburg in

1771 with three additional commissions and plans to visit Italy twice more (1771 and 1772): the *festa teatrale Ascanio in Alba* (1771) for a ducal wedding in Milan, where it outshone a **Johann Adolf Hasse** opera written for the same occasion; the opera seria *Lucio Silla* (1772, also Milan), which had a respectable run despite a lackluster production; and an oratorio for Padua, which was not performed.

Following their return to Salzburg in 1773, Wolfgang and Leopold remained there more consistently through the end of the decade, to a large extent because the new archbishop demanded greater attentiveness from them. At the same time, Colloredo's cutback of public vocal and instrumental music, his tendency to support Italian composers rather than natives, and his general rudeness and lack of appreciation for the Mozarts, notwithstanding the family's rising social status and Wolfgang's growing fame and productivity, frustrated their hopes for advancement. So, except for several months spent in Vienna (1773) fruitlessly pursuing a reputed opening at the imperial court and a second brief absence for the Munich premier of the opera buffa *La finta giardiniera* (*The Pretended Gardeness*, 1775), they mostly fumed in Salzburg, where the serenata *Il re pastore* was performed for an archducal visit (*The Shepherd King*, 1775).

Friction with Colloredo predictably resulted in the temporary discharge of both Leopold and Wolfgang in 1777. The latter went with his mother in search of a suitable position to Munich, Augsburg, and Mannheim, where he was well received but failed to find employment. They eventually ventured as far afield as Paris (1778), where Wolfgang found himself at odds with French taste, and where his mother sickened and died. Leopold blamed him for the tragedy, contributing to the disintegration of their relationship. After a position opened up in Salzburg, he returned home with stops in cities including Mannheim, where he probably began an incomplete **melodrama**, *Semiramis* (1778). He began serving as court organist shortly after his arrival in 1779, but was dismissed in 1781 because of supposed lackluster performance and inattention to his duties.

After the triumphant premier of the opera seria **Idomeneo, re di Creta** in Munich (1781), Mozart joined Colloredo and his entourage in Vienna for the celebration of Joseph II's accession as sole ruler of Austria and the Holy Roman Empire. Friction over his servile treatment and unjustified restrictions of his opportunities to perform in Vienna, as well as indications that he might succeed there as an independent musician, led to his definitive dismissal from the archbishop's service. In the imperial capital he at first earned a living from lessons for a few aristocratic pupils (he later, 1786–88, mentored the rising prodigy Johann Nepomuk Hummel, 1778–1837), aristocratic gifts, and publications. He gave public and private concerts, establishing himself as the leading keyboardist in the city, and composed frequently for the Freemasons lodge he joined in 1784. *Die Entführung aus dem Serail* (*The Abduction* *from the Seraglio*, 1782) became the acclaimed centerpiece of Joseph's German National-Singspiel (1778–83). Commissioned originally for a state visit but postponed, it is an important early example of **rescue opera**, in which a Spanish nobleman attempts to save his fiancé, his servant, and her maid (who is the servant's girlfriend), who are being held captive by a benevolent Turkish pasha who eventually releases all of them.

Mozart seized the opportunity created by Joseph's decision to revive Italian opera at the court theater in 1783. Following two aborted attempts at opera buffa—*L'oca del Cairo* (*The Cairo Goose*, 1783) and *Lo sposo deluso* (*The Deluded Bridegroom*, probably 1783–84)—and the one-act singspiel *Der Schauspieldirektor* (1786, performed in the Orangery of the Imperial Schönbrunn summer palace)—he created his first two operas with the celebrated **librettist Lorenzo Da Ponte**, which assured his legacy. Accolades for the initial performances of *Le nozze di Figaro* (1786) compelled Joseph to limit encores, and the opera was even more successful in Prague, leading to the commission for *Don Giovanni* (1787). These two monuments won Mozart's appointment as court chamber music composer, a modest sinecure devised by Joseph to give him limited financial security and keep him from moving elsewhere.

The death of Mozart's father prior to the premier of *Don Giovanni*, uncertainty about how to capitalize on the fame of the Da Ponte operas, and a decline in musical patronage during the Austro-Turkish War (1787–91) likely contributed to a compositional hiatus in all genres for several years. Continuing his perpetual quest for a prestigious position and possibly as a hedge against his shaky finances, Mozart toured northern Germany (Leipzig, Dresden, and Berlin) in mid-1789, during which time he improvised on the organ at Johann Sebastian Bach's (1685–1750) Thomaskirche and pocketed a chamber music commission from King Friedrich Wilhelm II.

Mozart's career ended with a resurgence of operatic activity that included three major new works. The opera buffa *Così fan tutte, ossia La scuola degli amanti* (*They All Do It, or The School for Lovers*, 1790), his third opera with Da Ponte, on a **libretto** proposed originally to **Antonio Salieri**, followed on a successful revival of *Figaro* in 1789. It played to enthusiastic crowds but drew fire for its edgy themes involving sexual manipulation and a wager over the fidelity of women. The Masonic singspiel *Die Zauberflöte* is arguably the most ambitious representative of its type ever created. Mozart's final stage work, the opera seria *La clemenza di Tito* (1791), was taken on after Salieri declined the commission for the coronation of Joseph's brother and successor Leopold II in Prague as king of Bohemia. Its outmoded genre and remodeled libretto by **Pietro Metastasio** (originally 1734) conformed to Leopold's projected agenda of reviving opera seria, demonstrating through the drastic reduction in the number of **arias** and the addition of numerous ensembles its potential for modernization. And its parable of noble restraint, in which Titus forgives his would-be assassins after they confess to save one another, celebrates Leopold's allegedly Enlightened attitudes.

The most likely cause of Mozart's death was rheumatic fever. He was buried in a plain grave with few attending the ceremony, according to Viennese practice.

Mozart's operatic output is distinguished by its uniformly high quality beginning with his earliest works, which demonstrate mastery of the stylistic idioms of opera buffa, opera seria, and singspiel comparable to that of his established contemporaries. As he matured, Mozart's unique melodic fecundity, creative treatment of **orchestral** accompaniments, and command of such Germanic elements as vivid instrumental color, richly textured counterpoint, and harmonic vigor and nuance gave his music extraordinary emotional breadth and subtlety. From this variegated palette he brilliantly chose musical affect and topic (*see* DOCTRINE OF THE AFFECTIONS), as well as localized expressive gestures, to clarify dramatic circumstances while filling entire operas with memorable music.

In his opere buffe, Mozart enlisted this plenitude of resources to convey compelling characters, varied situations, and flexibly paced action illustrating the social, moral, and personal entanglements of everyday life. And it allowed him to press the trend away from traditional, emotionally uniform arias toward psychologically mobile, episodic arias and dynamic ensembles that convey rapidly paced mood shifts and progressing action. In this regard, his deployment of expressively significant orchestral motives to underpin both solo singing and flexibly phrased dialogue in *parlante* or *nota e parola* style made a significant contribution. Mozart's virtuosity is particularly evident in his **finales**, which set aside conventional static sections in favor of thematically variegated movements that combine multiple ensemble modules and convey rapid changes of mood, situation, and character relationships. Broad dramatic arcs are often energized using elements of instrumental forms (such as sonata form) and long-range tonal progressions. This dramatically responsive approach contributed to the creation of scenes of breathtaking length, complexity, and psychological insight—most notably in the Act 2 finale of *Le nozze di Figaro*—that invite audience immersion and serve the late 18th-century goals of naturalness, individuality, and humanity.

Although in his opere serie Mozart mainly embraced the conventional alternation of real-time action in **recitatives** with suspended-time reflection in arias, he enlivened the traditional categories of affect and topic through his extraordinary musical inventiveness and his deft manipulation of the arsenal of late 18th-century aria forms, from various adaptations of symmetrical da capo form to the open-ended two-movement *rondò*. His commitment to aligning vocal idiom and technique with the idiosyncrasies of his singers made his works particularly effective concert operas. And in his "reform" opera *Idomeneo*—and to a lesser extent in *La clemenza di Tito*—he effectively incorporated numerous progressive trends of late 18th-century opera seria to create one of the greatest works in that genre. Mozart's most successful singspiels *Die Entführung aus dem Serail* and *Die Zauberflöte* made invaluable contributions to the development of German opera as a rival to Italian and French imports and spearheaded its exportation to other countries, giving it an international presence. They also arguably legitimized German opera as an art form capable of surpassing mere entertainment to engage significant social, political, and philosophical issues in the same manner as opera buffa and opera seria.

MUSORGSKY, MODEST PETROVICH. (1839, Karevo–1881, St. Petersburg.) Russian **composer** of one complete opera, the masterpiece of Russian nationalism *Boris Godunov*, as well as other vocal and instrumental music; bureaucrat and military officer.

Raised on the estate owned by his affluent family, Musorgsky showed promise as a pianist under his mother's tutelage. Dispatched to St. Petersburg (1849) to prepare for a military career, he pursued his piano studies, became a member of Tsar Peter I's regimental guard (1856), began associating with the other members of The Five (the Kuchka or Mighty Handful), and studied composition with Mily Balakirev (1837–1910). Intent on a career as a composer, he resigned from the military (1858) but was forced to resume government service as a petty bureaucrat when his family lost their wealth after their serfs were emancipated in 1861.

Early in his career, Musorgsky set scenes from two operas (*Salammbô*, 1863–66, and *Zhenit'ba*/*The Marriage*, 1868), which reflect the influences of his fellow Russians Aleksandr Serov (1820–1871)—the plot of *Salammbô* resembles that of Serov's *Judith* (1863)—and particularly of Aleksandr Dargomïzhsky (1813–1869) in Musorgsky's experimentation with naturalistic declamation that imitates the inflections of human speech. Musorgsky set *Boris Godunov* twice (1868–72), first as a *Literaturoper* dominated by realist declamation and focusing almost entirely on the title character. After it was rejected (1871), he completely revised it using a more traditional mix of declamation and set pieces modeled on Russian folk music, a version that premiered at the Mariinsky Theater in 1874. Although the opera was well received, César Cui's (1835–1918) criticism of it contributed to the subsequent disbandment of The Five. Also in the 1870s, before his death related to alcoholism, Musorgsky composed sections of a collaborative opera-**ballet** with other members of The Five and two other operas, which were eventually completed by **Nikolay Andreyevich Rimsky-Korsakov** and Cui.

N

NABUCCO. *Dramma lirico*; music by **Giuseppe Verdi**, **libretto** by Temistocle Solera (1815–1878) based on Antonio Cortesi's (1796–1879) **ballet** (1838) and Auguste Anicet-Bourgeois (1806–1870) and Francis Cornu's play (1836); four parts; premiered Milan, Teatro alla Scala, March 1842.

Verdi's first major triumph and first work to define his individual style, *Nabucco* rejuvenated his nearly aborted opera career following the failure of the **opera buffa** *Un giorno di regno* (1840) two years earlier and personal tragedies. Its nostalgic Act 3 choral hymn "Va pensiero" sung by the displaced Israelites became one of Verdi's most famous melodies and (later) an iconic representation of his involvement with the Risorgimento. At the premier, Verdi's future second wife Giuseppina Strepponi (1815–1897) and the eminent baritone (*see* BASS) **Giorgio Ronconi** played Abigaille and Nabucco, respectively.

Derived from the biblical history of the Babylonian captivity, *Nabucco* may be viewed as an outgrowth of the epic operas of **Gaspare Spontini**, **Gioachino Rossini**, and others. However, it also exemplifies the transition from the static conflict and alliance operas of the 1820s and 1830s (*see* *NORMA*) to more linear ones in combining a love triangle with a progressing series of events that plays out in four episodes. The opera begins at the Temple of Solomon as the terrified Israelites await the onslaught by the invading Babylonian king Nabucco and his army. Ismaele, nephew of the Israelite king, loves the Babylonian hostage Fenena, daughter of Nabucco, whom he met while imprisoned previously in Babylon. He is also pursued by Nabucco's other (supposed) daughter and Fenena's rival Abigaille, who arrives ahead of the army and confronts the lovers before her father makes his victorious entrance and orders the temple destroyed. In Part 2, having returned to Babylon, Abigaille stages a coup after her sister frees the enslaved Israelites. Nabucco thwarts her power play momentarily but is struck by lightning and rendered insane after declaring himself God. In Part 3, Abigaille presses her advantage, tricking her incapacitated father into ordering her sister's execution, and destroys proof of her ignoble birth. Part 4 brings

Nabucco's redemption: repenting his hubris and desperate to wrest power from his daughter, he converts to Judaism, recovering his senses in time to reclaim the throne from Abigaille, who has poisoned herself.

Although *Nabucco* has been considered Verdi's most Rossinian opera, it incorporates numerous forward-looking features. It ignores the **unities of time, place, and action** by shifting locales from Jerusalem to Babylon. Verdi dispensed almost entirely with **coloratura** passagework and, alongside his prevalent syllabic lyrical idiom, incorporated numerous examples of psychologically incisive declamatory song, most notably in Nabucco's mad scene to end Act 2. The extensive workloads for the baritone Nabucco and bass high priest Zaccharia demonstrate the mid-19th-century inclination toward lower, more realistic male vocal ranges. And the distribution and structure of set pieces also mirrors current trends. The frugally apportioned three-movement **arias** for Zaccharia (Act 1), Abigaille (Act 2), and Nabucco (Act 4) are dispersed across the opera rather than front-loaded. And they and other full-scale examples of the conventional set piece forms are offset by numerous one-movement numbers—the **choruses** in Acts 1 through 3 (most prominently "Va pensiero"), Zaccaria's prayer (Act 2) and prophesy (Act 3), and Fenena's prayer and Abigaille's *rondò finale* (both Act 4); by abbreviated forms (the two-movement Act 1 *terzettino* for Abigaille, Ismaele, and Fenena); and by such adaptations as the Act 2 finale, which ends with Nabucco's freely constructed mad scene instead of a traditional **stretta**.

NAPLES. Southwestern Italian coastal city, the glittering centerpiece of Italian opera in the 18th century. Isolated Roman operas first appeared in Naples in the 1640s, while adaptations of Venetian works were staged with increasing frequency and began to assume a social and political role under the Spanish viceroy, the 8th Count of Oñate (ruled 1648–53), who sought to ingratiate himself by lavishly entertaining his court. Operas probably including **Francesco Cavalli**'s *Didone* (1650, originally 1641) and **Claudio Monteverdi**'s *L'incoronazione di Poppea* (1651, originally 1643) were performed by a company of **Febiarmonici** in temporary quarters provided by the viceroy, relying on ticket sales to defray other expenses. In 1654 they moved to an established theater, the San Bartolomeo, which was attended by subsequent viceroys and thus became the premier venue for opera until the mid-18th century. Beginning in the 1680s the viceregal chapel reinforced this association between court and theater by hiring opera singers for its choir and opera **composers** as *maestri di cappella*, most notably **Alessandro Scarlatti**.

By producing a succession of his own works at the San Bartolomeo, Scarlatti initiated the practice of staging operas by local composers and through his own prestige drew attention to Naples as a center of operatic composition and **production**. Its four orphanage **conservatories** for boys, which trained many of the composers and singers who would dominate 18th-century Italian opera at home and across Europe, fueled this ascent. The Neapolitan cachet profited additionally, both locally and abroad, from replacement of the aging San Bartolomeo with the magnificent San Carlo Theater in 1737 (burned and rebuilt 1816–17). Constructed by Charles III next to his palace after the Spanish Bourbons retook Naples from the Austrian Habsburgs and reestablished the kingdom of Naples in 1734, it staged opulent productions of heroic operas composed to **Pietro Metastasio**'s **librettos**, which served approximately two-thirds of the works performed during its first four decades.

Alongside serious opera, Neapolitan composers also invented **opera buffa** written in Neapolitan dialect (until the last quarter of the 18th century), beginning with Michelangelo Faggioli's (1666–1733) *La Cilla* (1707). It flourished under the relatively tolerant Austrian occupation of Naples early in the century (1707–34), when three theaters specialized in the new genre: the Teatro dei Fiorentini, which began producing opera in 1706 and dedicated itself to comedy soon after *La Cilla* appeared there; the Teatro della Pace (built 1718), which staged comic opera from 1724 to ca. 1751; and the Teatro Nuovo, which opened in 1724 (partly burned and remodeled in 1861 for plays and light musical theater, burned and rebuilt as a movie theater 1935). King Ferdinand I (reigned 1759–1825) formally recognized opera buffa by authorizing palace performances (beginning 1767), personally attending the Teatro Nuovo (beginning 1776), and constructing the Teatro del Real Fondo di Separazione in 1779 (renamed the Real Teatro Mercadante, 1871) primarily for opera buffa, now sung in the more cosmopolitan Tuscan dialect rather than Neapolitan to reflect the genre's increased stature.

Following a decline in the late 18th century, Naples' glory resumed during the French occupation (1806–15) through consolidation of its foundering conservatories into the Real Collegio di Musica, revitalization of the San Carlo through extensive remodeling of its auditorium and improvement of its orchestra, and the introduction of gambling (until 1820) as a new and important revenue source. **Gioachino Rossini**'s involvement with the Neapolitan theaters in the 1810s and 1820s and **Gaetano Donizetti**'s dominance there from the 1820s through the 1840s restored Naples to the spotlight for several glorious decades. Subsequently, however, after establishment of the kingdom of Italy in 1861, the two royal theaters faded as government subsidies were withdrawn, **seasons** were shortened, and the numbers of new operas were drastically reduced. Under British occupation during World War II, the San Carlo was revitalized and subsequently regained government support, renewing its status as one of the premier opera houses in Italy.

NEO-CLASSICISM. Term applied to a range of 20th-century musical styles fashionable between the world wars, which mimic and adapt (mostly) 18th-century idioms of the **baroque** and classical eras. Neo-classical operas are characterized variously by elements of 18th-century form or local gesture, pseudo-tonal harmony and melody, regularly periodic phrase structure, discernible meter and energetic rhythms, **recitatives** and closed musical numbers (*see* NUMBER OPERA), avoidance of **leitmotifs** or other obvious long-range motivic integration, comparatively small **orchestras** and casts, modest length, and retrospective situations and plots sometimes reminiscent of the **commedia dell'arte**, **opera buffa**, or **ballad opera**. Primarily a rejection of the extreme intensity and apparent formlessness of post-romantic music, particularly **expressionism**, which seemed self-indulgent following World War I, its often witty and ironic recasting of archaic references distances its audience from the stage (e.g., in the "epic theater" of Bertolt Brecht and **Kurt Weill**'s *Die Dreigroschenoper*, based on John Gay's, 1685–1732, *The Beggar's Opera*). Its nostalgic recollection of an imagined musical past has also been viewed as a critique of then-current cultural maladies (global war, ensuing epidemics, totalitarianism, and the like). And its frugality reflected contemporary economic realities (inflation and depression).

The term "neo-classicism" was first associated with **Igor Stravinsky**'s music beginning with the **ballet** *Pulcinella* (1919–20), although earlier works such as Sergey Prokofiev's (1891–1953) *Classical Symphony* (1916–17) display the approach, which was championed by Ferrucio Busoni (1866–1924) in the 1910s. And it may be traced back to conservative opponents of **Richard Wagner** and the New German School (notably the Johannes Brahms and Edward Hanslick camp in the late 19th century) and to isolated classicizing works such as Edvard Grieg's (1843–1907) *Holberg Suite* (1884). In opera, Prokofiev's *The Love for Three Oranges* (composed 1919, premiered 1921) has been cited as first true neo-classical opera, following earlier precedents such as **Richard Strauss**'s *Der Rosenkavalier* and *Ariadne auf Naxos* (1912, revised 1916) and **Ralph Vaughan Williams**'s *Hugh the Drover* (composed 1910–14, premiered 1924), which turn away from expressionism. Stravinsky's first neo-classical opera was *Mavra* (1922), while his opera-oratorio *Oedipus Rex* (operatic premier 1928) and particularly *The Rake's Progress* are considered paradigms of the style, the latter being its ultimate important representative. Neo-classicism served as a highly influential predecessor to postmodernism following World War II.

NEW YORK CITY. Since 1790 the most populous city in the United States, and for a short time the republic's capital (1785–90). New York became one of the foremost world centers for the production of repertory opera during the second half of the 20th century thanks primarily to the Metropolitan Opera Company and the New York City Opera.

Ca. 1750, **ballad operas**, including *The Beggar's Opera*, were first performed at the Nassau Street Theater and were offered sporadically at various venues for the next three decades as an alternative to spoken plays. A **London** company that had a brief early run (1753–54) and was revived as the

American Company (later renamed the Old American Company) from 1767 to 1774 reopened following the Revolutionary War (1785) and featured ballad operas and **pasticcios** on a regular basis. Modified **opéras comiques**, including *Le devin du village*, were produced in the 1790s, sometimes in the original language.

While pasticcio remakes remained the norm, recurring short-lived efforts to produce Italian and French opera in recognizable form were made up to the late 19th century by a succession of companies that enjoyed marginal financial success. Legitimate Italian opera first appeared in 1825 at the Park Theater, beginning with **Gioachino Rossini**'s *Il barbiere di Siviglia* (originally 1816), the first opera performed in Italian in New York, in a production which included the young **Maria Malibran**. The touring company run by her father, Manuel García (1775–1832), which had come to town partly through the efforts of **Lorenzo Da Ponte**, mounted an extended season that included several other Rossini operas and *Don Giovanni* given in Italian with the original music more or less intact. Other notable ventures included French operas performed at the Park Theater in 1827 (among them Adrien Boieldieu's, 1775–1834, *La dame blanche*, originally 1825); visits by Italian and New Orleans–based French troupes (1832–33); the Italian Opera House (supported by Da Ponte, burned 1839), New York's first theater dedicated to opera, for one season in 1833, which included works by Rossini, **Saverio Mercadante**, and **Vincenzo Bellini**; Palmo's Opera House (four seasons of Italian operas, principally Bellini, **Gaetano Donizetti**, and **Giuseppe Verdi**, beginning 1844); the Astor Place Opera House (1847–52, scene of an infamous riot in 1849), which debuted with *Ernani*; and the Castle Garden Theater, which first brought **Jenny Lind** to the American public in the 1850s.

The Academy of Music, noted for its acoustics and the unprecedented size of its stage (opened 1854, burned and rebuilt 1866, rededicated to vaudeville 1888, torn down 1926), was the city's first long-standing opera theater and a noted gathering spot for old-money New Yorkers until it was superseded by the rival Metropolitan Opera House in 1883. **Richard Wagner**'s music made an unexpectedly early appearance with *Tannhäuser* at the Stadt Theater in 1859. Operettas—those of **Jacques Offenbach** in the 1860s, **William Schwenck Gilbert and Arthur Sullivan** beginning with *H.M.S. Pinafore* in 1879 (originally 1878), and others, and eventually works by American composers—drew sizable audiences.

However, New York's rise as a world-class operatic capital began with the opening of the original Metropolitan Opera House in 1883 (burned 1892, rebuilt 1893, remodeled 1903, torn down 1967), funded by nouveau-riche industrialists who had been shunned by members of the Academy of Music, which it quickly eclipsed in grandeur, popularity, and financial success, leading to the academy's demise as an opera house. The Metropolitan Opera raised the profile of opera in the United States through road performances in other cities that started in 1884, initially in Philadelphia, where Met productions continued until 1961. Under the directorship of Leopold Damrosch (1884) and Edmund Stanton (1885–91), the Met became a German opera company, even staging such Italian works as *Aida* in German. It began its current course as a venue for world-class singing within a broad, traditional repertory in 1891 under the stewardship of Maurice Grau (also the director at Covent Garden, *see* LONDON) who dazzled the public with brilliant casts. Over the years, the Met has hosted virtually all of the great singers of Europe and the United States, including Victor Maurel (1848–1923), Nellie Melba (1861–1931), **Fyodor Chaliapin**, **Enrico Caruso**, Birgit Nilsson (1918–2005), **Kirsten Flagstad**, **Marilyn Horne**, and **Luciano Pavarotti**, and has boasted such legendary musical directors as Gustav Mahler (1860–1911), **Arturo Toscanini**, and James Levine (born 1943), and such visionary (though not uncontroversial) managers as Rudolf Bing (1902–1997).

While primarily a repertory company, the Met has presented important premiers, particularly prior to 1920, among them **Giacomo Puccini**'s *La fanciulla del West* (1910) and *Il trittico* (1918), and has made an effort at various times to feature American operas (e.g., those of Samuel Barber, 1910–1981, and **Gian Carlo Menotti**). Along with its tours, it has broadened its audience through its groundbreaking series of Saturday matinee radio and (eventually) television broadcasts beginning in 1931 and has made a contribution to cultivating young talent with the Metropolitan Opera Auditions for young singers (beginning 1936). The company inaugurated its new quarters at Lincoln Center, where the possibilities for staging were much improved, in 1966 with the premier of Barber's *Antony and Cleopatra*. Long known for lavish productions with stellar casts mounted at high costs, it became even more entrenched in a conservative repertory following the move, 25 years elapsing between *Mourning Becomes Electra* (1967) by Marvin David Levy (born 1932) and its next premier (John Corigliano, born 1938, *The Ghosts of Versailles* in 1991). While efforts to bring new operas to the stage have been increasing recently, the list of premiers remains short, including **Philip Glass**'s *The Voyage* (1992), John Harbison's (born 1938) *The Great Gatsby* (1999), Tobias Picker's (born 1954) *An American Tragedy* (2005), **Tan Dun**'s *The First Emperor* (2006), and Jeremy Sams's (born 1957) pasticcio *The Enchanted Island* (2011).

Since dismissing the Academy of Music, the Met has had two principal rivals. The short-lived (1906–10) Manhattan Opera Company, founded by Oscar Hammerstein I, staged French productions including *Pelléas et Mélisande*, several featuring **Mary Garden**, at the Manhattan Opera House on 34th Street until it was bought out by the Met. The more permanent New York City Opera (opened in 1943 as the City Center Opera Company) moved from its original theater on West 55th Street to the New York State Theater at Lincoln Center in 1966 (renovated 1981–82; renamed the David H. Koch Theater in 2008), where until 2011 it offered a less familiar repertory, often in English, including baroque revivals (e.g., *Giulio Cesare*, 1966, and *L'incoronazione di Poppea*, 1973) and numerous works by American composers (Aaron Copland's, 1900–1990, *The Tender Land*, 1954; Jack Beeson's, 1921–2010, *Lizzie Bordon*, 1965; Ned Rorem's, born 1923, *Miss Julie*, 1965), frequently cast with fresh faces. Its schedule has included works that straddle the boundary between traditional opera and popular musical theater (such as **Leonard Bernstein**'s *Candide*, originally 1956, and Stephen Sondheim's, born 1930, *Sweeney Todd*, originally 1979). It has recently split two seasons between opera and established Broadway shows. New York's prolific theater scene has also included a host of smaller companies, for example, the Amato Opera Theater (1948–2009), the Bronx Opera Company (from 1967), and the New York Grand Opera (from 1973), as well as productions at conservatories (the Juilliard School) and universities. Operetta was led by the Light Opera of Manhattan from 1968 to 1989.

Currently a cultural crossroads for the United States and Europe, New York has served as a primary or secondary base of operations for numerous composers who have written operas. As a premier showcase for the spectrum of 20th-century styles—from the classical art music traditions to jazz, rock, folk, non-Western music, electronic media, popular musical theater and Broadway, alternative theater, and so forth—it has provided a hotbed of influences that have inspired many of the innovations and crossover syntheses of opera in the late 20th and 21st centuries.

See also MINIMALISM.

NICOLAI, OTTO. (1810, Königsberg, now Kaliningrad–1849, Berlin.) German **composer** of five operas during the 1830s and 1840s (one of them still important), pianist, and **conductor**.

Nicolai's father groomed him as a piano prodigy, resulting in his nervous breakdown at age 15. In Berlin after 1828 he studied singing, piano, and composition; composed songs and choral music; became involved with various vocal organizations; and won the support of numerous patrons. As organist at the Prussian embassy in **Rome** 1834–36, he attended operas and stayed on for a year as a freelance composer, hoping for a career in Italian *melodramma*. When nothing panned out, he moved to **Vienna** (1837) as assistant music director at the Kärntnertortheater, where he conducted and wrote his first opera, the *melodramma Rosmonda d'Inghilterra* (1839, lost). Its critical acclaim in Italy led to successful premiers of three subsequent operas in 1840 and 1841. Along the way he rejected the **libretto** of *Nabucco*, which launched **Giuseppe Verdi**'s international career.

Hired as principal conductor of the Vienna court opera (1841), Nicolai contracted to write German operas but was hamstrung by a dearth of librettos. He founded the high-minded Philharmonic Concerts, which performed works by classical masters, including a historically significant presentation of Ludwig van Beethoven's (1770–1827) *Ninth Symphony* in 1843. In Berlin at the behest of King Friedrich Wilhelm IV as music director of the royal Prussian opera house (beginning 1847), he produced his final and most successful opera and the only one for which he is currently known. *Die lustigen Weiber von Windsor* (*The Merry Wives of Windsor*, 1849), a **singspiel** based on William Shakespeare and a forerunner of Verdi's *Falstaff* (1893), blends Italianate lyricism and a flair for comedy with Germanic orchestration, harmony, and formal flexibility.

NINA, O SIA LA PAZZA PER AMORE. *Commedia in prosa ed in verso per musica*; music by **Giovanni Paisiello**, **libretto** by Giambattista Lorenzi (1719–1805) based on a translation of Benoît-Joseph Marsollier des Vivetières's (1750–1817) **opéra comique** *Nina, ou La folle par amour* (1786); one act revised as two acts; premiered Caserta, Palace Theater, June 1789, revised for **Naples**, Teatro dei Fiorentini, 1790. Paisiello set the translated opéra comique libretto in the French manner, incorporating spoken dialogues in both the one- and two-act versions. **Recitatives**, likely by another composer, were introduced in 1793 and 1795.

Nina, or Crazy for Love is the quintessential example of late 18th-century **sentimental opera**, its plot centering on the characteristic themes of marriage for love, true friendship, and family devotion. The heroine's father, the Count, revokes her engagement to Lindoro to pursue an arrangement with a wealthier prospect. Believing that Lindoro has been killed in a duel with his rival, Nina goes mad and is tended by loyal friends and the local villagers while devoting herself to good deeds. Regretting his decision, the Count defers to his daughter's longing and reconciles with Lindoro, enabling her recovery. Conforming to *Nina*'s rustic setting and its origins in opéra comique, Paisiello's music is appropriately simple, folklike, and inflected with Neapolitan regional references, including a canzone accompanied by the *zampogna* (bagpipe). *Nina*'s popularity likely contributed to the rise of *opera semiseria* in the 1790s.

NIXON IN CHINA. Opera; music by John Adams, **libretto** by the American poet Alice Goodman (born 1958); two acts; premiered Houston, Grand Opera, October 1987.

Envisioned by the director **Peter Sellars** in 1982, Adams's first and best-known stage work was commissioned jointly by the Brooklyn Academy of Music, the John F. Kennedy Center for the Performing Arts, and the Houston

Grand Opera and was composed over two years from 1985 to 1987. Initially dismissed by some as a banal derivative of **minimalist** operas by **Philip Glass** and others, along with *Einstein on the Beach* it became one of the most frequently produced operas of the late 20th century, spawning the genre of "CNN opera" (*see* ZEITOPER) and contributing to an upsurge of new operas in the United States that continues to the present day.

Like Adams's other stage works, *Nixon* reflects his politicized upbringing and belief that opera must be culturally relevant and contemporary. Its reenactment of the 37th president's visit to China in 1972 may be read as a cynical examination of diplomacy eroded by modern media, television in particular, which elevates image over substance. Scenes depicting airport ceremonies for Richard Nixon's arrival in Beijing (staged in front of a colossal replica of Air Force One), a private meeting of Nixon and National Security Advisor Henry Kissinger with Chairman Mao Zedong and Premier Zhou Enlai, and a magnificent banquet in which liquor warms relations contrast Nixon's preoccupations over the political symbolism of the occasion against Mao's more nuanced vision of China's relations with America. Photo ops and propaganda continue in the second act. The First Lady Pat Nixon's carefully orchestrated, televised tour of Chinese agriculture, industry, and communal life and the attendance of the entourage at a socialist allegorical **ballet**, a parable of the Cultural Revolution staged ridiculously with soldiers on point, expose the essential incompatibility of American and Chinese values. With no meaningful agreement in sight, the leads reminisce from their separate beds about formative experiences that account for their cultural conflicts and preclude reconciliation.

Nixon's popularity derives to a large extent from its eclecticism, comparative conservatism, and pop culture immediacy. Adam's post-minimalist approach combines a succession of cycling, gradually varied tonal motives with eclectic references to a variety of musical styles from Richard Wagner to Glass to quotes from the Red Army doctrine "The Three Main Rules of Discipline and Eight Points of Attention" and the propaganda ballet *The Red Detachment of Women* (originally 1964) performed for the visit. In contrast to Glass's *Einstein*, for example, it presents a traditional, reality-based, linear narrative using conventional singing accompanied by an extensive **orchestra** and spectacular staging. Adams's flexible handling of minimalism allows him to create canny representations of the various personalities, including a dead-on impression of Nixon's unmistakable speaking style.

NORMA. *Tragedia lirica*; music by **Vincenzo Bellini**, **libretto** by **Felice Romani** based on the play (1831) by Alexandre Soumet (1788–1845); two acts; premiered Milan, Teatro alla Scala, December 1831. Following a disappointing opening, *Norma* soon entered the repertory and has served as an important vehicle for such prominent sopranos as Rosa Ponselle (1897–1981) and **Maria Callas**.

Set in Roman-occupied Gaul, *Norma* provides an archetypal example of the schematically structured love-triangle opera of the second quarter of the 19th century, in which multimovement set pieces following conventional forms establish and resolve the central alliances and conflicts. Act 1 proceeds systematically toward comprehensive understanding of the situation by the characters. In his cavatina (*see* ARIA) with **chorus**, Norma's father Oroveso establishes his Druidic loyalties and hatred for the conquerors, who are led by the governor Pollione. The latter's scena (*see* SCENE) and cavatina reveals his prior assignation with the priestess Norma, who has secretly born his two sons, and his current love for the novice Adalgisa and fear of Norma's retribution. Norma's cavatina defines her religious persona, scorn for the Romans, and suspicions of Pollione's infidelity. In Adalgisa's **duet** with Pollione, she discloses her ambivalence about her religious duties and amorous yearnings. Norma's intrusion, turning the duet into a trio **finale**, makes manifest the existence of the love triangle and her awareness of Pollione's and Adalgisa's indiscretions.

The second act defuses these accumulated tensions through an equally methodical process. Norma's scena and subsequent duet with Adalgisa resolve her conflicted feelings about her boys, and the two **women** restore their friendship, Norma offering to let Adalgisa flee to **Rome** with Pollione, Adalgisa promising to renew her sacred vows and help Norma reclaim her lover. In a final scene that combines a duet for Pollione and Norma and her *rondò finale*, she confesses violating her Druidic oath, gives her father custody of her children, and with Pollione by her side prepares to atone for her forbidden love.

Individual scenes in *Norma* also illustrate characteristic approaches to musico-dramatic structure. Examples such as Norma's scena and four-movement duet with Adalgisa (Act 2), which runs more than 20 minutes, demonstrate the grand scale and psychological complexity reached through full development of the Rossinian designs for set pieces. Archetypal representatives of the broad **lyric prototype** melodies for which Bellini was famous serve both this structural expansion and the exposition of complementary psychological positions, as in the liquid **bel canto** slow movement "Casta diva" and energetic **cabaletta** "Ah bello a me ritorna" of her famous Act 1 aria. The opera also shows the effect of longer set pieces on singers' workloads by comparison with 18th-century norms. While a hierarchy is maintained through the distribution of arias—Norma has two, Pollione one, and Adalgisa none—the quantity of these showpieces is drastically reduced, a minimum number of prodigious solo scenes and the increasingly prevalent ensemble work taking the place of as many as a half dozen exit arias per character in the 18th century.

NOTA E PAROLA. *See* PARLANTE.

LE NOZZE DI FIGARO. **Opera buffa**; music by **Wolfgang Amadeus Mozart**, **libretto** by **Lorenzo Da Ponte** based on Pierre-Augustin Beaumarchais's (1732–1799) *La folle journée, ou Le mariage de Figaro* (1778); four acts; premiered **Vienna**, Burgtheater, May 1786.

In adapting the second of Beaumarchais's three Figaro plays, Mozart and Da Ponte conceived *The Marriage of Figaro* to trade on the overwhelming success of **Giovanni Paisiello**'s *Il barbiere di Siviglia* in Vienna (1783, originally St. Petersburg, 1782). After surmounting obstacles including Joseph II's initial resistance to the story, *Figaro* enjoyed modest initial recognition in Vienna before its triumphant restaging in Prague (1786), which resulted in the commission for *Don Giovanni*. Parts of it were heard in Italy as early as 1787. And like *Don Giovanni* it was performed frequently in Germany and France over the next decade with spoken dialogue. It remained in the repertory throughout the 19th and 20th centuries and currently holds pride of place as Mozart's most frequently staged opera and the summit of 18th-century opera buffa.

Figaro may be viewed as a **sentimental** parable of marriage embodying individual freedom and choice, an affectionate, voluntary partnership of complementary equals (Figaro and Susanna, Bartolo and Marcellina) versus a mismatch of competing wills and crossed purposes based on mere infatuation or social obligations (Almaviva and Rosina, and potentially Figaro and Marcellina). In a standard schema for mature opera buffa, the action unfolds in two phases, demonstrating the adoption of the intrigues and plot tangles increasingly excluded from serious opera (cf. **Christoph Willibald Gluck**'s *Orfeo ed Euridice*).

Acts 1 and 2 introduce three main problems faced by Figaro—barber, jack-of-all-trades, previously accomplice to the Count Almaviva in wooing his wife Rosina, and now his valet—and his companions. Despite renouncing his "noble's right," Almaviva remains unfaithful to his wife and slyly pursues Figaro's fiancée Susanna, making an expedited wedding imperative. The randy page Cherubino, whom Almaviva regards as a rival, must be rescued from conscription into the army by Almaviva's order. A contrived scheme to embarrass Almaviva by luring him to a supposed tryst with Susanna, her place to be taken by Cherubino in disguise, unravels when the count returns early from a hunt while Cherubino's dress is being fitted. As complications mount, the crone Marcellina and her ally Dr. Bartolo, who had previously lost Rosina to the count through Figaro's intervention, brandish her unfulfilled contract with Figaro, for which their marriage is collateral.

The second phase of action (Acts 3 and 4) resolves these concerns. Adjudication of Marcellina's contract reveals that she and Bartolo are Figaro's parents, freeing him to marry Susanna. Cherubino's girlfriend Barbarina saves him by threatening to betray Almaviva's prior attempt to bed her. And the conspirators shame Almaviva into mending his ways when he unwittingly tries to seduce his own wife, who has traded clothes with Susanna.

In *Figaro*, even more than in Paisiello's *Barbiere*, **commedia dell'arte** stereotypes, situations, and comedic formulas have evolved into credible interactions among humanized individuals, the variegated palette of Mozart's music playing an essential role in this transformation. Options range from the comic declamation, *parlante*, and **patter song** of Figaro, Susanna, the other comic characters, and even the count, who operates ignobly in his love life and music, to the sentimental lyricism of Rosina, who clings desperately to her aristocratic bearing, and Cherubino, in effect a romantic male lead. And it includes the mock **opera seria** numbers—the obbligato **recitatives** not only for the aristocrats Almaviva and Rosina (Act 3), but also for Figaro and Susanna (Act 4), as well as Barbarina's lament on the lost pin "L'ho perduta" (Act 4)—which project an equivalency between aristocratic and servant roles and symbolize Enlightened social leveling.

The internal organization of set pieces fosters this expressive range. **Arias** proceed as episodic series of melodies distinguished by their moods, topical associations, and styles of text setting (from comic idioms to sentimental **bel canto** lyricism), a spontaneous, psychologically persuasive mode of expression attuned to the late 18th-century aesthetic of natural, unscripted communication. Although many of these arias end with a framing return of the initial theme (see Figaro's "Se vuol ballare" and Cherubino's "Voi che sapete"), some remain asymmetrical musings (Rosina's "Porgi amor"). Frequent ensembles rely on the comic module of dialogue capped by reflection (*see* FINALE) as their basic unit of construction to allow similar flexibility within pieces of widely varying scale: the single module of Rosina and Susanna's billet-doux *duettino* "Che soave zeffiretto" (Act 3); the multiple modules of larger one-movement ensembles, such as the Act 1 trio "Cosa sento" during Cherubino's first run-in with Almaviva; and the even more numerous modules within the extended movements of the Act 2 and 4 finales. In these tours de force of musical inventiveness and energy, Mozart's music interweaves his characters in counterpoint that richly defines their distinct personalities, moods, attitudes, relationships, and concerns, earning *Figaro* its status as the consummate masterpiece of 18th-century opera.

NUMBER OPERA. Modern term for operas, mostly from the mid-17th century through the mid-19th century, in which self-contained lyric numbers/set pieces (**arias**, **duets**, **finales**, *introduzioni*, and the like) alternate with **recitatives** or spoken dialogues. Number operas may be distinguished from less conventionally organized early 17th-century operas and from more continuous late 19th-century Italian and French operas and the music dramas of **Richard Wagner** and his adherents. Such 20th-century throwbacks as **Igor Stravinsky**'s *The Rake's Progress* are also considered number operas.

OFFENBACH, JACQUES. (1819, Cologne–1880, Paris.) Prolific French **composer** of approximately 90 **operettas** (mostly from the 1850s through the 1870s), a genre that he popularized internationally, and several full-length **opéras comiques**, as well as numerous vaudevilles and other vocal and instrumental music; **conductor** and cellist. After a year's study at the Conservatoire (1834), Offenbach joined the **orchestra** of the Opéra-Comique (until 1838), during which time he studied composition with **Fromental Halévy** and performed as a cellist in the **Paris** salons, beginning a career as a soloist in which he appeared with the pianists Franz Liszt (1811–1886) and Anton Rubinstein (1829–1894).

Offenbach's activities as a stage composer had a fitful beginning. While serving as conductor at the Comédie-Française (from 1850), he saw only three short works performed at other theaters. His breakthrough came by his own devices when he founded the Bouffes-Parisiens in 1855 in conjunction with the Paris International Exhibition of that year and produced seven highly successful short comedies from July through October. Operating initially out of the tiny, ramshackle Théâtre Marigny, he was able to move to more respectable quarters in the Salle Choiseul during the winter of 1856. Relaxation of Offenbach's license for the theater, which originally limited his productions to three singers, allowed him to develop more complex productions beginning with *Orphée aux enfers* (1858) and later including *La belle Hélène* (1864) and *La vie parisienne* (1866), working with his principal collaborators Henri Meilhac (1831–1897) and Ludovic Halévy (1834–1908, nephew of **Fromental Halévy**).

Offenbach's popularity peaked during the International Exhibition of 1867, when *La Grande-Duchesse de Gérolstein* premiered. In 1873 he assumed management of the Théâtre de la Gaîté, which he bankrupted the next year with lavish productions of his own operas and others. In an effort at repaying his debts, he toured the United States as a cellist and conductor in conjunction with the Centennial Exhibition of 1876. Offenbach died before completing his most substantial work, the *opéra fantastique Les contes d'Hoffmann*. The success of his operettas in **Vienna** and **London** during the 1860s and 1870s paved the way for Johann Strauss the younger (1825–1899), **William Schwenck Gilbert and Arthur Sullivan**, and **Franz Lehár**.

OPÉRA-BALLET. Type of French musical theater fashionable during the first third of the 18th century, beginning with **André Campra**'s *L'Europe galante* (1697). An *opéra-ballet* consists of a **prologue** and three or four acts designated "entrées," each combining **airs, duets, choruses**, and **ballets** and at least one **divertissement**. Unlike **Jean-Baptiste Lully**'s *tragédies lyriques*, its acts have independent plots, characters, and locales only loosely related to a central theme, and contemporary characters pursue comic intrigues and spoof court manners in familiar settings. In their light subject matter and musical style, the first *opéras-ballets* provided an alternative to Lully's grandiose, politicized mythological paeans to French royalty, creating a musical counterpart to the charming *galant* style of Antoine Watteau's paintings and a rapprochement between the French and Italian manners that anticipated **Jean-Philippe Rameau**.

Beginning in the 1720s the format of the *opéra-ballet* was adapted to more serious purposes in the subgenre of *ballet-héroïque*, which discarded comic scenes to the *comédie en vaudevilles* and eventually **opéra comique**; introduced mythological, allegorical, and exotic subjects, for example in Rameau's *Les Indes galantes* (1735); and occasionally revived the regal veneration of the *tragédie lyrique* (Rameau's *Les fêtes de Polymnie*, 1745). The *acte de ballet* (e.g., Rameau's *Pigmalion*, 1748), which flourished during the third quarter of the 18th century, was equivalent to one entrée of an *opéra-ballet*—sometimes comprising literally one entrée of an existing *opéra-ballet*—combined with others to form an evening's entertainment. *Opéra-ballet* died out in the 1770s.

See also CATEGORIES OF OPERA.

OPERA BUFFA. Generic designation for Italian full-length, stand-alone comic opera, normally in two to four acts, and distinct from the much shorter **intermezzo**, which was performed between acts of an **opera seria** or spoken play and involved a smaller cast. The terms *commedia per musica* and *dramma giocoso* (and others) appear much more frequently in **librettos**. Opera buffa developed concurrently with the intermezzo during the first half of the 18th century and became the dominant Italian operatic genre during its last quarter.

While widespread use of comic *contrascene* in 17th-century serious operas made independent comic opera redundant, so-called learned comedies were present, particularly in Florence, and comic operas were also produced in **Rome** and Bologna (e.g., Virgilio Mazzocchi's *Chi soffre speri*, 1637).

True 18th-century opera buffa began in **Naples** as a private entertainment among aristocrats and jurists with the lawyer Michelangelo Faggioli's (1666–1733) *La Cilla* (1706). These performances soon spawned a new genre that proliferated in the minor theaters such as the Teatro dei Fiorentini, beginning in 1709 with Antonio Orefice's (active 1708–1734) *Patrò Calienno de la Costa*, and the Teatro Nuovo and the Teatro Pace (after 1724) and involved virtually all of the major Neapolitan composers as early as **Alessandro Scarlatti** (*Il trionfo dell'onore*, 1718). These initial opere buffe were set in Naples and sung in Neapolitan dialect, lending realism to the presentation. Based on the conventions of the **commedia dell'arte**, their plots centered on one or two pairs of lovers, treated as serious roles, whose lives are complicated by stock comic characters.

In the 1730s, opera buffa traveled north to Rome, a logical first step in its dissemination since comic opera was already familiar there. **Castratos** played the female roles owing to prohibitions against **women** onstage. By the 1740s it had reached a host of Italian and German cities, including **Venice**, where the second phase of its development began. Gaetano Latilla's (1711–1788) *Gismondo* (Naples, 1737), performed as *La finta cameriera* in Venice in 1743, was followed by frequent stagings of opere buffe written by Neapolitan composers at several theaters. Venetian composers joined in, most importantly **Baldassare Galuppi**, whose collaborations with the **librettist Carlo Goldoni**, beginning with *L'Arcadia in Brenta* (1749), took the genre in new directions.

Goldoni's librettos, consistently designated as *drammi giocosi*, made comic opera a more sophisticated type of social and psychological commentary by increasing the range of subjects; treating the interaction between serious, comic, and intermediate roles (*parti serie, parti buffe*, and *parti di mezzo carattere*) as a social parable; and adding a sentimental element (*see* SENTIMENTAL OPERA) as in Goldoni's *La buona figliuola*, set by **Egidio Duni** in 1756 and more famously by **Niccolò Piccinni** (1760). To enact his more linear plots, he and Galuppi added (alongside the **arias** and **duets** that had dominated previously) multisectional *introduzioni* and the extended **finales** that would become a hallmark of opera buffa in the late 18th century. Galuppi increased the flexibility and responsiveness of his music by giving the **orchestra** a more prominent role and casting arias as episodic series of melodies.

By the 1750s, opera buffa was heard everywhere including **Paris**, where it and the intermezzo fueled the infamous **War of the Comedians**. During the last quarter of the 18th century it surpassed opera seria in popularity, frequency of performance, social and political relevance, and artistic standing. In the hands of the most perceptive librettists, among them Giuseppe Petrosellini (1727–after 1797), Giovanni Bertati (1735–ca. 1815), and **Lorenzo Da Ponte**, and such composers as **Giovanni Paisiello**, **Domenico Cimarosa**, and **Wolfgang Amadeus Mozart**, who teamed up to produce masterworks such as *Il barbiere di Siviglia*, *Il matrimonio segreto*, and *Le nozze di Figaro*, opera buffa became a nuanced analysis of human interaction and a parable of class relationships and shifting balances of power and authority, particularly at **Vienna**'s Burgtheater in the 1780s. Composers increased musical differentiation of characters and heightened comic impact by broadening the range of melodic affect and topic and including **patter song** in comedic *lazzi* (*see* COMMEDIA DELL'ARTE). They gave more central roles to duets and larger ensembles, expanded them, and increased the flexibility of their dialogue by making greater use of *canto declamato*, **parlante**, and *nota e parole*, and experimented with unconventional forms. Even arias contributed to psychological development and plot progression.

Following the French Revolution, opera buffa lost relevance as an instrument of political and social commentary and change. And while it still could boast brilliantly entertaining trophies such as **Gioachino Rossini**'s remake of *Il barbiere di Siviglia* and **Gaetano Donizetti**'s *L'elisir d'amore* (1832) and *Don Pasquale*, it tended to lapse into simplified farcical situations, caricature, and antic humor, perhaps in a vain attempt to overcome the apathy of jaded audiences. Essentially exhausted and increasingly internalizing the virtuoso singing and conventional forms of *melodramma*, the genre lost its identity and died out following efforts in the 1840s and early 1850s by Donizetti, the brothers **Luigi and Federico Ricci**, and others to keep it alive. Nonetheless, echoes of opera buffa may be heard in the differently named comic operas (*commedia lirica*, *dramma comico*) of the late 19th and early 20th centuries, such as **Giuseppe Verdi**'s *Falstaff* (1893) and **Giacomo Puccini**'s *Gianni Schicchi* (1918).

See also BASS; CATEGORIES OF OPERA; CENSORSHIP; *DON GIOVANNI*; FARSA; LEO, LEONARDO; PACINI, GIOVANNI; RECITATIVE; STRETTA; TENOR; TRAETTA, TOMMASO.

OPÉRA COMIQUE. Term applied by the late 19th century to French opera combining spoken dialogue and vocal and instrumental music, in contrast to *opéra*, which is set to music throughout (as is Italian **opera buffa**). It is reserved for works of greater artistic merit than the popular entertainments (including **operettas**) of the so-called boulevard theaters. And it encompasses an array of designations that were employed as the genre developed during the 18th and 19th centuries. At various points, "Opéra-Comique" (distinguished by the hyphen) was also the name of companies or theaters that performed such works (*see* PARIS).

French opera with spoken dialogue originated in the theaters of the Parisian spring and summer trade fairs (the St. Germain and the St. Laurent), termed the Opéra-Comique after 1715, and the rival Comédie-Italienne or Nouveau Théâtre Italien (after 1716). Before 1750, their *comédies en vaude-*

villes and *opéras comiques en vaudevilles*—spoken plays that incorporate songs adapting preexisting, often popular melodies to new texts (**vaudevilles**)—traded in unsophisticated humor, social satire, and parody of the operas and plays of the official theaters (the Académie Royale de Musique, or Opéra, and the Comédie-Française). The first work to be designated "opéra comique" was Alain-René Lesage's (1668–1747) parody (1715) of André Destouches's (1672–1749) *Télémaque et Calypso* (1714).

Influenced by imported Italian **intermezzos** and opere buffe like those produced in Paris during the **War of the Comedians** (1752–54), and particularly by Jean-Jacques Rousseau's *Le devin du village*, a French approximation of the Italian intermezzo that contained no spoken words, composers provided newly composed songs in the *comédie mêlée d'ariettes* (play interspersed with little **arias**) or a combination of new and adapted songs in the *comédie en ariettes et en vaudevilles*. While most of these set pieces were simple songs resembling vaudevilles, by the 1760s others embraced a richer Italianate lyricism and even incorporated vocal display (for the female leads), and **duets** and larger ensembles sometimes occurred. Subject matter also became more varied, well mannered, and sophisticated, leading **librettists** to qualify *comédie* with descriptive modifiers: *féerie* (magical/fairy), *chevaleresque* (medieval knightly/chivalric), *larmoyant* (sentimental/tearful), and *villageois* (rustic). Leaders in this style of opéra comique were **Egidio Duni**; chess player and composer **François-André Danican Philidor** (famous for his *Tom Jones*, 1765, based on Henry Fielding's novel); **André-Ernest-Modeste Grétry**; and Nicolas-Marie Dalayrac (1753–1809, whose *Nina, ou La folle par amour*, 1786, was the source of **Giovanni Paisiello**'s *Nina*, 1789).

During the 1780s, serious subject matter appeared frequently, notably in Grétry's *Richard Coeur-de-lion* (1784), as the lighthearted *comédie mêlée d'ariettes* declined. This trend climaxed following the Revolution in the works of **Luigi Cherubini** and **Étienne-Nicolas Méhul**, in which imperiled protagonists confront violent situations in settings that range from Gothic to classical (e.g., Cherubini's *Lodoïska*, 1791, and *Médée*, 1797). They were designated as *comédie héroïque*, *drame lyrique*, *drame mêlé de chants* (drama interspersed with songs), *fait historique* (historical event, a recreation of a recent occurrence depicting the heroism of everyday people), or simply *opéra*. At this point the exception, truly comic operas often received the title *opéra bouffon*, particularly if they mimicked Italian opera buffa. Late 18th-century opéra comique anticipated 19th-century *grand opéra* not only in tone, but also in numerous other features, for example vocal writing that prioritizes passion over melodic elegance, lengthier musical numbers, unified scene complexes involving multiple set pieces, broader reliance on ensembles and **choruses** to carry action, enrichment of orchestral and harmonic color, and increased incorporation of spectacular effects, particularly after the Opéra-Comique moved to a more versatile theater in 1783.

Despite a reversal of Parisian taste during Napoleon's reign and the re-emergence of lighter sentimental or comic works, the Revolutionary period had demonstrated the broad potential for opera with spoken dialogue. Particularly during the lifespan of the Opéra-National (1847–72, housed after 1851 in the Théâtre Historique/Théâtre Lyrique), which presented a repertory of opéra comique dating back to Grétry, Parisian audiences could experience the entire spectrum of the genre, which could encompass works as diverse as **Gaetano Donizetti**'s jingoistic alpine romance *La fille du régiment* (1840), **Charles Gounod**'s supernatural psychodrama *Faust*, and **George Bizet**'s exotic-realist tragedy *Carmen*. The Opéra-Comique remained active into the 20th century as a venue for world premiers of progressive operas (e.g., *Pelléas et Mélisande*) and for French performances of operas that debuted elsewhere (*The Rake's Progress*, 1952, originally 1951).

See also AUBER, DANIEL-FRANÇOIS-ESPRIT; CARVALHO, LÉON; CATEGORIES OF OPERA; CENSORSHIP; FARSA; FINALE; GLUCK, CHRISTOPH WILLIBALD; HALÉVY, FROMENTAL; LEITMOTIF; MASSENET, JULES; MELODRAMA; OVERTURE; RAMEAU, JEAN-PHILIPPE; ROMANCE; SENTIMENTAL OPERA; SINGSPIEL; SMETANA, BEDŘICH; THOMAS, AMBROISE; VIENNA; ZARZUELA.

OPÉRA LYRIQUE. Modern generic term for mid- to late 19th-century French opera set to music throughout like *grand opéra*, and lacking the spoken dialogue of **opéra comique**, but shorter, less elaborately cast, less spectacular, and focused primarily on human relationships rather than their historical, social, or religious backdrops. The influence of **Richard Wagner** is often noted in the musical continuity, orchestral emphasis, **leitmotif**-like recurring motives, and chromatic harmonies of many of these works. Normally designated *opéra* or *drame lyrique* in scores or **librettos**, *opéra lyrique* was a specialty of the Opéra-National (1847–72)—established in competition with the Opéra and Opéra-Comique—particularly under the innovative director **Léon Carvalho** beginning in 1856. Housed in the Théâtre Historique/Théâtre Lyrique (and two other theaters) in **Paris** from 1851 to 1872, it also staged other types of new French opera, opéra comique from the 18th and early 19th centuries, and German and Italian opera in translation. Prominent examples of *opéra lyrique* include **Charles Gounod**'s *Faust* (1859, provided with **recitatives** for various productions the following year); **Georges Bizet**'s *Les pêcheurs de perles* (1863); **Hector Berlioz**'s *Les Troyens à Carthage* (1863); and **Jules Massenet**'s *Werther* (1892, Vienna).

See also CATEGORIES OF OPERA; THOMAS, AMBROISE; *YEVGENY ONEGIN*.

OPERA SEMISERIA. Italian outgrowth of French **rescue opera** and the *comédie larmoyante* (tearful comedy), **opéras comiques** of the 1760s through the 1790s that mix rusticism, sentimentality, and imminent violence. *Opera semiseria* also shows a relationship with the late 18th-century Italian *dramma giocoso* (*see* OPERA BUFFA), as illustrated by **Wolfgang Amadeus Mozart**'s *Don Giovanni*, which was frequently designated an *opera semiseria* in revivals.

The terms *opera semiseria* or *dramma semiserio* were applied, alongside such alternatives as *tragicomico* or *eroicomico*, beginning in the late 1790s to works that combine an imperiled hero and/or heroine, some comic characters and situations, and a happy ending (*see* LIETO FINE). Peasants, disenfranchised aristocrats or townspeople, or persecuted fugitives cope with coercive amorous advances, false criminal charges, unjust imprisonments, forced confessions, attempted assassinations, and madness. Vulnerable to abusive guardians, corrupt nobles, other unscrupulous authorities, and their loyal henchmen—typically buffo **basses**—they suffer in contemporary **pastoral** or Gothic settings ranging from country villages to underground dungeons, ruined castles, and asylums. Their stories play out against grotesque juxtapositions of horror and comedy: madness embodied both, and cross-gendered disguises were stock-in-trade. Averting potential tragedy, a benevolent authority legitimizes secret, disapproved marriages and brings salvation, recovery from madness, and reconciliation.

Initially most popular in cities directly or indirectly open to French influences—**Vienna**, Dresden, Parma, and Milan—*opera semiseria* was championed by the leading turn-of-the-century composers, **Simon Mayr** and especially **Ferdinando Paer**, whose touchstones of the genre included *Camilla, ossia Il sotterraneo* (*Camilla, or The Underground Vault*, 1799, Vienna); *Leonora, ossia L'amore conjugale* (*Leonora, or Marital Love*, 1804, Dresden), the prototype for Mayr's *L'amor coniugale* (1805) and Ludwig van Beethoven's (1770–1827) *Leonore/Fidelio*; and *Agnese* (1809). **Gioachino Rossini** also wrote several important examples, the most popular of which nowadays is *La gazza ladra* (*The Thieving Magpie*, 1817). After Donizetti's *melodramma semiserio Linda di Chamounix* (1842), the latest prominent example, *opera semiseria* merged with **melodramma**, and the designation apparently disappeared entirely with **Saverio Mercadante**'s *Violetta* (1853). In testing the limits of taste (without indulging **romantic** catharsis), *opera semiseria* took an important step toward such pastoral or Gothic tragedies as **Giuseppe Verdi**'s *Luisa Miller* (1849) and *Il trovatore* (1853).

See also CATEGORIES OF OPERA; RICCI, LUIGI AND FEDERICO; SENTIMENTAL OPERA.

OPERA SERIA. Modern designation for Italian heroic, primarily historical opera of the 18th and very early 19th centuries. Although the term appeared in **librettos** occasionally in the late 18th century, it mostly stands in nowadays for the more common *dramma per musica* and *dramma musicale*, which had already become commonplace in the 1640s, as in **Claudio Monteverdi's** *Il ritorno d'Ulisse in patria* (1640) and *L'incoronazione di Poppea* (1643), replacing the earlier *favola*.

Currently the term is applied mainly to operas descended from the reforms of the **Arcadian Academy**, an aesthetic most famously represented by the **librettists Apostolo Zeno** and **Pietro Metastasio**, who embraced the classicizing principles of simplicity, naturalness, and order and strove for verisimilitude through adherence to the **unities of time, place, and action**. And they embraced the *lieto fine*, which rewarded virtue, reasoned behavior, and social conformity; avoided onstage deaths as artistically ignoble; and relied on human resolutions of conflicts rather than supernatural ones involving an unnatural deus ex machina.

Arcadian librettists created an ideally rational, lawful operatic universe through adoption of various conventions. Each of three acts is divided into a series of approximately 6 to 18 small **scenes**—fewer than in the 17th century—defined by onstage personnel: an entrance or exit marks a new scene. Most scenes include a lengthy dialogue written in *versi sciolti* (*see* VERSIFICATION) set as simple **recitative**, and many end with *versi lirici* for set pieces, primarily exit **arias** in conventional da capo form or its variants, providing balanced, alternating emphasis of poetic and musical expression. A series of these small scenes presented in the same stage locale begins by gradually accumulating characters through recitative-only scenes and entrance arias, then disperses them through scenes ending with exit arias. The distribution of arias and a relatively few obbligato recitatives among roles of different rank was determined by a closely observed system of *convenienze* (theatrical conventions). The light *galant*, **bel canto** music developed from the 1720s on by **Leonardo Vinci, Giovanni Battista Pergolesi, Johann Adolf Hasse**, and others, which displaced the more learned style of **Alessandro Scarlatti** and the first generation of opera seria **composers**, projected a corresponding aesthetic of naturalness, decorum, and simplicity.

Beginning midcentury, these conventions were challenged increasingly by such progressives as the critic **Francesco Algarotti**; the librettists **Mattia Verazi** and **Ranieri Calzabigi**; and the composers **Niccolò Jommelli, Tommaso Traetta**, and **Christoph Willibald Gluck**. Innovations met the least resistance outside the conservative Italian orbit in artistically open-minded, often Francophile courts such as Mannheim, Stuttgart, **Vienna**, Dresden, St. Petersburg, and Parma and appeared most frequently in anything-goes genres such as the *festa teatrale* and *azione teatrale* (for example, Gluck's *Orfeo ed Euridice* for Vienna). But by the 1780s even formal opera seria written for

Naples and **Venice** routinely included progressive features: exploration of new, nonclassical subjects; reintroduction of staged deaths; more **duets** and other ensembles—including act-ending **finales**—at the expense of arias; development of less static set piece forms such as the *rondò* (*see* ARIA); and increased presence of **chorus** and **ballet**, larger **orchestras** and more colorful scoring, obbligato recitative, and recitative-like declamation within arias.

These stylistic shifts coupled with social changes following the French Revolution eventually expunged many of the conventions of the Arcadian style epitomized by Metastasio and Hasse and the premises on which it was founded, leading modern commentators to abandon the term "opera seria" for most works after 1800 and rely on the historically based *melodramma*, *tragedia*, and the perennial *dramma* when referencing serious opera.

See also ARNE, THOMAS AUGUSTINE; CASTRATO; CATEGORIES OF OPERA; CHERUBINI, LUIGI; DUNI, EGIDIO; GALUPPI, BALDAS-SARE; *GIULIO CESARE IN EGITTO*; GRAUN, CARL HEINRICH; HANDEL, GEORGE FRIDERIC; *IDOMENEO, RE DI CRETA*; LEO, LEONARDO; MAYR, SIMON; *IL MITRIDATE EUPATORE*; MOZART, WOLFGANG AMADEUS; PAISIELLO, GIOVANNI; PICCINNI, NICCOLÒ; PRODUCTION; *RINALDO*; SALIERI, ANTONIO; SET DESIGN; TENOR; VIVALDI, ANTONIO.

OPERETTA. Light opera combining spoken dialogue with tuneful songs and dances, written during the mid- to late 19th and early 20th centuries. Though operettas were sometimes shorter and less ambitious than full-length operas, no hard-and-fast stylistic distinction separates operetta from comic opera with spoken dialogue (**opéra comique**, **singspiel**) or musical comedy.

Operetta originated in **Paris** after 1850 to fill a void resulting from the increasingly serious repertory and snobbish atmosphere of the Opéra-Comique. Although efforts to establish an alternative entertainment had begun as early as the 1840s, the new genre became a craze overnight at **Jacques Offenbach**'s Théâtre des Bouffes-Parisiens during the 1855 International Exposition season. The popularity of his initial one-act social or theatrical farces and satires performed two or three per evening led Offenbach to create more ambitious stand-alone two- or three-act works such as *Orphée aux enfers* (1858).

Offenbach's operettas traveled to **Vienna** almost immediately in the late 1850s, where they were imitated beginning with Franz Suppé's (1819–1895) *Das Pensionat* (1860). In the 1870s, led by Johann Strauss the younger (1825–1899), Viennese operettas became more domestic and romantic and the music more infused with dances like the waltz, for example in *Die Fledermaus* (*The Bat*, 1874). Following a decline in Viennese operetta at the end of the century, **Franz Léhar** and others briefly revived the genre, most famously with *Die lustige Witwe* (*The Merry Widow*, 1905), while Berlin emerged as a new center of activity involving composers such as Paul Lincke (1866–1946; e.g., *Frau Luna*, 1899). In **London**, Arthur Sullivan traded on the Offenbach fever of the 1860s with the derivative *Cox and Box, or The Long-Lost Brothers* (1866) and soon began his noted collaboration with **William Schwenck Gilbert**, which extended from the 1870s through the 1880s. Operetta was sometimes mimicked by more traditional operas, for example **Giacomo Puccini**'s *commedia lirica La rondine* (1917). Between the wars, operetta declined in favor of musical comedy influenced by American vaudeville.

See also BIZET, GEORGES; CATEGORIES OF OPERA; MASCAGNI, PIETRO; PATTER SONG; VIARDOT, PAULINE; ZARZUELA.

ORCHESTRA. Instrumental ensemble, usually involving multiple players for each string part, which typically accompanies the singers and provides instrumental music such as the **overture** in an opera. (The term also applies more generally, of course, to any large group of instrumentalists.) "Orchestra" referred initially to the space in front of the stage occupied by the musicians, then (beginning in the late 17th century) to the ensemble itself. Across the history of opera, the corps of instrumentalists gradually expanded to embrace the resources of the modern orchestra and vastly increased its dramatic presence and responsiveness.

Contemporary documentation indicates that the earliest works, the *Euridice* operas of **Jacopo Peri** and **Giulio Caccini** and the *Rappresentatione di Anima, et di Corpo* (1600) of **Emilio de' Cavalieri**, were accompanied by a group limited primarily or perhaps exclusively to **basso continuo** instruments such as **harpsichord**, *chitarrone* and archlute (*see* LUTE), *lirone* (a fretted, bowed string instrument related to the viol), and (in Cavalieri's case) organ, playing offstage and out of sight. In *Orfeo*, **Claudio Monteverdi** amplified his scoring by drawing on the tradition of the *intermedio*, which used specific combinations of wind and string instruments to convey the atmosphere of different types of scenes (e.g., "infernal" cornetts, trombones, and reed organ versus "pastoral" violins and recorders). Thus he created a proto-orchestra of almost three dozen instruments, although unlike later orchestras it had no core of string instruments doubling their parts, and some instruments played offstage while others were onstage, to the side. While solo singing is accompanied primarily by basso continuo alone (with notable exceptions like Orfeo's "Possente spirto," Act 3), the instrumental corps plays a surrogate overture (toccata), a concluding dance (*moresca*), and numerous ritornellos (short instrumental sections within songs) and sinfonias (other short instrumental pieces), and doubles the voices in **choruses**.

In the second half of the 17th century in Italy, the instrumentalists were moved for the most part to the area in front of the stage. String instruments, two or more per part, led by the violins became the increasingly standardized core of a modest orchestra that served cost-conscious Venetian public theaters more economically than the variegated *intermedio* ensembles still sometimes employed for court opera. Public theater orchestras often included as few as two to four violins, a pair of violas, and two tenor/bass instruments plus continuo (one or two large lutes and/or harpsichords). Wind instruments—mostly flutes, oboes, or trumpets—were enlisted sparingly for color and topical associations as appropriate. Court operas regularly featured more impressive ensembles of about three dozen players and, according to contemporary reports, could number as high as 200 by the early 18th century for celebratory occasions. Although basso continuo remained the primary accompaniment for solo singing, the orchestra gradually infiltrated vocal sections of particularly important **arias**, providing echoes at ends of phrases and even playing along with singers (rarely). In the last quarter of the 17th century, cellos and/or basses joined the lutes and harpsichords for basso continuo accompaniments.

Early French productions of Italian operas in the mid-17th century were enhanced with **ballets**, entrusting a greater role to the orchestra than it saw in Italy, and apparently employed ensembles comparable to or exceeding those of Italian court orchestras in size. An imposing continuo group of as many as four harpsichords and eight lutes of various sorts could provide the foundation for the 24 Violons du Roi, the 18 Petits Violons du Roi, the oboes and bassoons of the Grande Ecurie, and additional chamber musicians, many or all of these forces coming to bear primarily in the overture, choruses, certain ritornellos, and the dances of the **divertissements**. Strings, often arranged famously in five-part textures (in which violas were divided among the three middle parts) or alternatively trios or quartets, and trios and quartets of oboes and bassoons (all parts played by multiple players in both cases) sounded separately or together. During the first half of the 18th century, the size of the orchestra was standardized at about four dozen players to fit the available space at the Palais Royal, where the Opéra was based (*see* PARIS), and scoring shifted in the direction of the modern four-part string texture, which eventually became standard across Europe. As in Italy the orchestra took an expanded role in solo vocal music, particularly the Italianate *ariettes* (*see* AIR) introduced by **Jean-Philippe Rameau** and others. And the wind band expanded to include horn (imported from Germany) and clarinets.

From the 18th century on, the development of the opera orchestra roughly paralleled that of the concert orchestra. Across that century its average size increased, more string instruments participating in an increasingly standardized arrangement of first and second violins, violas, and cellos and basses, although Italian orchestras continued to give minimal emphasis to the middle of the texture. Woodwinds and brass saw more action, particularly in German orchestras, and the transverse flute replaced the recorder, the *chalumeau/* clarinet and horns appeared with increasing frequency (particularly during the last quarter of the century), trumpets and timpani players were conscripted from military bands, and the lute family gradually disappeared from the continuo group. Overall, the size of the orchestra still varied considerably, depending on the location (city versus court, and type of theater) and occasion, from about two dozen to six dozen players. The entire ensemble participated in overtures, dances, and French-styled descriptive music such as battle and storm symphonies. Solo obbligato wind (or more rarely violin) parts sometimes interacted with the voice in arias, throughout or as brief interjections. In Italian theaters (and most others), responsibilities for directing the orchestra and singers were divided between the first violinist and harpsichordist, while in France a proto-**conductor**, the *batteur de mesure* who beat time with a wooden pole (or other implement), positioned himself on the stage apron (in front of the proscenium arch). There and elsewhere the orchestra played on the theater floor in front of the stage, the musicians arranged in rows in Italy, in a semicircle facing the stage in France.

During the 19th century the process of expanding the orchestra continued through a general increase in the number of players and more proportionate emphasis of violas and cellos in Italian houses. Low brass—trombone and less frequently a bass instrument such as the *ophicleide* or tuba—was often added; the capabilities of both brass and winds were enhanced through the introduction of valves and keys; and the percussion section was typically augmented with bass drum, snare drum, cymbals, and others. As obbligato **recitative** became standard and the trend toward musical continuity progressed, the orchestra was involved consistently throughout, and the continuo harpsichord or piano eventually disappeared. The directing role gradually passed to a standing conductor. And the modern arrangement of paired seatings facing the conductor won the day, as did the placement of the orchestra in a lowered pit, an innovation that began with the Bayreuth Festival Theater (*see* THEATER DESIGN) and was included in many new and remodeled houses. The role of the orchestra in conveying atmosphere and a sense of place and in contributing to emotional/psychological expression and illuminating characters' inner thoughts, motivations, and relationships (*see* LEIT-MOTIF) both expanded prodigiously and gained remarkable sophistication, first in France and Germany and eventually in Italy and elsewhere.

In the 20th century, further enrichment of the corps of available instruments to include the full array of pitched and nonpitched percussion (xylophone, gong, etc.), non-Western instruments, jazz and rock ensembles, and electronic resources, as well as novel treatments and combinations of traditional instruments, and nontraditional arrangements of instruments onstage, have turned the opera orchestra into a variegated palette of virtually unlimited sonic resources. The result has been a compendium of approaches to orchestration, ranging from the throwback styles of **neo-classical** operas such as *The Rake's Progress* and the more modernist economies of chamber operas by **Paul Hindemith** and **Benjamin Britten** to massive post-Wagnerian megaliths (**Richard Strauss**'s *Elektra*, 1909; **Hans Werner Henze**'s *The Bassarids*, 1966); scorings influenced by jazz, popular, rock, and/or non-Western musics (e.g., *Die Dreigroschenoper*, *Einstein on the Beach*, **John Adams**'s *I Was Looking at the Ceiling and Then I Saw the Sky*, 1995); and augmentations including electronically generated tracks (**John Eaton**'s *The Cry of Clytaemnestra*,1980, and *The Tempest*, 1985).

Beginning in the last quarter of the 20th century, numerous historically informed productions have enlisted orchestras of period instruments or replicas (violins with gut strings and lighter bows, winds with fewer keys, etc.) for 17th-, 18th-, and even 19th-century operas. Notable examples include the Monteverdi operas conducted by Nikolaus Harnoncourt (born 1929) and directed by Jean-Pierre Ponnelle (1932–1988) at the Zurich Opera House in the late 1970s, the series of **Wolfgang Amadeus Mozart** operas mounted by Arnold Östman (born 1939) at the Drottningholm Theater (Stockholm) in the 1980s, and John Eliot Gardiner's recent performances of **Carl Maria von Weber**'s *Oberon* (2002, originally1826) and *Carmen* (2009) with the Orchestre Révolutionnaire et Romantique.

ORFEO. Favola in musica; music by **Claudio Monteverdi**, **libretto** by Alessandro Striggio (ca. 1536–1592) based on the Orpheus legend following Ovid and Virgil; **prologue** and five acts, probably performed originally without intermissions; premiered Mantua, ducal palace, February 1607. Monteverdi's *Orfeo*, the most successful of a number of Orpheus operas that appeared during the initial quarter of the century, is considered the first masterpiece of early opera. Written as a court production for Carnival rather than to commemorate a political event, it probably resulted from competition between Duke Vincenzo Gonzaga's sons, Francesco Gonzaga in Mantua and his brother Ferdinando, who had ties to the Florentine court and **Jacopo Peri**. All or most of the female roles were sung by **castratos**.

Much more than Peri's *Euridice*, *Orfeo* demonstrates the potential of music for restoring the golden age of the arts. Appropriately, Monteverdi entrusted its prologue to the personification of Music instead of Tragedy. And although it shows similarities to *Euridice* in its distribution of different types of **recitatives** for analogous passages, its music is more elaborate and diverse, incorporating frequent *canzonette* (see the series of dance songs that begins Act 2), **madrigals**, and instrumental ritornellos and sinfonias and displaying richer treatments of the various recitative styles.

A mythological **pastoral** opera typical of the early 17th century, its action consists of a minimal number of events centered on the title character, who leads a very small cast, and proceeds through tableaux that focus on emotional responses to static situations. While celebrating his marriage to Euridice with shepherds and nymphs, Orfeo is blindsided by news of her death. In the underworld for Acts 3 and 4, he lulls the boatman Charon to sleep with his music and persuades Proserpina and Pluto to free Euridice. However, he fails to fulfill their requirement that he not look at her along the way and returns home without his wife. Printed librettos from 1607 end with Orfeo fleeing the Bacchantes, who end the opera with a frenzied **ballet**, whereas the 1609 printed score has a more celebratory ending in which Orfeo and Apollo ascend to the heavens on a cloud singing a virtuoso madrigal, followed by a *moresca* (Moorish dance) performed by his companions.

Monteverdi and Striggio's treatment includes light moments prior to Euridice's death that anticipate the later Venetian *contrascena*, as well as the most intensely moving passages heard in early opera: the Messenger's *recitativo espressivo* "In un fiorito prato" and the responding choral madrigal "Ahi, caso acerbo" (both Act 2), as well as Orfeo's plea to Charon, the hybrid strophic variation recitative-cum-**aria** "Possente spirto," which mimics Orpheus's virtuosity. Refrains within individual acts (the **choruses** "Vieni, Imeneo" and "Lasciate i monti" and two ritornellos in Act 1, for example) or across the entire opera (reappearances of the ritornello from the prologue in Acts 2 and 4) reinforce the narrative stasis of the tableaux structure and suggest a precocious concern for long-range architectural cohesion that would reappear no sooner than **Christoph Willibald Gluck**'s *Orfeo ed Euridice* (1762). Though evidence is uncertain, *Orfeo* appears to have played an important role in the early dissemination of opera across northern Italy and Austria within a decade or so of its premier.

ORFEO ED EURIDICE. *Azione teatrale* (*see* FESTA TEATRALE); music by **Christoph Willibald Gluck**, **libretto** by **Ranieri Calzabigi** based on the Orpheus legend as told by Ovid and Virgil; three acts; premiered **Vienna**, Burgtheater, October 1762. The first of three "reform" operas created with Calzabigi before Gluck relocated to **Paris** in the 1770s, *Orfeo* triumphed at its premier for the name day of Emperor Francis I. It was substantially enlarged for Paris as *Orphée et Eurydice* (1774), with expansive **divertissements**—a new one to end Orphée's scene with the Furies (Act 2) and extensions of those beginning the scene in Elysium (including the famous "Dance of the Blessed Spirits") and ending the opera—and additional **arias**: a **coloratura** showpiece for Orphée to end Act 1 ("L'espoir renaît") and a pastoral aria with **chorus** for Eurydice ("Cet asile") to conclude the Elysian divertissement. (Modern performances have typically adopted the French version in Italian translation.) Over the years, the role of Orfeo, composed for the **contralto castrato** Gaetano Guadagni (1728–1792), was transposed for **soprano** castrato Giuseppe Millico (1737–1802) in 1769, adapted and expanded for **tenor** *haute-contre* **Joseph Legros** in Paris, and sung by **women**, including the contralto **Pauline Viardot**, tenors, and even baritones (*see* BASS).

Gluck's most successful, influential, and familiar opera, *Orfeo* embodies principles later articulated in the preface to *Alceste*, centered on "noble simplicity" and on the service of music to drama as influenced by French practices. Calzabigi reduced the inherently simple tale to its bare essentials, devoid of **Metastasian** intrigue. Euridice already dead, Amore (Cupid) encourages Orfeo to rescue her. After the hero charms the furies of the underworld, reclaims her, and loses her a second time, Amore serves as deus ex machina and restores her to him, providing a *lieto fine* appropriate for the occasion of its premier. This action unfolds in four broad tableaux that mostly avoid the Metastasian litany of **recitatives** and exit arias and instead consist of spontaneous sequences of brief numbers linked musically through inconclusive cadences, thematic returns, and closely related keys (especially Orfeo's confrontation with the furies, Act 2). The cast comprises only three soloists, and their workloads are distributed unequally, Euridice receiving her only aria in the Viennese original ("Che fiero momento") no earlier than Act 3.

In line with Gluck's program, declamatory singing carries substantial expressive weight. Obbligato recitative reinforced by the **orchestra** appears to the exclusion of simple recitative, and most lyric set pieces incorporate recitative-like sections: the episodes that intersperse Orfeo's famous refrain "Che farò senza Euridice" (Act 3), the choral rejoinders within and between the three sections of his "Deh placatevi" (Act 2), and even the third section of that aria ("Men tiranno"), in which he abandons the Italianate **bel canto** of the previous sections for a more personally emotive—and more persuasive—style of rhetoric. Arias shun the most artificial conventions of the da capo tradition: the momentum killing opening ritornellos, unnatural word repetitions and rearrangements, and self-serving coloratura. The choice of genre—the myth-based *azione teatrale* instead of the historical *dramma per musica* (*see* OPERA SERIA)—allowed dance, chorus, and scenic instrumental music to play a prominent role in developing emotional context. The richness of Gluck's orchestration is stunning by comparison with traditional Italian scores, employing unaccustomed instruments such as harp, cornet, English horn, and *chalumeau* (related to the clarinet); novel effects (in Orfeo's scene with the furies, string pizzicatos with harp for his lyre and string glissandos for Cerberus's bark); and numerous solos for cello, bassoon, flute, and other instruments (see Orfeo's monologue "Che puro ciel") to characterize ritual, infernal, pastoral, and celebratory environments. Despite its disconnection from the mournful opening scene, even the festive **overture** plays a dramatic role by foreshadowing and to an extent rationalizing the happy ending.

Although Gluck backpedaled in certain respects when he revised *Orfeo* for Paris, lengthening it by a third, cutting down its recitatives, adding the virtuoso aria for Legros, and replacing unfamiliar instruments with more conventional ones, it exerted in all its versions an enormous influence on late 18th-century composers (e.g., **Wolfgang Amadeus Mozart** in *Idomeneo*) and set one crucial agenda for the development of Italian and German opera from the 1780s through the first half of the 19th century.

ORNAMENTATION. An outgrowth of virtuosic singing in the **madrigal** tradition of the 16th century, the embellishment of vocal lines with ornaments that were written out, indicated by conventional symbols, or added by performers (either rehearsed or extemporized) was standard practice in opera from the start. Endorsed by theoretical writings as an enhancement of text expression, ornamentation also demonstrated vocal accomplishment and contributed to individualized **singing style**, for example that of **Vittoria Archilei**, who reportedly enriched **monody** with frequent, elaborate flourishes to notable effect. That ornamentation was abused, resulting in melodic distortions and interruptions of text declamation that made the poetry less intelligible, is evident, for example, in **Giulio Caccini**'s attempt in *Le nuove musiche* (1602) to discourage excessive ornamentation by demonstrating proper usage.

Caccini and many others from the 17th through the early 19th centuries identified a panoply of ornaments, distinguishing between short *grazie* (graces, alternatively *accenti*, *affetti*, *maniere*) and *passaggi* (passagework), lengthier runs that fill in various melodic pitch intervals. Seventeenth-century *grazie* included the *trillo* (an accelerating repetition of a single note, sometimes mimicking sobbing); the *gruppo*, resembling either a modern trill (also *tremolo*) or later a turn (*gruppetto*); and various hairpin crescendos and decrescendo effects (e.g., *messa di voce*, the 18th-century term for a dynamic swell on a held note, a technique for which the **castrato Farinelli** was praised, or *esclamazione*, the opposite effect involving a decrescendo followed by a crescendo). Phrase-ending appoggiaturas (metered accented dissonances that resolve downward by step) became common, particularly in **recitatives** where they are indicated by repetition of the note of resolution, as did the *acciaccatura* (in the 19th century a quick, unmeasured grace note, generally on the beat), and other grace notes that anticipate the beat. Early writers also favored portamento (or *portamento della voce*), which involves "carrying the voice" (sliding) between successive notes, an effect exaggerated in the technique *cercar della nota* ("seeking out the note"), which involves starting a note as much as a fourth below the indicated pitch.

Added ornamentation was intrinsic to the 18th-century da capo **aria**. While most high-minded theorists advocated simple enhancements in the opening and middle sections and tasteful elaboration in the reprise, frequent complaints and rare examples of ornamentation written into manuscripts suggest that actual practice could be more extravagant. Slow arias that lacked passagework provided prime opportunities for embellishment. And a cadenza was expected at least at the final cadence of the reprise of any da capo aria, while others could be introduced to close additional sections. The proliferation of late 18th- and early 19th-century method books dealing with ornamentation indicates its continued significance. And assuming that **Gioachino Rossini**'s notated ornaments and *passaggi* in operas such as *Semiramide* were intended to rein in excesses, they indicate that embellishment could reach outrageous proportions, even in obbligato recitatives. Ornamentation decreased, beginning with male roles, in conjunction with the shift to a heavier, more frankly passionate singing style beginning in the 1830s, and was increasingly confined to turns at the ends of phrases. Slow movements of grand arias became the primary opportunity for enhancements, although brief cadenza-like elaborations of fermatas probably occurred within the **cabaletta** at the end of the main theme (particularly at its reprise) and in the coda.

A signature of the Italianate style, ornamentation was generally kept at arm's length in France, where **Jean-Baptiste Lully** notated sparse embellishments for his **airs** and prohibited additional elaboration. While it became more of a factor in the 18th and 19th centuries as *ariettes* in the Italian style and strophic songs became common, short graces were generally preferred over extended passagework. Elsewhere—primarily in Germany and England—it played a role in regional styles to the extent that they incorporated Italianate idioms. The cult of fidelity to the written score in the mid-20th century inhibited added embellishment, a tendency that has been reversed by performers familiar with recent musicological research.

ORONTEA. *Dramma musicale*; music by **Antonio Cesti, libretto** by Giacinto Andrea Cicognini (1606–ca. 1650); **prologue** and three acts; premiered Innsbruck, Teatro di Sala, February 1656; an earlier setting of the libretto for **Venice** (1649) may have been composed by Francesco Lucio (ca. 1628–1658). Alongside **Francesco Cavalli**'s *Giasone* (libretto also by Cicognini), *Orontea* was the most widely performed repertory opera of the 17th century and an influential paradigm of the midcentury Venetian public theater style.

Orontea's intricate plot, probably influenced by Spanish drama, combines multiple love entanglements and intrigues, disguises and mistaken identities (sometimes involving cross-dressing and cross-gendering in the assignment of roles—*see* TRAVESTY), lowbrow comic scenes integrated into the action, and modest attempts at human portraiture. In the allegorical **prologue**, Love and Philosophy contend for control of the action. Prince Floridano of Phoenicia, assumed to be the philandering painter Alidoro, is pursued by Orontea (queen of Egypt), Silandra (a lady-in-waiting), and Giacinta (a former lover, disguised as the boy Ismero, probably played by a **castrato**). Ismero catches the eye of the geriatric, libidinous nurse Aristea (the presumed mother of Alidoro, played by a male **tenor**), and Silandra temporarily rejects her lover Corindo. Giacinta/Ismero, Aristea, and Gelone (a drunken servant) provide comic relief. At the end of the opera, Orontea wins Alidoro/Floridano, and Silandra and Corindo are reunited in a *lieto fine*.

Composed in the **aria**-dominated Venetian manner, *Orontea* includes numerous examples of the main 17th-century forms and stylistic characteristics. ABB' or ABA arias in single or paired strophes display liquid melodies, metrical **coloratura**, word painting, and often antiphony between singers and the small "**orchestra**" of violins and **basso continuo**. And Cesti and Cicognini anticipated late 17th- and 18th-century practice through clearer delineation of their arias and **recitatives** in poetic (*see* VERSIFICATION) and musical style, although the typically sparse declamation of recitatives sometimes yields to more impassioned **arioso**.

OTELLO. *Dramma lirico* by **Giuseppe Verdi**, **libretto** by **Arrigo Boito** based on William Shakespeare's play *Othello, or The Moor of Venice*; four acts; Milan, Teatro alla Scala, February 1887.

Otello is Verdi's second to last opera; second of three Shakespearian works (along with *Macbeth*, 1847, and *Falstaff*, 1893); and one of his most sublime creations. It resulted from dogged diplomacy by Giulio **Ricordi** and Boito. For decades Verdi had been scouting Shakespearian projects to follow *Macbeth*—most prominently *Re Lear* in the 1850s—and they were able to entice him with a draft libretto in 1879, although startup was delayed because of work on revisions to *Simon Boccanegra* (1857, revised 1881) and *Don Carlos* (originally 1867, revised 1884). The long-anticipated premier with a stellar cast under the direction of superstar **conductor** Franco Faccio (1840–1891) was a popular triumph, and the opera soon made the rounds of European theaters and gained a secure place in the repertory, despite its considerable demands on singers and the **orchestra**.

Boito and Verdi crafted a much more faithful adaptation of the play than **Gioachino Rossini** and his **librettist** Francesco Maria Berio di Salsa (1765–1820) had in 1816, when they eliminated Cassio and shoved Rodrigo to the forefront, forcing Shakespeare's nuanced relationships and linear plot into a formulaic love triangle. Though Boito and Verdi excised Shakespeare's Venetian first act and set their opera entirely in Cyprus, they transplanted Otello and Desdemona's backstory to the love **duet** that ends Act 1 and provided an even more sympathetic baseline for the deterioration of their relationship. As in Shakespeare's play, Iago dispenses his poison as soon as Otello's fleet makes land, instigating the fight between Cassio and the nobleman Montano that results in his captain's demotion and, later, Desdemona's misconstrued petitions for his reinstatement. And his insidious designs mimic those in Shakespeare—he pricks Otello's jealousy with Desdemona and Cassio's innocent conversation, commandeers Desdemona's keepsake handkerchief, manufactures Cassio's incriminating dream about Desdemona, and encourages Otello to misinterpret Cassio's amorous braggadocio, incriminating him by planting the handkerchief in his possession—their progress culminating in Desdemona's humiliation in front of the Venetian ambassadors and her subsequent murder.

Otello's style constitutes an outgrowth of prior trends in Verdi's handling of both Italian and French elements. And in certain respects it anticipates **verismo** of the 1890s. Whether consciously attempting to position himself as a modern composer, responding to a particularly rich subject and libretto, profiting from a relaxed creative time frame, or simply reaping the fruits of decades of experience and maturity, with *Otello* (and later *Falstaff*), Verdi reached a remarkable level of sophistication as a composer and dramatist.

Otello demonstrates the prodigious expressive arsenal commanded by Verdi late in his career, which is capable of representing stunning psychological breadth as well as conveying a compelling sense of place and circumstance. Accommodating both Italian and French idioms, his primarily tonal, functional melodic and harmonic palette is enriched by the chromatic, pentatonic, and modal inflections, the nonfunctional juxtapositions of triads and seventh chords, and the distant key relations of French music. His instrumentation, also influenced by French practices, shows an extraordinary range of colors and nuances, from ethereal whispers to bombastic tantrums (as in the Act 1 love duet). Largely abandoning the unitized melodies of the 1850s, Verdi's music deflects from moment to moment as the characters' interactions and thought processes unfold. This expressive immediacy is evident, for example, in the opera's most famous piece, Desdemona's "Willow Song" ("Piangea cantando," Act 4). In the heroine's disjointed rendition of an archaic folk song, each of its stanzas consists of a series of disconnected, variable, and interchangeable melodic modules representing different fragments of her brittle psyche, her lack of focus and wistful resignation emphasized by its juxtaposition against her subsequent, more measured "Ave Maria." And this psychological acuity characterizes all of her interactions with Otello, from their love duet through their Act 2 quartet with Iago and Emilia, their Act 3 duet and the **finale** with the Venetian ambassadors, and the Act 4 murder.

In similar fashion, Verdi extended prior trends toward continuity and naturalness in handling the distribution and internal organization of set pieces. He eliminated entirely the conventional three-movement **aria**. The relatively few solo scenes involve single movements that are deployed not according to workload conventions but as the action suggests. They take the form of remnants from the traditional schema, such as Otello's **cabaletta** without repeat "Ora e per sempre addio" (Act 2) in which he abandons his marriage; **stage songs** (Cassio's drinking song "Inaffia l'ugola," joined by Iago and chorus, Act 1; Iago's *racconto* "Era la notte," his account of Cassio's purported dream, Act 2; and the "Willow Song"); or dramatic declamatory monologues, such as Iago's "Credo in un Dio crudel" (Act 1).

Distribution of set pieces is dominated instead by interactive ensembles, several of which betray their ancestry in four-movement set pieces: the opening storm scene in which lyric high points—the prayer "Dio, fulgor della bufera" and the celebration "Vittoria! Sterminio!"—suggest the *largo concertato* and **stretta** of an *introduzione*, or the aforementioned love duet, in which the lyrical points of relaxation "E tu m'amavi" and "Un baccio" hint at the reflective movements of a traditional duet. However, much more often single lyrical movements provide centerpieces for developing action, as in Otello and Iago's revenge cabaletta "Sì, pel ciel" (Act 2) or the *largo concertato* of the Act 3 finale "A terra! . . . sì . . . nel livido fango." When remnants of the standard schemata remain, their presence is less obtrusive than in operas as recent as *Aida* and the revised *Simon Boccanegra*. Verdi's pliable text-setting style, which distributes lyrical and declamatory singing uniformly, his avoidance of extended thematically and metrically uniform melodies, distribution of melodic phrases between characters to maintain dialogue, consistent orchestral presence, and continuity of action blend these traditional components with their surroundings. Applause breaks are infrequent, because the ends of set pieces tend to decay or elide their final cadences, as in Cassio's drinking song with Iago, a strophic arrangement that breaks down as Cassio becomes more inebriated and contentious.

Verdi's treatment of thematic integration in Otello combines two approaches rooted in French opera, which were gaining currency in Italy and would become centerpieces of **Giacomo Puccini**'s style. The ecstatic recollection of an incandescent phrase (heard previously in *Ernani*, 1844; *La traviata*, 1853; and elsewhere) appears to telling effect when the kiss theme, "Un baccio," from the end of the Act 1 love duet returns twice at the end of the opera as Otello kisses his sleeping wife and later at his own death to denote his conflicted passions. The more persistent network of short motifs associated with Iago (in the manner of the heroine, Amneris, and the priests of *Aida*) makes a subtler and yet more integral musical contribution to dramatic development and color. His array of snarling, chromatic, angular gestures, an infernal virus introduced surreptitiously in the fight scene and given unequivocal meaning in his "Credo," infects Otello's musical vocabulary as the villain's intrigues gradually dominate him.

Despite the continued presence of French aspects of melody, harmony, orchestration, and motivic integration, once the plot is under way, *Otello* gives considerably less play to spectacle, which had peaked with *Aida*. After an opening that recalls the cataclysms and atmospheric **divertissements** of **grand opéra** (storm, bonfire chorus "Fuoco di gioia," drinking song and duel, and Otello's intervention), arguably French elements appear less frequently and are more personal—the gentle homage to Desdemona "Dove guardi," Act 2; Cassio's caddish scherzo "Essa t'avvince" with Iago and Otello, Act 3; and possibly Desdemona's "Willow Song" and "Ave Maria"—as Iago's schemes play out in private dialogues.

OVERTURE. Generic designation for a substantial instrumental piece that introduces an opera or other dramatic work prior to the beginning of the staged action, or alternatively a similar concert piece.

The first operatic overtures were brass and wind fanfares that descended from openings to earlier court entertainments, for example, the toccata to **Claudio Monteverdi**'s *Orfeo*. As early as the Venetian operas of the1640s, the term "sinfonia," commonly associated with instrumental sections other than dances or ritornellos in predominantly vocal works, was applied to short opening pieces in a slow tempo for strings and **basso continuo**. By the 1660s, the sinfonia took the form of a pair of dance movements, in which a slow first movement in duple meter was followed by a faster movement in triple meter.

In France, a similar type of two-movement work, termed *ouverture*, introduced the *ballet de cour* (court **ballet**) beginning in the 1640s. **Jean-Baptiste Lully** developed this arrangement into the conventionalized French overture, normally scored for the five-part string ensemble of the 24 Violons du Roi plus oboes, beginning with his ballet *Alcidiane* (1658) and later in his *tragédies en musique* (e.g., *Alceste, ou Le triomphe d'Alcide*). Its standard form comprises two repeated sections: the first is processional, characterized by chordal texture, duple meter, and obsessive dotted rhythms exaggerated by overdotting, and ends with a half cadence; the second begins in a livelier triple meter and includes more linear and contrapuntal music before returning at the end to material resembling the first section. The French overture was adopted frequently in Germany and England (see the overture to *Giulio Cesare in Egitto*).

In contrast, late 17th-century Neapolitans such as **Alessandro Scarlatti** relied on the sinfonia in three tempos (fast-slow-fast) with increasing regularity. Its first and last movements often included trumpets echoed by violins in the manner of a concerto, and its last movement normally was a triple-meter dance in binary form. The Italian sinfonia gradually superseded the French overture as the standard type across Europe during the mid-18th century and was heard in several variants: the long-standing three-movement form, fast-slow-fast, with a dance finale and a first movement that often resembled sonata form; three movements, fast-slow-fast, with the finale drawing on materials from the opening movement (the so-called "reprise overture"); and two movements, fast-slow, for which the beginning of the first scene of the opera served as the finale of the overture. By the 1790s the sinfonia most often consisted of a single allegro in sonata form equivalent to the first movement of a symphony, sometimes beginning with a slow introduction but lacking a full-scale development section, as in the overtures to *Le nozze di Figaro* and *Die Zauberflöte*. This arrangement was conventionalized in **Gioachino Rossini**'s operas, where an extended slow introduction includes several contrasting sections and a simple retransition replaces the development section in the allegro (for example, the overture to *Il barbiere di Siviglia*).

In the wake of late 18th-century operatic "reforms" by **Christoph Willibald Gluck** and others (*see ALCESTE*), composers paid greater attention to relating the overture to the opera itself in various ways. In addition to the aforementioned two-movement overtures completed by the initial staged music, overtures attach themselves to the opening scene with transitions; set the mood and adopt musical topics appropriate for the entire opera (Asian or Turkish, for example) or the opening **scene** (storms, celebrations); and anticipate music from the opera, often in dramatically meaningful juxtapositions of themes associated with characters, relationships, or issues that encapsulate the drama. The overture to *Don Giovanni* plays all these roles, connecting to Leporello's *sortita*, establishing the opera's characteristic juxtaposition of dark and light, and foreshadowing the villain's fall in the slow introduction. Medley overtures, which dispense with gravitas and simply present a diverting introduction to the opera's most engaging tunes, existed in England by the 1780s and played an expanding role in mainstream opera in the 19th century. The gradual incursion of the medley impulse is seen, for example in the overture to *Nabucco*, in which themes taken from the opera—some having dramatic meaning, some not—pervade both an extended introduction and a fast conclusion with partial reprise.

During the mid-19th century the self-standing overture was often supplanted by a brief evocative prelude, roughly equivalent to the instrumental introductions to later acts. Shorter, less conventional in organization, and musically less conclusive, they typically include only one or two themes, which signify important elements of the ensuing drama (for example the curse motif in the prelude to *Rigoletto*, motifs associated with Aida and the priests in *Aida*, or those evoking the leads' yearning in *Tristan und Isolde*). By the end of the century, operas frequently launched the action with no overture or prelude (**Giuseppe Verdi**'s *Otello*) or with a bare minimum of evocative music (Scarpia's chords beginning *Tosca*). The medley overture remained popular in 19th-century **opéra comique** and **operetta** and their offspring in 20th-century musical comedy.

P

PACINI, GIOVANNI. (1796, Catania–1867, Pescia.) Prolific **composer** of over 80 Italian comic, semiserious, and serious operas (*see* CATEGORIES OF OPERA) from the 1810s through the 1860s, as well as sacred vocal and instrumental music.

Pacini studied singing, counterpoint, and composition beginning with his father, a famous **tenor**, and in Bologna and Venice, originally targeting a career in church music. Like many of his contemporaries, he paid his dues with comic opera, completing his first **opera buffa** at age 17 and staging a *farsa*, *Annetta e Lucindo*, that same year (1813), to begin a series of a dozen light works. His first major triumph came at La Scala in Milan with the *melodramma Il barone di Dolsheim* (1818), and (following **Gioachino Rossini**'s departure for Paris) he temporarily established himself in the 1820s as the leading Italian composer of serious opera with two relatively old-fashioned subjects, the **Pietro Metastasio** remake *Alessandro nelle Indie* (1824) and *L'ultimo giorno di Pompei* (1825) for **Naples**. Flush with success, he built a house in Viareggio, where he lived until 1855, and was tapped by **Domenico Barbaia** to succeed Rossini and **Saverio Mercadante** as director of Neapolitan theaters.

The 1830s brought setbacks. Pacini suffered from competition by a new generation of composers, particularly **Vincenzo Bellini** and **Gaetano Donizetti**, which contributed to a series of fiascos. They led him to retire from the theater (1835–39) and occupy himself as director of a **conservatory** he established in Viareggio and as *maestro di cappella* to the court of Lucca (beginning 1837). Following Bellini's death and noting the decline in Donizetti's popularity, Pacini resumed his career at the end of the decade, self-consciously determined to reinvent his style and overcome his prior typecasting as merely a prolific melodist. *Saffo* (1840), currently judged his best opera, demonstrates this second manner. Pacini avoided Rossinian **coloratura** and replaced freely phrased, episodic melodies with midcentury melodic forms (*see* LYRIC PROTOTYPE), adopted more frankly emotive vocal writing that reflects Bellini's and Donizetti's approaches, devised more expressive, atmospheric orchestrations, experimented with chromatic harmonies and key changes, smoothed the boundaries between **recitatives** and set pieces, and gave greater weight to the action movements of those set pieces (*see* TEMPO D'ATTACCO and TEMPO DI MEZZO).

Pacini moved to Pescia in 1855, where he concentrated on teaching and instrumental music. His operatic career essentially ended with *Il saltimbanco* (1858).

PAER, FERDINANDO. (1771, Parma–1839, Paris.) Italian **composer** of roughly 55 operas mostly from the 1790s to ca. 1820, as well as other vocal and instrumental music. Along with **Simon Mayr**, he was a leading composer of the generation prior to **Gioachino Rossini** and a central figure in the development of *opera semiseria*.

Paer began his career as adjunct *maestro di cappella* and music director of royal services in his hometown, positions of modest responsibilities that allowed him to tuck almost two dozen operas under his belt in the five years between *Circe* (1792), his first opera, and *Il principe di Taranto* (1797). He parlayed his successes in Parma and elsewhere with works such as the **opera buffa** *Saed, ossia Gl' intrighi del serraglio* (1795, Venice) into an appointment as music director of the Kärntnertortheater in **Vienna** (1797), which began a series of foreign positions that won him fame and fortune. As Kapellmeister in Dresden (beginning 1801), works including the **rescue opera** *Leonora, ossia L'amore conjugale* (1804), the prototype for operas by Mayr and Ludwig van Beethoven (1770–1827) the next year (*see FIDELIO*), caught the attention of Napoleon, who took him to Poland (1806) and installed him in **Paris** (beginning 1807) as his *maître de chapelle*, then director of the Théâtre Italien (1812), the latter post suspended by Rossini's appointment (1824–26), until Paer resigned in 1827. He ended his career in the 1830s as director of King Louis-Philippe's private chapel and superintendent and composition teacher at the Paris Conservatoire.

A prolific composer, particularly in his years in Parma, Paer wrote many traditional opere serie and opere buffe, as well as the *farse* fashionable around 1800 and a handful of **opéras comiques**, including the famous *Le maître de chapelle, ou Le souper imprévu* (*The Chapel Master, or The Unexpected Supper*), and an opéra, *Blanche de Provence* (both 1821) for Paris. However, his historical importance centers on his operas of mixed type. They range in their emphasis of serious and comic plotlines and characters from the mock-heroic *dramma eroicomico Sargino* (1803), which gives buffo and serious elements equal emphasis, to works like *Leonora* and *Agnese* (1809), essentially *melodrammas* in which comic servants and lovers relieve the tension of Gothic settings, imprisonments, and mad scenes.

PAGLIACCI. *Dramma*; music by **Ruggero Leoncavallo, libretto** by the **composer** based on a newspaper article; **prologue** and two acts; premiered Milan, Teatro Dal Verme, May 1892. Currently the most familiar early **verismo** opera.

A resounding success, the premier of *Clowns* was conducted by a youthful **Arturo Toscanini** and the leads taken by such notables as the French baritone Victor Maurel (1848–1923), Iago in **Giuseppe Verdi**'s *Otello* (and Falstaff the next year), who played Tonio. Within a few years it was performed across Europe, and it remains a mainstay of the repertory to the present, often paired in performance with *Cavalleria rusticana*.

Pagliacci's prologue is a verismo manifesto of aesthetic truthfulness and empathy, a microcosm of the opera in which melodic catharsis sells Tonio's proclamation that his fellow characters breathe air like the rest of us. And the opera presents a vision of life as coarse and violent, in which riffraff from an itinerant **commedia dell'arte** troupe and the local village are destroyed by lust, jealousy, grief, and rage. Nedda, wife of the company's leader, Canio, has an affair with the villager Silvio and mocks the hunchback Tonio, who lusts for her. After she strikes him when he tries to press his cause, he betrays her to Canio. That evening the company performs a play mirroring their own relationships, in which Canio portrays the cuckolded husband Pagliaccio, Nedda his adulterous wife Colombina, Tonio her rebuffed betrayer Taddeo, and the actor Beppe her lover Arlecchino. As their audience looks on in horror, Canio confronts Nedda, stabs her to flush his rival out of the audience, and kills Silvio as Tonio chalks up a morbid victory.

Leoncavallo's treatment of the story contributes to the audience's immersion in this sordid drama. A compact work lasting little more than an hour, *Pagliacci* compresses its action into the span of a single afternoon and evening. More than *Cavalleria* it integrates the set pieces of Act 1 (the ***introduzione*** with Canio's ***sortita*** and **choruses**, Nedda's one-movement flight **aria**, her **duets** with Tonio and Silvio, and Canio's scena—*see* SCENE—following his discovery of the lovers) with transitional lead-ins and departures and treats the entire second act as a single extended scene, creating continuous, rivetingly paced progressions in both acts from festivities to violent confrontation. Frequent melodic foreshadowings and recollections (e.g., those of the Act 1 celebrations, the love duet, and Canio's rage music) also contribute to this cohesion. Development of characters' individual motivations—Canio's hair-trigger rage, conveyed by chromaticism that echoes Iago, and belief that Nedda is obligated to him; her sense of imprisonment; and Tonio's humiliations—make them into credible objects of our empathy. And by imposing exaggerated impediments to the suspension of disbelief, the commedia dell'arte artifices of Tonio's opening monologue and the Act 2 play create a virtuoso vehicle for demonstrating the interpenetration of life and theater, as the musical style of the opera's reality intrudes on the contrived dance tunes of the play, the play's action becomes violent and spills into its audience, and the opera's audience becomes an extension of the play's audience.

PAISIELLO, GIOVANNI. (1740, Roccaforzata–1816, Naples.) **Composer** of nearly 90 **opera serias** and **opera buffas**, mostly from the 1760s through the 1790s; along with **Domenico Cimarosa**, one of the most important Italian composers of his time.

Trained primarily in **Naples** (1754–63), Paisiello based his activities there periodically throughout his career. Following his first position as music director for a small, newly formed theater in Bologna beginning in 1763, he moved back to Naples in 1766. Working at a furious pace, he composed about two dozen operas for Neapolitan theaters over the next decade, along with more than a dozen for other cities. Most were comic, but two heroic operas (*Lucio Papirio dittatore*, 1767, and *Olimpia*, 1768) received commissions for the royal San Carlo Theater, and numerous others premiered elsewhere. Royal support in Naples shriveled after 1768, apparently because Paisiello tried to break a marriage contract with a well-connected widow, to melodramatic effect: temporary imprisonment and a shotgun wedding. Seeking greener pastures, in 1776 he became *maestro di cappella* in St. Petersburg for Catherine the Great, who cultivated a lively Italian opera as an emblem of cultural prestige and cosmopolitanism. Among the dozen operas written for this position was the one best known today, *Il barbiere di Siviglia* (1782), prequel to **Wolfgang Amadeus Mozart**'s *Le nozze di Figaro* (1786) and predecessor to **Gioachino Rossini**'s *Barbiere* (1816).

After serving Catherine for six years, Paisiello accepted, with misgivings ascribed to court politics, a second renewal of his St. Petersburg contract, but he took a one-year paid leave (1783), returned to Naples in 1784 following a detour to **Vienna**, and never went back to Russia. By forwarding a portfolio that included *Il barbiere* and several other scores, he succeeded in winning an appointment as court theater composer shortly after that opera's Neapolitan premier (1783). His 1785 contract stipulated one serious opera per year for the San Carlo Theater, among other obligations that expanded when he became director of chamber music in 1787. Paisiello fulfilled these duties for five years until he experienced an apparent nervous breakdown (1790)—preparations for his famous **sentimental** comedy *Nina, o sia La pazza per amore* (*Nina, or Crazy for Love*, 1789) ironically seem to have been the last straw—after which King Ferdinando continued to compensate him without specific operatic obligations.

By that time, Paisiello had begun shifting his attention to religious music, becoming *maestro di cappella* of the Naples cathedral in 1796. When the French occupied Naples in 1799, Ferdinando fled, but Paisiello remained and was named *maestro di cappella* of the Parthenopean Republic and eventually

Napoleon's personal opera composer and director of sacred music in Paris. In these positions, Paisiello wrote one opera, *Proserpine* (1803), and a Mass for Napoleon's coronation (1804). Even after returning to Naples (1804), he continued to produce sacred music for Napoleon, who inducted him into the Legion of Honor (1806) and compensated him until the French defeat and Ferdinando's restoration in 1815.

Paisiello's output speaks for Italian mainstream trends in the last third of the 18th century. At a time when opera buffa was gaining sophistication and respectability, *L'idolo cinese* (1767), his first hit, received a command performance for the Neapolitan royals, gaining their earliest official acknowledgment of the genre. While opera seria remained largely a staged concert of **arias**, notwithstanding such experimenters as **Niccolò Jommelli** and **Christoph Willibald Gluck,** innovations are evident. For example, simple **recitatives** tend to be less prolix and give way more often to obbligato recitatives accompanied by **orchestra**. The full scale da capo aria may be replaced by adaptations that are often shorter, less repetitive, and share features with sonata form. Ensembles occur more frequently—*Pirro* (1787) includes *concertato* **introduzioni** and **finales.** Whether or not he invented *parlante* as his contemporaries claimed, Paisiello played a role in increasing its use and sophistication and that of *nota e parola.* His orchestration gives a greater role to the woodwinds, and he replaced the traditional three-movement **overture** with a single movement in quasi-sonata form.

PARIS. The largest city in France and centerpiece of French opera since the 17th century. Opera in Paris revolved around a core of companies that changed their titles and theaters frequently. Its history began in earnest when the system of royal administrative academies was expanded in the 1660s to include the Académies d'Opéra (1669) headed by Pierre Perrin (ca. 1620–1675), renamed the Académie Royale (Impériale during Napoleon's reign) de Musique (the Opéra) under **Jean-Baptiste Lully**'s directorship in 1672, through which Lully received exclusive rights to produce full-scale opera in France. Previously, various establishments had performed an assortment of theater works. Some involved music, such as *comédies-ballets*, spoken plays with music, *pièces à machines* (plays with special effects), and occasional imported Italian operas, the earliest probably being Francesco Sacrati's (1605–1650) *La finta pazza* (1645, originally 1641). Notable theaters included the Petit Bourbon (16th century, demolished 1660), which had staged *La finta pazza*, and the Théâtre des Machines of the Tuileries Palace (built 1659–62, abandoned after the 1660s), a magnificent, gargantuan hall said to hold 7,000 and equipped for stupendous aerialist effects but an acoustical disaster. It premiered **Francesco Cavalli**'s *Ercole amante* in 1662.

The initial academies run by Perrin and Lully refitted enclosed tennis courts until Lully set up his company at the theater of the Palais Royal in 1673 (built 1637, burned 1763, rebuilt 1770, burned 1781, third theater built at a new site 1781), previously home for Molière's theatrical troupe until his death and the site of performances of Cavalli's *Egisto* (originally 1643) and Luigi Rossi's (ca. 1597–1653) *Orfeo* in 1646 and 1647, respectively. It was remodeled for opera almost immediately (1674) and remained the public home of the Opéra through the 18th century, mounting works including Lully's and **Jean-Philippe Rameau**'s *tragédies en musique* and *opéras-ballets*.

The Opéra competed at the end of the 17th century with two other officially sanctioned companies. The Comédie-Française was founded (1680) by Louis XIV for French spoken plays, merging existing Parisian **acting** companies including the descendants of Molière's. The long-standing Comédie-Italienne (Ancien Théâtre Italien), originally an Italian **commedia dell'arte** troupe in the 16th century, performed French plays with music in violation of Lully's monopoly, some satirizing Lully's operas and the aristocracy, resulting in their disenfranchisement in 1697. The official theaters were bitter rivals of the unsanctioned fairground theaters of the Foire St. Germain (spring) and Foire St. Laurent (summer). In 1697 they took up the repertory of the dissolved Comédie-Italienne and repulsed attempts by the Opéra and Comédie-Française to prevent them from performing spoken plays with songs (**vaudevilles**) that were the ancestors of **opéra comique**.

In the 18th century the Opéra became in great part a conservative repertory theater for *tragédie en musique* and *opéra-ballet*, sustaining Lully's standing (and Rameau's) until the advent of **Christoph Willibald Gluck** in the 1770s, energized at times by the **War of the Comedians** in the 1750s and the controversy over Gluck and **Niccolò Piccinni** in the 1770s. The Comédie-Italienne was recalled to Paris in 1716 by Philippe d'Orléans, regent for Louis XV, following the death of Louis XIV, when it also became known as the Nouveau Théâtre Italien. As it had in the 17th century it resumed performing spoken plays, vaudeville comedies, and parodies of works performed at the Opéra, and also hosted the new *comédies mêlée d'ariettes* of **André-Ernest-Modeste Grétry** and others by the 1760s. The Opéra-Comique formed ca. 1715 through a merger of the fairground troupes and operated at the fairs as a fourth major (though unofficial) company. Their success in the 1750s after closure in the 1740s led to their amalgamation with the Nouveau Théâtre Italien in 1762 (under the name Théâtre Italien). Though still prohibited from including **recitatives** and **choruses** in their productions (the domain of the Opéra) or performing opera in Italian, their schedule improved from two fairground **seasons** to year round, first in the Italians' existing theater at the Hôtel de Bourgogne, then (beginning 1783) at the new

Salle Favart and the Théâtre Feydeau (opened 1791) after merger with the company there in 1801. They received official status as the Théâtre de l'Opéra-Comique in 1807.

Musical entertainments were also held at palaces outside Paris, two of which were particularly important for opera. The royal court moved to Versailles (about a dozen miles outside Paris) in 1682, which had been remodeled and expanded after 1661, and the earliest musical productions, the so-called grand **divertissements**, began in 1664. No sizable theater existed at Versailles during Louis XIV's reign, so operas and other spectacles were held as special occasions (and a condition of Lully's monopoly) in theaters constructed for specific performances in the marble court and elsewhere. These included a number of Lully's *tragédies en musique* (e.g., *Alceste, ou le triomphe d'Alcide*, 1674), **ballets**, and other works.

Louis XIV's social withdrawal in the later years of his reign (after ca. 1700) caused Versailles to fade as a theatrical center. Two decades after Louis XV restored Versailles as the official court, Madame de Pompadour (his mistress) founded the Théâtre des Petits Cabinets, which staged operas and *opéras-ballets* in the late 1740s. The first permanent major theater constructed at Versailles (1770) opened with Lully's *tragédie en musique Persée* (originally 1682) for the wedding of the future Louis XVI to Marie Antoinette. Her private theater in the Trianon was the scene of amateur performances of opéras comiques in which she participated. Fountainebleau, about 45 miles south of Paris, an important getaway since the early 16th century, staged operas by the Académie Royale de Musique and other companies as a frequent autumn event in the Salle de la Belle Cheminée (outfitted with machinery for special effects 1682, remodeled 1725 and 1754, inactive after 1786, burned 1856), France's finest opera theater until the Versailles opera house opened. Jean-Jacques Rousseau's (1712–1778) *Le devin du village* premiered there.

In 1791–92 the Revolutionary government eliminated theatrical monopolies, spawning a welter of competing companies until Napoleon reduced their number to eight in 1807. They included three officially recognized opera theaters, as well as other houses that had **orchestras** and included music in their productions. The Opéra cycled through a number of names until re-adopting its original title of Académie Royale de Musique after Napoleon's second defeat (by 1815). And it repeatedly changed theaters during the 19th century until arriving at its long-standing home at the Palais Garnier (1875–1987, now used mainly for ballet). Beginning with Napoleon's efforts to reestablish the Opéra as a symbol of French glory, it elevated its world status in the 19th century through its high performance standards; excellent orchestra and splendid staging, represented in particular by its productions of

French *grand opéra*, including **Gioachino Rossini**'s *Guillaume Tell* and **Giacomo Meyerbeer**'s *Les Huguenots*; and its cultivation of ballets, either embedded within operas or heard as accessory entertainments.

The reorganized Opéra-Comique, like the Opéra, migrated through a series of theaters, most prominently the Salle Feydeau (1805–29), the second Salle Favart (1840–87, burned), and its present home, the third Salle Favart (beginning 1898), and cultivated opéra comique and a version of *opéra lyrique*. The 19th-century Théâtre Italien—distinct from the 17th-century Ancien Théâtre Italien and the 18th-century Nouveau Théâtre Italien—was founded (1801) at Napoleon's behest to showcase the emperor's beloved Italian opera, providing official recognition for the influx of Italian composers that had begun with the War of the Comedians in the 1750s, and involved such luminaries as Piccinni, **Antonio Salieri**, and **Luigi Cherubini**. Like its competitors, it performed at a variety of locations, where it was run by famous **composers** including **Gaspare Spontini** (1810–12), **Ferdinando Paer** (1812–24 and 1826–27), and Rossini (1824–26). Its repertory was dominated by revivals and occasional newly commissioned works by the most prominent Italian composers—Rossini, **Vincenzo Bellini**, **Gaetano Donizetti**, **Giuseppe Verdi**, and others—until ceasing operations in 1878. The Opéra-National competed vigorously with the Opéra and Opéra-Comique beginning in 1847, particularly with the innovative director **Léon Carvalho** at its helm (1856–68, bankrupt 1868, continued sporadically until 1872). And these major theaters were challenged throughout the 19th century by a host of smaller popular venues—the so-called boulevard theaters—most prominently **Jacques Offenbach**'s houses for **operetta**.

Two principal companies, the Opéra and the Opéra-Comique, have survived into the new millennium as major European venues and have continued to host premiers of new works, particularly during the first half of the 20th century: notably **Igor Stravinsky**'s *Mavra* (1922) and *Perséphone* (1934) and the completed production of **Alban Berg**'s *Lulu* (Acts 1 and 2 composed 1928–35) at the Opéra, and *Pelléas et Mélisande*, Paul Dukas's (1865–1935) *Ariane et Barbe-bleue* (1907), **Maurice Ravel**'s *L'heure espagnole* (1911), **Darius Milhaud**'s *Le pauvre matelot* (1927), and **Francis Poulenc**'s *Les mamelles de Tirésias* (1947) and *La voix humaine* (1959) at the Opéra-Comique. The Opéra's newest home, the Opéra Bastille, opened in 1990 with a production of **Hector Berlioz**'s *Les Troyens* (composed 1856–58).

PARLANDO. *See* PARLANTE.

PARLANTE. A style of operatic text setting in which the **orchestra** carries the melody or the motivic substance of a passage, while vocalists sing freely paced dialogue along with it. *Parlante* ingeniously combines the flexibility of **recitative** and the musical substance and energy of a lyric set piece. The term, which literally means "spoken," appeared first in the 19th century, when *parlante melodico* ("melodic *parlante*"), in which the singers share parts of the orchestra's melody, was distinguished from *parlante armonico* ("harmonic *parlante*"), in which they provide declamatory counterpoint. Although the invention of *parlante* is sometimes credited to **Giovanni Paisiello** in the 1770s, its roots may be traced back to brief, orchestra-led passages in set pieces of early 18th-century comic opera (**Giovanni Pergolesi**'s *La serva padrona* has examples). It became a primary resource for the dramatically active movements of ensembles first in late 18th-century comic operas, then found a place in serious opera from the time of **Simon Mayr**'s and **Gioachino Rossini**'s generations through the motivically oriented *parlanti* of **Giacomo Puccini**. The Act 2 **finale** of *Le nozze di Figaro* and the opening revelry in the Act 1 *introduzione* of *Rigoletto* masterfully employ orchestral *parlante* melodies to characterize and create ambience.

Nota e parola ("music and speaking") is a related technique that alternates short phrases for orchestra alone with phrases that are sung. *Parlando* is a performance indication directing the voice to mimic speech in a manner similar to recitative.

PASTA, GIUDITTA. (1797, Saronno–1865, Como.) Preeminent Italian **soprano** of the 1820s and 1830s. Pasta was noted for her heartrending expressiveness, which included dramatically credible delivery of brilliant passagework. After **Paris** and **London** appearances in the late 1810s in operas by **Domenico Cimarosa**, **Niccolò Zingarelli**, **Wolfgang Amadeus Mozart**, and **Ferdinando Paer**, she gained international celebrity over the next decade beginning with performances of **Gioachino Rossini**'s *Otello* (originally 1816), *Tancredi* (originally 1813), and *Elisabetta, regina d'Inghilterra* (originally 1815) at the Théâtre Italien in Paris. In the 1830s she created the lead roles in **Gaetano Donizetti**'s *Anna Bolena* (1830) and *Ugo, conte di Parigi* (1832) and in **Vincenzo Bellini**'s *La sonnambula* (1831), *Norma*, and *Beatrice di Tenda* (1833). Her voice damaged from overuse, she retired from the theater in 1835.

PASTICCIO. A comic or serious opera, most often Italian, compiled from music not written originally for that opera and/or from music written by multiple composers. Pasticcios typically adapted a popular **libretto** (e.g., one by **Apostolo Zeno** or **Pietro Metastasio**), for which the arranger combined **arias** from previous settings of that opera or collected existing arias by himself and/or other **composers**, either retaining their original words or substituting new ones better suited to their current situations, and composed new **recitatives**. Alternatively, multiple composers collaborated on a medley of new or repurposed arias and recitatives. The pasticcio gained a certain legitimacy in the 18th century, the term being used commonly by theaters beginning ca. 1725 to acknowledge compilation operas. And numerous prominent composers produced or wrote music for pasticcios, among them **Antonio Vivaldi**, **Handel**, and **Joseph Haydn**. The main contemporary complaint regarding pasticcios involved the often haphazard distribution of affects among arias (*see* DOCTRINE OF THE AFFECTIONS).

The pasticcio had originated in 17th-century Italy out of the necessity of adapting operas in revival to the abilities of particular singers, which eventually involved singers substituting arias from their personal repertories ("suitcase arias"). In the 18th century, pasticcios became common in cities lacking a local tradition of Italian opera and appropriately skilled composers: in **London** they were the principal Italian operas heard prior to Handel's arrival. Even after alternatives became available, they fleshed out theater seasons alongside new operas and introduced music of trendy composers who were not locally available to create original works: for example, the King's Theater remained a prominent producer of pasticcios throughout the 18th century. By the very late 1700s, relatively few pasticcios were staged and the term fell out of use. (Jeremy Sams's, born 1957, recent **baroque** pasticcio *The Enchanted Island*, 2011, is a rare exception.) However, suitcase arias remained a troublesome fact of life through the mid-19th century.

PASTORALISM. A literary, dramatic, artistic, or musical style characterized by rustic subjects or images. References to pastoral music date at least to the sixth century B.C., and pastoral themes appear in the *pastourelles* (dialogues between knights and shepherdesses) of the 13th-century troubadours and trouvères; in chansons, *frottole*, **madrigals**, and *intermedi* of the 16th century; and in the cantatas and operas of the 17th century and after. By the 15th century, extended pastoral poems such as Angelo Poliziano's *Favola d'Orfeo* (1471), Torquato Tasso's *Aminta* (1581), and Giovanni Battista Guarini's *Il pastor fido* (1589) were performed as theater pieces with musical interludes and dances. These pastoral plays became increasingly popular festive entertainments in such Italian courts as Ferrara, Florence, and Mantua, where they exerted a decisive influence on madrigals and early operas. **Jacopo Peri**'s *Dafne* and *Euridice*, **Emilio de' Cavalieri**'s *Rappresentatione di Anima, e di Corpo* (1600), and **Claudio Monteverdi**'s *Orfeo* all have pastoral settings, as do some of the earliest operas outside of Italy, for example Heinrich Schütz's *Dafne* (1627) and **Jean-Baptiste Lully**'s *Les fêtes de l'Amour et de Bacchus* (1672). Having been displaced by historical and comic topics in the mid-17th century, pastoral operas experienced a revival beginning with the **Arcadian Academy** in the early 18th century, and pastoral episodes appear in operas into the 20th century. See, for example, Caesar's **aria** *concertante* "Se in fiorito ameno prato" (*Giulio Cesare in Egitto*, Act 2), the Wartburg scene in Act 1 of *Tannhäuser*, and (in an ironic manifestation) Wozzeck's murder of his wife and drowning (*Wozzeck*, Act 3).

In 17th- and 18th-century opera, pastoralism and references to the shepherds, nymphs, gods, and demigods of Arcadia typically symbolize the perceived privileged status of the arts in ancient Greek culture and reflect efforts by the **Florentine Camerata** and others to recreate a presumed golden age of the arts. During this period, pastoral settings also served religious or political allegories celebrating the "natural" legitimacy of a ruler or institution. In the 18th and 19th centuries, pastoralism evoked genuineness as opposed to the artificiality of cultured society, as in English **ballad opera**, German **singspiel**, and French **opéra comique**. To the **romantics** it represented devotion to nature and rejection of modern urbanization and industrialization, and it often had nationalist associations, for example in **Carl Maria von Weber**'s *Der Freischütz*. More generally, pastoral scenes can provide a nostalgic respite from crises and a background for action among the lower classes. In musical style, the pastoral topic (*see* DOCTRINE OF THE AFFECTIONS) is a folkish idiom characterized by pedal drones; repetitive, cycling melodies; obbligato wind instruments; melodic doublings at the third or sixth; and simple, diatonic functional harmonies.

PATTER SONG. Style of operatic singing—or a type of solo set piece featuring that style—in which words are delivered very rapidly for comic effect to a monotonous, repetitive melody and rhythm; patter song is a type of *parlando concitato* (excited speaking). Although its roots may be traced back to the early 18th century, patter song was not heard commonly until after 1770, when it became a mainstay of buffo **arias** and ensembles (for example, in *Le nozze di Figaro*, Bartolo's vengeance aria, Act 1, or the end of the Act 2 **finale**). Nineteenth-century composers accelerated and exaggerated the delivery, as in the concluding outburst of Figaro's "Largo al factotum" (**Gioachino Rossini**, *Il barbiere di Siviglia*, Act 1) and the **stretta** of the Act 2 finale of **Gaetano Donizetti**'s *Don Pasquale*. Most of **William Schwenck Gilbert and Arthur Sullivan**'s **operettas** feature a prominent patter song, such as "I Am the Very Model of a Modern Major-General" (*The Pirates of Penzance*, 1879, Act 1).

PAVAROTTI, LUCIANO. (1935, Modena–2007, Modena.) Italian **tenor**. Considered one of the greatest voices of the 20th century by his many adherents, Pavarotti was probably the most commercially successful opera singer in history.

Pavarotti debuted in 1961 in Reggio Emilia as Rodolfo in *La bohème* and immediately began appearing internationally. His career accelerated when **Joan Sutherland** made him her protégé in 1965 and toured with him across Australia, leading to a series of appearances at La Scala (as Rodolfo, the Duke in *Rigoletto*, and other **bel canto** roles) and at the Metropolitan Opera (*see* NEW YORK CITY) in 1968 (as Rodolfo, and subsequently as Manrico in **Giuseppe Verdi**'s *Il trovatore*, originally 1853; *Ernani*, originally 1844; Radames in *Aida*; and a host of other leads). His breakthrough performance as Tonio in **Gaetano Donizetti**'s *La fille du régiment* (originally 1840) at the Met in 1972 made him the champion of opera devotees, winning the appellation "King of the High Cs" for landing nine of them in a single aria. In his prime, his brilliant, distinctively colored cannon of a voice, a liquid high tenor capable of effortless high Cs (and Ds) that was particularly suited to the heroic love interests of Donizetti, early to mid-Verdi, and **Giacomo Puccini**, reigned supreme, although his commitment to acting often came into question.

Pavarotti made an equally significant contribution to opera by expanding the audience for operatic singing through his genius for media marketing and self-promotion. His status as a pop culture icon began with the maiden concert of the "Three Tenors" (along with Plácido Domingo, born 1941, and José Carreras, born 1946) in **Rome** prior to the soccer World Cup final in 1990 and his rendition of his signature aria "Nessun dorma" from Puccini's *Turandot* (originally 1926), which received wide play as a lead-in to broadcasts of matches throughout the tournament. The Three Tenors recording became the best-selling classical album of all time and led to successive concerts at the next three World Cups. Pavarotti also appeared at the outdoor opening ceremony of the 2006 Winter Olympics, lip-syncing "Nessun dorma" owing to the cold. In the 1990s he sang in a series of free outdoor concerts in **London**, New York, and **Paris**, which attracted estimated crowds of as many as half a million. An infectiously jovial, larger-than-life personality, he appeared on the television shows *Saturday Night Live* (the only opera singer to date) and *The Tonight Show*, in television commercials, and in a (poorly received) movie (*Yes, Giorgio*, 1982). He also founded the Pavarotti International Voice Competition in 1982 and spearheaded numerous charity concerts, appearing with rock stars for a range of causes and creating a crossover option for opera singers.

Pavarotti performed late into his sixties, giving his final operatic performance as Cavarodossi (*Tosca*) at the Met in 2004 and a farewell concert tour in 2005. Although in his last decades he gained a reputation as an egotistical glutton, womanizer, and publicity hound given to canceling appearances, he made unprecedented contributions to raising the profile of opera, and he retained a dedicated following throughout his career.

PELLÉAS ET MÉLISANDE. Literaturoper; music by **Claude Debussy**, **libretto** adapted by the **composer** from Maurice Maeterlinck's (1862–1949) play; five acts; premiered Paris, Opéra-Comique, April 1902. The preeminent example of **symbolist** opera.

Drawn to the dreamlike atmosphere and evocative language of *Pelléas* after reading the play and attending its premier in 1893, Debussy fashioned it into a **libretto** by cutting four scenes, all but eliminating the role of the servant woman, and streamlining the text by removing scenographic description that Maeterlinck had included in the dialogue. He immediately composed a continuity draft of the leading vocal and orchestral lines (1893–95), waiting to finish the score until an agreement to perform the opera was reached in 1898. *Pelléas* received mixed reviews at its premier, in which **Mary Garden** played Mélisande, opponents finding it pale and listless, supporters applauding Debussy's truthfully human interpretation of its characters. Performed frequently prior to World War I, it subsequently receded as symbolism became less fashionable.

A simple love triangle provides the pretext for the interplay between Maeterlinck's visceral images and Debussy's impressionist music. Golaud, the middle-aged grandson of Arkel, the blind king of Allemonde, marries Mélisande, an enigmatic maiden he met accidentally in the forest. After she falls in love with Golaud's much younger brother Pelléas, Golaud enlists his son by a previous relationship to spy on the lovers. When he discovers them together he kills Pelléas, and Mélisande dies following childbirth, leaving a baby daughter.

Stream-of-consciousness musings, particularly those of the lovers and Arkel, evoke a childlike immediacy of response to situations and surroundings. The resulting networks of metaphors—such as those related to light and darkness (lamps, beacons, and sunlight versus castle interiors and blindness); to injury (Golaud's fall from his horse), aging, death, and decay (the famine, the putrid waters under the castle) versus youth and rejuvenation (Mélisande as a vain tonic for Arkel, the birth of her daughter, and the well); or to loss (Mélisande's wedding ring and doves)—contribute to a wistful mood of resigned inevitability. Debussy's music provides a sensuous reinforcement of Maeterlinck's dreamlike landscape, ripe with nontraditional modal, pentatonic, whole-tone, and octatonic melodies; shimmering parallel triads and 7th and 9th chords; and ravishing orchestral sonorities. Vocal declamation prevails, even in such **aria**-like monologues as Pelléas's two love songs ("Je les tiens dans les mains," Act 3, and "On dirait que ta voix," Act 4), allowing variations in musical intensity and pacing that tellingly convey subtle psychological fluctuations.

While Debussy largely disavowed **Richard Wagner**'s influence on *Pelléas*, similarities with the latter's music dramas are obvious. They include musical continuity enhanced by transitions between scenes, emphasis on intimate dialogue over spectacle and massed ensembles with **chorus**, the prominence and psychological contribution of the **orchestra**, and the employment of networks of associative musical motifs (similar to **leitmotifs**) and associative keys.

PENDERECKI, KRZYSZTOF. (Born 1933, Dębica, Poland.) Prominent Polish **composer** of five operas (from the mid-1960s through the early 1990s), along with other vocal and instrumental music, and **conductor** of his own works. Penderecki trained at the Kraków Conservatory (1955–58) and eventually taught there, as well as in Germany and the United States. He first became known for his avant-garde experiments with searing atonal, dissonant blocks of violent string effects in such works as *Threnody for the Victims of Hiroshima* (1960).

Penderecki's best-known opera is the lurid *The Devils of Loudun* (1969), in which a 17th-century French priest is unjustly tried and burned for bewitching nuns. Its shocking themes of forbidden eroticism, physical torture, religious zealotry, and base motivations, and its construction in a series of numerous concise and extremely intense short **scenes**, the approach taken in all but his last opera, perfectly suit the extremities of his musical language. *Die schwarze Maske* (*The Black Mask*, 1986) explores similarly sensationalistic themes in a 17th-century Polish setting during a grotesque banquet attended by a social miscellany including an African intruder who has had a past relationship with a mayor's wife. Penderecki's other three operas are the children's opera *Najdzielniejszy z rycerzy* (*The Most Valiant of Knights*, 1965); the *rappresentazione sacra* Paradise Lost (1978), commissioned for the U.S. bicentennial by the Chicago Lyric Opera; and *Ubu Rex* (1991).

PERGOLESI, GIOVANNI BATTISTA. (1710, Lesi–1736, Pozzuoli.) Italian **composer** of at least nine operas during the early 1730s and other vocal and instrumental music, and violinist; his **intermezzo** *La serva padrona* (1733) was a landmark in the development of comic opera (*see* CATEGORIES OF OPERA) in the 18th century.

A sickly child, Pergolesi limped painfully because of a deformed leg, and his health plagued him until his untimely death from tuberculosis at age 26. Sent to **Naples** in his early teens, he studied with senior faculty at the Conservatorio dei Poveri di Gesù Cristo, one of Naples' famous orphanage **conser-**

vatories, including the opera composer **Leonardo Vinci** (in 1728) and the internationally known teacher **Francesco Durante** (after 1728). Pergolesi's first theater work, the **opera seria** *Salustia* on a revised **libretto** by **Apostolo Zeno**, premiered unsuccessfully in Naples in 1732. However, *Lo frate 'nnamorato*, a comedy, was unusually well received later that year (and in 1734) and suggested a fruitful alternative path. Pergolesi's professional positions included those of *maestro di cappella* to Prince Ferdinando Colonna Stigliano (beginning 1732) and—following the success of the opera seria *Il prigioniero superbo* and its intermezzo *La serva padrona* (1733)—deputy *maestro di cappella* for Naples and *maestro di cappella* to the Maddaloni family (previously patrons of **Alessandro Scarlatti**) beginning in 1734.

Along with Vinci, Pergolesi was one of the earliest and most popular proponents of musical naturalness, simplicity, and the ***galant*** style. His understandably slim output is divided almost equally between opera seria (four) and comic operas (three intermezzos and two **opera buffas**). The new style figures in both types. His comic masterpiece *La serva padrona* won a cult following through widespread performances across Europe and became the flashpoint for the **War of the Comedians** in **Paris**, 1752. Initially a disaster, his setting of **Pietro Metastasio**'s *L'Olimpiade* (**Rome**, 1735) was probably the most highly regarded of many versions written by such illustrious composers as **Johann Adolf Hasse**, **Niccolò Jommelli**, and **Giovanni Paisiello**. Sacred works, such as the *Salve Regina* and *Stabat mater* were also extremely popular and remain so.

PERI, JACOPO. (1561, Rome or Florence–1633, Florence.) Italian **tenor**, **composer**, lutenist (*see* LUTE), and keyboardist, and a pivotal figure in the early development of opera. By 1573 Peri had located in Florence, where he spent his entire career. His earliest compositions, a ricercare and a **madrigal**, appeared in 1577 and 1583 in printed collections of music by his teacher Cristofano Malvezzi (1547–1599). He was at least indirectly associated with the Medici court by 1583 and became their employee by 1588, composing music for and singing in ***intermedi*** for court celebrations.

It is likely that Peri attended at least some of the gatherings of the first **Florentine Camerata** led by Giovanni de' Bardi and was one of the principals in the later academy of Jacopo Corsi. Along with Corsi and the aristocratic poet Ottavio Rinuccini (1562–1621), he created the first complete opera, ***Dafne***, which was performed privately for Corsi's academy (1598). And he set another Rinuccini **libretto** for his most famous work, ***Euridice***, staged for the Florentine celebration of the wedding of Maria de' Medici and Henry IV of France (1600). In 1609 Peri published an important volume of songs, *Le varie musiche* (reprinted and expanded in 1619) and in the 1610s worked with other composers such as **Francesca Caccini** in creating music for spectacular court entertainments.

Widely praised for the subtle expressiveness of his singing, his reputation as a performer and composer extended to Mantua, where **Claudio Monteverdi** was employed, a court tied to Florence by marriage. He began two Mantuan operas, both incomplete and not performed; wrote songs on poems by Mantuan aristocrats; and corresponded extensively with the Mantuan Duke Ferdinando Gonzaga. In the late 1610s and 1620s, Peri collaborated with the Florentine Giovanni Battista da Gagliano (1594–1651) and his brother Marco (1582–1643) on three *rappresentazioni sacre* and two additional operas, *Lo sposalizio di Medoro ed Angelica* (1619), for the election of Emperor Ferdinand II, and *La Flora* (1628), for the wedding of Margherita de' Medici. As one of Florence's leading musicians, Peri was a target of intrigue by his rival **Giulio Caccini** and of an infamous poetic attack by the courtesan Francesco Ruspoli. Peri's slight build and shock of blond hair gave him the nickname Zazzerino ("little hair mop").

PETER GRIMES. Opera; music by **Benjamin Britten**, **libretto** by the **composer, tenor** Peter Pears (1910–1986), and Montagu Slater (1902–1956) based on George Crabbe's (1754–1832) poem *The Borough* (1810); **prologue** and three acts; premiered **London**, Sadler's Wells Theater, June 1945. *Grimes* received immediate acclaim for its revitalization of English opera as part of the 20th-century English musical renaissance, initiating Britten's international career as an opera composer. One of the most-performed 20th-century operas next to those of **Giacomo Puccini** and **Richard Strauss**, it has been staged frequently since the 1960s.

Grimes's scenario was developed by Britten and his companion Pears, who would create the lead role, as they returned shipboard from the United States to Great Britain in 1942, and its libretto was completed by Slater later that year. It introduces the theme of individual alienation from society common to several of Britten's operas. The fisherman and social misfit Grimes is a bipolar **romantic** visionary, abusive master to his apprentices, and companion to the schoolmistress Ellen Orford. Aloof from his fellow man, he nonetheless despairs of his isolation. Investigated and cleared (in the prologue) for the death of his former apprentice, Grimes is prohibited from hiring another, an order he ignores. At signs of renewed abuse, the townspeople set out to confront Grimes. As the men approach, he accuses his apprentice of betraying him, driving him out of their cliff-side hut to a fatal fall. Goaded by his neighbors, Grimes drowns himself at sea, ending his nightmare.

The popularity of *Grimes* stems in part from the familiarity of its style. Its straightforward linear narrative proceeds through a series of set pieces such as strophic songs (e.g., those for the innkeeper Auntie and the captain Balstrode, Act 1) and contrapuntal ensembles (the fugal reaction to the storm and Ned Keenes's canon "Old Joe Has Gone Fishing," also Act 1). Most of the singing is traditional, although there are examples of speechlike declamation at particularly intense moments, such as Grimes's climactic confrontation with his apprentice in Act 2. Britten's modally inflected, triad-based harmonic style is reminiscent of predecessors like **Ralph Vaughan Williams**. And linkages between **scenes** by shared motives and keys had been common currency since **Richard Wagner** and **Giuseppe Verdi** in the 19th century.

Diverse in its characters, situations, and atmospheric effects, *Grimes* provided an apt vehicle for Britten's variegated expressive palette. Its colorful cast of characters, which includes a retired sea captain, the mistress of the village inn, a Methodist preacher, a solicitor, a pharmacist, and two widows, richly evokes the ingrown society of a coastal village. And the evocative orchestral interludes that introduce each of its six scenes—depicting the dawn, a storm, a cheerful Sunday morning, Grimes's turmoil, a moonlit night, and a foggy seascape (four of which were offered separately as *Four Sea Interludes*)—establish the physical and emotional landscape of the action. In addition to his infrequent appearances together with the townspeople onstage, the rich expressive depth of Grimes's music sets him apart from the trivialities surrounding him.

PHILIDOR, FRANÇOIS-ANDRÉ DANICAN. (1726, Dreux–1795, London.) French **composer** of approximately 30 operas (mostly **opéras comiques** from the 1750s through the 1780s), best known in his day as a chess master. While serving as a page at Versailles, Philidor studied with the opera composer **André Campra**, then a *maître de chapelle*, and played chess with other musicians. The game gave him access to intellectual circles in **Paris** (beginning 1740) and facilitated an extended stay in England (1745–54), which remained a second home throughout his life.

Philidor's operatic career began after his return to Paris (1754), where he successfully introduced an Italianate melodic style in a series of opéras comiques beginning with *Blaise le savetier* (1759) and including *Le sorcier* (1764) and *Tom Jones* (1765). The notable *tragédie lyrique* (*see* TRAGÉDIE EN MUSIQUE) *Ernelinde, princesse de Norvège* (1767) became a centerpiece of controversy over his alleged (and probably unintentional) plagiarism of Italian melodies. As an opera composer, Philidor was eclipsed after ca. 1770 by **André-Ernest-Modeste Grétry** and **Christoph Willibald Gluck**.

PIAVE, FRANCESCO MARIA. (1810, Murano–1876, Milan.) Prominent Italian **librettist** of the 1840s through the mid-1860s. Born near **Venice**, Piave was first employed in his father's glass business and as a proofreader before moving to **Rome**, where he befriended the prominent librettist Jacopo

Ferretti (1784–1852) and other literary figures. He began his career as a librettist with works for the composers Samuel Levi and **Giovanni Pacini** (the last act of *Il duca d'Alba*, 1842).

Recommended to **Giuseppe Verdi** by an aristocratic mutual friend, he became the composer's chief librettist from *Ernani* (1844) through *La forza del destino* (1862) and including *Macbeth* (1847 and 1865), *Rigoletto*, *La traviata* (1853), and *Simon Boccanegra* (1857). Piave showed unwavering loyalty to Verdi, apparent obliviousness to his condescension, and unparalleled willingness to collaborate on projects from the earliest creative stages and to acquiesce by supplying economical verses on demand and revising them as directed. Piave served as poet and stage director at La Fenice in Venice and, on Verdi's recommendation, La Scala in Milan (beginning 1859). He experienced a stroke in 1867 that left him paralyzed for the final decade of his life.

PICCINNI, NICCOLÒ. (1728, Bari–1800, Passy.) Mythically productive **composer** of more than 110 operas from the 1750s into the 1790s (one report, no doubt tongue-in-cheek, claimed 300) and reluctant figurehead for opponents of **Christoph Willibald Gluck** in **Paris** in the late 1770s. Trained in **Naples** under **Leonardo Leo** and **Francesco Durante**, Piccinni began his career with three **opera buffas**, which led to his first **opera seria** commission *Zenobia* (1756) and a series of operas of both types and several **intermezzos**, first for Naples and later for **Rome** and other cities. His second Roman commission, the charming *dramma giocoso La buona figliuola* (1760) with the **librettist Carlo Goldoni**, based loosely on Samuel Richardson's sentimental novel *Pamela* (1740), took Europe by storm and became the cornerstone of Piccinni's career.

A corrosive rivalry with the composer Pasquale Anfossi (1727–1797) in Rome led Piccinni to try Paris in 1776. There he became the hero of proponents, led by the librettist and Piccinni's collaborator Jean-François Marmontel (1723–1799), of a reform of French opera that infused it with Italianate lyricism to a greater extent than Gluck's operas. In addition to staging performances of *La buona figliuola*, which became a flashpoint of the controversy, and its sequel *La buona figliuola maritata* (first performed 1761), Piccinni composed more than a dozen new *tragédies lyriques*—*Didon* (1783) was the most popular—**opéras comiques**, and opere buffe for France. Loss of popularity to Antonio Sacchini (1730–1786) and **Antonio Salieri** in the mid-1780s and the French Revolution, which eliminated his government stipend, led him to return to Naples in 1791, where in 1794 he found himself under extended house arrest after his daughter married a Revolutionary sympathizer. He returned to France for his final year.

Piccinni is credited with introducing **Baldassare Galuppi**'s Venetian multisectional comic **finale** to the south, beginning with *La buona figliuola*. His fusion of various comic modes, from slapstick to mock aristocratic to **sentimental**, his diversity of **aria** types that incorporate sonata-form elements, and his structural coordination of motivic and harmonic design all prefigure the late 18th-century classical style.

IL POMO D'ORO**. **Festa teatrale; music by **Antonio Cesti**, Emperor Leopold I (1640–1705, two scenes in Acts 2 and 5), and Johann Heinrich Schmelzer (after 1620–1680, ballets), **libretto** by Francesco Sbarra (1611–1668) based on the myth of the Judgment of Paris from Ovid and elsewhere; **prologue** and five acts; premiered **Vienna**, Hoftheater auf der Cortina, July 1668; most music for Acts 3 and 5 lost. *Il pomo d'oro* (*The Golden Apple*) was commissioned and mostly completed in 1666 for the marriage of Emperor Leopold I to his cousin Margarita Theresa of Spain. However, owing to delays in her travel and in construction of the new court theater, the premiere occurred two years later on her 17th birthday.

Pomo d'oro is the most wildly extravagant 17th-century court spectacle–opera ever staged. Presented across two evenings because of its eight-hour length, it featured 67 **scenes** involving 23 different sets. And it included a cast of almost 60 characters, among them approximately 40 gods, demigods, and other mythological and allegorical figures as well as 20 or so humans. Descended from the 16th-century *intermedio*, it dazzled its audience with numerous **ballets** and tableaux representing the Austrian territories, the underworld, the palaces of Jupiter and Aeolus (god of the winds), battles, and earthquakes. And it provided the obligatory comic *contrascene* in the Venetian style for the sardonic court jester Momo and the nurse Filaura.

Discordia (Discord) launches the plot, which is part morality play and social satire, when she crashes a banquet thrown by Giove (Jupiter) and baits the assembled goddesses with the golden apple intended for the greatest beauty. Venere (Venus), Pallade (Pallas Athena), and Giunone (Juno) contest the prize until Jupiter, who is unwilling to intercede, passes the responsibility to Paride (Paris, son of Priam of Troy). After Venus bribes Paris with Helen of Troy, he sets off to claim her, starting a series of intrigues aimed at deterring or assisting him. The conflict is resolved when Jupiter awards the golden apple to Empress Margarita for her birthday.

PONCHIELLI, AMILCARE. (1834, Paderno Fasolaro/Paderno Ponchielli, Lombardi–1886, Milan.) Italian **composer** of nine completed operas, **ballets**, and other vocal and instrumental music, active from the mid-1850s through the mid-1880s and the most prominent exponent of Italianized *grand opéra* during **Giuseppe Verdi**'s hiatus following *Aida* (1871).

A prodigious talent who composed a symphony at age 10, Ponchielli trained locally as an organist, then studied from 1843 to 1854 as a scholarship student at the Milan **Conservatory**. After graduating, he took a job as a church organist and music teacher in Cremona, which led to an assistantship at the local theater (1855) and opportunities to direct operas in Milan, and in the 1860s he worked as a bandmaster in Cremona and Piacenza. The late 1850s and 1860s brought a string of disappointments. His first opera, *I promessi sposi* (1856), based on Alessandro Manzoni's iconic novel, premiered successfully in Cremona but waited 16 years for broader distribution. Other projects were canceled, received only local notice, or had aborted runs. For one long-delayed opera (likely *Vico Bentivoglio*), his **librettist, Francesco Maria Piave**, died before completing the text. And he lost a prospective position at the Milan Conservatory to the *scapigliatura* **conductor** and composer Franco Faccio (1840–1891), probably due to Giulio **Ricordi**'s intervention

Ponchielli's fortunes turned in 1872 when *I promessi sposi*, revised with a new **libretto** by another *scapigliato*, the poet Emilio Praga (1839–1875), received an enthusiastic reception in Milan, convincing Ricordi to reverse course and adopt him as the successor to Verdi, eventually leading to a first-class production of *I lituani* at La Scala (1874). *La Gioconda* (premiered 1876, revised through 1879) represents the high point of Ponchielli's career and his one major contribution to the modern repertory, owing to its sensationalistic libretto by **Arrigo Boito**; spectacle in the style of *grand opéra*; captivating lyricism (e.g., Enzo's well-known "Cielo e mar," Act 2); and appealing ballet music (the popular *Dance of the Hours*). Despite his inability to repeat this success, now famous he was finally appointed professor of composition at the Milan Conservatory (beginning 1880), where he taught **Giacomo Puccini** and **Pietro Mascagni**, and organist at the church of Santa Maria Maggiore in Bergamo, for which he produced a number of sacred works. Ponchielli's last opera, *Marion Delorme* (1885), incorporated features of **opéra comique** with limited success, despite input from Verdi.

An unabashedly conservative composer invested in liquid, sometimes florid melody, Ponchielli's success may be attributed partly to an anti-Wagnerian backlash (*see* WAGNERISM) that met the dissemination of the latter's works in Italy. Ponchielli's popularization of broadly phrased vocal effusions suited to recapitulation by the **orchestra** at climactic moments, his experimentation with associative motifs akin to those in *Aida* (for example, that of

Barnaba—a precursor to Verdi's Iago—in *La Gioconda*), and his mastery of atmospheric modern orchestration prefigure the *giovane scuola* and his best student, Puccini.

PORPORA, NICOLA. (1686, Naples–1768, Naples.) Italian opera **composer** of over 40 operas (mostly from the 1710s through the early 1740s) and a singing teacher of international repute whose method books were used into the 19th century. Trained in **Naples**, he began his career as a composer with his first commissioned opera *L'Agrippina* (1708). Although he held several minor appointments—one of them as a singing teacher at the Conservatorio di Sant' Onofrio (1715), where he taught the **castratos Farinelli** and Caffarelli (1710–1783)—Porpora was overshadowed by **Alessandro Scarlatti** until Scarlatti left for **Rome** in 1719. After several successes in Naples and Rome, Porpora's peripatetic career took him to a host of major operatic centers where he found regular employment as a vocal or choral maestro at leading **conservatories**. (He would eventually teach at three of the Venetian *ospedali*.) A largely unproductive trip through Germany and Austria landed him in **Venice** (1725–33), where he wrote more than a dozen operas for that city and Rome, the majority on **Pietro Metastasio**'s **librettos**, and renewed a competition with **Leonardo Vinci** from their student days that continued until Vinci's death in 1730.

In 1733 Porpora pulled up roots and moved to **London** for three years, where he composed for the Opera of the Nobility in competition with **George Frideric Handel**'s Royal Academy. He had short-lived success with one of his five operas, *Arianna in Naxo* (1733), and composed *Polifemo* (1735) for Farinelli's London entrée. In Venice (beginning 1736) and Naples (beginning 1738) he continued writing operas until 1741, when they become infrequent and he focused on teaching. A rivalry with **Johann Adolf Hasse** that had simmered since 1730, when Hasse won the position of electoral Kapellmeister in Dresden sought by Porpora, resurfaced when Porpora moved to Dresden in 1747 and his young protégée Regina Mingotti (1722–1808) faced off against Hasse's more established wife, **Faustina Bordoni**. Porpora's appointment as Kapellmeister (1748) was trumped by Hasse's as *Ober-Kapellmeister* in 1750, eventually resulting in Porpora's departure for **Vienna** in 1752, where the young **Joseph Haydn** became his composition student, accompanist, and valet.

Porpora's preoccupation with vocal technique as a singing teacher perhaps led him to depend for success as a composer on conventional **arias** in extended da capo forms that tested singers' ranges, agility, and breath control. However, in London in competition with Handel, he attempted to loosen formal conventions and incorporated more frequent obbligato **recitatives**.

POULENC, FRANCIS. (1899, Paris–1963, Paris.) French **composer** of three operas for which he created two of the **librettos** (during the 1940s and 1950s), ballets, and film scores, as well as other instrumental and vocal music, and pianist. Although Poulenc was classically educated and studied piano with the acclaimed virtuoso Ricardo Viñes (1875–1943), he never attended a **conservatory** and learned composition on his own. He joined Jean Cocteau (1889–1963) and Erik Satie's (1866–1925) avant-garde coalition Les Six following the appearance of his vocal chamber piece *Rapsodie nègre* (1917).

While all of Poulenc's three operas, like his other works, remain true to the populist simplicity and iconoclasm championed by that circle, they display a stunning range of subjects, performing forces, and moods. His surreal comedy *Les mamelles de Tirésias* (*Tiresias's Breasts*, premiered 1947), an adaptation of the groundbreaking surrealist play by the French poet Guillaume Apollinaire featuring transgendering, cross-dressing, bondage, and random violence, reflects most clearly the rejection of traditional artistic values espoused by his colleagues. Its title character, a woman who wants to be a man, grows a beard, exposes her breasts (which turn into balloons and float away), and campaigns against sex with men, while her husband appropriates his wife's clothes and procreates prodigiously, causing overpopulation and famine.

Two subsequent operas represent the new psychological and spiritual intensity of Poulenc's style following his rediscovery of Catholicism in the 1930s. *Dialogues des Carmélites* (*Dialogues of the Carmelites*, premiered 1957), a historically based account of a convent of nuns martyred following the French Revolution, is his most traditional opera, featuring a populous cast of nuns and soldiers, recurring motives representing individual characters and personality traits, and musical inheritances from **Claudio Monteverdi**, **Modest Musorgsky**, **Claude Debussy**, and **Igor Stravinsky**. *La voix humaine* (1959) is one **woman**'s side of a three-quarter-hour phone call with her ex-lover that is interrupted constantly by the vagaries of the postwar phone system and ends with her distraught abandonment. It consists of mostly unaccompanied **recitative** punctuated by richly orchestrated connecting passages as she listens to her boyfriend's responses.

POUSSEUR, HENRI. (1929, Malmedy, Belgium–2009, Brussels.) Belgian **composer** of four innovative theater pieces involving serialism, electronic resources, indeterminacy (music in which the composer relinquishes control of substantial aspects of the performance), and collage structures, and **librettist** for several of these compositions.

Pousseur's best-known quasi-opera is the fantasy *Votre Faust* (written 1960–67, premiered 1969), in which a composer is commissioned by the devil to write a Faust opera. It examines the creative process and the nature of the genre by alluding to related operatic subjects such as the Orpheus myth and Don Juan and by inviting audience participation. In theory at least, members of the audience may interrupt the performers, who comprise five actors, four singers, an ensemble of 12 instrumentalists with percussion, and audiotapes of electronically distorted sounds, to decide the course of the plot, although at the Milan premier actors reportedly were planted to accomplish this interaction. Other hybrid theater works incorporating similar elements include *Die Erprobung des Petrus Hebraicus* (premiered 1978), *Leçons d'enfer* (1991), and *Don Juan à Gnide, ou les séductions de la chasteté* (1996).

PREGHIERA. *See* ARIA; STAGE SONG.

PRELUDE. *See* OVERTURE.

PRODUCTION. The presentation of an opera onstage and the process for preparing such a presentation.

The earliest Italian court operas were conceived as multimedia events that enlisted broad resources to move the passions and required extensive preparation and rehearsal led by a team of specialist contributors: in addition to the **librettist** and **composer**, a choreographer and/or fencing master to direct the dancers and *comparse* (nonsinging supernumeraries), machinist for special effects, scenographer (set painter), costumer, stage manager, and often many others. The coordinator of such an operation was seldom if ever a professional specialist assigned solely to that task, but instead was either one of the creators playing a secondary role or a watchful aristocrat. This approach was established as early as the composer and music director **Emilio de' Cavalieri**, who likely supervised the initial productions of his *Rappresentatione di Anima, et di Corpo* (1600) and of **Jacopo Peri**'s *Euridice* and set a precedent for including production guidelines in printed **librettos** and prefaces to scores to aid future revivals.

With the advent of Venetian public opera in the 1640s, Italian touring companies such as the **Febiarmonici**, and opera in France, production values could range from minimal to lavish, and the 17th-century producer's responsibilities could extend from coordinating and facilitating the work of others to dictatorial micromanagement, as in the case of **Jean-Baptiste Lully**'s supervision of his *tragédies en musique*. Owing to his stake as patent holder in the success not only of individual works but of the institution of opera, to the necessity of competing successfully with spoken stage productions and **ballet**, and to the organizational complexities of *tragédie en musique*, particularly in the **divertissements**, Lully personally supervised not only musical rehearsals but also the most minute details of **acting**, dancing, stage movements, **set design**, costuming, and special effects. Embedded in the repertory, these works set the style and standard for staging in 18th-century France, Lully's supervisory role institutionalized in part in the office of administrative *syndic* or *directeur*.

In 18th-century Italy, the formal simplicity and conventionality of **opera seria**, the absence of **chorus** and ballet integrated within acts, the minimization of special effects, and the reliance on a standardized vocabulary of set and costume types streamlined the task of production substantially. These tendencies made stage directions given in librettos largely sufficient for managing the action and reduced the process of preparing an opera to rehearsing singers, coaching their acting, establishing traffic patterns for entrances and exits to avoid collisions, and organizing any *comparse* in collaboration with a choreographer or fencing master. Responsibilities could be entrusted to the theater manager, music director, composer, or most often the theater poet (e.g., **Carlo Goldoni** in **Venice** or **Pietro Metastasio** in **Vienna**), in court theaters often under the supervision of an aristocratic authority (**Niccolò Jommelli** and Duke Carl Eugen of Württemberg in Stuttgart in the 1750s and 1760s, and **Joseph Haydn** and Nikolaus Esterházy at Eszterháza in the 1770s and 1780s). Supervision by the house librettist remained an important option through the mid-19th century, as evidenced by **Francesco Maria Piave**'s service as poet and stage manager at the Teatro La Fenice in Venice and La Scala in Milan.

In the 19th century an array of factors—the departure from **aria** opera and the adoption of complexities of interaction developed in comic opera (*see* CATEGORIES OF OPERA), the exploration of idiosyncratic situations and *scene* forms, greater expectations for operatic acting, the expansion of spectacle including chorus and dance, a renewed conception of opera as an integrated fusion of the arts in which production elements were inseparable from the composer's and the librettist's artistic visions—brought increasing responsibilities for the producer. For example, staging was integral to the conception of *grand opéra*, which demanded extensive attention to movement, gesture, characterization, scenery, costumes, props, and so on. The particulars of many productions were recorded in manuscript or printed *livrets de mise en scène* (production books) to ensure accurate revivals in Paris and faithful productions elsewhere, and the Comité de Mises en Scène pour l'Académie Royale de Musique was established in 1827 to maintain standards. French achievements raised expectations in Italian theaters, which had given increasing play to the chorus since the end of the 18th century and regularly included massed crowd scenes. **Giuseppe Verdi**'s emphasis of visual elements and stage movement is demonstrated by his adaptation of the French *livret* for *disposizione scenica* printed by **Ricordi** beginning with his own Parisian *grand opéra Les vêpres siciliennes* (1855).

Carl Maria von Weber in Prague (1813–16) and Dresden (1817–26) and **Richard Wagner** in Bayreuth (1876) set precedents for multifaceted involvement by the music director (e.g., **Arturo Toscanini**) in realizing a unified artistic conception. Wagner's collaboration with choreographer Richard Fricke became a model for modern independent directors, such as the Austrian theater and film director Max Reinhardt (1873–1943), working in close contact with composers and performers, as in his premier of *Der Rosenkavalier*. Reinhardt's eclectic productions, drawing on various modernist artistic idioms, were criticized as early examples of "director's operas" in which the presentation conflicts in certain respects with the operatic text. This approach was cultivated prominently in the sparing productions of post–World War II Bayreuth, which attempted to distance Wagner's operas from traditional stagings associated with the Nazis, and is represented more recently by the avant-garde productions of **Peter Sellars** and, for example, by Kenneth Branagh's (born 1960) film of *Die Zauberflöte* set during World War I (2006). A continuing traditionalist counterpoise is evident in the opulent filmed productions of such directors as Franco Zeffirelli (born 1923) and Jean-Pierre Ponnelle (1932–1988) in the 1980s.

PROLOGUE. An introductory **scene** prior to the opera proper, serving any number of functions. An operatic prologue may provide a conceptual or aesthetic foundation, claim credit for a stylistic or technical innovation, establish a rhetorical connection with the audience, introduce the action, or provide historical or narrative context. The earliest prologues were monologues or dialogues involving allegorical figures, gods, and goddesses rooted in such precedents as the **pastoral** play and the *intermedio*. For example, the prologues of **Jacopo Peri**'s and **Giulio Caccini**'s *Euridice* operas and **Claudio Monteverdi**'s *Orfeo* justified the new genre by citing classical forerunners and employing conventionalized poetic and musical forms, and established divergent emphases on tragedy and music, respectively, through their choice of characters. As opera gained artistic legitimacy by the mid-17th century, prologues became less theoretical and more narrative, staging debates among mythical figures concerning their own standing, their support for the contestants in the main action, the probable outcome of the action, or various moral imperatives, and at the same time glorifying aristocratic patrons and their exploits. This last function dominated the prologues of French *tragédie en musique*, which served as an arm of the state from **Jean-Baptiste Lully** through **Jean-Philippe Rameau**.

After ca. 1700, **Arcadian librettos** replaced prologues with an *argomento* ("argument") printed in the libretto distributed in the theater, or with a preface to a printed score (e.g., **Ranieri Calzabigi** and **Christoph Willibald Gluck**'s preface to *Alceste*). In the 19th century, prologues, which occur only rarely, may enact events prior to the main action, as in **Giuseppe Verdi**'s

Simon Boccanegra (1857) or **Richard Wagner**'s *Das Rheingold*, which serves as a prologue to the remainder of ***Der Ring des Nibelungen***. Late 19th- and 20th-century prologues draw, often self-consciously, on previously established approaches, as in Tonio's manifesto of **verismo** (***Pagliacci***). Sometimes they do so in conjunction with film techniques, for example the prologue to **Benjamin Britten**'s *Billy Budd* (1951), which casts the bulk of the opera as a flashback.

PUCCINI, GIACOMO. (1858, Lucca–1924, Brussels.) The foremost Italian opera **composer** after **Giuseppe Verdi**, and the last whose works (12 from the mid-1880s through the mid-1920s) play a major role in the modern repertory. Puccini was the most prominent member of the *giovane scuola* of the late 19th century.

Puccini's musical lineage in Lucca can be traced to the early 18th century. His father, Michele, was a composer, organist and choirmaster of the local cathedral, and director of the city music school, the Istituto Pacini, who died in 1864 before he could start his son's training in earnest and left little financial support. His mother, intent on having her son continue the family profession, had an uncle begin his music lessons, leading to formal studies at the Istituto (until 1880). Puccini subsequently received grants from the Italian queen consort and a wealthy cousin which allowed him to attend the Milan **Conservatory**, where he assembled a cadre of supporters. He studied with **Amilcare Ponchielli** and with the conservatory director, the famous violinist-composer Antonio Bazzini (1818–1897), a proponent of Germanic instrumental music. **Pietro Mascagni** was one of his classmates. And **Alfredo Catalani** introduced Puccini to the Milanese *scapigliatura* fraternity that included **Arrigo Boito** and the prominent conductor-composer Franco Faccio (1840–1891).

As a student, Puccini shared Bazzini's enthusiasm for instrumental music: his graduation project was a *Capriccio sinfonico*, in essence a tone poem, that was critically praised. However, said to have been influenced by a performance of *Aida* in 1876 and encouraged by Ponchielli, he decided to concentrate on opera and entered his first, *Le villi*, in the initial competition sponsored by the publisher Sonzogno in 1883. Although Puccini's submission was rejected ostensibly for its illegible score, Giulio **Ricordi** may have rigged the outcome to keep the opera out of his competitor's hands. Following a successful performance arranged by Puccini's friends, Ricordi gave him a stipend. And though his next opera flopped (*Edgar*, 1889), Ricordi kept the faith and was rewarded with *Manon Lescaut* (1893), an international triumph that—surprisingly to modern audiences—overshadowed his later successes. It was Puccini's first work with the fellow adventurer and **librettist Luigi Illica**, the **libretto** for which had previously made the rounds, passing among the poet Giuseppe Giacosa (*see* ILLICA, LUIGI, AND GIU-

SEPPE GIACOSA), a member of Boito's group; **Ruggero Leoncavallo**; and others. Financially solvent, Puccini rented and later built his own working retreat at Torre del Lago, on a resort lake between Lucca and the seashore, where he centered his activities until pollution of the lake led him to move to nearby Viareggio in 1921.

In 1893, Ricordi paired Illica with Giacosa, who collaborated with Puccini on three of his best-loved operas in succession: the Bohemian, sentimental tear-jerker *La bohème*; the violent melodrama *Tosca*; and the orientalizing tragedy *Madama Butterfly* (1904, revised three times). A turn-of-the-century man's man, Puccini hunted, raced cars, and chased women. His adultery ruined his marriage, and his wife's jealousy led to the suicide of an innocent maid, resulting in a lawsuit and scandal that complicated the composition of *La fanciulla del West* (*The Girl of the Golden West*, 1910). Although opportunities for performances contracted during World War I, he composed *La rondine* (staged in Monte Carlo, 1917) and the unique trilogy of one-act operas *Il trittico* (*Il tabarro*, *Suor Angelica*, and *Gianni Schicchi*) mounted in **New York** after the war (1918). It echoes the decadent Parisian avant-garde theater, the Grand Guignol, by juxtaposing episodes of horror, sentimentality, and comedy. Puccini died in Brussels following treatment for throat cancer before he could finish *Turandot*, his final opera, which was completed in several versions and first performed in 1926.

Puccini's style, which participates in the **verismo** movement to varying degrees, may be viewed as a culmination and exaggeration of trends observed in Italy, France, and Germany in the previous decades, and as a counterpoise to **Wagnerian** idealism, myth, and lyric inhibition. Although sometimes vilified for pandering to fin-de-siècle appetites for sensual titillation and the catharsis of despair, he embraces the verismo movement's empathy for human suffering, often expressed not only through the phosphorescent melodic outbursts that won him fame, but with intimate nuance. Following the leads of Ponchielli and Verdi, Puccini masterfully fused word, sound, and sight to create realistic detail that evokes atmosphere and a sense of place. To this end, he mustered the full turn-of-the-century French and German chromatic, modal, and pentatonic harmonic palette, as well as orchestration that ranges from opulent to delicate, strident to subtle. Puccini's operas demonstrate the continuity and nonconventionality of scene structure associated with late Verdi and the verismo composers. A *parlante* texture of spontaneously organized orchestral motives provides the matrix for a flexible, conversational declamatory dialogue of deflecting melodies that respond to textual meaning and mood phrase by phrase. Recurring across scenes or entire operas, these motifs or broader melodies, sometimes associated with characters or ideas, unify phases of drama, define new ones, or connect related scenes.

Puccini has been trivialized as a master of the Italian picturesque and accused of rehashing the same material from opera to opera. Yet his output belies such criticism. Its diversity of subject, musical style, and architecture are illustrated by the intimate proletarian realism of *La bohème* (descended from Verdi's *La traviata*, 1853), versus the grotesquely violent melodrama of *Tosca* (descended from *Il trovatore*, 1853), the social and personal imperialism of *Madama Butterfly*, the rustication of *La fanciulla del West*, the generic-structural experimentation of *Il trittico*, or the fairy-tale atmosphere of *Turandot*. From this standpoint, Puccini inherited Verdi's preoccupation with evoking individualized, memorably wrought situations, characterizations, and experiences, each having a unique power to move audiences.

PUPPET OPERA. Typically a work combining spoken dialogue and vocal and instrumental music performed on an appropriately constructed stage using hand or rod puppets or marionettes. Most are comic (*see* CATEGORIES OF OPERA), mock-serious, or parodies. Puppet theater already had a long history, dating back at least to **commedia dell'arte** performances of the Renaissance, before the earliest-known puppet operas appeared in the 1670s and 1680s in France and Italy. A pioneering effort to legitimize puppet opera was made in 1676 by the Parisian singer Dominique Normandin, who staged parodies of **Jean-Baptiste Lully**'s operas but was forced to shut down after a year because of Lully's intervention. In the early 18th century, puppet theaters in France and England served as refuges for disenfranchised actors, playwrights, directors, and singers. During this period, the marionette theaters of the two annual Parisian fairs produced about 40 surviving **opéras comiques**, while English companies staged parodies of **opera seria** given at the Royal Academy of Music (*see* HANDEL, GEORGE FRIDERIC) and **ballad operas** following the success of *The Beggar's Opera*. Italian puppet companies were popular in London as late as the 1790s. **Joseph Haydn** directed the music for numerous puppet operas at the Eszterháza palace and wrote at least five of his own in the 1770s. Although enthusiasm for puppet theater waned after 1800, a surprising number of 20th-century operas are indebted to it, among them **Paul Hindemith**'s *Das Nusch-Nuschi* (1921) and **Harrison Birtwistle**'s *Punch and Judy* (1968) and *The Mask of Orpheus* (1986).

PURCELL, HENRY. (Probably 1659, London–1695, London.) Preeminent English **composer** of one very significant opera, *Dido and Aeneas*; four semi-operas (*see* MASQUE); and incidental music for dozens of plays (mostly after 1689), as well as other vocal and instrumental music; organist.

After serving as a choirboy in the Chapel Royal (until 1673) and probably studying with the organist-composers **John Blow** and Christopher Gibbons (1615–1676), Purcell progressed through a series of royal appointments: court string composer (beginning 1677); organist at Westminster Abbey (beginning 1679), replacing Blow; organist at the Chapel Royal (1682); royal instrument keeper responsible for organs (beginning 1683); and court composer of sacred and ceremonial music under Charles II and James II during the 1680s. Although he retained his positions under William and Mary (beginning 1689), the court's musical profile was severely blunted under their austere reign, forcing Purcell and others to look more to composing for public theaters.

The earliest documented performance of Purcell's only true opera, the all-sung masque *Dido and Aeneas* (1689) at Josias Priest's boarding school, dates from this period, although he may well have composed it in the early 1680s for Charles II. Public indifference toward fully composed opera and the widespread belief that the English language was unsuited for opera confined his efforts in the public theater to incidental music for numerous plays—as many as 10 per year, including several by poet laureate John Dryden (1631–1700) and by Thomas D'Urfey (1653–1723), who wrote the epilogue to *Dido*—and semi-operas. Purcell wrote four of the latter for the Royal Theater company, beginning with *The Prophetess, or the History of Dioclesian* in 1690 and including *King Arthur* (1691), the only semi-opera of the period not based on an existing play, and *The Indian Queen* (1695), completed by Purcell's younger brother Daniel (ca. 1664–1717). Purcell's best-known venture in this genre was *The Fairy Queen* (1692), an adaptation of William Shakespeare's *A Midsummer Night's Dream*, for which he set none of Shakespeare's poetry, instead providing fairy masques for Acts 1 through 3 and 5 and a "Masque of the Four Seasons" for Act 4.

Although his operatic output was limited owing to cultural and economic factors—semi-opera was expensive to produce—as well as his untimely death in his mid-thirties, in *Dido* Purcell created one of the enduring monuments of Western music and one of very few prominent examples of true English opera prior to the 20th century.

QUERELLE DES BOUFFONS. *See* WAR OF THE COMEDIANS.

QUINAULT, PHILIPPE. (1635, Paris–1688, Paris.) French poet and play-wright; the foremost French **librettist** of the 17th century; and, with **Jean-Baptiste Lully**, the originator of French opera during the 1670s and 1680s. Quinault studied literature and poetry privately and became associated with the **Paris** salons before training for a legal career in the early 1650s. His appointment (1655) as private secretary to Henry II, Duke of Guise, gained him entry into Louis XIV's court, and he began building a reputation as an author of tragedies, tragicomedies, and especially comedies, beginning with *Les rivales* (1653). With *La grotte de Versailles* (1668), he joined Molière and Pierre Corneille in providing poetry for lavish court entertainments that extolled the king, making him a logical partner for Lully, and he entered the Académie Française (1670) and the Académie des Inscriptions et Belles-Lettres (1674), organizations responsible for approving his **librettos**. Quinault's collaboration with Lully started with his contribution to the libretto of the court spectacle *Psyché* (1671) and extended 15 years across 11 *tragédies en musiques*, from *Cadmus et Hermione* (1673) to *Armide* (1686) and Lully's last two **ballets**.

R

RACCONTO. *See* ARIA; STAGE SONG.

THE RAKE'S PROGRESS. Opera; music by **Igor Stravinsky**, **libretto** by Wystan Hugh (W. H.) Auden (1907–1973) and Chester Kallman (1921–1975) based on William Hogarth's paintings (1732–33); three acts; premiered **Venice**, Teatro La Fenice, September 1951. The most prominent **neo-classical** opera and Stravinsky's last true example of this style.

The Rake's Progress fulfilled Stravinsky's long-standing ambition to write an opera in English. It adapts Hogarth's series of eight paintings/engravings, which Stravinsky had viewed at an exhibit in Chicago (1947). In modifying its narrative, the creators rearranged, altered, added and deleted episodes and characters, for example, turning the old maid that Tom marries into the bearded lady Baba the Turk.

In the opera, the cad Tom Rakewell leaves his pure-hearted soul mate Anne Trulove in the country to pursue his fortunes in **London**. He unwittingly makes a Faustian deal with Nick Shadow—the devil in disguise—who grants him three wishes in exchange for his soul. Wealth comes through an unexpected inheritance that he sets about squandering on liquor and whores. On Nick's advice he pursues happiness by exorcising those base appetites and marrying the most unattractive woman he can find, a circus freak who turns into a violent shrew. Regretting his ill-conceived marriage and hoping to reclaim Anne, he seeks virtue represented by a redemptive good deed. But Nick again deceives him, touting investment in a bogus device purported to feed the world, which bankrupts him. Although Tom wins back his soul by beating Nick at cards and wheedles a fourth wish—to reclaim Anne's love— Nick steals his sanity. When Anne returns to him, he fails to recognize her and dies in the Bedlam asylum.

The Rake's Progress is a paradigm of 20th-century neo-classicism in its simplicity of means and stylistic retrospection. Its pervasively tonal score includes manifold references to 18th-century opera: distinct set piece **arias** including quasi-popular songs and Italianate **cabalettas**, **duets**, ensembles, and **choruses**, all introduced by harpsichord-accompanied **recitative**; an **or-**

chestra of 18th-century proportions; a moralizing epilogue reminiscent of *Don Giovanni*; and numerous other allusions to **Wolfgang Amadeus Mozart**'s music, particularly the **opera buffa** *Così fan tutte* (1790), and to other 18th- and 19th-century precedents. Its ingratiating style and the modest resources required for its performance have made it one of the most familiar post–World War II operas.

RAMEAU, JEAN-PHILIPPE. (1683, Dijon–1764, Paris.) Preeminent French **composer** of approximately 30 operatic works (most from the 1730s through the 1750s) and a music theorist whose influence resonates to the present day. Rameau was the most important opera composer in France between **Jean-Baptiste Lully** and **Christoph Willibald Gluck**.

Trained as an organist, Rameau's early interest in opera may have stemmed from his acquaintance with local Jesuit musical plays. He spent the first two decades of his career (ca. 1702–22) as a virtually unknown provincial organist, teacher, and independent musician, although he spent a brief stint in **Paris** (ca. 1706–09). Rameau moved permanently to Paris in 1722 after traveling there to oversee production of his influential *Traité de l'harmonie*. His operatic career began with contributions to early **opéras comiques** for the Parisian fair theaters during the 1720s.

Rameau's first complete opera, produced at age 50, was the epochal and highly controversial *tragédie en musique Hippolyte et Aricie* (1733), its musical complexity and dramatic intensity inspiring the pejorative appellation "**baroque**," and its popularity igniting debates between Rameau's supporters and those of Lully. The controversy escalated for six years, through otherwise successful premiers of his *opéra-ballet Les Indes galantes* (1735), *tragédie en musique Castor et Pollux* (1737), *opéra-ballet Les fêtes d'Hébé, ou Les talents lyriques* (1739), and *tragédie en musique Dardanus* (1739).

After a fallow period (1740–44), Rameau completed four commissions in the single year 1745, which were produced to celebrate the wedding of Louis XV's heir to the infanta of Spain (the *comédie-ballet La princesse de Navarre* and the *comédie lyrique Platée*) and to commemorate the recent French victory at the Battle of Fontenoy in the War of the Austrian Succession (the *opéras-ballets Les fêtes de Polymnie* and *Le temple de la Gloire*). These successes began an association with the royal court over the next six years that resulted in six additional full-scale operas, including *Naïs* and *Zoroastre* in 1749, as well as several shorter works. Rameau concentrated mainly on short *actes de ballet* in the 1750s, and his last major opera to be performed was the chronologically isolated *comédie lyrique Les Paladins* (1760).

Rameau's operas set 18th-century standards for all genres of French opera and tipped the balance between text and music in the latter direction. He intensified French **recitative** by making its rhythms more varied and responsive to mood, giving its vocal lines more angular and dramatic contours, and introducing more adventurous chord progressions (including 7th and 9th chords) and more distant modulations, while increasing the role of accompanied recitative and endowing it with a broader range of affects. His display **arias** became increasingly virtuosic, his dramatic arias more expressive in their declamatory vocal lines. **Choruses** shoulder more prominent roles and greater dramatic responsibilities, from commentary to participation in the action. And Rameau took Lully's emphasis of the French **orchestra** to a new level of brilliant color, particularly in his **ballets** and overtures, which play an increasing role in creating context for the initial action or prefiguring later scenes.

Despite these innovations and Rameau's early reputation as an anti-establishment troublemaker, his iconic status and association with the royal court made him a symbol of institutional entrenchment and an easy target for attacks by the *encyclopédistes* during the **War of the Comedians**. Beginning in 1752 he resumed his writings on music theory and aesthetics, in many cases to fend off criticisms, and eventually he was dethroned at the Opéra by Gluck's arrival in the 1770s.

RAPPRESENTAZIONE SACRA. A type of sacred theater production common in Florence in the 15th through the early 17th centuries, performed typically by costumed boys onstage with sets and even machinery for special effects. Dialogue set to melodic formulas alternated with various types of metered songs and **madrigals**, which often clustered in *intermedi*. **Emilio de' Cavalieri**'s *Rappresentatione di Anima, et di Corpo* (Rome, February 1600), the most famous example of the genre, set its dialogues with **recitatives**, bringing the *stile rappresentativo* from Florence to **Rome** and likely initiating the development of Roman religious opera. The designation has also been used occasionally in the 20th century, for example for **Luigi Dallapiccola**'s *Job* (1950) and **Krzysztof Penderecki**'s *Paradise Lost* (1978).

RASI, FRANCESCO. (1574, Arezzo–1621, Mantua.) Italian **tenor** and the most notable male singer of early opera, *chitarrone* player (*see* LUTE), **composer**, and **librettist**. A student of **Giulio Caccini**, Rasi spent his early career in **Rome**, Ferrara, **Venice**, and **Naples**. In 1598 he took a position with the Duke of Mantua and likely spent the rest of his career working for the Gonzaga family. Rasi sang in **Jacopo Peri**'s *Euridice* and Caccini's *Il rapimento di Cefalo* (1600) for Maria de' Medici's wedding, and in **Claudio Monteverdi**'s *Orfeo* (probably in the title role) and *Arianna* (1608). In 1608 he was convicted of murdering his stepmother's servant and attempting to murder his stepmother, escaping torture and execution with the help of the Gonzagas. His opera *Cibele, ed Ati* (1617, music lost) was composed, but not performed, for a Gonzaga wedding.

RAVEL, MAURICE. (1875, Ciboure–1937, Paris.) Prominent French **composer** of instrumental and vocal music, including two well-known operas. Ravel trained without great success as a pianist at the **Paris** Conservatoire (1889–95) and later (1898–1903) studied composition there with Gabriel Fauré (1845–1924), at which time he worked on his first opera, *Shéhérazade* (mostly lost).

Ravel's contribution to the current operatic repertory consists of two relatively brief light works in which furniture plays a central part. For *L'heure espagnole* (*The Spanish Hour*, composed 1907–09, premiered 1911), Ravel crafted a score ripe with exotic musical color for his adaptation of an extremely popular *risqué* comedy by Franc-Nohain (1872–1934), in which a clockmaker's adulterous wife entertains her lovers—concealing them to comic effect in her husband's creations—while he makes his weekly rounds servicing the municipal timepieces during her "Spanish hour." In *L'enfant et le sortilèges* (*The Child and the Magic Spells*, 1925), a fantasy opera on a **libretto** by the French writer Colette (1873–1954), a child's objects of abuse—pets and other animals, household furniture and accessories, a wallpaper shepherd and shepherdess, and so on—come to life and teach him to value others and behave charitably. The opera enlists a huge cast of soloists (some singing multiple roles) and a large **orchestra**, who perform an extended series of set pieces, including the infamous meowing **duet** said to parody **Richard Wagner**.

RECITATIVE. The most speechlike style of text setting in opera and in genres derived from opera (cantata and oratorio, for example). By the late 17th century, recitatives were distinguished from lyric set pieces not only by musical style but also, more definitively, because they set *versi sciolti* (free verses) rather than the *versi lirici* (lyric verses) used in lyric set pieces such as **arias** (*see* VERSIFICATION). Adoption of a looser poetic style incorporating lines of uneven lengths, irregular rhyme patterns, minimal repetitions, and no stanzas encouraged musical settings in which the melody moves more flexibly and often more rapidly than in true song, the tempo varies to suit the mood and pacing of the words, and the accompaniment avoids musical patterns, so that meter is relatively ambiguous. By ca. 1700 and continuing through the mid-19th century, composers adhered to a standard format for organizing **scenes**, in which a scena in recitative style precedes a lyric aria or other set piece.

Recitative began as a type of **monody** that was regarded by members of the **Florentine Camerata** as an approximation of the style used by the ancient Greeks for reciting tragedy, a method of "speaking in music" (*in armonia favellare*). Members of the academies referred to it as the *stile rappresentativo* ("theatrical style") and took credit for inventing it (**Giulio Caccini**) or implementing it in opera (**Jacopo Peri**). The Florentine music theorist **Gio-**

vanni Battista Doni distinguished three types of recitative in 1640: "narrative" recitative, the least affective, characterized by declamation lacking **ornamentation**, notable chromaticism, or intense dissonance with the bass line; "special" recitative, similar to the narrative style, used most frequently in the prologues of operas and marked by formulaic melody and strophic variation form; and "expressive" recitative, the most passionate, typified by freer melody and greater chromaticism, dissonance, and affective ornamentation. The last of these styles is close to that of solo **madrigals**, which often include recitative-like phrases.

In the late 17th century **composers** increasingly concentrated musical interest and dramatic expression in arias and set them off from their surroundings by cultivating the simplest, least emotive style of recitative. By the 18th century, commentators were distinguishing between two categories of recitative in **opera seria**. *Recitativo semplice* ("simple recitative") or alternatively *recitativo secco* ("dry recitative"), the descendent of Doni's narrative recitative, is accompanied only by **basso continuo**, is expressively and musically limited, and is used pervasively for active dialogue and plot movement. *Recitativo obbligato* ("obbligato recitative [with specified instruments]"), *recitativo stromentato* ("recitative with instruments"), or *recitativo accompagnato* ("accompanied recitative"), the descendent of Doni's expressive recitative, adds other instruments (normally strings in the 18th century) to the basso continuo, is musically and emotionally intense, and is invariably reserved for very few monologues in which principal characters experience their greatest crises.

Expanded use of obbligato recitative in the late 18th century by progressives such as **Christoph Willibald Gluck** led in the early 19th century to the elimination of recitative accompanied by basso continuo from operatic *melodramma* by **Gioachino Rossini** and his contemporaries (beginning with **Simon Mayr**'s *Medea in Corinto*, 1813). A shift in the meaning of *recitativo semplice* accompanied this development, as it now denoted musically and emotionally neutral recitative accompanied by orchestra, in contrast to *recitativo obbligato*, which was more expressive. In **opera buffa**, however, *recitativo semplice* accompanied by basso continuo persisted from the beginning until the genre withered in the middle of the 19th century. And *recitativo obbligato* occurred very rarely, often arguably in parody of the disproportionate pathos of the character singing.

National distinctions are evident in recitative styles from the late 17th century onward. The French distinguished between *récitatif ordinaire*, accompanied by basso continuo alone and flexible in its meter and tempo, and *récitatif mesuré*, accompanied also by strings and more melodious and regular in its meter and tempo. Both types tend to be more heavily accented and formalized and are given more dramatic and expressive weight than the increasingly streamlined Italian style. German recitative was noted for its intense harmonic progressions and unpredictable melodic contours, while the English version is sometimes compared to **arioso**. The absence of a true equivalent to Italian *recitativo semplice* in these national traditions probably related to the continued use of spoken dialogue largely to the exclusion of recitative in **opéra comique, singspiel**, and **ballad opera**. In the second half of the 19th century, composers of all nationalities tended to reduce the quantity of recitative and its polarization with respect to lyric sections, resulting in the more continuous styles of **Richard Wagner**'s music dramas and **Giuseppe Verdi**'s late masterworks. In the 20th century, derivatives of recitative are found in the *Sprechstimme* of the Second Viennese School and more literally in such diverse operas as *The Rake's Progress* and **Benjamin Britten**'s *Death in Venice* (1973).

RENZI, ANNA. (ca. 1620, Rome–after 1661.) Italian **soprano**, the most famous Venetian singer of the 1640s. Having begun her career in **Rome**, she relocated to the new operatic hotbed, **Venice**, in 1640. There her skill at psychological portraiture and her stamina as a performer contributed to her success in the public theaters and gained praise from Giovanni Francesco Loredano and other members of the avant-garde Accademia degli Incogniti (*see* BUSENELLO, GIOVANNI FRANCESCO). Her roles included Ottavia in **Claudio Monteverdi**'s *L'incoronazione di Poppea* and the title role in **Antonio Cesti**'s *La Cleopatra* (Innsbruck, 1654, originally *Il Cesare amante*, 1651–52).

RESCUE OPERA. Modern term for operas of the late 18th and early 19th centuries in which the hero or heroine escapes either politically motivated imprisonment by a tyrant or a natural or manmade catastrophe through the intervention of an individual or group. These works represent Enlightenment and Revolutionary ideals by emphasizing personal rights, justice, and freedom won through courage and sacrifice. And their rescue climaxes relate to the traditional operatic *lieto fine* produced through a deus ex machina. These characteristics developed initially in **opéras comiques** by the French **librettist** Michel-Jean Sedaine (1719–1797) such as Pierre-Alexandre Monsigny's (1729–1817) *Le déserteur* (1769) and **André-Ernest-Modeste Grétry**'s *Richard Coeur-de-lion* (1784), then spread to *opera semiseria* and **singspiel**. The type is most famously represented nowadays by Ludwig van Beethoven's (1770–1827) singspiel *Fidelio* and in its heyday by such works as **Luigi Cherubini**'s *comédie-héroïque Lodoïska* (1791).

See also CATEGORIES OF OPERA; *GUILLAUME TELL*; MOZART, WOLFGANG AMADEUS; PAER, FERDINANDO.

RICCI, LUIGI AND FEDERICO. (Luigi: 1805, probably Naples–1859, Prague; Federico: 1809, Naples–1877, Treviso.) Brothers whose works represented a final resurgence of Italian comic opera prior to ca. 1850. In total they produced more than two dozen works in the **categories** of *farsa*, **opera buffa**, *opera semiseria*, and their variants (most from the 1820s through the 1840s), four in collaboration.

Luigi and Federico both trained at the **Naples** Conservatory under the opera **composer** and pedagogue Niccolò Zingarelli (1752–1837), whose students included **Saverio Mercadante** and **Vincenzo Bellini**. Luigi's career began first, his operas in various genres vacillating between modest successes and outright flops until his breakout hit, the *opera semiseria Chiara di Rosembergh* (1831), after which he concentrated on comedy. The brothers collaborated from 1835 to 1850 on four successful comedies, beginning with *Il colonello*, Federico's first stage work, and culminating with the *melodramma fantastico-giocoso Crispino e la comare*, which remained popular throughout the century. During this same period they also premiered operas composed individually, most notably Luigi's disastrous *Le nozze di Figaro* (1838) and the more successful *La festa di Piedigrotta* (1852), and Federico's *Il marito e l'amante* (1852, a precursor of Johann Strauss's, 1825–1899, *Die Fledermaus*, 1874).

Beginning in 1844, Luigi began a flimsily disguised ménage à trois with twin **sopranos**, which apparently continued after he married one of them. Following the premier of his final opera in 1859, he became mentally unbalanced and died in a Prague asylum. Federico spent over a decade (1853 to 1869) as the *maestro di cappella* of imperial theaters in St. Petersburg, after which he found brief success writing light opera in **Paris**.

RICORDI. The dominant publisher of Italian operas and instrumental music in the 19th and 20th centuries and the Italian firm most responsible for the transition from circulating music in manuscript copies to printed editions.

Established in Milan in 1808 by Giovanni Ricordi (1785–1853), the Casa Ricordi remained a family concern throughout the 19th and early 20th centuries, passing from father to son at their deaths—from Giovanni to Tito (1811–1888), to Giulio (1840–1912), and to Giulio's son Tito (1865–1933)—until 1919, when the family relinquished management. It grew out of a manuscript copying business opened by Giovanni ca. 1803. After he learned the printing process with Breitkopf and Härtel in Leipzig (1807), Ricordi began printing music (1808). In 1811 he became the publisher for the Milan **Conservatory**, in 1814 publisher of works performed at La Scala, and by midcentury had contracts with other theaters in Milan, **Venice**, and **Naples**. The firm expanded rapidly by purchasing the inventory of the

Artaria publishing house (1837) and those of several other businesses by the end of the century, acquiring the Italian rights to **Richard Wagner**'s operas in the process.

Giovanni's earliest publications were piano arrangements of and sets of variations on hit operatic melodies. His first complete piano-vocal score was **Simon Mayr**'s *Adelasia ed Aleramo* (originally 1806, published by 1814). Eventually the business controlled the rights to about half of **Gioachino Rossini**'s operas and most of those by **Vincenzo Bellini, Gaetano Donizetti** (among those written after 1830), **Giuseppe Verdi**, and other luminaries. Giulio was instrumental in negotiating the truce between Verdi and the composer/**librettist Arrigo Boito** that resulted in Verdi's late works. And the Ricordi family ardently supported **Giacomo Puccini** and others in the late 19th and early 20th centuries, including **Amilcare Ponchielli, Boito, Alfredo Catalani**, and **Gian Francesco Malipiero**.

The Casa Ricordi also printed books for the Milan Conservatory and created several Italian musical journals, beginning with Italy's first, the *Gazzetta musicale di Milano* in 1842. The firm's archives are a treasure trove for operatic research, containing thousands of autograph music manuscripts, pieces of correspondence, and printed works. Ricordi currently participates in scholarly editions of the works of Rossini, Bellini, Donizetti, and Verdi.

RIGOLETTO. *Melodramma*; music by **Giuseppe Verdi, libretto** by **Francesco Maria Piave** based on Victor Hugo's (1802–1885) play *Le roi s'amuse* (1832); three acts; premiered **Venice**, Teatro La Fenice, March 1851. One of Verdi's most performed and beloved works, and one of the most innovative Italian operas of the mid-19th century. The title role was conceived for the eminent baritone (*see* BASS) Felice Varesi (1813–1889) who had played the lead in Verdi's *Macbeth* (1847).

Facing heightened theatrical **censorship** in Austrian-held Venice following the Revolutions of 1848, and choosing to adapt an explosive play that had already been banned in Paris and elsewhere, Verdi and Piave fought an uphill battle that almost ended the project. However, they engineered a compromise that distanced the opera from the play while retaining its most important elements. They shifted the locale from the French royal court of Francis I to the lesser duchy of Mantua, omitted the Duke's most nefarious activities, changed the names of the characters, and abandoned Verdi's preferred title *La maledizione* (*The Curse*). But the Duke remained an aristocratic philanderer and Rigoletto a hunchback, and they were able to keep his grisly discovery of his dying daughter. Despite continued censorship issues, *Rigoletto* received hundreds of performances over the next decades and soon won its lasting place in the repertory.

Rigoletto's plot illustrates the escalation of dramatic catharsis that characterizes mid-19th-century Italian opera. The deformed jester Rigoletto, butt of ridicule by courtesans of the licentious Duke, makes them pay for their cruelty by targeting new conquests for the Duke among their wives and daughters, leading them to plot their own revenge. After Rigoletto is confronted and cursed by Monterone, father of one of the girls the Duke has deflowered, he meets the hired assassin Sparafucile and idly inquires about his services. Despite shielding his daughter Gilda from the debauchery of the court by secluding her in his cottage, she meets and falls in love with the Duke, who masquerades as a student. As night falls, the courtesans launch their intrigue: thinking they are kidnapping Rigoletto's mistress for the Duke, they deceive Rigoletto into helping them abduct his daughter. When he discovers the ruse and realizes that the Duke has claimed her as his prize, he vows revenge, hiring Sparafucile to murder his master. Sparafucile's sister Maddalena seduces the Duke and lures him to their inn, but she becomes infatuated with him and convinces her brother to substitute another victim. In a scene featuring a famously innovative divided **set** that includes both the interior of the inn and the street outside, Gilda, who has disguised herself in male clothing and has eavesdropped on their conversation, sacrifices herself for her lover. Sparafucile delivers her body in a sack, leaving Rigoletto to discover his dying daughter instead of his nemesis.

Verdi judged *Rigoletto* one of his most successful and "revolutionary" operas, its intensity depending on both its libretto and its music. The opera recasts the timeworn Italian love triangle (*see NORMA*) with uniquely idiosyncratic and yet credibly human and conflicted individuals depicted with unaccustomed nuance—a charming, yet promiscuous and cynical leading man; his irrationally devoted paramour; and her doting but self-invested father—and sets it in the context of a debauched society lacking any moral compass. Its grotesque elements, such as the poetic justice of Rigoletto's unwitting complicity in the rape of his daughter, the minutia of the assassination contract, and the irreverent disposal of Gilda's body, are set jarringly against horrifying deformations of traditionally comic disguises, mistaken intentions, and Rigoletto's flesh-and-blood embodiment of the **commedia dell'arte** caricature, Punchinello, the fat humpbacked clown. And *Rigoletto*'s linear plotting, in which the action proceeds through a causally connected series of events, replaces the schematic exposition of conflicts and alliances common in the 1820s through 1840s and introduces interpersonal relationships gradually as the action unfolds, helping to immerse the audience in the emerging tragedy.

More than Verdi's previous works, *Rigoletto* presses the development of the Italian style by making the distribution of set pieces and their individual forms more spontaneous and by conveying atmosphere and characterization more incisively and coherently. **Arias** are demoted in favor of interactive ensembles. Gilda has only a single one-movement aria ("Caro nome," Act 1) as does Rigoletto, although his has multiple sections ("Cortigiani, vil razza dannata," Act 2), in addition to his self-reflexive monologue "Pari siamo" (Act 1). The Duke's best solos are his one-movement **stage songs** within bigger scenes (the *ballata* "Questa o quella," Act 1, and the canzone "La donna è mobile," Act 3), and he waits until Act 2 for a full three-movement aria ("Parmi veder le lagrime"). *Rigoletto*'s first and third acts consist almost exclusively of **duets** and larger action scenes rather than arias. Yet despite this emphasis on ensembles, Verdi and Piave included no conventional showstopping central **finale** in Act 1 or 2, instead creating the idiosyncratic abduction scene for **chorus** and Rigoletto (Act 1) and a duet in which Gilda confesses her relationship with the Duke and Rigoletto vows revenge (Act 2). Finale-like structures are situated more comfortably in the Act 1 party scene and the Act 3 quartet plus trio (Gilda's murder).

Within ensembles, both traditionally active movements (the *tempo d'attacco* and *tempo di mezzo*) and more lyrical ones (the slow movement and **cabaletta/stretta**) become primary plot vehicles (see the three duets for Rigoletto and Gilda), allowing **recitatives** to be minimized. And their traditional forms seem less obtrusive because the boundaries between their movements are announced less obviously, the personalities of the lyrical movements are adapted better to circumstances, and more cogent pretexts are provided for breaks in the music. For example, in the Act 1 *introduzione*, the extended *tempo d'attacco*, consisting of a sequence of episodes including the Duke's *ballata* and two dances, leads seamlessly into a rowdy, conspiratorial stretta that stands in for the expected *largo concertato*; Monterrone's fuming entrance to start the *tempo di mezzo* creates a naturalistic interruption; and his curse provides a credible coup de théâtre that launches the true stretta, which begins in a horrified whisper. The adaptability of ensembles is particularly evident in the one-movement duet for Rigoletto and Sparafucile "Quel vecchio maledivami" (Act 1) and in the deployment of the four-movement finale structure across the quartet and trio in Act 3.

Verdi viewed *Rigoletto* as a landmark in his development of the conception of musical and dramatic *tinta*, a signature style or styles that represent the essence of an opera's situation and atmosphere and gives it a cohesive texture. In *Rigoletto* it is heard in the juxtaposition of the opera's orchestral prelude, which introduces the ominous motive that represents Monterrone's curse throughout the opera, with the banal **stage band** music that begins the opening scene and conveys the crass gaiety of the Duke's court. The **orchestra** makes a more distinctive contribution to characterization in *Rigoletto* than in most of Verdi's prior operas, in the omnipresent *parlante* accompaniments, in the hunchback's disparaging sortie against Monterrone in the party **scene**, in his ensuing monologue, and in the calm before the storm: the scena (*see* SCENE)/*tempo di mezzo* "M'odi! ritorna a casa" that links the Act 3 quartet "Bella figlia dell'amore" and trio "Se pria ch'abbia il mezzo la notte." And Verdi's musical differentiation of characters, whether in solos like the Duke's brash stage songs, Gilda's naive love song, and Rigoletto's emotional polarities or in the lyrical movements of duets and ensembles—most famously "Bella figlia"—further contributes to *Rigoletto*'s unique tone and special status among the composer's emphatically individualized operas after 1850.

RIMSKY-KORSAKOV, NIKOLAY ANDREYEVICH. (1844, Tikhvin, Russia–1908, Lyubensk, Russia.) **Composer** of 15 operatic works (primarily during the 1870s and from about 1895 to 1905), **librettist** for 10 of them, editor/orchestrator, and **conductor**.

Born into the lesser nobility and educated privately, Rimsky attended the Naval College of St. Petersburg (1856–62), where he avidly attended operas, becoming familiar with the works of the Italians, **Giacomo Meyerbeer**, and **Mikhail Ivanovich Glinka**; studied composition with Mily Balakirev (1837–1910) beginning in 1861; and joined the other members of The Five (the Kuchka or Mighty Handful) and the critic Vladimir Stasov (1824–1906) as a leading figure in the Russian musical nationalist movement. Following a tour of duty at sea (1862–65), he wrote a number of orchestral pieces that contributed to his reputation as a symphonist in Russia and later in western Europe. An inspired orchestrator, he developed his alter ego as an editor of Russian nationalist music, which included scoring Aleksandr Sergeyevich Dargomïzhsky's (1813–1869) *The Stone Guest* in 1869, editing **Mikhail Ivanovich Glinka**'s operas, and completing *Boris Godunov*. His appointment at the St. Petersburg **Conservatory** (1871), where he would teach Aleksandr Glazunov (1865–1936), distanced him from the other members of The Five, who opposed institutional dogma, and led him to undertake a rigorous period of retraining (1874–76). He also compiled two collections of folk songs (1875–76) that provided materials for later operas. In addition to frequent conducting appearances, he served for a decade as Balakirev's assistant at the imperial chapel (1883–94).

Although best known in the West for his orchestral music, Rimsky devoted substantial time and effort to opera librettos and scores. His remarkably diverse style ranges from historically based sagas to fantastical folktales set in magical or exotic locales painted with his virtuosic orchestration and broad repertory of chromatic, modal, and whole-tone colors, from **number operas** constructed in set pieces and tableaux to continuous dialogue, from the severe realist declamation championed by The Five to brilliant vocalism, and from traditional lyricism Russianized with folk tunes to quasi-**Wagnerian** networks of reminiscence melodies.

Rimsky's first period of operatic activity began with *Pskovityanka* (*The Maid of Pskov*, premiered 1873, definitive version 1901), a historical drama based on the life of Ivan the Terrible that emphasizes continuity and naturalistic declamation. Ivan initially spares the city of Pskov because he had fathered a daughter there years before his murderous campaign, but she falls in love with a revolutionary and is killed in the fighting. *Snegurochka* (*The Snow Maiden*, composed 1880–81), a **Literaturoper** of sorts owing to Rimsky's faithful adaptation of a play by Alexander Nikolayevich Ostrovsky, was one of his greatest public triumphs and the opera he regarded as his best work. In a romantic nature myth populated by personifications of the seasons, peasants, and the tsar's court, the heroine melts in the spring sun after falling in love with a human.

Sadko (1897), Rimsky's finest opera from his second phase, is a medieval legend of sea gods, nymphs, traders from exotic lands, and wizards based on Russian epic ballads. In a succession of spectacular tableaux, the title character, a historical Russian singer akin to Orpheus, abandons his wife to seek a fortune using golden fish given to him by the daughter of the Sea King. Its production in 1897 by the Moscow company of the benefactor Savva Mamontov set an important precedent in using proto-modernist **set designs**. *Motsart i Sal'yeri* (*Mozart and Salieri*, 1898), on Aleksandr Pushkin's play (adapted by Rimsky) about **Antonio Salieri**'s supposed murder of **Wolfgang Amadeus Mozart**, is Rimsky's most thoroughgoing venture in the style of realist declamation. Its lyrical counterpoise is *Tsarskaya nevesta* (*The Tsar's Bride*, 1899), a fictionalized melodramatic treatment of Ivan the Terrible's third marriage.

The fairy-tale opera *Kashchey bessmertnïy* (*Kashchey the Immortal*, 1902) became a rallying point for the 1905 Revolution in St. Petersburg, during which Rimsky's support for student dissidents temporarily cost him his job at the conservatory. In *Skazaniye o nevidimom grade Kitezhe i deve Fevronii* (*The Legend of the Invisible City of Kitezh and the Maiden Fevroniya*, composed 1903–04, premiered 1907), which vies with *Sadko* among enthusiasts as Rimsky's best opera, the Christian God allied with various pantheistic, folkloric forces saves the city from the Mongol invasion of 1223. *Zolotoy petushok* (*Le coq d'Or*/*The Golden Cockerel*, composed 1906–07, premiered 1909 after Rimsky's death) is the composer's only opera to be assimilated into the Western repertory, aided in part by modernist performances by Sergey Diaghilev's (1872–1929) company in the 1910s. In this satirical fable, an inept king relies on a rooster to predict invasions but is seduced and conquered by a rival queen and pecked to death by the bird after he kills its astrologer master.

RINALDO. Opera seria; music by **George Frideric Handel**, libretto by Giacomo Rossi (active 1710–1731) based indirectly on Torquato Tasso's (1544–1595) *Gerusalemme liberata* (1581); three acts; premiered **London**, Queen's Theater, February 1711. The first Italian opera written specifically for London. Performed by a stellar cast with dazzling special effects, *Rinaldo* enjoyed public acclaim (despite a mixed critical reception) and was revived during five additional seasons as late as 1731. In 1984 it became the first Handel opera performed by the Metropolitan Opera in **New York**.

Rinaldo is spectacular theater in the traditions of Italian and Viennese court opera and French *tragédie en musique*. Set outside the walls of Jerusalem and in other fanciful locations, it pits Christian crusaders against Saracen defenders. During a three-day truce, the Saracen king Argante enlists the sorceress Armida to neutralize the Christian hero Rinaldo. She first kidnaps his fiancée Almirena, then captures Rinaldo as he and his companions Goffredo and Eustazio pursue her. Using magic wands supplied by a hermit, Goffredo and Eustazio rescue Almirena, and an assault led by Rinaldo wins Jerusalem. In a formulaic *lieto fine*, Rinaldo and Almirena reunite, Armida converts to Christianity, and she and Argante decide to marry. Spectacular scenes abound, including Armida's entrance in a chariot pulled by dragons, Rinaldo's entrapment by sirens, Armida's transformation into Almirena, Goffredo and Eustazio's treacherous passage to Armida's castle—during which they fight monsters, make a mountain vanish, and escape from a sea-swept rock—and a climactic battle.

DER RING DES NIBELUNGEN. *Bühnenfestspiel* (**festival** stage event) of four music dramas intended to be performed over four consecutive days; music by **Richard Wagner**, **librettos** by the **composer** based on 13th-century sources of northern European mythology (among them the *Poetic Edda* and *Prose Edda*, the *Völsunga Saga*, and *Das Nibelungenlied*), on more recent literary scholarship, and on Greek mythology (Aeschylus's *Oresteia* trilogy); first complete performance Bayreuth, Festspielhaus, August 1876. An extraordinarily influential operatic work and alongside *Licht* and **Philip Glass**'s *Portrait Trilogy* (1977–1983, *see EINSTEIN ON THE BEACH*) one of the most ambitious.

In 1848 Wagner began work on a prose scenario and wrote the libretto for *Siegfrieds Tod* (*Siegfried's Death*), which became *Götterdämmerung*. This initial foray involved such extensive narration of prior events that he subsequently enacted that background, working in reverse order through *Der junge Siegfried* (*Siegfried*), *Die Walküre*, and *Das Rheingold* (1851–52). He then revised *Junge Siegfried* and *Siegfrieds Tod*, making Wotan rather than Siegfried the protagonist and retargeting the outcome of Brünnhilde's death from saving the Gods to destroying them. The music was composed beginning with *Das Rheingold* and proceeding in narrative order through the remaining operas (1853–57 and 1869–74). He interrupted this process after Act 2 of *Siegfried* for composition of *Tristan und Isolde* and *Die Meistersinger von Nürnberg* (1868), resuming after financial support was secured from Ludwig of Bavaria (beginning 1864) and *Die Meistersinger* premiered. The complete cycle was performed as the first Bayreuth Festival, and cycles were heard in the late 1870s in various German-speaking cities and had reached Great Britain and the United States by 1890.

The Ring deploys a notoriously complex, epic cosmology that includes three levels of beings who inhabit different realms: the Gods, whose activities center on the newly constructed heavenly castle Valhalla; the Nibelungs, dwarves of subterranean Nibelheim; and the earthbound mortals and their offspring of mixed races. The Gods are ruled by Wotan, whose power stems from an artificial, and ultimately ill-conceived system of laws and contracts recorded on the spear he carries, which represents modern government and society. His companions include his wife Fricka, goddess of marriage and the home, who bristles at Wotan's infidelities and many illegitimate offspring; her sister Freia, who tends magical apples that ensure the Gods' immortality; his Walküre daughters—probably sired with the goddess Erda, and among whom his favorite is Brünnhilde—who recover the souls of dead heroes to guard Valhalla; and Loge, the crafty god of fire. The Nibelungs, who mine the riches of the underworld, are subjugated by the soulless Alberich, who exploits his brother Mime, an alchemical metalsmith empowered to create the Tarnhelm, which can enable its wearer to change shape and become invisible. Numerous races, some human, some half human, inhabit the earth: the Rhinemaidens, who guard the gold of the Rhine River in its natural state; the brother Giants Fafner and Fasolt, essentially the Ring's military-industrial complex, with whom he has contracted to build Valhalla; the Wälsungs Siegmund and Sieglinde, his twin son and daughter by a human woman, and their incestuous love child Siegfried; the white slave trader Hunding, unwanted husband of Sieglinde; the human Gibichung brother and sister Gunther and Gutrune; and their confident Hagen, Alberich's son with the mother of Gunther and Gutrune and his counterpart to Siegfried.

Characteristically high minded in its conception, Wagner's *Ring* attempts nothing less than an analysis of the decline of humanity and a proposal for reversing that decline through the exploits of a racially superior yet unsocialized hero and through the individual self-denial espoused by the philosopher Arthur Schopenhauer. *Das Rheingold* essays the corruption of human nature: greed and self-advancement lead loveless men to degrade their fellow beings and exploit nature within an expedient system of government based on laws and contracts instead of love and compassion. Alberich, teased for his lust by the Rhinemaidens, renounces love as a prerequisite for stealing the gold they guard and remaking it for his own purposes. The Ring, a perversion of the gold's pure beauty representing his wealth-based, sterile power, and the Tarnhelm, which allows him to operate unseen and unknown, enable him to exploit his fellow Nibelungs and fuel his ambition to destroy the Gods and dominate the world. His rival Wotan, confronted with paying his debt to the Giants for Valhalla and having failed to plan for the eventuality of its completion, yields his sister-in-law Freia to them as collateral, and the Gods begin to age immediately as the apples that have maintained their youth go untended. Unable to ignore his contract with the Giants, because doing so would undermine his credibility and his authority, for which laws are the basis, on Loge's advice Wotan picks out Alberich as a quarry toward whom he has no obligations. They abduct Alberich from Nibelheim by challenging him to use the Tarnhelm to change himself first into a dragon and then into a frog, which is easily caught. He is forced to ransom himself with his gold, the Tarnhelm, and the Ring, which he curses as he relinquishes it. The curse— and the inherent corruption of the Ring—take effect at once as Fafner quarrels with Fasolt, who loves Freia and resents giving her up; kills him; and takes the treasure to Riesenheim, where he turns himself into a dragon and secludes himself in a cave.

In *Die Walküre*, Wotan's commitment to power leads to further betrayals of his family. Cognizant of the threat represented by the Ring, recognizing the potential for Alberich or an equally cunning rival to steal the Ring from the thickheaded Fafner, and unable to reclaim it himself owing to their contract, he sires a surrogate, Siegmund (and incidentally his sister Sieglinde), to accomplish the task. Sieglinde has previously been abducted and forced into wedlock by Hunding, who with his accomplices has more recently overcome and disarmed Siegmund in battle. Siegmund stumbles upon Hunding's cottage, built around a mighty tree in which Wotan has implanted a sword, where he falls in love with Sieglinde and couples with her, recovers the sword he dubs Notung (Necessity) from the tree in an Arthurian moment, and fights Hunding. Meanwhile, Wotan is persuaded by Fricka that aiding Siegmund would violate his contract with Fafner, so he sends Brünnhilde to disarm him. Moved by Siegmund's devotion to Sieglinde, Brünnhilde declines to act, and Wotan intervenes himself, shattering his son's weapon and allowing Hunding to kill him. Amidst the chaos, Brünnhilde helps Sieglinde flee to Riesenheim with her unborn child and the remnants of the sword, and she takes Siegmund's body to a mountain rendezvous with her sisters. Wotan punishes her disobedience by entrancing her on a mountain top surrounded by Loge's magic fire, vulnerable to debasement by a hero sufficiently fearless to brave the flames.

Siegfried brings the initial virtuous, yet unwitting assault on the rule of the Gods and the power of the Ring. Determined to set about his career, Siegfried, whose mother Sieglinde died in childbirth and who has been raised by Alberich's brother Mime, reforges the remnants of Notung, accomplishing what his ineffectual tutor has failed to do. Profiting from his mistake with Siegmund, Wotan distances himself from Siegfried by contriving to thwart and destroy him. He manipulates Mime to set him against Fafner and poison him should he win the fight. But after Siegfried kills Fafner, taking the Ring and the Tarnhelm, he sees through Mime's plot—the violence of combat aligns him with nature, enabling him to understand a woodbird's warning—and kills him. Continuing his adventures he arrives at Brünnhilde's mountain, where he defeats Wotan who guards her, passes through the fire that encircles her, claims her, and gives her the Ring as a symbol of his love, undoing its corruption.

Götterdämmerung completes the cycle by demonstrating the futility of worldly love as an antidote to conflict and enacting the Schopenhauerian program of self-denial. The naive Siegfried is ensnared in a web of worldly intrigue at the court of the Gibichungs on the banks of the Rhine. Hagen administers a potion that makes Siegfried forget Brünnhilde, disguises himself as Gunther using the Tarnhelm, claims Brünnhilde as Gunther's bride, and marries Gutrune. After Brünnhilde recognizes Siegfried's betrayal, because he wears the Ring he stole from her disguised as Gunther, she takes her revenge by betraying his vulnerability to Hagen, who murders him on a hunting trip. In despair Brünnhilde reclaims the Ring, immolating it, herself, and the palace of the Gibichungs in a purifying fire that is quenched by the Rhine's overflowing waters, thus allowing nature to repossess the gold and ending the Gods' reign with her sacrifice.

The Ring served as an epochal proving ground for Wagner's theories of music drama and the *Gesamtkunstwerk*. Its focus on allegorical representation of philosophical, sociological, and political themes, as well as the gravity of the enterprise, is enhanced by marginalizing the distracting presence of **choruses** and other massed congregations and of spectacular scenic effects—for example the Rainbow Bridge (*Das Rheingold*, scene 4); the Walküre reunion and Brünnhilde's Magic Fire (*Die Walküre*, Act 3, and *Siegfried*, Act 3); and *Götterdämmerung*'s apocalyptic ending—and by elevating extended dialogue and monologue as the core of the action. Along with the work's grand scale, Wagner's "endless melody," which freely interchanges **arioso** and declamation supported by a vast system of **leitmotifs**, and orchestral transitions between **scenes** facilitate the audience's immersion in the grand, quasi-religious experience.

The presence of leitmotifs increases across the cycle, partly owing to their accumulation as the cast of characters expands and the plot thickens, and partly owing to Wagner's exposure to Schopenhauer's aesthetic theories, which prioritize music among the arts. Consequently the focus on music primarily at the start and finish of *Das Rheingold* (the Rhinemaidens and Rainbow Bridge) and at the beginnings and endings of acts in *Die Walküre* (Siegmund and Sieglinde's love **duet** ending Act 1, the Walküre scene and Wotan's farewell to Brünnhilde beginning and ending Act 3) gives way to more evenhanded musical distribution. Folkloric elements such as alliterative **Stabreim** and kenning (in which figurative language replaces simple nouns), the frequent bardic narratives of prior events, and freely constructed allusions to lied-like bar forms (AA'B, e.g., "Der Augen leuchtendes Paar") and quasi-strophic, sequentially modulating forms (AA'A", e.g., "Muss ich dich meid-en," both examples *Die Walküre*, Act 3, scene 3) enhance the cycle's mythic quality and Germanic cultural relevance.

ROMANCE. A type of operatic (or stand-alone) solo song similar to a ballad. Originally a French or Spanish narrative poem, by the 18th century the musical romance was characterized as a love song, often tragic, having an old-fashioned, rustic quality conveyed through naive poetry and simple, un-ornamented music in strophic (or later strophic variation) form (*see* ARIA). The romance appeared in the earliest **opéras comiques** (Colin's "Dans ma cabane obscure" in *Le devin du village*). It became a popular type of French **stage song** during the second half of the 18th century and a commonplace in German **singspiels** after ca. 1770 (e.g., Pedrillo's *Romanze* "In Mohrenland gefangen" in **Wolfgang Amadeus Mozart**'s *Die Entführung aus dem Serail*, 1782). In the 19th century it lost a measure of its individuality as the designa-tion expanded to include nostalgic one-movement arias in mainstream styles, often through-composed as single extended melodies (Riccardo's *romanza* "Ma se m'è forza perderti" in **Giuseppe Verdi**'s *Un ballo in maschera*, 1859, Act 3). Senta's ballad ("Johohoe," ***Der fliegende Holländer***, Act 2) may be regarded as a late Germanic representative of the genre. The term fell out of use by the end of the century.

ROMANI, FELICE. (1788, Genoa–1865, Moneglia.) Foremost Italian **li-brettist** of the second quarter of the 19th century and journalist. Romani produced over 90 **librettos** for all the prominent **composers** of the first half of the century, most from the 1810s through the mid-1830s and often at the prodigious rate of about five librettos per year. Over half of them were remodeled by other librettists for later operas.

Educated at the universities of Pisa and Genoa, he settled in Milan ca. 1812, beginning his career as a librettist in 1813 with **Simon Mayr**'s *La rosa bianca e la rosa rossa* and *Medea in Corinto*, and **Gioachino Rossini**'s *Aureliano in Palmira*, for Genoa, **Naples**, and Milan, respectively. He wrote two of **Giacomo Meyerbeer**'s early Italian works in 1820 and 1821 and eight librettos for **Gaetano Donizetti** between 1822 and 1834, among them *L'elisir d'amore* (1832) and *Lucrezia Borgia* (1833). His long-standing col-laboration with **Vincenzo Bellini** began with his revision of *Bianca e Fer-nando* for Genoa (1828, originally 1826) and produced seven new operas (the bulk of Bellini's output) through *Beatrice di Tenda* (1833), including *La sonnambula* and *Norma* (both 1831). Between 1834 and 1849 he served as lead editor and writer for the Savoy court house-organ in Turin, the *Gazzetta ufficiale piemontese*, responsibilities for which limited his operatic activities.

Romani's librettos are paradigms of early 19th-century **romantic *melodramma***. They draw on a spectrum of non-**Arcadian** sources from tragedy (Pierre Corneille, Voltaire, William Shakespeare) to the Parisian boulevard theater and romantic plays and novels (Victor Hugo, Lord Byron). And they minimize intrigue and linear plotting while centering on schematic exposition of alliance and conflict relationships among a limited number of principal characters in series of grand multimovement set pieces, in which reflective movements delineate decisive emotional positions. Romani's collaborative interactions with Bellini, which were exceptional for their day and which extended to aspects of plot, scene structure, and versification, anticipate **Giuseppe Verdi**'s creative involvement with his librettists.

ROMANTICISM. Literary, artistic, and musical style that developed concurrently with neoclassicism in the late 18th century, representing an alternative response to the revolutionary ethos of that period, and reached its greatest prominence in the first half of the 19th century. Alluding initially to the poetic and conceptual freedom of the medieval narrative romance, romanticism developed out of lines of Enlightenment social and cultural criticism represented particularly by Jean-Jacques Rousseau, as well as aspects of sentimental literature and art (*see* SENTIMENTAL OPERA) and literary Sturm und Drang (Storm and Stress), which include skepticism regarding science and society, faith in uncultivated wisdom and naturalness, and belief in intuitive, irrational emotional experience and expressive spontaneity in the arts. The romantic movement was led by critics, writers, and painters in Germany (such as August Wilhelm Schlegel, his younger brother Karl Wilhelm Friedrich Schlegel, and Caspar David Friedrich), in England (William Wordsworth and Joseph Mallord William Turner), and in France (Victor Hugo and Eugène Delacroix).

Romantics believed in the power of art—and for some, music in particular—to transcend logical thought, the boundaries of science and reason, and the mundane limitations of everyday life to penetrate the mysteries of the universe. Artworks can provide vicarious, potentially revelatory experiences involving unrestrained emotional responses to situations that are variously sexual, macabre, or violent; that explore alternative modes of consciousness or belief (our imagination and dreams, magic and the supernatural, and mystical aspects of religion); and that engage nontraditional, non-Eurocentric ideas and exoticisms. Romantic nature worship constituted another source of inspiration, providing a surrogate for conventional, institutionalized religion. Consider nature's sublime, awesome, terrifying aspects, its bucolic, joyous, nurturing aspects, and its connection to the infinite.

Nature worship and the anti-academic, anti-societal tendencies of romantic ideology triggered romantic nostalgia, a yearning for simplicity, clear values, and a more agrarian existence in an age of industrialization and perceived detachment from human existence through excessive socialization, and it spawned a number of historicist movements (e.g., the neo-Gothic and neo-baroque). Finally the fusion of personal and national identity in sundry 19th-century nationalist movements provided yet another source of intense experiences and led romantics to reject classical universality as an aesthetic goal, directing their work instead toward more culturally specific audiences by cultivating their regional artistic heritage and adapting elements of folk art to "high" art. Their pursuit of unique comprehension and understanding inclined them to value individualization of lifestyle and behavior, of creative process, and of particular artworks and to deify genius, the intuitive ability to penetrate the unknown and communicate insight through an artistic medium.

Italian romantics adopted many of these notions as they drew on models from Germany, France, and England in attempting to revitalize their own culture and to eliminate classical conventions by appropriating subjects from German, French, and English literature for their operas. Many of the characteristics noted above are evident in operas of diverse nationalities. See, for example, *Les Huguenots* and *Faust*; *Der Freischütz*, *Der fliegende Holländer*, *Tannhäuser*, and *Der Ring des Nibelungen*; *Lucia di Lammermoor* and *Rigoletto*; and **Mikhail Ivanovich Glinka**'s *A Life for the Tsar* (1836) and **Bedřich Smetana**'s *The Bartered Bride* (premiered 1866, standard version 1870).

ROMANZA. *See* ROMANCE.

ROME. Italian city, during the operatic era the capital of the Papal States, the Kingdom of Italy (beginning 1871), the Republic of Italy (beginning 1946), and the source of important developments in operatic style in the 17th and early 18th centuries.

Opera emerged in Rome in the 17th century alongside a tradition of spoken drama at the Jesuit colleges and in aristocratic homes. Throughout the first three-quarters of the century it was almost exclusively a court entertainment that drew on male singers from the Sistine Chapel. **Women** were excluded for the most part from performing in public theaters until the 19th century, leading native daughters who sought professional careers—most notably **Anna Renzi**—to relocate. Papal intervention at certain times both helped and hindered efforts to promote opera (e.g., through Barberini patronage, see below, and through theater closings and **censorship**, respectively).

Emilio de' Cavalieri's *Rappresentatione di Anima, et di Corpo* (1600) was the most notable among a half dozen or so operatic works, both sacred and secular (several showing ties to Florence), that were produced during the first quarter of the century. Rome's most active contribution to the repertory of new works and the development of operatic style came during the second quarter of the century thanks to the ascendency of the Barberini family as patrons of the arts, in particular the extravagant reign of Maffeo Barberini as Pope Urban VIII (1623–44). The establishment of a distinct Roman style of **libretto** featuring humanized characters wrestling with moral dilemmas, their tribulations interspersed with comic episodes, was led by **Giulio Rospigliosi**, whose best-known work is *Chi soffre speri* (1637), set by **Virgilio Mazzocchi** and Marco Marazzoli (after 1602–1662). Stefano Landi (1587–1639; *see SANT' ALESSIO*), Domenico Mazzocchi (ca. 1593–1665), and Luigi Rossi (ca. 1597–1653) were also important among a handful of **composers** who held primary responsibilities with the Church and at various courts or wrote music as an avocation. Performers from Rome introduced opera to Venetian theatergoers when they staged Giovanni Felice Sances's (ca. 1600–1679) *Ermiona* (lost) in nearby Padua in 1636, and the following year participated in **Francesco Manelli**'s *Andromeda* in **Venice**, the first public opera performance.

After a generation in which opera receded in prominence, two patrons returned it to the spotlight in the late 1660s and 1670s. The expatriate Queen Christina of Sweden, who had converted to Catholicism and emigrated to Rome (1655), funded three productions during that period and assembled a coalition of noblemen and clergy to build the Teatro Tordinona, which opened in 1671 as a public theater, presenting modified Venetian works from 1671 until it closed in 1675 (reopened 1690, torn down 1697; rebuilt 1733, remodeled 1762–64, burned down 1781; rebuilt 1795 for **opera buffa** and renamed the Teatro Apollo, remodeled 1820, 1830, and 1862, torn down 1889). Maria Mancini, matriarch of the Colonna family, also mounted a number of productions at their palace (from 1668). After the Tordinona shut down in 1675, Roman opera returned temporarily to being a private court enterprise, at which time the leading composers were Bernardo Pasquini (1637–1710) and the young **Alessandro Scarlatti**, who created a half dozen operas for Rome before moving to **Naples** in 1684, where he continued to supply new scores for Rome as well as remakes of his Neapolitan works. Opera was largely absent from 1698 to 1710 as a byproduct of Pope Innocent XII's disapproval and the War of the Spanish Succession.

In the early 18th century the most important Roman contribution to operatic development involved the style of the libretto rather than the music, which as elsewhere in Italy remained conservative for a time and then assimilated Neapolitan advances. The reforms of the **Arcadian Academy**, led by **Apostolo Zeno** and **Pietro Metastasio**, dominated productions across the peninsula and in foreign cities, whether in initial settings of librettos, remakes by other composers, or revivals of operas premiered elsewhere. In Rome, Pasquini and Scarlatti were eventually superseded in the 1720s by a new wave of (primarily) Neapolitan composers working in the more modern *galant* style, such as **Nicola Porpora** and **Leonardo Vinci**. And the city took its place among leading Italian centers for public opera through the construction and remodeling of a host of prominent theaters, which were managed by private families or coalitions of aristocrats and variously presented seasons of **opera seria**, opera buffa, and **intermezzos** (both new operas and remakes), serving Roman diplomacy and the burgeoning tourist industry.

In addition to the Teatro Tordinona noted above, these theaters included the Capranica (opened 1679, remodeled 1694–95, closed 1699, reopened 1711, remodeled 1713, 1802–03, 1853, closed 1881, in the 20th century reopened as a movie theater and lecture/recital hall), which like the Tordinona was capable of spectacular, state-of-the-art special effects by the end of the 17th century; the Pace (used for opera beginning 1694 and remodeled numerous times during the 18th century, no longer in use for opera by the 19th century); the Pallacorda di Firenze (built 1714, remodeled 1786, no longer in use for opera by the 19th century, demolished 1926); the Alibert (built 1716–18, enlarged and renamed the Teatro delle Dame 1726, rarely used for opera after 1811); the Valle (built 1726, remodeled 1765, 1791, 1821, and 1845, no longer in use for opera after the mid-19th century); and the Argentina (built 1732, little used for opera 1825–40, remodeled 1837, 1860–61, 1887).

By the late 1800s, Rome had lost ground as a center for new opera, and its theaters increasingly staged revivals of works originally composed for other cities. The Alibert, Pace, and Pallacorda theaters no longer served opera in the 19th century, nor did the Valle after midcentury. For a time only the Argentina, which still functions occasionally as an opera house, and the Apollo remained as opera facilities, varying their offerings across the century to include opera seria, opera buffa, *opera semiseria*, **ballet**, and spoken plays. While notable premieres still took place in these theaters (e.g., **Gioachino Rossini**'s *Il barbiere di Siviglia* and **Giuseppe Verdi**'s *I due Foscari*, 1844; *La battaglia di Legnano*, 1849; and *Il trovatore*, 1853), their seasons consisted mostly of revivals, including a Ring cycle (*see DER RING DES NIBELUNGEN*) in German in 1883.

Circa 1900 only the Argentina remained from the historical group. However, at the end of the 19th century the Roman operatic scene was supplemented by productions at other larger, multipurpose theaters, the Politeama Romano (built 1862, torn down 1883); the Teatro Manzoni (built 1876); the Teatro Drammatico Nazionale (built 1886, torn down 1929); and the Teatro Costanzi (opened 1880). The most lavish of the group and the most important for opera, the Costanzi hosted the premiers of *Cavalleria rusticana* and *Tosca* at the turn of the century. Remodeled 1926–28 as the Teatro Reale dell'Opera (later renamed the Teatro dell'Opera, 1946, remodeled 1958), it remains a centerpiece of operatic life in Rome, although it also hosts other entertainments.

See also CASTRATO; MELANI, ATTO; TRAVESTY; VITTORI, LO-RETO.

RONCONI, GIORGIO. (1810, Milan–1890, Madrid.) Preeminent Italian baritone (*see* BASS) of the second quarter of the 19th century, when the role of nemesis to the **tenor** hero came to prominence. Ronconi is associated primarily with **Gaetano Donizetti**, having created lead roles in seven of his operas, including *Torquato Tasso* (1833), *Maria Padilla* (1841), and *Maria di Rohan* (1843). He also sang the title role in the premier of *Nabucco* (1842). Between 1847 and 1866 he installed himself in **London**, performing a broad repertory that included operas by **Wolfgang Amadeus Mozart, Gioachino Rossini**, and **Giuseppe Verdi**, in particular the first British performance of *Rigoletto* (1853, originally 1851).

ROSENKAVALIER, DER. Komödie für Musik; music by **Richard Strauss, libretto** by Hugo von Hofmannsthal (1874–1929) based on Louvet de Couvrai's (1760–1797) novel *Les amours du chevalier de Faublas* (1787) and Molière's (1622–1673) *comédie-ballet Monsieur de Pourceaugnac* (1669); three acts; premiered Dresden, Königliches Opernhaus, January 1911. Following a triumphant premier, *The Rose Knight* quickly circulated among stages across Europe and remains steadfastly in the repertory to the present day.

The libretto of *Der Rosenkavalier*, concocted as in other Strauss-Hofmannsthal collaborations through persistent correspondence, combines the light humor of **operetta** with the pathos of **sentimental** drama. A homily on the decline of the old order, social climbing and the nouveau aristocracy, aging, and male inconstancy, its language reflects the diverse social classes intermingled in its romanticized recreation of 18th-century **Vienna**. In the tradition of *Le nozze di Figaro* and **Giuseppe Verdi**'s *Falstaff* (1893), it draws on such familiar comic plot elements as cross-dressing, disguise, real and feigned stupidity, philandering and coarse sexuality, buffoonish aristocrats, and a wacky household staff, and it even includes a descendent of the **opera buffa** catalog **aria** in Baron Ochs's seduction primer (Act 1).

Her husband absent, the Princess/Marschallin Marie Thérèse (not the empress) is luxuriating in an affair with the much younger Count Octavian Rofrano. When her oafish cousin Ochs (Ox) pays a surprise visit, Octavian, played in **travesty** by a female mezzo-soprano (*see* SOPRANO), disguises himself as a maid, Mariandel. She attracts Ochs's attention despite his intention to marry Sophie, daughter of the newly wealthy Faninal, to regain his fortune. In attempting to impress her father, Ochs has the Marschallin arrange for Octavian to deliver a silver rose symbolizing his proposal. Once Ochs is sent packing, she laments her declining looks and, anticipating Octavian's inevitable infidelity, breaks off their romance. Smitten by Octavian when he presents the rose, Sophie is equally revolted by the uncouth Ochs. Supporting her rejection of Ochs, Octavian superficially wounds him in a duel, leading Faninal to ban Octavian from his palace and threaten to cloister Sophie. The lovers resolve their dilemma by luring Ochs to an assignation with Mariandel/Octavian, who proves to be simpleminded and depressive. In a meticulously contrived trap, Ochs is assailed by servants costumed as ghosts, a pretended mistress and gaggle of illegitimate children, creditors, and hotel staff and police. Amidst the chaos Sophie and Faninal show up, much to Ochs's humiliation, as does the Marschallin, who dissolves the arranged marriage and blesses Octavian and Sophie's match.

In *Der Rosenkavalier*, aside from a few mock-**expressionist** tantrums, Strauss largely abandoned the dissonant chromaticism of *Salome* and *Elektra* (1909) and shifted back to the more traditional tonal vocabulary of his symphonic poems, appropriately saturated with Viennese waltzes in major mode. Within this glitzy topos, his music ranges from the poignant (the Marschallin's forlorn "Die Zeit," Act 1) to the ribald (beginning with the prelude's enthusiastic sex romp). And it receives rich support from an elaborate post-Wagnerian **orchestra**, which provides a sumptuous tapestry of **leitmotifs** (e.g., those for Octavian—akin to those of Strauss's own *Don Juan*—and the rose, a fairy-tale chord progression scored for celesta, harps, flutes, and solo violins). *Der Rosenkavalier* is hardly a **number opera**: each act consists of a single **scene** constructed mainly of spontaneous dialogue and climaxes in elaborately choreographed mayhem (the Marschallin's morning ritual, Act 1; Och's failed introduction to Sophie, Act 2; the spoiled assignation of Ochs and Mariandel, Act 3). Yet Strauss also made sparing use of distinguishable set pieces, such as Sophie and Octavian's encounter in Act 2 ("Ich kenn' Ihn"), and in Act 3 the soprano trio for the Marschallin, Octavian, and Sophie ("Hab mir's gelobt") and love **duet** "Ist ein Traum."

ROSPIGLIOSI, GIULIO. (1600, Pistoia–1669, Rome.) Italian cleric, poet, and **librettist**. Trained in law and philosophy, beginning in the 1620s Rospigliosi held a series of appointments under Pope Urban VIII and became active in Roman academies, in particular the group of theater enthusiasts led by Urban's nephew Cardinal Francesco Barberini. He wrote at least 11 **librettos** for operas and several more for *intermedi* produced at Barberini palaces between 1631 and 1656, which were composed by Stefano Landi (1587–1639), **Virgilio Mazzocchi**, Marco Marazzoli (after 1602–1662), and others. Following his election as Pope Clement IX (ruled 1667–69), he licensed the first public opera house in **Rome** (Teatro Tordinona, 1671).

In contrast to earlier mythological, **pastoral** librettos, Rospigliosi's were based on lives of saints (Landi's *Sant' Alessio*, 1631); classic literature (Mazzocchi and Marazzoli's *Chi soffre speri*, 1637, after Boccaccio's *Deca-*

meron); or traditional morality plays (Marazzoli's *La vita humana*, 1656). By presenting complex plots set in palaces (instead of elysian meadows) and enacted by large casts, by depicting the religious and psychological crises of flesh-and-blood humans, and by relieving the melancholy with comic *contrascene*, Rospigliosi played a pivotal role in the development of 17th-century Roman and (indirectly) Venetian opera.

ROSSINI, GIOACHINO. (1792, Pesaro–1868, Passy near Paris.) Along with **Giuseppe Verdi**, the foremost Italian opera **composer** of the 19th century. A northerner, his domination of **Naples** in the 1810s and 1820s ended the 18th-century hegemony of Neapolitan-trained composers. Although he is known to modern audiences primarily for a handful of comic and semiserious works, his serious operas for Naples and **Paris** had a more lasting impact on operatic development in the 19th century.

Born in a seaside town southeast of Bologna, he and his family moved first to Lugo in 1802, closer to the big city, and then to Bologna itself (1804). His first instruction came from his parents, both of whom were musicians. After studying voice and composition in Lugo with the local canon, in Bologna he sang professionally, successfully enough that he was inducted into the Accademia Filarmonica in 1806. He also served as a keyboardist in theaters, where he absorbed current operatic styles and wrote substitute **arias** (1804–11). He was admitted to Bologna's Liceo Musicale in 1806, taking lessons in singing, cello, piano, and (reluctantly) counterpoint—the last with the traditional composer-pedagogue Padre Stanislao Mattei (1750–1825)—and avidly absorbed the music of **Joseph Haydn** and **Wolfgang Amadeus Mozart**.

Following Rossini's first public production, the Venetian *farsa La cambiale di matrimonio* (late 1810), his career exploded from the starting gate, and he immediately found his niche as a composer of lighter works. He wrote eight operas for northern cities between 1810 and 1812—five in 1812 alone—of which six were comic or semiserious. Among these, the *farsa L'inganno felice* (1812, Venice) was his first lasting accomplishment, followed later that year by his most prestigious early commission, the *melodrama giocoso La pietra del paragone* for La Scala in Milan, which was on the verge of becoming the premier theater in Italy. Owing to the pace of composition and a compulsion to rescue good music from unsuccessful productions, Rossini engaged in substantial self-borrowing among these early works, at least one piece from which—a **duet** from his first opera, *Demetrio e Polibio* (written 1810, first performed 1812)—appeared in five other operas. This pace barely abated following his first two international successes, the heroic *melodramma Tancredi*, which established Rossini as a first-rank composer of serious opera, and the *dramma giocoso L'italiana in Algeri*, both for **Venice** in 1813, a year that brought four new operas in total.

Prior to 1815, and despite his glittering success elsewhere, Rossini had been shunned in parochial Naples, a situation remedied by the most powerful **impresario** of his day and manager of the Neapolitan royal opera houses, **Domenico Barbaia**, who signed him to a multiyear contract to compose new works, revive old ones, and co-manage the San Carlo theater's gambling operation (*see* THEATER DESIGN). The association produced 10 operas, the majority of them serious works for the richly endowed San Carlo, from the English historical psychodrama *Elisabetta, regina d'Inghilterra* (1815), his first opera to forego continuo **recitative**, through the **coloratura** showcase *Zelmira* (1822). These works draw on an expansive array of nontraditional sources, from Torquato Tasso (for the Renaissance epic *Armida*, 1819) to William Shakespeare (*Otello*, 1816, which has perhaps the most spontaneously constructed final act in early 19th-century opera); Sir Walter Scott (the Scottish **pastoral** *melodramma La donna del lago*, 1819); and Racine after Euripides (*Ermione*, 1819). And they are dominated by florid coloratura singing that was a specialty of Barbaia's company, which included **Isabella Colbran**, Barbaia's current mistress and Rossini's future wife (married 1822). During this period, his lighter operas opened elsewhere: for example, the archetypal **opera buffa** *Il barbiere di Siviglia* (1816), Rossini's most enduring masterpiece reportedly composed in as little as two weeks, and the rustic, **sentimental** *opera semiseria La Cenerentola* (1817) were both written for **Rome**.

In the 1820s Rossini extended his international reach. When Barbaia became director of the Kärntnertortheater in **Vienna** 1821, he held a Rossini festival (1822), for which six operas were performed to tremendous acclaim. After returning to Italy for his 34th opera, *Semiramide* (1823), his last for that country, he traveled to **London** for a Rossini season at the King's Theater. Though his performances received mixed receptions, he filled his pockets making appearances and giving lessons at the homes of wealthy aristocrats. He moved to Paris in 1824, where he contracted with the government to compose new works for the Opéra and the Théâtre Italien, to direct the latter, and to revive his older operas. Rossini's productivity had declined beginning in 1820, and his slower pace of about one opera per year continued in Paris until he stopped writing operas altogether in 1829. His productions at the Italian Theater included revivals of his own *Zelmira* and *Semiramide*; a premier, *Il viaggio a Reims* (1825), commemorating the coronation of Charles X; as well as operas by younger composers. Of particular importance, **Giacomo Meyerbeer**'s *Il crociato in Egitto* (1825, originally 1824) began the younger composer's domination of Paris. For the Opéra, he substantially adapted the massive historical epic *Maometto II* (1820) as *Le siège de Corinthe* (1826) and *Mosè in Egitto* (1818) as *Moïse* (1827), scaling back vocalization to suit French taste and simplifying the more complicated scenes. His final two stage works were the **opéra comique** *Le comte Ory* (1828, which reworks music from *Il viaggio a Reims*) and the pastoral patriotic saga *Guillaume Tell* (1829) based on Friedrich Schiller. Along with operas by **Daniel-François-Esprit Auber**, **Fromental Halévy**, and Meyerbeer, *Tell* set the standard for the development of French *grand opéra* in the 1830s.

Rossini's premature retirement from opera probably resulted from a range of issues. A lifetime annuity promised by Charles X's ministers was voided almost immediately by the Revolution of 1830 (while Rossini was vacationing in Bologna), management of the Opéra changed, chronic urinary and nervous disorders plagued him as early as 1832, and sensing that operatic taste had left him behind he apparently declined to compete with Meyerbeer and the younger Italians. Although still connected to the Théâtre Italien, where he mentored such composers as **Gaetano Donizetti** and **Vincenzo Bellini**, Rossini's heyday in Paris had passed. In 1836 he returned again to Bologna, where he became an advisor to the Liceo Musicale and attempted to restructure its curriculum. Following the Revolutions of 1848 he was effectively hounded out of town for his supposed lack of patriotism, first fleeing to Florence and then returning to Paris in 1855. The City of Light again favored him: his health improved dramatically, and he composed a flood of piano pieces, songs, and religious works over the next dozen years, until he died at age 76, 39 years after writing his last opera.

Rossini's style may be viewed as a brilliantly virtuosic intensification of **opera seria**, *opera semiseria*, and opera buffa traditions that had essentially run their course in the late 18th century. It involved both exaggeration of traditional approaches and incorporation of more recent novelties, some of them aspects of the **Christoph Willibald Gluck** agenda (*see ALCESTE*), a combination made enormously popular and influential because of Rossini's melodic ingenuity; mastery of rhythm, pacing, and timing at all levels of design; and theatrical instinct. And it depended on a multiplication of resources that made him unwilling to abandon old-fashioned aspects of his dramatic arsenal for the sake of mere currency. Echoing Arthur Schopenhauer, Rossini maintained that music needs to play to its strengths, creating metaphors for rather than representations of character, mood, situation, and events, and moving listeners through their responses to purely musical factors such as melodic gesture, rhythmic energy, orchestral color, and the like. Accordingly, in serious opera Rossini resisted the trend toward naturalism, emotional immediacy, and descriptive music at the expense of **bel canto** and emphatically reasserted the role of virtuoso singing in lyric set pieces, demonstrating its theatrical electricity by progressively increasing notated **ornamentation** in his Neapolitan operas, enveloping their lyric movements in coloratura.

Rossini's comic operas show a similarly exaggerated delineation of various conventional character types as he heroically sustained a genre that would in a matter of decades be socially irrelevant and artistically exhausted.

Drifting away from the realistic humanity of late 18th-century sentimental opera buffa, he verged on reestablishing **commedia dell'arte** caricatures in a less politicized environment through vibrantly overdrawn set pieces. Shamelessly surpassing the playfulness of **Giovanni Paisiello** and Mozart, his music paints an array of **categories**—slapstick, comic, sentimental, and even bel canto coloratura—in primary colors. Comic standbys like the *tirata* and *lazzo* become bravura displays of frenzied buffo **patter song** and slapstick *parlante*. Extravagantly disjunct melodies, suspended animation discharged by incendiary activity, and trademarks like the buffo crescendo ("Rossinian crescendo"), in which an energetic motif is repeated ad absurdum with progressively augmented orchestration, all contribute to the silliness.

While Rossini's expansion of resources in certain ways disconnected him from the Gluck reforms—in particular his reassertion of florid ornamentation—in others he crystallized their enactment by intermingling Italian and French practices, and comic and serious components, in the service of dramatic immediacy. He chose subjects that represent incipient Italian **romantic** interests in breaking the Arcadian stranglehold of the 18th century (*see* ARCADIAN ACADEMY and METASTASIO, PIETRO) and modestly reduced the artificiality of opera seria by replacing the **castrato** hero with female **contraltos** in pants roles (*see* TRAVESTY). He took a decisive step away from aria opera by increasing the number and size of ensembles and involving **chorus** within set pieces, other than duets. He gave the **orchestra** increased theatrical play by prefacing scenas (*see* SCENE) with extended orchestral preludes, motives from which are interjected within the recitative; by expanding the use of *parlante* texture in serious scenes; and by calling on the orchestra to define the coups de théâtre that motivate lyric reactions. His sensitivity to and cultivation of instrumental color and the woodwinds and brass (at least by Italian standards), apparently nurtured by his study of Haydn and Mozart, served as a model for later composers. He eliminated simple recitatives from his serious operas and maintained the late 18th-century commitment to invest obbligato recitatives with emotional weight. And having developed early on a signature style of lighthearted comic overture, he abandoned it in his Neapolitan serious operas in favor of shorter, more appropriately sober preludes.

Rossini has been criticized for conventionalizing scene structure and stalling the inevitable march toward Wagnerian continuity by popularizing an array of forms for multimovement set pieces—three-movement arias, four-movement duets, trios and central **finales**, and two types of *introduzioni*—suited to combine the palette of expressive resources from bel canto lyricism and coloratura to declamatory, orchestrally dominated realism that empowered his style. However, the inherently dynamic nature of those forms (by comparison with earlier static set pieces) and his reinterpretation of his nucleus of schemata through elaboration and adaptation to dramatic circumstances aligned him with Gluck's agenda of dramatic energy and naturalness and set the course for later architectural developments in Italian *melodramma* and French *grand opéra*.

RUBINI, GIOVANNI BATTISTA. (1794, Romano–1854, Romano.) Premier dramatic **tenor** of the period of **Vincenzo Bellini** and **Gaetano Donizetti**. A prodigious talent capable of performing a female operatic role in his hometown at age 12, Rubini debuted in Venice in a revival of **Gioachino Rossini**'s *L'italiana in Algeri* (1815, originally 1813), at which point the Neapolitan **impresario Domenico Barbaia** put him under contract for the next decade.

After appearances in **Vienna** and **Paris** singing Rossini (ca. 1825) won him an international reputation, Rubini played a key role in establishing the new, passionately expressive style of Italian **romantic** singing (*see* SINGING STYLE) by creating lead roles for Bellini's *Bianca e Gernando* (1826), *Il pirata* (1827), *La sonnambula* (1831), and *I puritani* (1835) and for numerous works by Donizetti, including *Anna Bolena* (1830) and *Marino Faliero* (1835). Between 1831 and 1843, Rubini centered his activities in **London** and Paris, then appeared for a season in St. Petersburg (1843–44) before retiring in 1845. In addition to the emotional intensity of his singing, Rubini was legendary for his extraordinary range, which extended to high f" (in falsetto).

S

SAINT-SAËNS, CAMILLE. (1835, Paris–1921, Algiers.) French **composer** of 13 operas from the 1870s through the first decade of the 20th century, of which *Samson et Dalila* (first performed 1877) remains in the repertory, as well as other vocal, instrumental, and keyboard music; pianist, organist, and **conductor**.

Like most prominent French 19th-century composers, Saint-Saëns trained (as a pianist) at the **Paris** Conservatoire (1848–52), where he studied composition with **Fromental Halévy** and was mentored by **Charles-François Gounod**, but was almost unique in not winning the Prix de Rome. A **Richard Wagner** disciple early in his career, he traveled to Bayreuth in 1876 to witness the first *Ring des Nibelungen*. Pigeonholed as a keyboard player and symphonist, prejudice against him in the opera world impeded production of his first two operas, *Le timbre d'argent* and *Samson et Dalila*, both partly composed in the 1860s but not staged until 1877 in Paris at the Théâtre Lyrique and in Weimar under Franz Liszt's oversight, respectively. Consequently his third opera, *La princesse jaune*, was the first to reach the public in 1872.

Samson, which originated as an oratorio, is an exotic religious ***grand opéra*** in four tableaux, in which the hero, blinded and enfeebled by Delila, recovers his strength through God's intervention and destroys the Philistine temple in a final cataclysm. Saint-Saëns specialized in historical settings ranging from Athens (*Phryné*, 1893) and **Rome** (*Les barbares*, 1901) to France (*Etienne Marcel*, 1879; *Ascanio*, 1890; and *L'ancêtre*, 1906); Italy (*Proserpine*, 1887); and England (*Henry VIII*, 1883). Other operas—*Déjanire* (1911), *Frédégonde* (1895), and *Hélène* (1904)—are based on classical or northern European myth.

Saint-Saëns traveled extensively late in life as a pianist and conductor and for revivals of his operas, ranging as far afield as North Africa and South America. He died in Algiers on one of those trips.

331

SALIERI, ANTONIO. (1750, Legnago–1825, Vienna.) Versatile **composer** of almost 40 comic and serious operas (*see* CATEGORIES OF OPERA) mostly from the 1770s through the 1790s, notable for adapting his style to a wide range of genres, subjects, and theatrical circumstances; his *tragédies lyriques* (*see* TRAGÉDIE EN MUSIQUE) were noteworthy successors to those of **Christoph Willibald Gluck.**

Orphaned at 15, Salieri was brought by an aristocrat (presumably) to **Venice** (1765) where he was "discovered" by the composer Florian Leopold Gassmann (1729–1774) who transplanted him to **Vienna** and began tutoring him the next year. Salieri was ambitious and adept at forging savvy political connections, among them friendships with **Pietro Metastasio**, Gluck, and Emperor Joseph II, the last of whom also would promote his career in Italy and **Paris** through family ties. Like most 18th-century composers, he cut his teeth on light works, beginning with the **opera buffa** *Le donne letterate* (1770), then received his first **opera seria** commission, *Armida*, in 1771. Salieri rose quickly through the ranks in Vienna and was promoted to *Kammerkomponist* and music director of the Italian opera (1774) and eventually *Hofkapellmeister* (1788 until his death).

Joseph's temporary disinterest in Italian opera (1776–83) led Salieri to try Italy, where he composed several, mostly comic operas (1778–80), including *La scuola de' gelosi* (1779), which established his international reputation. He also wrote a **singspiel**, *Der Rauchfangkehrer* (1781), for Joseph's German theater, which remained popular until it was overshadowed by **Wolfgang Amadeus Mozart**'s *Die Entführung aus dem Serail* (1782). Intervention by Gluck and Joseph led to three *tragédies lyriques* for France, of which *Tartare* (1787) was so popular that it was adapted for Vienna by **Lorenzo Da Ponte** as the *dramma tragicomico* (*see* OPERA SEMISERIA) *Axur re d'Ormus* (1788). Da Ponte, who had been appointed poet to the revived Italian theater in 1783, also collaborated with Salieri on three other operas, including his first original **libretto**, *Il ricco d'un giorno* (1784), which required extensive coaching by Salieri.

In the 1790s while he was *Hofkapellmeister*, Salieri's operatic output declined as he devoted more attention to administration, sacred music, and teaching, his students numbering Ludwig van Beethoven (1770–1827), **Franz Schubert**, Franz Liszt (1811–1886), and several important **sopranos**. His 11 operas after 1792 include the successful *dramma eroicomico* (*see* OPERA SEMISERIA) *Palmira regina di Persia* (1795) and the opera buffa *Falstaff* (1799). No evidence exists that Salieri felt professionally threatened by Mozart or in any way harmed him physically, as has been suggested in popular culture.

SALOME. Music drama by **Richard Strauss**, **libretto** adapted by the **composer** from a translation by Hedwig Lachmann (1865–1918) of Oscar Wilde's play, based loosely on biblical and historical accounts; one act with orchestral interlude; Dresden, Hofoper, December 1905. Strauss was immediately attracted to Wilde's play, which had triumphed in Germany in Lachmann's translation, when he saw it in 1903. Originally conceiving his adaptation as a companion piece to his previous opera, *Feuersnot* (1901), he set it virtually intact as a *Literaturoper* (1903–05). Its premier a phenomenal success, *Salome* traveled rapidly to other countries, despite initial puritanical opposition in Austria, England, and the United States. Strauss later thinned passages of orchestration (1930) to make the lead more suitable for **sopranos** who could both sing and dance the role themselves, creating the current standard version.

A paradigm of fin-de-siècle decadence, *Salome*'s themes of materialism, misogyny, revenge, lust, and necrophilia resonate with **symbolist** imagery of colors, textures, the moon, air, and flowers against a background of Jewish religious bickering, its grotesque plot advancing the post-**romantic** trend toward increasingly shocking and cathartic situations. The sultry beauty Salome, stepdaughter and niece of Herodes (Herod Antipas), Tetrarch of Judea, and daughter of his wife (and sister-in-law) Herodias, is captivated by the imprisoned proselytizer Jochanaan (John the Baptist), who makes apocalyptic prophesies condemning Herodias's immorality. She has entranced the captain Narraboth, who eventually kills himself when she ignores him, manipulating him to disobey orders and bring John to her. Obsessed by Jochanaan's aloofness, Salome begs to touch his skin, hair, and mouth, loathing each as he rejects her and vowing to kiss his mouth. Exploiting Herod's lust for her, she deflects his advances until he promises her anything she wants. After she performs the "Dance of the Seven Veils," removing them until she lies naked at his feet, she demands John's head, refusing Herod's alternative rewards as Herodias delights in her daughter's ploy. Salome fondles her grisly trophy and tastes the bitterness of John's lips before Herod orders her execution.

Salome constitutes the most prominent landmark of post-Wagnerian music drama and proto-**expressionist** opera, a precursor to *Wozzeck*. Its dissonant chromaticism bordering on atonality prefigures the modernist idiom of Arnold Schoenberg and the Second Viennese School, palpably conveying the opera's lurid atmosphere and the lead's deplorable self-indulgence and abuse of her allurements. Advancing **Richard Wagner**'s agenda of immersive continuous action, it lacks discernible set pieces (other than the instrumental interlude following Salome's attempt to seduce John, and her dance) or conventional spectacular elements (**choruses**, massed ensembles, **ballets**), and eliminates traditional distinctions between **recitatives** and lyric music. Instead, its spontaneous **arioso** setting of prose dialogue unfolds with the support of a gargantuan **orchestra**, reinforced with quadrupled woodwinds (famously including the *heckelphone*, close to a baritone oboe) and percussion (including xylophone, celesta, and harp), which deploys a dense web of evolving **leitmotifs** associated with characters or ideas.

SANT' ALESSIO. *Dramma musicale*; music by Stefano Landi (1587–1639), **libretto** by **Giulio Rospigliosi** based on the life of Saint Alexis; three acts; premiered **Rome**, Palazzo Barberini, 1631 and/or 1632. The 1632 performance of *Sant' Alessio* began the development of 17th-century Roman opera under the extravagant patronage of the Barberini family. Rospigliosi's libretto diverged from the mythological, **pastoral** orientation of earlier operas by examining human vulnerabilities and launched a succession of Barberini **productions** inspired by lives of saints or historical epics. Alessio returns after a long absence to his aristocratic family's home. Unrecognized by his parents or wife, he resists temptation and leads a life of poverty amidst opulence, inhabiting a closet underneath a stairway, despite the Devil's blandishments. While Landi's score includes traditional, **madrigal**-based **choruses** along the lines of **Claudio Monteverdi**'s *Orfeo*, it anticipates later trends in its incorporation of *contrascene*, secco **recitative**, and a string-dominated **orchestra** (with **basso continuo**), and in its incipient use of **arias** and other lyric set pieces alongside expressive recitative to represent personal reflection.

SCAPIGLIATURA. Avant-garde literary, artistic, social, and political movement active in northern Italy, particularly Milan, from the 1860s through the 1880s. The Scapigliati ("disheveled Bohemians") were led by the poet and painter Emilio Praga (1839–1875), the poet and **composer Arrigo Boito**, and the **conductor** and composer Franco Faccio (1840–1891), all of whom served briefly under the revolutionary general Giuseppe Garibaldi in 1866. Originally calling themselves *Avveniristi*, referring to the art of the future, Boito's poem *L'arte dell'avvenire*, and **Richard Wagner**'s essay *Das Kunstwerk der Zukunft* (1849), Praga and Boito popularized the term *scapigliatura*, which originated in the novel *La scapigliatura e il 6 febbraio* (1862) by Cletto Arrighi (Carlo Righetti), in their journal *Figaro* (beginning 1864).

Through their newspapers, pamphlets, and literary works the Scapigliati offended conservative Italians with their opposition to bourgeois complacency, Italian clericalism and militarism, the parliamentary monarchy of Vittorio Emanuele II, and the artistic status quo represented by moribund Italian **romanticism**. As alternatives, they championed unconventional attitudes and lifestyles dedicated to artistic idealism and the revitalization of Italian culture through assimilation of German romanticism, French realism and naturalism, and other current artistic movements; adoption of morbid and macabre subjects and nonconventional wordings and poetic versification; and promotion of connections among poetry, music, and the visual arts.

The leaders of the movement produced three modestly successful and influential operas: *I profughi fiamminghi* (*The Flemish Refugees*, 1863) composed by Faccio on a **libretto** by Praga, at the celebration for which Boito notoriously antagonized **Giuseppe Verdi** by calling for the restoration of Italian art to its altar; *Amleto* (1865) composed by Faccio on a libretto by Boito; and *Mefistofele* (1868) composed by Boito on his own libretto, embracing the Wagnerian precept of shared roles for composer and poet. The Scapigliati anticipated and supported a number of late 19th-century Italian causes, among which are decadentism, socialism, anarchism, and **verismo**.

See also CATALANI, ALFREDO; ILLICA, LUIGI, AND GIUSEPPE GIACOSA; PUCCINI, GIACOMO.

SCARLATTI, ALESSANDRO. (1660, Palermo–1725, Naples.) Italian **composer** of approximately 60 operas, mostly from the 1680s through the 1710s, and other vocal music (including hundreds of chamber cantatas and **serenatas**) who played a pivotal role in establishing **Naples** as an 18th-century operatic center and in popularizing conventions of **opera seria**. Member of an extended family of musicians, one of his sons was the keyboard composer Domenico Scarlatti (1685–1757).

In 1672, the death of a patron and a famine following his father's death led Scarlatti's mother to move their family from Palermo to **Rome**, where he began his career and familiarized himself with the pan-Italian style of late 17th-century Venetian opera as well as local Roman idiosyncrasies. Already exceptionally accomplished, he quickly rose to the upper levels of Roman musical circles. In 1678, he became *maestro di cappella* at the church of San Giacomo at the age of 18 and later San Girolamo (1682). He enjoyed the patronage of numerous aristocrats, including Queen Christina of Sweden, who hired him as her own *maestro di cappella*, and he and his new bride lived in the palace of the architect and sculptor Gian Lorenzo Bernini (beginning 1678).

Beginning with *Gli equivoci nel sembiante* (1679), a **pastoral** comedy, Scarlatti wrote five operas for Rome, including *Il Pompeo* (1683), a Roman historical drama of the type that would dominate his output. However, due to Pope Innocent XI's opposition to opera, their performances were limited to Queen Christina's circle, which included liberal cardinals, aristocrats such as the Neapolitan dukes of Maddaloni, and foreign diplomats. Seeking greater visibility, Scarlatti moved to Naples in 1684, probably with the encouragement of the Maddaloni and the support of the Neapolitan viceroy, who had heard Scarlatti's music while serving as ambassador to Rome and who appointed him *maestro di cappella* (1684–1702). Having survived initial resentments, intrigues, the resignation of the vice maestro, and a scandal involving his sister (a singer), Scarlatti settled into the task of writing his first 30 operas for Naples, which would establish the city as the premier operatic rival to **Venice**. Election of the liberal Pope Alexander VIII (ruled 1689–91), a Venetian, and the support for Scarlatti's music by his free-spending grandnephew Cardinal Pietro Ottoboni opened new opportunities in Rome, including several operas. Patronage by Ferdinando de' Medici, Grand Prince of Tuscany (beginning 1688), led to numerous revivals of his Neapolitan and Roman operas at the Medici villa at Pratolino north of Florence and eventually six new operas (1698–1706). When King Philip V of Spain visited Naples in 1702 during the War of the Spanish Succession, Scarlatti's *Tiberio Imperatore d'Oriente* and a serenata overshadowed performances by Arcangelo Corelli (1653–1713), who had been invited from Rome for the event.

Buoyed by his burgeoning reputation, dissatisfied with his compensation in Naples, and feeling underappreciated there, Scarlatti moved back to Rome in 1702. However, he found that Pope Clement XI's penitential reaction to the war stifled theater life, leaving the aforementioned Medici commissions as his only outlet in that genre while in Rome through 1706. One bright spot was his election to the **Arcadian Academy** as a musician and poet (1706), probably partly through the efforts of founding member Silvio Stampiglia (1664–1725), his **librettist** for *La caduta de' Decemviri* (1697) and subsequent operas.

At this time, despite the Venetian Ottoboni's patronage and the broad dissemination of Scarlatti's operas throughout most of Italy, they had not yet reached Venice, Italy's operatic mecca, largely owing to intrigues by his rivals. And whether hampered by Venetian parochialism, Scarlatti's mishandling of local theater management, or lack of appreciation by public audiences for the sophistication of his music, his attempt to establish himself in 1707 with two operas, his masterpiece *Il **Mitridate Eupatore*** and *Il trionfo della libertà*, met predictable resistance and even scathing ridicule (for *Mitridate*). When Scarlatti returned to Rome later that year the situation was worse than it had been previously, and he retreated again to Naples, where he wrote 11 more operas—among them *Tigrane* (1715), perhaps his most important late opera, and his single true **opera buffa** in the new Neapolitan style, *Il trionfo dell'onore* (1718)—in addition to four for Rome (including his last opera, *La Griselda*, 1721). Scarlatti's previous shabby treatment by the Neapolitan court apparently resumed during his final years and continued even after his death: pleas to the viceroy to pay him salary months in arrears went unanswered, and no attempt was made to relieve his widow of the family's considerable debts.

Scarlatti was the greatest composer connected with the early Arcadian Academy and its librettists Stampiglia and **Apostolo Zeno**. And while he resisted the progressive, simplifying trends of the nascent *galant* style, clinging instead to contrapuntal textures, chromatic harmonies, and continuous phrasing, he contributed to numerous other conventions of 18th-century *dramma per musica*. These included increased use of extended da capo **arias** involving Neapolitan "five-part" form, clearer separation of **recitative** and aria through more speechlike *recitativo semplice* and orchestral rather than **basso continuo** accompaniment for arias, more extensive use of obbligato recitative, and development of the three-movement Italian **overture**.

SCENE. Term (Italian *scena*, French *scène*, German *Szene*) that may designate the theatrical stage; a section of an opera taking place in a single locale; a section of an opera in which the complement of characters remains unchanged; or in Italian opera the setting of **recitative** verse (*see* VERSIFICATION), normally as musical recitative or **arioso**, which precedes a lyric set piece in a **number opera**.

SCHOENBERG, ARNOLD. (1874, Vienna–1951, Los Angeles.) Preeminent German Jewish composer of three completed one-act operas and an incomplete large-scale work from the first decade of the 20th century through the 1930s, as well as other vocal and instrumental music; **librettist** for two of his operas.

Schoenberg began violin lessons at age eight and soon composed music, but he was constrained to leave school and take a job as a bank clerk after his father died when he was 16. He received no institutional training, although he studied composition privately with his friend Alexander Zemlinsky (1871–1942), who had attended the **Vienna** Conservatory. Schoenberg taught composition at the Prussian Academy in Berlin (beginning 1926), a position from which he was discharged in 1933 after the Nazis came to power. He subsequently emigrated to Paris, then Boston, and finally settled at the University of California at Los Angeles, where he spent the remainder of his career.

Increasingly committed to Judaism, Schoenberg chose operatic subjects all of which, in one way or another, evince a neo-Wagnerian preoccupation with overcoming the impulses of material existence and achieving spirituality that is also apparent in his other works. The first two adopt his early post-**romantic** atonal chromaticism, extending the style of **Richard Strauss**'s *Salome* and *Elektra* (1909), in tremendously concentrated one-act **expressionist** psychodramas. The deranged monologue *Erwartung* (*Expectation*, composed 1909, premiered 1924) appropriates this anguished language for a **woman**'s nightmarish trek through an ominous forest toward the house in which her lover may be having an affair, her discovery of his body, and her resulting grief, jealousy, and emptiness. An athematic stream of consciousness responding moment by moment to her unstable emotions, *Erwartung* was composed in the improbably short period of 17 days. Its one-act companion piece, *Die glückliche Hand* (*The Hand of Fate*, composed 1910–13, premiered 1924, **libretto** by the composer), enlists more substantial resources—one singing and two mimed roles, a chorus of 12 soloists, and scenic effects coordinated with colored lighting that parallels the artist Wassily Kandinsky's theories of linkages between mood, color, and sound—to depict the fruitless struggle of a man who vainly seeks happiness through worldly love and is mocked by a woman who betrays him.

Schoenberg's last two operas belong to his initial wave of twelve-tone compositions, in which ordered rows of all the chromatic pitches become the thematic substance of the works and systematically undercut the establishment of perceptible keys. The half-comic *Von Heute auf Morgen* (*From Today to Tomorrow*, premiered 1930) is, oddly, the first opera to use the twelve-tone technique. Its domestic subject, which bears a resemblance to Strauss's *Intermezzo* (1924), may be viewed as an allegory of the superficiality of current fashion, in which a wife gives herself a makeover and threatens an affair to win back her straying husband, who is entranced by a "modern woman." Schoenberg's last opera, *Moses und Aron* (Acts 1 and 2 composed 1930–32, libretto by the composer) on the Exodus of Israel, his only one of full length, was left incomplete and lacking the final deliverance of the Jewish people.

SCHUBERT, FRANZ. (1797, Vienna–1828, Vienna.) Esteemed Austrian **composer** of instrumental and choral music and songs who attempted valiantly but unsuccessfully to establish himself in opera.

Schubert began music lessons with his father, brother, and a parish organist and began to compose as a boy. He continued his training as a choirboy in the Imperial chapel at **Antonio Salieri**'s recommendation (1808–12) until his voice broke, and studied composition with Salieri. He earned teacher certification and taught in the school run by his father (1815–18); explored the Viennese opera scene, which flourished in conjunction with the Congress of **Vienna**; and familiarized himself with works by **Christoph Willibald Gluck**, **Wolfgang Amadeus Mozart**, Ludwig van Beethoven (1770–1827), **Luigi Cherubini**, and **Gaspare Spontini**. His first complete opera, the three-act magic **singspiel** *Des Teufels Lustschloss*, was one of four written between 1813 and 1816 (none of them performed) while he was still a pupil of Salieri and a schoolteacher.

Attempting to make his way as a freelance composer (beginning 1816), Schubert turned from opera to smaller works that could be written more quickly and performed and marketed more easily. Having built a reputation in Vienna, he received commissions for the one-act farce *Die Zwillingsbrüder* and the magic play with music *Die Zauberharfe* (both 1820). This promising start encouraged him to pursue projects of his own choosing, but they fell victim to circumstances: economic downturns resulting from the Napoleonic Wars that hurt the theaters and began a long-term decline of opera in Vienna, **censorship** during the restoration following the Congress of Vienna, a continuing vogue for Italian opera sparked by **Gioachino Rossini** and sustained by the **impresario Domenico Barbaia**, and plain bad luck that included his premature death. As a result, six works, all on medieval or exotic themes, were either left incomplete or were completed but not performed until the 1850s or even the 20th century: the exotic opera *Sacontala* (partially sketched 1820–21); the grand **romantic** opera *Alfonso und Estrella* (written 1821–22, but refused by theaters in Vienna and performed in Weimar, 1854); the chivalric singspiel *Die Verschworenen* (written 1822–23, not performed until it enjoyed a heyday midcentury); *Rüdiger* (partially sketched); and the medieval grand heroic-romantic opera *Fierrabras* (commissioned by Barbaia, but abandoned following the failure of **Carl Maria von Weber**'s similarly themed *Euryanthe*, 1823, shortly after Schubert finished his own score). Schubert's final project, *Der Graf von Gleichen* (begun 1827), remained incomplete at his death.

SCRIBE, EUGÈNE. (1791, Paris–1861, Paris.) Preeminent and prolific mid-19th century French **librettist** and successful playwright. Trained as a lawyer, Scribe joined the lively Parisian theater scene in the 1810s, gradually winning a reputation as a capable craftsman of popular plays for the lesser theaters and of **librettos** well tailored to various types of opera and **ballet**. His first opera libretto was the **opéra comique** *La chambre à coucher* (1813), set by the obscure composer L. Guénée.

Beginning in the 1820s—often partnered with other writers—he collaborated with the major **composers** of the day on an impressive trove of Parisian operatic landmarks: three dozen librettos for **Daniel-François-Esprit Auber** beginning with *Leicester, ou Le château de Kenilworth* (1823) and including such warhorses as *La muette de Portici* (1828), *Fra Diavolo, ou L'hôtellerie de Terracine* (1830), and *Gustave III, ou Le bal masqué* (1833); Adrien Boieldieu (1775–1834), *La dame blanche* (1825); **Gioachino Rossini**'s *Le comte Ory* (1828); six librettos for **Giacomo Meyerbeer**, including all four of his *grands opéras Robert le diable* (1831), *Les Huguenots* (1836), *Le prophète* (1849), and *L'Africaine* (1865); 10 for **Fromental Halévy**, including *La Juive* (1835); **Gaetano Donizetti**'s *Les Martyrs* (1840) and *Dom Sébastien* (1843); **Charles-François Gounod**'s *La nonne sanglante* (1854); and **Giuseppe Verdi**'s *Les vêpres siciliennes* (1855). A national icon, Scribe was awarded the Legion of Honor (1827) and elected to the Académie Française (1836), which regulates usage of the French language.

Today, Scribe's historical importance centers on his co-creation, with Auber and particularly Meyerbeer, of mid-19th-century *grand opéra*. In librettos that apply his principle of the "well-made play," characters are propelled credibly and inevitably toward often cataclysmic disasters against a background of social or religious conflict depicted in spectacular crowd scenes. Sometimes faulted for pedestrian characterization and prosaic language, Scribe painted broad emotions with a palette of clear, direct wordings that could be understood in massed ensembles. And although his librettos broached controversial political, religious, and social themes, he succeeded with the bourgeois audiences who dominated theaters following the Revolution of 1830, primarily because he understood the theater to be a medium of entertainment rather than edification.

SEASON. Time of year in which performances of operas and other theatrical works were concentrated, occurring as many as five nights a week. Three principal seasons were observed in Italy and elsewhere in Italian-influenced cities: Carnival (*carnevale*), from St. Stephen's Day (December 26) to Lent (beginning Ash Wednesday); spring (*primavera*), from immediately after Easter into June; and autumn (*autunno*), from late August or September to Advent (ending Advent Sunday). The theatrical seasons developed among the public theaters as an alternative to court operas staged sporadically to celebrate birthdays, marriages, or other state occasions. They were timed to avoid religious holidays and summer heat, and the accompanying aristocratic exodus from cities, and to coincide with long-standing festivities. Their coordination among the various theaters enabled artists and audiences to plan their schedules.

Carnival was the preeminent operatic season. Established first in **Venice** (1637) to complement the traditional period of winter revelry and to profit from masked balls and banquets held at opera houses leading up to Lent, Carnival seasons existed in many cities by the end of the 17th century. As spring and autumn seasons developed later in conjunction with trade fairs (the *fiera* season), Carnival remained the most prestigious. Many theaters of the highest rank, the ones staging **opera seria** for predominantly aristocratic audiences, opened only for Carnival and featured two new offerings in addition to repertory works. Lower-ranking theaters dominated by nonaristocratic patrons and favoring lighter fare (in **Naples** the Teatro Nuovo versus the royal Teatro San Carlo) tended to be open a greater portion of the year. Secondary opera centers in Italy—Bologna for example—focused on spring or particularly autumn as a time when the best singers could be engaged more economically by avoiding competition with the wealthier theaters.

In a number of major cities outside of Italy—**Paris**, **London**, and **Vienna**, for example—a mostly continuous schedule of less frequent performances was followed. Even in 18th-century Italy, erosion of the prohibition against opera during Lent began with staged performances of sacred operas on biblical subjects. During Napoleonic occupations of some cities and again after

1830, secular productions continued into Lent, annexing it to Carnival. Most modern companies favor a continuous schedule running from fall through spring.

SECONDA PRATICA. The "second practice" or "modern style" (*stile moderno*) of the late 16th and early 17th centuries, in which music follows the meaning and delivery of the text, and traditional rules for handling dissonance, voice-leading, and rhythm may be broken for effective musical expression. It constituted an alternative to the strict counterpoint of the *prima pratica* ("first practice" or *stile antico*) defined by the theorist Gioseffe Zarlino (1517–1590) and exemplified by the works of Giovanni Pierluigi da Palestrina (ca. 1525–1594), who were concerned primarily with the luminous polish of their contrapuntal writing. Composers practiced the two styles concurrently during the late 16th and 17th centuries.

The *seconda pratica* probably originated in conjunction with the late 16th-century avant-garde madrigal in Ferrara and elsewhere, deemed a revival of ancient Greek musical rhetoric beginning with Cipriano de Rore (ca. 1515–1565). The term appeared in print and became common currency in the first decade of the 17th century thanks to a famous attack launched against **Claudio Monteverdi**'s madrigals by the conservative theorist Giovanni Maria Artusi (ca. 1540–1613). The premises of the *seconda pratica* informed the theory and style of the **Florentine Camerata** and early opera.

SELLARS, PETER. (Born 1957, Pittsburg.) American director known for his nontraditional stagings of plays and operas. Sellars's iconoclastic approach began while he was an undergraduate at Harvard University (graduated 1981) with avant-garde **productions** of plays—William Shakespeare's *Antony and Cleopatra* was performed in a campus swimming pool—and operas like **George Frideric Handel**'s *Orlando* (originally 1733), which cast characters as astronauts. Productions in the late 1980s of *Le nozze di Figaro*, *Don Giovanni*, and *Così fan tutte* (originally 1790), set in a high-rise apartment, a ghetto, and a diner on Cape Cod, respectively, gained him international notoriety. Sellars has been an important collaborator for composer **John Adams**, directing productions of *Nixon in China*, *The Death of Klinghoffer* (1991), and *Doctor Atomic* (2005), for which he wrote the libretto, and he also staged the premier of **Tan Dun**'s *Peony Pavilion* (1998). Sellars has served as director of the Boston Shakespeare Company (1983–84), the American National Theater at the Kennedy Center (1984–86), and the 1990 and 1993 Los Angeles **Festivals**; received a MacArthur Fellowship (1983) and the Dorothy and Lillian Gish Prize (2005); and is currently professor of world arts and cultures at the University of California at Los Angeles.

SEMI-OPERA. *See* MASQUE.

SEMIRAMIDE. *Melodramma tragico*; music by **Gioachino Rossini, libretto** by Gaetano Rossi (1774–1855) based on Voltaire's (1694–1778) *Sémiramis* (1749); two acts; premiered **Venice**, Teatro La Fenice, February 1823. *Semiramide* was Rossini's last opera for Italy and his most-produced serious opera through the 20th century.

Rossi deployed interlocked love triangles and political agendas to generate plot twists and intrigues reminiscent of 18th-century **opera seria**. Followers of the Assyrian queen Semiramide (Semiramis) gather to hear her finally name a successor to her husband Nino, who has been dead for 15 years. Although her confidant, the prince Assur, wants the throne, she intends to crown her general Arsace, who has spent years fighting distant wars. But he loves the princess Azema, who is in turn wooed by the Indian king Idreno. After the high priest Oroe reveals that Semiramide is Arsace's mother, Nino was his father, and she and Assur conspired to poison the king, Arsace plans to avenge his father by killing Assur. However, in the darkness of Nino's mausoleum, he mistakenly stabs his mother instead, inadvertently clearing the path for his own rule and his marriage to Azema.

Semiramide may be viewed as a magnificent bridge between 18th-century opera seria and 19th-century *melodramma*. It participates in the trend toward more sensationalistic subjects based on recent sources, subjects that incorporate brilliant coups de théâtre, such as those that twice derail the queen's plans (the bolt of light at the temple altar in the *introduzione*, Nino's apparition in the Act 1 **finale**) and her unexpected slaying in the *finale ultimo*. **Choruses** of Babylonians feature prominently in the majority of **scenes**— Semiramide's Act 1 aria, all the **arias** in Act 2, and the *introduzione* and both finales—creating monumental backdrops for the action in the manner of **Gaspare Spontini** and Napoleonic French opera. The **overture** introduces melodies from later in the opera (e.g., the duet for Semiramide and Arsace and the finale in Act 1). Obbligato **recitative** is adopted throughout. And set pieces display expansive, fully developed versions of the conventional 19th-century multimovement forms, for example Arsace's two-movement aria without *tempo di mezzo* "Ah quel giorno" (Act 1), his three-movement aria "In sì barbara sciagura" (Act 2), the Act 2 **duet** for Semiramide and Assur, and the ensemble *introduzione* and Act 1 finale.

Yet against these modern features, the lyrical slow movements, **cabalettas**, and **strettas** of these set pieces constitute a glorious, though somewhat exaggerated (perhaps even desperate) reassertion of **bel canto coloratura**, as a more psychologically cogent declamatory singing was making inroads. And the opera's intricate web of marital and murder intrigues centering on an ambiguously gendered hero—Arsace is a **contralto** pants role (*see* TRAVESTY)—seems a throwback to an earlier era.

SENESINO. (?, Sienna–before 1759, probably Sienna.) Italian **contralto castrato** born Francesco Bernardi and nicknamed for his birthplace. Along with **Farinelli**, Senesino was one of the most successful singers of the 18th century. Beginning as early as 1707, he performed in many of the most prestigious Italian centers, from **Venice** to Bologna, **Rome**, and **Naples**, in works by **Alessandro Scarlatti**, **Antonio Caldara**, and numerous others. A mercurial personality, while under contract in Dresden for an exorbitant sum (beginning 1717), he made a scene during at least one rehearsal and was dismissed in 1720. Immediately recruited by **George Frideric Handel** for his Royal Academy of Music in **London**, he performed in the almost three dozen operas staged subsequently until the academy disbanded in 1728 (including Caesar in *Giulio Cesare in Egitto*), and again from 1730 to 1733. Frequently at odds with Handel, he joined several other detractors to establish the rival Opera of the Nobility (1733–37). He finished his career in Naples (1740). In London, Senesino reportedly was even more highly regarded than the younger Farinelli, whom he admired and with whom he collaborated at the Opera of the Nobility.

SENTIMENTAL OPERA. A mixed genre of the second half of the 18th century that mediates between **opera seria** or *tragédie en musique* and **opera buffa** or **opéra comique** by combining serious situations with present-day characters, settings, and issues. Designated variously as opera buffa, *dramma giocoso*, or *comédie*, sentimental opera shows similarities to *opera semiseria*, though lacking its Gothic elements and sometimes grotesque juxtaposition of comedy and impending tragedy.

Sentimental opera stems from the 18th-century novel of sensibility represented by Antoine-François Prévost's *Manon Lescaut* (1731) and Samuel Richardson's *Pamela* (1740), and similarly styled plays (Denis Diderot's *Le père de famille*, 1758, and Pierre Beaumarchais's *Eugénie*, 1767) and paintings (Jean-Baptiste Greuze's *La cruche cassée*, 1773). Important examples are *Le devin du village*, **Niccolò Piccinni**'s *La buona figliuola* (1760), **André-Ernest-Modeste Grétry**'s *Lucile* (1769), Nicolas-Marie Dalayrac's (1753–1809) *Nina, ou La folle par amour* (1786), **Giovanni Paisiello**'s *Nina, o sia La pazza per amore*, and **Domenico Cimarosa**'s *Il matrimonio segreto*.

In these works the goal of moral edification and behavioral elevation depends on the fundamental goodness of human impulses and on emotional rather than intellectual responses as motivations for ethical behavior. Depictions of people, situations, and themes from private, everyday life—loyalty to family and friends, aristocratic benevolence and social harmony, uncultured wisdom, marriage for love, attainment of individual happiness and fulfillment, unwarranted distress of virtuous heroes and heroines, loss of innocence—are treated earnestly and sympathetically, without parody or trivialization, to arouse empathy for the lessons they illustrate and move readers, viewers, and listeners to self-improvement. A natural, spontaneous, folklike style of melody was believed to serve this goal by contributing to the immediacy of emotional communication.

An anti-sentimental response, in parodies that mock sentimental attitudes or depict them as disingenuous, developed immediately in the novel—for example Henry Fielding's *Shamela* (1741)—and later in opera, as in the exaggerated recognition scene for Figaro, Marcellina, and Bartolo in *Le nozze di Figaro* (Act 3), which parodies the sentimental preoccupations with family relationships and appellations.

SERENATA. A 17th- or 18th-century dramatic cantata for at least two singers and **orchestra**—sometimes a very large orchestra—normally performed outdoors at night by candlelight (literally under a "clear sky") in temporary theaters as part of more extensive celebrations of events such as weddings and treaties. Singers typically held their music and moved very little, but their performances were enhanced by costumes, sets, and stage machinery. Plots are minimal and characters tend to be allegorical or mythological figures involved in parables concerning the occasion being celebrated. Lengths vary from one set piece to two dozen (mostly **arias**). **Pietro Metastasio** wrote numerous works that were suitable for performance as serenatas. Notable examples of the genre include **George Frideric Handel**'s *Acis and Galatea* (1718) and **Wolfgang Amadeus Mozart**'s *Il re pastore* (1775) on a Metastasio **libretto**.

See also FESTA TEATRALE.

LA SERVA PADRONA. **Intermezzo**; music by **Giovanni Battista Pergolesi**, **libretto** by Gennaro Antonio Federico (active 1726–1743) based on the play (1709) by Jacopo Angello Nelli (1673–1767); two parts; premiered **Naples**, Teatro San Bartolomeo, September 1733, performed between acts of Pergolesi's **opera seria** *Il prigioniero superbo*.

La serva padrona (*The Servant as Mistress*), the second of Pergolesi's three intermezzos, is the paradigmatic example of the genre. As in many other intermezzos, its domestic plot is based on **commedia dell'arte** archetypes and is presented using only two characters—Uberto (a descendant of Pantalone) and the soubrette (*see* SOPRANO) Serpina (Little Serpent, from Columbina)—in very few **scenes** (just three **arias** and a **duet** in the first part, two arias and a duet in the second). Uberto's headstrong ward decides to marry her master and doggedly erodes his resistance, closing the deal when she threatens to elope with a soldier played by the servant Vespone (a nonsinging role) in disguise. Its music typifies the early 18th-century comic treatment of the *galant* style, which is characterized by melodies segmented into a series of short, rhythmically simple triadic motives and octave leaps interspersed with **patter song**, very light accompaniments in which doublings produce a two-voice texture, and flexible interaction between characters in the **recitatives** and duets.

La serva padrona played a central role in disseminating Italian comic opera and *galant* music across Europe. And it became a lightning rod in the **War of the Comedians** in Paris when it appeared between acts of **Jean-Baptiste Lully**'s *Acis et Galatée* (originally 1686) in 1752. Jean-Jacques Rousseau, one of Pergolesi's supporters, took it as a prototype for his own *intermède* **Le devin du village**. It was translated into French and English, adapted numerous times, and performed throughout Europe during the remainder of the 18th century.

SET DESIGN. The traditional conception of set design as a representational, illusionistic art form dedicated to creating a world distinct from that of the audience and to enhancing audience engagement with the action being represented onstage developed in the spoken theater in conjunction with realism in the arts and advances in the science of perspective in the 15th century. Large-scale backdrop painting adapted techniques of easel and mural painting, and the Italian perspective stage incorporated the technology of single-point perspective, its optimum vantage point being the centrally located boxes of the reigning aristocrat(s). Hierarchical generic standards developed in which tragedies were supported by representations of palace architecture, comedies by civic buildings, and pastoral plays by landscapes. Other elaborations of set design prior to the advent of opera included angled wing flats aligned with diagonal perspective lines pointing toward the central vanishing point, which extended the two-dimensional backdrop into three-dimensional space. For the Italian transformation stage, scene changes could be executed by exchanging flats that moved sideways, or by replacing the backdrop and wing flats with rotating, three-sided vertical prisms having segments of different **scenes** painted on their sides that could be realigned to shift locations.

In the 17th century these innovations were swiftly adapted for productions of court operas, and to a more limited extent for public operas in **Venice**, where interior settings, sometimes with ceilings added to enhance their realism, provided intimate surroundings for smaller casts. A proscenium arch often separated the illusionistic world from the audience and hid the stage equipment. Lighting was provided by candles and oil lamps. And an area in front of the stage was left free of seating for instruments. Innovations in stage machinery facilitated seamless transitions and the special effects—spectacular entrances of gods and goddesses and terrifying arrivals of monsters and storms—that had been associated with the *intermedio* and remained important particularly for myth-based operas. The Venetian **Giacomo Torelli** was the most prominent adaptor of Italian theater architecture and technology for opera and played a critical role in its exportation to France. Italianate perspective sets and machinery were widely employed elsewhere by the mid-17th century, for example in **Paris** initially for the *ballet de cour* (court **ballet**), then for imported Italian operas in the 1640s and for the *tragédie en musique* in the 1670s, which emphasized the *merveilleux* ("marvelous") even more than its Italian counterparts.

Reflecting the reforms of the **Arcadian Academy** and its followers, 18th-century **opera seria** minimized spectacular elements of production. Set design focused on the backdrop, which provided trompe l'oeil representation of interior and exterior architectural spaces using two-point perspective—the "scena per angolo" (scene observed at an angle) popular outside of France—sometimes from low or high points of view involving virtuoso foreshortening adapted from illusionist ceiling painting. These angled scenes incorporated multiple locations for action within a single setting, facilitating adherence to the classical principle of unity of space (*see* UNITIES OF TIME, PLACE, AND ACTION), although their creators sometimes indulged in bizarre architectural fantasies. In the developing forms of comic opera (*see* CATEGORIES OF OPERA), the aesthetic of simplicity and naturalness elicited more mundane, picturesque domestic and rural settings derived from genre painting and the *fête galante*, which furnished a suitable backdrop for prosaic interactions. In the 18th-century theater, lighting in the standard guises of chandeliers, footlights, and overhead and side lights behind the proscenium was still afforded by candles and oil lamps, the latter improved late in the century by the invention of the Argand lamp, which uses a cylindrical chimney to make its light more intense and constant.

Productions in the 19th century took advantage of the technological advances of the industrial age. Allocation of more space backstage accommodated the elaborate machinery necessary for increasingly ambitious, often cataclysmic special effects enjoyed particularly in **Paris** (*see* GRAND OPÉRA). Stage lighting improved first through the introduction of coal gas in **London** in the 1810s and Paris in the 1820s, which was safer and steadier than oil or candle light, then limelight (created by burning quicklime—calcium oxide), seen in theaters beginning in the 1830s; carbon arc electric lamps, which created the famous sunrise in Act 3 of **Giacomo Meyerbeer**'s *Le prophète* at the Opéra in 1849; and the incandescent lamp, used at the Opéra and other theaters in the 1880s.

Such innovations facilitated the adaptation of illusionist technology like the panorama (a wide-angle painting sometimes displayed on a cylindrical surface of 180 degrees or more), the moving panorama (an extended backdrop scrolled in front of the audience as if seen from a passing boat or train), and the diorama (a three-dimensional recreation of a specific scene). Demands for scenic accuracy and spectacle in Paris led to the development of specialized workshops for set design and construction which were capable of increasingly elaborate and dazzling projects, and to the historical or geographical research necessary to produce location-specific, culturally and historically accurate sets. These new capabilities were directed toward various aesthetic agendas, from the neoclassicism of Napoleonic opera to the Gothic, exotic, natural picturesque or sublime, or rustic sentimental themes of **romantic** opera, the historical settings of *grand opéra*, and the naturalism of late 19th-century **opéra comique**, **verismo**, and Russian realism (of **Modest Petrovich Musorgsky** and his contemporaries).

Extension at the turn of the century of the escapist strain of romanticism by the neo-romantics, symbolists, the German *Jugendstil*, and related movements both in operas that explore psychological abnormalities and traumas and in exotic fantasies, as well as efforts to achieve unified realizations of the Wagnerian *Gesamtkunstwerk* (*see* WAGNER, RICHARD), put increasing emphasis on staging to project inwardly oriented dramas of alternative worlds, existences, and consciousnesses and to create artistic unity. Consequently they gave the producer and director unprecedented importance in realizing a work's artistic conception. This modernist approach was promoted most influentially by the Swiss architect and set designer Adolphe Appia (1862–1928), known as the father of nonillusionist musical theater, who designed sets for a number of productions of Wagner's music dramas. Writing in the 1890s (*La mise en scène du drame Wagnérien*, 1895), Appia advocated creating a theatrical space independent of reality, in which mood and atmosphere are conveyed through expressive, nontraditional lighting, and the two-dimensional backdrop is replaced by three-dimensional abstract sets that emphasize the dimension of depth and promote dynamic spatial motions by the actors. Appia's theories were embraced by numerous followers, among them the English actor and set designer Edward Gordon Craig (1872–1966), who replaced painted scenery with colored screens, and by Vladimir Nemirovich-Danchenko (1858–1943), whose Moscow Art Theater Musical Studio (beginning 1919) emphasized meaningful physical movement engaging with nonrepresentational forms onstage.

Contributions by leading avant-garde artists brought derivatives of various modernisms in the visual arts to sets created for operas and ballets before and after World War I (e.g., expressionism, cubism, futurism, surrealism, and styles of geometric abstraction such as constructivism, de Stijl, and Bauhaus). These collaborations were prominent in Paris, where the modernist approach popularized by Sergey Diaghilev's Ballets Russes, through sets painted by Pablo Picasso and others, continued to be championed by Jacques Rouché as director of the Opéra (1915–45). In Bertolt Brecht's (1898–1956) "epic theater," seen in works by **Kurt Weill** ca. 1930, simplified, nonillusionistic sets and captions projected on the backdrop or displayed on placards or banners contributed to undermine the theatrical illusion, distance the audience from the action, and encourage a less emotive and more intellectual response to political and philosophical themes. As in previous centuries, technological advances facilitated the implementation of modernist creative visions. For example the incandescent bulb and such offshoots as the spotlight came into common usage in the early 20th century, along with electrically or hydraulically powered stage equipment for moving, raising, lowering, or rotating sets, backdrops, wing flats, and parts of the stage floor.

While traditional representational sets and backdrop painting had remained the norm for repertory operas prior to World War II, particularly in England and the United States and under repressive Nazi, Fascist, and Stalinist regimes, after the war a combination of factors contributed to a vogue for modernist reinterpretations and to anti-realist dogmatism in progressive circles. Financial realities and the economies of simplified sets and costuming, efforts to generate enthusiasm for shopworn operas, entrenchment of the interpretive producer-director (*see* PRODUCTION), and in Bayreuth after 1951 political distancing from the neo-romantic and neo-**baroque** stagings under the Nazis led to widespread postwar experimentation with radical "interventionist" agendas. These involved political and social commentary, present-day reinterpretations, and deconstructionist tension between the text of the opera and its presentation or within the text of the opera itself.

A virtually unlimited array of options was now available. As a result, anti-historicizing, modernist, deconstructionist productions vie—often at one and the same theater—with historicist productions that attempt to recreate the theatrical style of the period being depicted or the period in which the work was created. Postmodernist productions that synthesize modernist and historicist tendencies incorporate interplay between sets and costumes associated with the work, its intended milieu, and modern day to connect historical and contemporary issues and elucidate dramatic themes. And an arsenal of mechanical, multimedia, and digital electronic technologies—in particular projected translations of the **libretto** (surtitles or supertitles)—have enhanced spectacle, expression, and communication for current opera goers.

SHOSTAKOVICH, DMITRY. (1906, St. Petersburg–1975, Moscow.) Russian **composer** of instrumental and vocal music, including two complete operas in the 1930s, for which he contributed to the **librettos**; an **operetta** (*Moskva, Cheryomushki*, 1959); and numerous film scores and incidental music.

Shostakovich trained in piano and composition at the Petrograd Conservatory (1919–23). Now known primarily for his symphonies, he began his career as a promising composer of operas, until he fell victim to Soviet politics. Both of Shostakovich's operas are based on 19th-century Russian literature. *Nos* (*The Nose*, composed 1927–28, premiered 1930) is the composer's interpretation of a satirical short story (1835–36) by Nikolai Gogol, a parody of political careerism in which a Russian bureaucrat's nose becomes detached and carries on an independent existence, becoming a successful government official and refusing to return to its former face. In addition to six leads, it calls for an enormous cast of secondary singing characters (many of whom can be doubled or tripled by one performer) who come into contact with the titular proboscis. Its absurdist scenario echoes tendencies in Russian avant-garde theater and film, while its rhythmically energized, predominantly atonal and unmelodious music evokes in different ways the styles of **Igor Stravinsky** and **Alban Berg**, incorporating formalist musical devices like canons and parodies of folk and popular music as appropriate. Act 1 includes one of the earliest examples of music for nonpitched percussion ensemble.

Ledi Makbet Mtsenskogo uyezda (*Lady Macbeth of the Mtsensk District*, composed 1930–32, premiered 1934, and revised as *Katerina Izmaylova*, 1963), after a short story by Nikolay Leskov, is considered one of the operatic masterpieces of the 20th century. Its protagonist, the unfaithful, homicidal wife of a provincial businessman, poisons her father-in-law after he beats her lover, the couple strangle her husband when he finds them together, and she dies trying to kill a rival for her lover's affections while en route to a Siberian prison. More traditionally tonal than *The Nose*, it encourages empathy for a callous heroine by giving her expressive, lyrical melodies while mocking her companions with musical grotesqueries. A kind of Russian **verismo** opera, *Lady Macbeth* was wildly popular in Russia and internationally until Joseph Stalin and his journalistic mouthpiece *Pravda* made it a whipping boy for Soviet political aesthetics and socialist realism in 1936 (*see* CENSORSHIP), criticizing its "modernist formalism": its allegedly inaccessible music, crude natural language, and political pretensions. At that point it dropped from the repertory until it was revived in the 1960s.

Although Shostakovich had planned *Lady Macbeth* as the first of three or four operas depicting Russian **women** from various times, he turned in frustration from the theater to other pursuits. Despite considering a number of other projects and composing about a third of the music for *Igroki* (*The Gamblers*, 1941–42), he never fulfilled his considerable potential as an opera composer.

SIFACE. (1653, Chiesina Uzzanese–1697, Ferrara.) Italian **soprano**, born Giovanni Francesco Grossi, one of the first **castratos** to achieve international fame. His early success (1671) as Syphax in **Francesco Cavalli**'s *Scipione affricano* (originally 1664) won him his nickname. He sang in the papal chapel beginning 1675 and served Francesco II d'Este of Modena from 1679 until his death. He also performed in **Paris** for the dauphin and in **London** in James II's chapel in 1687, and at various Italian courts after his return to Modena that year. Siface was famous for the sweet beauty of his voice and his exquisite dynamic control of sustained notes, as well as for his arrogance and uncooperativeness. He was assassinated after boasting about an illicit affair with a member of a Bolognese family.

SINGING STYLE. According to contemporary reports a notable change in vocal mechanics occurred in the decades ca. 1800, resulting in a more modern style of operatic singing. Throughout the 17th and 18th centuries, Italian singers in all ranges, including **castratos,** cultivated two distinct vocal registers, *voce di petto* (chest voice, natural voice) and *voce di testa* (head voice, falsetto voice). Ideally an accomplished performer retained the distinct colors of the two registers while linking them with a smooth transition. Beginning in the late 18th century, non-Italians, who had traditionally segregated the chest and head registers, using transposition to maintain a single color as much as possible, extended the chest voice upward. The Irish **tenor** Michael Kelly (1762–1826) was one of the earliest singers reported to have used chest voice to the top of his range, while the extreme extension of this approach was accomplished notoriously by the French *tenore di forza* Gilbert Duprez (1806–1896). He employed the technique of *voix sombrée* ("covered" or "darkened" vowels) to sing full voice to c" above middle c' in the Italian premier of *Guillaume Tell* (1831) and later in **Paris** (1837)—to **Gioachino Rossini**'s apparent disdain—and continued to popularize the new style in Italy and France. Once it became the standard for singers of the generation of **Vincenzo Bellini** and **Gaetano Donizetti** (e.g., **Giovanni Battista Rubini**), it led to development of the "dramatic" vocal types (*see* SOPRANO, TENOR, and BASS) in the operas of **Giacomo Meyerbeer, Giuseppe Verdi, Richard Wagner,** and others.

This new approach reversed the traditional assumption that vocal sound should be lighter in the highest registers to avoid the often criticized shrillness of the falsetto, while the lowest notes should be strengthened, with singers instead increasing volume as they ascended. Greater power almost unavoidably resulted in more pervasive, heavier vibrato, which until this point had apparently been narrow and unobtrusive, except when introduced as a specific expressive enhancement or **ornament.** In the 19th century the trend toward greater power both encouraged and was increasingly necessitated by enlargement of theaters and the expanded presence of **orchestra** and **chorus.** It also accompanied the decline of **coloratura** ornamentation and the expansion of overtly impassioned *canto declamato* (declamatory, syllabic singing that intermingles **arioso** with **recitative**-like melody).

SINGSPIEL. Term applied commonly beginning in the 19th century to German opera, often comic or sentimental, combining spoken dialogue and vocal and instrumental music. In contrast, in the 17th and 18th centuries it was used most often as a synonym for *dramma per musica* (*see* OPERA SERIA), that is, for operas set entirely to music. During this period, German operas having spoken dialogue were usually designated by a range of other terms, including *komische Oper* (comic opera) and *Operette*, or else *Schauspiel mit Gesang* (play with singing), *Oper*, and *grosse Oper* (grand opera) when they had more elevated aspirations.

Prior to the mid-18th century, German spoken plays had included various songs and pieces of instrumental music for dances, processions, and the like as a minor enhancement. The development of entertainments in which music played a more significant role began in northern Germany with the translation of the Irishman Charles Coffey's (died 1745) **ballad opera** *The Devil to Pay* (1731) as *Der Teufel is los* for Berlin in 1743. It was retranslated by the poet Christian Felix Weisse (1726–1804) and set to new music by Johann Standfuss (died after ca. 1759) for Leipzig in 1752 as the first singspiel in the modern sense of the word, provoking an exchange of essays that drew attention to the new style of theater. A further revision by Weisse, renamed *Die verwandelten Weiber* (1766), with new music by **Johann Adam Hiller**, was even more successful, launching a series of collaborations for Leipzig, Weimar, and Berlin, many modeled on **opéra comique**, of which *Die Jagd* (1770) was most popular. Other prominent north German composers of late 18th-century singspiel were Georg Benda (1722–1795), Christian Gottlob Neefe (1748–1798), and Johann Friedrich Reichardt (1752–1814). The brevity and simplicity of the musical numbers suited German singing actors and made the genre accessible to a wide array of companies and popular with their audiences.

In southern Germany and Austria, singspiel spread through performances by traveling companies that had previously concentrated on translated opéras comiques. In the late 1770s and 1780s, concerted efforts were made in Munich and **Vienna** to raise the standards of German opera. Most prominently, Emperor Joseph II founded the National-Singspiel (1778–83) at the Burgtheater as a companion to the National Theater (beginning 1776) for German plays. It produced mediocre offerings, many on **librettos** by Gottlieb Stephanie the Younger (1741–1800)—the one glorious exception being **Wolfgang Amadeus Mozart**'s *Die Entführung aus dem Serail* (1782)—and was shut down in favor of Italian **opera buffa**. **Carl Ditters von Dittersdorf** contributed a series of popular successes during a second attempt to promote singspiel at the Kärntnertortheater (1785–88). Mozart's *Die Zauberflöte* represents the apex of a vogue for *Zauberoper* (magic opera) at the end of the 18th century, which continued into the 19th with works like **Franz Schubert**'s *Die Zauberharfe* (1820).

In the early 19th century, singspiel assimilated serious elements from Revolutionary **rescue opera** (e.g., *Fidelio*; *see* OPERA SEMISERIA) and northern **romanticism** (*Der Freischütz*), while maintaining ties to the 18th-century tradition in lighter romantic and comic scenes. Composers such as Wenzel Müller (1759–1835) and Adolf Müller (1801–1886) kept the genre alive until the vogue for Viennese **operetta** displaced it in the 1860s.

See also THE BEGGAR'S OPERA; CATEGORIES OF OPERA; COMMEDIA DELL'ARTE; HAYDN, JOSEPH; HOFFMANN, ERNST THEODOR AMADEUS; KODÁLY, ZOLTÁN; MARSCHNER, HEINRICH; MELODRAMA; PASTORALISM; ROMANCE; WEBER, CARL MARIA VON.

SMETANA, BEDŘICH. (1824, Litomyšl, Bohemia, now Czech Republic–1884, Prague.) **Composer** of eight operas that dominated the 19th-century Czech repertory, as well as instrumental and other vocal music; pianist and **conductor**. His best-known theater piece, *Prodaná nevěsta* (*The Bartered Bride*, standard version 1870), has also been popular outside Czechoslovakia.

Son of an affluent brewer, Smetana trained in Prague (1843–47), then ran a music school, taught piano, and directed a choral society in Göteborg, Sweden (1856–61). On his return to Prague, the opening of the Provisional Theater (1862) and a contest for a Czech opera arranged by a local aristocrat provided fresh opportunities at home. He wrote three operas from 1862 to 1867, including his first, which won the competition: *Braniboři v Čechách* (*The Brandenburgers in Bohemia*, composed 1862–63, performed 1866), modeled on **grand opéra** and harkening back to **Daniel-François-Esprit Auber**'s *La muette de Portici* (1828).

Smetana's Czech **opéra comique** *The Bartered Bride*, written beginning in 1863 and revised four times between its premier (1866) and the performance of its definitive version in 1870, gained momentum as he tinkered with it for successive performances and eventually replaced the original spoken dialogues with **recitatives**. Its **pastoral, sentimental** plot unfolds against a backdrop of local color that includes a tavern scene and a circus: to extricate the heroine Mařenka from an arranged marriage, her true love Jeník pretends to sell her to a marriage broker, but he words the contract so that he can reclaim her. Performed habitually in Prague, it became his most widely known stage work after his death.

As principal conductor at the Prague Provisional Theater (1866–74), Smetana cultivated Czech opera and produced two new works of his own (*Dalibor*, 1868, and *Dvě vdovy/The Two Widows*, 1874) and wrote a third, *Libuše* (composed 1869–72), for which the premier was delayed until 1881, when it inaugurated the new National Theater. Forced to give up his position in 1874 after becoming virtually deaf from syphilis, he spent his remaining years composing—completing three more operas—until he was confined in 1884 to the Prague asylum where he died. Although Smetana's operas served as paradigms of Czech nationalism, they were influenced variously by the Italian, French, and German styles and tend to avoid direct quotation of folk music in favor of original adaptations of the ethnic flavor of Czech dances.

SOPRANO. Highest female voice, covering the range from about middle c' to c''' two octaves above middle c'. During the early 17th and 18th centuries the term was also used for **castratos** and other high male voices. Seventeenth- and 18th-century operatic parts for soprano were generally oriented lower than later ones, and many singers were more or less equivalent in range and vocal quality to modern mezzo-sopranos (e.g., **Faustina Bordoni**). In France the designation *dessus* (treble) was used for native sopranos at least until the 1830s to distinguish them from Italians.

The earliest notable female operatic soprano was **Vittoria Archilei**, who likely sang the lead in **Jacopo Peri**'s *Euridice*. Castratos dominated the field in the early 17th century: for example, most if not all the female roles in **Claudio Monteverdi**'s *Orfeo* were taken by males, and **women** were excluded from the stage in **Rome** during that period. Female sopranos came into their own in midcentury **Venice**, led by **Anna Renzi**, who created the role of Ottavia in *L'incoronazione di Poppea*. In the 18th century, in additional to playing female leads (e.g., **Francesca Cuzzoni** as Cleopatra in *Giulio Cesare in Egitto*), some singers specialized in male parts (for example Margherita Durastanti, active 1700–1734, as Sesto in that opera).

Diversification of operatic styles and female vocal roles in the early 19th century—compare **Gioachino Rossini**'s heroines to Leonora in *Fidelio*—resulted in the development of specialized classifications for sopranos, comparable to those of other vocal types (*see* BASS, CONTRALTO, and TENOR). Gradual extension of the upper end of the range across the 18th century, the disappearance of castratos in the early 19th century, and their displacement by women in pants roles (who originally took the name *musico* from the castrato singers they replaced; *see* TRAVESTY) led to recognition of the mezzo-soprano category for women singing in the range from about a below middle c' to a'' two octaves above middle c'.

Both sopranos and mezzo-sopranos may be further subdivided into three main types: "**coloratura**" singers having the most brilliant and agile voices and specializing in roles involving acrobatic passagework and **ornamentation** (Norina in *Don Pasquale*); "lyric" singers (the "standard" type) characterized by voices of average weight and sustaining capability and a particularly beautiful tone for roles like Mimì in *La bohème*, Micaëla in *Carmen*, and Nedda in *Pagliacci*; and "dramatic" singers ("heroic," "Wagnerian," "falcon") possessed of tremendous richness and power throughout the entire range to project over heavy orchestration (the female leads in **Richard Wagner**'s operas from *Der fliegende Holländer* on, represented by singers like **Kirsten Flagstad**).

Numerous in-between and hybrid classifications also came into play and still exist, for example, the *soprano sfogato* having a phenomenally extended range and tessitura (e.g., **Isabella Colbran**); the lyric coloratura, represented by **Giuditta Pasta**—preeminent creator of roles by Rossini, **Vincenzo Bellini**, and **Gaetano Donizetti**—and **Jenny Lind**; the related but warmer *soprano leggiero*; the soubrette, characterized by a light, bright voice color suited to roles of spunky young women such as Susanna in *Le nozze di Figaro*; the dramatic coloratura capable of both agility and tremendous sustaining power for roles like the lead in *Norma* and Abigaille in *Nabucco* (represented by **Maria Callas** and **Joan Sutherland**); and *lirico-spinto* (pushed lyric), a somewhat darker voice than the lyric soprano capable of intense dramatic moments for such roles as the leads in *Aida* and *Tosca* and Desdemona in **Giuseppe Verdi**'s *Otello*.

See also CAVALIERI, CATARINA; FARINELLI; GARDEN, MARY; HORNE, MARILYN; MALIBRAN, MARIA; SIFACE; VELLUTI, GIOVANNI BATTISTA; VIARDOT, PAULINE; VITTORI, LORETO.

SORTITA. An **aria** or a prominent solo within an ensemble, which is sung by a lead at his or her first appearance onstage. Thus while all cavatinas (*see* ARIA) are *sortitas*, not all *sortitas* are cavatinas. Examples would include Norma's famous cavatina "Casta diva" (*Norma*, Act 1) and the Duke's *ballata* "Questa o quella" within the *introduzione* of *Rigoletto* (Act 1).

SPONTINI, GASPARE. (1774, Maiolati–1851, Maiolati.) Italian-born **composer** of about two dozen Italian, French, and German operas (from the late 1790s through the 1820s) as well as other vocal music, and historically important **conductor**. Spontini trained at the Turchini Conservatory in **Naples**, where he based the first phase of his career and wrote about a dozen mostly comic operas (*see* CATEGORIES OF OPERA) for that city, **Rome**, **Venice**, and Palermo, beginning with the *farsetta Li puntigli delle donne* (1796), before setting his sights on the French capital in 1802.

Although he produced two **opéras comiques**, a *fait historique* (an opera based on a heroic historical event), and an *opéra-ballet* in **Paris** with mixed success, Spontini's political and artistic trajectory there centered on four dramas for the Opéra. They, and one of his later German works for Berlin, anticipated the French *grands opéras* of **Giacomo Meyerbeer** and others in their depiction of personal tribulation against a background of historical pageantry and spectacle enacted in monumental tableaux studded with massed ensembles, **choruses**, and brilliant instrumental music. The subject of the *tragédie lyrique* (*see* TRAGÉDIE EN MUSIQUE) *La vestale* (1807), his fourth Parisian opera, anticipates **Vincenzo Bellini**'s *Norma* in its forbidden love between a priestess and a Roman general and provides ample opportunities for coups de théâtre, for example the lightning strike that reignites the temple flame, saving the heroine. Spontini's best-known work nowadays, its acclaimed premier facilitated by the Empress Josephine vaulted him to the forefront of the French opera. Prestigious political commissions followed. *Fernand Cortez, ou La conquête du Mexique* (1809, revised 1817, 1824, and 1832), in which the conquistador falls in love with an Aztec princess and saves her from being sacrificed by her people, and which featured horses onstage, the heroine's plunge into a lake, and the destruction of the Aztec temple, opened in conjunction with Napoleon's impending invasion of Spain. *Pélage, ou Le roi et la paix* (1814) celebrated the Bourbon restoration.

By the end of the decade, Spontini's luster had faded, and the spectacular premier of his classicizing *tragédie lyrique Olimpie* (1819, revised 1821 and 1826), which included elephants, was not surprisingly plagued by delays and poorly received. Its failure led him to move to Berlin (1820) as music director for Friedrich Wilhelm III, where he faced xenophobic resentment from rivals and friction with the director of the court opera. Although his Parisian standbys were performed repeatedly, his three new German works—the exotic fairy operas *Nurmahal* (1822) and *Alcidor* (1825), and the chivalric *Agnes von Hohenstaufen* (1827, revised 1829 and 1837), were unpopular, although he considered the last of these to be his best work. In the late 1820s he faced increasing criticism from the press. And after Friedrich's death in 1840 he was dismissed from his position and briefly imprisoned. Following a failed comeback in Paris—Spontini falsely blamed interference by Meyerbeer—he returned to his Italian hometown in 1850.

SPRECHGESANG. *See* SPRECHSTIMME.

SPRECHSTIMME. Partly vocalized heightened declamation halfway between speech and song particularly associated with the Second Viennese School and the composers **Arnold Schoenberg** and **Alban Berg**. In *Sprechstimme* (speaking voice) the singer performs rhythmically notated imprecise pitches that waver as a note is sustained, producing a moaning or wailing effect that conveys a magical, mysterious, macabre, or unearthly mood or psychological abnormality. The technique was first used continuously in Schoenberg's song cycle *Pierrot lunaire* (1912). In opera it figures prominently in Berg's *Wozzeck* and *Lulu* (composed 1928–35, completed and premiered 1979) and Schoenberg's *Moses und Aron* (incomplete, Acts 1 and 2 composed 1930–32). Since World War II, opera composers such as **Benjamin Britten** (*Death in Venice*, 1973) have continued to develop the technique.

Sprechgesang (speech song) is a related style closer to sung recitative. It can be heard in **Richard Wagner**'s music dramas—Kundry's wails in *Parsifal*—and was used extensively by Engelbert Humperdinck (1854–1921) in his musical play *Königskinder* (1897, developed as an opera 1910) alongside **melodrama** and true song.

STABREIM. "Stave-rhyme" is an alliterative technique in medieval Germanic poetry, in which the consonants of accented syllables (staves) within the first half of a poetic line reappear in accented syllables of the second half of the line. The practice was replaced by rhyming the ends of lines (end rhyme) in the late Middle Ages, but was revisited in modern times by the German baron and writer Friedrich de la Motte Fouqué (1777–1843) in *Der Held des Nordens* (1808–10), a retelling of the Nibelung saga. Influenced by Fouqué and believing that alliterative verse represented an innate expression of the spirit of Germanic folklore, **Richard Wagner** adopted *Stabreim* in the texts of his music dramas, particularly *Der Ring des Nibelungen*. At times he concentrated the effect to the extent that it involves two or more syllables per half line, as in Siegmund's "Winterstürme wichen/dem Wonnemond," and double alliteration, as in Wotan's "Muss ich dich meiden/und darf nicht minnig" (*Die Walküre*, Acts 1 and 3, respectively).

STAGE BAND. Termed *banda* (*sul palco*) in Italy, *fanfare téâtrale* in Paris, the stage band was normally a wind ensemble of about 20 miscellaneous pieces unspecified by the **composer**, some as unconventional as the saxhorn and bombardon, drawn from the local military garrison. Occasionally it also included strings. Located onstage, either costumed and visible to the audience or behind the scenes, it participated in processions, marches, ballroom revelries, or religious ceremonies. In most cases the composer provided a skeleton score that was then arranged by the bandmaster according to the resources available. The *banda* in Italian opera is said to have started with an onstage military marching band during an **aria** in Act 2 of **Giovanni Paisiello**'s *Pirro* (1787). Famous examples in which the *banda* provides melodies for *parlante* dialogues in party scenes, often in alternation with the pit **orchestra**, occur in **Wolfgang Amadeus Mozart**'s *Don Giovanni* (Acts 1 and 2) and **Giuseppe Verdi**'s *Rigoletto* (Act 1), *La traviata* (1853, Act 1), and *Un ballo in maschera* (1859, Act 3). Although this type of background music still occurs in the 20th century (for example in *Wozzeck*), by the end of the 19th century—with **Giacomo Puccini**, for example—it was typically fully scored and performed by the pit orchestra (as it had been in *La traviata*, Act 2).

STAGE SONG. A single-movement **aria**, **duet**, or **chorus** (or a movement within a larger set piece) presented as a performative event as part of the fictional world of an opera. Stage songs frequently follow strophic form, in which two (or more) stanzas of text are heard to the same music, sometimes with a refrain following each stanza. Instruments often mimic a guitar or other credible accompanying instrument.

Stage songs number many types of short arias: dance songs like the Italian ballata (often a lively, popular-sounding song in a fast triple meter like the Duke's "Questa o quella," *Rigoletto*, Act 1) or the Spanish habanera and seguidilla ("L'amour est un oiseau rebelle" and "Près des remparts de Séville," respectively, *Carmen*, Act 1); drinking songs like Violetta and Alfredo's *brindisi* "Libiamo ne' lieti calici" (**Giuseppe Verdi**, *La traviata*, 1853, Act 1); folklike or quasi-popular songs (Italian, canzone), for example the Duke's "La donna è mobile" (*Rigoletto*, Act 3) or Desdemona's "Willow Song" (*Otello*, Act 4); prayers (Italian, *preghiera*) such as Desdemona's "Ave Maria" (Act 4); narratives, normally of events prior to the opera (Italian, *racconto*), such as Ferrando's account of the supposed murder of the Count's brother, and Azucena's of the deaths of her mother and son (*Il trovatore*, 1853, Acts 1 and 2, respectively); and **romances** (Italian, *romanza*), such as Riccardo's "Ma se m'è forza perderti" (*Un ballo in maschera*, Act 3).

Performative songs appear in the earliest operas, for example Orfeo's *canzonetta* "Vi ricorda, o boschi ombrosi" (**Claudio Monteverdi**, *Orfeo*, Act 2) and in 18th-century comic opera, where the borrowed melodies and aphoristic texts of airs in **ballad operas** and the romances of mid-18th-century **opéra comique** and German **singspiel** conjure popular and folk music. Familiar examples from **Wolfgang Amadeus Mozart**'s operas include Pedrillo's "In Mohrenland gefangen" (*Die Entführung aus dem Serail*, 1782, Act 3) and Don Giovanni's serenade "Deh vieni alla finestra" (*Don Giovanni*, Act 2). Stage songs occur in serious opera in the early 19th century, for example the gondolier's barcarolle and Desdemona's "Willow Song" in **Gioachino Rossini**'s *Otello* (1816, Act 3). And they provide local color for the crowd scenes in such French *grands opéras* as **Giacomo Meyerbeer**'s *Les Huguenots* (for example the drinking chorus, Raoul's romance, and Marcel's renditions of the chorale "Ein feste Burg" and the folk song "Piff, paff," in Act 1 alone) and for opéras comiques and *opéras lyriques*. By midcentury they occur frequently in Italian crowd scenes (see the choruses for gypsies and matadors in the Act 2 finale of Verdi's *La traviata*) and remain a staple in the operas of the *giovane scuola* as late as **Giacomo Puccini**'s "Bevo al tuo fresco sorriso" (*La rondine*, 1917, Act 2). Familiar 20th-century examples of stage songs include Marie's lullaby and Wozzeck's folk song in the tavern (*Wozzeck*, Acts 1 and 3) and the "Ballad of Mac the Knife" (*Die Dreigroschenoper*, **prologue**).

STILE RAPPRESENTATIVO. Early 17th-century term meaning "representational style" or "theatrical style" applied originally by **Giulio Caccini** on the title page of his *Euridice* (and later, 1602, in the preface to his song collection *Le nuove musiche*) in reference to the new expressive manner of singing developed by the **Florentine Camerata**, purportedly in imitation of the ancient Greek manner of performing tragedy. Pietro de' Bardi (son of the Camerata's host Giovanni de' Bardi) later explained (1634) that Galilei had set a lament and sacred prayers using this style of singing, accompanied by a consort of viols, and that Caccini had sung "ariettas, sonnets, and other poems" to a single instrument (most likely a **lute**). Bardi credited **Jacopo Peri** with having first adapted this style to a stage work in *Dafne*. Ca. 1635, **Giovanni Battista Doni** associated the term *stile rappresentativo* with operatic music for the theater.

STORACE, STEPHEN. (1762, London–1796, London.) English composer of approximately 20 musical theater works during the 1780s and 1790s, as well as other vocal and instrumental music. Trained in **Naples**, Storace began his career composing **opera buffa**, two for **Vienna** (where he befriended **Wolfgang Amadeus Mozart)**, which were probably commissioned through the intervention of his sister Nancy (1765–1817), a prominent **soprano**, and one for **London** (*La cameriera astuta*, 1788). Beginning in 1788 he attached himself to the Drury Lane company in London. With the **librettists** James Cobb (1756–1818) and Prince Hoare (1755–1834) he created 14 mainpiece and afterpiece operas (full-length, principal entertainments and shorter works to be performed following mainpieces, respectively), which included spoken dialogue and some borrowed songs, in the English custom. With Cobb, Storace increasingly made musical numbers, particularly ensemble finales, more essential to the drama, culminating with *The Pirates* (1792) and *The Cherokee* (1794). And he extended the idiomatic range of songs from folklike to Italianate **coloratura**. His effort to give music a more integral role in English theater failed to influence other composers and librettists.

STRAUSS, RICHARD. (1864, Munich–1949, Garmisch-Partenkirchen.) German **composer** of 15 operas (mostly ca. 1900–40) and other vocal and instrumental music, **librettist** for three of his own operas, and **conductor**.

Strauss received most of his musical training from members of the Munich court **orchestra**, for which his father was principal horn player. He debuted as a conductor (1884) with the Meiningen Orchestra directed by Hans von Bülow (1830–1894) and became Bülow's assistant the next year, leading to a series of prestigious appointments in Weimar, Munich, and Berlin and including a stint as co-director of the **Vienna** State Opera (1919–24). The first phase of Strauss's career prior to 1903, during which he focused on instrumental music, particularly symphonic poems, also saw his first opera, *Guntram*, performed in Weimar (1894). Although written while Strauss was privy to the clique surrounding Cosima Wagner (1837–1930), and although Strauss's **libretto**, a medieval chivalric tale, recalls several of **Richard Wagner**'s operas, its assertion of the individuality of the hero derived from Friedrich Nietzsche and contradicted Wagnerian attitudes. Its disappointing revival in Munich (1895) discouraged further operas until the *Singgedicht* (sung poem) *Feuersnot* in 1900.

With the composition of two landmark works to start the century, Strauss reoriented his efforts toward opera. *Salome* (begun 1903, premiered 1905), is an **expressionist** interpretation of Oscar Wilde's psychodrama. In *Elektra* (1909), the first of six collaborations with the librettist Hugo von Hofmannsthal (1874–1929), the daughter of a murderous Queen and would-be stepfather who usurp the Mycenaean throne conspires with her once-exiled brother to kill her parents, and she consumes herself in a triumphal dance. The two operas show clear similarities: characters who indulge in horrific lust, violence, and emotional obsessions; continuous, intensively concise one-act structures; textures dominated by expanded orchestras; Wagnerian networks of **leitmotifs**; and dissonant extensions of late 19th-century chromaticism that anticipate the atonal idiom of **Arnold Schoenberg** and the Second Viennese School.

Der Rosenkavalier (*The Rose Knight*, 1911, also with Hofmannsthal)— Strauss's most popular opera—takes up the kind of lighter subject for which Strauss had been searching for several years. And in returning to a more traditional, nostalgic musical style punctuated by glittering waltzes, arching **romantic** melodies, and rich orchestration, it defines *Elektra* as the extremity of Strauss's exploration of modernism. Strauss composed four more operas with Hofmannsthal. *Ariadne auf Naxos* (1912, revised 1916), the first of this group, has the greatest historical significance, because it anticipates the neoclassicism of the 1920s in its comparatively light scoring for chamber orchestra. Like *Rosenkavalier*, it has a retrospective plot: in its original version, the one-act opera followed a spoken performance of Molière's *Le Bourgeois Gentilhomme* (with incidental music by Strauss), whose characters subsequently interacted with the **opera seria** and **commedia dell'arte** performers within the opera. The remaining Hofmannsthal operas are *Die Frau ohne Schatten* (1919), creation of which was interrupted by the poet's military service during World War I, *Die ägyptische Helena* (1928), and *Arabella* (1933). The early **Zeitoper** *Intermezzo* (1924), on a libretto by the composer, provided a counterpoise to Hofmannsthal's more high-minded essays, a semi-autobiographical farcical account of a marital flap set partly at an Austrian ski resort.

Although Strauss remained active as an opera composer after Hofmannsthal's death and his completion of *Arabella*, composing six additional theatrical projects (the last unfinished), he labored uncomfortably under the Nazi regime, was dismissed as president of the Reich's Music Bureau under Joseph Goebbels and was publicly discredited for his collaboration with the Jewish playwright Stefan Zweig (1881–1942) on *Die schweigsame Frau* (1935), which was swiftly banned in Germany. Remarkably, his last opera was one of his best. Written during World War II, the "conversation piece" *Capriccio* (1942) is a comic allegory on the merits of words and music in opera, in which a self-involved countess is unable to decide between two lovers, a poet and a composer.
See also CENSORSHIP.

STRAVINSKY, IGOR. (1882, Oranienbaum, Russia–1971, New York.) Preeminent **composer** of instrumental and vocal music including six operatic works from the second decade of the 20th century through the early 1950s and several hybrid theater pieces (*L'histoire du soldat*, 1918; *Les noces*, 1923; and *The Flood*, 1962), and **librettist** for one of his operas.

Following early training as a pianist and creation of numerous boyhood compositions, Stravinsky studied privately with **Nikolai Andreyevich Rimsky-Korsakov** (1903–06) and was influenced by a host of other composers, including **Pyotr Il'yich Tchaikovsky**, **Claude Debussy**, and Paul Dukas (1865–1935). He was persuaded by the **impresario** and founder of the Ballets Russes Sergei Dyagilev (1872–1929) and the scenographer Alexandre Benois (1870–1960) to prioritize **ballet** over opera, an orientation reflected in his initial focus on ballets and in the emphasis on dance in several of his operatic works.

His first, *Solovey* (*The Nightingale*, 1914), belongs to the strain of Russian fantasies popularized by Rimsky-Korsakov in operas like *The Golden Cockerel* (1909), Stravinsky's musical style mediating between Rimsky-Korsakov's and Debussy's. In this Orphic adaptation of Hans Christian Andersen's traditional fable, a songbird charms Death and saves the life of an emperor. At one point intended as a symphonic poem for **orchestra**, then retargeted for the opening of the Moscow Free Theater and ultimately produced by Dyagilev at the **Paris** Opéra, it presents its story in the guise of a ballet and ritual pageant with limited vocal music. A more sparing style appears in the "merry performance" on a **libretto** by Stravinsky, *Bayka pro lisu, petukha, kota da barana* (*Fable of the Vixen, the Cock, the Cat, and the Ram*, composed 1915–16, premiered 1922), best known as *Renard*, a hybrid chamber opera, in which singers stand with the instrumental ensemble, and the roles of a rooster, who is pursued by a fox, who is thwarted and eventually killed by a cat and a ram, are danced and mimed. *Mavra* (1922) is a small-scale farce after a poem by Aleksandr Pushkin, in which a daughter hides her lover under her mother's nose by disguising him as a female cook, until he is discovered shaving. A **number opera** with spoken dialogue, it parodies eastern European songs and dances and the styles of 19th-century Russian composers such as **Mikhail Ivanovich Glinka** and Tchaikovsky.

Although *Mavra* enjoyed no immediate success, it is regarded as a key work that mainstreamed Stravinsky's Russian style, its light musical affect and neo-tonal harmonic language marking a turning point in the development of the **neo-classical** idiom that would dominate his remaining operas. The next two, in which he turned from folklore and domestic comedy to ancient tragedy and myth, represent the most severe incarnations of this classicizing impulse. *Oedipus rex* (operatic premier 1928), director Jean Cocteau's (1889–1963) adaptation of Sophocles, is a cross between opera and oratorio in which the characters imitate statues on a frieze-like set and the action is framed by spoken narration and accompanied by an orchestra of winds, brass, and percussion. Also lying at the fringe of true opera, *Perséphone* (1934) includes only one solo singer (the priest-narrator Eumolpus) and gives predominant emphasis to ballet and **chorus**. The title role of the goddess abducted by Pluto, whose travels between earth and the underworld create the seasons, is normally split between a speaker and a dancer or mime. *The Rake's Progress* is one of Stravinsky's last neo-classical works before he turned to twelve-tone technique in the 1950s, his best-known opera, and the most produced 20th-century opera after those of **Giacomo Puccini**.

STRETTA. In Italian opera, a fast concluding section or movement of an ensemble of three or more voices, such as a central **finale** or ensemble *introduzione*. It presents agitated reaction to a startling event occurring in the previous section of the finale (the *tempo di mezzo* in the 19th century). The stretta developed in 18th-century **opera buffa** out of the *gliuòmmari* (tangles) of confusion and consternation that ended first acts of early comic operas, reflecting their ancestry in the **commedia dell'arte**. A familiar example is the *più allegro* "Son confusa, son stordita" that ends the Act 2 finale of **Wolfgang Amadeus Mozart**'s *Le nozze di Figaro*. It soon gained a foothold in serious opera as well, as in the *allegro con brio* "Deh cessi il scompiglio" of the trio in Act 2 of *Idomeneo*.

By the late 18th century, the stretta follows a conventional form which resembles that of the **cabaletta** in **arias** and **duets**. The entire cast may sing together from the start, or the principals may enter successively either with the same melody in quasi-canonic fashion or with separate melodies that differentiate characters and group them according to their interrelationships. Following an energetic transition, which often features a Rossinian crescendo (a phrase repeated with increasing volume and numbers of instruments), the stretta normally recapitulates all or part of this opening, then ends with a rousing coda. "Mi par d'esser con la testa" from the Act 1 finale of **Gioachino Rossini**'s *Il barbiere di Siviglia* illustrates this form perfectly.

As early as the 1840s, **composers** like **Giuseppe Verdi** and their **librettists** grew impatient with the repetitiveness of the stretta and with difficulties motivating it—as they had with the cabaletta—and increasingly eliminated the repeat or omitted the entire movement, ending with the *tempo di mezzo* or *largo concertato*.

STROPHIC ARIA. *See* ARIA.

SULLIVAN, ARTHUR. *See* GILBERT, WILLIAM SCHWENCK, AND ARTHUR SULLIVAN.

SUTHERLAND, JOAN. (1926, Sydney–2010 Montreux, Switzerland.) Australian dramatic **coloratura soprano**, who was instrumental in reviving the 18th- and particularly the 19th-century **bel canto** repertory beginning in the 1950s. Ardent admirers consider her voice to be the greatest of the 20th century.

Having learned to sing by imitating her mother, an accomplished amateur mezzo-**soprano**, Sutherland began formal training in Sydney in 1945. She debuted as Dido in a concert performance of *Dido and Aeneas* in 1947 and appeared first onstage in 1951 as the lead in Eugene Goossens's (1893–1962) *Judith* (originally 1929). That year she continued her studies in **London** at the Royal College of Music and joined the Covent Garden company in 1952, making her London debut as the First Lady in *Die Zauberflöte* and taking her first lead role as Amelia in **Giuseppe Verdi**'s *Un ballo in maschera* (originally 1859). Throughout her career, Sutherland flourished on a diet of early 19th-century bel canto roles, for example the leads in *Semiramide*, *Norma*, and particularly *Lucia di Lammermoor*, the breakthrough role with which she was most identified internationally. She also spearheaded the **George Frideric Handel** operatic revival, starring in *Alcina* in 1957 (originally 1735) and playing Cleopatra in *Giulio Cesare in Egitto* in 1963.

In her prime, Sutherland possessed an exceptional combination of rich tone, tremendous power, electrifying range extending to high f''', clean intonation, and the agility necessary for precise execution of extremely demanding passagework and **ornamentation**, her one weakness at times being unclear diction. Sutherland was made a Dame Commander of the Order of the British Empire in 1979 and received the Order of Merit in 1991.

SYMBOLISM. Style of French, Russian, and Belgian poetry said to have originated with Charles Baudelaire's (1821–1867) collection *Les fleurs du mal* (1857). Symbolism gained importance in the 1860s and 1870s through the work of the French poets Paul Verlaine (1844–1896) and Stéphane Mallarmé (1842–1898) and was adapted to the theater and the visual arts by such figures as the Belgian playwright Maurice Maeterlinck (1862–1949) and the Austrian painter Gustav Klimt (1862–1918). French composers set symbolist poems as songs and symphonic poems (e.g., **Claude Debussy**'s *Prélude à "L'après-midi d'un faune,"* 1894), and the style was explored in a limited number of operas, most notably Debussy's ***Pelléas et Mélisande*** (after Maeterlinck's play), Paul Dukas's (1865–1935) *Ariane et Barbe-bleue* (1907), and **Béla Bartók**'s *Bluebeard's Castle* (composed 1911, premiered 1918). Symbolism shared various goals and characteristics with the pre-Raphaelite, decadent, and art nouveau styles of the late 19th and early 20th centuries, and it would influence **expressionism** and surrealism.

In their mystical dreamscapes, symbolist writers confronted middle-class traditionalist expectations and created an alternative to the often politicized mundaneness of late 19th-century naturalism, enacting the philosopher Arthur Schopenhauer's aesthetics of art as unveiling spiritual existence. They saturated their fluid, free verse with psychologically ambiguous, allusive, sensory images of nature, sexuality, and mortality, exploiting the sensuous qualities of words. Symbolist opera may be viewed as both a reaction against the excesses of French ***grand opéra*** and Italian ***melodramma*** and **verismo** and as an ambivalent response to **Richard Wagner** that embraces his aesthetic of inner feelings while tempering orchestral bombast and the obsessive structuralism of **leitmotif** technique and replacing epic grandeur with intimacy and human vulnerability.

T

TAN DUN. (Born 1957, Simao, Hunan.) Chinese-born American **composer** of four operas during the 1990s and first decade of the 21st century, experimental stage works, movie scores, and other vocal and instrumental music. Following service at a commune where he became acquainted with traditional Chinese music through local peasants, Tan's musical career began as a violinist and arranger with a touring company of the **Beijing opera**. He entered the Central Conservatory of Music in Beijing in 1976 as the Cultural Revolution ended, Western music became increasingly available, and foreign composers began to visit China. He migrated to **New York** in 1986, completing the doctoral program in composition at Columbia University, where he familiarized himself with various types of American experimental music (e.g., **minimalism** and chance music) and began to fuse the diverse influences of Chinese folk music, traditional Western art music, and the avant-garde into a unique synthetic style.

Tan's operas *Marco Polo* (1996), *Peony Pavilion* (1998), *Tea: A Mirror of Soul* (2002), and *The First Emperor* (2006) explore aspects of Chinese history and cross-cultural intersections by combining Western atonality and experimental idioms with stylistic elements of Beijing opera, and Western instruments with counterparts from India and China. Tan's nonoperatic stage works, such as *Nine Songs* (1989) and *Orchestral Theatre I–IV* (1990–1999) are even more eclectic in their subject matter and musical and visual resources, which include jazz, rock, film, and even **puppets**.

TANNHÄUSER UND DER SÄNGERKRIEG AUF WARTBURG. Grosse romantische Oper; music by **Richard Wagner**, **libretto** by the **composer** based on 19th-century treatments of medieval legends; three acts; premiered Dresden, Hoftheater, October 1845, revised in conjunction with productions in Dresden (1847), **Paris** (1861), Munich (1867), and **Vienna** (1875).

One of three projects completed during Wagner's appointment in Dresden (libretto 1842–1843, music 1843–45), *Tannhäuser and the Singing Contest at the Wartburg Castle* received an indifferent response at its first presentation, partly owing to an inadequate performance, but gained its place in the

German repertory by the 1850s. It underwent several stages of revision resulting in two main versions commonly designated "Dresden" and "Paris." Currently performed more widely, the latter incorporated passages in a more sensuously chromatic and richly scored idiom (e.g., Venus's music in Acts 1 and 3), provided the obligatory **ballet** for the Opéra in the Venusberg orgy, and deleted passages from the Act 2 **finale**'s singing contest. Members of the Jockey Club disrupted the 1861 performance, apparently because they opposed both the Act 1 location of the ballet, which encroached on their dinners, and Wagner's unpopular sponsor, the Austrian princess Pauline von Metternich, effectively ending his hopes for stardom in Paris.

A stylistic hybrid, *Tannhäuser* synthesizes elements of French **grand opéra** and German **romantic** opera, as well as Italian features. Its plot is based in part on history: Tannhäuser (active ca. 1250) was commonly conflated in the 19th century with Heinrich von Ofterdingen (active ca. 1200), whose vocal prowess was rumored to be inspired by Satan; Wolfram von Eschenbach (active ca. 1170–1220) and Walther von der Vogelweide (active ca. 1200) were also historical *Minnesinger*; and the Wartburg song contest probably took place in the 13th century. But it overlays that background with romantic themes—myth, magic, the supernatural, and a nationalistic German locale— and recurring Wagnerian issues (social constraints versus individuality, perversion of true Christian charity by institutionalized religion, and redemption and unification of souls through spiritual versus carnal love.

Unfulfilled by Venus's sensual delights, Tannhäuser returns to his homeland in the Thuringian Wartburg Forest racked with guilt and is welcomed with some misgivings by his former companions, his warmest ally Wolfram, the standoffish Walter, his rival Biterolf, and the Landgrave (earl) and is later reunited with his beloved Elisabeth. Vying for her hand in a ritual contest introduced by spectacular courtly pageantry, the knights improvise songs on the topic of courtly love, which become increasingly combative concerning Tannhäuser's transgressions with Venus. In each of his rejoinders, Tannhäuser more vehemently extols physical love and, despite Wolfram's attempt to calm him, finally blurts his paean to the goddess (from the opening scene), to the horror of Elisabeth and the assembly. Exiled for his offense, he makes a pilgrimage to **Rome**, only to be rebuffed by the pope, who promises forgiveness only if his lifeless staff blooms. Tannhäuser is finally redeemed by the love-death of Elisabeth, as pilgrims deliver the flowering relic.

Tannhäuser's music similarly synthesizes various national styles and progressive tendencies. Wagner's vocal writing is freely molded to the action, its continuity increased through its emphasis of **arioso** over traditional **recitative**; its disintegration of regularly phrased melody into freer declamation; its elision of cadences; its frequent, spontaneous shifting among text-setting styles within a Germanic melodic/harmonic idiom; and its insertion of dialogue between more formal sections of set pieces. Scenic instrumental and vocal music—the Venusberg ballet (Act 1); the pentatonic shepherd's song accompanied by flute, English horn, and cowbell that opens the Wartburg scene (Act 2); and the pilgrims' hymn in the same scene—contribute to the sense of novelty, actuality, and specific locale, as well as providing a measured point of departure for the spectacular massed tableaux expected of *grand opéra*. Signature themes, most prominently the pilgrims' **chorus**, Venus's rapture, and Tannhäuser's ode to her, stem from both the German and French traditions and are introduced in a medley **overture** typical of the 1830s.

Organization of lyric numbers include lied-inspired forms such as the hero's strophic ode to Venus (Act 1), which is opened up by episodes of dialogue between stanzas (cf. the spinning chorus in Act 2 of *Der fliegende Holländer*), and episodic solos with returns (Wolfram's solo in the Act 2 singing contest, "Blick ich umher," or his evening star hymn "O du, mein holder Abendstern"). Also evident are the French-influenced crowd scenes popularized by **Giacomo Meyerbeer**, which adapt Italian grand finale form, camouflaging the conventional sequence of movements with transitions and secondary set pieces and *concertato* sections. In the Act 1 reunion scene in the Wartburg Forest, atmospheric components (the shepherd's song and pilgrims' chorus) and a series of dialogue and lyric ensemble passages (like the one beginning "Gegrüsst sei uns") in the manner of an elaborate *tempo d'attacco*, lead to a *largo concertato* (beginning with Wolfram's "Als du in kühnem Sange"), which is connected by a line of recitative ("Zu ihr!") to a **stretta** ("Ha, jetzt erkenne ich sie wieder"). The singing contest follows a more expansive version of this schema, which climaxes in the *largo concertato* beginning with Elisabeth's "Der Unglücksel'ge, den gefangen" and concludes with the stretta "Versammelt sind aus meinen Landen."

TCHAIKOVSKY, PYOTR IL'YICH. (1840, Votkinsk–1893, St. Petersburg.) Russian **composer** of 10 completed operas (beginning in the late 1860s), for which he wrote or contributed to six **librettos**, as well as other vocal and instrumental music. Although he is known more for his **orchestral** works, two of his operas—*Yevgeny Onegin* and *Pikovaya dama* (*The Queen of Spades*, 1890)—are mainstays of the modern repertory.

A member of the first graduating class of the St. Petersburg Conservatory (1866), Tchaikovsky immediately relocated to teach at the new companion **conservatory** in Moscow, where he spent the rest of his life, resigning the position once long-term patronage by a baroness began in 1876, making him Russia's first full-time composer. A host of factors—his conservative politics, acceptance by the aristocracy, success at the mainstream national theaters, status as the de facto imperial composer under Tsar Alexander III (r. 1881–94), sexual orientation, and particularly his professional status—distinguished and alienated him from the Kuchka (The Five), who leaned left and distrusted institutional training, believing that it undermined artistic and nationalist integrity. His relatively traditional operatic style reflected this position in its continued reliance on set pieces, lyricism, linear plotting, visual effects, technical polish, and ambivalence toward the Russian realism of Alexander Sergeyevich Dargomïzhsky (1813–1869) and **Modest Petrovich Musorgsky.**

Tchaikovsky's operatic career began in 1869 with the premier of *Voyevoda* (*The Provincial Governor*, lost), for which he completed the libretto after his interference caused a falling out with his collaborator, an experience that led him to write two other librettos and contribute to three more. A forgettable semiserious drama, in which a love triangle involving the title character is resolved improbably by the arrival of a new governor, Tchaikovsky withdrew it after a brief run, reusing parts of the score for later works and discarding the rest. *Oprichnik* (composed 1870–72, premiered 1874, on his own libretto) was Tchaikovsky's first enduring success and his first opera to survive intact. It is a melodramatic work in the style of *grand opéra* featuring numerous folk songs cannibalized from *Voyevoda*, in which a Boyar joins Ivan the Terrible's secret police to avenge a family dishonor, but is entrapped and executed in front of his mother. *Kuznets Vakula* (*Vakula the Smith*, 1876), composed for a contest, steps back from Russian realism, particularly in its revision as the comic-fantastic opera *Cherevichki* (*The Fancy Slippers*, 1887), and is more sparing in its use of folk tunes.

Western familiarity with Tchaikovsky's operas tends to begin with *Yevgeny Onegin* (conservatory premier 1879, professional premier 1881), which renews his realist inclinations in adapting Aleksandr Pushkin's (1799–1837) well-known verse novel. A domestic drama developed as a series of lyric vignettes, *Onegin*'s music imitates the songs and dances of the middle class and peasants and the conventions of the salon. *Orleanskaya deva* (*The Maid of Orléans*, 1881, on Tchaikovsky's libretto), which shows affinities to *grand opéra* and *opéra lyrique*, suffered a short-lived triumph owing to the assassination of Alexander II, which closed theaters two weeks after the premier. Appropriately for the subject of *Mazepa* (1884, after Pushkin), Tchaikovsky swung back toward Russian realism by incorporating folk songs, working on a more personal scale, and adopting a somber affect. It depicts an early 18th-century Ukranian uprising against Peter the Great, a subject that had already captured **romantic** revolutionary imaginations across Europe, but which the composer treated as an affirmation of imperial rule.

Tchaikovsky's last two operas depart from the traditional and Russian realist approaches of his previous works in the direction of surrealism. Written in only 44 days, *Pikovaya dama* (*The Queen of Spades*, 1890, libretto by Tchaikovsky and his brother, Modest, after Pushkin) has steadily overtaken the popularity of *Yevgeny Onegin*. It is a discourse on social relations and their emotional fallout in which a military officer feigns love for the granddaughter of a countess (the Queen of Spades) to learn her secret for winning at cards, eventually precipitating the deaths of all three characters. Orchestration, pointed musical cross-references, and purposefully corrupted allusions to anachronistic musical idioms contribute to the work's hallucinatory atmosphere. Tchaikovsky died a year after the premier of his final opera, *Iolanta* (1892), a medieval romance in which the blindness of a heroine kept ignorant of her disability is miraculously cured through love.

TEMPO D'ATTACCO. The "starting movement" or "attaching movement" that opens a standard 19th-century Italian multimovement **duet** or a larger ensemble such as a **finale**. It begins when the **libretto** shifts from the *versi sciolti* (*see* VERSIFICATION) of the scena (*see* SCENE) to the *versi lirici* of the set piece proper. In the early 19th century (as handled by **Gioachino Rossini** and others), the principals often began with solos before interacting more spontaneously. However, by midcentury the *tempo d'attacco* more commonly consisted of dialogue throughout, interspersing passages of **recitative**-like declamation, *parlante*, and **arioso**, and in ensemble crowd scenes it may incorporate **stage songs** and **choruses**. Whereas early *tempi d'attacco* normally restate conflicts or alliances among characters that have previously been established in the scena, by midcentury they increasingly present new developments and carry the action forward.

TEMPO DI MEZZO. Interactive "middle movement" that links the slow movement or *largo concertato* of a 19th-century Italian multimovement **aria**, **duet**, or ensemble (such as a **finale**) to the ensuing **cabaletta** or **stretta**. The *tempo di mezzo* normally presents an event, announcement, or shift of attitude or relationships among characters—frequently a breathtaking coup de théâtre in finales—that prompts a reaction in the next movement. It follows no conventional form, ranges tremendously in length and complexity, and consists primarily of dialogue set in some combination of **recitative**-like declamation, **arioso**, and *parlante*. The *tempi di mezzo* of arias and finales often involve **chorus** and secondary characters.

TENOR. Highest of the standard male voices, covering the range from approximately c below middle c' to a' (or higher) above middle c'. Tenors played the male heroes of the first operas (Orfeo in **Jacopo Peri**'s and **Giulio Caccini**'s *Euridice* operas and **Claudio Monteverdi**'s *Orfeo*) and continued to take leads through the 1640s (e.g., Ulysses in Monteverdi's *Il ritorno d'Ulisse in patria*, 1640) as well as lesser roles. However, they faded in importance with the rise of the **castrato** in the mid-17th century and were increasingly consigned to supporting or comic roles as servants and other minor parts (the soldiers in *L'incoronazione di Poppea*) or even **travesty**

nurses. In France, the castrato voice was deemed unnatural. Consequently male leads in the *tragédie en musique* were assigned to *hautes-contres*, high tenors who sang in full voice up to b' or more above middle c' by contracting the throat (whereas a conventional 18th-century tenor would sing in falsetto above g'; *see* SINGING STYLE). The tenor voice was also popular in Germany (the lead in **George Frideric Handel**'s *Nero* for Hamburg, 1705). And important secondary roles for tenor returned to **opera seria** in the early 1700s (the Turkish emperor Bajazete in Handel's *Tamerlano*, 1724).

However, the emergence of the tenor voice begins in earnest in the late 18th century, as demonstrated by **Wolfgang Amadeus Mozart**'s operas, where tenors play leads in opera seria (the title roles in *Idomeneo* and *La clemenza di Tito*, 1791); comic supporting characters in **opera buffa** (Basilio in *Le nozze di Figaro*); and the male love interest in **singspiel** (Tamino in *Die Zauberflöte*). Ca. 1800, disparagement of the castrato voice led to its replacement for male romantic and heroic leads by female **contraltos** in travesty (Arsace in *Semiramide*) and by tenors (the title character in **Gioachino Rossini**'s *Otello*, 1816), who also took romantic leads in opera buffa (Almaviva in Rossini's *Il barbiere di Siviglia*). As tenors became a primary option for male roles in all types of opera, different styles developed in response to varying circumstances. Leggiero (light) or **coloratura** tenor roles demand an agile, lyric instrument capable of negotiating difficult passagework and **ornamentation** and a range extending as high as f" (second octave above middle c) in falsetto (Arturo in **Vincenzo Bellini**'s *I puritani*,1835, as performed originally by **Giovanni Battista Rubini**).

The turn toward more overtly dramatic vocal writing in the 1830s coupled with extension of the chest voice from g' above middle c' to as high as c", famously demonstrated by Gilbert Duprez's (1806–1896) performances of Arnold in *Guillaume Tell* beginning in 1831 (originally 1829), resulted in a number of species characterized less by agility than by sustained lyricism, power, brilliance, range or color, emotional gravity, and/or endurance. Examples include the middleweight lyric tenor (Edgardo in *Lucia di Lammermoor*) and the various dramatic subspecialties such as the Italian *tenore di forza* or *tenore robusto* (Radames in *Aida* and Otello in **Giuseppe Verdi**'s *Otello*), epitomized at the turn of the 20th century by **Enrico Caruso**, and the German Heldentenor (heroic tenor, for example **Richard Wagner**'s Tannhäuser or Siegfried).

See also DAVIDE, GIOVANNI; LEGROS, JOSEPH; PAVAROTTI, LUCIANO; RASI, FRANCESCO.

THEATER DESIGN. Italian operatic theater design, developed in the city opera houses of Venice and elsewhere during the 17th century, dominated everywhere except France through the late 19th century. It served the function of the theater as a social gathering place where the same circle attended night after night and interacted much as they would in a drawing room at home.

The seating area was laid out in a U or horseshoe shape flanked by as many as six tiers of superimposed balconies, which were divided by solid partitions into rows of boxes. Although these boxes were typically owned by families and could be sold, rented, or loaned (like a modern condominium) and were privately furnished and decorated, attendees paid an admission fee every night like other patrons. Dressing rooms across the hall were used by servants to prepare food and by box holders as powder rooms. In many theaters patrons could close off their box by drawing a curtain, facilitating a range of activities from conversation to eating, card playing, and even sexual escapades (sometimes with prostitutes). The floor of the theater (*platea, poltrone*, or pit stalls) provided a mix of standing room and benches for less-privileged patrons and those who wanted to focus on the performance. Beginning in the late 18th century, some theaters set up the highest balcony as an unpartitioned gallery (*loggione*) furnished with backless benches, accessible to the general public through a separate entrance and stairs and allowing no entry to the rest of the theater.

Distribution of seating reflected the social order. Typically the center box in the first or second balcony belonged to the reigning aristocrat. Other boxes occupied by noblemen and upper-middle-class bankers, lawyers, and wealthy merchants, who had became more of a factor by the end of the 18th century, were assigned according to rank. Less-distinguished members of the middle class, tradesmen, students, servants of box holders, and tourists who lacked aristocratic connections occupied the floor and gallery. In some cities the foremost rows of the floor were reserved for the military, who notoriously abused the privilege with their boorish behavior. Admission prices also mirrored social standing, nobles paying more than commoners.

Foyers hosted various casino games until the Restoration—an essential revenue supplement—and provided food service and other amenities. Chamber pots used in changing rooms but parked in the corridors were the primary sanitary facilities for box holders—unpleasant conditions that persisted in many theaters throughout the 19th century—until British water closets and other improvements appeared during the Napoleonic era. Theaters remained lighted throughout performances, at first by candles and oil lamps, then increasingly by gas lighting after the 1830s, until electricity became common around the turn of the century (*see* SET DESIGN). The orchestra sat at the front of the platea, at the same level as the spectators.

A trend in the 18th century toward increased seating capacity is represented by the San Carlo in Naples (1737, rebuilt following a fire in1816) and La Scala in Milan (1778), which contain over 3,000 seats each. Richard Wagner's Bayreuth Festival House (1876) revolutionized theater design by arranging seats in long, curved rows without aisles on a sloped, fan-shaped floor and mostly eliminating boxes and nonoperatic distractions. The theater was darkened during performances and the orchestra was hidden in a sunken pit that extended under the stage. Wagner's single-level amphitheater provided egalitarian seating with unobstructed sight lines. It led in the 20th century to construction of new theaters having fewer balconies and no boxes, and to remodeling of old theaters, which replaced benches and standing room on the floor with individual seats and cut down or removed partitions between boxes.

THOMAS, AMBROISE. (1811, Metz–1896, Paris.) French **composer** of 20 operas, all but four of them **operás comiques** (mostly between the late 1830s and 1870), as well as other vocal and instrumental music; teacher.

Trained by family members to play the piano and violin, Thomas enrolled at the **Paris** Conservatoire (beginning 1828) and studied piano with Frédéric Kalkbrenner (1785–1849) and composition with Jean-François Le Sueur (1760–1837). He won the Prix de Rome (1832), traveling to **Rome** and Germany and returning in 1835. His most auspicious early operas were his first, *La double échelle* (1837), and *Le panier fleuri* (1839). *Le Caïd* (1849) was the most popular of his operas next to *Mignon* during his lifetime. Thomas taught composition at the Conservatoire beginning in the late 1850s and followed **Daniel-François-Esprit Auber** as its director (1871).

Currently Thomas's reputation rests on two operas that appeared in close succession. His *opéra lyrique Mignon* (1866), based on Johann Wolfgang von Goethe's *Wilhelm Meisters Lehrjahre*, premiered with the role of the heroine created by Célestine Galli-Marié (1840–1905)—who later starred in *Carmen*—and gained international standing with **recitatives** by Thomas that replaced the original spoken dialogues (London, 1870). After Wilhelm buys Mignon's freedom from the gypsies who had kidnapped her as a young girl, her jealousy toward him leads her to consider suicide, and she almost dies in a fire set at her suggestion by another of her admirers. She is finally united with Wilhelm in a happy ending that preempted the tragic original after it was poorly received. *Hamlet* (1868), Thomas's only truly successful work for the Opéra, presented reasonable likenesses of the conflicted hero and his mother, but ended with Hamlet's coronation, a *lieto fine* later changed for **London** (1869).

TIPPETT, MICHAEL. (1905, London–1998, London.) English **composer** of instrumental and vocal music including six operas (from the 1930s through the 1980s), for which he wrote the **librettos**. Following early piano lessons and a preparatory school education, Tippett trained at the Royal College of Music (1923–28 and again 1930–32), after graduating gaining experience with opera by serving as **conductor** for minor opera societies. His earliest theatrical projects in the 1930s included the folk-song opera *Robin Hood* (1934) and two children's plays with music (1938–39).

Tippett's mature operas exhibit a striking diversity of subject and musical style, which ranges from structural continuity to fragmentation, post-**romantic** lyricism to realist declamation, rich to sparse scoring, modal tonality to Second Viennese atonality, popular to art music references, and cinematic realism to surreal episodes, all targeted for dramatic impact. *The Midsummer Marriage* (composed 1946–52, premiered 1955) combines elements of Jungian psychology, pagan ritual, and Celtic lore in a mythic comedy that shows resemblances to William Shakespeare's *Midsummer Night's Dream* and *Die Zauberflöte*. With a ruined temple as its backdrop, it presents a journey of development and self-realization through ceremonial trials and involves two couples of different classes, an overbearing parent, and a society of benevolent priests. *King Priam* (premiered 1962) takes a completely different course. A Trojan War epic, it depicts episodes including the rescue of Paris as an infant, his courtship of Helen, the siege of Troy, and the deaths of Hector and Priam.

Tippett again changed directions with *The Knot Garden* (1970), which is regarded as his best opera, on a contemporary subject alluding again to Shakespeare (*The Tempest*) and to **Wolfgang Amadeus Mozart**'s *Così fan tutte* (1790). The shrubbery maze that serves as a backdrop symbolizes the complex interrelationships connecting two couples (one of them gay) and two other **women** as they confront issues of neurosis, sexual orientation, race, disfigurement, pedophilia, sexual violence, and marital decline. *The Ice Break* (1977), perhaps the composer's most modern score and subject—the opera opens in an airport lounge—also explores realistic interpersonal dynamics through racial, cultural, and generational conflicts involving a Russian gulag survivor, his wife and son, and their friends. The eclectic psychological fantasy *New Year* (premiered 1989) about an agoraphobic cured by time-traveling aliens, retains the popular orientation of its original conception as a musical in its references to jazz, rap, and other modern idioms.

TONADILLA. A musical entertainment (literally "little song") performed between acts of a play or, less frequently, opera, sometimes called a *tonadilla escénica* (theatrical *tonadilla*). It originated in mid-18th-century Madrid; peaked during the 1770s and 1780s, as popularized by Pablo Esteve y Grimau (ca. 1734–1794) and others; and essentially disappeared by 1850. At its height a *tonadilla escénica* was a brief Spanish comic opera (*see* CATEGORIES OF OPERA) normally involving one to four nonaristocratic characters, performed during the intermission of a play or an opera like a one-part Italian

intermezzo. Its three or four set pieces included songs, ensembles, **choruses**, instrumental sections, and possibly **recitatives**, and its music often mimicked Spanish dances and used regional instruments like the guitar and castanets.

TORELLI, GIACOMO. (1608, probably Fano–1678, Fano.) Italian architect and the most innovative and influential designer of sets and stage machinery in the 17th century. Torelli created **Venice**'s fourth public opera house, the Teatro Novissimo (built 1641), where he pioneered innovations attuned to Venice's small public theaters and their plot-oriented operas: the single-point perspective set, which remained state-of-the-art through the 18th century; interior sets (with a ceiling) appropriate for limited casts; and a mechanical system for making instantaneous scene transformations using movable parallel wing flats (*see* SET DESIGN), which facilitated an increased number of locales. Nicknamed the "great magician," he also introduced effects for levitation and weather and incorporated fashionable aspects of gardening such as grottos and rows of potted shrubs. Torelli's inventions influenced generations of followers who took them to Italian courts and other countries, most notably Ludovico Burnacini's (1636–1707) stupendous production of **Antonio Cesti**'s *Il pomo d'oro*. Torelli himself worked for the French royal court (1645–1661), designing sets and machinery for Italian operas, plays, and the *ballet de cour* (*see* BALLET).

TORREJÓN Y VELASCO, TOMÁS DE. (1644, probably Villarrobledo, Spain–1728, Lima.) Spanish-born **composer** of sacred choral music and one particularly significant opera. A page to the Spanish Count of Lemos, who took him to the New World when he became Viceroy of Peru (beginning 1667), Torrejón rose through administrative ranks to the post of choirmaster of the Lima Cathedral (1676). His one surviving secular work is his opera *La púrpura de la rosa* (1701), a remake of **Juan Hidalgo** and Pedro Calderón de la Barca's (1600–1681) Madrid version (ca. 1660). Created for festivities celebrating King Philip V's birthday, it is assumed to be the first surviving opera written and premiered in the Americas.

TOSCA. *Melodramma*; music by **Giacomo Puccini**, libretto by **Luigi Illica and Giuseppe Giacosa** based on Victorien Sardou's (1831–1908) play (1887); three acts; premiered **Rome**, Teatro Costanzi, January 1900. Puccini's enthusiasm for Sardou's play took root at least as early as 1889 and piqued again after he attended a performance in 1895. Although a libretto had been written and consigned by Giulio **Ricordi** to another composer, Puccini's contemporary Alberto Franchetti (1860–1942), Puccini easily re-

claimed the project and began work in 1898. Despite opposition of conservative critics to its lurid tone, *Tosca* triumphed with the public and has held a
secure place in the repertory ever since.

Set in 1800 as the impending return of Napoleon's army threatens the
Neapolitan occupation of Rome, Tosca is a grisly potboiler of attempted
rape, coercion, murder, execution, and suicide. The wealthy painter Mario
Cavaradossi loves the prima donna Floria Tosca, who is also coveted by the
Roman chief of police Scarpia. When Scarpia suspects that Cavaradossi has
aided the escape of the political prisoner Cesare Angelotti, he has Cavaradossi tortured in an adjacent room with Tosca present to bully her into revealing
Angelotti's hiding place at Cavaradossi's villa and bartering sex for Cavaradossi's freedom. After Scarpia promises that Cavaradossi's execution will be
faked—but surreptitiously tells his agent Spoletta the opposite—and hands
her a letter of safe passage, she stabs him and mocks his corpse. When
Cavaradossi's execution on the ramparts of the Castel Sant' Angelo proves
all too real, and with Spoletta in pursuit for Scarpia's murder, Tosca leaps to
her death.

The most fervid of Puccini's operas, *Tosca* may be viewed as both a
logical outcome of trends in 19th-century *melodramma* toward progressive
escalation of salaciousness and cathartic violence seen, for example, in **Giuseppe Verdi**'s *Rigoletto*, and a representation of the **verismo** posture that life
is inherently corrosive and degrading. The verismo agenda is also apparent in
Puccini's obsession with authenticity of locale and environment. The opera's
Napoleonic political background lends urgency to Scarpia's abuse of political power directed toward Angelotti, Cavaradossi, and Tosca. Puccini personally researched Roman carillons, chant variants, ceremonial processions,
and costuming; he probably based the character of Angelotti on the historical
Consul Libero Angelucci; and he wrote for Tosca a historically credible
cantata imitating **Giovanni Paisiello**. Attention to such mundane details as
the minutia of Cavaradossi's and Tosca's occupations, the Sacristan's activities and irreverence for Cavaradossi's Madonna, and the painter's betrayal
by his food basket left for Angelotti at times creates telling juxtapositions, for
example the domestic setting for Cavaradossi's interrogation and torture,
Tosca's performance heard during the interrogation, and the church bells and
shepherd's song preceding the execution (Act 3). The specifics enhance credibility and enlist the audience's empathy, legitimizing both the gratuitous
violence and the characters' extravagant melodic outbursts.

In *Tosca*, Puccini's concern with credibility included self-conscious avoidance of conventional set pieces. He fended off Ricordi's request for a quartet
during Cavaradossi's torture and for an effusive Act 3 love **duet**, keeping
instead the original duet in which Tosca coaches Cavaradossi's performance
at his supposed mock execution. And like most of Puccini's operas, *Tosca* is
much more continuous than such early verismo forays as *Cavalleria rustica-*

na and *Pagliacci*, which are essentially **number operas**. Pervasive dialogue, led by the orchestra in *parlante* style or interspersed with associative orchestral motifs as characters exchange melodic phrases that avoid clear distinctions between declamation and lyricism, advances the trend toward continuous action heard in earlier operas like Verdi's *Otello*. In the few ersatz set pieces, identifiable by their broader melodic arches, music unfolds spontaneously according to the sense of the text, the level of lyricism rising and falling appropriately. For example, Cavaradossi's "Recondita armonia" (Act 1) is punctuated by the Sacristan's mutterings, its deflecting phrases avoiding any predictable melodic schemata. And such other lyrical centerpieces as Cavaradossi's duet with Tosca "Qual'occhio" (also Act 1), her "Vissi d'arte" (Act 2), and his "E lucevan le stelle" (Act 3) include substantial expanses of declamatory singing.

TOSCANINI, ARTURO. (1867, Parma–1957, New York.) Italian **conductor**, the most celebrated and progressive operatic artistic director of the first quarter of the 20th century. Toscanini caused a sensation in 1886 with his unscheduled debut in Rio de Janeiro conducting *Aida* at age 19. After gaining notoriety in Italy with the premieres of *Pagliacci* and *La bohème*, he became artistic director at La Scala in Milan (1898–1903 and 1906–08), where he promoted the works of **Giuseppe Verdi** and **Richard Wagner** and arranged notable Italian premieres such as those of *Yevgeny Onegin* and *Pelléas et Mélisande*. An ardent reformer, Toscanini attempted with mixed results to raise artistic standards and improve audience behavior by taking control of all aspects of production: he rehearsed singers himself, supervised staging, dimmed the lights during performances, and discouraged encores.

Ultimately frustrated by contentious responses to these initiatives, he left La Scala and soon landed as artistic director of the Metropolitan Opera (1908–15), where he premiered **Giacomo Puccini**'s *La fanciulla del West* (1910), among others, but was as dissatisfied in **New York** as he had been in Milan with his company's inconsistent progress, and returned to Italy in 1915 and eventually to La Scala (1920–29). After resigning from La Scala for artistic and political reasons, he concentrated almost exclusively on the symphonic repertory with the New York Philharmonic Orchestra (1926–36) and the NBC Symphony Orchestra (1937–1954).

TRAETTA, TOMMASO. (1727, Bitonto–1779, Venice.) Along with **Niccolò Jommelli** and **Christoph Willibald Gluck**, one of the most important progressive composers of Italian serious opera (*see* CATEGORIES OF OPERA) in the mid-18th century. In **Naples** under **Nicola Porpora** and the internationally reputed teacher **Francesco Durante**, Traetta received traditional instruction in strict, chromatic counterpoint. His first dozen operas (1751–1758) are split evenly between **opera buffa** and **opera seria**, the latter including five settings of **librettos** by **Pietro Metastasio**.

Having acquainted himself with Jommelli's forward-looking operas in the early 1750s, he won an appointment in Parma (1758), a Bourbon court where the prime minister Guillaume Du Tillot called on Traetta to enact his program for merging French *tragédie lyrique* with Italian opera seria using a translation of **Jean-Philippe Rameau**'s *Hippolyte et Aricie* (1733) adapted as *Ippolito ed Aricia* (1759). It included **choruses, ballets,** programmatic instrumental music involving an expanded orchestral palette, spectacular effects, and more frequent obbligato **recitatives** in the French manner championed by the theater critic **Francesco Algarotti**. And like several of his later works, it anticipated the reforms of Gluck and **Ranieri Calzabigi** while retaining an Italianate focus on lengthy exit **arias**.

Ippolito launched a series of 10 diverse operas for various cities (1759–63). Several written for conservative centers were traditional, for example the Metastasio warhorses *Zenobia* for Lucca and Rome (1761 and 1762, originally 1740) and *Alessandro nell'Indie* for Reggio Emilia (1762, originally 1729). However, others for more progressive centers carried Traetta's agenda forward, including *Armida* (**Vienna**, 1761), *Sofonisba* (Mannheim, 1762), which included gladiatorial and equestrian scenes, and *Ifigenia in Tauride* (Vienna, 1763), his most famous opera seria, which was probably influenced by Gluck's ***Orfeo ed Euridice***.

Economic constrictions in Parma led Traetta to move to a teaching position in **Venice** (1765), then an appointment as opera director in Catherine the Great's St. Petersburg (1768), which produced his acclaimed masterwork *Antigona* (1772). In declining health during his final years, Traetta moved back to Venice (1775), to **London** and **Paris**, and again to Venice (1777), unable to reclaim his lost popularity.

TRAGÉDIE EN MUSIQUE. Also termed *tragédie lyrique* beginning in the 1770s, "musical tragedy" was the earliest and most prestigious type of true French opera from **Jean-Baptiste Lully** through **Jean-Philippe Rameau** and the 18th century. It was established by Lully and his **librettist Philippe Quinault** beginning with *Cadmus et Hermione* (1673) after Lully obtained the royal monopoly for opera in France, and was delineated decisively by *Alceste, ou Le Triomphe d'Alcide* (1764).

For the French **baroque** theater, *tragédie en musique* provided a complement to spoken tragedy and the *ballet de cour* (*see* BALLET) by combining aspects of each. An integrated plot deployed over five acts and the concept of heightened declamation derived from tragedy joined the laudatory political function and elements of the *merveilleux* (the "wonderful" or "marvelous") derived from the ballet. Adoption of serious subjects from myth, legend, or medieval romance encouraged freedoms considered inappropriate for historical tragedy, such as departures from the Aristotelian **unities**, and plots centered on amorous couples and rivals. Elaborate **divertissements** (entertainments), normally one per act, provide relief from the succession of dramatic scenes dominated by **recitative**. At the same time, they contribute to the action by depicting dazzling events or defining groups of characters or locations through songs, dances, **choruses**, and descriptive instrumental music combined with machinery for special effects. Particularly during the age of Louis XIV, a substantial **prologue** framed the story as an allegory of the king's glory and of allegiance to duty and honor, in part by alluding to contemporary events.

In many of its characteristics, *tragédie en musique* constituted a competitive cultural foil to the international style of Italian opera. Its five acts—versus the standard three for **opera seria**—incorporate a broader range of components, not only recitatives and **airs**, but also ensembles, choruses, and instrumental music for ballets and mimed action. And these structural elements, which tend to be shorter than their Italian equivalents, appear in much less conventional arrangements, link more continuously, and create less distinct strata of real time and suspended time. In contrast to Italian da capo **arias**, French airs draw on a wider repertory of forms and generally avoid vocalization, sometimes resembling recitative in their vocal style. French recitatives tend to be more flexible and more active in melody and rhythm than the Italian secco recitative dominant by the late 17th century, and far more of them are accompanied by **orchestra** (beginning with Lully's *Bellérophon*, 1679). Rather than the Italian three-movement symphony, *tragédies en musique* begin with the type of binary "French" **overture** in three metrically differentiated tempos developed by Lully for the *ballet de cour*.

Even after Lully's death, his 13 *tragédies* dominated the repertory in revivals until Gluck's operas appeared in Paris in the 1770s. Their primacy was challenged only by Rameau's operas of the 1730s and 1740s (*see HIPPOLYTE ET ARICIE*), which partially revived the genre as new works were becoming less frequent, and by isolated works by other composers (for example, **Marc-Antoine Charpentier**'s *Médée*, 1693). Although *tragédie en musique* was attacked by the liberal philosophes during the **War of the Comedians** in the 1750s for its antiquated musical style and its associations with the French academies and the cultural status quo, it influenced mid-18th-century adaptations of Italian opera by **Christoph Willibald Gluck** and others. And, ironically, critical controversy prompted a second renewal of interest in the genre. Gluck's arrival in the 1770s brought a rapprochement between the French and Italian traditions, establishing a more international musical idiom that prevailed in French serious opera into the 19th century, when the designation *opéra* replaced *tragédie lyrique*. The combination of mythological or legendary subject matter, flexible dramatic organization, and utilization of the full spectrum of theatrical resources in *tragédie en musique* anticipated **Richard Wagner**'s conception of the *Gesamtkunstwerk* by almost two centuries.

See also CAMPRA, ANDRÉ; CATEGORIES OF OPERA; CONDUCTOR; DUET; PARIS; PRODUCTION; SALIERI, ANTONIO; SET DESIGN; SPONTINI, GASPARE; TENOR.

TRAGÉDIE LYRIQUE. *See* TRAGÉDIE EN MUSIQUE.

TRAVESTY. An operatic role involving cross-dressing. Italian and French equivalents of the term (*travesti*) may apply either to men or **women**; in English and German, "pants role" (breeches role, *Hosenrolle*) more commonly denotes women dressed like men.

Travesty roles appeared in the earliest operas: Dafne in **Jacopo Peri**'s *Euridice* was sung by a boy, while most, or possibly all, of the female characters in **Orfeo** were taken by **castratos**, a practice observed especially in Rome, where women were excluded from performing. In early Venetian opera, male **contraltos** or **tenors** depicted lecherous old women to comic effect (Ottavia's nurse in *L'incoronazione di Poppea*), a role that continued in Neapolitan comic operas after comic *contrascene* were removed from 18th-century **opera seria**. *Haute-contre* singers (*see* TENOR) occasionally took similar parts in 18th-century France. Male travesty roles became rare after 1800.

Female pants roles occurred fairly often in the 17th and 18th centuries, either for heroic or romantic leads or secondaries (Annio in **Wolfgang Amadeus Mozart**'s *La clemenza di Tito*, 1791) or for boys (Sesto in *Giulio Cesare in Egitto*). During the first quarter of the 19th century, a female contralto or mezzo-**soprano**, termed *primo musico* or *musico* after the conventional designation for a castrato, became a standard option for male lead characters as the castrato waned (for example, Arsace in *Semiramide*). Unlike males in drag, female pants roles continued to appear with some frequency during the 19th and even the 20th centuries (e.g., Oscar in **Giuseppe Verdi**'s *Un ballo in maschera*, 1859; Siébel in *Faust*; Octavian in *Der Rosenkavalier*; and Caliban in **John Eaton**'s *The Tempest*, 1985).

Travesty is related to (but distinct from) the practice of male or female characters (who may already be cross-dressed or ambivalently gendered) cross-dressing to disguise themselves as part of the plot. Familiar examples include Ottone (castrato) in *Poppea*, Cherubino (female mezzo-soprano) in *Le nozze di Figaro*, Leonora in *Fidelio*, and Gilda in *Rigoletto*.

TRISTAN UND ISOLDE. Music drama (*Handlung*); music by **Richard Wagner**, **libretto** by the **composer** based primarily on Gottfried von Strassburg's (died ca. 1210) courtly **romance** (early 13th century); three acts; premiered Munich, Königliches Hof- und Nationaltheater, June 1865.

Wagner became interested in the subject in 1854 in conjunction with his (probably unfulfilled) affair with Mathilde Wesendonck, wife of his Swiss patron during his exile. He began work in earnest in 1857 and completed the score in 1859, interrupting work on *Der Ring des Nibelungen* after Act 2 of *Siegfried*. Projected as a modest project of practical length intended to offset costs of *The Ring* and increase his reputation, it grew to epic proportions, lasting over four hours, its initial **production** dependent on funding from Ludwig II of Bavaria. The prelude (*see* OVERTURE) was performed in **Paris** (1860), probably as a calling card for an eventual staging of the entire opera there, which was not to happen following the *Tannhäuser* fiasco (1861). As with many of Wagner's works, the premier, conducted by Wagner's proponent Hans von Bülow (1830–1894), prompted ardent but polarized reactions, in part owing to opposition by Ludwig's detractors.

Tristan may be viewed as a metaphysical allegory inspired by the German philosopher Arthur Schopenhauer's conception of the "Will," explicated in *Die Welt als Wille und Vorstellung* (*The World as Will and Representation*, 1818, revised 1844). Worldly love is a beguiling serendipity—in the opera it depends on misuse of a magic potion—and physical union provides only a superficial, and ultimately futile solution to human conflict, represented by the hero's betrayal of the Irish princess and objectification of her as a prize, and by their jockeying to gain the upper hand in Act 1. Such destructive alienation, self-interest, and ambition are virtually inevitable, being rooted in the delusional sense impressions that are imposed on us by the light that the couple so fervidly wishes to escape, and can only be negated through denial of the individual will, as demonstrated ultimately by the hero and heroine.

Prior to the opening curtain, the knight Tristan, nephew of King Marke of Cornwall, defeated the Irish champion Morold, Isolde's betrothed, who had demanded tribute. In Ireland to claim counter-tribute for England, Tristan, disguised as "Tantris," was wounded in battle and subsequently nursed back to health by Isolde. Despite discovering his true identity and role in Morold's death, she nonetheless shielded him from Irish retribution and refrained from killing him herself. Valuing career over friendship, Tristan repaid her favor by claiming her as his uncle's bride.

The opera begins on the return voyage: feeling betrayed and playing on Tristan's guilt, Isolde goads him to join her in a suicide pact. Intending to take poison, they unwittingly drink a love potion substituted by her maid Brangäne and lose themselves in amorous rapture, oblivious to their arrival in England for Isolde's royal wedding. With Marke off hunting, and unable to contain their ardor, the couple consummate their love, ignoring

Brangäne's warnings, and are discovered by Marke and his men when they return. Challenging the courtier Melot, who also loves Isolde, Tristan allows himself to be fatally wounded in their fight. Tended in Brittany by his squire Kurwenal, Tristan dies awaiting a reunion with Isolde. Subsequently Marke and Melot arrive intending to forgive the lovers, but are challenged by Kurwenal, who kills Melot and himself dies in the melee. In an ecstatic transfiguration Isolde joins Tristan in death.

Wagner's first publicly produced music drama, *Tristan* exerted an extraordinary influence on the later development of opera and instrumental music in the 19th and early 20th centuries in Germany, France, and to a lesser extent Italy (*see*, for example, *PELLÉAS ET MÉLISANDE*) and became a centerpiece of **Wagnerism** in the sister arts. Having reconceptualized opera as philosophical allegory enacted through continuous psychological dialogue, Wagner minimized enacted plot events along with **chorus** and massed spectacle, which are confined to the extreme ends of acts (the disembarkation at Cornwall, Act 1, Tristan's fight with Melot, Act 2, and the arrival of Marke's retinue, Act 3). And the few vestigial allusions to the scenic **stage songs** of *grand opéra* (the unaccompanied sailor's chanty "Westwärts schweift der Blick," Act 1, and Brangäne's tower song "Einsam wachend in der Nacht," Act 2) are much less fully developed and are more integrated into the flow of the music than in preceding operas.

Responding to his recent encounter with Schopenhauer's aesthetics, which privilege music among the arts, Wagner entrusted his "endless" **arioso** supported by dense, voluptuous orchestration with a more intensive and omnipresent expressive role and with a more uniform contribution to structural cohesiveness than in the *Ring* operas he had already composed. Thoroughgoing exploration of the far reaches of chromaticism and unresolved 7th- and 9th-chord dissonance, emblemized by the much examined evocative "Tristan chord" heard at the start of the prelude, communicates the vortex of emotions experienced by the lovers. Also by comparison with the early *Ring* operas, *Tristan* shows a more sophisticated treatment of **leitmotif** technique: musical ideas associated in a general way with the characters' yearning, passion, and disillusionment are otherwise ambiguous and multidirectional in their specific meanings, providing an expressively diverse array of gestures that may appear almost interchangeably to create appropriate affects. And more thoroughgoing deployment of those motifs results in a remarkably coherent score.

Finally, Wagner's acknowledged indebtedness to Ludwig van Beethoven (1770–1827) is apparent in the extent to which dramatic tension is sustained across an expansive musical landscape, a feature that influenced such followers as Anton Bruckner (1824–1896), Gustav Mahler (1860–1911), and **Richard Strauss**. This aspect of style is illustrated particularly in the 20 or so minutes of cyclically intensifying groundswells of Tristan and Isolde's assignation (Act 2) beginning "O sink hernieder, Nacht der Liebe"—and especially the final surge at "So starben wir, um ungetrennt"—which regroups at various points of articulation but avoids closure entirely. Conveying the lovers' desire and ultimate frustration when its momentum is broken and its cadential drive left unresolved by Marke's intrusion, it resonates uncomfortably until its resumption and fulfillment by Isolde's love-death (Act 3), in perhaps the most cathartic example of long-range musical rhetoric in all of opera.

U

UNITIES OF TIME, PLACE, AND ACTION. Dramatic principle, observed in certain styles of opera, that the action should begin and end within a day, take place in related locations within walking distance of one another, and center on a single central plot, avoiding unrelated subplots. It was espoused by classicizing aestheticians, beginning with the Italian Lodovico Castelvetro (ca. 1505–71) and echoed by 17th- and 18th-century French and English critics, who treated observations by Aristotle in his *Poetics* as imperatives serving more fundamental goals: verisimilitude within the limitations of a theatrical performance, since credibility is strained by depicting spans of weeks or months, remote locales, and events unlikely to take place in the same place at the same time; practicality, since set changes and lighting effects were necessarily limited in **baroque** theaters; and adherence to classical authority. This orientation was most prominently represented by the dramas of Pierre Corneille (1606–1684) and Jean Racine (1639–1699) at the court of Louis XIV.

Although the earliest operas, for example **Claudio Monteverdi**'s *Orfeo*, tend to observe these rules, 17th-century Roman and Venetian **librettos** for both public and court productions (for example, **Francesco Cavalli**'s *Giasone*), influenced by freely conceived Spanish drama, often self-consciously detach themselves from classical rules in their *argomenti* (explanatory prefaces) and include extended time frames, distant locations, and extraneous comic subplots. A reaction in Italy against this "undisciplined" approach is evident as early as Vincenzo Grimani's (after 1652–1710) libretto *Orazio* (1688, music probably by Giuseppe Felice Tosi, 1619–1693), which is based on Corneille. Beginning in the 1690s, **Apostolo Zeno**'s Accademia degli Animosi and the **Arcadian Academy**, which eventually included **Pietro Metastasio**, embraced an agenda that involved simplifying plots and minimizing subplots, centralizing locations, and abbreviating time lines, pointing ultimately toward Spartan narratives such as **Christoph Willibald Gluck**'s *Orfeo ed Euridice* in the mid- to late 18th century. In France, while the *tragédie en musique* at first provided a counterpoise to spoken tragedy by including romantic and comic subplots, magical transformations, and epic voyages within extended time frames (e.g., **Jean-Baptiste Lully**'s *Alceste, ou Le Triomphe d'Alcide*), it gravitated increasingly toward classical prescriptions in the early 18th century, sufficiently so that the more freely conceived *opéra-ballet* emerged to fill the void.

The authority of the unities was challenged beginning in the late 18th century as part of an anti-classical rebellion against the prescriptions of the artistic academies. Operatic adaptation of literary or historical sources that themselves violated the rules resulted in the unfettered storytelling of such **romantic** operas as **Giuseppe Verdi**'s *Nabucco* and **Richard Wagner**'s *Der Ring des Nibelungen*.

V

VAUDEVILLE. French term derived from the 16th-century *voix de ville* ("city voices"), an urban or courtly love song resembling the midcentury Parisian chanson. By the mid-1600s, "vaudeville" referenced the simplest of popular, strophic dance, drinking, and/or satirical songs. Outfitted with new words, these melodies took on a theatrical role in the *comédies en vaudevilles* (plays with music) of the 18th-century Parisian fair theaters that were the ancestors of **opéra comique**, in which such retexted popular songs were increasingly elbowed aside by *ariettes* (newly composed songs; *see* AIR) and more extended ensembles. The strophic form of the vaudeville supplied the framework for the so-called vaudeville **finale**. An ensemble that ended numerous comic operas, it enlisted the principal characters to sing solo stanzas (sometimes with choral refrains) that presented epigrammatic morals related to their situations, as in the final numbers of *Le devin du village* and *Don Giovanni*. By the 1790s, comedy with vaudevilles detached from opéra comique and eventually evolved into the music hall vaudeville ca. 1900, a variety show mixing songs, dances, comedy routines and sketches, and other entertainments.

VAUGHAN WILLIAMS, RALPH. (1872, Down Ampney, England–1958, London.) English composer of orchestral and vocal music including five true operas (1920s through ca. 1950), and **librettist** for three of them.

Vaughan Williams received a conventional formal education at Trinity College, Cambridge (in history) and the Royal College of Music (through 1897). Influenced by his composition teacher Charles Stanford (1852–1924), he collected hundreds of British folk songs and edited *The English Hymnal*, dedicating himself to promoting the tradition of English music as an alternative to those of Germany and France, despite his admiration for **Richard Wagner** and study with **Maurice Ravel** in **Paris** (1908). A number of his theater works reflect traditional English genres dating as far back as the 17th century—**masque** (*On Christmas Night*, 1926, and *Job*, premiered 1929), **ballad opera**, and **operetta** (*The Poisoned Kiss*, 1927–29, premiered

1936)—as well as mainstream operatic categories; are steeped in British literature, lore, and ambience; and adopt traditional English music or Vaughan Williams's own facsimiles.

Hugh the Drover, or Love in the Stocks (composed 1910–14, premiered 1924)—designated a ballad opera although it contains **recitatives**—employs folk songs and pseudo–folk songs amidst a sentimental plot set in an English village during the Napoleonic Wars, in which a herder falls in love with a woman committed to an arranged marriage, wins a fight with her fiancé, but is falsely accused of spying for the French and temporarily pilloried. *Sir John in Love* (premiered 1929), an adaptation of William Shakespeare's *The Merry Wives of Windsor* and other plays, quotes numerous folk melodies, including "Greensleeves," as well as Vaughan Williams's replicas. In the miniature *Riders to the Sea* (composed 1925–32, premiered 1937), a mother living in a fishing community on a barren Scottish island loses her sons to the ocean, the last when his horse throws him into the water. *The Pilgrim's Progress* (1951), a moral parable after the English preacher John Bunyan's fable (1678), recycled music from as early as 1906—including the one-act opera *The Shepherds of the Delectable Mountains* (1922)—and provided castoff themes for the composer's *Fifth Symphony*. Its burdened title character meets a host of allegorical figures on his journey, faces tests including a fight for his soul, and ultimately wins redemption, gaining entrance to the Celestial City.

VELLUTI, GIOVANNI BATTISTA. (1780, Montolmo–1861, Venice.) Italian **soprano** and last of the star operatic **castratos**. Velluti trained in Bologna and Ravenna and debuted in nearby Forlì (1801). His career centered on heroic male soprano roles in operas of the era of **Domenico Cimarosa**, **Simon Mayr**, and **Gioachino Rossini**, including the premier of Rossini's *Aureliano in Palmira* (1813). Velluti is famous for having created the part of Armando in **Giacomo Meyerbeer**'s *Il crociato in Egitto* (1824), the last significant opera to include a castrato role. He retired from the stage after appearing in a revival of Giuseppe Nicolini's (1762–1842) *Il conte di Lennox* in Venice (1830).

VENICE. Northeastern Italian coastal city. Venice led the development of operatic style during the second half of the 17th century, pioneered the system of public opera given in regularly scheduled **seasons**, and remained a rival to the dominance of **Naples** throughout most of the 18th century. Long-standing theatrical precedents for opera included private spectacles, the **commedia dell'arte**, elaborate civic rituals, and even isolated operatic palace entertainments such as **Claudio Monteverdi**'s *Combattimento di Tancredi e Clorinda* (1624 or 1625) and *Proserpina rapita* (1630). However, the lack of a centralized court and a focus on music connected with St. Mark's Basilica meant that the new art form, like the commedia dell'arte, would depend on sales of tickets to moneyed Venetians and foreign tourists rather than state subsidies, and the first **composers**, such as Monteverdi and **Francesco Cavalli**, were *maestri di cappella* and organists who moonlighted as opera composers. This commercialization was engineered by **impresarios**, many of them **librettists**, who put opera on a predictable calendar of productions staged by a pool of competing theaters, developed a plot-driven style that appealed to a broad audience (*see L'INCORONAZIONE DI POPPEA* and *GIASONE*), and initiated the cult of star singers performing virtuoso **bel canto arias**.

As early as the 1640s Venice had four opera theaters, and in its heyday from the 1670s through the 18th century boasted as many as half a dozen companies offering operas. The Teatro San Cassiano opened in 1637 (closed 1804) as the first opera house for a paying public with **Francesco Manelli** and Benedetto Ferrari's (after 1603–1681) *Andromeda* (1637), premiered Claudio Monteverdi's *Il ritorno d'Ulisse in patria* (1639), and was the venue most associated with Francesco Cavalli in the 1640s. The Teatro Santi Giovanni e Paolo was remodeled to stage operas in 1639 (closed 1699) by the Grimani family, beginning their extended involvement with Venetian opera. It held pride of place as the most active and highly regarded theater during this decade, staging *L'incoronazione di Poppea* in 1642–43. In 1640, Ferrari's company moved to the new Teatro San Moisè (closed 1818), which was joined by the short-lived, aristocratic Teatro Novissimo in 1641 (closed 1647), distinguished by the revolutionary stagecraft of **Giacomo Torelli** and the Venetian debut of the singer **Anna Renzi**.

Waning interest in the 1650s and 1660s was addressed through drastic reductions in ticket prices, resulting in a boom of activity beginning in the 1670s and the construction of new theaters. The most magnificent, the Teatro San Giovanni Grisostomo, was opened in 1678 by the Grimani family (renamed for **Maria Malibran** in 1834, converted to a movie house by the 1920s). At this point Venice's largest and most glamorous theater, its elevated repertory, lavish scenery and special effects, and parade of celebrity singers entertained an elite clientele of local and foreign luminaries. The San Salvatore, noted for its fine company, premiered numerous operas of **Giovanni Legrenzi** in the 1670s and 1680s. **Antonio Vivaldi** was associated with the rival Teatro Sant' Angelo (opened 1677, closed 1803) as well as the established San Moisè.

The advent of the **intermezzo** in the first decade of the 18th century and the rise of **opera buffa** in Venice in the 1740s encouraged both old and new theaters to cultivate specialties. The existing San Cassiano and Sant' Angelo were most associated with the early development of the intermezzo as entr'acte entertainment for serious opera. The San Samuele, which the Grimani had opened in 1710 (burned and rebuilt in 1747, renamed the Camploy in the second half of the 19th century and repurposed for nonoperatic entertainment, closed 1894) devoted itself to establishing opera buffa in the 1750s, alongside the San Moisè. The Grimani also constructed the San Benedetto in the 1750s (burned and rebuilt 1774, renamed the Gallo in the 1820s and the Rossini in 1868, converted to a movie theater in 1937), which served as the leading theater for **opera seria** until the end of the century. This segregation of purpose is demonstrated by **Baldassare Galuppi**'s devotion to the San Moisè and San Samuele for his comic works, to other theaters for serious ones. After the Teatro La Fenice opened in 1792 (burned and rebuilt 1836–37, burned 1996 and rebuilt 2001–03), it usurped the preeminence of the San Benedetto and became the premier Venetian venue in the 19th century, introducing such masterworks of **Gioachino Rossini** and **Giuseppe Verdi** as *Semiramide* and *Rigoletto*, and as part of the theater's resurgence after World War II, **Igor Stravinsky**'s *The Rake's Progress* and **Benjamin Britten**'s *The Turn of the Screw* (1954).

Venice's four *ospedali* (orphanage **conservatories** for girls)—the Incurabili, bankrupted in 1776, followed shortly by the Mendicanti and Ospedaletto, and the Pietà, which survived into the 1800s—reached their apex in the early 18th century. Because they trained girls, whose professional opportunities were limited and whose involvement with the theater was discouraged, the ospedali claimed no first-rank composers and had a considerably lower profile in the operatic world than their Neapolitan counterparts. Nonetheless, along with hordes of choir singers and string players, they also produced virtuoso vocal soloists, a number of whom had opera careers (e.g., **Faustina Bordoni**).

VERAZI, MATTIA. (ca. 1730, probably Rome–1794, Munich.) Italian **librettist** and a leader of the mid-18th-century movement directed at fusing Italian and French characteristics in **opera seria**, pushing it in the direction of 19th-century *melodramma*. His operas *Enea nel Lazio* and *Pelope* with **Niccolò Jommelli** for Stuttgart (1755) anticipate by several years reform works by **Tommaso Traetta** and **Christoph Willibald Gluck**.

Verazi served in Mannheim for most of his career (1756–78) as court poet and secretary to the Elector and Duke of Bavaria Karl Theodor. From this base he wrote mainly for the progressive theaters there and in nearby Stuttgart and Ludwigsburg. He collaborated with Jommelli on seven operas from *Ifigenia in Aulide* (1751) to *Ifigenia in Tauride* (1771), including Jommelli's most innovative work, *Fetonte* (1768), and with Traetta, Johann Christian Bach (1735–1782), and others. Verazi's most forward-looking **librettos** present dark, horrific situations that sometimes involve deaths onstage, challenging **Arcadian pastoralism**. In various operas he simplified and tightened the plot, departed from set piece conventions by reducing the number of exit **arias** and bringing secondary characters into set pieces, and created climactic act endings involving ensemble **finales** and **scene** complexes that combine short arias with dramatically significant **choruses**, **ballets**, and spectacular effects.

VERDI, GIUSEPPE. (1813, Roncole near Busseto–1901, Milan.) Along with **Gioachino Rossini** the foremost Italian opera **composer** of the 19th century. Many of Verdi's 28 operas (1839–93) have long served as mainstays of the repertory, and he remains the most dominant presence on modern stages.

Born in a small town northwest of Parma to a lower-middle-class family, Verdi was trained by local clergy and was serving as the organist at a local church by 1822. He was sent to Busseto in 1823, where he received musical instruction from the church organist and composer Ferdinando Provesi (1770–1833), who directed the town music school, along with a classical education, and composed frequently for church services and other local events. In 1831, Verdi moved in with the businessman Antonio Barezzi, an avid musician who supported his career, and fell in love with his daughter Margherita. Barezzi paid for Verdi to travel to Milan in 1832, where he applied unsuccessfully for admission to the **conservatory**, his rejection attributed to his nonresidency in Lombardy, advanced age (18), and unconventional keyboard technique. Subsequently he studied counterpoint and free composition privately (1832–35) with the composer Vincenzo Lavigna (1776–1836), frequented the opera, made social contacts, and participated in various musical events, including his co-direction with Pietro Massini of a performance of Rossini's *La Cenerentola* (originally 1817).

Unable to make further inroads in Milan, Verdi returned to Busseto as director of the Philharmonic Society (1836) and married Margherita. He composed his first opera, *Oberto, conte di San Bonifacio* in Busseto and (probably through Massini's intervention) had it staged at La Scala, moving to Milan in 1839 prior to the premier. *Oberto*'s modest success won a contract for three more Milanese operas. The *melodramma giocoso* (*see* OPERA BUFFA) *Un giorno di regno* (1840) flopped owing to a poor production and ended after the first night. This professional setback, coupled with the recent deaths of his wife and two children, led Verdi to withdraw temporarily from the theater, apart from participating in revivals of *Oberto*. When he resumed activity after an 18-month hiatus with *Nabucco* in 1842, its unequivocal triumph established Verdi as the premier prospect of his generation.

During the ensuing decade (1843–53), Verdi settled into a businesslike, yet taxing cycle of negotiating contracts with theater managers, arranging for effective casts, choosing subjects with those casts in mind, devising **librettos** in collaboration with his **librettists**, composing scores, and supervising rehearsals and productions. He traveled constantly among the major Italian centers (Milan, Venice, **Rome**, **Naples**, Florence, and Trieste) and to **London** (1847) and **Paris** (1847–49) for revivals as well as premiers, frequently adapting scores to fit new performers. This unremitting cycle of work, which he would later deem his years as a galley slave, resulted in 16 operas on librettos by **Francesco Maria Piave**, Salvatore Cammarano (1801–1852), and others from *I Lombardi all prima crociata* (1843, the third opera of the La Scala contract) to *La traviata* (1853), as many as three per year (*Macbeth*, *I masnadieri*, and *Jérusalem*, the Parisian revision of *I Lombardi*, in 1847). These included several of his most enduring works (in addition to *Macbeth* and *La traviata*): *Ernani* (1844), *Luisa Miller* (1849), **Rigoletto**, and *Il trovatore* (1853).

By the mid-1850s, Verdi had eclipsed Rossini and **Gaetano Donizetti** as the most familiar and lauded Italian opera composer in the world. A celebrity and popular icon, darling of the Milanese salons, he could now pick and choose his opportunities, turn down unwanted commissions, and exert greater control over aspects of his librettos, from their subject matter to choices of poetic meters for individual set pieces and the distribution of those set pieces among singers, allowing their arrangement to be determined by dramatic circumstances. Now earning unprecedented commissions, his growing wealth enabled him to rein in the frenetic pace, which had taken its toll on his health during the mid-1840s, and to buy his family's ancestral farm, Sant' Agata near Busseto (1848), which he extensively expanded in the 1850s and 1860s. During the 1840s he began his decades-long relationship with the **soprano** Giuseppina Strepponi (1815–1897), who had created Abigaille in *Nabucco* and was close to her early retirement in 1846. After living together while in Paris, they returned (unmarried) to Bussetto in 1849 to the disapproval of local busybodies and soon fled to Sant' Agata (1851). Verdi married Strepponi in 1859.

With the exception of 1857, which produced the original *Simon Boccanegra* and the adaptation of *Stiffelio* (1850) as *Aroldo*, he composed only a single opera every two to five years, totaling seven between *Les vêpres siciliennes* (1855) and *Aida* (1871), and including *Un ballo in maschera* (1859), *La forza del destino* (1862), and *Don Carlos* (1867). Now less profuse, his premiers became blockbuster events that generated international interest. Moreover, by the 1860s Verdi was viewed not only as an artistic icon, but also as a figurehead for the Risorgimento and Italy's struggle for national sovereignty, his name serving as a patriotic acrostic (the slogan "Viva VERDI" abbreviating "Viva Vittorio Emanuele Re D'Italia"). He served (1861–65) as a deputy to the first Italian parliament during the process of Italian emancipation and unification. At the same time, however, he was targeted in the 1860s and 1870s as an uncomprehending whipping boy for the avant-garde **scapigliati**, to whom he symbolized a bourgeois artistic inertia that prevented Italy from embracing progress represented by composers such as **Richard Wagner** and **Jules Massenet**.

Independently wealthy and disillusioned by this perceived lack of appreciation and respect, he retreated to his farm and a self-constructed rustic myth of peasant roots and unsophisticated anti-cosmopolitanism. Apart from the String Quartet (1873), the Requiem Mass (1874)—the latter, to be sure, an astounding accomplishment that took him on a tour of Paris, London, and **Vienna** in 1875—and minor works, as well as revisions of *Simon Boccanegra* (1881) and *Don Carlos* (1884), he withdrew into retirement and produced no new operas until *Otello* in 1887, which had proceeded sporadically after Giulio **Ricordi** and **Arrigo Boito** broached the subject in 1879. Verdi began work on his final opera, *Falstaff* (1893), adapted primarily from William Shakespeare's *The Merry Wives of Windsor*, in 1889, again at Boito's suggestion. Other than these projects, he tended his farm and spearheaded two charitable initiatives, a hospital in Villanova sull'Arda near Sant' Agata and the Casa di Riposo retirement home for musicians in Milan. He died following a stroke and was commemorated by a Milanese funeral procession that numbered hundreds of thousands of devoted followers.

Verdi's operas adapt, enrich, and humanize Rossini's grand heroic style, Donizetti's drama of interpersonal conflict, and formal experiments by **Saverio Mercadante** and others, and synthesize contributions from French opera, to enhance naturalness, audience immersion, and catharsis. Despite protests that he would prefer to write continuous operas, a sentiment evident in early efforts such as Act 3 of *Ernani*, Verdi wrote **number operas** through *Aida*, the conventional forms of the grand **aria**, **duet**, *introduzione*, and **finale** providing the starting points for his set pieces. Yet adaptations of these schemata begin as early as *Nabucco*. They include increasing reliance on single-movement arias, many of them stage songs within ensembles; abbreviation and elimination of **cabalettas** and **strettas**; and development of stylistic variants of those movements that emphasize lyricism and passion rather than virtuosity. Moreover, Verdi and his librettists gradually eroded the traditional alternation of action and reflection within different strata of dramatic time (*see* METASTASIO, PIETRO) through expansion and emphasis of spontaneous lyricism in the action-oriented movements of those forms (the *tempo d'attacco* and *tempo di mezzo*); through more convincing motivation of lyrical movements (the slow movement/*largo concertato* and cabaletta/stretta)—in part through their introduction by a *parola scenica* (an incisive word or phrase emphasized by music, which encapsulates a dramatic turning point that invites prolonged reaction); and through integration of those movements into the narrative of foreground events.

Verdi's melodic style has been deemed populist, hit tunes like "La donna è mobile" (*Rigoletto*, Act 3) bearing out that assessment, and through midcareer he tended to treat the punctuation of the **lyric prototype** in two-, four-, and eight-measure subdivisions more predictably than his predecessors. Yet, at the same time, he frequently modified the arrangement and number of phrases across the form to produce melodies that were less predictable in their expressive profiles and responsive to what characters have on their minds. The result was both expansive melodies that could encompass multiple phases of dramatic expression (Violetta's "Ah! fors'è lui," *La traviata*, Act 1) and abbreviated versions of the lyric prototype that are incorporated within broader designs (Radames, "Celeste Aida," *Aida*, Act 1). By the 1850s, Verdi had largely fulfilled the trend toward marginalizing **coloratura**, tending to confine **ornamentation** to brief punctuation points at the ends of phrases. And as his career proceeded he increasingly sought from his librettists longer and more varied poetic lines—even passages of *versi sciolti* (*see* VERSIFICATION) within lyric set pieces—that would facilitate less rigidly metrical phrasing.

After adhering in the 1840s, for the most part, to the long-standing *convenienze* (customs) for assigning singers' workloads—a sizable entrance aria for each of the principals and their participation in a proportional number of duets and other ensembles—Verdi began to diverge from these requirements as his status increased and he became empowered to impose his artistic will, while still remaining sensitive to the strengths and limitations of his singers. In *Rigoletto*, for example, the title character's first solo is a **recitative** scena (*see* SCENE), following his initial appearance in the ensemble *introduzione*, and his only aria comes in Act 2; Gilda's one-movement aria (her only solo scene in the opera) follows her duet with him; and the Duke's one-movement *sortita* occurs within the *introduzione*. Verdi's reinforcement of the ongoing trend toward throwing more emphasis on duets and other ensembles (e.g., the duets in Act 1 of *Rigoletto*) and of the trend toward giving greater dramatic and musical presence to the **chorus** in arias, ensembles, and freestanding set pieces (for example, Verdi's popularization of the unison chorus that represents an assembled people, such as the Israelites in *Nabucco*) both contributed to and benefited from this realignment of singers' and audiences' expectations.

Verdi's preeminence also allowed him to choose subjects endowed with distinctive roles, locales, historical backgrounds, or literary associations, and to press his librettists to emphasize each work's uniqueness through evocative poetic imagery and wording and through idiosyncratic character development. For his part he created a characteristic musical *tinta* or *tinte* ("color"/ "colors") by manipulating both broad features, such as the forms of scenes and individual melodies (for example the adaptations of the lyric prototype noted above) and styles of vocal writing, and more localized ones such as specific melodic, rhythmic, or harmonic gestures, vocal tessituras, and even prominent single pitches. Verdi's preoccupation with individualizing his operas is noted in his three warhorses of the 1850s, in which his music differentiates the crass amorality of *Rigoletto*, the more glamorous decadence of *La traviata*, and the Gothic chiaroscuro of *Il trovatore*, as well as in the Middle Eastern idioms of *Aida* and the nautical references in *Simon Boccanegra*.

Verdi at times reinforced the internal coherence provided by a work's *tinta* with constellations of recurring melodic motifs and related keys. Electrifying reprises of climactic melodic phrases appear famously in the last acts of *Ernani*, *La traviata*, and *Otello*. And more broad-based melodic networking connected to particular characters and their attributes, launched in *I due foscari* (1844) and probably drawing on French practices, occurs famously in the dirge motif signifying Monterrone's curse in *Rigoletto*, the "fate" theme in *La forza del destino*, and motifs associated with Aida, Amneris, and the Priests. And evidence has been advanced to suggest Verdi's possible engagement with long-range tonal planning beginning in the 1850s, involving various relationships such as the use of tonal mobility in set pieces to reflect progressing action or psychology; associations among individual keys, constellations of keys, or recurring progressions and characters, groups, or subplots; and even long-range tonal progressions supporting phases of action or plotlines.

In conjunction with his prolonged exposure to French opera in the late 1840s, Verdi and his librettists infused his operas with French-inspired elements beginning with strophic arias (with or without short refrains at the end of each stanza) in *Il corsaro* (1848) and *La battaglia di Legnano* (1849). Various features contribute to the equivalent of French *actualité* and *lisibilité* ("reality" and "legibility"; *see* GRAND OPÉRA): local color and distinctive ambiance (e.g., the party scenes in *Rigoletto* and *La traviata*) created in part through colloquial dialogue and dance; increased definition of atmosphere or character through idiosyncratic orchestration (Rigoletto's Act 1 monologue and the Act 3 storm); unconventional scene structures determined by the action (the abduction in Rigoletto, Act 1, which replaces the standard central finale); deflecting melodies that incorporate declamation and arioso phrases and mirror the immediate psychology of the character singing (Desdemona's "Willow Song," *Otello*, Act 3); and local chromaticism, non-major/minor modalities, and distant key relationships within functional harmonic outlines (particularly beginning with *Aida*). Inclusion of the comic and the grotesque as a foil to tragedy (the witches in *Macbeth*, the character of Rigoletto, banter in the crowd scenes in *La traviata*, *Un ballo in maschera*, and *La forza del destino*) reflects the presence of elements of **opéra comique** in *grand opéra*. Verdi's forays into the latter genre—as well as his adaptations of its style for Italian works—at times produced expansive, sometimes politically charged panoramas against which the exploration of personal relationships unfolds, as in *Les vêpres siciliennes*, *La forza del destino*, *Don Carlos*, and *Aida*, in which a synthetic style mediates between French pomp and Italianate lyricism and intimacy.

VERISMO. Term meaning "realism" or, more literally, "truthfulness." It first appeared in the 1860s in connection with the visual arts, then referred to a type of literary realism espoused by the Italian writers Luigi Capuana (1839–1915) and Giovanni Verga (1840–1922) in the 1870s and 1880s and was applied to prose literature, drama, and poetry during that period. Verismo enacted a post-*scapigliatura* renewal of Italian culture by attempting to depict life as it is through a quasi-objective portrayal of nonidealized characters and their environments. It acknowledged regional idiosyncrasies and the pervasiveness of poverty, violence, failure, despair, and ordinariness while avoiding the distortion and distance created by artistic conventions.

The term was initially attached to a new type of Italian opera beginning with *Cavalleria rusticana* (1890), based on a play by Verga, and was popularized as an operatic term subject to varying interpretations in the early 20th century. In addition to *Cavalleria*, prominent examples of verismo opera include *Pagliacci* and **Giacomo Puccini**'s operas to varying degrees and in different ways (e.g., *La bohème* and *Tosca*). Almost immediately the style spread outside Italy, for example in **Jules Massenet**'s *La Navarraise* (1894) and Ermanno Wolf-Ferrari's (1876–1948) *I gioielli della Madonna* (1911). Beginning in the 1920s, Italian film superseded verismo opera and appropriated many of its characteristics.

The verismo style in opera may be viewed as an extension of characteristics apparent in such antecedents as **Giuseppe Verdi**'s middle and late operas (for example, *Rigoletto*; *La traviata*, 1853; and *Otello*); Italian operas by other composers after *Aida* (**Amilcare Ponchielli**'s *La Gioconda*, 1876); and French **opéra comique** and *opéra lyrique*, which were translated and revived in Italy from the 1860s through the 1880s, among which **Georges Bizet**'s *Carmen* (1875) was a critical influence. From these prototypes, **librettists** and **composers** developed the mundane, psychologically individualized, often disreputable characters who succumb to decadent, base impulses in commonplace locales and enact themes of powerlessness, futility, and doomed love capped by unceremonious deaths that horrify audiences and beg for empathy.

Numerous stylistic features enhance intensity and immediacy. Stark contrasts between intimate tenderness and graphic violence played out across compressed time frames exaggerate the shock value of the coups de théâtre popularized in 19th-century *melodramma*, serving the ultimate goal of emotional catharsis. Verismo librettists reduced the artificiality of their language by employing irregular poetic meters centered on *versi sciolti* (*see* VERSIFICATION) and nonsymmetrical stanzas while avoiding archaic, idealized wordings and metaphors. At their best, verismo **productions** heightened realism and immersion by giving increased attention to the visual aspects of production. They adopted a more spontaneous, physical, and psychologically communicative style of acting and a more naturalistic style of singing that at times sacrificed vocal beauty for frank communication of crude passion, developed authentic **sets** and costumes that served the depiction of poverty and other previously marginalized social conditions, and experimented with evocative lighting and other effects.

In music, characteristic, recurring orchestral motives that chatter underneath *parlante* dialogues, particularly in Puccini's operas, contribute to the sense of place that is critical to verismo. He and others cultivated expressively intense **arioso** and declamatory singing devoid of **coloratura** to create unconventionally structured, emotionally impetuous melodies, which spawn the incandescent phrases reprised in the orchestra at moments of crisis or resolution. They also assimilated the fin-de-siècle chromatic, pentatonic, and modal palette, as well as nonfunctional chord juxtapositions and abrupt tonal digressions. The scarcity of self-contained, formal **arias**, which are mostly displaced by interactive **duets** and ensembles, rationalized as **stage songs**, or carried within the psychological flow of their situations, and the abandonment of mid-19th-century **scene** forms contribute to the accelerated pacing, continuity, naturalness, and unconventionality intrinsic to the verismo style.

See also GIORDANO, UMBERTO; GIOVANE SCUOLA; ILLICA, LUIGI, AND GIUSEPPE GIACOSA; LEONCAVALLO, RUGGERO; MASCAGNI, PIETRO; SHOSTAKOVICH, DMITRY; ZARZUELA.

VERSIFICATION. From the 17th century through much of the 19th, poetic conventions for the **libretto** were dominated by the Italian and French traditions, the Italian being more standardized. Italian poetic meters are designated by the number of syllables in a standard (*piano*) line, which ends with an accent followed by a non-accent. Syllables are counted through the non-accent, whether or not a given line actually lacks the final non-accent (*tronco*, "truncated" lines) or includes an additional one (*sdrucciolo*, "slippery" lines). Through the mid-19th century, Italian librettos distinguish *versi sciolti* ("**recitative** verse") used for the scena that begins each small **scene** from *versi lirici* ("lyric verse") for set pieces such as **arias**, **duets**, and ensembles (e.g., **finales**). Whereas recitative verse is characterized by free alternation between 11- and 7- syllable lines, flexibly arranged and intermittent rhymes, and absence of defined stanzas, lyric verse has lines of consistent length (mostly from 5 to 10 syllables), regularly and often conventionally patterned rhymes, and clear stanzaic divisions.

After recitative verse dominated the earliest operas, reflecting the aesthetic importance of the *stile rappresentativo*, lyric verse gained importance in conjunction with the rise of the aria in the mid-17th century. The standard small scene, institutionalized by the **Arcadian Academy** and **Pietro Metastasio** in the 18th century and maintained as a norm through the mid-19th century, consists of a scena in recitative verse followed by two or more stanzas of lyric verse for an aria or other lyric set piece. Only in the late 19th century, under the influence of the **Scapigliati** and a propensity for naturalness, did this habitual segregation of poetic and musical categories diminish in the operas of **Arrigo Boito, Giuseppe Verdi, Giacomo Puccini**, and others.

In contrast to the conventionality of their Italian counterparts, French librettos adopted a style of *vers libres* ("free verse") which mixes 12-syllable alexandrines with lines of 8, 10, or other numbers of syllables. Syllable count also differs in French poetry: syllables are counted through the final accent, and the count ignores the final mute *e* if one occurs. Librettos are rhymed throughout using traditional patterns that alternate strong (without the mute *e*) and weak (with the mute *e*) line endings. And they make no hard-and-fast distinction between poetry for recitatives versus **airs**. These practices remained in effect from the earliest *tragédies en musiques* of **Philippe Quinault** and **Jean-Baptiste Lully** in the 1670s through **Eugène Scribe**'s librettos for **grands opéras** of the mid-19th century, until greater liberties were introduced by the **symbolist** poets in the 1880s.

No comparable system of universal conventions developed in Germany, owing mainly to the late development of native German opera, the use of prose for spoken dialogue in **singspiel**, and the consequent delayed adoption of recitative for 19th-century German grand opera. This absence of institutionalized norms is reflected in the free treatment of line length, accentuation, rhyme, and stanzaic structure in **Richard Wagner**'s poetry for even his earliest operas and his idiosyncratic adoption of *Stabreim* as a prominent poetic device in *Der Ring des Nibelungen*.

VIARDOT, PAULINE. (1821, Paris–1910, Paris.) French mezzo-**soprano**, pianist, **composer**, and teacher born Pauline García to a musical family of Spanish origin that included the singer **Maria Malibran**, her older sister. Trained by her parents, she made her debut as a concert singer in 1837 and her opera debut in 1839 in the role of Desdemona in **Gioachino Rossini**'s *Otello* (originally 1816). She married the writer and director of the **Paris** Théâtre Italien, Louis Viardot (1800–1883), in 1840. Possessed of countless male admirers, while located in St. Petersburg (1843–46) she entranced the novelist Ivan Turgenev, beginning a (probably platonic) companionship that lasted the rest of her life.

Viardot commanded a three-octave range and tremendous musical versatility, and her passionate acting was lauded by a host of composers including **Giacomo Meyerbeer, Hector Berlioz, Richard Wagner**, and **Camille Saint-Saëns**. She won her greatest acclaim for the lead in **Christoph Willi-**

bald Gluck's *Orphée et Eurydice* (originally 1774, *see ORFEO ED EURI-DICE*), adapted for her by Berlioz, and for the role of Fidès in Meyerbeer's *Le prophète* (1849). In 1863 she retired as an opera singer and relocated in Baden-Baden, eventually returning to Paris via **London** (1871). An accomplished composer, Viardot wrote eight **operettas** and other stage works (three on Turgenev librettos), one of which was performed in Weimar in 1869 (*Le dernier sorcier*). She also composed over 100 songs, as well as vocal arrangements of piano music by Fryderyk Chopin (1810–1849), **Franz Schubert**, and Johannes Brahms (1833–1897).

VIENNA. Capital of Austria and, previously, the Holy Roman Empire and Austro-Hungarian Empire. An operatic city since the 17th century and a unique stylistic crossroads that intertwined French, Italian, and German culture, Vienna became a hotbed of innovation in both serious and comic opera (particularly **opera buffa**) in the second half of the 18th century. It remains one of the major world centers for repertory opera.

Opera had appeared in Austria as early as a performance of an *Orfeo*, likely **Claudio Monteverdi**'s, in 1619 (originally 1607) with the emperor in attendance, which was followed in 1627 by the first true operatic performance at the imperial court (in Prague, *Calisto e Arcade*, 1627, composer unknown). Subsequent operas were mounted sporadically for special events, productions occurring with increasing regularity under Emperor Leopold I (ruled 1658–1705). They were presented as private aristocratic entertainments in rooms of the imperial palace in Vienna (the Hofburg), particularly its ballroom (Tanzsaal; built 1630, remodeled as a theater 1658, 1666, and 1698–1700; in use for operas and plays until 1744 as the Teatro Grande) and at other residences. Vienna's earliest permanent theater designed for opera, the Hoftheater auf der Cortina (Court Theater at the City Wall), was constructed (1666–67) for **Antonio Cesti**'s extravagant *Il pomo d'oro* in celebration of the emperor's wedding, but remained active only to 1679 and was destroyed during the Turkish siege of 1683. Opera was introduced to the general public by the Kärntnertortheater (Carinthian Gate Theater), intended originally as a nonimperial, public theater (built 1709, burned 1761; rebuilt as the Kaiserlishes und Königliches Hoftheater zu Wien; torn down 1870) that presented modified Italian operas (beginning 1728) and German-language light spoken plays, some including music (after ca. 1750).

Following almost a decade spent consolidating her political power, Empress Maria Theresa (reigned 1740–65) inaugurated the golden age of Viennese opera after remodeling the Burgtheater in 1748 as her palace theater (originally an enclosed tennis court converted to a theater in 1741; renamed the German Nationaltheater, 1776; renamed the Kaiserlich-Königliches Hoftheater nächst der Burg, 1794; no longer used by the court opera after 1810; demolished in 1888 after a new theater was built on the Ringstrasse). It opened with **Christoph Willibald Gluck**'s *Semiramide riconosciuta* (1748) and hosted Italian **opera seria**, until the empress imported a French troupe (1752 to 1765), which performed spoken plays and arrangements (often by Gluck) of **opéras comiques** under the innovative Francophile manager **Giacomo Durazzo**. Italian opera returned in the 1760s, which saw a number of *feste teatrali* and opere serie by **Johann Adolf Hasse** on **librettos** by **Pietro Metastasio**, who had been court poet since 1729, beginning with *Alcide al bivio* (1760) for Archduke Joseph's first wedding. *Alcide* initiated the Viennese reform movement represented more prominently by Gluck's operas with **Ranieri Calzabigi**, who had arrived in 1761: *Orfeo ed Euridice*, *Alceste*, and *Paride ed Elena* (1770).

The death of Maria's husband, Emperor Francis I (ruled 1745–65), and Joseph's accession (ruled 1765–90) resulted in eliminating the French company and closing theaters while his mother mourned. By the 1770s the Viennese stage was increasingly devoted to **ballet** and to opera buffa, a state of affairs reversed in 1776 by Joseph's establishment of a German national spoken-theater company at the Burgtheater and, beginning in 1778, the National-Singspiel at the same theater. Unfortunately the **singspiels** that resulted suffered by comparison with the more familiar and glamorous Italian and French repertory, a notable exception being **Wolfgang Amadeus Mozart**'s *Die Entführung aus dem Serail* (1782). In addition to promoting singspiel, Joseph made the Burgtheater available (on open nights), as well as the Kärntnertortheater and other houses, to alternative companies, rescinding a court monopoly on theater that had been imposed by Maria Theresa in 1752. This new policy resulted in the construction of numerous suburban theaters, among them the Theater in der Leopoldstadt, home to Wenzel Müller's (1759–1835) singspiels (opened 1781; demolished and rebuilt 1847 as the Carltheater, which would feature **operettas**; closed 1929); the Theater auf der Wieden, where *Die Zauberflöte* premiered (active 1787–1801); and the Theater an der Wien, which replaced it in 1801 (still active), where *Fidelio* premiered.

In 1783 a disappointed Joseph reestablished opera buffa at the Burgtheater, hiring the **librettist Lorenzo Da Ponte** to collaborate with court composer **Antonio Salieri** and others including Mozart and creating what was considered by some to be the best comic troupe in Europe. Unable to forego his earlier commitment to German opera, he subsequently reinstated singspiel as the Deutsche Opéra Comique at the Kärntnertortheater (1785–88). This initiative was more successful artistically than the first—owing largely to the successes of **Carl Ditters von Dittersdorf**—but it fell victim to the financial realities of the Austro-Turkish War (1787–91) and other factors.

Following the war, Joseph's brother and successor Leopold II reopened the Kärntnertortheater, which had temporarily closed after the singspiel left (1788–91), primarily for ballet and opera seria, staging opera buffa for financial support. From Leopold's reign (1790–92) to the Revolutions of 1830, the Hofoper—at both the Burgtheater (until 1810) and Kärntnertortheater—produced little notable native opera, focusing instead on repertory operas and Italian and French imports, most prominently the premier of **Domenico Cimarosa**'s *Il matrimonio segreto* (1792). Its repertory in the early 19th century was dominated by **Gioachino Rossini**'s operas in the 1810s and 1820s (initially with *L'inganno felice* in 1816, originally 1812) and works by **Luigi Cherubini** and **Gaspare Spontini**, and later by those of **Gaetano Donizetti** and **Vincenzo Bellini**. Although beginning in the 1830s the Hofoper at the Kärntnertortheater was mainly leased to Italian **impresarios** who put on Italian **seasons** (*stagioni*) through the end of the century, **Richard Wagner**'s operas came to Vienna starting with *Lohengrin* in 1858 (originally 1850).

As part of the development of the Ringstrasse (beginning 1857), Vienna built a magnificent new opera house, the Kaiserlich-Königliches Hofoperntheater, now the Vienna State Opera (constructed 1861–69; renamed the Staatsoper after World War I; bombed 1945; reconstructed 1946–55), which saw productions of *Aida* conducted by **Giuseppe Verdi** (1875, originally 1871) and a complete performance of the *Ring des Nibelungen* in 1879 (originally 1876). Beginning at the turn of the century, the Hofoper was led by an extraordinary series of directors that included Gustav Mahler (1897–1907), Felix Weingartner (1908–11), **Richard Strauss** (1919–24), Karl Böhm (1943–45 and 1954–56), and Herbert von Karajan (1956–64). The Theater an der Wien continued to field operas in the 19th century, turning to operettas by **Jacques Offenbach**, Johann Strauss the younger (1825–1899), and others as its bread and butter by the mid-1860s. The Volksoper (after 1938 the Städtische Volksoper) opened in 1898 for spoken plays, but evolved into a less expensive operatic alternative to the Hofoper. Not subject to the same restrictions of subject matter, it was able to produce works like *Tosca* and *Salome* that were edgy for their day. The Staatsoper and Volksoper (specializing in lighter fare) remain the two principal companies in Vienna, accompanied since 2006 by the Theater an der Wien.

VINCI, LEONARDO. (ca. 1696, Strongoli–1730, Naples.) The most influential opera **composer** of the 1720s. A product of **Naples**' orphanage **conservatory** system, Vinci dominated the Neapolitan comic theater from 1719 until the premier of his first *dramma per musica Publio Cornelio Scipione* in 1722, after which he composed **opera seria** for Naples, **Rome**, and to a lesser extent **Venice** and Parma almost exclusively, 20 in all during the eight years prior to his death. Beginning with *Didone abbandonata* and *Siroe re di Persia* (both 1726), he became **Pietro Metastasio**'s principal collaborator, setting six of his eight early **librettos** (five of them premiers) through *Alessandro nell' Indie* and *Artaserse* (both 1730). He was reportedly poisoned following a love affair.

Famed for his graceful, segmented melodies, Vinci was one of the originators and popularizers of the **galant** style, first in **opera buffa**, then in opera seria, which through his efforts became closely associated with the **Arcadian** reform movement. His works influenced younger composers such as **Giovanni Battista Pergolesi** (whom he taught) and **Johann Adolf Hasse**, as well as the late works of **Antonio Vivaldi** and **George Frideric Handel**.

VITTORI, LORETO. (1600, Spoleto–1670, Rome.) **Soprano** singer, **composer**, and poet. One of the earliest operatic **castratos**, Vittori was among the most renowned virtuosos during the heyday of Roman heroic sacred opera under the Barberini family. From his late teens, Vittori served a series of wealthy and powerful patrons: Bishop Maffeo Barberini (later Pope Urban VIII) in **Rome** ca. 1617; Cosimo II de' Medici in Florence, where he took a lead role in **Jacopo Peri** and Marco da Gagliano's (1582–1643) *Lo sposalizio di Medoro ed Angelica* (1619); and Cardinal Lodovico Ludovisi (nephew of Pope Gregory XV) in Rome (ca. 1621–32), where he sang in the papal choir from 1622 to 1647. Vittori's career illustrates the division of duties between church and theater that was typical of castratos during the early decades of opera. In 1642, a year before he was ordained as a priest, he took a lead role in a blockbuster production of Luigi Rossi's (ca. 1597–1653) *Il palazzo incantato* at the Barberini palace.

VIVALDI, ANTONIO. (1678, Venice–1741, Vienna.) Italian **composer** of instrumental music, sacred vocal music, and **opera seria**; violinist, teacher, and theatrical producer. He was active as an opera composer from the 1710s through the 1730s, when he wrote about 40 documented operas (more than 90 by his own account), the majority for **Venice**, and contributed to several **pasticcios**.

The son of a violinist at St. Mark's Basilica, who probably trained him, Vivaldi was ordained a priest in 1703 (although he almost immediately stopped leading Masses), an occupation that created friction concerning his theatrical activities. The same year he began teaching violin at the Pio Ospedale della Pietà, one of the four Venetian girls' orphanage **conservatories**. His first opera, the *dramma per musica Ottone in villa* premiered in Vicenza (1713). His Venetian debut occurred the next year with *Orlando finto pazzo* at the Teatro Sant' Angelo, which he managed with his father and where more than a third of his operas would be staged.

Leaves of absence from the conservatory over the next decades allowed him to travel widely and stage operas in Florence, Milan, **Rome**, Verona, **Vienna**, Prague (where he wrote or contributed to five works, 1730–32), and elsewhere. His appointment as *maestro di cappella da camera* to the governor of Mantua (1718–21) led (reportedly) to seven operatic productions. As opera director at the Sant' Angelo from 1726 to 1728, he began his scandalous relationship with the young mezzo-**soprano** Anna Girò (ca. 1710–after 1747), who sang approximately 30 of his productions. His affiliation with the Sant' Angelo had largely run its course with his setting of **Pietro Metastasio**'s *L'Olimpiade* (1734) as he lost popularity to composers writing in the more current *galant* style, including **Johann Adolf Hasse**. Bowing to fashion, some of his late scores are pasticcios mixing **arias** by these more current composers with his own. Failed negotiations with Ferrara (1736–39) resulted in performances in which his music was replaced by Hasse's, canceled productions, legal action, and Vivaldi's banishment from the city by the archbishop. The death of his supporter Charles VI in 1740 thwarted a last-ditch effort to establish himself in Vienna.

Vivaldi's operas were comparatively traditional three-act opere serie dominated by simple **recitatives** and da capo exit arias. He chose mostly old-fashioned **librettos**, although works by the **Arcadians** Silvio Stampiglia (1664–1725), **Apostolo Zeno**, and even Pietro Metastasio are represented, and in 1735 he collaborated on at least one opera with the young **Carlo Goldoni** (*Griselda*) and possibly a second. His scores benefitted from his experience as a composer of concertos: prior to the mid-1720s his orchestration is notable for its inclusion of obbligato wind, brass, and string parts, and he employed tone painting when suggested by poetic metaphor. By all accounts a flamboyant personality emblemized by his brilliant red hair (a family trait), Vivaldi's unconventional priestly behavior—his vanity, arrogance, materialism, and zest for life—both colored his music and brought him into frequent conflicts with the directors of the Pietà and other associates, sometimes limiting his professional opportunities.

WAGNER, RICHARD. (1813, Leipzig–1883, Venice.) Preeminent **composer** and **librettist** of 13 completed operas, the majority of them mainstays of the current repertory. Wagner pressed the campaign begun by **Carl Maria von Weber** and **Heinrich Marschner** to elevate German opera and became one of the most influential, controversial, and, alongside **Gioachino Rossini** and **Giuseppe Verdi**, prominent opera composers of the 19th century.

Wagner was adopted and raised by the actor and painter Ludwig Geyer (1779–1821), who may have been his biological parent, after his father of record (the bureaucrat Carl Friedrich Wagner, 1770–1813) died at the end of 1813. Educated in Dresden (beginning 1822) and Leipzig (beginning 1828), where he enrolled at the university in 1831, he studied music surreptitiously at first. His devotion to Ludwig van Beethoven (1770–1827) inspired the early C major symphony (1832). And his passion for the theater resulted in a grandiose tragic **libretto** or spoken play *Leubald* (1826–28) and two incomplete operas *Schäferoper* (*Pastoral Opera*, 1830) and *Die Hochzeit* (*The Wedding*, 1832–33), for which he began his lifelong practice of writing his own librettos.

Wagner spent the first decade and a half of his career as a journeyman moving frequently from city to city, often with debtors at his heels. His first job as director of the theater choir in Würzburg, northern Bavaria (1833–34), familiarized him with early 19th-century Italian, German, and French repertory including Rossini, Weber, and **Daniel-François-Esprit Auber** and prompted him to compose his first extant complete stage work, the magical **romantic** opera *Die Feen* (*The Fairies*, 1833–34), which was not produced until after his death. Wagner returned to Leipzig in 1834, where he joined the liberal and libertine movement Junges Deutschland ("Young Germany"), which opposed both classicism and trite romanticism and looked in opera to Italian **bel canto** and French **opéra comique** for inspiration. These influences are apparent in *Das Liebesverbot* (*The Ban on Love*, 1835–36), which transplants William Shakespeare's *Measure for Measure* to a rapturous Sicilian paradise.

Infatuated with the actress Minna Planer (1809–1866), whom he would marry in 1836, he became musical director of the troupe with which she performed (1834–36), developing skill as a **conductor** and suffering a disastrous premier of *Das Liebesverbot*. He followed Minna to Königsberg (then East Prussia, now Kaliningrad, Russian Federation), then took the position of music director at the theater in Riga, Latvia (1837). After abandoning a second comic opera (*see* CATEGORIES OF OPERA), he began *Rienzi, der Letzte der Tribunen* (*Rienzi, the Last of the Tribunes*) in the style of French **grand opéra**. In 14th-century Rome, the title character, a commoner who harnesses the city's amoral nobles, declines a call for his coronation and, serving as tribune to the Roman senate, overcomes intrigues by aristocrats and the pope until his capricious supporters finally expel him as they burn the city in revolt.

With uncertain job prospects and deeply in debt, he made a surreptitious exit on foot from Riga into Prussia in the middle of the night with Minna and their dog. There they boarded a ship headed for **London** (1839), surviving a stormy passage that Wagner later credited as inspiration for *Der fliegende Holländer* (*The Flying Dutchman*), then proceeded to **Paris**. During almost three years in the French capital (1839–42), he was unable to gain a foothold in Parisian society and secure a coveted production of *Rienzi* (completed 1840) despite **Giacomo Meyerbeer**'s acknowledged support, eking out a living by arranging excerpts from other composers' operas for publication and attacking the declining standards of the Opéra in published reviews while he composed *Holländer* (1840–41).

Again in debt and disgruntled by his lack of headway, he left Paris in 1842 after *Rienzi* was accepted for staging in Dresden. Its triumphant premier (1842) and *Holländer*'s less auspicious one (1843) gave Wagner a leg up for the position of second royal Kapellmeister (beginning 1843), which involved conducting the opera and orchestra and composing occasional music for the court. Between 1842 and 1848 he began contemplating the subjects for *Die Meistersinger* and *Parsifal* and completed *Tannhäuser* (1842–45) and *Lohengrin* (1845–48). The latter, a religious-chivalric epic, is set in the 10th-century Antwerp of King Henry the Fowler amidst an impending invasion, a disputed succession at the court of Brabant, and a confrontation between pagans and Christians. Lohengrin, a legendary Swan Knight and seeker of the Holy Grail, defends Elsa of Brabant against charges that she murdered her brother to claim his throne.

While in Dresden, Wagner again aligned himself with liberal politics, probably becoming acquainted with the communist and anarchist doctrines of Karl Marx, Friedrich Engels, and Mikhail Bakunin; supported the Paris and **Vienna** revolts of 1848; and joined the Dresden uprising of 1849. His contributions to the unrest included an agenda for democratically restructuring the court theater with an elected director and expanded **orchestra** and an inflammatory speech opposing capitalist materialism, forecasting the decline of absolutism, and supporting a constitutional monarchy. He incorporated related themes of social reform—for example, communal ownership of property, and society and religion based on compassion rather than law and dogma—into projects launched and scuttled such as the planned opera *Jesus von Nazareth* and his draft scenario and incipient libretto for **Der Ring des Nibelungen**.

Forced to flee when the army intervened to suppress the unrest, Wagner first took refuge with Franz Liszt (1811–1886) in Weimar, then immigrated to Switzerland (1849) where he was supported by wealthy expatriates and would remain in exile from Germany until 1860. While in Switzerland he began his authorship (which would continue into the 1880s) of voluminous prose essays on topics ranging from the history of humanity, government, and religion to psychology, animal rights, vegetarianism, and perceived shortcomings of Judaism. Postulating the decline of art since ancient Greece, he proposed its rebirth in a projected artwork of the future, which would reunite all media in a total work of art (*Gesamtkunstwerk*) combining poetry, singing, and instrumental music with dance, architecture, and painting in a communal religious-philosophical experience (*Das Kunstwerk der Zukunft*, 1849, and *Oper und Drama*, 1850–51). In this type of music drama, music would constitute an integral extension of poetry and visual elements, conveying content and coherence through a system of recurring associative **leitmotifs** devoted primarily to the orchestra; alliterative poetic **Stabreim** would evoke Germanic folk culture; and performers would show equal skill in singing, acting, and physical movement. Also during his Swiss sojourn, Wagner arranged the premier of *Lohengrin* in Weimar with Liszt conducting (1850), completed the libretto of the Ring (1852), printed and recited it for a private audience (1853), and performed concert excerpts of his music. By 1853 his endeavors were supported financially by the merchant Otto Wesendonck, who assumed his considerable debts (1854) in exchange for future royalties and provided accommodations. His new acquaintance with the philosophy of self-denial espoused by Arthur Schopenhauer, together with his apparently unfulfilled romance with Wesendonck's wife Mathilde, inspired *Tristan und Isolde* (begun 1857).

After a second foray in Paris (late 1859–61), which included a calamitous production of *Tannhäuser* revised for the Opéra (1861), and having been pardoned (1860) for his Dresden indiscretions, Wagner set himself up in Beibrich (Wiesbaden) where he began composing *Die Meistersinger von Nürnberg* in 1862 and separated from Minna. He relocated to Penzing, Austria, near Vienna, but again fell into debt and fled in 1864. Fortunately his luck would soon turn.

When he published his *Ring* librettos in 1863, he included an appeal for financial support, which elicited a windfall in 1864 from the newly crowned king of Bavaria, the eccentric youth Ludwig II. Seconding Wesendonck's prior patronage, Ludwig paid Wagner's remaining debts, provided a generous annual stipend and a comfortable house, bankrolled production of *Tristan* in Munich at the National Theater (1865), and eventually funded construction of the Bayreuth **Festival** Theater and the first two Bayreuth Festivals, in 1876 for the premier of the *Ring* and in 1882 for the premier of *Parsifal*. During this period Wagner began his affair with Liszt's daughter Cosima, who was unhappily married to the conductor Hans von Bülow (1830–1894), eventually divorced her husband, and married Wagner in 1870. (Minna had died in 1866.) Under pressure from his court, Ludwig dismissed Wagner from Munich at the end of 1865 but continued financial support for the rest of the composer's life. Wagner relocated to a house on Lake Lucerne in Switzerland.

Die Meistersinger premiered with Bülow conducting in Munich at the National Theater (1868) to tremendous acclaim, a much more positive reception than *Tristan* had received three years earlier. Like Verdi's *Falstaff* (1893), it is Wagner's only comedy as an established composer. Historically based on a guild of mastersingers—it includes Hans Sachs of Nuremberg (1494–1576)—and set in the picturesque narrow streets and half-timbered shops of the 16th-century Bavarian city, it may be read as an autobiographical allegory of Wagner's professed struggles against artistic orthodoxy, which dramatizes his program for revitalizing and purifying German culture proposed in the essays *Was ist deutsch?* (1865) and *Deutsche Kunst und deutsche Politik* (1867). Its hero Walter must become a mastersinger to win his beloved Eva but fails initially because his test song violates their rules. Under Sachs's mentoring he matures, adapting his genius to artistic realities, and the expressive fervor of his "Prize Song" overcomes aesthetic dogma.

Wagner relocated to Bayreuth to oversee construction of the festival theater (beginning 1872), built his permanent home of "Wahnfried," and settled there in 1874. The score of the *Ring* was completed in 1874, and three *Ring* cycles were given to mixed reviews in the first festival held in 1876. The second Bayreuth Festival (1882) was devoted to Wagner's final opera *Parsifal*, an allegorical amalgam of elements ranging from Christian imagery and ritual to Buddhist teachings and the writings of philosopher Arthur Schopenhauer concerning empathy and compassion, the polarity of chastity and sexuality, Aryan purification, and Wagner's conception of human regeneration through a natural lifestyle and worship of true Christianity. Sent on a quest by the Knights of the Grail, the pure fool Parsifal resists the blandishments of flower maidens and the seductress Kundry, who suffers eternal torment because she mocked Christ, and repels an attempt by her master Klingsor to kill him with the spear that afflicted Christ on the cross. Having learned compassion through his encounter with Kundry and subsequent wanderings, Parsifal returns the spear to the knights and miraculously uses it to heal their king Amfortas and release Kundry from her curse. Redeemed through self-denial, love, and freedom from society's constraints, he becomes the priestly guardian of the Grail and spear. Wagner died after moving to **Venice** (1882) and suffering a second heart attack. He was buried at Wahnfried in Bayreuth.

Wagner's operas prior to his Swiss exile represent outgrowths of existing traditions of Italian and French comic opera (*Das Liebesverbot*), French *grand opéra* (*Rienzi*), and German romantic opera (*Die Feen* and *Der fliegende Holländer*) or synthesize German and French features (*Tannhäuser* and *Lohengrin*). At the same time his adaptation of traditional elements of these genres laid the foundation for a more idiosyncratic, philosophical/mythological music drama conceived during that exile, many characteristics of which were prefigured in his earlier works. From the beginning, Wagner wrote his own librettos, partly out of necessity and partly believing that level of involvement to be necessary for a complete synthesis of purpose and effect. The last three of the traditional operas, *Der fliegende Holländer*, *Tannhäuser*, and *Lohengrin* initiate Wagner's commitment to Germanic myth, legend, and history and anticipate the religious philosophical orientation of the music dramas. They adopt themes that would preoccupy him throughout the remainder of his career: redemption through love and self-denial, the corrupt dogmatism of institutionalized religion and the imperative to reinstate fundamental Christian ideals, the inhibiting inflexibility of society and civilization, and the inadequacy of physical, mortal love.

These operas of the first phase of Wagner's career anticipate the monumental scale of the music dramas, though relying to a great extent on extended crowd **scenes** of sailors, maidens, knights, and pilgrims (the singing contest and other scenes from *Tannhäuser*) that he would later minimize. Some of these scenes involve flexible treatments of Italian forms in the French manner, and strophic designs suggesting folk origins (*see* ARIA) that are interspersed with declamatory episodes between stanzas (as in Senta's ballade from *Der fliegende Holländer*). Increasing continuity at a local level results from more flexible interchange of **arioso**, declamation, and formal lyricism, and from adoption of episodic deflecting melody in the French style that veers among different moods in response to express or implicit sentiments and inflections of the text. On a broader scale, elision of boundaries within and between set pieces heralds the disintegration of **number opera**, while extensive employment of reminiscence motives anticipates leitmotif technique. The orchestra plays a heightened dramatic role in transitions between scenes; in ritual, processional, or other atmospheric music; and in the general matrix of vocal accompaniments. It joins Wagner's expanding melodic and harmonic vocabulary in providing distinctive characterization of individuals and groups. Abandonment of the medley **overture** in *Lohengrin* in favor of a prelude that sets the action in motion points toward the evocative openings of the later works.

Wagner's music dramas—the *Ring, Tristan, Die Meistersinger*, and *Parsifal*—distinguish themselves from his preceding operas through their more pronounced commitment to the progressive features discussed above, taking the ultimate step toward through-composed, organically conceived opera in which structure is generated through associative relationships between music and text. Having assumed the romantic mantle of artist as savior and dedicated his music dramas to the grandiose philosophical, religious, and social goal of redeeming humanity and the arts, Wagner indulged his ideological agenda more openly. He emphasized its nationalistic orientation and the folkloric nature of his subject matter by saturating his poetry with medieval *Stabreim* alliteration and by referencing in musical shorthand the bar forms of traditional Germanic song. And he facilitated audience immersion in his rituals of enlightenment by eliminating regularly phrased tuneful melodies and traditional set piece divisions in favor of a continuous synthesis of orchestral and vocal music dominated by "endless melody."

Spectacle and massed crowd scenes play more peripheral roles, particularly in the *Ring*, the discourse being reoriented toward broadly paced monologues devoted to feelings, motivations, and justifications as well as mythic antecedents and narrative perorations. The orchestra takes the lead in sustaining momentum and continuity, in creating dramatic weight through its titanic sound, and in deploying sprawling networks of leitmotifs. Its expansion to include multiple harps, massive brass sections including contrabass trombones and tubas, and augmentation of the normal winds with bass clarinet and English horn facilitated increasingly sophisticated scorings culminating in the luminosity of *Parsifal*. And it demanded a new brand of vibrato-fueled, high-octane singing (*see* SINGING STYLE) to compete with its volume. Constantly modulating chromatic harmony, which reaches its apex in *Tristan*, broadens Wagner's palette of connotative relationships and perpetuates instability and forward motion by avoiding distinct cadential closure. At Bayreuth, introduction of stadium-style seating, darkened house lights during performances, retraction of the orchestra under the stage, stricter expectations regarding audience behavior and attentiveness, and various other practices (*see* THEATER DESIGN) reduced distractions and enhanced the quasi-religious atmosphere.

Wagner promoted the ideals of the music drama in a cogent doctrine that influenced the development of opera in all countries during the late 19th century, his shadow falling across national boundaries to France, Italy, eastern Europe, and America (*see* WAGNERISM). Like Ludwig van Beethoven (1770–1827), Wagner exerted a profound and often constricting influence on his disciples from music to the other arts. His operas and his prose writings became centerpieces for aesthetic polemics in the 19th century—for example, between advocates of the classicizing absolute music of Johannes Brahms (1833–1897) and his followers and those of descriptive music centered on Franz Liszt's circle in Weimar—and they remained objects of critical and political adulation and invective well into the 20th century.

WAGNERISM. Late 19th-century tide of enthusiasm for the music of **Richard Wagner**, his operatic aesthetics, and/or his political, social, and religious ideology. Obsessive devotion, fueled initially by such luminaries as Franz Liszt (1811–1886), who conducted the premier of *Lohengrin* in Weimar (1850), grew exponentially in Germany following the premier of *Die Meistersinger von Nürnberg* (1868) and in response to ***Der Ring des Nibelungen***, unveiled at the first Bayreuth Festival in 1876. The festival's enshrinement of Wagner was perpetuated by his second wife Cosima (Liszt's daughter) and by the *Bayreuther Blätter* that Wagner co-founded (beginning 1878), which became a forum for prominent Aryan anti-Semites such as Houston Stewart Chamberlain. Wagnerism continued in Germany and Austria through World War II as the artistic fulcrum of the National Socialists, who appropriated the Wagner repertory, *Parsifal* (1882) in particular, for their racist agenda.

Beginning in the 1880s, fervid devotees formed quasi-religious Wagner societies and journals across Europe and in the United States, where the conductor Anton Seidl (1850–1898) and East Coast matriarchs of the Gilded Age such as Isabella Stewart Gardner (1840–1924) took lead roles. Features of Wagner's style—**leitmotifs**, voluptuous chromatic harmony, spontaneous endless melody, replacement of set pieces with broader continuous structures, mythological religious subjects and symbolism, and massive artistic/philosophical ambition—were adopted variously by composers as diverse as Anton Bruckner (1824–1896), Gustav Mahler (1860–1911), **Richard Strauss**, **Claude Debussy**, and members of the Second Viennese School (e.g., **Arnold Schoenberg** and **Alban Berg**). Wagner's operas were introduced to Italy by the **conductor** and **composer** Franco Faccio (1840–1891) beginning with *Lohengrin* in 1871 (originally 1850), and Wagner's aesthetics were supported by a number of the *Scapigliati*. In Italy and France, Wagnerism was a charge leveled at composers thought to have betrayed their national identities by adopting "Germanic" elements such as chromatic harmony, expanded brassy orchestration, recurring themes, and transitions to obscure formal boundaries, for example **Giuseppe Verdi** in *Don Carlos* (1867) and *Aida*. Opposition to Wagnerism inspired parodies involving famous passages in unflattering contexts, for example in **Paul Hindemith**'s *Das Nusch-Nuschi* (1921).

WALTON, WILLIAM. (1902, Oldham, England–1983, Ischia, Italy.) English **composer** of orchestral and vocal music, including two relatively traditional operas from the 1950s and 1960s. Walton began composing as a choirboy in Oxford (1912–18). After failing to complete his degree at Oxford University, he was supported within the artistic circle centered in **London** on the Sitwell siblings (Osbert, Sacheverell, and particularly Edith) and briefly explored atonal chromaticism in the manner of **Arnold Schoenberg** before turning to his characteristic mixture of post-romantic tonal lyricism and populist influences. He settled in southern Italy in the 1950s.

Walton's attempt at an opera about the late Renaissance composer Carlo Gesualdo (ca. 1561–1613) never proceeded beyond a **libretto** written by the music critic Cecil Gray (1895–1951) in 1941. A commission from the British Broadcasting Corporation produced his only major work in the genre, *Troilus and Cressida* (1954, revised 1963 and 1972–76) based on Geoffrey Chaucer's poem about tragic lovers during the Trojan War. Its lyrical, richly scored, often passionate music and epic plot represent a traditionalist return to the aesthetics of *grand opéra*. Equally conservative from a different perspective, *The Bear* (1967), after Anton Chekhov, is a breezy one-act "extravaganza," for two principals and a servant character, in which a virtuous Russian widow is wooed and won by a brusque neighbor (the Bear) in the course of negotiating an unpaid debt and debating social expectations for men versus **women**.

WAR OF THE COMEDIANS. The Querelle des Bouffons (or Guerre des Bouffons) was a **Parisian** dispute between supporters of French versus Italian opera that lasted from 1752 to 1754. Extended polemics, involving over 50 published letters and pamphlets by some of the most prominent writers of the time, took as their lightning rod an Italian company known locally as Les Bouffons, led by the **impresario** Eustacio Bambini (1697–1770). Their performances of more than a dozen **intermezzos** and **opera buffas** during the period in question, most notoriously **Giovanni Battista Pergolesi**'s *La serva padrona* (1752, originally 1733), fueled the controversy and inspired a first wave of **opéra comique** composers, including **Egidio Duni**.

Since French opera had been identified with the monarchy and its allied institutions since its inception in the late 17th century (*see* LULLY, JEAN-BAPTISTE), the war provided a surrogate forum for polemics between royalists and *encyclopédiste* critics, and engaged a host of political, religious, national, and linguistic issues. Proponents of traditional *tragédie en musique* included the composer **Jean-Philippe Rameau** and the king's official mistress, Madame de Pompadour, who embraced its grandiose homages to royalty on mythological subjects cast with outsized characters, its dramatically declaimed **recitative** that marries words and music, and its emphasis of drama over vocalism. Their most prominent adversaries, who supported the more modest intermezzo, opera buffa, and the budding opéra comique, were the Swiss philosophe Jean-Jacques Rousseau (1712–1778), whose *Le devin du village* had just premiered (1752); German literary critic Friedrich Melchior Grimm (1723–1807); and the queen. They preferred an Enlightened emphasis of lyrical Italianate music sung by humanized characters in unassuming, contemporary settings, and mostly regarded the French language as unsuited for opera.

WEBER, CARL MARIA VON. (1786, Eutin–1826, London.) German **composer** of 10 operas during the first three decades of the 19th century, as well as other stage, vocal, piano, orchestral, and chamber works; pianist, **conductor**, and critic. Weber led the development of German **romantic** opera and crusaded for raising the status of German opera and standards of operatic repertory and performance in Germany and Prague.

Weber's father led an itinerant family theater troupe that performed spoken plays and **singspiels** in southern Germany, obliging Weber to cobble together training in piano, singing, and composition from one of his brothers and local musicians as he traveled from town to town. In Munich (beginning 1798) Weber heard a broad array of German and French operas and wrote his first, *Die Macht der Liebe und des Weins* (1798–99, lost) with guidance from the court organist. His first staged opera, *Das Waldmädchen*, set a **libretto** by the director of the company that performed it in 1800. Weber studied (1803–04) with the German theorist and composer Georg Joseph (Abbé) Vogler (1749–1814), who apparently stimulated his interest in folk music and nontraditional, exotic scenarios and who recommended him for his first significant position as music director for the Breslau theater (1804) at age 17.

Bucking resistance to his initiatives by established musicians and managers, he attempted to improve the quality of productions in Breslau by enlarging the **orchestra** and changing its seating arrangement, paying higher salaries, demanding more disciplined rehearsals and performances, and programming a more challenging menu of works from **Vienna** (including **Wolfgang Amadeus Mozart**'s operas) and Berlin, as well as Italian operas and **opéras comiques** in translation. While sidelined under suspicious circumstances after drinking engraving acid from a wine bottle (1806), his reforms were reversed and he resigned and moved first to Poland, then to Stuttgart as court secretary. There he completed his fifth opera, *Silvana* (1810), which recycled some of the music and text from *Das Waldmädchen*, but was exiled the same year—after he and his father embezzled money from the Duke of Württemberg—and had the work produced in Frankfurt.

In between jobs, Weber founded the Harmonischer Verein, a secret society that included **Giacomo Meyerbeer**, which was intended both to improve musical taste through unbiased reviews and to foster the careers of its members. *Abu Hassan*, a singspiel based on a story from the *Thousand and One*

Nights and Weber's first work to remain in the repertory, premiered in 1811, followed by an acclaimed production of *Silvana* in Berlin (1812). Notoriety from these successes helped Weber win the position of music director of the Prague opera (beginning 1813), where he again began to rebuild and raise the profile of a floundering company by recruiting new soloists and **chorus** and orchestra members. He launched an extremely ambitious schedule of German operas, including Ludwig van Beethoven's (1770–1827) *Fidelio* and Louis Spohr's (1784–1859) *Faust* (1816), as well as translated Italian and French works by **André-Ernest-Modeste Grétry, Luigi Cherubini, Gaspare Spontini**, and Meyerbeer among others, which left little time or energy for opera composition.

Compelled to resign because of conflicts with theater management, Weber moved to Dresden in 1817, again hired to revive a lethargic opera company as a royal theater and raise the status of German opera with respect to the imported opera that dominated there. A less frenetic schedule than in Prague allowed him to compose again. In 1817 he began work in earnest on *Der Freischütz*, a subject he had considered as early as 1810. After several delays, *Der Freischütz* finally premiered successfully in Berlin in 1821 and began a brilliant and highly influential run of performances in most of the major European capitals. With *Euryanthe* (1823, Vienna), a grand romantic opera on a medieval chivalric subject, Weber further attempted to legitimize German opera by abandoning the spoken dialogue of singspiel in favor of obbligato **recitative**. Weber's most ambitious work, considered by some to be his musical masterpiece, its echoes and those of *Der Freischütz* may be heard in German romantic operas as late as **Richard Wagner**'s *Lohengrin* (1850). Taxing work completing the fairy opera *Oberon* for **London** (1826) led to Weber's death. While Weber's last two operas are still performed, a combination of worsening health—he was plagued by tuberculosis much of his life—and mediocre librettos kept him from matching the success of *Der Freischütz*.

WEILL, KURT. (1900, Dessau–1950, New York.) German Jewish **composer** of a dozen operas, two **operettas**, and about 20 musicals, plays with music, and hybrid operatic works (mostly from the 1920s through the 1940s), and other instrumental and vocal music. Weill's reputation as a theater composer rivaled that of **Paul Hindemith** during the Weimar Republic between World War I and the Nazi rise to power in the 1930s.

Weill trained at the Berlin Music Academy (1918–19) with the opera composer Engelbert Humperdinck (1854–1921) and later (1921–24) with Ferruccio Busoni (1866–1924). His style initially mediated between postromantic dissonant chromaticism and the neo-classicism pioneered by **Igor Stravinsky** and others, adopting the example of **Wolfgang Amadeus Mozart**'s **number operas** as an antidote to **Richard Wagner**'s music dramas.

The plot of Weill's first surviving opera, *Der Protagonist* (1926), shows affinities to Italian **verismo** and the **expressionist** subject matter of **Arnold Schoenberg** and **Alban Berg**: an actor kills his sister, for whom he has incestuous longings, during a performance when he discovers her affair. Musical polarities distinguish the post-romantic "real world" within the opera from pantomimed plays, which are accompanied by grotesque neo-classical **stage band** music.

One of a number of composers invested in popularizing art music in the early 20th century and making it a socially inclusive medium, his orientation differed from Hindemith's *Gebrauchsmusik* in treating music as an agent for political change by examining social issues and satirizing the social depravity of the period. His ***Zeitopern*** began during a famous, and sometimes conflicted collaboration with the playwright Bertolt Brecht (1898–1956) from 1927 to 1933. Brecht's "epic theater" incorporates anti-illusionist devices, dividing the action into self-contained episodes that are announced and interpreted by placards and projected captions and images that break the "fourth wall" between stage and audience and encourage audience awareness of the artificiality of the play and attentiveness to its social and political symbolism. And although Weill's music seldom took the subservient role detached from dramatic content advocated by Brecht, it did avoid artifices like virtuosic singing and orchestral tone painting, instead adopting a sophisticated recasting of the most accomplished styles of American jazz and popular song.

This program of politically charged popular opera appears in Weill's first opera with Brecht, ***Die Dreigroschenoper*** (*The Threepenny Opera*, 1928), based on the story of ***The Beggar's Opera***. In 1930 they produced their *Aufstieg und Fall der Stadt Mahagonny* (*Rise and Fall of the City of Mahagonny*), an expansion of the *Mahagonny-Songspiel* (1927) with its triadic harmony further popularized by reducing dissonance. A political satire banned by the Nazis in 1933, in which criminals found an Alaskan pleasure city—a sort of Las Vegas North of booze, gambling, and whores for the miners—that sees temporary success but is ultimately burned to the ground, its plot is announced by projected captions and montages, its music an eclectic blend of jazz and popular motifs. Weill's other significant operas include *Die Bürgschaft* (*The Pledge*, 1932) and *Der Silbersee* (*The Silver Lake*, 1933).

Denounced by the Nazis for his socialist leanings, Weill emigrated to **Paris** (1933) and to **London** and the United States (1935), becoming an American citizen in 1943. He wrote film music for Hollywood and during the 1940s devoted most of his efforts to popular and often controversial Broadway musicals, such as *Lady in the Dark* (1940), *Street Scene* (1946), and *Lost in the Stars* (1949), which had an important influence on **Leonard Bernstein** and Stephen Sondheim (born 1930).

See also CENSORSHIP.

WERTHER. *Drame lyrique*; music by **Jules Massenet**, **libretto** by Édouard Blau (1836–1906) and Paul Milliet (1848–1924) probably based on a scenario by Massenet's publisher Georges Hartmann (1843–1900) after Johann Wolfgang von Goethe's (1749–1832) novel *Die Leiden des jungen Werthers* (1774); four acts; premiered **Vienna**, Hofoper, February 1892. Along with *Manon* (1884), it is currently Massenet's most popular opera and the best representative of the genre of *opéra lyrique*. Massenet became interested in the subject as early as 1880 and composed the score between 1885 and 1887. Originally intended for the Opéra-Comique (*see* PARIS), it was rejected as too morose and set aside for *Esclarmonde* (1889). Eventually staged in Vienna on the heels of the triumphant production of *Manon* there in 1890, it appeared in Paris (1893) only after its Viennese success.

Werther's story unfolds from July through Christmas near Frankfurt in the 1780s. The sensitive **romantic** poet and diplomat falls in love with Charlotte, daughter of the local Bailli (prince's steward), when he escorts her to a ball in the absence of her fiancé Albert, whom Charlotte had agreed to marry at the behest of her dying mother. Despite his obsession, Werther agrees to honor her prior commitment. Unsuccessfully attempting to coexist for three tortured months while Charlotte begins her loveless marriage to Albert, she and Werther decide that he will leave until Christmas, hoping that the separation will cool their passion. After a heartbreaking reunion on Christmas Eve, Werther borrows pistols from Albert, who recognizes his wife's feelings for Werther and is all too happy to oblige, and shoots himself. Charlotte declares her love as he dies in her arms.

A paradigm of the intimacy of *opéra lyrique*, *Werther* centers almost exclusively on the alternately bittersweet and turbulent pathos of its hero, represented by the two themes of its prelude (*see* OVERTURE), which recur throughout the score. And it avoids the spectacular crowd scenes—the presence of the **chorus** is minimal even in the Wetzlar Square act (Act 2)—and the historical, political, religious, or philosophical subtext of *grand opéra* or **Richard Wagner**'s music dramas. Werther is suffocated by his circle's preoccupation with love, marriage, and family, from Werther's friend Brühlmann's luckless betrothal to the Bailli's loss of his wife, the pastor's 50th wedding anniversary celebration, and Charlotte's sister Sophie's crush on him. And his emptiness festers amidst the bourgeois domesticity of his surroundings, represented particularly by the settings of Acts 1 and 3 in the garden and the Christmas-bedecked parlor, respectively, by the children's carol rehearsal (Act 1), by Charlotte's role as surrogate mother to her siblings and Werther's love for her in that role, by Sophie's doting protectiveness, and by the mundane pleasantries and forced civility of his everyday interactions.

Werther also differs in significant respects from **opéra comique**. Its light-hearted moments fail to cheer the principals and only underscore their relentless sadness. It lacks spoken dialogue or even distinct **recitative**, setting most conversations as a continuous mixture of declamatory or **arioso** singing over fluidly phrased orchestral melody. And its solos consist mainly of single through-composed melodies (e.g., Werther's "O Nature, pleine de grâce," Act 1, or the climactic "Lied d'Ossian," Act 3); often incorporate considerable declamation, as in Charlotte's "Letter Song" (Act 3); and emerge from their contexts as comparatively realistic monologues (cf. *Carmen*). In a rare symmetrical form, Sophie's ABA' "Du gai soleil," the outer sections frame dialogue. And while final cadences create applause breaks, the ensuing music provides a cohesive motivic exit out of the set piece.

WOMEN AND OPERA. Women have participated in opera as subjects and singers, and have also been involved at times as **composers**; contributors to **production** (in the latter case, notably Sara Caldwell, 1924–2006, beginning with the Boston Opera Group in 1958); and occasionally **librettists** (e.g., Julie Candeille, 1767–1834, for her own operas, and Myfanwy Piper, 1911–1997, for **Benjamin Britten**).

Female characters have frequently been objectified and victimized in opera, beginning with the earliest heroines from myth, legend, and history, including the nymph Dafne, target of Apollo's lust in the first opera (**Jacopo Peri**'s *Dafne*); Euridice, snakebite casualty and object of Orpheus's quest (*Euridice* and *Orfeo*); the abandoned queen Dido, prey to witches' spells and Aeneas's destiny (*Dido and Aeneas*); and countless other love interests and murder and suicide victims who demonstrate varying degrees of passivity and helplessness across the next four centuries. But more robust, self-actualizing women, often demonized as scheming villainesses, also appear as early as the sorceresses of **Francesca Caccini**'s *La liberazione di Ruggiero* (1625), which takes the issue of women in power as its subject, and count among the most fascinating operatic leads from the 17th century on: the ambitious seductress Poppea of *L'incoronazione di Poppea*; the libidinous witch Armida in *Armide* operas by **Jean-Baptiste Lully** and **Christoph Willibald Gluck** (1686 and 1777, respectively) and in **George Frideric Handel**'s *Rinaldo*; the incestuous stepmother and suicide Phaedra, in *Hippolyte et Aricie*; or the more heroic, self-sacrificing wife Alcestis in Lully's and Gluck's versions of *Alceste*. Secondary roles broadened the range of character types from the earliest days of opera, supporting the principals as confidants and celebrants of their activities (Poppea's nurse Arnalta, the shepherdesses in *Orfeo*); as goddesses or allegorical figures (Venus, Athena, Juno, Discord, personifications of various countries, and so on in *Il pomo d'oro*); or as figures of comic relief, caricatures drawn from the **commedia dell' arte** frequently played by men (Aristea in *Orontea*).

During the Enlightenment, Revolutionary, and Napoleonic eras, particularly in the less conventionalized genres of **opera buffa**, **opéra comique**, and **singspiel**, female leads appear increasingly individualized, human, intelligent, vigorous, and in their own ways as heroic as their male companions. Myriad examples exist: Susanna in *Le nozze di Figaro*, Pamina in *Die Zauberflöte*, Leonora in *Fidelio*, or Rosina in *Il barbiere di Siviglia*. And the range of characterization is evident in an opera like *Don Giovanni*, which contrasts the vengeful firebrand Donna Anna against the lovelorn groupie Elvira and the randy peasant Zerlina. Women even played men with some frequency as they replaced **castratos** in heroic roles (Arsace in *Semiramide*; *see* TRAVESTY).

In the 19th century this trend toward diversification of female roles infiltrated even the more high-minded types of opera (Italian *melodramma*, French *grand opéra*, the Wagnerian music drama) and contributed to realizing the **romantic** goal of idiosyncrasy. Passive, unwitting victims (Desdemona in **Gioachino Rossini**'s and **Giuseppe Verdi**'s *Otello* operas, the former composed 1816) and self-sacrificing redeemers (Senta, idealistic social outcast, willing token of her father's ambitious barter, and her beloved's deliverer in *Der fliegende Holländer*) trade turns onstage with political operatives (Margaret of Valois in *Les Huguenots*), vengeful harpies (Amneris in *Aida*), and full-blown sociopaths (Lucrezia Borgia in **Gaetano Donizetti**'s opera of the same name, 1833). They represent the panoply of European society, from royalty and the moneyed classes (Violetta in Giuseppe Verdi's *La traviata*, 1853) to its lowest strata (Azucena in Verdi's *Il trovatore*, 1853, *Carmen*). And they face irresolvable quandaries leading to unthinkable tragedies: in *Lucia di Lammermoor*, the heroine, victim of a vindictive and socially ambitious brother, becomes a murderess and suicide; Brünnhilde, torn between her father's needs and wants, ultimately destroys him (*Der Ring des Nibelungen*); in *Werther*, Charlotte succumbs to an arranged marriage and expedites her true love's suicide.

This new range of characterization results in stark juxtapositions of contrasting roles within operas, for example the genocidal anti-Semite Abigaille versus the more traditional love interest Fenena in *Nabucco*, the cloistered paradigm of misguided self-sacrifice Gilda versus the prostitute Maddalena in *Rigoletto*, the seductive sorceress Venus versus the sanctified redeemer Elisabeth in *Tannhäuser*, or the henpecking guardian of household morality Fricka versus the visionary heroine Brünnhilde. And it facilitates character development—for better or worse—as illustrated by Tatyana's metamorphosis from Yevgeny's doormat to self-realization (*Yevgeny Onegin*) or Santuzza's from innocence to bloodlust (*Cavalleria rusticana*).

In the 20th century this trend toward individualization reaches its logical outcome in characters who embody such diverse themes as psychological disturbances ranging from the benign—Mélisande's inscrutable dissociation

(*Pelléas et Mélisande*) or the Marschallin's nostalgic melancholy (*Der Rosenkavalier*)—to the destructive—the obsessive psychosis of *Salome* or the Woman in **Arnold Schoenberg**'s *Erwartung* (composed 1909, premiered 1924); contemporary domestic issues (the wives, mothers, and daughters in **Richard Strauss**'s *Intermezzo*, 1924, or **Leonard Bernstein**'s *Trouble in Tahiti*, 1952, and *A Quiet Place*, 1983; the political figures Pat Nixon and Madam Mao in *Nixon in China*); the bizarre and grotesque (the shrewish circus freak Baba the Turk in *The Rake's Progress* and Thérèse in **Francis Poulenc**'s *Les Mamelles de Tirésias*, 1947); anthropomorphism (the fox Bystrouška in **Leoš Janáček**'s *The Cunning Little Vixen*, 1924, and characters in **Sergey Prokofiev**'s *The Love for Three Oranges*, 1921); or the mythic (Strauss's *Elektra*, 1909, and Jocasta in **Igor Stravinsky**'s *Oedipus rex*, 1928).

Having previously gained entry to the stage through the commedia dell'arte, women rose to prominence as virtuoso singers in the Farrarese *concerto delle donne* and its offshoots in northern Italy in the last quarter of the 16th century. Their participation in the earliest operas was limited, and although several women reportedly performed in Jacopo Peri and **Giulio Caccini**'s *Euridice* (among them probably Caccini's daughter Francesca), most if not all the female roles in **Claudio Monteverdi**'s *Orfeo* were sung by castratos, and women were banned from the stage in **Rome**. Women became stars in the public theaters of **Venice** in the mid-17th century, led by the **soprano Anna Renzi**, who set the standard for the operatic prima donna, and the city's *ospedale* (orphanage **conservatories** for girls) likely contributed to the development of opera singers (notably **Faustina Bordoni**). Largely because castratos were unpopular at the Opéra in **Paris**, female singers enjoyed opportunities there that were otherwise restricted for them at the 17th-century French court. Among women who enjoyed international renown in the 18th century were Bordoni and **Francesca Cuzzoni**, the notorious rivals of Handel's Royal Academy of Music in **London**. Leading female singers of the 19th century included the sopranos **Isabella Colbran**, **Giuditta Pasta**, and **Jenny Lind**, and the mezzo-soprano/**contralto Pauline Viardot**. **Kirsten Flagstad**, **Maria Callas**, **Joan Sutherland**, **Marilyn Horne**, and Leontyne Price (b. 1927), the first widely recognized African American opera singer, are considered giants of the 20th century.

Judging by current scholarship, female composers have written comparatively few operas, owing initially to limited opportunities for training as composers and subsequently for productions of their works, although their contributions have increased across the 20th century and isolated individuals were active earlier. Francesca Caccini, singer, composer, and daughter of Giulio, wrote music for court entertainments in Florence. Her *La liberazione di Ruggiero*, the first opera by a female composer to survive, was commissioned by Maria Magdalena of Austria, for whom the work had personal political significance since it deals metaphorically with the issue of women in power. Otherwise, female composers apparently made little if any headway in the Italian theater system. While 17th-century scholarly academies and later 18th-century urban salons saw performances of **arias** and cantatas, some by female composers, they generally lacked the resources to mount entire operas. And the Venetian *ospedali* discouraged composition, prescribing marriage or service to the Church for their graduates, rather than professional careers.

In Paris, although operatic composition remained an overwhelmingly male pursuit, beginning at the end of the 17th century women enjoyed sporadic opportunities at the Académie Royale de Musique. In 1694, the ***tragédie en musique*** *Céphale et Procris* (1694) by the harpsichordist and composer of instrumental music and cantatas Elisabeth Jacquet de La Guerre (1665–1729) became the first work by a female composer performed at the Opéra; *Les Génies, ou Les caractères de l'Amour* (1736), by the harpsichordist, composer, and dancer Mlle Duval (1718–after 1775), was the second. The Venetian singer and vocal music composer Antonia Bembo (ca. 1640–ca. 1720), working under the patronage of Louis XIV, wrote an *Ercole amante* in 1707, though it was never performed. Lucile Grétry (1772–1790), daughter of prominent opera composer **André-Ernest-Modeste Grétry**, wrote the very popular opéra comique *Le mariage d'Antonio* (1786), as well as the failed *Toinette et Louis* the next year. At least two women were sufficiently successful to number among the professional opera composers of their day. Henriette de Beaumesnil (1748–1813) composed a handful of operas, among them *Anacréon* (1781), *Tibulle et Délie, ou Les Saturnales* (1784), and *Plaire, cest commander* (1792), which were performed privately at the Opéra and at Versailles, respectively, while Candeille, who wrote her own **librettos**, produced eight light operas, most prominently *Cathérine, ou La belle fermière* (1792).

A few other operas written by women were performed at Germanic courts aligned with France: Wilhelmina, Princess of Prussia (1709–1758), the sister of Frederick the Great who built the theater in Bayreuth that predated **Richard Wagner's Festival** Theater, composed *Argenore* in 1740 (lost); Maria Antonia Walpurgis, Electress of Saxony (1724–1780), who trained with **Nicola Porpora** and **Johann Adolf Hasse**, sang in two of her own operas, for which she wrote text and music (*Il trionfo della fedeltà*, 1754, and Talestri, regina delle amazzoni, 1760); Maria Theresia von Paradis (1759–1824), an Austrian composer and performer supported by the Empress Maria Theresa, composed five German operas between 1791 and 1805.

Despite feminist advances that brought expanded opportunities for training in all areas of music, chances for women to have operas staged professionally remained next to nonexistent throughout the 19th century. With one exception (*Le dernier sorcier*, 1869), Viardot's eight operettas and other stage works were performed only in her own private theater. Consequently even the most recognized women composers, such as Fanny Mendelssohn (1805–1847) and Clara Schumann (1819–1896) confined themselves to instrumental and nonoperatic vocal music. Around 1900, however, the situation began to change after secular conservatories selectively opened their doors to women. Notably, Ethel Smyth (1858–1944), the English feminist, suffragette, and composer trained at the Leipzig Conservatory, had six German-, French-, and English-language operas performed in Weimar, Berlin, London, Leipzig, and elsewhere between 1898 and 1926, ranging in dramatic intensity from the well-regarded tragedy *Les Naufrageurs* (*The Wreckers*, 1906) to the lighthearted *The Boatswain's Mate* (1916). Germaine Tailleferre (1892–1983), member of the avant-garde cadre Les Six in Paris, composed a dozen light operas from the 1930s to 1960. Nonetheless, this level of involvement with full-scale opera remained exceptional during the first half of the century. The prominent impressionist composer Lili Boulanger's (1893–1918) only opera, *La princesse Maleine* on a libretto by Maurice Maeterlinck and Tito Ricordi, remained incomplete and unperformed at her premature death. The American **neo-classicist** Louise Talma's (1906–1996) single opera, *The Alcestiad*, appeared in 1962. And the well-known English-born American modernist composer Ruth Crawford Seeger (1901–1953) wrote no operas.

A watershed of sorts occurred in the 1970s and 1980s, when renewed feminism and affirmative action facilitated the formation of women's professional societies and performing groups and won an increased presence for women in academia and for women composers in general. And although the field is still dominated by men—and women have found their voice at a time when the specialist opera composer is a thing of the past, opportunities for producing new full-scale operas being limited across the board—some inroads have been made. At least a dozen international notables have contributed to a growing portfolio of operas that incorporate the full range of compositional idioms available to contemporary composers, from traditional styles to radical experiments involving microtonal and electronic resources.

Scottish-American composer Thea Musgrave (born 1928) has composed about a dozen children's, radio, chamber, and full-scale operas beginning in the 1950s, including *The Abbot of Drimrock* (1955), *Mary, Queen of Scots* (1977), and most recently *Pontalba* (2003). Nancy Van de Vate (born 1930), an American based in Austria, produced several operas in the 1990s (e.g., *In the Shadow of the Glen*, 1994, and *All Quiet on the Western Front*, 1998), and in 2005 her chamber opera *Where the Cross Is Made* won a National Opera Association award. The Australian Moya Henderson's (born 1941) opera *Lindy* (1997), based on a notorious wrongful filicide conviction, accompanies several other musical theater pieces. Meredith Monk (American, born 1942), whose style is related to **minimalism**, has composed a relatively traditional opera (*Atlas*, 1991), along with several quasi-operatic works. Marta Ptaszyńska (1943–), a Polish-born composer who has taught in the United States since the 1970s, has a television opera, *Oskar z Alwy* (*Oscar from Alva*, 1971) and two children's operas to her credit.

Most indicative of a trend toward increased opportunities for women are two individuals, both English, whose extensive oeuvres hearken back to the heyday of the career opera composer: Nicola LeFanu (born 1947), seven operas including a chamber opera, a monodrama, a radio opera, a children's opera, and three full-scale works (*Blood Wedding*, 1992; *The Wildman*, 1995; and *Light Passing*, 2004); and Judith Weir (born 1954), nine operatic works for which she wrote both score and libretto, among them *Night at the Chinese Opera* (1987), *The Vanishing Bridegroom* (1990), *Blond Eckbert* (1994), and *Miss Fortune* (2011). *Alice in Wonderland* by the South Korean based in Germany Unsuk Chin (born 1961) created a sensation at its Munich premier in 2007.

See also ARCHILEI, VITTORIA; *BOHÈME, LA*; CAVALIERI, CATARINA; GARDEN, MARY; *LUCIA DI LAMMERMOOR*; MALIBRAN, MARIA.

WOZZECK. Opera by Alban Berg, **libretto** by the **composer** based on Georg Büchner's play *Woyzeck* (incomplete, 1836–37, completed and published 1879, first performed 1913); three acts; Berlin, Staatsoper, December 1925. Berg's only completed stage work, *Wozzeck* is one of the monuments of the Second Viennese School prior to the advent of serialism, regarded as the first large-scale atonal opera.

Work on *Wozzeck* proceeded slowly. Although Berg wrote the draft libretto in 1914, the same year in which he had attended the **Vienna** premier of Büchner's play, composition was delayed until 1917 owing to Berg's service in World War I and took five years to complete (1922). The Berlin premier was followed by productions in Prague, Leningrad, and various German houses up to 1932, until the Nazi's banned "degenerate" art.

In Berg's post-Wagnerian parable of social decay and individual alienation, Wozzeck is a common soldier ill suited to his lot in life. His common-law wife Marie betrays him for a flashy Drum Major. His companions—the captain whom he shaves, the doctor who performs experiments on him, and the Drum Major with whom he shares quarters—ridicule him for his wife's affair, the illegitimacy of their child, his personal habits, and his apocalyptic visions, and physically abuse him. Overcome by rage, despair, and delusions, he takes Marie into the woods and stabs her, then, oblivious to his circumstances, retires to the local tavern to drown his guilt. Fleeing after his bloody hands are discovered, he accidentally drowns trying to retrieve the murder weapon from the pond where he left his wife's body. Their child learns about his parents' deaths from playmates.

Berg's score synthesizes numerous compositional traditions. The post-Wagnerian, **expressionist** intensity and spontaneity of his vocal writing ranges from quasi-tonal lyricism through violently dissonant atonal and proto-serial constructions (the 12-tone passacaglia, Act 1, **scene** 4) in haunting **arioso**, declamation, and *Sprechstimme*. Also indebted to **Richard Wagner** are the convention of linking scenes with orchestral transitions, which recall and develop motifs introduced previously and generate ideas for the upcoming scene, and the system of recurring **leitmotifs** associated with the various characters, such as those recapitulated when Marie dies in Act 3, scene 2. The precisely descriptive music heard in scenes in the taverns, woods, and fields has its roots in the lied and symphonic poem.

At the same time, Berg's allegiance to Brahmsian classicism and Second Viennese constructivist impulses resulted in a symmetrical and historically based structure that imposes order on a surface of apparent disarray. In each act, five scenes are based on a single category of instrumental music. Act 1's character pieces—a suite of dances and cadenzas, rhapsody, march and lullaby, passacaglia variations, and rondo—are matched to the characters they introduce, for example the march for Marie's incipient infatuation with the Drum Major, the lullaby for her maternal devotion. In Act 2, movements appropriate to an instrumental cycle that Berg characterized as "symphonic" (sonata form, fantasia and fugue, largo, scherzo, introduction, and rondo) similarly reflect the situation—for example, the scherzo for the **stage band** music of the dance hall (scene 4)—as does the set of five inventions on a theme, a note, a rhythm, a chord, and perpetual eighth-note motion in Act 3.

Y

YEVGENY ONEGIN. Lyric **scenes**; music by **Pyotr Il'yich Tchaikovsky**, **libretto** by the **composer** and Konstantin Shilovsky (1849–1893) based on Alexander Pushkin's (1799–1837) verse novel (1833); three acts; student premier Moscow, Malïy Theater, March 1879, public premier Moscow, Bol'shoy Theater, January 1881. *Eugene Onegin* has been Tchaikovsky's most performed opera outside Russia.

A *Literaturoper* of sorts for which Tchaikovsky and Shilovsky combined original material with extracts from Pushkin's novel, this domestic tearjerker benefits from the close adaptation of its literary source in its depth of characterization. Larina's two daughters—the outgoing, free-spirited Ol'ga and the introverted, contemplative Tatyana—experience very different romantic entanglements. Ol'ga has been attached to the naive Lensky since they were paired off as children by their parents. Tatyana meets and is smitten by the smug, urbane Yevgeny, who initially rejects both her and the monotony of a committed relationship. For sport Yevgeny dances and flirts with Ol'ga, who humiliates Lensky by ignoring him, leading to a duel with Yevgeny in which Lensky is killed. When Yevgeny returns after a healing absence, Tatyana has metamorphosed into a glowing aristocratic presence happily married to a wealthy prince (Gremin). He falls in love with her, but is himself rejected even though she admits she still loves him.

Onegin illustrates Tchaikovsky's detachment from the Russian realists Aleksandr Sergeyevich Dargomïzhsky (1813–1869) and **Modest Petrovich Musorgsky** and his mainstream allegiances to the traditions of *opéra lyrique* and Italian *melodramma*. (Resemblances to **Giuseppe Verdi**'s *La traviata*, 1853, are evident.) Drab vocal declamation finds little space amidst his rich melodic writing. Folklike divergences from major and minor modes and traditional functional harmony are few. The Russian dances and songs, both authentic and simulated, which accompany the peasants of Larina's estate are not a pervasive part of the opera's musical language, which is characterized equally by the ballroom dances of its two glittering party scenes. And the intimately drawn characters rehearse their personal preoccupations absent any broader historical, political, or religious backdrop. A **number opera**,

Onegin includes numerous traditional set pieces (**arias**, ensembles, **choruses**, dances) ranging from spontaneous episodic designs such as the quartet for the two couples and Tatyana's letter monologue "Puskai pogibnu ya" (both Act 1) to the Italianate party scene of Act 2 and Gremin's aria "Lyubvi vse vozrastï pokornï" (Act 3).

See also WOMEN AND OPERA.

Z

ZARZUELA. The most esteemed type of Spanish musical theater. Combining spoken dialogue and singing, the zarzuela was cultivated almost continuously for three centuries (ca. 1650 to 1950) and comes closest to a native operatic tradition in Spain.

The earliest zarzuelas, performed at the king's Palacio Real de la Zarzuela outside Madrid, were short two-act pastoral-mythological fables written by the poet Pedro Calderón de la Barca (1600–1681) and the court composer **Juan Hidalgo**, beginning with Calderón's *El laurel de Apolo* (1657, music lost). Immensely popular, the zarzuela dominated the court theater in the late 17th century during the last years of Habsburg rule in Spain. Because their Bourbon successors (following the War of Spanish Succession, 1701–14) preferred Italian opera, the 18th-century zarzuela relocated from the court to the public theaters of Madrid, and alongside Spanish songs incorporated more Italianate international elements such as da capo **arias**, limited numbers of **recitatives**, and mannerisms of **opera buffa**. Landmark works in this new style were José Nebra's (1702–1768) *Viento es la dicha de Amor* (1743) and Antonio Rosales's (ca. 1740–1801) *El tío y la tía* (1767).

Following an ebb in the late 18th and early 19th centuries, the zarzuela enjoyed a mid-19th-century revival led by Rafael Hernando's (1822–1888) immensely popular *Colegiales y soldados* (1849). Hernando and his colleagues in the Sociedad Artistica of Madrid promoted zarzuelas with sufficient success to build a new specialty theater, the Teatro de la Zarzuela (1856). The vogue spread to Barcelona, which competed with Madrid for primacy from the 1850s through the 1920s, and throughout South and Central America and Mexico. These productions adapted the contemporary themes—and even the **librettos**—of **opéra comique** and late opera buffa, and in the **operetta**-zarzuela imitated **Jacques Offenbach** (beginning in the 1860s) and later **Franz Lehár**. At the end of the century they also show relationships to Italian **verismo**, particularly in the one-act *género chico*, set in the proletarian neighborhoods of Madrid, which developed after the Glorious Revolution of 1868. The zarzuela declined during the Spanish Civil War

(1936–39) and World War II and never fully recovered, ending for all intents and purposes with Federico Moreno Torroba's (1891–1982) *Maria Manuela* (1957).

DIE ZAUBERFLÖTE. Singspiel; music by **Wolfgang Amadeus Mozart**, **libretto** by Emanuel Schikaneder (1751–1812) based in part on August Jacob Liebeskind's (1758–1793) *Lulu, oder Die Zauberflöte* (1788); two acts; premiered **Vienna**, Theater auf der Wieden, September 1791. As was often the case in suburban popular theaters, many of the participants in the initial production of *The Magic Flute* were close acquaintances: the singing actor Schikaneder managed the company and played Papageno; Mozart's sister-in-law Josepha Hofer (nee Weber, 1758–1819) the Queen of the Night; the original Tamino and Sarastro also wrote music for Schikaneder's entertainments. *Die Zauberflöte* immediately delighted Viennese audiences and traveled quickly throughout German-speaking countries, appearing as far away as St. Petersburg by the end of the century and in **London** and **New York** (in translation) by the 1830s, and has remained in the repertory to the present.

The preeminent example of late 18th-century singspiel, *The Magic Flute* represents an ambitious rejuvenation of efforts by Mozart and others in the 1770s and 1780s to elevate German opera. It was likely inspired by Mozart's and Schikaneder's familiarity with Freemasonry and communications with Frederick William II, the Masonic king of Prussia, and they infused its plot with references to Masonic initiation rites and post-Enlightenment philosophy.

In a wild and exotic landscape, the prince Tamino is rescued from a serpent by the Three Ladies of the Queen of the Night and meets Papageno, her simple-minded bird catcher. The Queen sends Tamino and Papageno on a quest to rescue her kidnapped daughter Pamina—Tamino is smitten by her picture—with a magic flute for protection. They find her guarded by the libidinous Moor Monostatos at the palace of Pamina's father, the virtuous priest Sarastro, near his temples of Nature, Reason, and Wisdom. At his behest, Tamino undergoes three trials of character and courage: accompanied by Papageno, who fails miserably, a trial by silence in which they must resist the blandishments of the Three Ladies; and accompanied by Pamina and armed with the flute, surprisingly mild trials by fire and water. The Queen, who has infiltrated the temple with the help of the jealous Monostatos, is vanquished. Papageno, despite his failings, is rewarded with the bird woman Papagena. And Tamina and Pamino are elevated to priesthood, light triumphing over darkness.

Die Zauberflöte may be read as a post-Enlightenment allegory acknowledging the presence of true evil in the world (the Queen and her minions) and in each of us, which must be overcome through heroic acts and personal development leading to wisdom. Wisdom results from understanding nature through reason, a dyad symbolized by the Egyptian deities Isis and Osiris, respectively, the triad of nature, reason, and wisdom being represented by Sarastro's three temples. Merely reclaiming nature is insufficient, as illustrated by the cowardly Papageno and the lustful Monostatos, Rousseauvian "natural men" driven by instinctual desires and fears. Social reform depends on an elite class of educated, primarily aristocratic leaders counseled by idealist artists, all of whom have resisted regression into a comfortable childlike naturalness (Papageno and Papagena) and attained wisdom through intellectual cultivation and character building in tests of adversity (the trials of the aristocratic Tamino and Pamina, and Zarastro).

The spiritual marriage represented by the union of the hero and heroine completes the actualization of individuals seen in Tamino and Pamina's effortless passage through fire and water. In such partnerships, **women** play a supporting role defined by their innate strengths and weaknesses: their emotional, loving nature makes them potentially virtuous moral compasses but at the same time leads to irrational, erratic, and often deceitful behavior (particularly in public arenas, as demonstrated by the Queen and her Ladies) limiting them to supporting roles and necessitating their guidance by rational men (Pamina must learn wisdom from Zarastro's male society).

Mozart's audience was quick to draw parallels with contemporary leaders. The Queen of the Night may have represented the Holy Roman Empress Maria Theresa (ruled with Francis I, 1745–65), an intolerant Roman Catholic whose reign was characterized as arbitrary, bigoted, and superstitious. Tamino stood in for her son Joseph II, her successor as Holy Roman Emperor (1765–1790), one of the most beloved Enlightened despots of the late 18th century, a religiously tolerant, ardent reformer and patron of the arts. And Sarastro perhaps impersonated Ignaz von Born (1742–1791), an influential scientist during the 1770s, Mozart's mentor in the Freemason's lodge "Benevolence," and master of the Viennese lodge of the Bavarian Illuminati.

Mozart's music also ignores the traditional limitations of the genre, drawing on his full palette of idioms and affects. Quasi-**baroque** lament and rage **arias** for the Queen (e.g., "O zittre nicht," Act 1) convey her aristocratic egoism, self-importance, and lack of true humanity. Sentimental episodic melody distinguishes Tamino's acculturated naturalness ("Dies Bildnis ist bezaubernd schön") from Papageno's folklike naiveté ("Der Vogelfänger bin ich ja") and **opera buffa** slapstick (for example, the Act 1 quintet in which Papageno's mouth is padlocked), and from the hymnic style of Sarastro and his priests ("O Isis und Osiris," Act 2). While the miniature set pieces adhere to singspiel tradition, they combine in magnificent scene complexes at the ends of acts for Sarastro's ritual introduction (Act 1) and the trials and expulsion of the dark Queen (Act 2). Furthermore, Mozart devoted the same attention to ensembles and **choruses** as in his opere buffe, and the **overture** is a symphonic tour de force integrated into the opera by introducing the recurring Masonic motive of the three chords.

ZEITOPER. "Opera of the times" popular in Weimar Germany during the 1920s and early 1930s. **Richard Strauss**'s *Intermezzo* (1924) may be viewed as an early example. *Zeitoper* involves contemporary characters and situations; explores current social and political issues (normally in a comic or satirical vein); features references to modern business, industry, and technology; and incorporates popular-sounding music often flavored by jazz. For example, the title character of **Ernst Krenek**'s *Jonny spielt auf* (*Jonny Strikes Up the Band*, 1927) is a jazz musician and person of color, and the opera's settings include city streets and a train station. In **Paul Hindemith**'s *Neues vom Tage* (*News of the Day*, 1929), a couple whose marriage is falling apart becomes media fodder when the husband is imprisoned for attacking his presumed rival with a priceless museum piece, and she is later discovered in the bathtub of her hotel room with her supposed lover present. *Zeitopern* were suppressed under Nazi rule beginning in the mid-1930s as instruments of social criticism and decadence. The genre is related to more recent, so-called CNN (Cable News Network) operas based on contemporary news events, such as **John Adams**'s *Nixon in China* and *The Death of Klinghoffer* (1991), and celebrity operas (*People Magazine* operas?) such as Mark-Anthony Turnage's (born 1960) *Anna Nicole* (2011).

See also EATON, JOHN C; WEILL, KURT.

ZENO, APOSTOLO. (1668, Venice–1750, Venice.) Italian poet, **librettist**, and historian; one of the leading figures in the **Arcadian** reform movement ca. 1700. He founded the Accademia degli Animosi (Academy of the Bold) with his Venetian patron and employer Giovanni Carlo Grimani in 1691. Zeno served as imperial Italian court poet in **Vienna** (1718–29)—he had previously refused the position in 1705—until he was replaced by **Pietro Metastasio**. His almost four dozen **librettos**, written from the 1690s through the 1720s, were set multiple times by virtually all the leading composers of the early 18th century and were adapted as late as the 1790s.

Zeno's academy shared with the **Arcadian Academy**, by which it would eventually be absorbed, the goal of reforming poetry and the theater, and legitimizing and ennobling the opera libretto, taking cues from the naturalness of ancient **pastoral** drama; the refined language of the 16th-century poet Giovanni Battista Guarini (e.g., *Il pastor fido*, 1590); the architectural clarity of the classicizing French **baroque** tragedies of Pierre Corneille and Jean Racine; and the simplifying **unities** recommended by Aristotle.

Zeno's librettos follow these principles throughout his *drammi per musica* beginning with his first, *Gl'inganni felici* (1696), set by Carlo Francesco Pollarolo (ca. 1653–1723). Moralizing stories that encourage aristocratic audiences to temper impulse with reason and to respect the social hierarchy are taken from the history or myth of ancient Greece or Rome, the Middle Ages, or occasionally exotic locales such as China, India, or Persia. Their happy endings (*see* LIETO FINE) reward ethical behavior. Fewer subplots (particularly comic ones), scene changes, and disguises intrude to complicate and trivialize the discourse. Accordingly, Zeno's librettos are populated by relatively few characters, a greater majority of them aristocrats absent the comic servants, nurses, or soldiers who had accompanied them in the late 17th century. Zeno followed the current trend toward conventionalized short **scenes**: most begin with a **recitative** written in loose *versi sciolti* (*see* VERSIFICATION) that presents real-time, expository interaction among the characters; an exit **aria**, normally in two stanzas of *versi lirici* appropriate for da capo form; and then provides a generalized, reflective, often moralizing aside. Expanded recitatives allow for literary and philosophical development, while the formalized arias create a more universal emotional and ethical context through commentary similar to that of a Greek chorus.

Bibliography

CONTENTS

INTRODUCTION

The current body of operatic scholarship is immense, having grown prodigiously beginning in the 1970s as opera gained increasing legitimacy as a musicological subspecialty for historical research and interpretation, and is far too extensive for a complete account to be given in a compact printed volume. For that reason, the present bibliography is limited to major studies in English from the last three decades that are pertinent to entries included in the dictionary; essays that appear within collections are not cited individually; publications of primary source materials (manuscripts and printed scores and editions of operas and librettos, collections of letters, and other documents) have not been included; and admittedly subjective decisions to omit overly specialized or insufficiently appropriate publications were necessarily made. In short, it is intended simply as a sample of the available literature, an entry point for further reading concerning the many topics introduced in this volume.

Broader investigation of these topics and related literature may be pursued beginning with *The New Grove Dictionary of Opera* and *The New Grove Dictionary of Music and Musicians* (both Stanley Sadie, ed., available online at Oxford Music Online, www.oxfordmusiconline.com), the most authoritative encyclopedic reference tools for musical topics, and the bibliographies of their individual entries. RILM (Répertoire International de Littérature Musicale) Abstracts of Music Literature, the standard bibliographical search engine for music research (available online at www.rilm.org), gives an exhaustive account of recent scholarship. Also helpful are the printed annotated composer bibliographies released by General Music and (more recently) Routledge (and others), the most up-to-date of which include Stephen A. Willier, *Vincenzo Bellini: A Research and Information Guide*; Bryan R. Simms, *Alban Berg: A Research and Information Guide*; Peter J. Hodgson, *Benjamin Britten: A Guide to Research*; James P. Cassaro, *Gaetano Donizetti: A Guide to Research*; Patricia Howard, *Christoph Willibald Gluck: A Guide to Research*; Mary Ann Parker, *G. F. Handel: A Guide to Research*; Robert Ignatius Letellier and Marco Clemente Pellegrini, *Giacomo Meyerbeer: A Guide to Research*; Linda B. Fairtile, *Giacomo Puccini: A Guide to Research*; Denise P. Gallo, *Gioachino Rossini: A Research and Information Guide*; Gregory W. Harwood, *Giuseppe Verdi: A Research and Information Guide*; and Michael Saffle, *Richard Wagner: A Research and Information Guide.*

Overviews such as Donald Jay Grout, *A Short History of Opera*, in its 4th edition still the standard textbook survey of opera history, and Patrick J. Smith, *The Tenth Muse: A Historical Study of the Opera Libretto*; period studies—such as Anthony R. DelDonna and Pierpaolo Polzonetti, eds., *The Cambridge Companion to Eighteenth-Century Opera*, and Mervyn Cooke, ed., *The Cambridge Companion to Twentieth-Century Opera*; and Marion Kant, ed., *The Cambridge Companion to Ballet*, provide informative background for pursuing more specialized topics. Alongside the Grove dictionaries, John Warrack and Ewan West, *The Oxford Dictionary of Opera*; Michael Kennedy, ed., *Who's Who in Opera: A Guide to Opera Characters*; and Ken Wlaschin, *Encyclopedia of Opera on Screen: A Guide to More Than 100 Years of Opera Films, Videos, and DVDs*, are useful reference tools. Novices may find Robert Cannon, *Opera*; Denise P. Gallo, *Opera: The Basics*; David Pogue and Scott Speck, *Opera for Dummies*; and Alexandra Wilson, *Opera: A Beginner's Guide*, to be user-friendly entry points.

Interested readers might turn next to more specialized studies of national, regional, or local traditions, which deal variously with social, political, literary, aesthetic, artistic, philosophical, and theatrical contexts for the development of operatic music and the libretto, aspects of production, and dance. Excellent starting points for Italy include David Kimbell, *Italian Opera* (through Puccini); Ellen Rosand, *Opera in Seventeenth-Century Venice: The Creation of a Genre* (covering the period 1637–1678); Michael Robinson, *Naples and Neapolitan Opera* (in the 18th century); Alan Mallach, *The Autumn of Italian Opera: From Verismo to Modernism (1890–1915)*; Deirdre

O'Grady, *The Last Troubadours: Poetic Drama in Italian Opera, 1597–1887* (the history of the libretto); and John Rosselli, *The Opera Industry in Italy from Cimarosa to Verdi: The Role of the Impresario.* For France, see Vincent Giroud, *French Opera: A Short History*; Downing A. Thomas, *Aesthetics of Opera in the* Ancien Régime, *1647–1785*; Caroline Wood, *Music and Drama in the "Tragédie en musique," 1673–1715: Jean-Baptiste Lully and His Successors*; Georgia Cowart, *The Triumph of Pleasure: Louis XIV and the Politics of Spectacle*; Paul F. Rice, *Fontainebleau Operas for the Court of Louis XV of France by Jean-Philippe Rameau (1683–1764)*; David Charlton, *Grétry and the Growth of the Opéra-comique*; Jane F. Fulcher, *The Nation's Image: French Grand Opera as Politics and Politicized Art*; David Charlton, ed., *The Cambridge Companion to Grand Opera* (including chapters on *grand opéra* outside of France); Marian Smith, *Ballet and Opera in the Age of Giselle* (mid-19th-century Paris); and Steven Huebner, *French Opera at the* Fin de siècle: *Wagnerism, Nationalism, and Style* (late 19th century).

For Germany, alongside John Hamilton Warrack's indispensable survey, *German Opera: From the Beginnings to Wagner*, are several more narrowly focused studies: Thomas Bauman, *North German Opera in the Age of Goethe* (second half of the 18th century); Gundula Kreuzer, *Verdi and the Germans: From Unification to the Third Reich* (the challenge of Italian opera to late 19th- and 20th-century perceptions of Germanic musical supremacy); and Michael Meyer, *The Politics of Music in the Third Reich* (not exclusively opera). Viennese opera is represented by Bruce Alan Brown, *Gluck and the French Theater in Vienna*; John A. Rice, *Antonio Salieri and Viennese Opera*; and Mary Hunter, *The Culture of Opera Buffa in Mozart's Vienna: A Poetics of Entertainment* (all broader studies of late 18th-century Viennese opera and social institutions than their titles might suggest). Eric Walter White's *A History of English Opera* provides a framework for studies of specific English historical periods such as Carl Steven LaRue, *Handel and His Singers: The Creation of the Royal Academy Operas, 1720–1728*; Roger Fiske, *English Theater Music in the Eighteenth Century* (Purcell to the end of the 18th century); Jane Girdham, *English Opera in Late Eighteenth-Century London: Stephen Storace at Drury Lane* (the last decade of the 18th century); and Jennifer L. Hall-Witt, *Fashionable Acts: Opera and Elite Culture in London, 1780–1880.* Other national traditions are examined in John Tyrrell, *Czech Opera* (Smetana to Janáček); Brian Locke, *Opera and Ideology in Prague* (1900–World War II); Judit Frigyesi, *Béla Bartók and Turn-of-the-Century Budapest*; Mikuláš Bek et al., eds., *Socialist Realism and Music* (numerous essays on 20th-century Russia); Colin Mackerras, *Peking Opera*; and Ken Wlaschin, *Encyclopedia of American Opera.*

Composer (and librettist) biographies are plentiful, boasting a history that extends back to the 19th century, and a number of the more recent ones are cited in this bibliography under composer names. Cambridge University

Press's growing series of *Companions* to composers, either opera specialists—e.g., Emanuele Senici, ed., *The Cambridge Companion to Rossini*, and *Companions* for Verdi (Scott L Balthazar, ed.); Wagner (Thomas Grey, ed.); Richard Strauss (Charles Youmans, ed.); and Britten (Mervyn Cooke, ed.)—or generalists who made important contributions to the genre—e.g., Monteverdi (John Whenham and Richard Wistreich, eds.); Handel (Donald James Burrows, ed.); and Mozart (Simon P. Keefe, ed.)—are readily accessible and provide wide-ranging biographical, cultural, theatrical, and stylistic context. So too do a number of other composer companions and dictionaries, such as William Weaver and Simonetta Puccini, eds., *The Puccini Companion*, and Roberta M. Marvin, ed., *The Cambridge Verdi Encyclopedia* (forthcoming 2013). Recent monographs on the works of specific 17th-century composers include Tim Carter, *Monteverdi's Musical Theater*; Ellen Rosand, *Monteverdi's Last Operas: A Venetian Trilogy*; and Jane Glover, *Cavalli*. For 18th-century figures, see Rodney Bolt, *The Librettist of Venice: The Remarkable Life of Lorenzo Da Ponte, Mozart's Poet, Casanova's Friend, and Italian Opera's Impresario in America*; Eric Cross, *The Late Operas of Antonio Vivaldi*; Donald Jay Grout, *Alessandro Scarlatti: An Introduction to his Operas*; and Anthony Holden, *The Man Who Wrote Mozart: The Extraordinary Life of Lorenzo Da Ponte*. Mozart is, of course, well represented, for example by Daniel Heartz, *Mozart's Operas*; William Mann, *The Operas of Mozart*; Charles Osborne, *The Complete Operas of Mozart: A Critical Guide*; John A. Rice, *Mozart on the Stage*; and Andrew Steptoe, *The Mozart–Da Ponte Operas: The Cultural and Musical Background to* Le nozze di Figaro, Don Giovanni, *and* Così fan tutte. Readers interested in the 19th century may enjoy William Ashbrook, *Donizetti and His Operas*; John Black, *The Italian Romantic Libretto: A Study of Salvadore Cammarano*; Julian Budden, *The Operas of Verdi*; John Deathridge, *Wagner Beyond Good and Evil*; Steven Huebner, *The Operas of Charles Gounod*; Knud Arne Jürgensen, *The Verdi Ballets*; David R. B. Kimbell, *Verdi in the Age of Italian Romanticism*; and Benjamin Walton, *Rossini in Restoration Paris: The Sound of Modern Life*. For the 20th century, see Daniel Albright, *Stravinsky: The Music Box and the Nightingale*; Joanna Bottenberg, *Shared Creation: Words and Music in the Hofmannsthal-Strauss Operas*; Foster Hirsch, *Kurt Weill on Stage: From Berlin to Broadway*; Charles Osborne, *The Complete Operas of Puccini: A Critical Guide*; and Philip Rupprecht, *Britten's Musical Language*.

Monographs on individual operas are led by the expanding library of Cambridge University Press companions to iconic works from the 18th through the 20th centuries (e.g., Tim Carter, *W. A. Mozart:* Le nozze di Figaro; James A. Hepokoski, *Giuseppe Verdi:* Otello; Mosco Carner, *Giacomo Puccini:* Tosca; and Philip Brett, *Benjamin Britten:* Peter Grimes), many of which are cited in this bibliography. They consider such wide-ranging issues as social, political, theatrical, literary, and musical-stylistic context; the creative process; and staging and reception, and provide close analysis of text and music. Other fine studies of this sort include Eric Chafe, *The Tragic and the Ecstatic: The Musical Revolution of Wagner's* Tristan und Isolde; Caryl Emerson, Boris Godunov: *Transpositions of a Russian Theme*; Bryan Gilliam, *Richard Strauss's* Elektra; William Ashbrook and Harold Powers, *Puccini's* Turandot: *The End of the Great Tradition*; and Nicholas John, ed., *Benjamin Britten:* Peter Grimes *and* Gloriana.

Scholarship that examines connections between opera and literature and spoken drama, politics, psychology, philosophy, and the other arts, including cinema in the 20th century, contributes provocative interdisciplinary perspectives. Books providing broad overviews of such topics across multiple centuries include John Bokina, *Opera and Politics: From Monteverdi to Henze*; Milton Brener, *Opera Offstage: Passion and Politics behind the Great Operas* (examines the historical and theatrical background of two dozen iconic operas); Robert Donington, *Opera and Its Symbols: The Unity of Words, Music, and Staging* (psychological foundations of paradigmatic images and themes in opera); Gloria Flaherty, *Opera in the Development of German Critical Thought*; Herbert Samuel Lindenberger, *Opera in History: From Monteverdi to Cage* and *Situating Opera: Period, Genre, Reception* (social, political, intellectual, and psychological preconditions of opera); Joseph Kerman, *Opera as Drama* (a venerable classic, one of the first to take opera seriously as a topic of comparative analysis and criticism); Frits Noske, *The Signifier and the Signified: Studies in the Operas of Mozart and Verdi* (semiotic study of select masterworks); Eric A. Plaut, *Grand Opera: Mirror of the Western Mind* (psychiatric study of operas from Mozart through Richard Strauss); Paul Robinson, *Opera and Ideas: From Mozart to Strauss*; Gary Schmidgall, *Shakespeare and Opera*; Daniel Snowman, *The Gilded Stage: A Social History of Opera*; and Gary Tomlinson, *Metaphysical Song: An Essay in Opera* (opera as intellectual history).

Excellent interdisciplinary studies focused specifically on the 18th century include David J. Buch, *Magic Flutes and Enchanted Forests: The Supernatural in Eighteenth-Century Musical Theater*; Charles William Dill, *Monstrous Opera: Rameau and the Tragic Tradition*; Martha Feldman, *Opera and Sovereignty: Transforming Myths in Eighteenth-Century Italy* (opera seria); Edmund J. Goehring, *Three Modes of Perception in Mozart: The Philosophical, Pastoral, and Comic in* Così fan tutte; Ellen T. Harris, *Handel and the Pastoral Tradition*; Nicholas Till, *Mozart and the Enlightenment: Truth, Virtue, and Beauty in Mozart's Operas*; Jessica P. Waldoff, *Recognition in Mozart's Operas*; and Adrienne Ward, *Pagodas in Play: China on the Eighteenth-Century Italian Opera Stage*. For the 19th century, see Carolyn Abbate, *Unsung Voices: Opera and Musical Narrative in the 19th Century*; Sandra Corse, *Wagner and the New Consciousness: Language and Love in the* Ring; Laurence Dreyfus, *Wagner and the Erotic Impulse*; Barry Emslie,

Richard Wagner and the Centrality of Love; Cormac Newark, *Opera in the Novel from Balzac to Proust*; Susan Vandiver Nicassio, *Tosca's Rome: The Play and Opera in Historical Perspective*; Mary Ann Smart, *Mimomania: Music and Gesture in Nineteenth-Century Opera* (Auber through Wagner); and James Treadwell, *Interpreting Wagner* (recurring themes in Wagner's prose writings and operas). And for the 20th century, the reader may be interested in Elliot Antokoletz, *Musical Symbolism in the Operas of Debussy and Bartók: Trauma, Gender, and the Unfolding Unconscious*; Marcia J. Citron, *Opera on Screen*; and David P. Schroeder, *Cinema's Illusions, Opera's Allure: The Operatic Impulse in Film*.

Increasing attention has been paid over the past two decades to issues of gender and ethnicity in opera, including aspects of patronage, social expectations, the law, literary characterization, sexuality, and training and professional opportunities. Noteworthy studies include for the 17th century Kelley Harness, *Echoes of Women's Voices: Music, Art, and Female Patronage in Early Modern Florence*, and Wendy Heller, *Emblems of Eloquence: Opera and Women's Voices in Seventeenth-Century Venice*; for the 18th, Kristi Brown-Montesano, *Understanding the Women of Mozart's Operas*; and for the 19th, Emanuele Senici, *Landscape and Gender in Italian Opera: The Alpine Virgin from Bellini to Puccini*; Jeffrey Peter Bauer, *Woman and the Changing Concept of Salvation in the Operas of Richard Wagner*; Ryan Edwards and Geoffrey Edwards, *Verdi and Puccini Heroines: Dramatic Characterization in Great Soprano Roles*; Nila Parly, *Vocal Victories: Wagner's Female Characters from Senta to Kundry*; and Eva Rieger, *Richard Wagner's Women*. While not exclusively operatic in orientation, Jane L Baldauf-Berdes, *Women Musicians of Venice: Musical Foundations, 1525–1855*, examines professional training for women in a particularly significant conservatory system. Eric Ledell Smith, *Blacks in Opera: An Encyclopedia of People and Companies, 1873–1993*, is an important resource on more than a century of involvement in opera by persons of color, while Naomi André et al., eds., *Blackness in Opera: How Race and Blackness Play Out in Opera*, explores numerous provocative topics involving race.

Also relatively recently, studies of contemporary performance practice and staging, particularly collections of essays on the 19th century, have emphasized the intrinsic role played by the musical and visual interpretation of the score in establishing an opera's identity. See, for example, Philip Gossett, *Divas and Scholars: Performing Italian Opera*; Alison Latham and Roger Parker, eds., *Verdi in Performance*; Barry Millington and Stewart Spencer, eds., *Wagner in Performance*; Hilary Poriss, *Changing the Score: Arias, Prima Donnas, and the Authority of Performance* (on 19th-century aria substitution); Rudolf Hartmann, *Richard Strauss: The Staging of His Operas and Ballets*; and Martha Elliott, *Singing in Style: A Guide to Vocal Performance Practices* (not exclusively operatic).

On singers, numerous biographies, some of which have been included in this bibliography, are available. Broader reference books, monographs, and collections of essays include Laura Macy, *The Grove Book of Opera Singers* (which contains entries in addition to those appearing in the *New Grove* dictionaries); John Rosselli, *Singers of Italian Opera: The History of a Profession* (confined to the industry as it developed in Italy 1600 to the late 20th century); Rodolfo Celletti, *A History of Bel Canto*; Rachel Cowgill and Hilary Poriss, eds., *The Arts of the Prima Donna in the Long Nineteenth Century*; Susan Rutherford, *The Prima Donna and Opera, 1815–1930*; Richard Somerset-Ward, *Angels and Monsters: Male and Female Sopranos in the Story of Opera, 1600–1900*; and John Potter, *Tenor: History of a Voice*.

In addition to Oxford Music Online and RILM (mentioned above), several among the hundreds of opera-related websites provide especially rich troves of information, links, and other materials. OperaGlass (opera. stanford.edu) is a huge site that includes full texts of hundreds of librettos and literary sources for many operas, historical background (including performance histories and lists of roles and their creators), plot summaries, discographies, and links to dozens of opera company home pages worldwide. The Aria Database (www.aria-database.com) provides information, texts and translations, and partial sound files for approximately 1,300 arias by Mozart, Berlioz, Verdi, Wagner, and Puccini and roughly 50 additional composers. Italian Opera (www.italianopera.org) contains information regarding hundreds of composers and operas, including scene-by-scene plot summaries (in Italian). Modern editions of hundreds of librettos are available at www.librettidopera.it and www.naxos.com/education. Among composer society websites, that of the Donizetti Society (www.donizettisociety.com) has much to offer. Finally, though not specifically operatic, more general research tools—such as WorldCat (www.worldcat.org), the international union library catalog, and IMSLP (www.imslp.org), the International Musical Score Library Project/Petrucci Music Library, a rapidly expanding online repository of music in the public domain that contains a myriad of printed scores and manuscripts of operas and music files for download—are indispensable resources for accessing hard-to-find items.

STUDIES SPANNING MORE THAN ONE CENTURY

Abbate, Carolyn. "'Tristan' in the Composition of 'Pelleas.'" *19th-Century Music* 5 (1981): 117–41.
Aldrich-Moodie, James Dunbar. *Toward a Sociology of Opera and Literature: Three Case Studies*. Ph.D. dissertation, Stanford University, 1998.

Anderson, James. *The Complete Dictionary of Opera and Operetta*. New York: Wings, 1993.

André, Naomi, et al., eds. *Blackness in Opera: How Race and Blackness Play Out in Opera*. Urbana: University of Illinois Press, 2012.

Anthony, James R. "Air and Aria Added to French Opera from the Death of Lully to 1720." *Revue de musicologie* 77 (1991): 201–19.

Arnold, Denis. "Orphans and Ladies: The Venetian Conservatories (1680–1790)." *Proceedings of the Royal Musical Association* 89 (1962–63): 31–47.

Bacht, Nikolaus, ed. *Music, Theater, and Politics in Germany: 1848 to the Third Reich*. Aldershot, England: Ashgate, 2006.

Baldauf-Berdes, Jane L. *Women Musicians of Venice: Musical Foundations, 1525–1855*. Oxford: Clarendon, 1996; originally 1993.

Baragwanath, Nicholas. "Alban Berg, Richard Wagner, and Leitmotivs of Symmetry." *19th-Century Music* 23 (1999): 62–83.

———. *The Italian Traditions and Puccini: Compositional Theory and Practice in Nineteenth-Century Opera*. Bloomington: Indiana University Press, 2011.

Barbieri, Patrizio. "The Acoustics of Italian Opera Houses and Auditoriums (ca. 1450–1900)." In Marco Di Pasquale and Fabrizio Della Seta, eds., *In Memoria di Nino Pirrotta. Recercare: Rivista per lo Studio e la Pratica Della Musica Antica* 10 (1998): 263–328.

Batta, András, and Sigrid Neef. *Opera: Composers, Works, Performers*. Translated by Paul Aston. Cologne: Könemann, 2000.

Benzecry, Claudio E. *The Opera Fanatic: Ethnography of an Obsession*. Chicago: University of Chicago Press, 2011.

Bianconi, Lorenzo, and Giorgio Pestelli, eds. *The History of Italian Opera, Part II: Systems*. Vol. 4, *Opera Production and Its Resources*. Vol. 5, *Opera on Stage*. Vol. 6, *Opera in Theory and Practice, Image, and Myth*. Translated by Lydia G. Cochrane. Chicago: University of Chicago Press, 1998–2003.

Blackburn, Bonnie J., ed. *Music and Culture in Eighteenth-Century Europe: A Source Book*. Chicago: University of Chicago Press, 1994.

Blackmer, Corinne E., and Patricia Juliana Smith, eds. *En travesti: Women, Gender Subversion, Opera*. New York: Columbia University Press, 1995.

Blažeković, Zdravko, ed. *Music, Body, and Stage: The Iconography of Music Theater and Opera*. New York: City University of New York, 2009.

Bokina, John. *Opera and Politics: From Monteverdi to Henze*. New Haven, Conn.: Yale University Press, 1997.

Bordman, Gerald. *American Operetta*. New York: Oxford University Press, 1981.

Bourne, Joyce. *Opera: The Great Composers and Their Masterworks*. London: Mitchell Beazley, 2008.

Bowen, José Antonio, ed. *The Cambridge Companion to Conducting*. Cambridge: Cambridge University Press, 2003.

Boyden, Matthew. *The Rough Guide to Opera*. London: Rough Guides, 2007.

Branscombe, Peter. "Music in the Viennese Popular Theater of the Eighteenth and Nineteenth Centuries." *Proceedings of the Royal Musical Association* 98 (1971): 101–12.

Brener, Milton. *Opera Offstage: Passion and Politics behind the Great Operas*. New York: Walker, 1996.

Bucciarelli, Melania. *Italian Opera and European Theater, 1680–1720: Plots, Performers, Dramaturgies*. Turnhout, Belgium: Brepols, 2000.

Burgess, Geoffrey. *Ritual in the* Tragédie en musique *from Lully's* Cadmus et Hermione *(1673) to Rameau's* Zoroastre *(1749)*. Ph.D. dissertation, Cornell University, 1998.

Cannon, Robert. *Opera*. New York: Cambridge University Press, 2012.

Carter, Tim. *Music in Late Renaissance and Early Baroque Italy*. London: Batsford, 1992.

Celletti, Rodolfo. *A History of Bel Canto*. Translated by Frederick Fuller. Oxford: Clarendon Press, 1991.

Charlton, David. *French Opera 1730–1830: Meaning and Media*. Aldershot, England: Ashgate, 2000.

———. *Orchestration and Orchestral Practice in Paris, 1789–1810*. Ph.D. dissertation, University of Cambridge, 1974.

Christiansen, Rupert. *A Pocket Guide to Opera*. London: Faber and Faber, 2002.

Chua, Daniel K. L. "Untimely Reflections on Operatic Echoes: How Sound Travels in Monteverdi's *L'Orfeo* and Beethoven's *Fidelio* with a Short Instrumental Interlude." *Opera Quarterly* 21 (2005): 573–96.

Clark, Caryl, and Linda Hutcheon, eds. "Opera and Interdisciplinarity." *University of Toronto Quarterly* 72 (2003): 769–869.

Coeyman, Barbara. "Theaters for Opera and Ballet during the Reign of Louis XIV and Louis XV." *Early Music* 18 (1990): 22–37.

Conrad, Peter. *Verdi and/or Wagner: Two Men, Two Worlds, Two Centuries*. London: Thames and Hudson, 2011.

Cowgill, Rachel, et al., eds. *Art and Ideology in European Opera: Essays in Honor of Julian Rushton*. Woodbridge, England: Boydell, 2010.

Deane, Basil. "The French Operatic Overture from Grétry to Berlioz." *Proceedings of the Royal Musical Association* 99 (1972): 67–80.

Dellamora, Richard, and Daniel Fischlin, eds. *The Work of Opera: Genre, Nationhood, and Sexual Difference*. New York: Columbia University Press, 1997.

DeMarco, Laura E. "The Fact of the Castrato and the Myth of the Countertenor." *Musical Quarterly* 86 (2002): 174–85.

Donington, Robert. *Opera and Its Symbols: The Unity of Words, Music, and Staging.* New Haven, Conn.: Yale University Press, 1990.

Dowling, John. "Fortunes and Misfortunes of the Spanish Lyric Theater in the Eighteenth Century." *Comparative Drama* 31 (1997): 129–57.

Downey, Charles. *Musical-Dramatic Productions Derived from Ariosto and Tasso in the City of Paris, 1600–1800.* Ph.D. dissertation, Catholic University of America, 1998.

Edwards, Ryan, and Geoffrey Edwards. *Verdi and Puccini Heroines: Dramatic Characterization in Great Soprano Roles.* Lanham, Md.: Scarecrow Press, 2001.

Elliott, Martha. *Singing in Style: A Guide to Vocal Performance Practices.* New Haven, Conn.: Yale University Press, 2006.

Esse, Melina Elizabeth. *Sospirare, Tremare, Piangere: Conventions of the Body in Italian Opera.* Ph.D. dissertation, University of California, Berkeley, 2004.

Ewen, David. *The New Encyclopedia of the Opera.* New York: Hill and Wang, 1971.

Fader, Donald James. *Musical Thought and Patronage of the Italian Style at the Court of Philippe II, Duc d'Orleans (1674–1723).* Ph.D. dissertation, Stanford University, 2000.

Fauser, Annegret, and Mark Everist, eds. *Music, Theater, and Cultural Transfer: Paris, 1830–1914.* Chicago: University of Chicago Press, 2009.

Fenlon, Iain, and Tim Carter, eds. *Con che soavità: Studies in Italian Opera, Song, and Dance, 1580–1740.* Oxford: Clarendon, 1995.

Flaherty, Gloria. *Opera in the Development of German Critical Thought.* Princeton, N.J.: Princeton University Press, 1978.

Frassà, Lorenzo, ed. *The Opéra-Comique in the Eighteenth and Nineteenth Centuries.* Turnhout, Belgium: Brepols, 2011.

Freeman, Robert. *Opera without Drama: Currents of Change in Italian Opera 1675–1725.* Ann Arbor, Mich.: UMI Research Press, 1981.

Freitas, Roger. "The Eroticism of Emasculation: Confronting the Baroque Body of the Castrato." *Journal of Musicology* 20 (2003): 196–249.

Galkin, Elliott W. *A History of Orchestral Conducting: In Theory and Practice.* Stuyvesant, N.Y.: Pendragon, 1988.

Gallo, Denise P. *Opera: The Basics.* New York: Routledge, 2006.

Gattey, Charles Neilson. *Queens of Song.* London: Barrie and Jenkins, 1979.

Gibbons, William. *Eighteenth-Century Opera and the Construction of National Identity in France, 1875–1918.* Ph.D. dissertation, University of North Carolina, 2010.

Gier, Albert. "Guillaume Tell in French Opera: From Grétry to Rossini." In Suzanne M. Lodato et al., eds., *Essays in Honor of Steven Paul Scher and on Cultural Identity and the Musical Stage,* 229–44. Amsterdam: Rodopi, 2002.

Giroud, Vincent. *French Opera: A Short History*. New Haven, Conn.: Yale University Press, 2010.

Goehr, Lydia, and Daniel A. Herwitz, eds. *The Don Giovanni Moment: Essays on the Legacy of an Opera*. New York: Columbia University Press, 2006.

Griffel, Margaret Ross. *Operas in English: A Dictionary*. Westport, Conn.: Greenwood, 1999.

Griffin, Robert A. *High Baroque Culture and Theatre in Vienna*. New York: Humanities Press, 1972.

Grout, Donald Jay. *A Short History of Opera*. Rev. 4th ed. Edited by Hermine Weigel Williams. New York: Columbia University Press, 2003.

Grover-Friedlander, Michal. *Operatic Afterlives*. Brooklyn, N.Y.: Zone, 2011.

Guest, Ivor Forbes. *The Paris Opéra Ballet*. Alton, U.K.: Dance Books, 2006.

Guinn, John, and Les Stone, eds. *The St. James Opera Encyclopedia: A Guide to People and Works*. Detroit, Mich.: Visible Ink, 1997.

Haldey, Olga. *Mamontov's Private Opera: The Search for Modernism in Russian Theater*. Bloomington: Indiana University Press, 2010.

Hall-Witt, Jennifer L. *Fashionable Acts: Opera and Elite Culture in London, 1780–1880*. Durham: University of New Hampshire, 2007.

Hamilton, David, ed. *The Metropolitan Opera Encyclopedia: A Comprehensive Guide to the World of Opera*. New York: Simon and Schuster, 1987.

Helfgot, Daniel, and William O. Beeman. *The Third Line: The Opera Performer as Interpreter*. New York: Schirmer, 1993.

Hill, John W. *Baroque Music: Music in Western Europe, 1580–1750*. New York: Norton, 2005.

Holden, Amanda. *The Penguin Concise Guide to Opera*. London: Penguin, 2005.

Hosford, Desmond. *Redefining Perfection: The Lullian Aesthetic and Its 18th-Century Development*. Ph.D. dissertation, City University of New York, 2004.

Hughes, Derek. *Culture and Sacrifice: Ritual Death in Literature and Opera*. Cambridge: Cambridge University Press, 2007.

Hutcheon, Linda, and Michael Hutcheon. *Opera: Desire, Disease, and Death*. Lincoln: University of Nebraska Press, 1996.

Hyman, Alan. *Sullivan and His Satellites: A Study of English Operettas, 1860–1914*. London: Chappell, 1978.

Jander, Owen Hughes. "The Three Chapters of the Orpheus Myth as They Figure in Librettos of Operas: The Favorite Episode, the Subject Avoided, and the Theme Cultivated." In David Rosen and Claire Brook, eds., *Words on Music: Essays in Honor of Andrew Porter on the Occasion of His 75th Birthday*, 152–70. Hillsdale, N.Y.: Pendragon, 2003.

Jensen, Niels Martin, and Franco Piperno, eds. *The Opera Orchestra in 18th- and 19th-Century Europe*. 2 vols. Berlin: Berliner Wissenschafts-Verlag, 2008.

Joe, Jeongwon. *Opera on Film, Film in Opera: Postmodern Implications of the Cinematic Influence on Opera*. Ph.D. dissertation, Northwestern University, 1998.

Joe, Jeongwon, and Rose Theresa, eds. *Between Opera and Cinema*. New York: Routledge, 2002.

Johnson, James H. *Listening in Paris: A Cultural History*. Berkeley: University of California Press, 1995.

Johnson, Victoria, et al., eds. *Opera and Society in Italy and France from Monteverdi to Bourdieu*. Cambridge: Cambridge University Press, 2007.

Kant, Marion, ed. *The Cambridge Companion to Ballet*. Cambridge: Cambridge University Press, 2007.

Kelly, Thomas Forrest. *First Nights at the Opera*. New Haven, Conn.: Yale University Press, 2004.

Kennedy, Michael, ed. *Who's Who in Opera: A Guide to Opera Characters*. New York: Oxford University Press, 1998.

Kerman, Joseph. *Opera as Drama*. New York: Random House, 1952.

Ketterer, Robert C. *Ancient Rome in Early Opera*. Urbana: University of Illinois Press, 2009.

Kimbell, David. *Italian Opera*. Cambridge: Cambridge University Press, 1991.

Kirkendale, Warren. *The Court Musicians in Florence during the Principate of the Medici, with a Reconstruction of the Artistic Establishment*. Florence: Olschki, 1993.

Kramer, Lawrence. *Opera and Modern Culture: Wagner and Strauss*. Berkeley: University of California Press, 2004.

Kuhn, Laura, ed. *Baker's Dictionary of Opera*. New York: Schirmer, 2000.

Lamb, Andrew. *150 Years of Popular Musical Theater*. New Haven, Conn.: Yale University Press, 2000.

LaRue, Carl Steven, and Leanda Shrimpton, eds. *International Dictionary of Opera*. Detroit, Mich.: St. James Press, 1993.

Latham, Alison, ed. *The Oxford Companion to Music*. Oxford: Oxford University Press, 2002.

Levin, David J. *Unsettling Opera: Staging Mozart, Verdi, Wagner, and Zemlinsky*. Chicago: University of Chicago Press, 2007.

Lewis, Anthony, and Nigel Fortune, eds. *The New Oxford History of Music*. Vol. 5. *Opera and Church Music 1630–1750*. London: Oxford University Press, 1975.

Lindenberger, Herbert Samuel. *Opera in History: From Monteverdi to Cage*. Stanford, Calif.: Stanford University Press, 1998.

————. *Situating Opera: Period, Genre, Reception*. Cambridge: Cambridge University Press, 2010.

Littlejohn, David. *The Ultimate Art: Essays around and about Opera*. Berkeley: University of California Press, 1992.

Macneil, Anne. *Music and Women of the* Commedia dell'arte *in the Late Sixteenth Century*. Oxford: Oxford University Press, 2003.

Macy, Laura. *The Grove Book of Opera Singers*. New York: Oxford University Press, 2008.

Maes, Francis. *A History of Russian Music: From* Kamarinskaya *to* Babi Yar. Translated by Arnold J. Pomerans and Erica Pomerans. Berkeley: University of California Press, 2002.

Major, Leon, and Michael Laing. *The Empty Voice: Acting Opera*. Milwaukee, Wis.: Amadeus, 2011.

Mallach, Alan. *The Autumn of Italian Opera: From Verismo to Modernism (1890–1915)*. Boston: Northeastern University Press, 2007.

Martin, George Whitney. *Verdi in America*: Oberto *through* Rigoletto. Rochester, N.Y.: University of Rochester, 2011.

Marvin, Roberta Montemorra, and Downing A. Thomas, eds. *Operatic Migrations: Transforming Works and Crossing Boundaries*. Aldershot, England: Ashgate, 2006.

McClary, Susan. *Feminine Endings: Music, Gender, and Sexuality*. Minneapolis: University of Minnesota, 1991.

McDonald, Marianne. *Sing Sorrow: Classics, History, and Heroines in Opera*. Westport, Conn.: Greenwood, 2001.

McGregor, Cynthia Annmarie. *The Musical Language of Dramatic Monologues: A Study of Wotan, Tristan, Salome, Boris, and Grimes*. Ph.D. dissertation, Northwestern University, 2001.

Meldrum Brown, Hilda. *Leitmotiv and Drama: Wagner, Brecht, and the Limits of Epic Theater*. Oxford: Clarendon, 1991.

Meyer, Stephen C. "Terror and Transcendence in the Operatic Prison, 1790–1815." *Journal of the American Musicological Society* 55 (2002): 477–523.

Mezzanotte, Riccardo, ed. *Phaidon Book of Opera: A Survey of 780 Operas from 1597*. Oxford: Phaidon, 1979.

Milhous, Judith. "Opera Finances in London, 1674–1738." *Journal of the American Musicological Society* 37 (1984): 567–92.

Miller, Jonathan, ed. *Don Giovanni: Myths of Seduction and Betrayal*. New York: Schocken, 1990.

Monelle, Raymond. *The Musical Topic: Hunt, Military, and Pastoral*. Bloomington: Indiana University Press, 2006.

Monson, Craig A. "*Giulio Cesare in Egitto*: From Sartorio (1677) to Handel (1724)." *Music and Letters* 66 (1985): 313–43.

Morey, Carl. *An Opera Sampler: Miscellaneous Essays on Opera*. Toronto: Dundurn, 1998.

Morris, Christopher. *Reading Opera between the Lines: Orchestral Interludes and Cultural Meaning from Wagner to Berg*. Cambridge: Cambridge University Press, 2002.

Nalbach, Daniel. *The King's Theatre, 1704–1867: London's First Italian Opera House*. London: Society for Theater Research, 1972.

Naroditskaya, Inna. *Bewitching Russian Opera: The Tsarina from State to Stage*. New York: Oxford University Press, 2012.

Nauman, Philip. *Sirènes, Spectres, Ombres: Dramatic Vocalization in the Nineteenth and Twentieth Centuries*. Ph.D. dissertation, Boston University, 2009.

Newark, Cormac. *Opera in the Novel from Balzac to Proust*. Cambridge: Cambridge University Press, 2011.

Noske, Frits. *The Signifier and the Signified: Studies in the Operas of Mozart and Verdi*. Oxford: Clarendon, 1990; originally 1977.

O'Grady, Deirdre. *The Last Troubadours: Poetic Drama in Italian Opera, 1597–1887*. London: Routledge, 1991.

Orrey, Leslie, ed. *The Encyclopedia of Opera*. New York: Scribner, 1976.

Osborne, Charles. *The Dictionary of the Opera*. New York: Simon and Schuster, 1983.

Parker, Roger. *Remaking the Song: Operatic Visions and Revisions from Handel to Berio*. Berkeley: University of California Press, 2006.

———, ed. *The Oxford History of Opera*. Oxford: Oxford University Press, 1996.

Parsons, Charles H. *Opera Composers and Their Works*. Lewiston, N.Y.: Mellen, 1986.

Pitou, Spire. *The Paris Opéra: An Encyclopedia of Operas, Ballets, Composers, and Performers*. 3 vols. Westport, Conn.: Greenwood, 1983–1990.

Plaut, Eric A. *Grand Opera: Mirror of the Western Mind*. Chicago: Dee, 1993.

Pleasants, Henry. *Opera in Crisis: Tradition, Present, Future*. London: Thames and Hudson, 1989.

Pogue, David, and Scott Speck. *Opera for Dummies*. Foster City, Calif.: Wiley, 1997.

Potter, John. *Tenor: History of a Voice*. New Haven, Conn.: Yale University Press, 2009.

Powers, David M. *The* Pastorale héroique*: Origins and Developments of a Genre of French Opera in the Seventeenth and Eighteenth Centuries*. Ph.D. dissertation, University of Chicago, 1988.

Radice, Mark A., ed. *Opera in Context: Essays on Historical Staging from the Late Renaissance to the Time of Puccini*. Portland, Ore.: Amadeus, 1998.

Robinson, Paul. *Opera and Ideas: From Mozart to Strauss*. New York: Harper and Row, 1985.

———. *Opera, Sex, and Other Vital Matters*. Chicago: University of Chicago Press, 2002.

Rosand, Ellen. "Operatic Madness: A Challenge to Convention." In Steven Paul Scher, ed., *Music and Text: Critical Inquiries*, 241–87. Cambridge: Cambridge University Press, 1992.

———, ed. *The Garland Library of the History of Western Music*. Vol. 11, *Opera I: Up to Mozart*. New York: Garland, 1985.

Rosselli, John. "The Castrati as a Professional Group and a Social Phenomenon, 1550–1850." *Acta Musicologica* 60 (1988): 143–79.

———. "Grand Opera: Nineteenth-Century Revolution and Twentieth-Century Tradition." In John Potter, ed., *The Cambridge Companion to Singing*, 96–108. New York: Cambridge University Press, 2000.

———. The Opera Industry in Italy from Cimarosa to Verdi: The Role of the Impresario. Cambridge: Cambridge University Press, 1984.

———. *Singers of Italian Opera: The History of a Profession*. New York: Cambridge University Press, 1992.

Rutherford, Susan. *The Prima Donna and Opera, 1815–1930*. Cambridge: Cambridge University Press, 2006.

Sadie, Stanley, ed. *The Billboard Illustrated Encyclopedia of Opera*. New York: Billboard Books, 2004.

———. *History of Opera*. New York: Norton, 1989.

———. *The New Grove Book of Operas*. London: Macmillan, 1996.

———. *The New Grove Dictionary of Music and Musicians*. London: Macmillan, 2001.

———. *The New Grove Dictionary of Opera*. London: Macmillan, 1992.

Saint, Andrew John, et al. *A History of the Royal Opera House Covent Garden, 1732–1982*. London: Royal Opera House, 1982.

Schmidgall, Gary. *Shakespeare and Opera*. New York: Oxford University Press, 1990.

Shapiro, Anne Dhu. "Action Music in American Pantomime and Melodrama, 1730–1913." *American Music* 2 (1984): 49–72.

Smart, Mary Ann, ed. *Siren Songs: Representations of Gender and Sexuality in Opera*. Princeton, N.J.: Princeton University Press, 2000.

Smart, Mary Ann, and Roger Parker, eds. *Reading Critics Reading Opera: Opera and Ballet Criticism in France from the Revolution to 1848*. New York: Oxford University Press, 2001.

Smeed, John William. *Don Juan: Variations on a Theme*. London: Routledge, 1990.

Smith, Eric Ledell. *Blacks in Opera: An Encyclopedia of People and Companies, 1873–1993*. 2nd ed. Jefferson, N.C.: McFarland, 1995.

Smith, Patrick J. *The Tenth Muse: A Historical Study of the Opera Libretto.* New York: Knopf, 1970.

Snowman, Daniel. *The Gilded Stage: A Social History of Opera.* London: Atlantic Books, 2010.

Somerset-Ward, Richard. *Angels and Monsters: Male and Female Sopranos in the Story of Opera, 1600–1900.* New Haven, Conn.: Yale University Press, 2004.

Sternfeld, Frederick. "Orpheus, Ovid, and Opera." *Journal of the Royal Musical Association* 113 (1988): 172–202.

Strunk, Oliver, et al., eds. *Source Readings in Music History.* Rev. ed. New York: Norton, 1998.

Sturman, Janet L. *Zarzuela: Spanish Operetta, American Stage.* Urbana: University of Illinois Press, 2000.

Sutcliff, Tom, ed. *The Faber Book of Opera.* London: Faber and Faber, 2000.

Swanston, Hamish F. G. *In Defense of Opera.* London: Allen Lane, 1978.

Tallián, Tibor. "From Singspiel to Post-modern: Two Hundred Years of Hungarian Opera." *Hungarian Quarterly* 42 (2003): 144–56.

Tartak, Marvin. "The Two *Barbieri.*" *Music and Letters* 50 (1969): 453–69.

Taruskin, Richard. *Defining Russia Musically: Historical and Hermeneutical Essays.* Princeton, N.J.: Princeton University Press, 1997.

Tcharos, Stefanie. *Opera's Orbit: Musical Drama and the Influence of Opera in Arcadian Rome.* Cambridge: Cambridge University Press, 2011.

Termini, Olga. "The Role of Diction and Gesture in Italian Baroque Opera." *Performance Practice Review* 6 (1993): 146–57.

Thomas, Downing A. *Aesthetics of Opera in the Ancien Régime, 1647–1785.* Cambridge: Cambridge University Press, 2002.

Tomlinson, Gary. *Metaphysical Song: An Essay in Opera.* Princeton, N.J.: Princeton University Press, 1999.

Tyrrell, John. *Czech Opera.* Cambridge: Cambridge University Press, 2005; originally 1988.

Varwig, Bettina. "Schütz's *Dafne* and the German Operatic Imagination." In Nikolaus Bacht, ed., *Music, Theater, and Politics in Germany: 1848 to the Third Reich*, 115–36. Aldershot, England: Ashgate, 2006.

Warrack, John Hamilton. *German Opera: From the Beginnings to Wagner.* Cambridge: Cambridge University Press, 2001.

Warrack, John Hamilton, and Ewan West, eds. *The Concise Oxford Dictionary of Opera.* New York: Oxford University Press, 1996.

———, ed. *The Oxford Dictionary of Opera.* New York: Oxford University Press, 1992.

Warren, Raymond. *Opera Workshop: Studies in Understanding and Interpretation.* Aldershot, England: Scolar, 1995.

Watanabe-O'Kelly, Helen, and Pierre Béhar, eds. *Spectaculum Europaeum: Theater and Spectacle in Europe/Histoire du spectacle en Europe (1580–1750)*. Wiesbaden, Germany: Harrassowitz, 1999.

Weaver, Robert Lamar, and Norma Wright Weaver. *A Chronology of Music in the Florentine Theater 1590–1750*. Detroit, Mich.: Harmonie Park, 1993.

Webber, Christopher. *The Zarzuela Companion*. Lanham, Md.: Scarecrow Press, 2002.

Webster, James. "To Understand Verdi and Wagner We Must Understand Mozart." *19th-Century Music* 11 (1987–88): 175–93.

White, Eric Walter. *A History of English Opera*. London: Faber and Faber, 1983.

Williams, Bernard. *On Opera*. New Haven, Conn.: Yale University Press, 2006.

Wilson, Alexandra. *Opera: A Beginner's Guide*. Oxford: Oneworld, 2010.

Wlaschin, Ken. *Encyclopedia of American Opera*. Jefferson, N.C.: McFarland, 2006.

———. *Encyclopedia of Opera on Screen: A Guide to More Than 100 Years of Opera Films, Videos, and DVDs*. New Haven, Conn.: Yale University Press, 2004.

Wood, Caroline. "Orchestra and Spectacle in the *Tragédie en musique*, 1673–1715: *Oracle*, *Sommeil*, and *Tempête*." *Proceedings of the Royal Musical Association* 108 (1981): 25–46.

Yeazell, Ruth Bernard. "Harems for Mozart and Rossini." *Raritan* 16 (1997): 86–105.

Zietz, Karyl Lynn. *Opera Companies and Houses of the United States: A Comprehensive, Illustrated Reference*. Jefferson, N.C.: McFarland, 1994.

17TH CENTURY: COMPOSERS

Cavalieri, Emilio de'

Bradshaw, Murray C. "Cavalieri and Early Monody." *Journal of Musicology* 9 (1991): 238–53.

———. "Character and Meaning in Cavalieri's Opera *The Play of Soul and Body (1600)*." In Colleen Reardon and Susan Parisi, eds., *Music Observed: Studies in Memory of William C. Holmes*, 15–30. Warren, Mich.: Harmonie Park, 2004.

———. "Salvation, Right Thinking, and Cavalieri's *Rappresentatione di Anima, et di Corpo*." *Musica disciplina* 52 (1998): 233–50.

Kirkendale, Warren. "The Myth of the 'Birth of Opera' in the *Florentine Camerata* Debunked by Emilio de' Cavalieri—A Commemorative Lecture." *Opera Quarterly* 19 (2003): 631–43. Reprinted in Ursula Kirkendale and Warren Kirkendale. *Music and Meaning: Studies in Music History and the Neighbouring Disciplines*. Florence: Olschki, 2007.

Cavalli, Francesco

Calcagno, Mauro P. *Staging Musical Discourses in Seventeenth-Century Venice: Francesco Cavalli's* Eliogabalo *(1667)*. Ph.D. dissertation, Yale University, 2000.

Glover, Jane. *Cavalli*. London: Batsford, 1978.

Oster, Andrew. "Melisma as Malady: Cavalli's *Il Giasone* (1649) and Opera's Earliest Stuttering Role." In Neil Lerner and Joseph N. Strauss, eds., *Sounding Off: Theorizing Disability in Music*, 157–71. New York: Routledge, 2006.

Rosand, Ellen. "Comic Contrast and Dramatic Continuity: Observations on the Form and Function of Aria in the Operas of Francesco Cavalli." *Music Review* 37 (1976): 92–105.

Scgulze, Hendrik. "Dramaturgical Setting, Representation of Characters, and the Mythological Basis in Giacinto Andrea Cicognini's and Francesco Cavalli's *Giasone*." In Metoda Kokole et al., eds., *Mediterranean Myths from Classical Antiquity to the Eighteenth Century*, 119–30. Ljubljana, Slovenia: Slovenska Akademija in Umetnosti Ljubljana, 2006.

Cesti, Antonio

Holmes, William C. "Giacinto Andrea Cicognini's and Antonio Cesti's *Orontea* (1649)." In William W. Austin, ed., *New Looks at Italian Opera: Essays in Honor of Donald J. Grout*, 108–32. Ithaca, N.Y.: Cornell University Press, 1968.

Schmidt, Carl Brandon. "Antonio Cesti's *Il pomo d'oro*: A Re-examination of a Famous Hapsburg Court Spectacle." *Journal of the American Musicological Society* 29 (1976): 381–412.

———. "Antonio Cesti's *La Dori*: A Study of Sources, Performance Traditions, and Musical Style." *Rivista italiana di musicologia* 10 (1975): 455–98.

———. *The Operas of Antonio Cesti*. Ph.D. dissertation, Harvard University, 1973.

Grabu, Louis

Holman, Peter. "Valentinian, Rochester, and Louis Grabu." In Edward D. Olleson et al., eds., *The Well Enchanting Skill: Music, Poetry, and Drama in the Culture of the Renaissance*, 127–41. Oxford: Clarendon, 1990.

White, Bryan. "Grabu's *Albion and Albanius* and the Operas of Lully: 'Acquainted with All the Performances of the French Operas.'" *Early Music* 30 (2002): 410–27.

———. *The Life and Works of Louis Grabu*. Ph.D. dissertation, University of Wales, Bangor, 1998.

Zimmerman, Franklin B. "Louis Grabu in England." In H. T. Swedenberg et al., eds., *The Works of John Dryden*, vol. 15, *Plays:* Albion and Albanius, Don Sebastian, Amphitryon, 336–61. Berkeley: University of California Press, 1976.

Lully, Jean-Baptiste

Anthony, James R. "The Musical Structure of Lully's Operatic Airs." In Jérôme La Gorce and Herbert Schneider, eds., *Jean-Baptiste Lully*, 65–76. Laaber, Germany: Laaber, 1990.

Baillargeon, Kathryn Anne. *"Of Bodies Chang'd to Various Forms, I Sing":* Ovid's Metamorphoses *in Lully/Quinault Operas*. Ph.D. dissertation, University of California, Santa Barbara, 2008.

Gordon-Seifert, Catherine. "Heroism Undone in the Erotic (Manuscript) Parodies of Jean-Baptiste Lully's *Tragédies lyriques*." In Linda Phyllis Austern, ed., *Music, Sensation, and Sensuality*, 137–63. New York: Routledge, 2002.

———. "Strong Men, Weak Women: Gender Representation and the Influence of Lully's 'Operatic Style' on French *Airs sérieux* (1650–1700)." In Thomasin Lemay, ed., *Musical Voices of Early Modern Women: Many-Headed Melodies*, 135–67. Aldershot, England: Ashgate, 2005.

Harris-Warrick, Rebecca. "Magnificence in Motion: Stage Musicians in Lully's Ballets and Operas." *Cambridge Opera Journal* 6 (1994): 189–203.

Heyer, John Hajdu, ed. *Jean-Baptiste Lully and the Music of the French Baroque: Essays in Honor of James R. Anthony*. Cambridge: Cambridge University Press, 1989.

———. *Lully Studies*. Cambridge: Cambridge University Press, 2000.

Howard, Patricia. "The Influence of the *Précieuses* on Content and Structure in Quinault's and Lully's *Tragédies lyriques*." *Acta Musicologica* 63 (1991): 57–72.

———. "Lully and the Ironic Convention." *Cambridge Opera Journal* 1 (1989): 139–53.

————. "The Positioning of Woman in Quinault's World Picture." In Jérôme La Gorce and Herbert Schneider, eds., *Jean-Baptiste Lully*, 193–99. Laaber, Germany: Laaber, 1990.

————. "Quinault, Lully, and the *Précieuses*: Images of Women in Seventeenth Century France." In Susan Cook et al., eds., *Cecelia Reclaimed: Feminist Perspectives on Gender and Music*, 70–89. Urbana: University of Illinois Press, 1994.

Newman, Joyce Enith. *Formal Structure and Recitative in the* Tragédie lyrique *of Jean-Baptiste de Lully*. Ph.D. dissertation, University of Michigan, 1974.

Norman, Buford. "Ancients and Moderns, Tragedy and Opera: The Quarrel over *Alceste*." In Georgia Cowart, ed., *French Musical Thought, 1600–1800*, 177–96. Ann Arbor, Mich.: University Microfilms International, 1989.

————. *Touched by the Graces: The Libretti of Philippe Quinault in the Context of French Classicism*. Birmingham, Ala.: Summa, 2001.

————. "The *Tragédie-lyrique* of Lully and Quinault: Representation and Recognition of Emotion." *Continuum* 5 (1993): 111–42.

Powell, John S. "Appropriation, Parody, and the Birth of French Opera: Lully's *Les festes de l'Amour et de Bacchus* and Molière's *Le malade imaginaire*." *Recherches sur la musique française classique* 29 (1996): 3–26.

Rosow, Lois. "*Le Théâtre de sa Gloire*: Essays on *Persée, Tragédie en musique* by Quinault and Lully." *Journal of Seventeenth-Century Music* 10 (2004).

Seares, Margaret. "Aspects of Performance Practice in the Recitatives of Jean-Baptiste Lully." *Studies in Music Australia* 8 (1974): 8–16.

Turnbull, Michael. "The Metamorphosis of *Psyché*." *Music and Letters* 64 (1983): 12–24.

Wood, Caroline. *Music and Drama in the "Tragédie en musique," 1673–1715: Jean-Baptiste Lully and His Successors*. New York: Garland, 1996.

Monteverdi, Claudio

Adams, Gary K., and Dyke Kiel. *Claudio Monteverdi: A Guide to Research*. New York: Garland, 1989.

Arnold, Denis. "*Intermedio*, Ballet, and Opera in the Oeuvre of Monteverdi." In Marc Honegger et al., eds., *La musique et le rite sacré et profane*, 363–70. Strasbourg, France: University of Strasbourg, 1986.

Arnold, Denis, and Nigel Fortune, eds. *The New Monteverdi Companion*. London: Faber and Faber, 1985.

Carter, Tim. "Artusi, Monteverdi, and the Poetics of Modern Music." In Nancy Kovaleff Baker and Barbara Russano Hanning, eds., *Musical Humanism and Its Legacy: Essays in Honor of Claude Palisca*, 171–94. Stuyvesant, N.Y.: Pendragon, 1992.

————. *Monteverdi and His Contemporaries*. Aldershot, England: Ashgate, 2000.

————. *Monteverdi's Musical Theater*. New Haven, Conn.: Yale University Press, 2002.

————. "Re-reading Poppea: Some Thoughts on Music and Meaning in Monteverdi's Last Opera." *Journal of the Royal Musical Association* 122 (1997): 173–204.

Curtis, Alan. "*La Poppea Impasticciata* or, Who Wrote the Music to *L'Incoronazione?*" *Journal of the American Musicological Society* 42 (1989): 23–54.

Cusick, Suzanne G. "Gendering Modern Music: Thoughts on the Monteverdi-Artusi Controversy." *Journal of the American Musicological Society* 46 (1993): 1–25.

————. "'There Was Not One Lady Who Failed to Shed a Tear': Arianna's Lament and the Construction of Modern Womanhood." *Early Music* 22 (1994): 21–41.

Fabbri, Paolo. *Monteverdi*. Translated by Tim Carter. Cambridge: Cambridge University Press, 1994.

Fenlon, Iain, and Peter. N. Miller. *The Song of the Soul: Understanding "Poppea."* London: Royal Musical Association, 1992.

Fortune, Nigel. "Monteverdi and the *Seconda prattica*, ii: From Madrigal to Duet." In Denis Arnold and Nigel Fortune, eds., *The New Monteverdi Companion*, 198–215. London: Faber and Faber, 1985.

Gordon, Bonnie Susan. *Singing the Female Body: Monteverdi, Subjectivity, Sensuality*. Ph.D. dissertation, University of Pennsylvania, 1998.

John, Nicholas, ed. *The Operas of Monteverdi*. London: Calder, 1992.

Kurtzman, Jeffrey G. "Deconstructing Gender in Monteverdi's *L'Orfeo*." *Journal of Seventeenth-Century Music* 9 (2003).

McClary, Susan. "Constructions of Gender in Monteverdi's Dramatic Music." *Cambridge Opera Journal* 1 (1989): 202–23.

Ossi, Massimo. "Claudio Monteverdi's *Ordine novo, bello, et gustevole*: The Canzonetta as Dramatic Module and Formal Archetype." *Journal of the American Musicological Society* 45 (1992): 261–304.

————. *Divining the Oracle: Aspects of Monteverdi's Seconda prattica*. Chicago: University of Chicago Press, 2003.

Palisca, Claude. "The Artusi-Monteverdi Controversy." In Denis Arnold and Nigel Fortune, eds., *The Monteverdi Companion*, 127–58. New York: Norton, 1968. Reprinted in Claude V. Palisca, ed., *Studies in the History of Italian Music and Music Theory*, 54–87. Oxford: Oxford University Press, 1994.

Pirrotta, Nino, and Elena Povoledo. *Music and Theater from Poliziano to Monteverdi*. Cambridge: Cambridge University Press, 1981.

Ridler, Anne. *The Operas of Monteverdi*. London: Calder, 1992.

Rosand, Ellen. "The Bow of Ulysses." *Journal of Musicology* 12 (1994): 376–95.

———. *Monteverdi's Last Operas: A Venetian Trilogy*. Berkeley: University of California Press, 2007.

———. "Monteverdi's Mimetic Art: *L'incoronazione di Poppea*." *Cambridge Opera Journal* 1 (1989): 113–37.

———. "Seneca and the Interpretation of *L'incoronazione di Poppea*." *Journal of the American Musicological Society* 38 (1985): 34–71.

Solomon, Jon D. "The Neoplatonic Apotheosis in Monteverdi's *Orfeo*." *Studi musicali* 24 (1995): 24–47.

Stubbs, Stephen. "*L'armonia sonora*: Continuo Orchestration in Monteverdi's *Orfeo*." *Early Music* 22 (1994): 87–98.

Tomlinson, Gary A. "Madrigal, Monody, and Monteverdi's *via naturale alla immitatione*." *Journal of the American Musicological Society* 34 (1981): 60–108.

———. *Monteverdi and the End of the Renaissance*. Berkeley: University of California Press, 1987.

Whenham, John, ed. *Claudio Monteverdi: Orfeo*. Cambridge: Cambridge University Press, 1986.

———. *Duet and Dialogue in the Age of Monteverdi*. Ann Arbor, Mich.: University Microfilms International, 1982.

Whenham, John, and Richard Wistreich, eds. *The Cambridge Companion to Monteverdi*. Cambridge: Cambridge University Press, 2007.

Peri, Jacopo

Carter, Tim. *Jacopo Peri (1561–1633): Aspects of His Life and Works*. New York: Garland, 1989.

Harness, Kelley. "*Le tre Euridici*: Characterizations and Allegory in the *Euridici* of Peri and Caccini." *Journal of Seventeenth-Century Music* 9 (2003).

Palisca, Claude. "Peri and the Theory of Recitative." *Studies in Music* 15 (1981): 51–61. Reprinted in Claude V. Palisca, ed. *Studies in the History of Italian Music and Music Theory*, 452–66. Oxford: Oxford University Press, 1994.

Purcell, Henry

Adams, Martin Howard. *Henry Purcell: The Origins and Development of His Musical Style*. Cambridge: Cambridge University Press, 1995.

Burden, Michael, ed. *The Purcell Companion*. London: Faber and Faber, 1994.

Duffy, Maureen. *Henry Purcell*. London: Fourth Estate, 1994.

Harris, Ellen T. *Henry Purcell's "Dido and Aeneas."* Oxford: Clarendon, 1987.

Holman, Peter. *Henry Purcell*. Oxford: Oxford University Press, 1994.

Moore, Robert Etheridge. *Henry Purcell and the Restoration Theatre*. Cambridge, Mass.: Harvard University Press, 1961.

Price, Curtis A. *Henry Purcell and the London Stage*. Cambridge: Cambridge University Press, 1984.

Zimmerman, Franklin B. *Henry Purcell, 1659–1695: His Life and Times*. London: Macmillan, 1967; revised 1983.

———. *Henry Purcell: A Guide to Research*. New York: General, 1989.

17TH CENTURY: LOCATIONS

England

Buttrey, John. "New Light on Robert Cambert in London, and His *Ballet et musique*." *Early Music* 23 (1995): 198–220.

Hume, Robert D. "The Politics of Opera in Late-Seventeenth-Century London." *Cambridge Opera Journal* 10 (1998): 15–43.

Neufeldt, Tim. "Italian Pastoral Opera and Pastoral Politics in England, 1705–1712." *Discourses in Music* 5 (2004).

Price, Curtis A. "Political Allegory in Late Seventeenth-Century English Opera." In Nigel Fortune, ed., *Music and Theatre: Essays in Honour of Winton Dean*, 1–29. Cambridge: Cambridge University Press, 1987.

Vos, Wesley Marvin. *English Dramatic Recitative before ca. 1685*. Ph.D. diss., Washington University, 1967.

Florence

Carlton, Richard A. "Florentine Humanism and the Birth of Opera: The Roots of Operatic 'Conventions.'" *International Review of the Aesthetics and Sociology of Music* 31 (2000): 67–78.

Coelho, Victor Anand. "The Players of Florentine Monody in Context and in History, and a Newly Recognized Source for *Le nuove musiche*." *Journal of Seventeenth-Century Music* 9 (2003).

Cusick, Suzanne G. *Francesca Caccini at the Medici Court: Music and the Circulation of Power*. Chicago: University of Chicago Press, 2009.

Hanning, Barbara Russano. "Glorious Apollo: Poetic and Political Themes in the First Opera." *Renaissance Quarterly* 32 (1979): 485–513.

———. *Of Poetry and Music's Power: Humanism and the Creation of Opera*. Ann Arbor, Mich.: University Microfilms International, 1980.

Hansen, Jette Barnholt. "From Invention to Interpretation: The Prologues of the First Court Operas Where Oral and Written Cultures Meet." *Journal of Musicology* 20 (2003): 556–96.

Harness, Kelley. *Amazzoni di Dio: Florentine Musical Spectacle under Maria Maddalena d'Austria and Cristina di Lorena, 1620–1630*. Ph.D. dissertation, University of Illinois, 1996.

———. *Echoes of Women's Voices: Music, Art, and Female Patronage in Early Modern Florence*. Chicago: University of Chicago Press, 2006.

Hill, John Walter. "Florence: Musical Spectacle and Drama, 1570–1650." In Curtis A. Price, ed., *The Early Baroque Era: From the Late 16th Century to the 1660s*. Englewood Cliffs, N.J.: Prentice-Hall, 1994.

———. "Realized Continuo Accompaniments from Florence c. 1600." *Early Music* 11 (1983): 194–208.

Katz, Ruth. *Divining the Powers of Music: Aesthetic Theory and the Origins of Opera*. New York: Pendragon, 1986.

Palisca, Claude V. "The 'Camerata Fiorentina': A Reappraisal." *Studi musicali* 1 (1972): 203–36. Reprinted in Ellen Rosand, ed. *Opera. I: Up to Mozart. The Garland Library of the History of Western Music*. Vol. 11, pp. 45–80. New York: Garland, 1985.

———. *The Florentine Camerata: Documentary Studies and Translations*. New Haven, Conn.: Yale University Press, 1989.

———. *Humanism in Italian Musical Thought*. New Haven, Conn.: Yale University Press, 1985.

———. "Vincenzo Galilei and Some Links between 'Pseudo-Monody' and 'Monody.'" *Musical Quarterly* 46 (1960): 344–60. Reprinted in Claude V. Palisca, ed. *Studies in the History of Italian Music and Music Theory*, 346–63. Oxford: Oxford University Press, 1994.

Saslaw, J. M. *The Medici Wedding of 1589: Florentine Festival as Theatrum Mundi*. New Haven, Conn.: Yale University Press, 1996.

Sternfeld, Frederick W. "The First Printed Opera Libretto." *Music and Letters* 59 (1978): 121–38.

Tomlinson, Gary A. *Rinuccini, Peri, Monteverdi, and the Humanist Heritage of Opera*. Ph.D. dissertation, University of California, Berkeley, 1979.

France

Auld, Louis E. "'Dealing in Shepherds': The Pastoral Ploy in Nascent French Opera." In Cowart, Georgia, ed., *French Musical Thought, 1600–1800*, 53–80. Ann Arbor, Mich.: University Microfilms International, 1989.

———. *The Lyric Art of Pierre Perrin, Founder of French Opera*. Henryville, Pa.: Institute of Medieval Music, 1986.

Banducci, Antonia L. "Staging and Its Dramatic Effect in French Baroque Opera: Evidence from Prompt Notes." *Eighteenth-Century Music* 1 (2004): 5–28.

Bashford, Christina M. "Perrin and Cambert's *Arianne, ou Le Mariage de Bacchus* Re-examined." *Music and Letters* 72 (1991): 1–26.

Chae, Donald Baird. *Music, Festival, and Power in Louis XIV's France: Court Divertissements and the Musical Construction of Sovereign Authority and Noble Identity (1661–1674)*. Ph.D. dissertation, University of Chicago, 2003.

Cowart, Georgia. *The Triumph of Pleasure: Louis XIV and the Politics of Spectacle*. Chicago: University of Chicago Press, 2008.

Cronk, Nicholas. "Marc-Antoine Charpentier's *Le malade imaginaire*: The First *Opéra-comique*." *Forum for Modern Language Studies* (1993): 216–31.

Hitchcock, H. Wiley. *Marc-Antoine Charpentier*. Oxford: Oxford University Press, 1990.

Jaffee, Kay C. *Medea among the Ancients and Moderns: Morality and Magic in French Musical Theater of the Seventeenth Century*. Ph.D. dissertation, New York University, 2001.

Lefkowitz, Murray. "Shadwell and Locke's *Psyche*: The French Connection." *Proceedings of the Royal Musical Association* 106 (1979): 42–55.

McCleave, Sarah, ed. *Dance and Music in French Baroque Theater: Sources and Interpretations*. London: University of London, 1998.

Murata, Margaret. "Why the First Opera Given in Paris Wasn't Roman." *Cambridge Opera Journal* 7 (1995): 87–105.

Rosow, Lois. "French Baroque Recitative as an Expression of Tragic Declamation." *Early Music* 11 (1983): 468–79.

Sadler, Graham. "The Role of the Keyboard Continuo in French Opera 1673–1776." *Early Music* 8 (1980): 148–57.

Sadler, Graham, and Caroline Wood, eds. *French Baroque Opera: A Reader.* Aldershot, England: Ashgate, 2000.

Thomas, Downing A. "Opera, Dispossession, and the Sublime: The Case of *Armide.*" *Theatre Journal* 49 (1997): 168–88.

Rome

Hammond, Frederick. *Music and Spectacle in Baroque Rome: Barberini Patronage under Urban VIII.* New Haven, Conn.: Yale University Press, 1994.

———. *The Ruined Bridge: Studies in Barberini Patronage of Music and Spectacle 1631–1679.* Sterling Heights, Mich.: Harmonie Park, 2010.

Hill, John Walter. *Roman Monody, Cantata, and Opera from the Circles around Cardinal Montalto.* Oxford: Oxford University Press, 1997.

Lamothe, Virginia Christy. *The Theater of Piety: Sacred Operas for the Barberini Family (Rome, 1632–1643).* Ph.D. dissertation, University of North Carolina, Chapel Hill, 2009.

Murata, Margaret. *Operas for the Papal Court 1631–1668.* Ann Arbor, Mich.: University Microfilms International, 1981.

Tcharos, Stefanie. *Beyond the Boundaries of Opera: Conceptions of Musical Drama in Rome, 1676–1710.* Ph.D. dissertation, Princeton University, 2002.

Spain

Harney, Lucy D. "*Zarzuela* and the Pastoral." *Modern Language Notes* 123 (2008): 252–73.

Stein, Louise K. *Music in the Seventeenth-Century Spanish Secular Theater.* Ph.D. dissertation, University of Chicago, 1987.

———. "Opera and the Spanish Political Agenda." *Acta Musicologica* 63 (1991): 125–67.

Venice

Alm, Irene. *Theatrical Dance in Seventeenth-Century Venetian Opera.* Ph.D. dissertation, University of California, Los Angeles, 1993.

Calcagno, Mauro. "Signifying Nothing: On the Aesthetics of Pure Voice in Early Venetian Opera." *Journal of Musicology* 20 (2003): 461–97.

Glixon, Beth L. *Recitative in Seventeenth-Century Venetion Opera: Its Dramatic Function and Musical Language.* Ph.D. dissertation, Rutgers University, 1985.

Glixon, Beth L., and Jonathan E. Glixon. *Inventing the Business of Opera: The Impresario and His World in Seventeenth-Century Venice*. Oxford: Oxford University Press, 2006.

————. "Marco Faustini and Venetian Opera Production in the 1650s: Recent Archival Discoveries." *Journal of Musicology* 10 (1992): 48–73.

Heller, Wendy. *Chastity, Heroism, and Allure: Women in the Opera of Seventeenth-Century Venice*. Ph.D. dissertation, Brandeis University, 1995.

————. *Emblems of Eloquence: Opera and Women's Voices in Seventeenth-Century Venice*. Berkeley: University of California Press, 2003.

Macklem, Mary Sue. *Reforming Opera and Its Public in Early Modern Venice*. Ph.D. dissertation, University of Pennsylvania, 2003.

Rosand, Ellen. "In Defense of the Venetian Libretto." *Studi musicali* 9 (1980): 271–85.

————. *Opera in Seventeenth-Century Venice: The Creation of a Genre*. Berkeley: University of California Press, 1991.

Thorburn, Hugh A. *Seventeenth-Century Venetian Opera: The Collaborative Context of a Commercial, Synaesthesic Art Form*. Ph.D. dissertation, University of Toronto, 2006.

17TH CENTURY: COMPARATIVE AND OTHER TOPICS

Aikin, Judith P. *A Language for German Opera: The Development of Forms and Formulas for Recitative and Aria in Seventeenth-Century German Libretti*. Wiesbaden, Germany: Harrassowitz, 2002.

Assenza, Concetta. *La Canzonetta dal 1570 al 1615*. Lucca: Libreria Editrice Musicale, 1997.

Baron, John H. "Monody: A Study in Terminology." *Musical Quarterly* 54 (1968): 462–74.

Bianconi, Lorenzo. "Production, Consumption, and Political Function of Seventeenth-Century Opera." *Early Music History* 4 (1984): 209–96.

Bjurström, Per. *Giacomo Torelli and Baroque Stage Design*. Stockholm: Nationalmuseum, 1961; revised 1962.

Borgir, Tharald. *The Performance of the Basso Continuo in Italian Baroque Music*. Ann Arbor, Mich.: UMI Research Press, 1987.

Brown, Howard Mayer, and Stanley Sadie, eds. *Performance Practice: Music after 1600*. New York: Norton, 1989.

Brown, Jennifer Williams. "On the Road with the 'Suitcase Aria': The Transmission of Borrowed Arias in Late Seventeenth-Century Italian Opera Revivals." *Journal of Musicological Research* 15 (1995): 3–23.

Bucciarelli, Melania. *Italian Opera and European Theatre, 1680–1720: Plots, Performers, Dramaturgies.* Turnhout, Belgium: Brepols, 2000.

Buller, Jeffrey L. "Looking Backwards: Baroque Opera and the Ending of the Orpheus Myth." *International Journal of the Classical Tradition* 1 (1995): 57–79.

Carter, Stewart. *A Performer's Guide to Seventeenth-Century Music.* New York: Schirmer, 1997.

Carter, Tim. "'An Air New and Grateful to the Ear': The Concept of *Aria* in Late Renaissance and Early Baroque Italy." *Music Analysis* 12 (1993): 127–45.

Carter, Tim, and John Butt, eds. *The Cambridge History of Seventeenth-Century Music.* Cambridge: Cambridge University Press, 2005.

Donington, Robert. *A Performer's Guide to Baroque Music.* London: Faber and Faber, 1973.

———. *The Rise of Opera.* London: Faber and Faber, 1981.

Fortune, Nigel. "Italian Secular Monody from 1600 to 1635: An Introductory Survey." *Musical Quarterly* 39 (1953): 171–95. Reprinted as "Italian Secular Monody from 1600 to 1635: An Introductory Study." In Ellen Rosand, ed., *Baroque Music I: Seventeenth Century. The Garland Library of the History of Western Music*, vol. 5. New York: Garland, 1985.

Freitas, Roger. *Portrait of a Castrato: Politics, Patronage, and Music in the Life of Atto Melani.* New York: Cambridge University Press, 2009.

Gianturco, Carolyn M. "Accompanied Recitative and Alessandro Stradella: Experiments in Expression." In Nicole Ristow, ed., *"Critica musica": Studien zum 17. und 18. Jahrhundert. Festschrift Hans Joachim Marx zum 65. Geburtstag*, 83–96. Stuttgart, Germany: Metzler, 2001.

Glixon, Beth, ed. *Studies in Seventeenth-Century Opera.* Farnham, England: Ashgate, 2010.

Holzer, Robert. "'Sono d'altro garbo... le canzonette che si cantano oggi': Pietro della Valle on Music and Modernity in the Seventeenth Century." *Studi musicali* 21 (1992): 253–306.

Leve, James Samuel. *Humor and Intrigue: A Comparative Study of Comic Opera in Florence and Rome during the Late Seventeenth Century.* Ph.D. dissertation, Yale University, 1998.

Muir, Edward. *The Culture Wars of the Late Renaissance: Skeptics, Libertines, and Opera.* Cambridge, Mass.: Harvard University Press, 2007.

Murata, Margaret. "The Recitative Soliloquy." *Journal of the American Musicological Society* 32 (1979): 45–73.

North, Nigel. *Continuo Playing on the Lute, Archlute, and Theorbo.* Bloomington: Indiana University Press, 1987.

Palisca, Claude V. "Aria Types in the Earliest Operas." *Journal of Seventeenth-Century Music* 9 (2003).

————. *Studies in the History of Italian Music and Music Theory.* Oxford: Oxford University Press, 1994.

Peschel, Enid Rhodes, and Richard E. Peschel. "Medicine and Music: The *Castrati* in Opera." *Opera Quarterly* 4 (1986): 21–38.

Price, Curtis A., ed. *The Early Baroque Era: From the Late 16th Century to the 1660s.* Englewood Cliffs, N.J.: Prentice-Hall, 1994.

————. *Music in the Restoration Theatre.* Ann Arbor, Mich.; University Microfilms International, 1979.

Purciello, Maria Anne. *And Dionysus Laughed: Opera, Comedy, and Carnival in Seventeenth-Century Venice and Rome.* Ph.D. dissertation, Princeton University, 2005.

Rosand, Ellen. "The Descending Tetrachord: An Emblem of Lament." *Musical Quarterly* 65 (1979): 346–59.

Savage, Roger, and Matteo Sansone. "*Il corago* and the Staging of Early Opera: Four Chapters from an Anonymous Treatise Circa 1630." *Early Music* 17 (1989): 495–511.

Silke, Leopold, and Irene Zedlacher. "The Orchestra in Early Opera." *Musical Quarterly* 80 (1996): 265–68.

Stubbs, Stephen. "The Theory and Practice of Basso Continuo in the 17th Century and Today." In Johann Trummer, ed., *Alte Musik—Lehren, Forschen, Hören: Perspektiven der Aufführungspraxis*, 99–109. Regensburg, Germany: ConBrio, 1994.

Thompson, Shirley, ed. *New Perspectives on Marc-Antoine Charpentier.* Farnham, England: Ashgate, 2010.

Vavoulis, Vassilis. "An Approach to the Expressive Content of Late Seventeenth-Century Arias: Antonio Sartorio's *Giulio Cesare in Egitto* (1677)." In Alberto Colzani et al., eds., *Il teatro musicale italiano nel Sacro Romano Impero nei secoli XVII e XVIII*, 53–66. Como, Italy: Antiquae Musicae Italicae Studiosi, 1999.

Weaver, Robert L. "The Orchestra in Early Italian Opera." *Journal of the American Musicological Society* 17 (1964): 83–89.

18TH CENTURY: COMPOSERS AND LIBRETTISTS

Arne, Thomas Augustine

Adas, Jane H. *Arne's Progress: An English Composer in Eighteenth Century London.* Ph.D. dissertation, Rutgers University, 1993.

Aspden, Suzanne. "Arne's Paradox: National Opera in Eighteenth-Century Britain." In Suzanne M. Lodato et al., eds., *Essays in Honor of Steven Paul Scher and on Cultural Identity and the Musical Stage*, 195–215. Amsterdam: Rodopi, 2002.
Parkinson, John A. *Thomas Arne: Master of a Scurvy Profession*. London: Toccata, 2008.

Benda, Georg

Bauman, Thomas. "Benda, the Germans, and Simple Recitative." *Journal of the American Musicological Society* 34 (1981): 119–31.

Caldara, Antonio

Kirkendale, Ursula. *Antonio Caldara: Life and Venetian-Roman Oratorios*. Translated by Warren Kirdendale. Florence: Olschki, 2007.
Pritchard, Brian W. *Antonio Caldara: Essays on His Life and Times*. Aldershot, England: Scolar, 1987.

Campra, André

Brown, Leslie Ellen. *The Tragédie lyrique of André Campra and His Contemporaries*. Ph.D. dissertation, University of North Carolina, 1978.

Cherubini, Luigi

Deane, Basil. *Cherubini*. Oxford: Oxford University Press, 1965.
Fend, Michael. "Literary Motifs, Musical Form, and the Quest for the 'Sublime': Cherubini's *Eliza, ou Le voyage au glaciers du Mont St. Bernard*." *Cambridge Opera Journal* 5 (1993): 17–38.
Pencak, William. "Cherubini Stages a Revolution." *Opera Quarterly* 8 (1991): 8–27.
Ringer, Alexander L. "Cherubini's *Médée* and the Spirit of French Revolutionary Opera." In Gustave Reese and Robert J. Snow, eds., *Essays in Musicology in Honor of Dragan Plamenac on His 70th Birthday*, 281–99. Pittsburgh, Pa.: University of Pittsburg Press, 1969.
Willis, Stephen. *Luigi Cherubini: A Study of His Life and Dramatic Music 1795–1815*. Ph.D. dissertation, Columbia University, 1975.

Cimarosa, Domenico

Rossi, Nick, and Talmage Fauntleroy. *Domenico Cimarosa: His Life and Operas*. Westport, Conn.: Greenwood, 1999.

Da Ponte, Lorenzo

Bolt, Rodney. *The Librettist of Venice: The Remarkable Life of Lorenzo Da Ponte, Mozart's Poet, Casanova's Friend, and Italian Opera's Impresario in America*. New York: Bloomsbury, 2006.
Holden, Anthony. *The Man Who Wrote Mozart: The Extraordinary Life of Lorenzo Da Ponte*. London: Weidenfeld and Nicolson, 2006.
Lachmayer, Herbert, and Reinhard Eisendle. *Lorenzo Da Ponte: Opera and Enlightenment in Late 18th Century Vienna*. Kassel, Germany: Bärenreiter, 2005.

Dittersdorf, Carl Ditters von

Horsley, Paul Joseph. *Dittersdorf and the Finale in Late-Eighteenth-Century German Comic Opera*. Ph.D. dissertation, Cornell University, 1988.
Tsai, Shunmei. *The Viennese Singspiele of Karl Ditters von Dittersdorf*. Ph.D. dissertation, University of Kansas, 1990.

Duni, Egidio

Smith, Kent Maynard. *Egidio Duni and the Development of the Opéra comique from 1753 to 1770*. Ph.D. dissertation, Cornell University, 1980.

Gay, John

Barlow, Jeremy. *The Music of John Gay's* The Beggar's Opera. Oxford: Oxford University Press, 1990.
Heartz, Daniel. "*The Beggar's Opera* and *Opéra-comique en vaudevilles*." *Early Music* 27 (1999): 42–53.
Richardson, John. "John Gay, *The Beggar's Opera*, and Forms of Resistance." *Eighteenth-Century Life* 24 (2000): 19–30.

Gluck, Christoph Willibald

Brown, Bruce Alan. *Gluck and the French Theater in Vienna.* Oxford: Clarendon, 1991.

Einstein, Alfred. *Gluck.* Translated by Eric Blom. New York: Collier, 1962.

Heartz, Daniel; John A. Rice, ed. *From Garrick to Gluck: Essays on Opera in the Age of Enlightenment.* Hillsdale, N.Y.: Pendragon, 2004.

Howard, Patricia. *Christoph Willibald Gluck: A Guide to Research.* New York: Routledge, 2003.

———, ed. C. W. von Gluck: Orfeo. Cambridge: Cambridge University Press, 1981.

———. *Gluck and the Birth of Modern Opera.* London: Barrie and Rockliff, 1963.

Monelle, Raymond. "Gluck and the *festa teatrale.*" *Music and Letters* 54 (1973): 308–25.

Newman, Ernest. *Gluck and the Opera: A Study in Musical History.* London: Gollancz, 1967.

Goldoni, Carlo

Pietropaolo, Domenico, ed. *Goldoni and the Musical Theatre.* Ottawa: Legas, 1995.

Grétry, André-Ernest-Modeste

Bartlet, M. Elizabeth C. "Patriotism at the Opéra-Comique during the Revolution: Grétry's *Callias, ou nature et patrie.*" In Angelo Pompilio, ed., *Atti del XIV Congresso della Società Internazionale di Musicologia, Bologna, 1987,* 839–52. Turin, Italy: Edizioni di Torino, 1990.

Charlton, David. *Grétry and the Growth of the Opéra-Comique.* Cambridge: Cambridge University Press, 1986.

Pendle, Karin S. "The Opéras Comiques of Grétry and Marmontel." *Musical Quarterly* 62 (1976): 409–34.

Handel, George Frideric

Aspden, Suzanne. "The 'Rival Queens' and the Play of Identity in Handel's *Admeto.*" *Cambridge Opera Journal* 18 (2006): 301–31.

Bucchianeri, E. A. *Handel's Path to Covent Garden: A Rocky Journey.* Bloomington, Ind.: 1stBooks, 2002.

Burrows, Donald James, ed. *The Cambridge Companion to Handel.* Cambridge: Cambridge University Press, 1997.

————. "Handel and the London Opera Companies in the 1730s: Venues, Programmes, Patronage, and Performers." *Göttinger Handel-Beiträge* 10 (2004): 149–65.

Dean, Winton. *Handel's Operas, 1726–1741.* Woodbridge, England: Boydell, 2006.

Dean, Winton, and J. Merrill Knapp. *Handel's Operas, 1704–1726.* Oxford: Clarendon, 1995; originally 1987.

Emslie, Barry. "Handel the Postmodernist." *Cambridge Opera Journal* 15 (2003): 185–98.

Gargiulo, Piero. "The Pastorale in Handel's *Serse.*" In Hans Joachim Marx, ed., *Händels italianità,* 73–80. Göttingen, Germany: Göttinger Händel-Festspiele, 1998.

Goldin-Folena, Daniela. "Orlando in Händel." In Belinda Cannone and Michel Orcel, eds., *Figures de Roland,* 185–99. Paris: Klincksieck, 1998.

Gutknecht, Dieter. "Performance Practice of *recitativo secco* in the First Half of the 18th Century: A Contribution to the Debate over the Interpretation of Recitative, Particularly in Handel's Operas." *Early Music* 33 (2005): 473–93.

Harris, Ellen T. *Handel and the Pastoral Tradition.* New York: Oxford University Press, 1980.

————. "Harmonic Patterns in Handel's Operas." In Mary Ann Parker, ed., *Eighteenth-Century Music in Theory and Practice: Essays in Honor of Alfred Mann,* 77–118. Stuyvesant, N.Y.: Pendragon, 1994.

————. "The Italian Influence in Handel's Operatic Dramaturgy." *Händel-Jahrbuch* 37 (1991): 15–36.

————. "With Eyes on the East and Ears on the West: Handel's Orientalist Operas." *Journal of Interdisciplinary History* 26 (2006): 419–43.

Heller, Wendy. "The Beloved's Image: Handel's *Admeto* and the Statue of Alcestis." *Journal of the American Musicological Society* 58 (2005): 559–637.

Hume, Robert. "Handel and Opera Management in London in the 1730s." *Music and Letters* 67 (1986): 347–62.

LaRue, Carl Steven. *Handel and His Singers: The Creation of the Royal Academy Operas, 1720–1728.* Oxford: Clarendon, 1995.

Leon, Donna. *Handel's Bestiary: In Search of Animals in Handel's Operas.* New York: Atlantic Monthly, 2010.

Link, Nathan. "The Orchestra as Choric Voice in Handel's Opera Arias." *Göttinger Händel-Beiträge* 12 (2008): 163–81.

————. *Story and Representation in Handel's Operas.* Ph.D. dissertation, Yale University, 2006.

McCleave, Sarah Yuill. *Dance in Handel's Italian Operas: The Collaboration with Marie Sallé*. Ph.D. dissertation, King's College, University of London, 1993.

Meynell, Hugo Anthony. *The Art of Handel's Operas*. Lewiston, N.Y.: Mellen, 1986.

Monod, Paul. "The Politics of Handel's Early London Operas, 1711–1719." *Journal of Interdisciplinary History* 26 (2006): 445–72.

Parker, Mary Ann. *G. F. Handel: A Guide to Research*. New York: Routledge, 2005.

Timms, Colin. "What Did Handel Learn from Steffani's Operas?" *Göttinger Händel-Beiträge* 9 (2002): 55–72.

Hasse, Johann Adolf

Millner, Frederick Lewis. *The Operas of Johann Adolf Hasse*. Ph.D. dissertation, University of California, Berkeley, 1976.

Haydn, Joseph

Clark, Caryl Leslie, ed. *The Cambridge Companion to Haydn*. Cambridge: Cambridge University Press, 2005.

Debly, Patricia Anne. "Social Commentary in the Music of Haydn's Goldoni Operas." In Jamie Croy Kassler, ed., *Metaphor: A Musical Dimension; Melbourne 1988*, 51–68. Sydney: Currency, 1991.

Hunter, Mary. *Haydn's Aria Forms: A Study of the Arias in the Italian Operas Written at Eszterháza, 1766–1783*. Ph.D. dissertation, Cornell University, 1982.

———. "Haydn's Sonata-Form Arias." *Current Musicology* 37–38 (1984): 19–32.

———. "Text, Music and Drama in Haydn's Italian Opera Arias: Four Case Studies." *Journal of Musicology* 7 (1989): 29–57.

Jones, David Wyn. *The Life of Haydn*. Cambridge: Cambridge University Press, 2009.

Landon, H. C. Robbins. "Haydn's Marionette Operas and the Repertoire of the Marionette Theatre at Esterháza Castle." *Haydn Yearbook*, 1962, 111–99.

Rice, John A. "Sarti's *Giulio Sabino*, Haydn's *Armida*, and the Arrival of *Opera Seria* at Eszterháza." *Haydn Yearbook* 15 (1984): 181–98.

Waldoff, Jessica P. "Sentiment and Sensibility in *La vera constanza*." *Haydn Studies*, 1998, 70–119.

Hiller, Johann Adam

Joubert, Estelle. "Songs to Shape a German Nation: Hiller's Comic Operas and the Public Sphere." *Eighteenth-Century Music* 3 (2006): 213–30.

Jommelli, Niccolò

McClymonds, Marita Petzolt. "The Evolution of Jommelli's Operatic Style." *Journal of the American Musicological Society* 33 (1980): 326–55.
———. *Niccolò Jommelli: The Last Years, 1769–1774.* Ann Arbor, Mich.: University Microfilms International, 1980.

Méhul, Etienne-Nicolas

Bartlet, M. Elizabeth C. "On the Freedom of the Theater and Censorship: The *Adrien* Controversy (1792)." In Antoine Hennion, ed., *1789–1989: Musique, Histoire, Démocratie*, 15–30. Paris: Maison des Sciences de l'Homme, 1992.
Charlton, David. "Motive and Motif: Méhul before 1791." *Music and Letters* 57 (1976): 362–69.
Grace, Michael D. "Méhul's *Ariodant* and the Early Leitmotif." In Michael D. Grace, ed., *A Festschrift for Albert Seay: Essays by His Friends and Colleagues*, 173–93. Colorado Springs: Colorado College Press, 1982.
Miller, William J. "Étienne Nicolas Méhul: The Revolution's Significant Yet Obscure Composer." In Donald D. Horward et al., eds., *The Consortium on Revolutionary Europe, 1750–1850: Selected Papers, 1994*, 579–86. Tallahassee: Florida State University Press, 1994.

Metastasio, Pietro

Harris, Ellen T. "Metastasio and Sonata Form." *Händel-Jahrbuch* 45 (1999): 19–36.
Neville, Don J. "Metastasio and the Image of Majesty in the Austro-Italian Baroque." In Shearer West, ed., *Italian Culture in Northern Europe in the Eighteenth Century*, 140–58. Cambridge: Cambridge University Press, 1999.
———. "Metastasio: Poet and Preacher in Vienna." In Andrea Sommer-Mathis and Elisabeth T. Hilscher, eds., *Pietro Metastasio: Uomo universale (1698–1782)*, 47–62. Vienna: Österreichische Akademie der Wissenschaften, 2000.

Savage, Roger. "Staging an Opera: Letters from the Cesarian Poet." *Early Music* 26 (1998): 583–95.

Sprague, Cheryl Ruth. *A Comparison of Five Musical Settings of Metastasio's* Artaserse. Ph.D. dissertation, University of California, Los Angeles, 1979.

Stonehouse, Alison A. *The Attitude of the French towards Metastasio as Poet and Dramatist in the Second Half of the Eighteenth Century.* Ph.D. dissertation, University of Western Ontario, 1997.

Mozart, Wolfgang Amadeus

Allanbrook, Wye Jamison. "Human Nature in the Unnatural Garden: *Figaro* as Pastoral." *Current Musicology* 51 (1991): 82–93.

————. "Mozart's Happy Endings: A New Look at the 'Convention' of the 'Lieto Fine.'" *Mozart-Jahrbuch* (1984–5): 1–5.

Allanbrook, Wye Jamison, and Wendy Hilton. "Dance Rhythms in Mozart's Arias." *Early Music* 20 (1992): 142–49.

Andrews, Richard. "From Beaumarchais to Da Ponte: A New View of the Sexual Politics of *Figaro*." *Music and Letters* 82 (2001): 214–33.

Baker, Felicity R. "The Figures of Hell in the *Don Giovanni* Libretto." In Dorothea Link and Judith Nagley, eds., *Words about Mozart: Essays in Honour of Stanley Sadie*, 77–106. Woodbridge, England: Boydell, 2005.

Baker, Nicole. "The Relationship between Aria Forms in Mozart's *Idomeneo* and Reform Operas in Mannheim." In Theodor Göllner and Stephan Hörner, eds., *Mozart's Idomeneo und die Musik in München zur Zeit Karl Theodors*, 131–41. Munich: C. H. Beck, 2001.

Baron-Woods, Kristina. "Strength and Defiance in the Seraglio: Coloratura as Characterization in Mozart's *Die Entführung aus dem Serail*." *Music Research Forum* 23 (2008): 27–51.

Barry, Barbara R. "The Spider's Stratagem: The Motif of Masking in *Don Giovanni*." In Barbara R. Barry, *The Philosopher's Stone: Essays in the Transformation of Musical Structure*, 53–72. Hillsdale, N.Y.: Pendragon, 2000.

Bartel, Kate. "Pamina, Portraits, and the Feminine in Mozart and Schikaneder's *Die Zauberflöte*." *Musicology Australia* 22 (1999): 31–45.

Bauman, Thomas. *W. A. Mozart: Die Entführung aus dem Serail.* Cambridge: Cambridge University Press, 1987.

Beckerman, Michael Brim. "Mozart's Pastoral." *Mozart-Jahrbuch* 93 (1991): 93–102.

Berk, Matheus Franciscus Maria van den. The Magic Flute/Die Zauberflöte: *An Alchemical Allegory.* Leiden, Netherlands: E. J. Brill, 2004.

Branscombe, Peter. "The Literary Afterlife of *Die Zauberflöte*." In David Rosen and Claire Brook, eds., *Words on Music: Essays in Honor of Andrew Porter on the Occasion of His 75th Birthday*, 14–29. Hillsdale, N.Y.: Pendragon, 2003.

Brown, Bruce Alan. *W. A. Mozart:* Così fan tutte. Cambridge: Cambridge University Press, 1995.

Brown, Jane K. "The Queen of the Night and the Crisis of Allegory in *The Magic Flute*." *Goethe Yearbook* 8 (1996): 142–56.

Brown, Kristi Ann. *A Critical Study of the Female Characters in Mozart's* Don Giovanni *and* Die Zauberflöte. Ph.D. dissertation, University of California, Berkeley, 1997.

Brown-Montesano, Kristi. *Understanding the Women of Mozart's Operas*. Berkeley: University of California Press, 2007.

Buch, David J. *Die Zauberflöte*, Masonic Opera, and Other Fairy Tales." *Acta Musicologica* 76 (2004): 193–219.

———. "Fairy-Tale Literature and *Die Zauberflöte*." *Acta Musicologica* 64 (1992): 30–49.

———. *Magic Flutes and Enchanted Forests: The Supernatural in Eighteenth-Century Musical Theater*. Chicago: University of Chicago Press, 2008.

———. "Mozart and the Theater auf der Wieden: New Attributions and Perspectives." *Cambridge Opera Journal* 9 (1997): 195–232.

———. "The Otherworld as Past: Operatic Conventions for the Supernatural in the Eighteenth Century and Mozart's *Don Giovanni*." In László Dobszay, ed., *The Past in the Present: Papers Read at the IMS Intercongressional Symposium and the 10th Meeting of the Cantus Planus, Budapest and Visegrád, 2000*, 193–206. Budapest: Liszt Ferenc Zeneművészeti, 2003.

Cairns, David. *Mozart and His Operas*. London: Allen Lane, 2006.

Campana, Alessandra. "The Performance of *Opera buffa*: Le nozze di Figaro and the Act IV Finale." In Stefano La Via and Roger Parker, eds., *Pensieri per un Maestro: Studi in Onore di Pierluigi Petrobelli*, 125–34. Turin, Italy: Edizioni di Torino, 2002.

Canfield, J. Douglas. "The Classical Treatment of Don Juan in Tirso, Molière, and Mozart: What Cultural Work Does It Perform?" *Comparative Drama* 31 (1997): 42–64.

Carter, Tim. "Mozart, Da Ponte, and the Ensemble: Methods in Progress?" In Stanley Sadie, ed., *Wolfgang Amadé Mozart: Essays on His Life and His Music*, 241–49. New York: Oxford University Press, 1996.

———. *W. A. Mozart:* Le nozze di Figaro. Cambridge: Cambridge University Press, 1987.

Castelvecchi, Stefano. "Sentimental and Anti-sentimental in *Le nozze di Figaro*." *Journal of the American Musicological Society* 53 (2000): 1–24.

Cole, Malcolm S. "Monostatos and His 'Sister': Racial Stereotype in *Die Zauberflöte* and Its Sequel." *Opera Quarterly* 21 (2005): 2–26.

Corneilson, Paul E. "Mozart's Ilia and Elettra: New Perspectives on *Idomeneo*." In Theodor Göllner and Stephan Hörner, eds., *Mozart's* Idomeneo *und die Musik in München zur Zeit Karl Theodors*, 97–113. Munich: C. H. Beck, 2001.

Eckelmeyer, Judith A. *The Cultural Context of Mozart's* Magic Flute: *Social, Aesthetic, Philosophical*. Translated by Renata Cinti and Joachim Werner Kiwi. Lewiston, N.Y.: Edwin Mellen, 1991.

Edge, Dexter. "Mozart's Viennese Orchestras." *Early Music* 20 (1992): 64–88.

Fredman, Myer. *From* Idomeneo *to* Die Zauberflöte: *A Conductor's Commentary on the Operas of Wolfgang Amadeus Mozart*. Portland, Ore.: Sussex Academic, 2002.

Goehring, Edmund J. "Despina, Cupid, and the Pastoral Mode of *Così fan tutte*." *Cambridge Opera Journal* 7 (1995): 107–33.

———. "*Don Giovanni* at the Crossroads of Pleasure and Virtue." *Current Musicology* 84 (2007): 101–16.

———. *Three Modes of Perception in Mozart: The Philosophical, Pastoral, and Comic in* Così fan tutte. Cambridge: Cambridge University Press, 2004.

Grout, Donald Jay. *Mozart in the History of Opera*. Washington, D.C.: Library of Congress, 1972.

Heartz, Daniel. "Mozart and Da Ponte." *Musical Quarterly* 79 (1995): 700–18.

———. "Raaff's Last Aria: A Mozartian Idyll in the Spirit of Hasse." *Musical Quarterly* 60 (1974): 517–43.

Heartz, Daniel; Thomas Bauman, ed. *Mozart's Operas*. Berkeley: University of California Press, 1990.

Herwitz, Daniel A. "The Cook, His Wife, the Philosopher, and the Librettist." *Musical Quarterly* 78 (1994): 48–76.

Hunter, Mary. *The Culture of Opera Buffa in Mozart's Vienna: A Poetics of Entertainment*. Princeton, N.J.: Princeton University Press, 1999.

———. *Mozart's Operas: A Companion*. New Haven, Conn.: Yale University Press, 2008.

Irmen, Hans-Josef. *Mozart's Masonry and* The Magic Flute. Translated by Ruth Ohm. Zülpich, Germany: Prisca, 1996.

Kaminsky, Peter. "How to Do Things with Words and Music: Towards an Analysis of Selected Ensembles in Mozart's *Don Giovanni*." *Theory and Practice* 21 (1996): 55–78.

Keefe, Simon P., ed. *The Cambridge Companion to Mozart*. Cambridge: Cambridge University Press, 2003.

Lewin, David. "Figaro's Mistakes." *Current Musicology* 57 (1995): 45–60.

Lewy Gidwitz, Patricia. "'Ich bin die erste Sängerin': Vocal Profiles of Two Mozart Sopranos." *Early Music* 19 (1991): 565–74.

———. *Vocal Profiles of Four Mozart Sopranos.* Ph.D. dissertation, University of California, Berkeley, 1991.

Link, Dorothea. "The Fandango Scene in Mozart's *Le nozze di Figaro.*" *Journal of the Royal Musical Association* 133 (2008): 69–92.

———. *The National Court Theatre in Mozart's Vienna: Sources and Documents, 1783–1792.* Oxford: Clarendon, 1998.

Lütteken, Laurenz. "Negating Opera through Opera: *Così fan tutte* and the Reverse of the Enlightenment." *Eighteenth-Century Music* 6 (2009): 229–42.

Mann, William. *The Operas of Mozart.* New York: Oxford University Press, 1982; originally 1977.

McClymonds, Marita P. "*La clemenza di Tito* and the Action Ensemble Finale in Opera Seria before 1791." *Mozart-Jahrbuch* (1991): 766–72.

———. "The Great Quartet in *Idomeneo* and the Italian Opera seria Tradition." In Stanley Sadie, ed., *Wolfgang Amadé Mozart: Essays on His Life and His Music*, 449–76. New York: Oxford University Press, 1996.

———. "Mannheim, *Idomeneo*, and the Franco-Italian Synthesis in Opera seria." In Ludwig Finscher et al., eds., *Mozart und Mannheim*, 187–96. Berlin: Peter Lang, 1994.

———. "Mozart and His Contemporaries: Action Trios by Paisiello, Cimarosa, Martin, and Mozart." In Axel Beer et al., eds., *Festschrift Christoph-Hellmut Mahling zum 65. Geburtstag*, 853–82. Tutzing, Germany: Schneider, 1997.

Nedbal, Martin. "Mozart as a Viennese Moralist: *Die Zauberflöte* and Its Maxims." *Acta Musicologica* 81 (2009): 123–57.

Neumann, Frederick. *Ornamentation and Improvisation in Mozart.* Princeton, N.J.: Princeton University Press, 1986.

Osborne, Charles. *The Complete Operas of Mozart: A Critical Guide.* London: Gollancz, 1986; originally 1978.

Platoff, John. "The Buffa Aria in Mozart's Vienna." *Cambridge Opera Journal* 2 (1990): 99–120.

———. "Catalog Arias and the 'Catalogue Aria.'" In Stanley Sadie, ed., *Wolfgang Amadé Mozart: Essays on His Life and His Music*, 296–311. New York: Oxford University Press, 1996.

———. "How Original Was Mozart? Evidence from Opera Buffa." *Early Music* 20 (1992): 105–17.

———. *Music and Drama in the Opera Buffa Finale: Mozart and His Contemporaries in Vienna, 1781–1790.* Ph.D. dissertation, University of Pennsylvania, 1984.

———. "Myths and Realities about Tonal Planning in Mozart's Operas." *Cambridge Opera Journal* 8 (1996): 3–15.

————. "Tonal Organization in Buffo Finales and the Act II Finale of *Le nozze di Figaro*." *Music and Letters* 72 (1991): 387–403.

————. "Tonal Organization in the Opera buffa of Mozart's Time." *Mozart Studies* 2 (1997): 139–74.

Rice, John A. *Mozart on the Stage*. Cambridge: Cambridge University Press, 2009.

————. *W. A. Mozart:* La clemenza di Tito. Cambridge: Cambridge University Press, 1991.

Rushton, Julian. *The New Grove Guide to Mozart and His Operas*. New York: Oxford University Press, 2007.

————. "Tonality in Act Three of *Idomeneo*." In Alison Stonehouse et al., eds., *Mozart in History, Theory, and Practice: Selected Papers from the International Symposium. Studies in Music from the University of Western Ontario* 14 (1993): 17–48.

————. *W. A. Mozart:* Don Giovanni. Cambridge: Cambridge University Press, 1981.

————. *W. A. Mozart:* Idomeneo. Cambridge: Cambridge University Press, 1993.

Sadie, Stanley, ed. *Wolfgang Amadé Mozart: Essays on His Life and His Music*. New York: Oxford University Press, 1996.

Schenbeck, Lawrence. "Leporello, *Don Giovanni*, and the Picaresque." *Opera Quarterly* 11 (1995): 3–16.

Sisman, Elaine R. "The Marriages of *Don Giovanni*: Persuasion, Impersonation, and Personal Responsibility." In Simon P. Keefe, ed., *Mozart Studies*, 163–92. Cambridge: Cambridge University Press, 2006.

Solomon, Maynard. *Mozart: A Life*. New York: HarperCollins, 1995.

Steinberg, Michael P. "*Don Giovanni* against the Baroque, or, The Culture Punished." In James M. Morris, ed., *On Mozart*, 187–203. Washington, D.C.: Woodrow Wilson Center for Scholars, 1994.

Steptoe, Andrew. *The Mozart–Da Ponte Operas: The Cultural and Musical Background to* Le nozze di Figaro, Don Giovanni, *and* Così fan tutte. Oxford: Clarendon, 1988.

Subotnik, Rose Rosengard. "Whose *Magic Flute*? Intimations of Reality at the Gates of Enlightenment." *19th Century Music* 15 (1991–92): 132–50.

Taylor, Raphael. *Mozart's Carnival: Opera Masquerade and the World Turned Upside-Down*. Ph.D. dissertation, King's College, 2005.

Thomson, Ian. *Mozart's Opera* Die Zauberflöte: *An Analysis of the Historical and Literary Sources of the Libretto*. Ph.D. dissertation, University of East Anglia, 2003.

Till, Nicholas. *Mozart and the Enlightenment: Truth, Virtue, and Beauty in Mozart's Operas*. London: Faber and Faber, 1992.

Waldoff, Jessica P. "The Music of Recognition: Operatic Enlightenment in *The Magic Flute*." *Music and Letters* 75 (1994): 214–35.

———. "Reading Mozart's Operas 'For the Sentiment.'" In Simon P. Keefe, ed., *Mozart Studies*, 74–108. Cambridge: Cambridge University Press, 2006.

———. *Recognition in Mozart's Operas*. New York: Oxford University Press, 2006.

Weber, William. "The Myth of Mozart the Revolutionary." *Musical Quarterly* 78 (1994): 34–47.

Webster, James. "The Analysis of Mozart's Arias." In Cliff Eisen, ed., *Mozart Studies*, 101–99. Oxford: Clarendon, 1991.

———. "Mozart's Operas and the Myth of Musical Unity." *Cambridge Opera Journal* 2 (1990): 197–218.

Woodfield, Ian. *Performing Operas for Mozart: Impresarios, Singers, and Troupes*. Cambridge: Cambridge University Press, 2012.

———. *The Vienna* Don Giovanni. Woodbridge, England: Boydell, 2010.

Zeiss, Laurel Elizabeth. *Accompanied Recitative in Mozart's Operas: "The* chef d'oeuvre *of the Composer's Art."* Ph.D. dissertation, University of North Carolina. Ann Arbor, Mich.: University Microfilms International, 1999.

———. "Permeable Boundaries in Mozart's *Don Giovanni*." *Cambridge Opera Journal* 13 (2001): 115–39.

Paisiello, Giovanni

Castelvecchi, Stefano. "From *Nina* to *Nina*: Psychodrama, Absorption, and Sentiment in the 1780s." *Cambridge Opera Journal* 8 (1996): 91–112.

Hunt, Jno Leland. *Giovanni Paisiello: His Life as an Opera Composer*. National Opera Association, 1975.

Zwiebach, Michael Howard. *Marriage of Wits: Comic Archetypes and the Staging of Ideas in Five Comic Operas by Giovanni Paisiello*. Ph.D. dissertation, University of California, Berkeley, 2000.

Pergolesi, Giovanni Battista

Lazarevich, Gordana. "Pergolesi and the Querre des Bouffons." *Pergolesi Studies* 2 (1988): 195–203.

Mackenzie, Barbara Dobbs. "Neapolitan Comic Opera in Naples and Rome: Pergolesi's *Lo frate 'nnamorato* and Latilla's *La finta cameriera*." *Studi pergolesiani/Pergolesi Studies* 3 (1999): 183–99.

Monson, D. E. Recitativo semplice *in the opere serie of G. B. Pergolesi and His Contemporaries*. Ph.D. dissertation, Columbia University, 1982.

Paymer, Marvin E., and Hermine W. Williams. *Giovanni Battista Pergolesi: A Guide to Research*. New York: Garland, 1989.

Piccinni, Niccolò

Rushton, Julian. "The Theory and Practice of Piccinnisme." *Proceedings of the Royal Musical Association* 98 (1971–72): 31–46.

Porpora, Nicola

Robinson, Michael. "Porpora's Operas for London, 1733–1736." *Soundings* 2 (1971): 57–87.
Walker, Frank. "A Chronology of the Life and Works of Nicola Porpora." *Italian Studies* 6 (1951): 29–62.

Rameau, Jean-Philippe

Burgess, Geoffrey. "'Le théâtre ne change qu'à la troisième scène': The Hand of the Author and Unity of Place, Act V of *Hippolyte et Aricie*." *Cambridge Opera Journal* 10 (1998): 275–87.
Cyr, Mary. "Eighteenth-Century French and Italian Singing: Rameau's Writing for the Voice." *Music and Letters* 61 (1980): 318–37.
———. "The Paris Opéra Chorus during the Time of Rameau." *Music and Letters* 76 (1995): 32–51.
Dill, Charles William. *Monstrous Opera: Rameau and the Tragic Tradition*. Princeton, N.J.: Princeton University Press, 1998.
———. "Pellegrin, Opera, and Tragedy." *Cambridge Opera Journal* 10 (1998): 247–57.
———. "Rameau Reading Lully: Meaning and System in Rameau's Recitative Tradition." *Cambridge Opera Journal* 6 (1994): 1–17.
———. "Rameau's Imaginary Monsters: Knowledge, Theory, and Chromaticism in *Hippolyte et Aricie*." *Journal of the American Musicological Society* 55 (2002): 433–76.
Downing, Thomas A. "Rameau's *Platée* Returns: A Case of Double Identity in the Querelle des Bouffons." *Cambridge Opera Journal* 18 (2006): 1–19.
Harris-Warrick, Rebecca. "Ballet, Pantomime, and the Sung Word in the Operas of Rameau." In Cliff Eisen, ed., *Coll'astuzia, col giudizio: Essays in Honor of Neal Zaslaw*, 31–61. Ann Arbor, Mich.: Steglein, 2009.
Rice, Paul Francis. *Fontainebleau Operas for the Court of Louis XV of France by Jean-Philippe Rameau (1683–1764)*. Lewiston, N.Y.: Mellon, 2004.
———. "The Fontainebleau Operas of Jean-Philippe Rameau." *Journal of Musicology* 6 (1988): 227–44.

———. "Mid-eighteenth Century Changes in French Opera: The Two Versions of Rameau's *Zoroastre*." *Recherches sur la musique française classique* 21 (1983): 128–44.

Rosow, Lois. "Structure and Expression in the *Scènes* of Rameau's *Hippolyte et Aricie*." *Cambridge Opera Journal* 10 (1998): 259–73.

Verba, Cynthia. "What Recitatives Owe to the Airs: A Look at the Dialogue Scene, Act I Scene 2 of Rameau's *Hippolyte et Aricie*—Version with Airs." *Cambridge Opera Journal* 11 (1999): 103–34.

Rousseau, Jean-Jacques

Gay-White, Pamela. "Rousseau and the Lyric Natural: The Representation of *Le Devin du village*." In Claude Dauphin, ed., *Musique et langage chez Rousseau*, 211–19. Oxford: Voltaire Foundation, 2004.

Heartz, Daniel. "The Beginnings of the Operatic *Romance*: Rousseau, Sedaine, and Monsigny." *Eighteenth-Century Studies* 15 (1981): 149–78.

Salieri, Antonio

Rice, John A. *Antonio Salieri and Viennese Opera*. Chicago: University of Chicago Press, 1998.

———. "The Operas of Antonio Salieri as a Reflection of Viennese Opera, 1770–1800." In David Wyn Jones, ed., *Music in Eighteenth-Century Austria*, 210–20. New York: Oxford University Press, 1996.

Scarlatti, Alessandro

D'Accone, Frank A. *The History of a Baroque Opera: Alessandro Scarlatti's Gli equivoci nel sembiante*. New York: Pendragon, 1985.

Grout, Donald Jay. *Alessandro Scarlatti: An Introduction to His Operas*. Berkeley: University of California Press, 1979.

Vidale, Carole Franklin. *Alessandro and Domenico Scarlatti: A Guide to Research*. New York: General, 1993.

Storace, Stephen

Durham, Linda Eileen. *Stephen Storace and Prince Hoare's* No Song, No Supper*: Influences and Reception*. Ph.D. dissertation, Florida State University, 1998.

Girdham, Jane. *English Opera in Late Eighteenth-Century London: Stephen Storace at Drury Lane*. Oxford: Clarendon, 1997.

Traetta, Tommaso

Loomis, George W. *Tommaso Traetta's Operas for Parma*. Ph.D. dissertation, Yale University, 1999.

Verazi, Mattia

McClymonds, Marita Petzolt. "Mattia Verazi and the Opera at Mannheim, Stuttgart, and Ludwigsburg." *Studies in Music from the University of Western Ontario* 7 (1982): 99–136.

Vinci, Leonardo

Markstrom, Kurt S. *The Operas of Leonardo Vinci, Napoletano*. Hillsdale, N.Y.: Pendragon, 2007.

Vivaldi, Antonio

Collins, Michael, and Elise K. Kirk, eds. *Opera and Vivaldi: Dallas 1980*. Austin: University of Texas, 1984.

Cross, Eric. *The Late Operas of Antonio Vivaldi*. Ann Arbor, Mich.: University Microfilms International, 1981.

———. "Vivaldi's Operatic Borrowings." *Music and Letters* 59 (1978): 429–39.

Rosand, Ellen. "Vivaldi's Stage." *Journal of Musicology* 18 (2001): 8–30.

Strohm, Reinhard. *The Operas of Antonio Vivaldi*. Florence: Olschki, 2008.

Talbot, Michael. "Vivaldi's Serenatas: Long Cantatas or Short Operas?" In *Venetian Music in the Age of Vivaldi*, 67–96. Aldershot, England: Ashgate, 1999.

Zeno, Apostolo

Freeman, Robert. "Apostolo Zeno's Reform of the Libretto." *Journal of the American Musicological Society* 21 (1968): 321–41.

18TH CENTURY: LOCATIONS

Austria and Germany

Bauman, Thomas. *North German Opera in the Age of Goethe.* Cambridge: Cambridge University Press, 1985.

Corneilson, Paul E. *Opera at Mannheim, 1770–1778.* Ph.D. dissertation, University of North Carolina, 1992.

Dunlap, Susanne Emily. Armida *and* Rinaldo *in Eighteenth-Century Vienna: Context, Content, and Tonal Coding in Viennese Italian Reform Operas, 1761–1782.* Ph.D. dissertation, Yale University, 1999.

Heartz, Daniel. *Haydn, Mozart, and the Viennese School, 1740–1780.* New York: Norton, 1995.

Hunter, Mary, and James Webster, eds. *Opera Buffa in Mozart's Vienna.* Cambridge: Cambridge University Press, 1997.

Platoff, John. "Musical and Dramatic Structure in the Opera Buffa Finale." *Journal of Musicology* 7 (1989): 191–230.

Rabin, Ronald Jay. *Mozart, Da Ponte, and the Dramaturgy of Opera buffa: Italian Comic Opera in Vienna, 1783–1791.* Ph.D. dissertation, Cornell University, 1996.

Rice, John A. *Emperor and Impresario: Leopold II and the Transformation of Viennese Musical Theater, 1790–1792.* Ph.D. dissertation, University of California, Berkeley, 1987.

Swack, Jeanne. "Anti-Semitism at the Opera: The Portrayal of Jews in the Singspiels of Reinhard Keiser." *Musical Quarterly* 84 (2000): 389–416.

Wade, Mara R. *The German Baroque Pastoral "Singspiel."* Berne: Peter Lang, 1990.

Wallace, Robin. "Myth, Gender, and Musical Meaning: *The Magic Flute*, Beethoven, and 19th-Century Sonata Form Revisited." *Journal of Musicological Research* 19 (1999): 1–26.

England

Armondino, Gail Miller. *The Opéra Comique in London, or, Transforming French Comic Opera for the English Stage, 1770–1789.* Ph.D. dissertation, Catholic University, 2000.

Dircks, Phyllis T. *David Garrick.* Boston: Twayne, 1985.

Fiske, Roger. *English Theater Music in the Eighteenth Century.* London: Oxford University Press, 1973.

Gibson, Elizabeth Anne. *The Royal Academy of Music 1719–1728: The Institution and Its Directors.* New York: General, 1989.

Hodges, Sheila. "A Nest of Nightingales." *Music Review* 54 (1993): 79–94.

Hume, Robert D. *Henry Fielding and the London Theatre, 1728–1737.* Oxford: Oxford University Press, 1988.

Joncus, Berta. *A Star Is Born: Kitty Clive and Female Representation in Eighteenth-Century English Musical Theater.* Ph.D. dissertation, Oxford University, 2004.

McGeary, Thomas Nelson. "'Warbling Eunuchs': Opera, Gender, and Sexuality on the London Stage, 1705–1742." *Restoration and Eighteenth-Century Theatre Research* 7 (1992): 1–22.

Milhous, Judith, and Robert D. Hume. "Opera Salaries in Eighteenth-Century London." *Journal of the American Musicological Society* 46 (1993): 26–83.

Petty, Fred C. *Italian Opera in London, 1760–1800.* Ph.D. dissertation, Yale University, 1971.

Price, Curtis A. "Italian Opera and Arson in Late Eighteenth-Century London." *Journal of the American Musicological Society* 42 (1989): 55–107.

Stone, George Winchester, Jr., and George M. Kahrl. *David Garrick: A Critical Biography.* Carbondale: Southern Illinois University Press, 1979.

Wierzbicki, James. "Dethroning the Divas: Satire Directed at Cuzzoni and Faustina." *Opera Quarterly* 17 (2001): 175–96.

Willaert, Saskia. *Italian Comic Opera in London, 1760–1770.* Ph.D. dissertation, University of London, 1999.

Woodfield, Ian. *Opera and Drama in Eighteenth-Century London: The King's Theater, Garrick, and the Business of Performance.* Cambridge: Cambridge University Press, 2006.

France

Banducci, Antonia. "Staging and Its Dramatic Effect in French Baroque Opera: Evidence from Prompt Notes." *Eighteenth-Century Music* 1 (2004): 5–28.

Bartlet, M. Elizabeth C. "The New Repertory at the Opéra during the Reign of Terror: Revolutionary Rhetoric and Operatic Consequences." In Malcolm Boyd, ed., *Music and the French Revolution*, 107–56. Cambridge: Cambridge University Press, 1992.

Betzwieser, Thomas. "Musical Setting and Scenic Movement: Chorus and *Choeur dansé* in Eighteenth-Century Parisian Opéra." *Cambridge Opera Journal* 12 (2000): 1–28.

Boyd, Malcolm, ed. *Music and the French Revolution.* Cambridge: Cambridge University Press, 1992.

Brown, Leslie Ellen. "Departures from the Lullian Convention in the *Tragédie lyrique* of the *Préramiste* Era." *Recherches sur la musique française classique* 22 (1984): 59–78.

————. "The *récit* in the Eighteenth-Century *Tragédie en musique.*" *Music Review* 45 (1984): 96–111.

Charlton, David. "On Redefinitions of 'Rescue Opera.'" In Malcolm Boyd, ed., *Music and the French Revolution*, 169–88. Cambridge: Cambridge University Press, 1992.

————. "Orchestra and Chorus at the Comédie-Italienne (Opéra-Comique), 1755–1799." In Malcolm Hamrick Brown and Roland John Wiley, eds., *Slavonic and Western Music: Essays for Gerald Abraham*, 87–108. Ann Arbor, Mich.: University Microfilms International, 1985.

Cole, Catherine Jean. *"Nature" at the Opera: Sound and Social Change in France, 1750–1779*. Ph.D. dissertation, University of Chicago, 2003.

Cook, Elisabeth A. "Challenging the Ancien Régime: The Hidden Politics of the Querelle des Bouffons." In Andrea Fabiano and Sylvie Bouissou, eds., *La Querelle des Bouffons dans la vie culturelle française du XVIIIiem Siècle*, 141–60. Paris: Éditions du Centre National de la Richerche Scientifique, 2005.

————. *Duet and Ensemble in the Early* Opéra comique. New York: General, 1995.

————. *The Operatic Ensemble in France, 1673–1775*. Ph.D. dissertation, University of East Anglia, 1990.

Cowart, Georgia. "Of Women, Sex, and Folly: Opera under the Old Regime." *Cambridge Opera Journal* 6 (1994): 205–20.

Dill, Charles William. "Eighteenth-Century Models of French Recitative." *Journal of the Royal Musical Association* 120 (1995): 232–50.

Darlow, Mark. "Repertory Reforms at the Paris Opéra on the Eve of the Revolution." *Journal for Eighteenth-Century Studies* 32 (2009): 563–76.

————. *Staging the French Revolution: Cultural Politics and the Paris Opéra (1789–1794)*. Oxford: Oxford University Press, 2012.

Isherwood, Robert M. "Nationalism and the Querelle des Bouffons." In Jean Gribenski et al., eds., *D'un Opéra L'autre: Hommage à Jean Mongrédien*, 323–30. Paris: Presses Universitaires de France, 1996.

Koch, Charles Edmund, Jr. "The Dramatic Ensemble Finale in the *Opéra comique* of the Eighteenth Century." *Acta Musicologica* 39 (1967): 72–83.

Kopp, James Butler. *The* Drame lyrique *: A Study in the Esthetics of* Opéra comique*, 1762–1791*. Ph.D. dissertation, University of Pennsylvania, 1982.

Ledbury, Mark, and David Charlton, eds. *Michel-Jean Sedaine (1719–1797): Theater, Opera, and Art*. Aldershot, England: Ashgate, 2000.

Letzter, Jacqueline. "Making a Spectacle of Oneself: French Revolutionary Opera by Women." *Cambridge Opera Journal* 11 (1999): 215–32.

McClellan, Michael E. "The Italian Menace: Opera *buffa* in Revolutionary France." *Eighteenth-Century Music* 1 (2004): 249–63.

Norman, Buford. "Remaking a Cultural Icon: *Phèdre* and the Operatic Stage." *Cambridge Opera Journal* 10 (1998): 225–45.

Pękacz, Jolanta T. "Gender as a Political Orientation: Parisian Salonnières and the Querelle des Bouffons." *Canadian Journal of History* 32 (1997): 405–14.

———. "Salon Women and the Quarrels about Opera in Eighteenth-Century Paris." *The European Legacy: Toward New Paradigms* 1 (1996): 1608–14.

Stilwell, Jama. "A New View of the Eighteenth-Century 'Abduction' Opera: Edification and Escape at the Parisian Théâtres de la Foire." *Music and Letters* 91 (2010): 51–82.

———. *"A Story Altogether Foolish, Bizarre, and Buffoonish": The Theatres de la Foire and the Eighteenth-Century Captivity Opera.* Ph.D. dissertation, University of Iowa, 2003.

Italy

Bergeron, Katherine. "The Castrato as History." *Cambridge Opera Journal* 8 (1996): 167–84.

Buelow, George J. "A Lesson in Operatic Performance Practice by Madame Faustina Bordoni." In Edward H. Clinkscale and Claire Brook, eds., *A Musical Offering: Essays in Honor of Martin Bernstein*, 79–96. New York: Pendragon, 1977.

Butler, Margaret R. "Producing the Operatic Chorus at Parma's Teatro Ducale, 1759–1769." *Eighteenth-Century Music* 3 (2006): 231–51.

Collins, Michael. "Dramatic Theory and the Italian Baroque Libretto." In Michael Collins and Elise K. Kirk, eds., *Opera and Vivaldi*, 15–40. Austin: University of Texas, 1984.

Crosscurrents and the Mainstream of Italian Serious Opera 1730–1790. Studies in Music from the University of Western Ontario 7 (1984).

Dame, Joke. "Unveiled Voices: Sexual Difference and the Castrato." In Philip Brett et al., eds., *Queering the Pitch: The New Gay and Lesbian Musicology*, 139–53. New York: Routledge, 1994.

DelDonna, Anthony R. "Behind the Scenes: The Musical Life and Organizational Structure of the San Carlo Opera Orchestra in Late 18th-Century Naples." In Paologiovanni Maione, ed., *Fonti d'archivio per la storia della musica e dello spettacolo a Napoli tra XVI e XVIII secolo*, 427–48. Naples: Editoriale scientifica, 2001.

———. "Eighteenth-Century Politics and Patronage: Music and the Republican Revolution of Naples." *Eighteenth-Century Music* 4 (2007): 211–50.

———. "Production Practices at the Teatro di San Carlo, Naples, in the Late 18th Century." *Early Music* 30 (2002): 429–45.

Downes, Edward O. D. "Secco Recitative in Early Classical Opera Seria (1720–80)." *Journal of the American Musicological Society* 14 (1961): 50–69.

Feldman, Martha. "Magic Mirrors and the *Seria* Stage: Thoughts toward a Ritual View." *Journal of the American Musicological Society* 48 (1995): 423–84.

————. *Opera and Sovereignty: Transforming Myths in Eighteenth-Century Italy.* Chicago: University of Chicago Press, 2007.

Freitas, Roger. "The Eroticism of Emasculation: Confronting the Baroque Body of the Castrato." *Journal of Musicology* 20 (2003): 196–249.

Hansell, Kathleen Kuzmick. *Opera and Ballet at the Regio Ducal Teatro of Milan, 1771–1776.* Ph.D. dissertation, University of California, Berkeley, 1980.

Heartz, Daniel. "Caffarelli's Caprices." In Colleen Reardon and Susan Parisi, eds., *Music Observed: Studies in Memory of William C. Holmes*, 195–208. Warren, Mich.: Harmonie Park, 2004.

————. "The Creation of the Buffo Finale in Italian Opera." *Proceedings of the Royal Musical Association* 104 (1977–78): 67–78.

————. "Farinelli Revisited." *Early Music* 18 (1990): 430–43.

Hunter, Mary. "Some Representations of Opera seria in Opera buffa." *Cambridge Opera Journal* 3 (1991): 89–108.

Mackenzie, Barbara Dobbs. *The Creation of a Genre: Comic Opera's Dissemination in Italy in the 1740s.* Ph.D. dissertation, University of Michigan, 1993.

Macklem, Mary Sue. *Reforming Opera and Its Public in Early Modern Venice.* Ph.D. dissertation, University of Pennsylvania, 2003.

McClymonds, Marita Petzoldt. "The Role of Innovation and Reform in the Florentine Opera seria Repertory: 1760 to 1800." In Collen Reardon and Susan Parisi, eds., *Music Observed: Studies in Memory of William C. Holmes*, 281–300. Warren, Mich.: Harmonie Park, 2004.

————. "Style as a Sign in Some *Opere serie* of Hasse and Jommelli." In Rheinhard Wiesend, ed., *Johann Adolf Hasse in seiner Zeit: Bericht über das Symposium vom 23. bis 26. März 1999 in Hamburg*, 179–92. Stuttgart, Germany: Carus, 2006.

Milhous, Judith, et al. *Italian Opera in Late Eighteenth-Century London.* 2 vols. Oxford: Oxford University Press, 1995, 2001.

Monelle, Raymond. "Recitative and Dramaturgy in the *Dramma per musica.*" *Music and Letters* 59 (1978): 245–67.

Monson, Dale E. "*Semplice o secco*: Continuo Declamation in Early 18th-Century Italian Recitative." Francesco Degrada, ed., *Lo stato attuale degli studi su Pergolesi e il suo tempo. Studi pergolesiani/Pergolesi Studies I*, 107–15. Scandicci, Italy: Nuova Italia, 1986.

Petrobelli, Pierluigi. "The Italian Years of Anton Raaff." *Mozart-Jahrbuch* (1973–74): 233–73.

Polzonetti, Pierpaolo. *Italian Opera in the Age of the American Revolution.* Cambridge: Cambridge University Press, 2011.

Robinson, Michael F. "The Da Capo Aria as Symbol of Rationality." In Raffaele Pozzi, ed., *La musica come linguaggio universale: Genesi e storia de un'idea*, 51–63. Florence: Olschki, 1990.

———. *Naples and Neapolitan Opera.* London: Oxford University Press, 1972.

Selfridge-Field, Eleanor. "Music at the Pietà before Vivaldi." *Early Music* 14 (1986): 373–86.

Strohm, Reinhard. Dramma per musica*: Italian Opera seria of the Eighteenth Century.* New Haven, Conn.: Yale University Press, 1997.

Talbot, Michael. "The Serenata in Eighteenth-Century Venice." *Royal Musical Association Research Chronicle* 18 (1982): 1–50.

———. "Tenors and Basses at the Venetian Ospedali." *Acta Musicologica* 66 (1994): 123–38.

Tcharos, Stefanie. "The Serenata in Early 18th-Century Rome: Sight, Sound, Ritual, and the Signification of Meaning." *Journal of Musicology* 23 (2006): 528–68.

Troy, Charles. *The Comic Intermezzo: A Study in the History of Eighteenth-Century Opera.* Ann Arbor, Mich.: University Microfilms International, 1979.

Vogelaar, Peter W. "Castrati in Western Art Music." *Medical Problems of Performing Artists* 13 (1998): 94–99.

Ward, Adrienne. *Pagodas in Play: China on the Eighteenth-Century Italian Opera Stage.* Lewisburg, Pa.: Bucknell University, 2010.

Weimer, Eric. *Opera seria and the Evolution of Classical Style.* Ann Arbor, Mich.: University Microfilms International, 1984.

Werr, Sebastian. "Neapolitan Elements and Comedy in Nineteenth-Century Opera buffa." Translated by Mary Hunter. *Cambridge Opera Journal* 14 (2002): 297–311.

Other Locations

Lamas, Rafael. "*Zarzuel* and the Anti-musical Prejudice of the Spanish Enlightenment." *Hispanic Review* 74 (2006): 39–58.

Rytsarev, Marina, and Anna L. Porfir'eva. "The Italian Diaspora in Eighteenth-Century Russia." In Reinhard Strohm, ed., *The Eighteenth-Century Diaspora of Italian Music and Musicians*, 211–53. Turnhout, Belgium: Brepols, 2001.

Stein, Louise K. "'La miúsica de dos orbes': A Context for the First Opera of the Americas." *Opera Quarterly* 22 (2006): 433–58.

18TH CENTURY: COMPARATIVE AND OTHER TOPICS

Bauman, Thomas, and Marita Petzolt McClymonds, eds. *Opera and the Enlightenment*. Cambridge: Cambridge University Press, 1995.

Castelvecchi, Stefano. *Sentimental Opera: The Emergence of a Genre, 1760–1790*. Ph.D. dissertation, University of Chicago, 1996.

Dean, Winton. "The Performance of Recitative in Late Baroque Opera." *Music and Letters* 58 (1977): 389–402.

DelDonna, Anthony R., and Pierpaolo Polzonetti, eds. *The Cambridge Companion to Eighteenth-Century Opera*. Cambridge: Cambridge University Press, 2009.

DeMarco, Laura E. "The Fact of the Castrato and the Myth of the Countertenor." *Musical Quarterly* 86 (2002): 174–85.

Dill, Charles, ed. *Opera Remade, 1700–1750*. Farnham, England: Ashgate, 2010.

Gjerdingen, Robert O. *Music in the Galant Style*. New York: Oxford University Press, 2007.

Heartz, Daniel. *Music in European Capitals: The Galant Style, 1720–1780*. New York: Norton, 2003.

Letzter, Jacqueline, and Robert Adelson. "Reconstructing the Author-Function: Naming the Forgotten Women of Eighteenth-Century Opera." *Women of Note Quarterly* 5 (1997): 13–27.

McClelland, Clive. *Ombra Music in the Eighteenth Century: Context, Style, and Signification*. Ph.D. dissertation, University of Leeds, 2001.

Minniear, J. M. *Marionette Opera: Its History and Literature*. Ph.D. dissertation, North Texas State University, 1971.

Rice, John A., ed. *Essays on Opera, 1750–1800*. Aldershot, England: Ashgate, 2010.

Robinson, Michael. *Opera before Mozart*. London: Hutchinson, 1966.

Russo, Paolo. "Visions of Medea: Musico-dramatic Transformations of a Myth." *Cambridge Opera Journal* 6 (1994): 113–24.

Taylor, Timothy D. "Peopling the Stage: Opera, Otherness, and New Musical Representations in the Eighteenth Century." *Cultural Critique* 36 (1997): 65–88.

Van Boer, Bertil H., Jr. "Coffey's *The Devil to Pay*, the Comic War, and the Emergence of the German Singspiel." *Journal of Musicological Research* 8 (1988): 119–39.

Vickers, David. "The Good, the Bad, and the Ugly: Representation of Amorous Behaviour at the Court of Queen Partenope." *Händel-Jarhbuch* 49 (2003): 59–68.

19TH CENTURY: COMPOSERS AND LIBRETTISTS

Auber, Daniel-François-Esprit

Clark, Maribeth. *Understanding French Grand Opera through Dance*. Ph.D. dissertation, University of Pennsylvania, 1998.

Jacobshagen, Arnold. "Staging at the Opéra-Comique in Nineteenth-Century Paris: Auber's *Fra Diavolo* and the *Livrets de mise-en-scène*." Translated by Mary Hunter. *Cambridge Opera Journal* 13 (2001): 239–60.

Letellier, Robert Ignatius. *Daniel-François-Esprit Auber: The Man and His Music*. Newcastle upon Tyne, England: Cambridge Scholars, 2010.

Mordey, Delphine. "Auber's Horses: L'année terrible and Apocalyptic Narratives." *19th-Century Music* 30 (2007): 213–29.

Beethoven, Ludwig van

Griffel, L. Michael, and John Potter. "Transcending Gender and Cross-Dressing: Leonore as Romantic Revolutionary." *Beethoven Journal* 11 (1996): 8–11.

Kaleva, Daniela. "Beethoven and Melodrama." *Musicology Australia* 23 (2000): 49–75.

Lockwood, Lewis. "Beethoven's *Leonore* and *Fidelio*." *Journal of Interdisciplinary History* 36 (2006): 473–82.

Robinson, Paul, ed. *Ludwig van Beethoven:* Fidelio. Cambridge: Cambridge University Press, 1996.

Tusa, Michael C. "Beethoven and Opera: The Grave-Digging Duet in *Leonore* (1805)." *Beethoven Forum* 5 (1996): 1–64.

———. "Beethoven's Essay in Opera: Historical, Text-Critical, and Interpretive Issues in *Fidelio*." In Glenn Stanley, ed., *The Cambridge Companion to Beethoven*, 200–17. New York: Cambridge University Press, 2000.

Whittall, Arnold. "Against the Operatic Grain? *Fidelio* in History and Theory." *Beethoven Forum* 8 (2000): 195–206.

Bellini, Vincenzo

Brauner, Charles S. "Textual Problems in Bellini's *Norma* and *Beatrice di Tenda.*" *Journal of the American Musicological Society* 29 (1976): 99–118.

Kimbell, David R. B. *Vincenzo Bellini:* Norma. Cambridge: Cambridge University Press, 1998.

Maguire, John S. E. *Vincenzo Bellini and the Aesthetics of Early Nineteenth-Century Italian Opera.* Ph.D. dissertation, Oxford University, 1985. New York: General, 1989.

Rosselli, John. *The Life of Bellini.* Cambridge: Cambridge University Press, 1996.

Smart, Mary Ann. "In Praise of Convention: Formula and Experiment in Bellini's Self-Borrowings." *Journal of the American Musicological Society* 53 (2000): 25–68.

Weinstock, Herbert. *Vincenzo Bellini: His Life and Operas.* New York: Knopf, 1971.

Willier, Stephen A. *Vincenzo Bellini: A Research and Information Guide.* New York: Routledge, 2009.

Berlioz, Hector

Albright, Daniel. *Berlioz's Semi-operas:* Roméo et Juliette *and* La damnation de Faust. Rochester, N.Y.: University of Rochester, 2001.

Bloom, Peter Anthony, ed. *The Cambridge Companion to Berlioz.* Cambridge: Cambridge University Press, 2000.

Hart, Beth. "The Loves of Hector Berlioz, in His Life and in *Les troyens.*" *Opera Quarterly* 19 (2003): 331–56.

Holoman, D. Kern. *Berlioz.* Cambridge, Mass.: Harvard University Press, 1989.

Kemp, Ian. *Hector Berlioz:* Les Troyens. Cambridge: Cambridge University Press, 1988.

Rij, Inge van. "'There Is No Anachronism': Indian Dancing Girls in Ancient Carthage in Berlioz's *Les Troyens.*" *19th-Century Music* 33 (2009): 3–24.

Saloman, Ora Frishberg. "'The Harmony of Opposites': Characterizing Cellini's Apprentice." *Journal of Musicological Research* 24 (2005): 27–47.

———. "Literary and Musical Aspects of the Hero's Romance in Berlioz's *Benvenuto Cellini.*" *Opera Quarterly* 19 (2003): 401–16.

Bizet, Georges

Baker, Evan. "The Scene Designs for the First Performance of Bizet's *Carmen*." *19th-Century Music* 13 (1990): 230–42.

Curtiss, Mina Stein Kirstein. *Bizet and His World*. Westport, Conn.: Greenwood, 1977; originally 1958.

Gould, Evlyn. *The Fate of Carmen*. Baltimore, Md.: Johns Hopkins University Press, 1996.

Lavielle, Gail Milgram. Carmen: *The Seduction of the Century*. Seattle, Wash.: Caldwell, 1997.

McClary, Susan, ed. *Georges Bizet:* Carmen. Cambridge: Cambridge University Press, 1992.

Rabinowitz, Peter J. "Singing for Myself: Carmen and the Rhetoric of Musical Resistance." In Lydia Hamessley and Elaine Barkin, eds., *Audible Traces: Gender, Identity, and Music*, 134–51. Zurich: Carciofoli, 1999.

Wright, Leslie A. "Gounod and Bizet: A Study in Musical Paternity." *Journal of Musicological Research* 13 (1993): 31–48.

Boito, Arrigo

Morelli, Giovanni, ed. *Arrigo Boito*. Florence: Olschki, 1994.

Nicolaisen, Jay. "The First *Mefistofele*." *19th-Century Music* 1 (1978): 221–32.

Solinas, Rosa. *Arrigo Boito: The Legacy of Scapigliatura*. Ph.D. dissertation, Oxford University, 1999.

Termini, Olga. "Language and Meaning in the 'Prologue in Heaven': Goethe's *Faust* and Boito's *Mefistofele*." In John Koegel and Malcolm S. Cole, eds., *Music in Performance and Society: Essays in Honor of Roland Jackson*, 355–79. Warren, Mich.: Harmonie Park, 1997.

Borodin, Aleksandr Porfir'yevich

Bumpass, Kathryn, and George B. Kauffman. "Nationalism and Realism in Nineteenth-Century Russian Music: 'The Five' and Borodin's *Prince Igor*." *Music Review* 49 (1988): 43–51.

Domokos, Zsuzsanna. "The Epic Dimension in Borodin's *Prince Igor*." *Studia Musicologica Academiae Scientiarum Hungaricae* 33 (1991): 131–49.

Fuller, Jennifer. "Epic Melodies: An Examination of Folk Motifs in the Text and Music of *Prince Igor*." In Andrew Baruch Wachtel, ed., *Intersections and Transpositions: Russian Music, Literature, and Society*, 33–57. Evanston, Ill.: Northwestern University Press, 1998.

Robinson, Harold Loomis. "'If You're Afraid of Wolves Don't Go into the Forest': On the History of Borodin's *Prince Igor.*" *Opera Quarterly* 7 (1990): 1–12.

Cammarano, Salvatore

Black, John. *The Italian Romantic Libretto: A Study of Salvadore Cammarano.* Edinburgh: Edinburgh University Press, 1984.

Catalani, Alfredo

Pardini, Domenico Luigi. *Alfredo Catalani: Composer of Lucca.* Norfolk, England: Durrant, 2010.

Donizetti, Gaetano

Alitt, John Stewart. "*The Bride of Lammermoor*: Scott and Donizetti—Novel and Opera." *Bergomum* 92 (1997): 17–30.
———. *Donizetti: In the Light of Romanticism and the Teaching of Johann Simon Mayr.* Rockport, Mass.: Element, 1991.
Ashbrook, William. *Donizetti and His Operas.* Cambridge: Cambridge University Press, 1982.
———. "Donizetti and Romani." *Italica* 64 (1987): 606–31.
———. "The Evolution of the Donizettian Tenor-Persona." *Opera Quarterly* 14 (1998): 24–32.
Black, John N. "Cammarano's Notes for the Staging of *Lucia di Lammermoor.*" *Donizetti Society Journal* 4 (1980): 29–44.
———. "Librettist, Composer, and Censor: The Text of *Roberto Devereux.*" *Bergomum* 92 (1997): 65–74.
Budden, Julian. "Aspects of the Development of Donizetti's Musical Dramaturgy." In Francesco Bellotto, ed., *L'opera teatrale di Gaetano Donizetti: Atti del convegno internazionale di studio/Proceedings of the International Conference on the Operas of Gaetano Donizetti,* 121–33. Bergamo, Italy: Commune di Bergamo, 1993.
Cassaro, James P. *Gaetano Donizetti: A Guide to Research.* New York: General, 2000.
Cronin, Charles Patrick Desmond. *The Comic Operas of Gaetano Donizetti and the End of the Opera buffa Tradition.* Ph.D. dissertation, Stanford University, 1993.
———. "Stefano Pavesi's *Ser Marcantonio* and Donizetti's *Don Pasquale.*" *Opera Quarterly* 11 (1995): 39–53.

Deasy, Martin Joseph. *Donizetti and Naples in the 1830s*. Ph.D. dissertation, University of California, Berkeley, 2005.

Izzo, Francesco. "Donizetti's *Don Pasquale* and the Conventions of Mid-Nineteenth-Century Opera buffa." *Studi musicali* 33 (2004): 387–431.

Poriss, Hilary. "A Madwoman's Choice: Aria Substitution in *Lucia di Lammermoor*." *Cambridge Opera Journal* 13 (2001): 1–28.

Smart, Mary Ann. "The Silencing of Lucia." *Cambridge Opera Journal* 4 (1992): 119–41.

Weinstock, Herbert. *Donizetti and the World of Opera in Italy, Paris and Vienna in the First Half of the Nineteenth Century*. New York: Pantheon, 1963.

Dvořák, Antonin

Beckerman, Michael Brim. *Dvořák and His World*. Princeton, N.J.: Princeton University Press, 1993.

Hallová, Markéta, et al., eds. *Musical Dramatic Works by Antonin Dvořák: Papers from an International Conference*. Prague: Česká Hudební Společnost, 1989.

Houtchens, Henry Alan. *A Critical Study of Antonin Dvořák's* Vanda. Ph.D. dissertation, University of California, Santa Barbara, 1987.

Smaczny, Jan. "'Alfred': Dvořák's Operatic Endeavour Surveyed." *Journal of the Royal Musical Association* 115 (1990): 80–106.

———. *A Study of the First Six Operas of Antonin Dvořák: The Foundations of an Operatic Style*. Ph.D. dissertation, Oxford University, 1990.

Gilbert, William Schwenck, and Arthur Sullivan

Ainger, Michael. *Gilbert and Sullivan: A Dual Biography*. Oxford: Oxford University Press, 2002.

Crowther, Andrew. *Gilbert of Gilbert and Sullivan: His Life and Character*. Stroud, England: History Press, 2011.

Dunn, George. *A Gilbert and Sullivan Dictionary*. Philadelphia, Pa.: West, 1977.

Eden, David, and Meinhard Saremba, eds. *The Cambridge Companion to Gilbert and Sullivan*. Cambridge: Cambridge University Press, 2009.

Heylar, James, ed. *Gilbert and Sullivan*. Lawrence: University of Kansas, 1971.

Hubbard, Andrew. *Musico-dramatic Techniques in the Late Operas of Sullivan*. Ph.D. dissertation, University of Nottingham, 1983.

Jefferson, Alan. *The Complete Gilbert and Sullivan Opera Guide*. New York: Facts on File, 1984.

Lee, Josephine. *The Japan of Pure Invention: Gilbert and Sullivan's* The Mikado. Minneapolis: University of Minnesota Press, 2010.

Stedman, Jane W. *W. S. Gilbert: A Classic Victorian and His Theater*. New York: Oxford University Press, 1996.

Williams, Carolyn. *Gilbert and Sullivan: Gender, Genre, Parody*. New York: Columbia University Press, 2010.

Wilson, Robin, and Frederic Lloyd. *Gilbert and Sullivan: The D'Oyly Carte Years*. London: Weidenfeld and Nicolson, 1984.

Wren, Gayden. *A Most Ingenious Paradox: The Art of Gilbert and Sullivan*. New York: Oxford University Press, 2001.

Glinka, Mikhail Ivanovich

Brown, David. *Mikhail Glinka: A Biographical and Critical Study*. London: Oxford University Press, 1973.

Frolova-Walker, Marina. "On *Ruslan* and Russianness." *Cambridge Opera Journal* 9 (1997): 21–45.

Gounod, Charles

Gann, Andrew G. "Théophile Gautier, Charles Gounod, and the Massacre of *La nonne sanglante*." *Journal of Musicological Research* 13 (1993): 49–66.

Harding, James. *Gounod*. London: Stein and Day, 1973.

Huebner, Steven. *The Operas of Charles Gounod*. New York: Oxford University Press, 1990.

Rustman, Mark Manfred. *Lyric Opera: A Study of the Contributions of Charles Gounod*. Ph.D. dissertation, University of Kansas, 1986.

Halévy, Fromental

Hallman, Diana R. *The French Grand Opera* La Juive *(1835): A Socio-historical Study*. Ph.D. dissertation, City University of New York, 1995.

Jordan, Ruth. *Fromental Halévy: His Life and Music, 1799–1862*. London: Kahn and Averill, 1994.

Hoffmann, Ernst Theodor Amadeus

Garlington, Aubrey S. "E.T.A. Hoffmann's *Der Dichter und der Komponist* and the Creation of the German Romantic Opera." *Musical Quarterly* 65 (1979): 22–47.

——. "Notes on Dramatic Motives in Opera: Hoffmann's *Undine*." *Music Review* 32 (1971): 136–45.

Negus, Kenneth. *E.T.A. Hoffmann's Other World*. Philadelphia: University of Pennsylvania Press, 1965.

Leoncavallo, Ruggero

Basini, Laura. "Masks, Minuets, and Murder: Images of Italy in Leoncavallo's *Pagliacci*." *Journal of the Royal Musical Association* 133 (2008): 32–68.

Dryden, Konrad. *Leoncavallo: Life and Works*. Lanham, Md.: Scarecrow Press, 2007.

Sansone, Matteo. "The 'Verismo' of Ruggero Leoncavallo: A Source Study of *Pagliacci*." *Music and Letters* 70 (1989): 342–62.

Marschner, Heinrich

Weisstein, Ulrich. "Heinrich Marschner's 'romantische Oper' *Hans Heiling*: A Bridge between Weber and Wagner." In James M. McGlathery, ed., *Music and German Literature: Their Relationship since the Middle Ages*, 154–79. Columbia, S.C.: Camden House, 1992.

White, Pamela Cynthis. "Two Vampires of 1828." *Opera Quarterly* 5 (1987): 22–57.

Mascagni, Pietro

Luraghi, Silvia. "Mascagni's *Guglielmo Ratcliff*: How Dream Affects Reality." In Peter Csobádi et al., eds., *Dream and Reality in the Theater and Music Theater: Lecture and Discussions at the Salzburger Symposion, 2004*, 322–29. Salzburg, Austria: Mueller-Speiser, 2006.

Mallach, Alan. "Mascagni, Marat, and Mussolini: A Study in Ambivalence and Accommodation." *Opera Quarterly* 11 (1995): 55–80.

——. *Pietro Mascagni and His Operas*. Boston: Northeastern University Press, 2002.

Sansone, Matteo. "Verga and Mascagni: The Critics' Response to *Cavalleria rusticana*." *Music and Letters* 71 (1990): 198–214.

Massenet, Jules

Dibbern, Mary. Manon: *A Performance Guide*. Hillsdale, N.Y.: Pendragon Press, 2011.

Harding, James. *Massenet*. London: Dent, 1970.

Irvine, Demar. *Massenet: A Chronicle of His Life and Times*. Portland, Ore.: Amadeus, 1994.

Lorenzo, Elizabeth Ann. *Opera and the Ordered Nation: Massenet's Esclarmonde in Performance at the 1889 Paris Exposition*. Ph.D. dissertation, University of California, Los Angeles, 2005.

Rowden, Clair. "*Hérodiade*: Church, State, and the Feminist Movement." In Jim Samson and Bennett Zon, eds., *19th-Century Music: Selected Proceedings of the Tenth International Conference*, 250–78. Aldershot, England: Ashgate, 2002.

———. *Massenet, Marianne, and Mary: Republican Morality and Catholic Tradition at the Opera*. Ph.D. dissertation, City University, London, 2001.

———. "Opera and Caricature in the French Fin-de-Siècle Press: Massenet's *Thaïs*, a Case Study." *Music in Art* 34 (2009): 274–90.

———. *Republican Morality and Catholic Tradition in the Opera: Massenet's Hérodiade and* Thaïs. Weinsberg, Germany: Lucie Galland, 2004.

Mayr, Simon

Allitt, John Stewart. *J. S. Mayr: Father of 19th Century Italian Music*. Shaftesbury: Element, 1989.

Balthazar, Scott L. "Mayr and the Development of the Two-Movement Aria." In Francesco Bellotto, ed., *Giovanni Simone Mayr: L'opera teatrale e la musica sacra*, 229–51. Bergamo, Italy: Stefanoni, 1997.

Mercadante, Saverio

Bryan, Karen McGaha. *An Experiment in Form: The Reform Operas of Saverio Mercadante*. Ph.D. dissertation, Indiana University, 1994.

Kowals, Rebecca R. *Issues of Style in Saverio Mercadante's Mature Operas*. Ph.D. dissertation, Brandeis University, 1997.

Meyerbeer, Giacomo

Brooks, L. Jeanice, and Mark Everist. "Giacomo Meyerbeer's *Les Huguenots*: Staging the History of the French Renaissance." In Yannick Portebois and Nicholas Terpstra, eds., *The Renaissance in the Nineteenth Century*, 121–42. Toronto: Centre for Reformation and Renaissance Studies.

Cruz, Gabriela Gomes da. *Giacomo Meyerbeer's L'Africaine and the End of Grand Opera*. Ph.D. dissertation, Princeton University, 1999.

———. "Meyerbeer's Music of the Future." *Opera Quarterly* 25 (2009): 169–202.

Everist, Mark. *Giacomo Meyerbeer and Music Drama in Nineteenth-Century Paris.* Aldershot, England: Ashgate, 2005.

———. "Meyerbeer's *Il crociato in Egitto*: *Mélodrame, Opéra,* Orientalism." *Cambridge Opera Journal* 8 (1996): 215–50.

———. "The Name of the Rose: Meyerbeer's *Opéra comique, Robert le diable.*" *Revue de musicologie* 80 (1994): 211–50.

Fulcher, Jane F. "Meyerbeer and the Music of Society." *Musical Quarterly* 67 (1981): 213–29.

Gibson, Robert Wayne. *Meyerbeer's* Le prophète: *A Study in Operatic Style.* Ph.D. dissertation, Northwestern University, 1972.

Huebner, Steven. "Italianate Duets in Meyerbeer's Grand Operas." *Journal of Musicological Research* 8 (1989): 203–58.

Jackson, Jennifer. *Giacomo Meyerbeer: Reputation without Cause? A Composer and His Critics.* Newcastle upon Tyne, England: Cambridge Scholars, 2011.

Letellier, Robert Ignatius. "History, Myth, and Music in a Theme of Exploration: Some Reflections on the Musico-Dramatic Language of *L'Africaine.*" In Arnold Jacobshagen and Sieghard Döhring, eds., *Meyerbeer und das Europäische Musiktheater,* 148–68. Laaber, Germany: Laaber, 1998.

———. *The Operas of Giacomo Meyerbeer.* Madison, N.J.: Fairleigh Dickinson University, 2006.

Letellier, Robert Ignatius, and Marco Clemente Pellegrini. *Giacomo Meyerbeer: A Guide to Research.* Newcastle upon Tyne, England: Cambridge Scholars, 2007.

Roberts, John. *The Genesis of Meyerbeer's L'Africaine.* Ph.D. dissertation, University of California, Berkeley, 1977.

Smith, Marian. "Ballet and the Opera at the Time of Meyerbeer." In Hans Moeller and Gunhild Oberzaucher-Schüller, eds., *Meyerbeer und der Tanz,* 15–35. Feldkirchen, Austria: Ricordi, 1998.

Wilberg, Rebecca S. *The Mise-en-Scène at the Paris Opera—Salle Le Peletier (1821–1872) and the Staging of the First French Grand Opéra: Meyerbeer's* Robert le diable. Ph.D. dissertation, Brigham Young University, 1990.

Moniuszko, Stanislaw

Maciejewski, Boguslaw. *Moniuszko: Father of Polish Opera.* London: Allegro, 1979.

Murphy, Michael. *Moniuszko and Musical Nationalism in Poland.* In Harry M. White and Michael Murphy, eds., *Musical Constructions of Nationalism: Essays on the History and Ideology of European Musical Culture, 1800–1945*, 163–80. Cork, Ireland: Cork University, 2001.

Prosnak, Jan. *Moniuszko.* Cracow: Polskie Wydawnictwo Muzyczne, 1980; trans. of 1968.

Musorgsky, Modest Petrovich

Brown, David. *Musorgsky: His Life and Works.* Oxford: Oxford University Press, 2002.

Emerson, Caryl. Boris Godunov: *Transpositions of a Russian Theme.* Bloomington: Indiana University Press, 1986.

———. *The Life of Musorgsky.* New York: Cambridge University Press, 1999.

Emerson, Caryl, and Robert William Oldani Jr. *Modest Musorgsky and* Boris Godunov: *Myths, Realities, Reconsiderations.* New York: Cambridge University Press, 1994.

Morosan, Vladimir. "Musorgsky's Choral Style: Folk and Chant Elements in Musorgsky's Choral Writing." In Malcolm Hamrick Brown, ed., *Musorgsky in Memorium 1881–1981*, 95–133. Ann Arbor, Mich.: University Microfilms International, 1982.

Oldani, Robert William, Jr. "*Boris Godunov* and the Censor." *19th-Century Music* 2 (1979): 245–53.

Taruskin, Richard. "Musorgsky vs. Musorgsky: The Versions of *Boris Godunov.*" *19th-Century Music* 8 (1984): 91–118.

———. "Serov and Musorgsky." In Malcolm Hamrick Brown and Roland John Wiley, eds., *Slavonic and Western Music: Essays for Gerald Abraham*, 139–61. Ann Arbor, Mich.: University Microfilms, 1985.

Turner, June. "Musorgsky." *Music Review* 47 (1986): 153–75.

Nicolai, Otto

Greenwald, Helen M. "Otto Nicolai's *Italienische Reise*: A Diary in Exile." In Peter Csobádi et al., eds., *Das (Musik-)Theater in Exil und Diktatur*, 224–38. Salzburg, Austria: Mueller-Speiser, 2005.

Offenbach, Jacques

Faris, Alexander. *Jacques Offenbach.* New York: Scribner's, 1981.

Gammond, Peter. *Offenbach.* London: Omnibus, 1986.

Hadlock, Heather. *Mad Loves: Women and Music in Offenbach's* Les Contes d'Hoffman. Princeton, N.J.: Princeton University Press, 2000.

Peschel, Enid Rhodes, and Richard Peschel. "Medicine, Music, and Literature: The Figure of Dr. Miracle in Offenbach's *Les contes d'Hoffman.*" *Opera Quarterly* 3 (1985): 59–71.

Rimsky-Korsakov, Nikolay Andreyevich

Griffiths, Steven. *A Critical Study of the Music of Rimsky-Korsakov, 1844–1890.* New York: General, 1982.

Halbe, Gregory A. *Music, Drama, and Folklore in Nikolai Rimsky-Korsakov's Opera* Snegurochka *(*Snowmaiden*)*. Ph.D. dissertation, Ohio State University, 2004.

Muir, Stephen Phillip Katongo. *The Operas of N. A. Rimsky-Korsakov from 1897 to 1904.* Ph.D. dissertation, University of Birmingham, 2000.

Neff, Lyle K. "Close to Prose or Worse Than Verse? Rimsky-Korsakov's Intermediate Type of Opera Text." *Opera Quarterly* 15 (1999): 238–50.

Reeve, Brian. *Nikolai Rimsky-Korsakov's Use of the* Byliny *(Russian Oral Epic Narratives) in his Opera* Sadko. Ph.D. dissertation, University of Nottingham, 2005.

Zin'kevič, Elena Sergeevna, ed. *Anton Rubenstein and Nikolaj Rimsky-Korsakov: Selected Operas.* Heilbronn, Germany: Galland, 1997.

Romani, Felice

Black, John N. "The Central Finale in the Libretti of Felice Romani: A Contribution to the Dramaturgy of the Libretto." In Andrea Sommariva, ed., *Felice Romani: Melodrammi, poesie, documenti*, 183–202. Florence: Olschki, 1996.

Roccatagliati, Alessandro. "Felice Romani: Librettist by Trade." Translated by Karen Henson. *Cambridge Opera Journal* 8 (1996): 113–45.

Rossini, Gioachino

Balthazar, Scott L. "Rossini and the Development of the Mid-century Lyric Form." *Journal of the American Musicological Society* 41 (1988): 102–25.

Bartlett, M. Elizabeth C. "Staging French *Grand opéra*: Rossini's *Guillaume Tell* (1829)." In Paolo Fabbri, ed., *Gioachino Rossini 1792–1992: Il Testo e la Scena*, 623–48. Pesaro, Italy: Fondazione G. Rossini.

Demarco, Laura Elizabeth. *Rossini and the Emergence of Dramatic Male Roles in Italian and French Opera.* Ph.D. dissertation, Columbia University, 1998.

Esse, Melina. "Rossini's Noisy Bodies." *Cambridge Opera Journal* 21 (2009): 27–64.

Gallo, Denise P. *Gioachino Rossini: A Research and Information Guide.* New York: Routledge, 2010.

Gossett, Philip. "The Overtures of Rossini." *19th-Century Music* 3 (1979): 3–31.

Kimbell, David. "Some Observations on *Tempi d'attacco* and *Tempi di mezzo* in Rossini's *Otello.*" In Daniel Brandenburg and Thomas Lindner, eds., *Belliniana et alia musicologica: Festschrift für Friedrich Lippmann zum 70. Geburtstag,* 190–211. Vienna: Praesens, 2004.

Senici, Emanuele, ed. *The Cambridge Companion to Rossini.* Cambridge: Cambridge University Press, 2004.

Walton, Benjamin. "Looking for Revolution in Rossini's *Guillaume Tell.*" *Cambridge Opera Journal* 15 (2003): 127–51.

———. *Rossini in Restoration Paris: The Sound of Modern Life.* Cambridge: Cambridge University Press, 2007.

Weinstock, Herbert. *Rossini: A Biography.* New York: Limelight, 1987; originally 1968.

Saint-Saëns, Camille

Locke, Ralph P. "Constructing the Oriental 'Other': Saint-Saëns's *Samson et Dalila.*" *Cambridge Opera Journal* 3 (1991): 261–302.

Schubert, Franz

Denny, Thomas A. "Schubert's Operas: 'The Judgment of History.'" In Christopher H. Gibbs, ed., *The Cambridge Companion to Schubert,* 224–38. New York: Cambridge University Press, 1997.

McKay, Elizabeth Norman. *Franz Schubert's Music for the Theatre.* Tutzing: Schneider, 1991.

———. "Schubert as a Composer of Operas." In Eva Badura-Scoda and Peter Branscombe, eds., *Schubert Studies: Problems of Style and Chronology,* 85–104. Cambridge: Cambridge University Press, 1982.

Williams, Simon. "The Viennese Theater." In Raymond Erickson, ed., *Schubert's Vienna,* 214–45. New Haven, Conn.: Yale University Press, 1997.

Scribe, Eugène

Pendle, Karin S. *Eugène Scribe and French Opera of the Nineteenth Century*. Ann Arbor, Mich.: University Microfilms International, 1979.

Smetana, Bedřich

Clapham, John. *Smetana*. London: Dent, 1972.

Spontini, Gaspare

Libby, Dennis Albert. *Gaspare Spontini and His French and German Operas*. Ph.D. dissertation, Princeton University, 1969.

Tchaikovsky, Pyotr Il'yich

Brown, David. *Tchaikovsky: A Biographical and Critical Study*. Vol. 1, *The Early Years (1840–74)*. London: Gollancz, 1978.

Čerkašina, Marina Romanovna. "Tchaikovsky, *The Maid of Orléans*: The Problem of the Genre and the Specific Treatment of the Subject." *International Journal of Musicology* 3 (1994): 175–85.

Holden, Anthony. *Tchaikovsky*. Toronto: Viking, 1995.

John, Nicholas, and David Lloyd-Jones. *Peter Tchaikovsky:* Eugene Onegin. New York: Riverrun, 1988.

Kearney, Leslie, ed. *Tchaikovsky and His World*. Princeton, N.J.: Princeton University Press, 1998.

Mihailovic, Alexander, ed. *Tchaikovsky and His Contemporaries: A Centennial Symposium*. Westport, Conn.: Greenwood, 1999.

Zajaczkowski, Henry. *An Introduction to Tchaikovsky's Operas*. Westport, Conn.: Praeger, 2005.

Thomas, Ambroise

Achter, Morton Jay. *Felicien David, Ambroise Thomas, and French* Opéra lyrique*, 1850–1870*. Ph.D. dissertation, University of Michigan, 1972.

Harrison, John. "Deconstructive Melodrama in the *Hamlet* of Ambroise Thomas." In Paul-André Bempéchat, ed., *Liber amicorum Isabelle Cazeaux: Symbols, Parallels, and Discoveries in Her Honor*, 129–44. Hillsdale, N.Y.: Pendragon, 2005.

Verdi, Giuseppe

Andre, Naomi Adele. *Azucena, Eboli, and Amneris: Verdi's Writing for Women's Lower Voices*. Ph.D. dissertation, Harvard University, 1996.

Baldini, Gabriele. *The Story of Giuseppe Verdi: "Oberto" to "Un ballo in maschera."* Translated by Roger Parker. Cambridge: Cambridge University Press, 1980.

Balthazar, Scott L. "Analytic Contexts and Mediated Influences: The Rossinian *convenienze* and Verdi's Middle and Late Duets." *Journal of Musicological Research* 10 (1990): 19–45.

———, ed. *The Cambridge Companion to Verdi*. Cambridge: Cambridge University Press, 2004.

———. "Plot and Tonal Design as Compositional Constraints in *Il trovatore*." *Current Musicology* 60–61 (1996): 51–77.

Budden, Julian. *The Operas of Verdi*. 3 vols. London: Cassell, 1973–81.

———. *Verdi*. Rev. ed. London: Dent, 1993.

Chusid, Martin. "Drama and the Key of F Major in *La traviata*." In Mario Medici and Marcello Pavarani, eds., *Atti del III Congresso internazionale di studi verdiani, Milano, 12–17 giugno, 1972*, 89–121. Parma: Istituto di Studi Verdiani, 1974.

———. "Rigoletto and Monterone: A Study in Musical Dramaturgy." *Verdi: Bollettino dell'Istituto di Studi Verdiani* 3 (1982): 1544–58.

———, ed. *Verdi's Middle Period, 1849–1859: Source Studies, Analysis, and Performance Practice*. Chicago: University of Chicago Press, 1997.

Conner, Theodore A. *Towards an Interpretive Model of Text–Music Relations: An Analysis of Selected Scenes from Verdi's Otello*. Ph.D. dissertation, University of Connecticut, 1997.

Crutchfield, Will. "Vocal Ornamentation in Verdi: The Phonographic Evidence." *19th-Century Music* 7 (1983–84): 3–54.

Della Seta, Fabrizio. "'O cieli azzurri': Exoticism and Dramatic Discourse in *Aida*." *Cambridge Opera Journal* 3 (1990): 49–62.

Della Seta, Fabrizio et al., eds. *Verdi 2001: Atti del Convegno internazionale/Proceedings of the International Conference, Parma, New York, New Haven, 24 gennaio–1 febbraio 2001*. 2 vols. Florence: Olschki, 2003.

Drabkin, William. "Characters, Key Relations, and Tonal Structure in *Il trovatore*." *Music Analysis* 1 (1982): 143–53.

Edwards, Ryan, and Geoffrey. *The Verdi Baritone: Studies in the Development of Dramatic Character*. Bloomington: Indiana University Press, 1994.

Elliott, Jan Claire. *Amneris and Aida: Their Vocal and Rhetorical Portraits Conveyed by Tessitura*. Ph.D. dissertation, University of California, Los Angeles, 2000.

Gable, David. *Mode Mixture and Lyric Form in the Operas of Giuseppe Verdi*. Ph.D. dissertation, University of Chicago, 1997.

Giger, Andreas. *The Role of Giuseppe Verdi's French Operas in the Transformation of His Melodic Style*. Ph.D. dissertation, Indiana University, 1999.

———. "Social Control and the Censorship of Giuseppe Verdi's Operas in Rome (1844–1859)." *Cambridge Opera Journal* 11 (1999): 233–65.

———. *Verdi and the French Aesthetic: Verse, Stanza, and Melody in Nineteenth-Century Opera*. New York: Cambridge University Press, 2008.

Goehr, Lydia. "*Aida* and the Empire of Emotions (Theodor W. Adorno, Edward Said, and Alexander Kluge)." *Current Musicology* 87 (2009): 133–59.

Gossett, Philip. "Verdi, Ghislanzoni, and *Aida*: The Uses of Convention." *Critical Inquiry* 1 (1974–75): 291–334.

Greenwood, Joanna. "Musical and Dramatic Motion in Verdi's *Il trovatore*." *Jahrbuch für Opernforschung* 2 (1986): 59–73.

Grover, Michal. *Voicing Death in Verdi's Operas*. Ph.D. dissertation, Brandeis University, 1997.

Hadlock, Heather. "'The Firmness of a Female Hand' in *The Corsair* and *Il corsaro*." *Cambridge Opera Journal* 14 (2002): 47–57.

Harwood, Gregory W. *Giuseppe Verdi: A Research and Information Guide*. New York: Routledge, 2012.

———. "Verdi's Reform of the Italian Opera Orchestra." *19th-Century Music* 10 (1986–87): 108–34.

Hawes, Jane Delap. *An Examination of Verdi's* Otello *and Its Faithfulness to Shakespeare*. Lewiston, N.Y.: Mellen, 1994.

Hepokoski, James A. "Genre and Content in Mid-century Verdi: 'Addio del passato' (*La traviata*, Act III)." *Cambridge Opera Journal* 1 (1989): 249–76.

———. *Giuseppe Verdi:* Falstaff. Cambridge: Cambridge University Press, 1983.

———. *Giuseppe Verdi:* Otello. Cambridge: Cambridge University Press, 1987.

Hudson, Elizabeth. "Gilda Seduced: A Tale Untold." *Cambridge Opera Journal* 4 (1992): 229–51.

———. *Narrative in Verdi: Perspectives on His Musical Dramaturgy*. Ph.D. dissertation, Cornell University, 1993.

Izzo, Francesco. "Verdi, the Virgin, and the Censor: The Politics of the Cult of Mary in *I Lombardi alla prima crociata*." *Journal of the American Musicological Society* 60 (2007): 557–97.

Jensen, Luke. *Giuseppe Verdi and the Milanese Publishers of His Music: From* Oberto *to* La traviata. Ph.D. dissertation, New York University, 1987.

Jürgensen, Knud Arne. *The Verdi Ballets*. Parma: Istituto Nazionale di Studi Verdiani, 1995.

Kerman, Joseph. "Lyric Form and Flexibility in *Simon Boccanegra*." *Studi verdiani* 1 (1982): 47–62.

———. "Verdi and the Undoing of Women." *Cambridge Opera Journal* 18 (2006): 21–31.

Kimbell, David R. B. *Verdi in the Age of Italian Romanticism*. Cambridge: Cambridge University Press, 1981.

Kreuzer, Gundula. *Verdi and the Germans: From Unification to the Third Reich*. Cambridge: Cambridge University Press, 2010.

———. "Voices from Beyond: Verdi's *Don Carlos* and the Modern Stage." *Cambridge Opera Journal* 18 (2006): 151–79.

Kurtzman, Jeffrey G. "The Iagoization of Otello: A Study in Verdi's Musical Translation of Shakespeare's Linguistic Dramaturgy." In Siglind Bruhn, ed., *Sonic Transformations of Literary Texts: From Program Music to Musical Ekphrasis*, 69–101. Hillsdale, N.Y.: Pendragon, 2008.

Kwa, Shiamin. "The Unbearable Lightness of Meaning in Verdi's *Rigoletto*." *Verdi Forum* 30–31 (2003): 26–36.

Latham, Alison, and Roger Parker, eds. *Verdi in Performance*. Oxford: Oxford University Press, 2001.

Lawton, David. "On the 'Bacio' Theme in *Otello*." *19th-Century Music* 1 (1977–78): 211–20.

———. "Tonal Structure and Dramatic Action in *Rigoletto*." *Verdi: Bollettino dell'Istituto di studi verdiani* 3 (1982): 1559–81.

———. *Tonality and Drama in Verdi's Early Operas*. 2 vols. Ph.D. dissertation, University of California, Berkeley, 1973.

Lendvai, Ernö. *The Unity of Artistic Creation in Verdi's* Aida. Translated by Antonia Eliason. Budapest, 2003; originally 2002.

Locke, Ralph P. "*Aida* and Nine Readings of Empire." *Nineteenth-Century Music Review* 3 (2006): 45–72.

———. "Beyond the Exotic: How 'Eastern' is *Aida?*" *Cambridge Opera Journal* 17 (2005): 105–39.

Marcozzi, Rudy T. *The Interaction of Large-Scale Harmonic and Dramatic Structure in the Verdi Operas Adapted from Shakespeare*. Ph.D. dissertation, Indiana University, 1992.

Martin, George Whitney. *Aspects of Verdi*. New York: Dodd Mead, 1988.

———. "Verdi, Politics, and 'Va, pensiero': The Scholars Squabble." *Opera Quarterly* 21 (2005): 109–32.

Marvin, Roberta Montemora, ed. *The Cambridge Verdi Encyclopedia*. Cambridge: Cambridge University Press, forthcoming.

———. "The Censorship of Verdi's Operas in Victorian London." *Music and Letters* 82 (2001): 582–610.

———. *Verdi the Student—Verdi the Teacher*. Parma: Istituto Nazionale di Studi verdiani, 2010.

Marvin, Roberta Montemora, et al., eds. *Verdi 2001*. Florence: Olschki, 2003.

McCants, Clyde T. Rigoletto, Trovatore, *and* Traviata: *Verdi's Middle Period Masterpieces On and Off the Stage*. Jefferson, N.C.: McFarland, 2009.

———. *Verdi's* Aida: *A Record of the Life of the Opera On and Off the Stage*. Jefferson, N.C.: McFarland, 2006.

Moreen, Robert. *Integration of Text Forms and Musical Forms in Verdi's Early Operas*. Ph.D. dissertation, Princeton University, 1975.

Osborne, Charles. *The Complete Operas of Verdi*. Cambridge, Mass.: Da Capo, 1977; originally 1969.

———. *Verdi: A Life in the Theatre*. New York: Knopf, 1987.

Parker, Roger. *Leonora's Last Act: Essays in Verdian Discourse*. Princeton, N.J.: Princeton University Press, 1997.

———. *The New Grove Guide to Verdi and His Operas*. New York: Oxford University Press, 2007.

———. "Reading the *Livrets*, or, The Chimera of Authentic Staging." In Fabrizio Della Seta and Pierluigi Petrobelli, eds., *La realizzazione scenica dello spettacolo verdiano*, 345–66. Parma: Istituto di Studi Verdiani, 1996.

———. *Studies in Early Verdi, 1832–1844: New Information and Perspectives in the Milanese Musical Milieu and the Operas from "Oberto" to "Ernani."* New York: Garland, 1989.

———. "Verdi and Verismo: The Case of *La traviata*." In James P. Cassaro, ed., *Music, Libraries, and the Academy: Essays in Honor of Lenore Coral*, 215–22. Middleton, Wis.: A-R Editions, 2007.

Parker, Roger, and Matthew Brown. "'Ancora un bacio': Three Scenes from Verdi's *Otello*." *19th-Century Music* 9 (1985–86): 50–62.

———. "Motivic and Tonal Interaction in Verdi's *Un ballo in maschera*." *Journal of the American Musicological Society* 36 (1983): 243–65.

Petrobelli, Pierluigi, ed. *"Ernani" Yesterday and Today: Proceedings of the International Congress, Modena, Teatro San Carlo, 9–10 December 1984*. Parma, Italy: Istituto di Studi Verdiani, 1989.

Phillips-Matz, Mary Jane. *Verdi: A Biography*. Oxford: Oxford University Press, 1993.

Powers, Harold S. "'La solita forma' and 'The Uses of Convention.'" *Acta Musicologica* 59 (1987): 65–90.

———. "*Tempo di mezzo*: Three Ongoing Episodes in Verdian Musical Dramaturgy." *Verdi Newsletter* 19 (1991): 6–36.

———. "Verdi's Monometric Cabaletta-Driven Duets: A Study in Rhythmic Texture and Generic Design." *Il Saggiatore Musicale: Rivista Semestrale di Musicologia* 7 (2000): 281–323.

Robinson, Paul. "Is *Aida* an Orientalist Opera?" *Cambridge Opera Journal* 5 (1993): 133–40.

Rosen, David. "How Verdi's Operas Begin: An Introduction to the *Introduzioni*." In Giovanni Morelli, ed., *Tornando a Stiffelio: Popolarità, Rifacimenti, Messinscena, Effettismo e Altre "Cure,"* 203–21. Florence: Olschki, 1987.

———. "How Verdi's Serious Operas End." In Angelo Pompilio et al., eds., *Atti del XIV Congresso della Società internazionale di musicologia*, 3:443–50. Turin, Italy: Edizione di Torino, 1990.

———. "The Staging of Verdi's Operas: An Introduction to the Ricordi *Disposizioni sceniche*." In Daniel Heartz et al., eds., *International Musicological Society: Report of the Twelfth Congress, Berkeley, 1977*, 444–53. Kassel, Germany: Bärenreiter, 1981.

Rosen, David, and Andrew Porter, eds. *Verdi's "Macbeth": A Sourcebook*. New York: Norton, 1984.

Rosselli, John. *The Life of Verdi*. New York: Cambridge University Press, 2000.

Sala, Emilio. "Verdi and the Parisian Boulevard Theater, 1847–9." Translated by Mary Ann Smart. *Cambridge Opera Journal* 7 (1995): 185–205.

Schneider, Magnus, and Nicolai Elver Anthon. "Gilda's Voices: On Potential Meanings, Intertextuality, and Vocal Performance in Verdi's *Rigoletto*." *Nordic Theater Studies* 17 (2005): 24–37.

Senici, Emanuele. "Verdi's Luisa, a Semiserious Alpine Virgin." *19th-Century Music* 22 (1998–99): 144–68.

Smart, Mary Ann, ed. *Primal Scenes. Cambridge Opera Journal* 14 (2002).

———. "Verdi Sings Erminia Frezzolini." *Women and Music* 1 (1997): 33–45.

Toliver, Brooks. "Grieving in the Mirrors of Verdi's Willow Song: Desdemona, Barbara, and a 'Feeble, Strange Voice.'" *Cambridge Opera Journal* 10 (1998): 289–305.

Tomlinson, Gary. "Verdi after Budden." *19th-Century Music* 5 (1981–82): 170–82.

Van, Gilles de. *Verdi's Theater: Creating Drama through Music*. Translated by Gilda Roberts. Chicago: University of Chicago Press, 1998; originally 1992.

Weaver, William, and Martin Chusid, eds. *The Verdi Companion*. New York: Norton, 1979.

Weiss, Piero. "Verdi and the Fusion of Genres." *Journal of the American Musicological Society* 35 (1982): 138–56.

Wagner, Richard

Abbate, Carolyn. *The "Parisian" Tannhäuser*. Ph.D. dissertation, Princeton University, 1984.

―――. "The Parisian Venus and the Paris *Tannhäuser*." *Journal of the American Musicological Society* 36 (1983): 73–123.

―――. "Wagner, Cinema, and Redemptive Glee." *Opera Quarterly* 21 (2005): 597–611.

―――. "Wagner, 'On Modulation,' and 'Tristan.'" *Cambridge Opera Journal* 1 (1989): 33–58.

Barker, John W. *Wagner and Venice*. Rochester, N.Y.: University of Rochester Press, 2008.

Bartlett, Rosamund. *Wagner and Russia*. Cambridge: Cambridge University Press, 1995.

Bassett, Peter. *Richard Wagner's* Tristan und Isolde. Kent Town, Australia: Wakefield, 2006.

―――. *A* Ring *for the Millennium: A Guide to Wagner's* Der Ring des Nibelungen. Kent Town, Australia: Wakefield, 1998.

Bauer, Jeffrey Peter. *Woman and the Changing Concept of Salvation in the Operas of Richard Wagner*. Salzburg: Müller-Speiser Anif, 1994.

Beckett, Lucy. *Richard Wagner:* Parsifal. Cambridge: Cambridge University Press, 1981.

Berry, Mark. *The Political and Religious Thought of Wagner's* Ring of the Nibelungen. Ph.D. dissertation, Cambridge University, 2002.

―――. "Wagner's Idea of Power in the *Ring*." *Wagner* 19 (1998): 47–57.

Binder, Benjamin Alan. "Kundry and the Jewish Voice: Anti-Semitism and Musical Transcendence in Wagner's *Parsifal*." *Current Musicology* 87 (2009): 47–131.

Bolen, Jean Shinoda. *Ring of Power: Symbols and Themes, Love vs. Power in Wagner's* Ring *Cycle and in Us—A Jungian-Feminist Perspective*. York Beach, Maine: Nicholas-Hays, 1999; originally 1992.

Borchmeyer, Dieter. *Drama and the World of Richard Wagner*. Translated by Daphne Ellis. Princeton, N.J.: Princeton University Press, 2003.

Bribitzer-Stull, Matthew Prescott. "'Did You Hear Love's Fond Farewell?' Some Examples of Thematic Irony in Wagner's *Ring*." *Journal of Musicological Research* 23 (2004): 123–57.

―――. *Thematic Development and Dramatic Association in Wagner's* Der Ring des Nibelungen. Ph.D. dissertation, University of Rochester, 2001.

Bribitzer-Stull, Matthew Prescott, et al., eds. *Richard Wagner for the New Millennium: Essays in Music and Culture*. New York: Palgrave Macmillan, 2007.

Budden, Julian. "Wagnerian Tendencies in Italian Opera." In Nigel Fortune, ed., *Music and Theater: Essays in Honour of Winton Dean*, 299–332. Cambridge: Cambridge University Press, 1987.

Buller, Jeffry Lynn. *Classically Romantic: Classical Form and Meaning in Wagner's* Ring. Philadelphia, Pa.: Xlibris, 2001.

———. "The Messianic Hero in Wagner's *Ring*." *Opera Quarterly* 13 (1996): 21–38.

———. "Sleep in the *Ring*." *Opera Quarterly* 12 (1995): 3–22.

———. "Spectacle in the *Ring*." *Opera Quarterly* 14 (1998): 41–57.

———. "The Thematic Role of *Stabreim* in Richard Wagner's *Der Ring des Nibelungen*." *Opera Quarterly* 11 (1995): 59–76.

Busch, Justin E. A. "Foreshadows of 'Fate' in *Das Rheingold*." *Wagner* 22 (2001): 93–96.

Carnegy, Patrick. *Wagner and the Art of the Theatre*. New Haven, Conn.: Yale University Press, 2006.

Chafe, Eric. *The Tragic and the Ecstatic: The Musical Revolution of Wagner's* Tristan und Isolde. New York: Oxford University Press, 2005.

Cicora, Mary A. *From History to Myth: Wagner's* Tannhäuser *and Its Literary Sources*. New York: Peter Lang, 1992.

———. *Modern Myths and Wagnerian Deconstructions: Hermeneutic Approaches to Wagner's Music-Dramas*. Westport, Conn.: Greenwood, 2000.

———. *Mythology as Metaphor: Romantic Irony, Critical Theory, and Wagner's* Ring. Westport, Conn.: Greenwood, 1998.

———. *Wagner's* Ring *and German Drama: Comparative Studies in Mythology and History in Drama*. Westport, Conn.: Greenwood, 1999.

Cooke, Deryck. *I Saw the World End: A Study of Wagner's* Ring. London: Oxford University Press, 1979.

Cord, William O. *An Introduction to Wagner's* Der Ring des Nibelungen. 2nd ed. Athens: Ohio University Press, 1995.

———. *Richard Wagner's Literary Journey to the* Ring: *An Inquiry into the Nibelung Myth as Sketch for a Drama and Related Matters*. Philadelphia, Pa.: Xlibris, 2004.

Corse, Sandra. *Wagner and the New Consciousness: Language and Love in the* Ring. Rutherford, N.J.: Farleigh Dickinson University, 1990.

Dana, Margaret E. "Orchestrating the Wasteland: Wagner, *Leitmotiv*, and the Play of Passion." In John Xiros Cooper, ed., *T. S. Eliot's Orchestra: Critical Essays on Poetry and Music*, 267–94. New York: General, 2000.

Danuser, Hermann. "Musical Manifestations of the End in Wagner and in Post-Wagnerian *Weltanschauungsmusik*." *19th-Century Music* 18 (1994): 64–82.

———. "Powerless Crowds: On the 'Collective Units' Appearing in the *Ring of the Nibelung*." Translated by Claudia R. Kalay. *Wagner* 23 (2002): 3–16.

Darcy, Warren. "*Creatio ex nihilo*: The Genesis, Structure, and Meaning of the *Rheingold* Prelude." *19th-Century Music* 13 (1989–90): 79–100.

———. "The Pessimism of the *Ring*." *Opera Quarterly* 4 (1986): 24–48.

Daub, Adrian. "Mother Mime: Siegfried, the Fairy Tale, and the Metaphysics of Sexual Difference." *19th-Century Music* 32 (2008): 160–77.

Deathridge, John. *Wagner Beyond Good and Evil*. Berkeley: University of California Press, 2008.

Dennison, Peter. *The Richard Wagner Centenary in Australia. Miscellanea musicologica: Adelaide Studies in Musicology* (Australia) 14 (1985).

DiGaetani, John Louis, ed. *Inside the* Ring: *Essays on Wagner's Opera Cycle*. Jefferson, N.C.: McFarland, 2006.

———. *Wagner and Suicide*. Jefferson, N.C.: McFarland, 2003.

———, ed. *Wagner Outside the* Ring: *Essays on the Operas, Their Performance, and Their Connections with Other Arts*. Jefferson, N.C.: McFarland, 2009.

Dreyfus, Laurence. *Wagner and the Erotic Impulse*. Cambridge, Mass.: Harvard University Press, 2010.

Emslie, Barry. *Richard Wagner and the Centrality of Love*. Woodbridge, England: Boydell, 2010.

Foster, Daniel H. *Wagner's* Ring *Cycle and the Greeks*. Cambridge: Cambridge University Press, 2010.

Fuchs, Hanns. "Parsifal and Eroticism in Wagner's Music." Translated by John Urang. *Opera Quarterly* 22 (2006): 328–44.

Grey, Thomas Spencer, ed. *The Cambridge Companion to Wagner*. Cambridge: Cambridge University Press, 2008.

———. "Leading Motives and Narrative Threads: Notes on the *Leitfaden* Metaphor and the Critical Pre-history of the Wagnerian *Leitmotiv*." In Tobias Plebuch and Hermann Danuser, eds., *Musik als Text*, 352–58. Kassel, Germany: Bärenreiter, 1998.

———, ed. *Richard Wagner and His World*. Princeton, N.J.: Princeton University Press, 2009.

———. *Richard Wagner and the Aesthetics of Form in the Mid-19th Century (1840–1860)*. Ph.D. dissertation, University of California, Berkeley, 1988.

———. *Richard Wagner: Der fliegende Holländer*. Cambridge: Cambridge University Press, 2000.

———. "Wagner the Degenerate: *Fin de siècle* 'Pathology' and the Anxiety of Modernism." *Nineteenth-Century Studies* 16 (2002): 73–92.

———. "Wagner, the Overture, and the Aesthetics of Musical Form." *19th-Century Music* 12 (1988): 3–22.

———. "Wagner's *Die Meistersinger* as National Opera (1868–1945)." In Celia Applegate and Pamela Maxine Potter, eds., *Music and German National Identity*, 78–104. Chicago: University of Chicago Press, 2002.

Grimm, Reinhold, and Jost Hermand, eds. *Re-reading Wagner*. Madison: University of Wisconsin Press, 1993.

Groos, Arthur. "Back to the Future: Hermeneutic Fantasies in *Der fliegende Holländer*." *19th-Century Music* 19 (1995): 191–211.

———, ed. *Richard Wagner*: Tristan und Isolde. Cambridge: Cambridge University Press, 2011.

HaCohen, Ruth, and Naphtali Wagner. "The Communicative Force of Wagner's Leitmotifs: Complementary Relationships between Their Connotations and Denotations." *Music Perception* 14 (1997): 445–76.

Harper-Scott, John Paul Edward. "Medieval Romance and Wagner's Musical Narrative in the *Ring*." *19th-Century Music* 32 (2009): 211–34.

Hatch, Christopher. "Dramatic and Musical Intricacies in Wagner's *Die Meistersinger*." *Opera Quarterly* 17 (2001): 197–217.

Herbert, James, D. "The Debts of Divine Music in Wagner's *Ring des Nibelungen*." *Critical Inquiry* 28 (2002): 677–708.

Hoeckner, Berthold. "Elsa Screams, or, The Birth of Music Drama." *Cambridge Opera Journal* 9 (1997): 97–132.

———. "Wagner and the Origin of Evil." *Opera Quarterly* 23 (2007): 151–83.

Holman, J. K. *Wagner's* Ring: *A Listener's Companion and Concordance*. Portland, Ore.: Amadeus, 1996.

Huckvale, David. "Wagner and Vampires." *Wagner* 18 (1997): 127–41.

Hunt, Graham Gregory. *"Ever New Formal Structures": The Evolution of the Dialogue Scene in Wagner's* Lohengrin. Ph.D. dissertation, Duke University, 2001.

Joe, Jeongwon, and Sander Gilman, eds. *Wagner and Cinema*. Bloomington: Indiana University Press, 2010.

Karnes, Kevin C. "Wagner, Klimt, and the Metaphysics of Creativity in Fin-de-siècle Vienna." *Journal of the American Musicological Society* 62 (2009): 647–97.

Kennaway, James Gordon. *Musical Pathology in the Nineteenth Century: Richard Wagner and Degeneration*. Ph.D. dissertation, University of California, Los Angeles, 2004.

Kinderman, William, and Katherine R. Syer, eds. *A Companion to Wagner's* Parsifal. Rochester, N.Y.: Camden House, 2005.

Kirby, Frank E. *Wagner's Themes: A Study in Musical Expression*. Warren, Mich.: Harmonie Park, 2004.

Kitcher, Philip, and Richard Schacht. *Finding an Ending: Reflections on Wagner's* Ring. Oxford: Oxford University Press, 2004.

Köhler, Joachim. *Nietzsche and Wagner: A Lesson in Subjugation.* Translated by Ronald Taylor. New Haven, Conn.: Yale University Press, 1998.

———. *Richard Wagner: The Last of the Titans.* Translated by Stewart Spencer. New Haven, Conn.: Yale University Press, 2004.

———. *Wagner's Hitler: The Prophet and His Disciple.* Translated by Ronald Taylor. Cambridge: Polity, 2000.

Kozlowski, Krzystof, and John Comber. "Salvation in Love: *Tristan und Isolde* by Richard Wagner." *Interdisciplinary Studies in Musicology* 6 (2007): 107–27.

Kramer, Lawrence. "Contesting Wagner: The *Lohengrin* Prelude and Anti-anti-Semitism." *19th-Century Music* 25 (2001–02): 190–211.

———. "*Tannhäuser* and the General Equivalent." *Cambridge Opera Journal* 21 (2009): 139–58.

Lee, M. Owen. *Athena Sings: Wagner and the Greeks.* Toronto: University of Toronto Press, 2003.

———. *Wagner and the Wonder of Art: An Introduction to* Die Meistersinger. Toronto: University of Toronto Press, 2007.

———. *Wagner: The Terrible Man and His Truthful Art.* Toronto: University of Toronto Press, 1999.

———. *Wagner's* Ring: *Turning the Sky Round.* New York: Summit Books, 1990.

Lees, Heath. *Mallarmé and Wagner: Music and Poetic Language.* Translated by Rosemary Lloyd. Aldershot, England: Ashgate, 2007.

Levin, David J. *Richard Wagner, Fritz Lang, and the Nibelungen: The Dramaturgy of Disavowal.* Princeton, N.J.: Princeton University Press, 1998.

———, ed. *Richard Wagner:* The Flying Dutchman/Der Fliegende Holländer—*New Perspectives on Wagner's* Flying Dutchman. *Opera Quarterly* 21 (2005): 416–521.

Livingstone, Ernest. "The *Ring* as a Classical Drama of Individual and Social Tragedy." *Pendragon Review* 1 (2001): 33–44.

Lüdecke, Johannes. "Ways of Understanding Leitmotive." In Eero Tarasti et al., eds., *Musical Semiotics Revisited*, 376–85. Helsinki, Finland: International Semiotics Institute, 2003.

Magee, Bryan. *Aspects of Wagner.* New York: Oxford University Press, 1988; originally 1970.

———. *The* Tristan *Chord: Wagner and Philosophy.* New York: Henry Holt, 2001; originally 2000.

———. *Wagner and Philosophy.* London: Allen Lane, 2000.

May, Thomas. *Decoding Wagner: An Invitation to His World of Music Drama.* Pompton Plains, N.J.: Amadeus, 2004.

McClatchie, Stephen C. *Analyzing Wagner's Operas: Alfred Lorenz and German Nationalist Ideology.* Rochester, N.Y.: University of Rochester Press, 1998.

McCredie, Andrew D. "Leitmotive: Wagner's Points of Departure and Their Antecedents." *Miscellanea musicologica* 14 (1985): 1–28.

McGlathery, James M. *Wagner's Operas and Desire.* New York: Peter Lang, 1998.

Meyer, Stephen C. "Illustrating Transcendence: *Parsifal*, Franz Stassen, and the Leitmotif." *Musical Quarterly* 92 (2009): 9–32.

Millington, Barry. *The New Grove Guide to Wagner and His Operas.* Oxford: Oxford University Press, 2006.

———. *Wagner.* Princeton, N.J.: Princeton University Press, 1992; originally 1984.

———, ed. *The Wagner Compendium: A Guide to Wagner's Life and Music.* London: Thames and Hudson, 2001; originally 1992.

———. "Wagner's Anti-Semitism." *Wagner* 18 (1997): 83–90.

Millington, Barry, and Stewart Spencer, eds. *Wagner in Performance.* New Haven, Conn.: Yale University Press, 1992.

Miner, Margaret. *Resonant Gaps: Between Baudelaire and Wagner.* Athens: University of Georgia Press, 1995.

Minor, Ryan. "Parsifal's Promise or Parsifal's Reality? On the Politics of Voice Exchange in Wagner's Grail Operas." *Opera Quarterly* 22 (2006): 249–68.

———. "Wagner's Last Chorus: Consecrating Space and Spectatorship in *Parsifal.*" *Cambridge Opera Journal* 17 (2005): 1–36.

Morgan, Robert P. "Circular Form in the *Tristan* Prelude." *Journal of the American Musicological Society* 53 (2000): 69–103.

Nattiez, Jean-Jacques. *Wagner Androgyne: A Study in Interpretation.* Translated by Stewart Spencer. Princeton, N.J.: Princeton University Press, 1993; originally 1990.

Nicholson, Peter. "Orpheus Ascending: A Reassessment of Wagner and Wagnerism." *Wagner* 22 (2001): 3–37.

North, Roger. *Wagner's Most Subtle Art: An Analytic Study of* Tristan und Isolde. London: 1999; originally 1996.

Nussbaum, Rachel. "Wagner's *Rienzi* and the Creation of a People." *Musical Quarterly* 84 (2000): 417–25.

Osborne, Charles. *The Complete Operas of Richard Wagner.* Cambridge, Mass.: Da Capo, 1993; originally 1990.

Painter, Karen. "Ritual Time in Wagner and Wagnerian Opera." In Sven Oliver Müller et al., eds., *Oper im Wandel der Gesellschaft: Kulturtransfers und Netzwerke des Musiktheaters im modernen Europa,* 179–96. Vienna: Böhlau, 2010.

Parly, Nila. "Plot versus Music: Elisabeth and Venus in Wagner's *Tannhäuser.*" *Nordic Theater Studies* 17 (2005): 16–23.

———. *Vocal Victories: Wagner's Female Characters from Senta to Kundry.* Translated by Gaye Kynoch. Copenhagen: Museum Tusculanum, 2011.

Petty, Jonathan Christian, and Marshall Tuttle. "The Genealogy of Chaos: Multiple Coherence in Wagnerian Music Drama." *Music and Letters* 79 (1998): 72–98.

Rather, L. J. *The Dream of Self-Destruction: Wagner's* Ring *and the Modern World.* Baton Rouge: Louisiana State University, 1979.

Reale, Steven M. *Cyclic Structure and Dramatic Recapitulation in Richard Wagner's* Der Ring des Nibelungen. Ph.D. dissertation, University of Michigan, 2009.

Richardson, Herbert, ed. *New Studies in Richard Wagner's* The Ring of the Nibelung. Lewiston, N.Y.: Mellon, 1991.

Richey, John. "A Short History of the Sequence in Wagner's Music." *Journal of the American Liszt Society* 48 (2000): 17–34.

Riedlbauer, Jörg. "*Erinnerungsmotive* in Wagner's *Der Ring des Nibelungen.*" *Musical Quarterly* 74 (1990): 18–30.

Rieger, Eva. *Richard Wagner's Women.* Translated by Chris Walton. Woodbridge, England: Boydell and Brewer, 2011.

Rose, Paul Lawrence. "Wagner and Hitler: After the Holocaust." *Wagner* 22 (2001): 37–49.

Russell, Peter. "The Prisoner of Gender: Woman-Power and Man-Power in Wagner's *Tannhäuser.*" *Wagner* 20 (1999): 63–77.

Sabor, Rudolph. *Richard Wagner:* Der Ring des Nibelungen. London: Phaidon, 1997.

Saffle, Michael. *Richard Wagner: A Research and Information Guide.* New York: Routledge, 2010.

Salmi, Hannu. *Imagined Germany: Richard Wagner's National Utopia.* New York: Peter Lang, 1999.

Schofield, Paul. *The Redeemer Reborn:* Parsifal *as the Fifth Opera of Wagner's* Ring. New York: Amadeus, 2007.

Schopf, Jane. "Senta: A Reappraisal." *Wagner* 17 (1996): 103–13.

Scruton, Roger. *Death-Devoted Heart: Sex and the Sacred in Wagner's* Tristan und Isolde. Oxford: Oxford University Press, 2004.

Shaw, Leroy R., et al., eds. *Wagner in Retrospect: A Centennial Reappraisal.* Amsterdam: Rodopi, 1987.

Sheffi, Na'ama. *The Ring of Myths: The Israelis, Wagner, and the Nazis.* Translated by Martha Grenzeback. Brighton, England: Sussex, 2001.

Skelton, Geoffrey. *Wagner in Thought and Practice.* Portland, Ore.: Amadeus, 1992; originally 1991.

Spotts, Frederic. *Bayreuth: A History of the Wagner Festival*. New Haven, Conn.: Yale University Press, 1994.

Suschitzky, Anya Catherine. *The Nation on Stage: Wagner and French Opera at the End of the Nineteenth Century*. Ph.D. dissertation, University of California, Berkeley, 1999.

Syer, Katherine Rae. *Altered States: Musical and Psychological Processes in Wagner*. Ph.D. dissertation, McMaster University, 1999.

Tanner, Michael. *Wagner*. Princeton, N.J.: Princeton University Press, 2002; originally 1996.

Tarasti, Eero. "Do Wagner's Leitmotifs Have a System?" In Jan Stęszewski and Maciej Jabloński, eds., *Interdisciplinary Studies in Musicology*, 257–80. Poznań, Poland: Wydawnictwo Poznańskiego Towarzystwa Przyjaciól, 1997.

Tietz, John. *Redemption or Annihilation? Love versus Power in Wagner's Ring*. New York: Peter Lang, 1999.

Treadwell, James. *Interpreting Wagner*. New Haven, Conn.: Yale University Press, 2003.

———. "The *Ring* and the Conditions of Interpretation: Wagner's Writing, 1848–1852." *Cambridge Opera Journal* 7 (1995): 207–31.

Tuttle, Marshall. *Musical Structures in Wagnerian Opera*. Lewiston, N.Y.: Mellen, 2000.

Vazsonyi, Nicholas. *Richard Wagner: Self-Promotion and the Making of a Brand*. Cambridge: Cambridge University Press, 2010.

———, ed. *Wagner's* Meistersinger: *Performance, History, Representation*. Rochester, N.Y.: University of Rochester Press, 2003.

Wagner, Nike. *The Wagners: The Dramas of a Musical Dynasty*. Translated by Ewald Osers and Michael Downes. Princeton, N.J.: Princeton University Press, 1998.

Walton, Chris. *Richard Wagner's Zurich: The Muse of Place*. Rochester, N.Y.: Camden House, 2007.

Warrack, John Hamilton. "The Influence of Grand Opera on Wagner." In Peter Anthony Bloom, ed., *Music in Paris in the Eighteen-Thirties*, 575–87. Stuyvesant, N.Y.: Pendragon, 1987.

———. *Richard Wagner:* Die Meistersinger von Nürnberg. Cambridge: Cambridge University Press, 1994.

White, Andrew. "Toward an Understanding of Wagnerian Music Drama: An Examination of *Tristan und Isolde*." *Music Research Forum* 14 (1999): 27–58.

White, David A. *The Turning Wheel: A Study of Contracts and Oaths in Wagner's Ring*. Selinsgrove, Pa.: Susquehanna University Press, 1988.

Williams, Simon. *Wagner and the Romantic Hero*. Cambridge: Cambridge University Press, 2004.

————. "The Writing of Exoticism in the Libretti of the Opéra-Comique, 1825–1862." Translated by Peter Glidden. *Cambridge Opera Journal* 11 (1999): 135–58.

Laurance, Emily Rose. *Varieties of Operatic Realism in Nineteenth-Century France: The Case of Gustave Charpentier's* Louise *(1900)*. Ph.D. dissertation, University of North Carolina, 2003.

Letelier, Robert Ignatius. "Hector Berlioz and Giacomo Meyerbeer: A Complex Friendship Revisited." *Opera Quarterly* 19 (2003): 357–92.

Mcquinn, Julie. *Unofficial Discourses of Gender and Sexuality at the Opéra-Comique during the Belle Epoque*. Ph.D. dissertation, Northwestern University, 2003.

Miner, Margaret. "Phantoms of Genius: Women and the Fantastic in the Opera-House Mystery." *19th-Century Music* 18 (1994): 121–35.

Newark, Cormac. *Staging* Grand opéra*: History and the Imagination in Nineteenth-Century Paris*. Ph.D. dissertation, Oxford University, 1999.

Pendle, Karin S. "The Boulevard Theaters and Continuity in French Opera of the 19th Century." In Peter Anthony Bloom, ed., *Music in Paris in the Eighteen-Thirties*, 509–35. Stuyvesant, N.Y.: Pendragon, 1987.

Pottinger, Mark Ainsworth. *The Staging of History in France: Characterizations of Historical Figures in French Grand Opera during the Reign of Louis Philippe*. Ph.D. dissertation, City University of New York, 2005.

Runyan, William Edward. *Orchestration in Five French Grand Operas*. Ph.D. dissertation, University of Rochester, 1983.

Smart, Mary Ann, and Roger Parker, eds. *Reading Critics Reading: Opera and Ballet Criticism in France from the Revolution to 1848*. New York: Oxford University Press, 2001.

Smith, Marian. *Ballet and Opera in the Age of Giselle*. Princeton, N.J.: Princeton University Press, 2000.

————. "Ballet, Opera, and Staging Practices at the Paris Opéra." In Fabrizio Della Seta and Pierluigi Petrobelli, eds., *La realizzazione scenica dello spettacolo verdiano*, 273–318. Parma, Italy: Istituto di Studi Verdiani, 1996.

————. "Three Hybrid Works at the Paris Opéra, circa 1830." *Dance Chronicle: Studies in Dance and the Related Arts* 24 (2001): 7–53.

Speagle, John. *Opera and Parisian Boulevard Theatre, 1800–1850*. Ph.D. dissertation, Princeton University, 2006.

Speare, Mary Jean. "Convention and Structure in Opéra comique at Mid-century." In Arnold Jacobshagen and Milan Pospíšil, eds., *Meyerbeer und die Opéra comique*, 63–80. Laaber, Germany: Laaber, 2004.

————. *The Transformation of Opéra comique: 1850–1880*. Ph.D. dissertation, Washington University, St. Louis, 1997.

Spies, André Michael. *Opera, State, and Society in the Third Republic, 1875–1914*. New York: Lang, 1998.

Theresa, Rose M. *Spectacle and Enchantment: Envisioning Opera in Late Nineteenth-Century Paris*. Ph.D. dissertation, University of Pennsylvania, 2000.

Traubner, Richard. *Operetta: A Theatrical History*. New York: Oxford University Press, 1989; originally 1983.

Walsh, Thomas Joseph. *Second Empire Opera: The Théâtre Lyrique, Paris, 1851–1870*. London: Calder, 1981.

Walton, Benjamin Toby. *Romanticisms and Nationalisms in Restoration France*. Ph.D. dissertation, University of California, Berkeley, 2000.

Germany and Austria

Crittenden, Camille. *Johann Strauss and Vienna: Operetta and the Politics of Popular Culture*. Cambridge: Cambridge University Press, 2000.

Daverio, John. *Nineteenth-Century Music and the German Romantic Ideology*. New York: Macmillan, 1993.

Doerner, Mark F. "German Romantic Opera? A Critical Reappraisal of *Undine* and *Der Freischütz*." *Opera Quarterly* 10 (1993): 10–26.

Federhofer-Königs, Renate. "The Joining of Words and Music in Late Romantic Melodrama." *Musical Quarterly* 62 (1976): 571–90.

Hughes, Derek. "'Wie die Hans Heilings': Weber, Marschner, and Thomas Mann's *Doktor Faustus*." *Cambridge Opera Journal* 10 (1998): 179–204.

Meyer, Stephen Conrad. *Performing Identity: The Search for a German Opera in Dresden, 1798–1832*. Ph.D. dissertation, State University of New York, Stony Brook, 1996.

Scher, Steven Paul. "Hoffmann, Weber, Wagner: The Birth of Romantic Opera from the Spirit of Literature?" In Steven Paul Scher et al., eds., *Essays on Literature and Music (1967–2004)*, 367–85. Amsterdam: Rodopi, 2004.

Tusa, Michael C. "Richard Wagner and Weber's *Euryanthe*." *19th-Century Music* 9 (1986): 206–21.

Williams, Simon. "Bayreuth Festspielhaus: Enchaining the Audience." *Theatre Survey: The American Journal of Theatre History* 33 (1992): 65–73.

Žižek, Slavoj, and Mladen Dolar. *Opera's Second Death*. New York: Routledge, 2002.

Italy

André, Naomi. *Voicing Gender: Castrati, Travesti, and the Second Woman in Early-Nineteenth-Century Italian Opera*. Bloomington: Indiana University Press, 2006.

Ashbrook, William. "Whatever Happened to the Cabaletta? Intensity, Brevity, and the Transformation of the Cabaletta from Form to Function." In Jürgen Maehder and Lorenza Guiot, eds., *Letteratura, musica, e teatro al Tempo di Ruggero Leoncavallo*, 83–87. Milan: Casa Musicale Sonzogno di Piero Ostali, 1995.

Balthazar, Scott L. "Aspects of Form in the *Ottocento* Libretto." *Cambridge Opera Journal* 7 (1995): 23–35.

———. *Evolving Conventions in Italian Serious Opera: Scene Structure in the Works of Rossini, Bellini, Donizetti, and Verdi, 1810–1850*. Ph.D. dissertation, University of Pennsylvania, 1985.

———. "Mayr, Rossini, and the Development of the Early Concertato Finale." *Journal of the Royal Musical Association* 116 (1991): 236–66.

———. "The *Primo Ottocento* Duet and the Transformation of the Rossinian Code." *Journal of Musicology* 7 (1989): 471–97.

———. "Tectonic and Linear Form in the *Ottocento* Libretto: The Case of the Two *Otellos*." *Opera Journal* 28 (1995): 2–14.

Capra, Marco. "Aspects of the Use of the Chorus in 19th-Century Italian Opera." *Polifonie: Storia e teoria della coralità/History and Theory of Choral Music* 3 (2003): 157–73.

Davis, John A. "Opera and Absolutism in Restoration Italy, 1815–1860." *Journal of Interdisciplinary History* 36 (2006): 569–94.

Dunstone, Prudence. "Italian Vocal Music in the Early Nineteenth Century: Historical versus Modern Interpretive Approaches." In Michael Ewans et al., eds., *Music Research: New Directions for a New Century*, 40–53. London: Cambridge Scholars, 2004.

Giger, Andreas. "*Verismo*: Origin, Corruption, and Redemption of an Operatic Term." *Journal of the American Musicological Society* 60 (2007): 271–315.

Gossett, Philip. "Becoming a Citizen: The Chorus in *Risorgimento* Opera." *Cambridge Opera Journal* 2 (1990): 41–64.

———. *Divas and Scholars: Performing Italian Opera*. Chicago: University of Chicago Press, 2006.

Guarnieri Corazzol, Adriana. "Opera and Verismo: Regressive Points of View and the Artifice of Alienation." Translated by Roger Parker. *Cambridge Opera Journal* 5 (1993): 39–53.

Hadlock, Heather. "Women Playing Men in Italian Opera, 1810–1835." In Jane A. Bernstein, ed., *Women's Voices across Musical Worlds*, 285–307. Boston: Northeastern University, 2004.

Huebner, Steven. "Lyric Form in *Ottocento* Opera." *Journal of the Royal Musical Association* 117 (1992): 123–47.

Izzo, Francesco. "Comedy between Two Revolutions: Opera buffa and the Risorgimento, 1831–48." *Journal of Musicology* 21 (2004): 127–74.

————. *Laughter between Two Revolutions: Opera buffa in Italy, 1831–1848*. Ph.D. dissertation, New York University, 2003.

Jensen, Luke. "The Emergence of the Modern Conductor in 19th-Century Italian Opera." *Performance Practice Review* 4 (1991): 34–63.

Kaufman, Thomas G. "Giorgio Ronconi." *Donizetti Society Journal* 5 (1984): 169–206.

————. "Mercadante and Verdi." *Opera Quarterly* 13 (1997): 41–56.

Marvin, Roberta Montemorra, and Hilary Poriss, eds. *Fashions and Legacies of Nineteenth-Century Italian Opera*. Cambridge: Cambridge University Press, 2010.

Newark, Cormac. "'In Italy We Don't Have the Means for Illusion': *Grand opéra* in Nineteenth-Century Bologna." *Cambridge Opera Journal* 19 (2007): 199–222.

Nicolaisen, Jay R. *Italian Opera in Transition, 1871–1893*. Ann Arbor, Mich.: University Microfilms International, 1980.

Pleasants, Henry. "Giovanni Battista Rubini (1794–1854)." *Opera Quarterly* 10 (1993): 100–104.

Poriss, Hilary. *Artistic License: Aria Interpolation and the Italian Operatic World, 1815–1850*. Ph.D. dissertation, University of Chicago, 2000.

————. *Changing the Score: Arias, Prima Donnas, and the Authority of Performance*. New York: Oxford University Press, 2009.

Powers, Harold S. "One Halfstep at a Time: Tonal Transposition and 'Split Association' in Italian Opera." *Cambridge Opera Journal* 7 (1995): 135–64.

Rutherford, Susan. "'La cantante delle passioni': Giuditta Pasta and the Idea of Operatic Performance." *Cambridge Opera Journal* 19 (2007): 107–38.

Sansone, Matteo. Verismo*: From Literature to Opera*. Ph.D. dissertation, University of Edinburgh, 1987.

Senici, Emanuele. *Landscape and Gender in Italian Opera: The Alpine Virgin from Bellini to Puccini*. Cambridge: Cambridge University Press, 2005.

Toelle, Jutta. "Venice and Its Opera House: Hope and Despair at the Teatro La Fenice, 1866–97." *Journal of Musicological Research* 26 (2007): 33–54.

Tomlinson, Gary. "Italian Romanticism and Italian Opera: An Essay in Their Affinities." *19th-Century Music* 10 (1986): 43–60.

————. "Learning to Curse at Sixty-Seven." *Cambridge Opera Journal* 14 (2003): 229–41.

————. "Opera and Drame: Hugo, Donizetti, and Verdi." In Studies in the History of Music, 2:171–92. New York: Broude, 1988.

Zoppelli, Luca. "'Stage Music' in Early Nineteenth-Century Italian Opera." *Cambridge Opera Journal* 2 (1990): 29–39.

Other Locales

Buckler, Julie A. *The Literary Lorgnette: Attending Opera in Imperial Russia.* Stanford, Calif.: Stanford University Press, 2000.

Burghauser, Jarmil. "Dvořák and Smetana: Some Thoughts on Sources, Influences, and Relationships." *Czech Music* 17 (1991–92): 16–24.

Butler, Jennifer Ann. *Ambiguity in Nineteenth-Century Russian Literature and Opera.* Ph.D. dissertation, University of New South Wales, 2005.

Caswell, Austin B. "Jenny Lind's Tour of America: A Discourse of Gender and Class." In Thomas J. Mathiesen and Benito V. Rivera, eds., *Festa musicologica: Essays in Honor of George J. Buelow*, 319–37. Stuyvesant, N.Y.: Pendragon, 1995.

Cunningham, Thomas Thurston. *Terrible Visions: The Sublime Image of Ivan the Terrible in Russian Opera.* Ph.D. dissertation, Princeton University, 1999.

Dideriksen, Gabriella. *Repertory and Rivalry: Opera and the Second Covent Garden, 1830–56.* Ph.D. dissertation, University of London, 1997.

Kalil, Mary Helena. *Reports from Offstage: Representations of Slavic History in Russian and Czech Opera.* Ph.D. dissertation, Princeton University, 2002.

Öhrström, Eva. W. E. Ottercrans, trans. *Jenny Lind: The Swedish Nightingale.* Stockholm: Swedish Institute Stockholm, 2000.

Taruskin, Richard. *Opera and Drama in Russia as Preached and Practiced in the 1860s.* Ann Arbor, Mich.: University Microfilms International, 1981.

———. "'The Present in the Past': Russian Opera and Russian Historiography, ca. 1870." In Malcolm Hamrick Brown, ed., *Russian and Soviet Music: Essays for Boris Schwarz*, 77–146. Ann Arbor, Mich.: University Microfilms International, 1984.

Taylor, Philip. *Gogolian Interludes: Gogol's Story "Christmas Eve" as the Subject of the Operas by Tchaikovsky and Rimsky-Korsakov.* London: Collets, 1984.

Vázquez, Roland J. *The Quest for National Opera in Spain and the Reinvention of the Zarzuela (1808–1849).* Ph.D. dissertation, Cornell University, 1992.

Volpe, Maria Alice. "Remaking the Brazilian Myth of National Foundation: *Il Guarany.*" *Latin American Music Review* 23 (2002): 179–94.

Ware, W. Porter, and Thaddeus C. Lockard Jr. *P. T. Barnum Presents Jenny Lind: The American Tour of the Swedish Nightingale.* Baton Rouge: Louisiana State University, 1980.

19 CENTURY: COMPARATIVE AND OTHER TOPICS

Abbate, Carolyn. *Unsung Voices: Opera and Musical Narrative in the 19th Century*. Princeton, N.J.: Princeton University Press, 1991.

Budden, Julian. "Verdi and Meyerbeer in Relation to *Les vêpres siciliennes*." *Studi verdiani* 1 (1983): 11–20.

Bushnell, Howard. *Maria Malibran: A Biography of the Singer*. University Park: Pennsylvania State University Press, 1979.

Caswell, Austin B., ed. *Embellished Opera Arias*. Madison, Wis.: A-R Editions, 1989.

Corman, Brian, ed. "Voices of Opera: Performance, Production, Interpretation." *University of Toronto Quarterly* 67 (1998): 739–840.

Cowgill, Rachel, and Hilary Poriss, eds. *The Arts of the Prima Donna in the Long Nineteenth Century*. Oxford: Oxford University Press, 2012.

Edgecombe, Rodney Stenning. "The Influence of Auber's *Le domino noir* on *La traviata*." *Opera Quarterly* 20 (2004): 166–70.

Emslie, Barry. "The Domestication of Opera." *Cambridge Opera Journal* 5 (1993): 167–77.

Fitzlyon, April. *Maria Malibran: Diva of the Romantic Age*. London: Souvenir, 1988.

Foster, Dina Grundemann. *Manon Lescaut and Her Representation in Nineteenth-Century Literature, Criticism, and Opera*. Ph.D. dissertation, University of Michigan, 1998.

Goldhill, Simon. *Victorian Culture and Classical Antiquity: Art, Opera, Fiction, and the Proclamation of Modernity*. Princeton, N.J.: Princeton University Press, 2011.

Goldstein, Robert Justin. *Political Censorship of the Arts and the Press in Nineteenth-Century Europe*. New York: Macmillan, 1989.

Greenwald, Helen. "Comic Opera and National Identity in the Late Nineteenth Century: Verdi, Wagner, and the 'Restoration of a Proper Society.'" In Peter Csobádi and Gernot Gruber, eds., *Politische Mythen und nationale Identitäten im (Musik-)Theater: Vorträge und Gespräche des Salzburger Symposions 2001*, 545–55. Salzburg, Austria: Mueller-Speiser, 2003.

Groos, Arthur, and Roger Parker, eds. *Reading Opera*. Princeton, N.J.: Princeton University Press, 1988.

Hansen, Jack Winsor. *The Sibyl Sanderson Story: Requiem for a Diva*. Pompton Plains, N.J.: Amadeus, 2005.

Henson, Karen. *Of Men, Women, and Others: Exotic Opera in the Late Nineteenth Century*. Ph.D. dissertation, Oxford University, 1999.

Heuscher, Julius E. "*Don Pasquale, Fidelio*, and Psychiatry." *American Journal of Psychoanalysis* 52 (1992): 161–73.

Huebner, Steven. "Massenet and Wagner: Bridling the Influence." *Cambridge Opera Journal* 5 (1993): 223–38.

Johnson, James H. "The Myth of Venice in Nineteenth-Century Opera." *Journal of Interdisciplinary History* 36 (2006): 533–54.

Katalinić, Vjera, et al., eds. *Musical Theatre as High Culture? The Cultural Discourse on Opera and Operetta in the 19th Century.* Zagreb, Croatia: Hrvatsko Muzikološko Društvo, 2011.

Kaufman, Tom. "Wagner vs. Meyerbeer." *Opera Quarterly* 19 (2003): 644–69.

Kendall-Davies, Barbara. *The Life and Works of Pauline Viardot García.* Vol. 1, *The Years of Fame, 1836–1863.* London: Cambridge Scholars, 2003.

Kolb, Katherine. "Flying Leaves: Between Berlioz and Wagner." *19th-Century Music* 33 (2009): 25–61.

Laudon, Robert Tallant. *Sources of the Wagnerian Synthesis: A Study of the Franco-German Tradition in 19th-Century Opera.* Munich: Katzbichler, 1979.

Letellier, Robert Ignatius. "Bellini and Meyerbeer." *Opera Quarterly* 17 (2001): 361–79.

Locke, Ralphe P. "Cutthroats and Casbah Dancers, Muezzins and Timeless Sands: Musical Images of the Middle East." *19th-Century Music* 22 (1998): 20–53.

———. "Reflections on Orientalism in Opera (and Musical Theater)." *Revista di musicologia* 16 (1993): 3122–34.

Miller, Andrew J. *Manon and Her Daughters: Literary Representations and Musical Adaptations of Three Femmes Fatales.* Ph.D. dissertation, Duke University, 2002.

Parker, Roger, and Carolyn Abbate, eds. *Analyzing Opera: Verdi and Wagner.* Berkeley: University of California Press, 1989.

Parr, Sean M. *Melismatic Madness: Coloratura and Female Vocality in Mid Nineteenth-Century French and Italian Opera.* Ph.D. dissertation, Columbia University, 2009.

Payne, Linda. "Lovesickness: Female Insanity in Nineteenth-Century Opera." In William A. Everett and Paul R. Laird, eds., *On Bunker's Hill: Essays in Honor of J. Bunker Clark,* 235–43. Sterling Heights, Mich.: Harmonie Park, 2007.

Petrobelli, Pierluigi. *Music in the Theater: Essays on Verdi and Other Composers.* Translated by Roger Parker. Princeton, N.J.: Princeton University Press, 1994.

Riggs, Geoffrey S. *The Assoluta Voice in Opera 1797–1847.* Jefferson, N.C.: McFarland, 2003.

Rosen, Charles. *The Romantic Generation.* Cambridge, Mass.: Harvard University Press, 1995.

Sala, Emilio. "Women Crazed by Love: An Aspect of Romantic Opera." Translated by William Ashbrook. *Opera Quarterly* 10 (1994): 19–41.

Samson, Jim, ed. *The Cambridge History of Nineteenth-Century Music.* Cambridge: Cambridge University Press, 2002.

Smart, Mary Ann. *Mimomania: Music and Gesture in Nineteenth-Century Opera.* Berkeley: University of California Press, 2004.

Wittmann, Michael. "Meyerbeer and Mercadante? The Reception of Meyerbeer in Italy." Translated by Stewart Spencer. *Cambridge Opera Journal* 5 (1993): 115–32.

20TH CENTURY: COMPOSERS

Adams, John

Burkhardt, Rebecca Louise. *The Development of Style in the Music of John Adams from 1978 to 1989.* Ph.D. dissertation, University of Texas, Austin, 1993.

Daines, Matthew N. *Telling the Truth about Nixon: Parody, Cultural Representation, and Gender Politics in John Adams's Opera* Nixon in China. Ph.D. dissertation, University of California, Davis, 1995.

Fink, Robert. "Klinghoffer in Brooklyn Heights." *Cambridge Opera Journal* 17 (2005): 173–213.

Johnson, Timothy Alan. *Harmony in the Music of John Adams: From* Phrygian Gates *to* Nixon in China. Ph.D. dissertation, State University of New York, Buffalo, 1991.

———. *John Adams's* Nixon in China: *Musical Analysis, Historical, Political Perspectives.* Farnham, England: Ashgate, 2011.

May, Thomas, ed. *The John Adams Reader: Essential Writings on an American Composer.* Pompton Plains, N.J.: Amadeus, 2006.

Schwarz, David. "Postmodernism, the Subject, and the Real in John Adams's *Nixon in China.*" *Indiana Theory Review* 13 (1992): 107–35.

Bartók, Béla

Frigyesi, Judit. *Béla Bartók and Turn-of-the-Century Budapest.* Berkeley: University of California Press, 1998.

Gilmore, Britta. *Bartók as Dramatist.* Ph.D. dissertation, Princeton University, 2004.

John, Nicholas, ed. *The Stage Works of Béla Bartók.* New York: Riverrun, 1991.

Leafstedt, Carl S. *Inside* Bluebeard's Castle*: Music and Drama in Béla Bartók's Opera*. New York: Oxford University Press, 1999.

Vazsonyi, Nicholas. "*Bluebeard's Castle*: The Birth of Cinema from the Spirit of Opera." *Hungarian Quarterly* 46 (2005): 132–44.

Berg, Alban

Adorno, Theodor W. "The Opera *Wozzeck*." In *Essays on Music*, trans. Susan Gillespie, 619–26. Berkeley: University of California Press, 2002.

Bruhn, Siglind, ed. *Encrypted Messages in Alban Berg's Music*. New York: General, 1998.

Dos Santos, Silvio José. "Marriage as Prostitution in Berg's *Lulu*." *Journal of Musicology* 25 (2008): 143–82.

———. *Portraying* Lulu*: Desire and Identity in Alban Berg's* Lulu. Ph.D. dissertation, Brandeis University, 2003.

Fukunaka, Fuyuko. "The Use of Symmetry in Alban Berg's *Wozzeck*." In Jürgen Kühnel et al., eds., *Alban Bergs Wozzeck un di Zwanziger Jahre*, 311–27. Salzburg, Austria: Mueller-Speiser Anif, 1999.

Gilman, Sander L. "Alban Berg, the Jews, and the Anxiety of Genius." In Ronald Michael Radano and Philip V. Bohlman, eds., *Music and the Racial Imagination*, 483–509. Chicago: University of Chicago Press, 2000.

Hall, Patricia. *Berg's* Wozzeck. New York: Oxford University Press, 2011.

Headlam, Dave. *The Music of Alban Berg*. New Haven, Conn.: Yale University Press, 1996.

Jarman, Douglas. *Alban Berg:* Lulu. Cambridge: Cambridge University Press, 1991.

———. *Alban Berg:* Wozzeck. Cambridge: Cambridge University Press, 1989.

———, ed. *The Berg Companion*. Basingstoke, England: Macmillan, 1989.

Morris, Christopher. "'Sympathy with Death': Narcissism and Nostalgia in the Post-Wagnerian Orchestra." *Musical Quarterly* 85 (2001): 85–116.

Pople, Anthony, ed. *The Cambridge Companion to Berg*. Cambridge: Cambridge University Press, 1997.

Schmalfeldt, Janet. *Berg's* Wozzeck*: Harmonic Language and Dramatic Design*. New Haven, Conn.: Yale University Press, 1983.

Schroeder, David P. "Opera, Apocalypse, and the Dance of Death: Berg's Indebtedness to Krauss." *Mosaic* 25 (1992): 91–105.

Simms, Bryan R. *Alban Berg: A Research and Information Guide*. New York: Routledge, 2009.

Spies, Bertha. "Alban Berg's *Wozzeck*: Revisiting a Historically Sedimented Metaphor." *SAMUS: South African Journal of Musicology* 22 (2002): 47–61.

Bernstein, Leonard

Burton, Humphrey. *Leonard Bernstein*. New York: Doubleday, 1994.
Everett, William A. "*Candide* and the Tradition of American Operetta." *Studies in Musical Theater* 3 (2009): 53–59.

Birtwistle, Harrison

Adlington, Robert. *The Music of Harrison Birtwistle*. Cambridge: Cambridge University Press, 2000.
Beard, David. "'A Face Like Music': Shaping Images into Sound in *The Second Mrs. Kong*." *Cambridge Opera Journal* 18 (2006): 273–300.
———. "Meta-narratives and Multidimensional Opera: Harrison Birtwistle's *The Mask of Orpheus*." In Tatjana Marković and Vesna Mikić, eds., *Music and Networking*, 143–53. Belgrade, Serbia: Fakultet Muzičke Umetnosti, 2005.
———. "The Shadow of Opera: Dramatic Narrative and Musical Discourse in *Gawain*." *Twentieth-Century Music* 2 (2005), 159–95.

Britten, Benjamin

Allen, Stephen Arthur. "*Billy Budd*: Temporary Salvation and the Faustian Pact." *Journal of Musicological Research* 25 (2006): 43–73.
Banks, Paul, ed. *Britten's* Gloriana*: Essay and Sources*. Woodbridge, England: Boydell and Brewer, 1993.
Brett, Philip. *Benjamin Britten: Peter Grimes*. Cambridge: Cambridge University Press, 1983.
———. "Eros and Orientalism in Britten's Operas." In Phillip Brett et al., eds., *Queering the Pitch: The New Gay and Lesbian Musicology*, 235–56. New York: Routledge, 1994.
———. "Salvation at Sea: Britten's *Billy Budd*." In Philip Brett and George E. Haggerty, eds., *Music and Sexuality in Britten: Selected Essays*, 70–80. Berkeley: University of California Press, 2006.
Cooke, Mervyn, ed. *The Cambridge Companion to Benjamin Britten*. New York: Cambridge University Press, 1999.
Cooke, Mervyn, and Philip Reed, eds. *Benjamin Britten: Billy Budd*. Cambridge: Cambridge University Press, 1993.
Diana, Barbara A. *Benjamin Britten's "Holy Theatre": From Opera-oratorio to Theatre-parable*. London: Travis and Emery, 2011.
Emslie, Barry. "*Billy Budd* and the Fear of Words." *Cambridge Opera Journal* 4 (1992): 43–59.

Fuller, Michael. "The Far-Shining Sail: A Glimpse of Salvation in Britten's *Billy Budd*." *Musical Times* 147 (2006): 17–24.

Godsalve, William H. L. *Britten's* A Midsummer Night's Dream: *Making an Opera from Shakespeare's Comedy*. Madison, N.J.: Fairleigh Dickinson University, 1995.

Hindley, Clifford. "Homosexual Self-Affirmation and Self-Oppression in Two Britten Operas." *Musical Quarterly* 76 (1992): 143–68.

———. "Why Does Miles Die? A Study of Britten's *The Turn of the Screw*." *Musical Quarterly* 74 (1990): 1–17.

Hodgson, Peter J. *Benjamin Britten: A Guide to Research*. New York: General, 1996.

Howard, Patricia, ed. *Benjamin Britten:* The Turn of the Screw. Cambridge: Cambridge University Press, 1985.

John, Nicholas, ed. *Benjamin Britten:* Peter Grimes *and* Gloriana. London: Calder, 1983.

McKellar, Shannon. "Re-visioning the 'Missing' Scene: Critical and Tonal Trajectories in Britten's *Billy Budd*." *Journal of the Royal Musical Association* 122 (1997): 258–80.

Mitchell, Donald, ed. *Benjamin Britten:* Death in Venice. Cambridge: Cambridge University Press, 1987.

Palmer, Christopher, ed. *The Britten Companion*. Cambridge: Cambridge University Press, 1984.

Rupprecht, Philip. *Britten's Musical Language*. Cambridge: Cambridge University Press, 2001.

———. "Tonal Stratification and Uncertainty in Britten's Music." *Journal of Music Theory* 40 (1996): 311–46.

Whittall, Arnold. "'Twisted Relations': Method and Meaning in Britten's *Billy Budd*." *Cambridge Opera Journal* 2 (1990): 145–71.

Dallapiccola, Luigi

Fearn, Raymond. "Homer, Dante, Joyce, Dallapiccola: Four Artists in Search of Ulysses." *Irish Musical Studies* 4 (1996): 411–21.

———. "Those Magnificent Men in Their Flying Machines: The Ideology of Luigi Dallapiccola's *Volo di notte*." *Journal of Musicological Research* 16 (1997): 283–99.

Samuel, Jamuna S. *Music, Text, and Drama in Dallapiccola's* Il Prigioniero. Ph.D. dissertation, City University of New York, 2005.

Debussy, Claude

Abbate, Carolyn. "Debussy's Phantom Sounds." *Cambridge Opera Journal* 10 (1998): 67–96.

Grayson, David A. "Debussy on Stage." In Simon Trezise, ed., *The Cambridge Companion to Debussy*, 61–83. Cambridge: Cambridge University Press, 2003.

———. "Waiting for Golaud: The Concept of Time in *Pelléas*." In Richard Langham Smith, ed., *Debussy Studies*, 26–50. Cambridge: Cambridge University Press, 1997.

Latham, Edward D. "Reuniting the Muses: Cross-Disciplinary Analysis of Debussy's *Pelléas* and *L'après-midi d'un faune*." *Ex tempore* 12 (2005): 25–46.

Nichols, Roger, and Richard Langham Smith, eds. *Claude Debussy:* Pelléas et Mélisande. Cambridge: Cambridge University Press, 1989.

Giordano, Umberto

Alverà, Pierluigi. *Giordano*. New York: Treves, 1986.

Sansone, Matteo. "Giordano's *Mala vita*: A 'Verismo' Opera Too True to Be Good." *Music and Letters* 75 (1994): 381–400.

Glass, Philip

Flemming, Robert, and Richard Kostelanetz, eds. *Writings on Glass: Essays, Interviews, Criticism*. New York: Schirmer, 1997.

Glass, Philip. *Music by Philip Glass*. New York: Harper and Row, 1987.

———. *Opera on the Beach: Philip Glass on His New World of Music Theater*. London: Faber and Faber, 1988.

Haskins, Rob. "Another Look at Philip Glass: Aspects of Harmony and Formal Design in Early Works and *Einstein on the Beach*." *JEMS: An Online Journal of Experimental Music Studies* (2005).

Raickovich, Milos. Einstein on the Beach *by Philip Glass: A Musical Analysis*. Ph.D. dissertation, City University of New York, 1994.

Richardson, John. *Singing Archaeology: Philip Glass's* Akhnaten. Hanover, N.H.: University Press of New England, 1999.

Hindemith, Paul

Arndt, Jennifer Lee. *Paul Hindemith's* Hin und Zuruck: *A Study and a Rationale for a Cinematographic Approach.* Ph.D. dissertation, University of Texas, Austin, 1988.

Bruhn, Siglind. *The Temptation of Paul Hindemith:* Mathis der Maler *as a Spiritual Testimony.* Stuyvesant, N.Y.: Pendragon, 1998.

D'Angelo, James. "Tonality Symbolism in Hindemith's Opera *Die Harmonie der Welt.*" *Hindemith Jahrbuch* 14 (1985): 99–128.

Haney, Joel. "Slaying the Wagnerian Monster: Hindemith, *Das Nusch-Nuschi,* and Musical Germanness after the Great War." *Journal of Musicology* 25 (2008): 339–93.

Inwood, Mary B. *The Long Christmas Dinner.* Ph.D. dissertation, New York University, 1997.

Jackson, Timothy L. "Representations of 'Exile' and 'Consolation' in Hindemith's *Mathis der Maler.*" In Chris Walton and Antonio Baldassarre, eds., *Musik im Exil: Die Schweiz und das Ausland 1918–1945,* 141–87. Bern: Peter Lang, 2005.

Neumeyer, David. *The Music of Paul Hindemith.* New Haven, Conn.: Yale University Press, 1986.

Paulding, James E. "*Mathis der Maler.* The Politics of Music." *Hindemith-Jahrbuch* 5 (1977): 102–22.

Janáček, Leoš

Beckerman, Michael Brim, ed. *Janáček and His World.* Princeton, N.J.: Princeton University Press, 2003.

Beckerman, Michael Brim, and Glen Bauer, eds. *Janáček and Czech Music: Proceedings of the International Conference.* Stuyvesant, N.Y.: Pendragon, 1995.

Chisholm, Erik. *The Operas of Leoš Janáček.* New York: Pergamon, 1971.

Merti, Gretory. *Janáček's Interconnected World with a Closer Look at* The Cunning Little Vixen. Ph.D. dissertation, University of Rochester, 2005.

Paige, Diane Marie. *Women in the Operas of Leoš Janáček.* Ph.D. dissertation, University of California, Santa Barbara, 2000.

Stamogiannou, D. G. *The Genesis of Leoš Janáček's Opera* Kát'a Kabanová. Ph.D. dissertation, University of Cambridge, 2004.

Tyrrell, John. *Janáček's Operas: A Documentary Account.* Princeton, N.J.: Princeton University Press, 1992.

Wingfield, Paul, ed. *Janáček Studies.* Cambridge: Cambridge University Press, 1999.

Krenek, Ernst

Stewart, John Lincoln. *Ernst Krenek: The Man and His Music.* Berkeley: University of California Press, 1991.

Lehár, Franz

Grun, Bernard. *Gold and Silver: The Life and Times of Franz Lehár.* New York: McKay, 1970.

Ligeti, György

Beckles Willson, Rachel. *Ligeti, Kurtág, and Hungarian Music during the Cold War.* Cambridge: Cambridge University Press, 2007.
Everett, Yayoi Uno. "Signification of Parody and the Grotesque in György Ligeti's *Le grand Macabre.*" *Music Theory Spectrum* 31 (2009): 26–56.
Steinitz, Richard. *György Ligeti: Music of the Imagination.* London: Faber and Faber, 2003.

Malipiero, Gian Francesco

Waterhouse, John C. G. *Gian Francesco Malipiero (1882–1973): The Life, Times, and Music of a Wayward Genius.* Amsterdam: Harwood, 1999.

Milhaud, Darius

Drake, Jeremy. *The Operas of Darius Milhaud.* New York: Garland, 1989.

Poulenc, Francis

Buckland, Sydney, and Myriam Chimènes, eds. *Francis Poulenc: Music, Art, and Literature.* Aldershot, England: Ashgate, 1999.

Puccini, Giacomo

Ashbrook, William, and Harold Powers. *Puccini's* Turandot: *The End of the Great Tradition.* Princeton, N.J.: Princeton University Press, 1991.
Bernardoni, Virgilio, et al., eds. *'L'insolita forma': Structure and Analytical Processes in Italian Opera at the Time of Puccini. Studi pucciniani* 3 (2004).

Budden, Julian. *Puccini: His Life and Works*. Oxford: Oxford University Press, 2002.

Burton, Deborah Ellen. *An Analysis of Puccini's Tosca: A Heuristic Approach to the Unifying Elements of the Opera*. Ph.D. dissertation, University of Michigan, 1995.

————. "The Real Scarpia: Historical Sources for *Tosca*." *Opera Quarterly* 10 (1993): 67–86.

Carner, Mosco. *Giacomo Puccini:* Tosca. Cambridge: Cambridge University Press, 1985.

Cheng, Ya-Hui. *The Harmonic Representation of the Feminine in Puccini*. Ph.D. dissertation, Florida State University, 2008.

Davis, Andrew. *Il trittico,* Turandot, *and Puccini's Late Style*. Bloomington: Indiana University Press, 2010.

Fairtile, Linda B. *Giacomo Puccini: A Guide to Research*. New York: General, 1999.

Gentry, Theodore L. "Musical Symbols of Death in *Tosca*." *Opera Quarterly* 14 (1998): 59–69.

Groos, Arthur. "Luigi Illica's Libretto for *Madama Butterfly* (1901)." In Virgilio Bernardoni et al., eds., *John Rosselli In Memorium: Studi Pucciniani* 2 (2000): 91–204.

————. "TB, Mimì, and the Anxiety of Influence." *Studi pucciniani* 1 (1998): 67–81.

Groos, Arthur, and Roger Parker, eds. *Giacomo Puccini:* La bohème. Cambridge: Cambridge University Press, 1986.

Ho, Min. *The Leitmotif Technique in Puccini's* La bohème, Tosca, *and* Madama Butterfly*: A Critical Examination of Transformation Procedures*. Ph.D. dissertation, University of Saskatchewan, 1994.

Lippmann, Friedrich. "Remarks on Puccini's Melodic Style: *La bohème*, *Tosca*, and *Madama Butterfly*." *Studi musicali* 37 (2008): 529–39.

Nicassio, Susan Vandiver. *Tosca's Rome: The Play and Opera in Historical Perspective*. Chicago: University of Chicago Press, 1999.

Osborne, Charles. *The Complete Operas of Puccini: A Critical Guide*. Cambridge, Mass.: Da Capo, 1983; originally 1982.

Schoffman, Nachum. "Puccini's *Tosca*: An Essay on Wagnerism." *Music Review* 53 (1992): 268–90.

Schwartz, Arman. "Rough Music: *Tosca* and Verismo Reconsidered." *19th-Century Music* 31 (2008): 228–44.

Weaver, William, and Simonetta Puccini, eds. *The Puccini Companion*. New York: Norton, 1994.

Wilson, Conrad. *Giacomo Puccini*. London: Phaidon, 1997.

Zhong, Mei. *Tempo in the Soprano Arias of Puccini's* La bohème, Tosca, *and* Madama Butterfly. Lewiston, N.Y.: Mellen, 2002.

Ravel, Maurice

Abbate, Carolyn. "Outside Ravel's Tomb." *Journal of the American Musicological Society* 52 (1999): 465–531.
Huebner, Steven. "Laughter: In Ravel's Time." *Cambridge Opera Journal* 18 (2006): 225–46.
Mawer, Deborah, ed. *The Cambridge Companion to Ravel*. Cambridge: Cambridge University Press, 2000.

Schoenberg, Arnold

Batnitzky, Leora. "Schoenberg's *Moses und Aron* and the Judaic Ban on Images." *Journal for the Study of the Old Testament* 92 (2001): 73–90.
Buchanan, Herbert H. "A Key to Schoenberg's 'Erwartung' (Op. 17)." *Journal of the American Musicological Society* 20 (1967): 434–49.
Haimo, Ethan. "Schoenberg, Numerology, and *Moses und Aron*." *Opera Quarterly* 23 (2007): 385–94.
Jackson, Roland. "Schoenberg as Performer of His Own Music." *Journal of Musicological Research* 24 (2005): 49–69.
Yerushalmi, Yosef Hayim. "The Moses of Freud and the Moses of Schoenberg." *Psychoanalytic Study of the Child* 47 (1992): 1–20.
Zakim, Eric. "The Dialectics of Nerves and Muscles: Schoenberg's Moses as the New Jew." *Opera Quarterly* 23 (2007): 455–77.

Shostakovich, Dmitry

Čerkašina, Marina Romanovna. "Gogol and Leskov in Shostakovich's Interpretation." *International Journal of Musicology* 1 (1992): 229–44.
Fairclough, Pauline, and David Fanning, eds. *The Cambridge Companion to Shostakovich*. Cambridge: Cambridge University Press, 2008.
Fanning, David. "Leitmotif in *Lady Macbeth*." In Philip Furia, ed., *Shostakovich Studies*, 137–59. Cambridge: Cambridge University Press, 1995.
Fay, Laurel E., ed. *Shostakovich and His World*. Princeton, N.J.: Princeton University Press, 2004.
Fitzpatrick, Sheila. "The 'Lady Macbeth' Affair: Shostakovich and the Soviet Puritans." In *The Cultural Front: Power and Culture in Revolutionary Russia*, 183–215. Ithaca, N.Y.: Cornell University Press, 1992.
Merrill, Reed. "The Grotesque in Music: Shostakovich's *Nose*." *Russian Literature Triquarterly* 23 (1990): 303–14.
Taruskin, Richard. "Entr'acte: The Lessons of Lady M." In *Defining Russia Musically: Historical and Hermeneutical Essays*. Princeton, N.J.: Princeton University Press, 1997.

Stockhausen, Karlheinz

Kohl, Jerome. "Into the Middleground: Formula Syntax in Stockhausen's *Licht*." *Perspectives of New Music* 28 (1989–90): 262–91.
———. "Time and Light." *Contemporary Music Review* 7 (1993): 203–19.
Thomas, Helen C. "Morphologies of Time in Stockhausen's *Licht*." *Tempo* 62 (2008): 2–16.

Strauss, Richard

Birken, Kenneth. Friedenstag *and* Daphne*: An Interpretive Study of the Literary and Dramatic Sources of Two Operas by Richard Strauss*. New York: General, 1982.
———, ed. *Richard Strauss:* Arabella. Cambridge: Cambridge University Press, 1989.
Bottenberg, Joanna. *Shared Creation: Words and Music in the Hofmannsthal-Strauss Operas*. Frankfurt am Main: Peter Lang, 1993.
Caddy, Davinia. "Variations on the Dance of the Seven Veils." *Cambridge Opera Journal* 17 (2005): 37–58.
Forsyth, Karen. Ariadne auf Naxos *by Hugo von Hofmannsthal and Richard Strauss: Its Genesis and Meaning*. Oxford: Oxford University Press, 1982.
Gilliam, Bryan. "*Ariadne, Dafne*, and the Problem of *Verwandlung*." *Cambridge Opera Journal* 15 (2003): 67–81.
———. *The Life of Richard Strauss*. Cambridge: Cambridge University Press, 1999.
———, ed. *Richard Strauss and His World*. Princeton, N.J.: Princeton University Press, 1992.
———, ed. *Richard Strauss: New Perspectives on the Composer and His Work*. Durham, N.C.: Duke University Press, 1992.
———. *Richard Strauss's* Elektra. Oxford: Clarendon, 1991.
Hart, Beth. "Strauss and Hofmannsthal's Accidental Heroine: The Psychohistorical Meaning of the Marschallin." *Opera Quarterly* 15 (1999): 414–34.
Hartmann, Rudolf. *Richard Strauss: The Staging of His Operas and Ballets*. Translated by Graham Davies. New York: Oxford University Press, 1981.
Jefferson, Alan. *Richard Strauss:* Der Rosenkavalier. Cambridge: Cambridge University Press, 1985.
Kennedy, Michael. *Richard Strauss: Man, Musician, Enigma*. Cambridge: Cambridge University Press, 1999.
Kristiansen, Morten. *Richard Strauss's Feuersnot in Its Aesthetic and Cultural Context: A Modernist Critique of Musical Idealism*. Ph.D. dissertation, Yale University, 2000.

Murphy, Edward W. "Tonality and Form in *Salome.*" *Music Review* 50 (1989): 215–30.

Osborne, Charles. *The Complete Operas of Richard Strauss.* Pomfret: Trafalgar Square, 1988.

Puffett, Derrick, ed. *Richard Strauss:* Elektra. Cambridge: Cambridge University Press, 1990.

———, ed. *Richard Strauss:* Salome. Cambridge: Cambridge University Press, 1989.

Schmid, Mark-Daniel, ed. *The Richard Strauss Companion.* Westport, Conn.: Praeger, 2003.

Seshadri, Anne Marie Lineback. *Richard Strauss,* Salome, *and the "Jewish Question."* Ph.D. dissertation, University of Maryland, 1998.

———. "The Taste of Love: Salome's Transfiguration." *Women and Music* 10 (2006): 24–44.

Thomas, David Wayne. "The 'Strange Music' of *Salome*: Oscar Wilde's Rhetoric of Verbal Musicality." *Mosaic* 33 (2000): 15–38.

Wikshåland, Ståle. "Elektra's Oceanic Time: Voice and Identity in Richard Strauss." *19th-Century Music* 31 (2007): 164–74.

Youmans, Charles Dowell, ed. *The Cambridge Companion to Richard Strauss.* Cambridge: Cambridge University Press, 2010.

———. *Richard Strauss's* Guntram *and the Dismantling of Wagnerian Musical Metaphysics.* Ph.D. dissertation, Duke University, 1996.

Stravinsky, Igor

Albright, Daniel. *Stravinsky:* The Music Box and the Nightingale. New York: Gordon and Breach, 1989.

Campbell, Stuart. "The *Mavra*s of Puskin, Kochno, and Stravinsky." *Music and Letters* 58 (1977): 304–17.

Carter, Lee Chandler. *The Progress in the Rake's Return.* Ph.D. dissertation, City University of New York, 1995.

———. "The Rake's (and Stravinsky's) Progress." *American Journal of Semiotics* 13 (1996): 183–225.

———. "Stravinsky's Special Sense: The Rhetorical Use of Tonality in *The Rake's Progress.*" *Music Theory Spectrum* 19 (1997): 55–80.

Chew, Geoffrey. "Pastoralism and Neoclassicism: A Reinterpretation of Auden's and Stravinsky's *Rake's Progress.*" *Cambridge Opera Journal* 5 (1993): 239–63.

Cross, Jonathan, ed. *The Cambridge Companion to Stravinsky.* Cambridge: Cambridge University Press, 2003.

Griffiths, Paul. *Igor Stravinsky:* The Rake's Progress. Cambridge: Cambridge University Press, 1982.

Hunter, Mary. "Igor and Tom: History and Destiny in *The Rake's Progress*." *Opera Quarterly* 7 (1990): 38–52.

Neytcheva, Svetlana. "Dream as Agent of Myth in Stravinsky's Opera *The Rake's Progress*." In Peter Csobádi, ed., *Traum und Wirklichkeit in Theater und Musiktheater: Vorträge und Gespräche des Salzburger Symposions 2004*, 365–81. Salzburg: Mueller-Speiser, 2006.

Paulson, Ronald. "Auden, Hogarth, and *The Rake's Progress*." *Raritan* 16 (1996): 22–51.

Straus, Joseph N. "The Progress of a Motive in Stravinsky's *The Rake's Progress*." *Journal of Musicology* 9 (1991): 165–85.

Taruskin, Richard. "In *The Rake's Progress*, Love Conquers (Almost) All." In *The Danger of Music and Other Anti-utopian Essays*, 109–17. Berkeley: University of California Press, 2009.

Walsh, Stephen, et al. *Stravinsky:* Oedipus rex. New York: Cambridge University Press, 1993.

Wiebe, Heather. "*The Rake's Progress* as Opera Museum." *Opera Quarterly* 25 (2009): 6–27.

Tan Dunn

Sheppard, W. Anthony. "Blurring the Boundaries: Tan Dunn's *Tinte* and *The First Emperor*." *Journal of Musicology* 26 (2009): 285–326.

———. "Tan Dun and Zhang Yimou between Film and Opera." *Journal of Musicological Research* 29 (2010): 1–33.

Young, Samson. "The Voicing of the Voiceless in Tan Dun's *The Map*: Horizon of Expectation and the Rhetoric of National Style." *Asian Music* 40 (2009): 83–99.

Tippett, Michael

Bowen, Meirion. *Michael Tippett*. New York: Robson, 1998.

Clarke, David. *Tippett Studies*. New York: Cambridge University Press, 1999.

Gloag, Kenneth. *Tippett: A Child of Our Time*. Cambridge: Cambridge University Press, 1999.

Robinson, Suzanne, ed. *Michael Tippett: Music and Literature*. Aldershot, England: Ashgate, 2002.

Scheppach, Margaret A. *Dramatic Parallels in Michael Tippett's Operas: Analytical Essays on the Musico-Dramatic Techniques*. Lewiston, N.Y.: Mellon, 1990.

Vaughan Williams, Ralph

Adams, Byron, and Robin Wells, eds. *Vaughan Williams Essays*. Aldershot, England: Ashgate, 2003.

Forbes, Anne-Marie H. "Motivic Unity in Ralph Vaughan Williams's *Riders to the Sea*." *Music Review* 44 (1983): 234–45.

Meares, Stan. "*The Pilgrim's Progress*: An Investigation." *British Music Society Journal* 5 (1983): 1–26.

Savage, Roger. "Vaughan Williams, the Romany Ryes, and the Cambridge Ritualists." *Music and Letters* 83 (2002): 383–418.

Weltzien, O. Alan. "Notes and Lineaments: Vaughan William's *Job, A Masque for Dancing* and Blake's Illustrations." *Musical Quarterly* 76 (1992): 301–36.

Walton, William

Price, Scott. "'A Lost Child': A Study of the Genesis of *Troilus and Cressida*." In Stewart R. Craggs, ed., *William Walton: Music and Literature*, 182–208. Aldershot, England: Ashgate, 1999.

Weill, Kurt

Albright, Daniel. "Kurt Weill as Modernist." *Modernism/Modernity* 7 (2000): 273–84.

Fuegi, John. *Brecht and Company: Sex, Politics, and the Making of the Modern Drama*. New York: Grove, 1994.

Gilliam, Bryan. "Stage and Screen: Kurt Weill and Operatic Reform in the 1920s." In Bryan Gilliam, ed., *Music and Performance during the Weimar Republic*, 1–12. Cambridge: Cambridge University Press, 1994.

Hinton, Stephen. *Kurt Weill:* The Threepenny Opera. Cambridge: Cambridge University Press, 1990.

Hirsch, Foster. *Kurt Weill on Stage: From Berlin to Broadway*. New York: Knopf, 2002.

Kowalke, Kim H. *Kurt Weill in Europe, 1900–1935: A Study of His Music and Writings*. Ph.D. dissertation, Yale University, 1977.

Kowalke, Kim H., and Hort Edler, eds. *"A Stranger Here Myself": Kurt Weill-Studien*. Hildesheim: Olns, 1993.

Thornhill, William Robert. *Kurt Weill's* Street Scene. Ph.D. dissertation, University of North Carolina, Chapel Hill, 1990.

Willett, John. "Three Elements of *Mahagonny*." In Christine Tretwo and Helmut Gier, eds., *Caspar Neher: The Greatest Stage Designer of Our Time*, 73–89. Opladen, Germany: Westdeutscher, 1997.

20TH CENTURY: COMPARATIVE AND OTHER TOPICS

Antokoletz, Elliot. *Musical Symbolism in the Operas of Debussy and Bartók: Trauma, Gender, and the Unfolding Unconscious*. New York: Oxford University Press, 2004.

Atlas, Allan W. "Mimì's Death: Mourning in Puccini and Leoncavallo." *Journal of Musicology* 14 (1996): 52–79.

Babcock, Renee Elizabeth. *The Operas of Hindemith, Krenek, and Weill: Cultural Trends in the Weimar Republic, 1918–1933*. Ph.D. dissertation, University of Texas, Austin, 1996.

Bek, Mikuláš, et al., eds. *Socialist Realism and Music*. Prague: Konizsch Latin Press, 2004.

Bendikas, Kristina. *Opera Productions of Jean-Piere Ponnelle: The American Years (1958–1987)*. Ph.D. dissertation, University of Toronto, 1999.

Bonds, Alexandra B. *Beijing Opera Costumes: The Visual Communication of Character and Culture*. Honolulu: University of Hawaii Press, 2008.

Borovsky, Victor. *Chaliapin: A Critical Biography*. New York: Knopf, 1988.

Breckbill, David. *The Bayreuth Singing Style around 1900*. Ph.D. dissertation, University of California, Berkeley, 1991.

Breslin, Herbert H., ed. *The Tenors*. New York: Macmillan, 1974.

Caruso, Dorothy. *Enrico Caruso: His Life and Death*. Westport, Conn.: Greenwood, 1987.

Chapin, Schuyler. *Sopranos, Mezzos, Tenors, Basses, and Other Friends*. New York: Crown, 1995.

Citron, Marcia J. *Opera on Screen*. New Haven, Conn.: Yale University Press, 2000.

———. *When Opera Meets Film*. Cambridge: Cambridge University Press, 2010.

Cook, Susan Carol. *Opera for a New Republic: The Zeitopern of Krenek, Weill, and Hindemith*. Ann Arbor, Mich.: University Microfilms International, 1988.

Cooke, Mervyn, ed. *The Cambridge Companion to Twentieth-Century Opera*. Cambridge: Cambridge University Press, 2007.

Edwards, Anne. *Maria Callas: An Intimate Biography*. New York: St. Martin's, 2001.

Everett, William A., and Paul R. Laird, eds. *The Cambridge Companion to the Musical*. 2nd ed. New York: Cambridge University Press, 2008.

Farkas, Andrew. "Enrico Caruso: Tenor, Baritone, Bass." *Opera Quarterly* 4 (1986): 53–60.

Farkas, Andrew, and Enrico Caruso Jr. *Enrico Caruso: My Father and My Family*. Portland, Ore.: Amadeus, 1997; originally 1991.

Fritz, Rebekka. *Text and Music in German Operas of the 1920s: A Study of the Relationship between Compositional Style and Text-Setting in Richard Strauss'* Die Ägyptische Helena, *Alban Berg's* Wozzeck, *and Arnold Schoenberg's* Von Heute auf Morgen. Ph.D. dissertation, Trinity College, Dublin, 1997.

Fullerton, James Graeme. *The Grotesque in Twentieth-Century Opera*. Ph.D. dissertation, City University of New York, 2006.

Gann, Kyle. *American Music in the Twentieth Century*. New York: Schirmer, 1997.

Garafola, Lynn, and Nancy Van Norman Baer, eds. *The Ballets Russes and Its World*. New Haven, Conn.: Yale University Press, 1999.

Hamberlin, Larry. *Tin Pan Opera: Operatic Novelty Songs in the Ragtime Era*. New York: Oxford University Press, 2011.

Horne, Marilyn, and Jane Scovell. *Marilyn Horne: The Song Continues*. Fort Worth, Texas: Baskerville, 2004.

Illiano, Roberto, ed. *Italian Music during the Fascist Period*. Turnhout, Belgium: Brepols, 2004.

Kennedy, Michael. *Glyndebourne: A Short History*. Oxford: Shire, 2010.

Kornick, Rebecca Hodell. *Recent American Opera: A Production Guide*. New York: Columbia University Press, 1991.

Law, Joe K. "Sutherland before *Lucia*: The 1948–1958 Recordings." *Opera Quarterly* 20 (2004): 603–23.

Levi, Erik. "Towards an Aesthetic of Fascist Opera." In Günter Berghaus, ed., *Fascism and Theater: Comparative Studies on the Aesthetics and Politics of Performance in Europe, 1925–1945*, 260–76. Oxford: Berghahn, 1996.

Levine, Robert. *Maria Callas: A Musical Biography*. New York: Black Dog and Leventhal, 2003.

Lew, Nathaniel Geoffrey. *A New and Glorious Age: Constructions of National Opera in Britain, 1945–1951*. Ph.D. dissertation, University of California, Berkeley, 2001.

Li, Siu Leung. *Cross-Dressing in Chinese Opera*. Hong Kong: Hong Kong University, 2003.

Lindenberger, Herbert. "Anti-theatricality in Twentieth-Century Opera." *Modern Drama* 44 (2001): 300–18.

Locke, Brian. *Opera and Ideology in Prague*. Rochester, N.Y.: University of Rochester, 2006.

Mackerras, Colin. *Peking Opera*. Oxford: Oxford University Press, 1997.

Major, Norma. *Joan Sutherland: The Authorized Biography*. Boston: Little, Brown, 1994; originally 1987.

Matheopoulos, Helena. *Fashion Designers at the Opera*. London: Thames and Hudson, 2011.

Mehring, Frank. "Welcome to the Machine! The Representation of Technology in *Zeitopern*." *Cambridge Opera Journal* 11 (1999): 159–77.

Meyer, Michael. *The Politics of Music in the Third Reich*. New York: Lang, 1991.

Morra, Irene Mary. *The Muddying of the Wells: Twentieth-Century British Opera and the Literary Librettist*. Ph.D. dissertation, University of Toronto, 2002.

Morrison, Elizabeth Aileen Carmen. *The Deadly Feminine: Violence and Eroticism in Three Expressionist Operas*. Ph.D. dissertation, McGill University, 2002.

Newark, Cormac. "'Vous qui faites l'endormie': *The Phantom* and the Buried Voices of the Paris Opéra." *19th-Century Music* 33 (2009): 62–78.

Novak, Jelena. "Opera in the Age of Media." In Vesna Mikić and Tatjana Marković, eds., *Music and Media: Sixth International Symposium Folklore-Music-Work of Art*, 89–98. Belgrade, Serbia: Fakultet Muzičke Umetnosti, 2004.

O'Loughlin, Niall. "Crossing the Language Barrier: Hidden Meanings in Early 20th-c. European Opera." In Peter Andraschke and Edelgard Spaude, eds., *Kunstgespräche: Musikalische Begegnungen zwischen Ost und West*, 295–317. Freiburg, Germany: Rombach, 1998.

Pan, Xiafeng. *The Stagecraft of Peking Opera*. Beijing: New World, 1995.

Potter, Keith. *Four Musical Minimalists*. Cambridge: Cambridge University Press, 2000.

Ringer, Alexander L. "Schoenberg, Weill, and Epic Theater." *Journal of the Arnold Schoenberg Institute* 4 (1980): 77–98.

Sachs, Harvey. *Toscanini*. Rocklin, Calif.: Prima, 1995; originally 1978.

Schroeder, David P. *Cinema's Illusions, Opera's Allure: The Operatic Impulse in Film*. New York: Continuum, 2002.

Schwartz, K. Robert. *Minimalists*. London: Phaidon, 1996.

Seletsky, Robert. "The Performance Practice of Maria Callas: Interpretation and Instinct." *Opera Quarterly* 20 (2004): 587–602.

Steane, John Barry. *The Grand Tradition: Seventy Years of Singing on Record*. London: Duckworth, 1974.

———. *Singers of the Century*. 3 vols. Portland, Ore.: Amadeus, 1996, 1998, 2000.

Stock, Jonathan P. "A Reassessment of the Relationship between Text, Speech Tone, Melody, and Aria Structure in Beijing Opera." *Journal of Musicological Research* 18 (1999): 183–206.

Sutherland, Joan. *A Prima Donna's Progress: The Autobiography of Joan Sutherland*. London: Random House, 1997.

Taylor-Jay, Claire. *The Artist-Operas of Pfitzner, Krenek, and Hindemith: Politics and the Ideology of the Artist*. Aldershot, England: Ashgate, 2004.

Turnbull, Michael. *Mary Garden*. Portland, Ore.: Amadeus, 1997.

Vogt, Howard. *Flagstad: Singer of the Century*. London: Secker and Warburg, 1987.

Warren, Raymond. "The Composer and Opera Performance." In Thomas Wyndham, ed., *Composition—Performance—Reception: Studies in the Creative Process*, 17–34. Aldershot, England: Ashgate, 1998.

Wichmann, Elizabeth. *Listening to Theatre: The Aural Dimension of Beijing Opera*. Honolulu: University of Hawaii Press, 1989.

Williams, James B. *Visual Rhetoric in Staging: Peter Sellars and the Mozart/Da Ponte Trilogy*. Ph.D. dissertation, Bowling Green State University, 1999.

Young, Samson. "Reconsidering Cultural Politics in the Analysis of Contemporary Chinese Music: The Case of *Ghost Opera*." *Contemporary Music Review* 26 (2007): 605–18.

About the Author

Scott L. Balthazar is professor of music history at West Chester University of Pennsylvania, where he has been a member of the faculty since 1991; he taught previously at the University of Virginia. Balthazar received his Ph.D. in music history and theory from the University of Pennsylvania in 1985 and has lectured and published on stylistic aspects of 19th-century Italian opera and contemporary theories of instrumental form in the 18th and 19th centuries. Balthazar is a contributor to the *New Grove Dictionary of Music*, the *New Grove Dictionary of Opera*, and the forthcoming *Cambridge Verdi Encyclopedia*. He edited and wrote two chapters for the *Cambridge Companion to Verdi* for Cambridge University Press (2004), and his articles and reviews have appeared in the *Journal of the American Musicological Society*, *Journal of Musicological Research*, *Journal of Musicology*, *Opera Journal*, *Cambridge Opera Journal*, *Journal of the Royal Musical Association*, *Current Musicology*, *Opera Quarterly*, *Music and Letters*, and *Music Library Association Notes*.

DATE DUE	RETURNED